The Writings of David Thompson
VOLUME I

The *Travels*, 1850 Version

"Map of the North West Territory of the Province of Canada," Archives of Ontario, F443-6. Thompson's Great Map was commissioned upon his retirement from the fur trade in 1812 and hung in the Great Hall at Fort William. His most masterful and expansive work of cartography, 2.13 metres high x 3.30 metres wide, it depicts the West from Hudson Bay to the Pacific and from the Athabasca to the Missouri. Two copies have survived: the one reproduced here and a second at The National Archives (TNA) in London. Five details of the TNA's copy of the Great Map are found at the end of the book, preceding map 5.

The Writings of David Thompson

VOLUME I

The *Travels*, 1850 Version

EDITED WITH AN INTRODUCTION BY
WILLIAM E. MOREAU

McGILL-QUEEN'S UNIVERSITY PRESS · Montreal & Kingston
UNIVERSITY OF WASHINGTON PRESS · Seattle
and THE CHAMPLAIN SOCIETY · Toronto
in association with
the Centre for Rupert's Land Studies at the University of Winnipeg

© The Champlain Society 2009
ISBN 978-0-7735-3558-9

Legal deposit third quarter 2009
Bibliothèque nationale du Québec

Printed in Canada on acid-free paper that
is 100% ancient forest free (100% post-
consumer recycled), processed chlorine free

McGill-Queen's University Press acknowledges the support of the Canada Council
for the Arts for our publishing program. We
also acknowledge the financial support of the
Government of Canada through the Book
Publishing Industry Development Program
(BPIDP) for our publishing activities.

This book has been published with the help
of a grant from the Canadian Federation
for the Humanities and Social Sciences,
through the Aid to Scholarly Publications
Programme, using funds provided by the
Social Sciences and Humanities Research
Council of Canada

LIBRARY AND ARCHIVES CANADA
CATALOGUING IN PUBLICATION

Thompson, David, 1770–1857
The writings of David Thompson / edited
with an introduction by William E. Moreau.

(The publications of the Champlain Society)
Contents: v. 1. The Travels, 1850 version.
ISBN 978-0-7735-3558-9 (v. 1)

1. Thompson, David, 1770–1857 –
Travel – Canada, Western. 2. Thompson,
David, 1770–1857 – Travel – Northwest,
Pacific. 3. Hudson's Bay Company – History. 4. North West Company – History.
5. Northwest, Canadian – Description and
travel. 6. Northwest, Pacific – Description
and travel. 7. Explorers – Canada – Biography. 8. Surveyors – Canada – Biography.
9. Cartographers – Canada – Biography.
10. Fur traders – Canada – Biography.
11. Pioneers – Canada – Biography.
I. Moreau, William, 1969– II. Champlain
Society III. Centre for Rupert's Land
Studies IV. Title. V. Series: Publications of
the Champlain Society

FC3212.1.T46A3 2009   917.1204'1
C2009-900473-9

University of Washington Press
PO Box 50096
Seattle, WA 98145-5096
www.washington.edu/uwpress

LIBRARY OF CONGRESS
CATALOGING-IN-PUBLICATION DATA

Thompson, David, 1770–1857.
The writings of David Thompson : the
Travels, 1850 version / edited with an
introduction by William E. Moreau.
p. cm.
Includes bibliographical references
and index.
ISBN 978-0-295-98936-5 (pbk. : alk. paper)

1. Thompson, David, 1770–1857—Travel—
Canada, Western. 2. Thompson, David,
1770–1857—Travel—Northwest, Pacific.
3. Canada, Western—Description and
Travel. 4. Northwest, Pacific—Description
and Travel. 5. Pioneers—Canada—Biography. 6. Explorers—Canada—Biography.
7. Cartographers—Canada—Biography.
8. Fur traders—Canada—Biography. 9. Hudson's Bay Company—History. 10. North
West Company—History. I. Moreau,
William, 1969– II. Champlain Society.
III. Centre for Rupert's Land Studies.
IV. Title.

F1060.7.T48A3 2009
917.1204'1—dc22   2009010168

Set in 10/13 Sabon by Garet Markvoort

CONTENTS

PREFACE AND ACKNOWLEDGMENTS

This edition had its genesis in 1997, when representatives from the University of Washington Press and McGill-Queen's University Press approached the Champlain Society with a proposal to republish its 1962 text of Thompson's *Travels*, edited by Richard Glover. After some consultation, the presses became partners with the Society in sponsoring a new and complete edition of Thompson's work, based on a fresh transcription from the original manuscript, and meeting modern standards of documentary editing. It was then that I was invited to become editor. The *Travels* was written over the course of five years, and this edition has now been twice as long in its preparation, so first I must thank the editors at the University of Washington Press and McGill-Queen's University Press and the Council of the Champlain Society for their unflagging confidence and patience.

This work has come to fruition only with the guidance, generosity, insights, hard work, and support of others, and whatever is of value in this edition is a credit to them. First and foremost, I wish to thank Germaine Warkentin, who as my thesis director first steered me towards Thompson some fifteen years ago and who has shepherded this edition along, providing guidance, reading and commenting on countless drafts, and advocating for this work.

Financial and material support have come from several sources. The Centre for Rupert's Land Studies at the University of Winnipeg provided a substantial research grant, which enabled Anne Lindsay to dig up a horde of valuable information at the Hudson's Bay Company Archives in Winnipeg. Early on in this project, the Basilian Fathers of Toronto generously freed my summers for research, travel, and writing, while the John M. Kelly Library at St Michael's College provided study space.

Jennifer Brown kindly read an earlier draft of this work, and her comments on Cree cosmology were especially helpful. David Malaher showed uncommon generosity and shared his own ideas about what Thompson was up to. Ian Wilson and Michael Moir were faithful supporters at the Champlain Society. Jack Nisbet shared insights into Thompson's world and provided constant good counsel and perspective. John Warkentin lent his considerable expertise to the development of the maps, which were prepared by Byron Moldofsky and Mariange Beaudry of the cartography office of the University of Toronto Press. Ted Binnema assisted with Native material, and with the Native culture areas map, and Andy Korsos shared his meticulous research into Thompson's travels, providing the foundation for the maps of these journeys.

Thanks are due to the Thomas Fisher Rare Book Library at the University of Toronto and to the Archives of Ontario, keepers of the manuscripts of the *Travels*, for granting access to and permission to publish the work. I am especially grateful to Sandra Alston, Anne Dondertman, P.J. Carefoote, and Albert Masters at Thomas Fisher and to Corrado Santoro at the Archives of Ontario. I have been assisted greatly by Ian Wilson, Patricia Kennedy, and Ghislain Malette at Library and Archives Canada and by Anne Morton at the Hudson's Bay Company Archives. Special thanks to Rose Mitchell at the National Archives of the United Kingdom for providing a fresh, high-quality scan of their copy of Thompson's "Map of the North West Territory of the Province of Canada." Thank you to Roger Hall and Bill Harnum at the Champlain Society and Joan McGilvray and Carlotta Lemieux at McGill-Queen's University Press for their help in shepherding the manuscript of this edition to publication.

For helping to shed light on different aspects of Thompson's life, work, and world, I thank David Anderson, Fiona Black, Roland Bohr, Jim Boyle, Lyle Campbell, J.A. Chartres, Ed Dahl, Rick Dobson, Mike Dove, Harry Duckworth, William Dumas, Peter Flood, George Fulford, Bob Gaba, Mark Gallop, Keith Goulet, John C. Jackson, D'Arcy Jenish, Bruce Johanson, Lloyd Keith, Bill Layman, Ross MacDonald, Ian MacLaren, Mary Malainey, David Nicandri, Carolyn Podruchny, Marsha Rooney, Dale Russell, George Sibley, and Sylvia Van Kirk.

I thank my parents Bill and Angela Moreau, my in-laws Pina and Armando Filippelli, the Basilian Fathers of Toronto, Maria Moreau and Bill Boyle, René and Debbie Lachmansingh, and the children. The deepest debt of gratitude is due to my wife Daiana, who has been endlessly patient and supportive and who served as a fine research assistant. The last thank-you is for our son William, who joined this project in its final stages and to whom this work is dedicated.

William E. Moreau
October 2008

HISTORICAL INTRODUCTION

I WITNESS

In his long life, David Thompson both witnessed and contributed to the transformation of a continent. When he was born in Westminster in 1770, Britain ruled a string of burgeoning colonies, extending along the Atlantic seaboard from Newfoundland to Florida, and the Hudson's Bay Company was making its first tentative forays into the interior of North America to meet the challenge of Montreal-based fur traders. Still, the intimate contours of the West were known to few non-aboriginal people. By the time Thompson died in Longueuil in 1857, many parts of the American West were being occupied by settlers and prospectors: the Oregon Trail had been inaugurated in 1841, the first Mormon communities in Utah date from 1847, and the California Gold Rush began a year later. North of the forty-ninth parallel, the Red River Colony had been settled in 1812 but remained, as Thompson stated in his *Travels*, "an isolated Settlement" (iv.188, 228).[1] As Thompson himself predicted, this would not be the case for long. The Assiniboine River, he wrote, "every where flows thro' a pleasant country of good soil, and in time to come will no doubt, be covered with an agricultural population" (iv.147, 198); Ojibwa lands in the Upper Mississippi would "in time be in the hands of those that cultivate the soil" (iv.183, 224).[2] In the summer following Thompson's death, John Palliser departed for the West as head of

1 Pages of the *Travels* manuscript are identified by the number assigned them in the David Thompson Papers, MS21, Thomas Fisher Rare Book Library, University of Toronto. These numbers consist of an arabic and a roman numeral. The former refers to the draft to which the page was thought to belong and was probably assigned by J.B. Tyrrell, while the second is the number that each page bears at its head, in Thompson's hand. Page numbers may not be sequential in this edition, as our understanding of the history of Thompson's composition of the work has evolved since numbers were assigned. For the twenty-nine *Travels* pages housed at the Archives of Ontario, see note on 47. For a complete discussion of the manuscript, see "Textual Introduction."

2 Gerald Friesen estimates that, of the 480,000,000 acres (194,250,000 hectares) that make up the modern provinces of Manitoba, Saskatchewan, and Alberta, a mere 9,000 were under cultivation in 1857. Gerald Friesen, *The Canadian Prairies: A History* (Toronto: University of Toronto Press, 1987), 9.

the British North American Exploring Expedition, a reconnaisance mission sponsored by the British Colonial Office to investigate whether the northern Plains could be settled, and the next year the geologist Henry Youle Hind travelled over the same region, assessing its agricultural potential on behalf of the Legislature of Canada. The transformation that Thompson foresaw was definitively initiated by the transfer of Hudson's Bay Company lands to Canada in 1870, and a world was thus lost as, in the words of Irene Spry, the region underwent a transition from "common property resources, to open access resources, and finally to private property."[3] Thompson played a pivotal role in the prelude to this drama, in his writings preserving the memory of what was and in his activities preparing the way for what would be.

Now, one hundred and fifty years after Thompson's death, his presence continues to pervade the places of the West, and he occupies such a place of prominence in the popular imagination that one may speak of a David Thompson awakening. Already memorialized in a river, town, mountain, highway, tourist region, and monuments and historical markers, during the current bicentennial celebrations of his activities west of the Rocky Mountains he has been the subject of renewed and intense popular and scholarly interest. Because of his prolific production of documents and the broad scope of his activities, he serves as a point of reference for people as diverse as canoe enthusiasts, local historians, epidemiologists, and linguists. He has been made and remade in several images, from mountain man to philosopher, hailed by J.B Tyrrell as "the greatest practical land geographer that the world has produced"[4] and by Victor Hopwood as "the foundation mythmaker of the Canadian West."[5]

3 Irene Spry, "The Tragedy of the Loss of the Commons in Western Canada," in *As Long as the Sun Shines and the Water Flows*, ed. Ian A.L. Getty and Antoine S. Lussier (Vancouver: University of British Columbia Press, 1983), 203. Not all regarded this process as inevitable. One voice raised in opposition to white settlement belonged to Thompson's brother-in-law, John McDonald of Garth, who argued that a Native "confederacy" ought to be established west of the Mississippi. This scheme is described in Germaine Warkentin's "John McDonald of Garth and the Dream of a Native North-West," in Laura Peers and Carolyn Podruchny, eds, *Gathering Places: Essays on Aboriginal and Fur Trade Histories* (forthcoming, University of British Columbia Press).

4 J.B. Tyrrell, introduction to *David Thompson's Narrative of His Explorations in Western America, 1784–1812*, ed. Tyrrell (Toronto: Champlain Society, 1916), xxxii.

5 Victor G. Hopwood, introduction to *Travels in Western North America 1784–1812*, ed. Hopwood (Toronto: Macmillan, 1971), 34.

The general shape of his life is well known. At the age of seven Thompson entered the Grey Coat School in Westminster, where he received an education for the Royal Navy; he was instead apprenticed to the Hudson's Bay Company (HBC) and in 1784 was sent to the bayside post of Churchill. Thompson remained thirteen years in the HBC's employ, first as a clerk and later as a trader and surveyor, spending much of his energies in the attempt to develop an easterly route to the fur-rich Athabasca region. Frustrated in this endeavour, in 1797 he left the HBC for the rival North West Company (NWC), where he worked for the next fifteen years, after 1804 as an NWC partner. His career with the Nor'westers gave Thompson broader scope for his activities, and his achievements included a visit to the villages of the Mandans on the Missouri in 1797–98 and expansion of the fur trade west of the Continental Divide in 1807–12. In 1799 Thompson had married Charlotte Small, and in 1812 he brought her and their growing family east to the vicinity of Montreal, retiring from active participation in the fur trade. In 1815 the family moved to a farm at Williamstown in Upper Canada, where Thompson was active as a landowner and merchant, and from 1817 to 1827 he served as astronomer and surveyor on the International Boundary Commission (IBC), which delineated the boundary between British North America and the United States in what is now the province of Ontario. Because of factors that were largely beyond his control, including a global recession, his financial fortunes began to fail during the late 1820s, and by 1836 he had moved to the city of Montreal. Here he did occasional surveying jobs, petitioned unsuccessfully for pensions and public employment, and from 1845 to 1850 composed his *Travels* narrative, a project he ultimately abandoned when he lost his sight. Thompson died on 10 February 1857. Charlotte survived him by less than three months.

2 LEGACY

Thompson left behind him a world of works, both textual and material. One hundred and eighteen notebooks in his hand survive in archival collections. They date from 13 September 1786, when as a sixteen-year-old HBC apprentice he began to keep the South Branch House post journal for the trader Mitchell Oman,[6] and continued until 28 February 1851, when as an eighty-year-old patriarch he penned a journal entry describing blustery Montreal

6 South Branch House, Post Journal, 13 September 1786 to 30 May 1787, B.205/a/1, Hudson's Bay Company Archives, Provincial Archives of Manitoba, Winnipeg (hereafter HBCA).

weather.[7] The notebooks include such diverse material as fur post inventories, astronomical observations, traverse tables, descriptions of water courses, personal journals, drafts of correspondence, and miscellaneous prose sketches.[8] Thompson also wrote several reports for his employers, including the HBC, NWC, and IBC, made more than three dozen contributions to the Montreal *Gazette* and *Montreal Herald*, and drafted hundreds of maps.[9] And he created more than documents: in an 1847 letter to HBC governor Sir George Simpson he called himself "a maker of nets and canoes";[10] he also designed and constructed showshoes, a model cannon frame, and a desk, and he built several fur-trading posts.

Late in life Thompson fretted that his works were "soon to perish in oblivion,"[11] but happily, one of his final acts salvaged his memory from obscurity. From 1845 to 1850, while in his late seventies, he composed the narrative he called his *Travels* – the work, along with his great map, on which his reputation rests. Although Thompson was unable to finish the *Travels* to his satisfaction, the manuscript has subsequently formed the basis of three editions: *David Thompson's Narrative of His Explorations in Western America, 1784–1812*, edited by J.B. Tyrrell and published by the Champlain Society (1916), a second Champlain Society edition, entitled *David Thompson's Narrative, 1784–1812*, and edited by Richard Glover (1962), and *Travels in Western North America, 1784–1812*, edited by Victor G. Hopwood and published by Macmillan of Canada (1971).[12]

The current edition is based on a fresh transcription of Thompson's manuscript and a careful study of the evolution of the work through its various drafts, the full details of which may be found in the "Textual Introduction." The text found here in Volume I consists of a draft that Thompson was working on when he had to suspend composition definitively in 1850, and it parallels part 1 of Tyrrell's and Glover's Champlain editions. This text, the *1850 Travels*, includes Thompson's account of his HBC years and his early

---

7 Notebook 61b, page 32, David Thompson Fonds, F443, Archives of Ontario, Toronto (hereafter abbreviated in the style AO. 61b.32).

8 A complete list of Thompson's manuscript materials will be found in Volume III.

9 Thompson's reports, letters, and contributions to newspapers will be the focus of Volume III and will be treated at greater length there.

10 David Thompson to Sir George Simpson, 17 August 1847, D.5/20: f. 116–17, HBCA.

11 David Thompson to James Alexander, 9 May 1845, FO5/441: 101r–102v, The National Archives of the United Kingdom (hereafter TNA).

12 For a fuller treatment of these editions, see "Textual Introduction"; the publication of other works by Thompson will be discussed in the introduction to Volume III.

NWC career, with extended sections on the Cree, the Plains, and the Piegan. Volume II, forthcoming, contains earlier versions of much of this material and an account, which Thompson had concluded in 1848, of his activities west of the Continental Divide between 1807 and 1812. This text, the *1848 Travels*, parallels part 2 of the Tyrrell and Glover editions, and contains the conclusion with which we have become familiar: Thompson's 1812 coming down to Montreal. In addition, Volume II contains an account of Thompson's activities between February 1811 and January 1812, written in 1847, and a brief description of Hudson Bay, written in 1845. Volume III consists of other writings, such as letters, reports, and contributions to newspapers.

At one level, the *Travels* is an account of the author's activities as an HBC and NWC trader and surveyor between 1784 and 1812, including such key episodes as a winter's residence with the Piegan near present-day Calgary in 1787–88, a 1796 journey to the east end of Lake Athabasca, an arduous survey of the Red River basin, the Upper Mississippi, and Lake Superior in 1797–98, and the extension of the fur trade into the Columbia Plateau during 1807–12, climaxing in the 1811 journey down the Columbia River to visit the Pacific Fur Company post of Astoria at its mouth.

But the chronological recounting of personal exploits is only one of the *Travels'* elements. Its content, structure, and style are complex and nuanced, and the work is treasured for its historical significance, topical breadth, literary excellence, and intellectual force. The *Travels* is a rich source of information, not only about Thompson's career, but about western geography, natural history, Native peoples, and the business of the fur trade, and as the writer's eye ranges over this world, it settles on topics as diverse as caribou and copper mines, smallpox and the Sasquatch. An extended meditation on the land and peoples of the West, the *Travels* reflects many of the central preoccupations of nineteenth-century discourse: the conflicting claims of theology and geology about the origin and nature of the Earth, questions about human migrations and cultural difference, and considerations about the future of the New World and its relationship to the Old. And while the *Travels* generally follows Thompson from childhood to retirement, it is also structured spatially, as a series of regional vignettes that synthesize the geography of the West as the author's journeys unfold. Finally, the *Travels* is a distinguished literary work, alternating between the empirical and expository prose of the scientist, and the immediate and vivid language of the storyteller, animated throughout by a restless spirit of inquiry and sense of wonder.

The breadth of the *Travels* is reflected in the many ways in which the work has been approached. It was first employed as a geographical source, providing data for Charles Lindsey's 1873 *Investigation of the Unsettled Boundar-*

ies of Ontario,[13] though geographers have generally had recourse more to Thompson's notebooks and maps than to his narrative. It is as a historical primary source that the *Travels* has been used most frequently. In a narrow sense, the work has provided biographical material about Thompson himself. The two most influential treatments of Thompson's life and career remain Tyrrell's and Glover's introductions to their editions of the *Travels*, each of which relies heavily on the narrative it prefaces; to these works should be added Catherine M. White's fine biographical introduction to her edition of Thompson's Montana journals.[14] In addition, the *Travels* has provided source material for over a dozen single-volume biographies of its author.[15] Thompson's biographers, particularly his first two editors, have been especially concerned with his personal character and professional competence. At one end of the spectrum, Tyrrell wrote of Thompson's technical skill, piety, and strong sense of morality, claiming that he lived "the white flower of a blameless life,"[16] while at the other end Glover, emphasizing Thompson's

---

13 Charles Lindsey, *An Investigation of the Unsettled Boundaries of Ontario* (Toronto: Hunter, Rose and Company, 1873).

14 Catherine M. White, ed., *David Thompson's Journals relating to Montana and Adjacent Regions, 1808–1812* (Missoula, MT: Montana State University Press, 1950).

15 In chronological order of publication, these works are J.B. Tyrrell, *A Brief Narrative of the Journeys of David Thompson in North-Western America* (Toronto: Copp, Clark, 1888); Charles Norris Cochrane, *David Thompson the Explorer* (Toronto: Macmillan, 1924); Arthur Silver Morton, *David Thompson* (Toronto: Ryerson Press, 1930); Hubert Evans, *North to the Unknown: The Achievements and Adventures of David Thompson* (Toronto: McClelland & Stewart, 1949); Kerry Wood, *The Map-Maker: The Story of David Thompson* (Toronto: Macmillan, 1955); James K. Smith, *David Thompson: Fur Trader, Explorer, Geographer* (Toronto: Oxford University Press, 1971); James K. Smith, *David Thompson* (Don Mills: Fitzhenry & Whiteside, 1975); Stan Garrod, *David Thompson* (Toronto: Grolier, 1989); Jack Nisbet, *Sources of the River: Tracking David Thompson across Western North America* (Seattle: Sasquatch, 1994); D'Arcy Jenish, *Epic Wanderer: David Thompson and the Mapping of the Canadian West* (Scarborough, ON: Doubleday Canada, 2003); Graeme Pole, *David Thompson: The Epic Expeditions of a Great Canadian Explorer* (Canmore, AB: Altitude Pub Canada, 2003); Frieda Wishinsky, *David Thompson: Map-Maker* (Don Mills, ON: Pearson Educational, 2005); Tom Shardlow, *David Thompson: A Trail by Stars* (Lantzville, BC: XYZ Publishing, 2006). Thompson is also the subject of several biographical reference entries, the most important of which is John Nicks, "David Thompson," in *Dictionary of Canadian Biography* (Toronto: University of Toronto Press, 1985), 8:878–84. Biographical components also feature in several more specialized studies of Thompson.

16 Tyrrell, introduction, lviii.

personal faults and professional failings, argued against the "beatification of a historical character."[17]

More broadly, the *Travels* is a key source for scores of works on the history of the fur trade and of western North America, including such seminal texts as A.S. Morton's *History of the Canadian West to 1870–71*[18] and E.E. Rich's *The Fur Trade and the Northwest to 1857*.[19] The question of character links writing on Thompson's life with general treatments of western North American history, for Thompson has played the role of both hero and anti-hero to historians, lauded by some as intrepid and pure hearted, indicted by others as cowardly and irresolute. Debate amongst biographers and historians has centred on two especially controversial episodes. Thompson's abrupt transfer from the HBC to the NWC in 1797 has been regarded by some as a reasonable response to the continued obstruction of his surveying projects, and by others as base treachery against his erstwhile employers.[20] His 1811 arrival at the mouth of the Columbia River *after* the employees of John Jacob Astor's Pacific Fur Company has been considered a failure of will and dereliction of duty by those who frame his journey as a "race to the sea" by employees of rival firms; it has been seen as simply inconsequential by those who argue that there was at that time no rivalry and hence no race.[21] Debate often centres around Thompson's representation of himself and his actions, and many have concurred in the assessment reported by Francis H. Baddeley, a member of the commission that hired Thompson to survey the Muskoka region in 1837: "[T]here are rumours abroad that Mr. T. is not trustworthy as to reporting of facts."[22] Indeed, Thompson's accounts of certain episodes

17 Glover, introduction, xii.
18 Arthur Silver Morton, *A History of the Canadian West to 1870–71: Being a History of Rupert's Land (The Hudson's Bay Company's Territory) and of the North-West Territory (including the Pacific Slope)* (London: T. Nelson and Sons, 1939).
19 E.E. Rich, *The Fur Trade and the Northwest to 1857* (Toronto: McClelland & Stewart, 1967).
20 Again, Tyrrell and Glover represent the opposing sides in this debate. In his introduction to Thompson's narrative, Tyrrell writes of the lack of support Thompson had received from his HBC superiors (xli–xliii). Glover, in his introduction, argues that Thompson's action constituted "desertion" (xl–xliii).
21 The former assessment has been expressed most forcefully by A.S. Morton, primarily in "The North West Company's Columbian Enterprise and David Thompson," *Canadian Historical Review* 17 (1936): 266–88. His thesis has been rebutted with equal force by Barbara Belyea in "The 'Columbian Enterprise' and A.S. Morton: A Historical Exemplum," *BC Studies* 86 (Summer 1990): 3–27.
22 Francis H. Baddeley to John Macaulay, 2 October 1837, Macaulay Family Fonds, F32, AO. In his introduction, Glover assiduously details instances of this unreliabil-

in the *Travels*, such as Samuel Hearne's actions at the fall of Prince of Wales's Fort in 1782 (10–11), leave him vulnerable to the criticism that he wilfully misrepresented facts.

Thompson's narrative has nevertheless proved to be a fruitful source of information for writers in an array of specialized fields, from Native studies and fur trade social history, to natural history and epidemiology. While much of this discourse has taken place in doctoral theses and learned journals, the *Travels* has also informed many influential works of more general interest, including such recent volumes as *Common and Contested Ground*, Theodore Binnema's revisionist account of the ecological and ethnographic history of the northwest Plains,[23] Robert Brightman's study of the Cree cosmology of animals, *Grateful Prey*,[24] and *Pox Americana*, Elizabeth Fenn's popular history of the smallpox epidemic of the early 1780s.[25]

Finally, exploration texts such as Thompson's have come to be appreciated as literary works (despite Northrop Frye's statement that Canada's explorers were "as innocent of literary intention as a mating loon"),[26] and Thompson appears regularly in anthologies of Canadian literature and on course syllabi.[27] Literary critics have focused particular attention on Thompson's

ity, stating that Thompson was a master of "*suppressio veri et suggestio falsi*" (xiii). To the episodes he cites there may be added his discussion of Thompson's portrayal of Samuel Hearne, in "The Witness of David Thompson," *Canadian Historical Review* 31 (1950): 25–38.

23 Theodore Binnema, *Common and Contested Ground: A Human and Environmental History of the Northwestern Plains* (Toronto: University of Toronto Press, 2004).

24 Robert Brightman, *Grateful Prey: Rock Cree Human-Animal Relationships* (Regina: Canadian Plains Research Centre, 2002).

25 Elizabeth Fenn, *Pox Americana: The Great Smallpox Epidemic of 1775–82* (New York: Hill and Wang, 2001).

26 Northrop Frye, conclusion to *Literary History of Canada: Canadian Literature in English*, ed. Carl F. Klinck (Toronto: University of Toronto Press, 1965), 822.

27 Significant literary treatments of the *Travels* are Victor Hopwood, "David Thompson: Mapmaker and Mythmaker,"*Canadian Literature* 38 (Autumn 1968): 5–17; Hopwood's introduction to his 1971 edition of the narrative, *Travels in Western North America, 1784–1812*; T.D. MacLulich, "The Explorer as Sage: David Thompson's Narrative," *Journal of Canadian Fiction* 4, no. 4 (1976): 97–107; Germaine Warkentin, "David Thompson," in *Profiles in Canadian Literature* (Toronto: Dundurn Press, 1980), 1:1–8; Ian MacLaren, "David Thompson's Imaginative Mapping of the Canadian Northwest, 1784–1812," *Ariel* 15 (1984): 89–106. The most influential literary analysis of exploration texts is Bruce Greenfield, *Narrating Discovery: The Romantic Explorer in American Literature, 1790–1855* (New York: Columbia University Press, 1992).

juxtaposition of the prose of objective exposition and that of subjective narration, and on the closely related question of the work's structural unity. T.D. MacLulich argued that the *Travels'* thematic passages are more important than the chronological narratives they adjoin, and that the work possesses a unity of vision that brings together all apparent disjunctions and digressions,[28] while Germaine Warkentin comments that Thompson "often moves with unexpected rapidity from the factual descriptiveness of the scientific observer to the colourful recreation of fur trade life,"[29] concluding that the "passionate activity of Thompson's mind ... shapes his narrative."[30] The *Travels* has gradually attained a place of preeminence in the canon of early Canadian literature; W.J. Keith claims Thompson as the "best" of the travellers and explorers,[31] and Warkentin states that Thompson produced "the best writing, of whatever sort, in Canada before the twentieth century."[32] Thompson has in turn inspired a number of literary works: Bliss Carman's romantic poem "David Thompson,"[33] Marion R. Smith's verses in *Koo-koo-sint: David Thompson in Western Canada*,[34] and Elizabeth Clutton-Brock's novel *Woman of the Paddle Song*, focusing on the figure of Charlotte.[35]

3 CONTEXT

On 30 September 1809, while attempting to unravel the intricacies of the geography of what is now northeast Washington State, Thompson met a group of Kalispel along the Pend Oreille River. The Natives supplied his party with provisions, including twelve pounds of camas bulbs. Thirty-eight years later, Thompson recounted the event in the *Travels*:

These Roots are about the size of a Nutmeg, they are near the surface, and turned up with a pointed Stick, they are farinaceous, of a pleas-

28 MacLulich, "The Explorer as Sage."
29 Warkentin, "David Thompson," 4.
30 Ibid., 5.
31 W.J. Keith, *Canadian Literature in English* (London: Longman, 1985), 13.
32 Germaine Warkentin, ed., *Canadian Exploration Literature: An Anthology, 1660–1860* (Toronto: Oxford University Press, 1993), xviii.
33 Bliss Carman, "David Thompson," *Far Horizons* (Toronto: McClelland & Stewart, 1925), 7–13.
34 Marion R. Smith, *Koo-koo-sint: David Thompson in Western Canada* (Red Deer, AB: Red Deer College Press, 1976).
35 Elizabeth Clutton-Brock, *Woman of the Paddle Song* (Vancouver: Copp Clark, 1972).

ant taste, easily masticated, and nutritive, they are found in the small
meadows of short grass, in a rich soil, and a short exposure to the Sun
dries them sufficiently to keep for years. (I have some by me which were
dug up in 1811 and are now thirty six years old, 1847) and are in good
preservation, I showed them to the late Lord Metcalfe who eat two of
them, and found them some thing like bread; but although in good
preservation, they, in two years lost their fine aromatic smell.

(iii.217; Volume II)[36]

Imagining the scene as this passage was composed, Jack Nisbet writes: "As
he sniffed the camas roots, Thompson transported himself back to the blue-
petaled meadows of the Pen Oreille, and the shriveled relics on his desk
brought back the taste of the whole place."[37]

The *Travels* is punctuated by many such moments, revealing the gap
between experience and narration, and allowing us to glimpse the Montreal
writer of the 1840s behind the western explorer and trader of a half-century
earlier. Thompson refers to a conversation on digestion with Dr Henry
Howard, a prominent Montreal eye surgeon who in 1848 had treated his cat-
aracts (iv.208, 243–4), and states of the Assiniboine River country that "the
climate is as mild as Montreal" (iv.182, 223). After writing of his 1798 travels on the Red River, Thompson describes the status of the Assiniboia colony
in 1848 (iv.187–8, 227–8), while his account of Lake Superior is informed
not only by his 1798 circuit of that lake but also by his surveys of the 1820s
(iv.226–32, 257–61). Thompson's story had been shaping itself for decades,
evolving in its author's mind. This quality lends the work a mature and wide
perspective, but also reminds us that the *Travels* does not necessarily present
what *was*; rather, it presents what was *remembered*.

If the *Travels* is to be appreciated anew, it must be placed in a similarly
broad context and must be understood as a work of retrospection and synthesis. The context is certainly that of the life of its author, especially his
fur trade career of 1784 to 1812, which provides its subject matter, and his

36 Thompson had at least seven personal audiences with Charles Theophilus Metcalfe
during the latter's tenure as governor of the Province of Canada, 1843–45. Thompson
applied for public employment, solicited a government pension, gave advice on public
works projects, offered to draft maps, and provided information about the Oregon
Territory at a time when the fate of that region was being decided by the United
States and Great Britain, its joint occupants since 1818. It was perhaps in the context
of a conversation about Oregon that Thompson proffered the camas bulbs.

37 Nisbet, *Sources of the River*, 257.

retirement years of 1845 to 1850, during which it was composed. But the context is also that of Thompson's historical moment. Too often viewed in isolation or within the overly narrow confines of the North American fur trade, Thompson's work must find its place within more ample horizons.

Let us trace him back to his origins. Thompson was born on 30 April 1770 in the parish of St John the Evangelist in Westminster, the first child of Ann and David Thompson.[38] Thompson is often identified as being of Welsh descent, but he does not appear to have made this claim himself,[39] and although Thompson's father had lived on Marsham Street, Westminster, since 1759, his prior whereabouts remain unknown. Thompson Sr paid poor rates of between twelve and fourteen pounds per year, indicating a comfortable social standing.[40] A second son, John, was born on 25 January 1772,[41] and just over a month later, on 28 February, Thompson Sr died,[42] and the family moved to new quarters.[43]

38 The Register Book of Births and Baptisms Belonging to the Parish of Saint John the Evangelist Westminster in the County of Middlesex, vol. 2, 1755–1791: 137, City of Westminster Archives, Westminster.

39 Evidence of Thompson's Welshness consists of John Jeremiah Bigsby's comment in *The Shoe and Canoe* that his "speech betrayed the Welshman, although he left his native hills when very young" (J.J. Bigsby. *The Shoe and Canoe; or Pictures of Travels in the Canadas* [London: Chapman and Hall, 1850], 1:113); a statement by Thompson's daughter Mary in an 1888 letter to J.B. Tyrrell that "David Thompson's parents lived in Swansee, Wales" (M.E. Shaw to J.B. Tyrrell, 23 January 1888, Joseph Burr Tyrrell Papers, MG30 D49, vol. 1, Library and Archives Canada [hereafter LAC]); and, most intriguingly, his entry in the 1852 census, in which his birthplace is identified as "Wales" (1852 Census: Canada East, Subdistrict 430, Melbourne Township, Brompton Gore: 10a, LAC). It is nonetheless suggestive that Thompson's Christian name is that of the patron saint of Wales.

40 The poor rate was a form of property tax, paid by the tenant of a dwelling rather than its owner. Poor Rate Books, St Margaret's and St John's, 1759–1772, vols. E410, E414, E418, E422, E426, E430, E434, E438, E442, E446, E450, E454, E458, E465, City of Westminster Archives, Westminster.

41 The Register Book of Births and Baptisms Belonging to the Parish of Saint John the Evangelist Westminster in the County of Middlesex, vol. 2, 1755–1791: 153, City of Westminster Archives, Westminster.

42 A Register of the Burials in the Parish of St John the Evangelist Westminster, 1754–75, City of Westminster Archives, Westminster.

43 The site of their new residence has not been identified. John Thompson was employed with the HBC from 1789 to 1795, working his way up to bowsman (York Factory, List of Servants, 1783–1795, B.239/f/1, HBCA). David Thompson continued to send money to his mother until at least 1802 from his HBC account, which remained

During the 1700s, Westminster was largely subsumed into the expanding metropolis of London, which was home to some 675,000 inhabitants by mid-century.[44] Still, Westminster retained its own local government and a distinct character. Then as now, the two great anchors of the district were Westminster Abbey and the Palace of Westminster, the former the principal ceremonial and monumental church in England, site of the coronation and burial of monarchs, and the latter the seat of the British Houses of Parliament. The area was socially diverse; several thousand career officals made their homes in Westminster, near some of the city's worst slums, huddled in the narrow streets close to the abbey.[45]

As Marsham Street makes its way north, it becomes Smith Street, and here lived one of these officials, Abraham Acworth, a clerk in the office of the Exchequer.[46] Acworth served as a member of the board of governors of Westminster's Grey Coat Hospital, a charity school dedicated to the preparation of poor and orphaned children for apprenticeships and for their growth in Christian virtue. He recommended Thompson for admission, and the boy entered on 29 April 1777, a day shy of his seventh birthday.[47] Thompson remained at the Grey Coat School for seven years, and in the hospital's mathematical school he received an education designed to prepare him for Royal Navy service.[48]

One of the most personal moments in the *Travels* occurs when Thompson reflects on the activities and influences of these schoolboy years. He reports that he enjoyed exploring the places of his city, walking the short distance to Westminster Abbey and St James's Park or travelling farther afield, to London Bridge, Chelsea and across the Thames to Vauxhall. He and his friends entertained themselves by reading and discussing the *Arabian Nights Entertain-*

active after he left the company (Officers' and Servants' Ledger, York, 1797–1813, A. 16/34: 46v–47r, HBCA).

44 For this figure, see Roy Porter, *London: A Social History* (London: Hamish Hamilton, 1994), 131.

45 Liza Picard, *Dr. Johnson's London: Life in London 1740–1770* (London: Weidenfeld and Nicolson, 2000), 15.

46 W.A. Green, *Pedigree of Acworth of Bedfordshire* (London: Mitchell Hughes and Clarke, 1905), 41.

47 Fair Minute Book of Meetings of Board of Governors, 1775–1791, 1648/11, Grey Coat School Records, City of Westminster Archives, Westminster. The Grey Coat School was one of thousands of such instititions in late-eighteenth-century Britain.

48 For a discussion of the nature and function of the Grey Coat School and similar instititions, see Richard I. Ruggles, "Hospital Boys of the Bay," *Beaver* 308 (Autumn 1977): 4–11.

ments, *The Thousand and One Days*, *Robinson Crusoe*, *Gulliver's Travels*, and *The Tales of the Genii*. The environment and activities of Thompson's Westminster boyhood initiated the unique life of discovery and learning that he would lead. But they also situate him in the broader political, economic, intellectual, and scientific currents of his time.

A short distance east of the Grey Coat Hospital, the Palace of Westminster served as the political hub of a nation that in 1770 was on its way to becoming the world's predominant military and commercial power. Victorious over France and its allies in the Seven Years War (1756–63), Britain had acquired colonies in North America and India; although the American Revolution (1775–83) for a time reduced Britain's territorial holdings, in its wake arose a new emphasis on the development of trading networks rather than the mere acquisition of territory, which soon led to a considerable expansion of Britain's commercial sphere. Although Thompson emigrated before the full flowering of the Industrial Revolution, during the decade before his birth Britain's economy had already begun to shift from an agrarian to an industrial base. Agricultural lands were rapidly being enclosed for pasture, workers were beginning to congregate in cities and become integrated into the factory system, while an entrepreneurial middle class grew significantly.

The education that Thompson received at Westminster's Grey Coat Hospital was largely designed to support this expansion. The curriculum of the mathematical school included mathematics proper (particularly trigonometry and geometry), practical navigation (the use of nautical instruments, the taking of latitude, and the observation of sun, moon, and tides), and cartography (the use and drawing of maps and charts, land measurement, and the sketching of landscape features).[49] This kind of education would ensure a supply of competent young men to the Royal Navy, merchant ships, and commercial enterprises such as the HBC.

Britain's military and commercial ascendancy was thus partly a product of the rapid expansion of scientific knowledge and of the revolution in scientific method that began in the late eighteenth century and continued during the first half of the nineteenth. This period, roughly coterminous with Thompson's life, saw the grand project of the collection and ordering of all knowledge about the world, as in every discipline, data from around the globe was amassed and synthesized. Explorers and cartographers sought to chart lands and oceans; geologists probed the formation of the Earth; anthropologists and philologists searched for the origins of and relationships between peoples; naturalists collected and classified organic species; and meteorolo-

49 Ruggles, "Hospital Boys of the Bay," 10.

gists investigated atmospheric phenomena. Of particular importance in the British context were the three voyages of Captain James Cook (1768–79), which were consciously carried out as scientific endeavours, contributing to the development of all of these fields of knowledge, and the systematizing work of the botanist Sir Joseph Banks, who as president of the Royal Society from 1778 to 1820, linked science, exploration, and imperialism.[50]

Just as important as Cook's voyages are the texts they produced, which stand as exemplars of the tradition of rationalistic, enumerative exploration writing to which Thompson would contribute. No longer fanciful tales, the accounts of travellers became scientific documents, bearing a burden of proof and playing a key role in the dissemination of data about the Earth and its diverse peoples, plants, and animals. As Thompson writes after having calculated the elevation of Turtle Lake, "the age of guessing is passed away, and the traveller is expected to give his reasons for what he asserts" (iv.226, 256).

But scientific rationalism was not the only mode that would influence Thompson. His formative reading belonged to an earlier age, and if the five texts he mentions share many qualities with exploration texts – such as voyages to unknown lands, encounters with diverse peoples, exposure to grave danger, and the accomplishment of tasks through perseverance and ingenuity – they are also (the narrative realism of *Robinson Crusoe* aside) fantastic fictions.[51] Moreover, beginning at the turn of the nineteenth century, exploration accounts began to inspire, and be subverted by, key Romantic literary texts such as Samuel Taylor Coleridge's "Rime of the Ancient Mariner" and Mary Shelley's *Frankenstein*, which value emotion and express fascination with the supernatural. The careful reader of the *Travels* will discern the influence both of scientific rationalism, with its emphasis on objectivity and proof, and of the non-rational, the subjective, and the fantastic.

Thompson and his schoolmates often discussed how each "would behave on [the] various occasions" presented in their favourite books (iv.3, 7). Thompson soon had his chance to find out. On 20 May 1784, a few weeks after his fourteenth birthday, his time at the Grey Coat Hospital came to an end, and he was bound to the HBC as an apprentice. The Grey Coat treasurer

50 For a thorough treatment of these themes, see Tim Fulford, Debbie Lee, and Peter J. Kitson, *Literature, Science, and Exploration in the Romantic Era* (Cambridge: Cambridge University Press, 2004).

51 These works are emblematic of late-eighteenth- and early-nineteenth-century childhood; Charlotte Brönte has Jane Eyre read *Gulliver's Travels* and *Arabian Nights*, while Charles Dickens supplies David Copperfield with *Robinson Crusoe*, *Arabian Nights*, and *Tales of the Genii*.

paid the HBC five pounds, upon which Thompson became the company's indentured servant, theirs to keep, guide, and instruct for a period of seven years.[52] The HBC governors determined that Thompson would be trained as a clerk, and on 29 May 1784 the fourteen-year-old boy was placed on board the HBC vessel *Prince of Wales* at Gravesend. After a sojourn at Stromness in the Orkney Islands, the ship arrived at Churchill Factory on 2 September 1784.

In the *Travels* account of this outbound voyage, Thompson reflects ironically on his reading: "With such an account of the several regions of the Earth and on such credible authority, I conceived myself to have knowledge to say something of any place I might come to" (iv.3, 7). But Lemuel Gulliver, Robinson Crusoe, and Sinbad had not served him well, and while he was still in Britain he was confronted by the unknown. He recalls: "[T]he blue hills of Scotland were so distant as to leave to imagination to paint them as she pleased. When I awoke in the morning and went upon deck, I could not help staring to see if [what] was before me was reality for I had never read of such a place, and at length exclaimed, 'I see no trees,' to which a Sailor answered 'No no. people here do not spoil their clothes by climbing up trees'" (iv.3–4, 7).

When Thompson arrived at Churchill, a still stranger world awaited him. He felt his alienation from England deeply, reflecting in an early draft of the *Travels* that, as the *Prince Rupert* sailed away, he "bid a long and sad farewell to [his] noble, [his] sacred country, an exile for ever" (i.3, Volume II). But he soon came to know the land, people, and history of western North America and gradually assimilated his experiences into a system. This great intellectual synthesis is expressed most fully in the *Travels*, with its dual regional and chronological structure, capsule geographies, accounts of Native material culture, society, and beliefs, passages of historical information, and overarching awareness of the forces of change.

Thompson was probably the first to see the geography of western North America whole, perceiving the physical regions of the West and understanding how they affect organic life, economy, and human society.[53] He arrived in the Hudson Bay Lowlands (his "alluvials"), the band of low boggy land around the south and west shores of the bay. Beyond the bayside lay the Canadian Shield (the "Great Stoney Region"), the rocky swath of boreal

---

52 Fair Minute Book of Meetings of the Board of Governors, 1775–1791, 1648/11, Grey Coat School Records, City of Westminster Archives, Westminster; Register Book of Wills and Administrations of Proprietors, 1717–1819, A.44/1: 82, HBCA.

53 See the map "Physical Landscape and Thompson's Regions," following page lxiv.

forest arcing in a broad crescent from the Great Lakes to the Arctic, with its intricate system of waterways and rich population of fur-bearing animals; here Thompson spent much of his early trading career. This region is bounded on the west and south by a chain of large bodies of water (the "Great Valley of the Lakes"), through which Thompson ranged during those years, from the east end of Lake Athabasca to the shores of Lake Superior. After crossing these, he saw the transitional Parklands (aptly termed "Hills and Plains, Forests and Meadows"), with their bluffs of poplar, aspen, and oak interspersed with tall grasses. Finally he emerged onto the Prairie (the "Great Plains"), the vast region of shortgrass vegetation stretching across the heart of the continent, dominated by the bison, and the subject of the finest of the *Travels*' regional geographies (iv.125–33, 180–7). After 1807, Thompson travelled still farther west, crossing the Continental Divide and exploring the mountains and plateaus of the interior, before descending the Columbia to the Pacific.[54]

This land had been inhabited for millennia by diverse groups of Native peoples,[55] and during his HBC and NWC career Thompson travelled, traded, and visited with Natives belonging to most of the groups represented in the West. Indeed, much of our historical knowledge about many of these peoples comes from Thompson. He had his first and most abiding contact with the Cree (his "Nahathaways"), whom he encountered at the HBC's bayside settlements in the country north of Lake Winnipeg (the "Musk Rat Country") and inland along the Saskatchewan River. Thompson's familiarity with the Cree language is reflected in the scores of Cree words found in the *Travels*, while his wife Charlotte's maternal ancestry gave Thompson a personal connection to the group. North of the Cree, he met the Caribou Inuit who visited Churchill, as well as the Chipewyan north of Reindeer Lake. As he ventured west onto the Plains, Thompson met groups friendly to the Cree: the Assiniboine west of Red River, and the Piegan, Blood, and Siksika, members of the Blackfoot alliance, on the western prairie towards the Continental Divide. In the region between the Red River and Lake Superior he travelled among the Ojibwa, also allied with the Cree, and during his 1797–98 visit to the Missouri River he stayed at the agricultural villages of the Mandan and Hidatsa. Thompson is one of those responsible for fostering the migration of Iroquois,

54 For fuller consideration of these Far West regions, see the introduction to Volume II.
55 The pre-contact population of the region between the Great Lakes and the Rockies, and from the Arctic to the Missouri, has been estimated at between 15,000 and 50,000 (Friesen, *The Canadian Prairies*, 15). See the map "Native Culture Areas 1784–1807," following page lxiv.

Algonquin, and Nipissing hunters onto the Plains, having in 1800 received permission from the Piegan to introduce Iroquois hunters to the foothills of the Rockies. After crossing the Continental Divide, Thompson encountered the Kootenai and Flathead in the interior plateau, and Sahaptin and Chinookan groups along the Columbia.[56] Tellingly, Thompson had little or no direct contact with Sioux, Gros Ventre, or Shoshone people, reflecting their outsider status in the fur trade world.

The *Travels'* descriptions of these Native groups are complemented by scores of portraits of individuated Natives. Hosts, chiefs, hunters, companions, and guides, these figures range from the adolescent Chipewyans Paddy and Kozdaw who accompany Thompson on his arduous journey to Lake Athabasca to the two Cree elders on Duck Mountain who describe ancient traditions about the beaver. Among the most illustrious are the Piegan trio of the war chief Kootenae Appee, civil chief Sakatow, and the elder Saukamappee (in fact Cree by birth), and the Ojibwa leader Sheshepaskut. It is important to remember that there are Native voices and perspectives that do not appear in the *Travels*, which would complement or at times contradict Thompson's own and which, unlike European discourse, have not survived in written form.[57]

By the late eighteenth century, the Native groups Thompson encountered had become involved in the fur trade in degrees related to their proximity to Hudson Bay and the Great Lakes. The HBC had been founded in 1670, when a group of eighteen London investors received a royal charter granting them the exclusive right to trade and commerce over an area encompassing the entire drainage basin of Hudson Bay (although its parameters were then only vaguely understood). For the first century of its existence, the HBC conducted its business primarily through bayside establishments, which acted as trading posts for furs brought from the interior by Cree hunters and middlemen. Of particular importance were the factories at which Thompson spent his first two years in North America: York, founded in 1682 on a low peninsula between the mouths of the Nelson and Hayes Rivers, and Churchill, a site at the mouth of the Churchill River occupied definitively by 1717. Although the

56 For these groups, see the introduction to Volume II.
57 For example, Plateau oral traditions collected by Jack Nisbet suggest the insights that might still be gained by further work in this area. The testimony of the Kalispel Salish elder Alice Blackbear Ignace is particularly rich, including information about Thompson's first encounter with the tribe, the development of trading relationships, and Kalispel attitudes towards Thompson's Iroquois companions (Alice Blackbear Ignace, interview with Jack Nisbet at Usk, WA, 12 January and 10 August 1996, 25 September 1999, and 3 March 2000).

HBC made some isolated forays inland, with the journeys of Henry Kelsey in 1690–91 and Anthony Henday in 1754–55, for the most part it was content to wait for Cree traders to come down to the bay. But the initial success of this policy was short-lived, and the Company's perceived lethargy was frequently criticized in London, even leading to an official investigation by a House of Commons committee in 1749.

The HBC also began to encounter competitors more frequently. Beginning in the 1730s, with the activities of Pierre Gaultier de Varennes, Sieur de la Vérendrye, and his sons, the western interior was penetrated by traders working in the service of the merchants of New France, who travelled the long, arduous route from the St Lawrence Valley, up the Ottawa and French Rivers, through the Great Lakes, and so on to the West. The French fur trade differed from the English in that it was intended to function as a fluid, entrepreneurial network, rather than a colony or monopoly. Trade from New France soon led to the establishment of several posts throughout the Great Lakes and west onto the Plains as far as the forks of the Saskatchewan River.

Events in the North American theatre of the Seven Years War had profound implications for the fur trade, as the British conquest of New France, confirmed by the 1763 Treaty of Paris, briefly cut off trade from the St Lawrence Valley. Soon, however, the route from Montreal was again alive with commerce as established networks (and seasoned labourers) were taken on by newly arrived British merchants. With fresh capital, trade was prosecuted with new vigour, and the proliferation of inland posts cut deeply into the HBC's business. By the early 1780s, these several Montreal-based traders began to coalesce into a greater body, which came to be known as the North West Company. Unlike the chartered HBC, which was in the hands of a small group of English investors, with decisions made by a London committee, the NWC was operated by shareholding partners, many of whom worked directly in the western trade and who met annually at the rendezvous on the shores of Lake Superior. As an entity, the NWC may be dated from 1783, when a sixteen-share partnership was established, but it was in fact a rather fluid concern, for partners were brought in and others withdrew over the course of several reorganizations. The HBC could no longer afford, in the words of the prominent critic Joseph Robson, to "[sleep] at the edge of a frozen sea,"[58] and it had already spent a decade attempting to counter the moves of its rivals when Thompson arrived at Churchill. In 1774 Samuel Hearne had established Cumberland House at Pine Island Lake near the Sas-

58 Joseph Robson, *An Account of Six Years Residence in Hudson's-Bay, from 1733 to 1736, and 1744 to 1747* (London: J. Payne and J. Bouquet, 1752), 6.

katchewan, and Hudson House was built farther upstream in 1779. With the actual transactions of the trade now taking place inland, the HBC's bayside posts were developing into transhipment points and the headquarters for vast inland districts.

Just as Thompson came to know the Native peoples of the West, so he encountered the diverse peoples of the fur trade: the HBC's factors and post masters, appointed by the London Committee, the clerks and labourers under their command, the NWC's partners, and their workforce of French Canadian voyageurs.[59] Again, the *Travels* is studded with vivid portraits of individuals connected to the fur trade, such as William Tomison, the parsimonious Orkneyman who served as the HBC inland master, the profane veteran NWC voyageur François Babue, and the classically educated NWC trader Jean-Baptiste Cadotte *fils*, of mixed French-Ojibwa heritage.

Gerald Friesen writes aptly of the existence of two fur trades: the first, involving Native hunters and middlemen, was the means by which many furs passed to the second, shared by Natives and Europeans.[60] Still, the imperatives of the European economy remained peripheral to Native life across much of the West late into the eighteenth century.[61] But three significant forces of change had already preceded the Europeans from whom they emanated, spreading relentlessly from one group to the next through the West. Guns, entering the region from British and French posts in the northeast and east, had a profound effect on the efficiency of big-game hunting and the prosecution of warfare, while horses, entering from Spanish settlements in the southwest, had a comparable effect on mobility, hunting, and war. As Saukamappee relates in his narrative, guns and horses met on the Plains in the early eighteenth century, and the members of the Blackfoot alliance, the first to possess both, assumed a distinct power advantage in the region. But the most profound impact of the arrival of Europeans was the introduction of diseases new to the Native peoples of the Americas, such as smallpox, measles, and whooping cough, and Thompson arrived in the immediate aftermath of a devastating smallpox epidemic. Thought to have originated in 1779 in Mexico City, the epidemic reached Hudson House on the Saskatchewan River in October 1781, and in early 1782 spread north and east from

59 See Carolyn Podruchny, *Making the Voyageur World: Travelers and Traders in the North American Fur Trade* (Lincoln: University of Nebraska Press, 2006).

60 Friesen, *The Canadian Prairies*, 45.

61 For a useful discussion of Native-European trade relationships, see Richard White, *The Middle Ground: Indians, Empires, and Republics in the Great Lakes Region, 1650–1815* (Cambridge: Cambridge University Press, 1991).

Cumberland House, causing catastrophic population losses and leading to profound social and economic dislocation.[62]

4 IN THE WEST, 1784–1812

Thompson's first two years on the Bay, under Hearne at Churchill (2 September 1784 – 4 September 1785) and Humphrey Marten at York (14 September 1785 – 22 July 1786) marked his initiation into the world of work. Officially, Thompson was being trained as a clerk, or writer, which would qualify him to keep post journals, maintain records of accounts, and copy correspondence. But there was little to be done in this line, as Thompson recalled in the *Travels*: "On my complaining that I should lose my writing for want of practice, Mr Hearne employed me a few days on his manuscript, entitled 'A Journey to the North,' and at another time I copied an Invoice" (iii.9a, 27). For his part, Hearne mentions Thompson nine times in the Churchill post journal (usually as "Boy"), indicating that in addition to writing, the apprentice wove fishing nets and tied up ptarmigan quills.[63] Despite the HBC Council's request that Thompson "be kept from the common Men & employed in the Writings, Accounts and Warehouse Duty,"[64] Marten seems to have made scant use of Thompson's clerical skills, employing him mainly in hunting small game.[65]

It was the HBC's policy of developing its inland trade that drew Thompson from the bayside. Leaving York Factory on 22 July 1786, he did not return to the post until 7 July 1790. These four inland years are worth dwelling on, for as Thompson matured from adolescence to adulthood, he had several formative experiences that resonated throughout his personal and professional life: responsibility for keeping a post journal, a conversion episode, a winter spent learning a new language and listening to a Native elder, a crippling accident, and training in the art of surveying. Not coincidentally, the *Travels*' account of these years (27a–zd, 47–74) is the freshest and most vivid part of the entire work. The importance of this period can hardly be overestimated.

62 Two recent studies of this epidemic are found in Fenn, *Pox Americana*, and Paul Hackett, *A Very Remarkable Sickness: Epidemics in the Petit Nord, 1670–1846* (Winnipeg: University of Manitoba Press, 2002).

63 Churchill Factory, Post Journal, 12 September 1784 to 1 September 1785, B.42/a/104, HBCA.

64 London Correspondence Book Outwards, H.B.C. Official, 1781–1786, A.6/13: 128v–129r, HBCA.

65 York Factory, Post Journal, 12 September 1785 to 29 August 1786, B.239/a/86, HBCA.

The HBC's immediate need was for a writer to keep the first post journal at South Branch House, which was to be under the direction of the unlettered trader Mitchell Oman.[66] Thompson took his part in the building and running of the post and kept its records in the careful hand of a youthful clerk. After signing off on the log on 30 May 1787, he and his companions went downstream to Cumberland House. That summer, Thompson had an intriguing waking encounter with the devil, who appeared while he was passing the time alone playing draughts. While the episode, which is fully described in the *Travels*, is not rationally explicable, its symbolism sheds light on its function in the narrative and also in Thompson's understanding of his life. In several Celtic folktales, the playing of a game with a mysterious stranger (sometimes revealed to be the devil) often serves as a device to send the hero on a course of adventures.[67] While the most obvious meaning of the black-and-white draughts table is the action of opposed forces, the board may also symbolize the role of Divine Providence, as it does in Thompson's keystone text, *Robinson Crusoe*, in which the hero exclaims, "How strange a Chequer Work of Providence is the Life of Man!"[68] The incident seemed to serve as the seventeen-year-old's rite of passage into the world of adult responsibility, for it was time for him to put aside the thoughtless ways of childhood and enter seriously upon his life's work.

Appropriately, the apprentice's next assignment presented his greatest challenge yet; he was chosen to spend the winter of 1787–88 with a group of Piegan, acquiring their language and thus assisting in the HBC's development of direct trade with this group and its allies. The winter is notable not so much for Thompson's linguistic achievements as for the relationship that developed between the young man and his host, the revered elder Saukamappee. Cree by birth, Saukamappee had, like his guest, been exiled from home in his youth. He was probably in his eighties when Thompson met him, and he spent his old age much as Thompson later would, in telling stories of his life. For the apprentice, this was an opportunity to cultivate his listening ear and drink in tales of the region's past; and for the future writer of the *Travels*, the "narrative old man" (iv.277, 298) served as a model and touchstone.

Thompson passed the summer of 1788 at Hudson House, enjoying his second opportunity to keep a post journal, and in October he went upstream

---

66 For the location of South Branch House and other HBC posts, see the map "Thompson's Hudson's Bay Company Journeys 1785–1796," following page 166.

67 Tom Peete Cross, *Motif-Index of Early Irish Literature* (Bloomington, IN: Indiana University Press, 1952), 405.

68 Daniel Defoe, *Robinson Crusoe* (London: W. Taylor, 1719), 184.

to Manchester House, where an event occured that would alter the course of his professional career. On 23 December 1788 the youth fell down a river-bank while hauling a sled of meat back to the post; and as he tumbled, his leg became caught between the sled and a branch, breaking the tibia.[69] He was confined to a cradle bed for more than three months, and in May 1789 was sent down to Cumberland House, where he remained, unable to continue to York. He took his first steps with crutches on 17 August but only slowly and painfully recovered use of his leg, which on 1 February 1790 was still reported to be "bad."[70]

Looking back, Thompson discerned Providence's checker-work in this traumatic event, writing in the *Travels* that the accident "by the mercy of God turned out to be the best thing that ever happened to me" (27zc, 72–3). On 7 October 1789, while the young apprentice was still reported to be "lame," Philip Turnor arrived at Cumberland House. Turnor, the first HBC employee to be hired specifically as a surveyor (or, in the usage of the time, a "practical astronomer"), was engaged in the quest for a feasible trade route between the Saskatchewan country and the fur-rich Athabasca region. His appearance was a happy coincidence for Thompson, for over that winter of 1789–90 he "learned practical astronomy under an excellent master of the science" (27zd, 73). This was a decisive event, for the training bore fruit in his life's vocation. Observing the heavens, measuring the land, and using this data to create maps, Thompson would travel from the hills of Quebec's Eastern Townships to Cape Disappointment on the Pacific, from the shores of Lake Athabasca to the banks of the Missouri. He was known to Natives as the man who gazed at stars, and described as travelling "more like a geographer than a fur-trader;"[71] in later life, he proudly annotated his signature with the words "Astronomer and Surveyor." Thompson had also become a record keeper, for on 9 June 1790, the day he began his journey back to York Factory, he wrote the opening entry of his first regular personal journal; he sustained this activity for the next sixty-two years.

---

69 For a convincing analysis of this injury, see Jack Nisbet, "Breaking a Leg," *Pacific Northwest Inlander*, 11 April 2007.

70 Manchester House, Post Journal, 24 May 1788 to 2 July 1789, B.121/a/3: 29r, 51v, HBCA; Cumberland House, Post Journal, 9 June 1789 to 9 June 1790, B.49/a/21: 10r, 38v, HBCA.

71 This remark was made by the Pacific Fur Company clerk Gabriel Franchère on Thompson's 15 July 1811 arrival at Astoria, the PFC post at the mouth of the Columbia. See Gabriel Franchère, *Narrative of a Voyage to the Northwest Coast of America, in the Years 1811, 1812, 1813, and 1814* (New York: Redfield, 1854), 121.

On 7 July 1790, Thompson emerged at the coast, and he remained at York Factory for the next two years. In May 1791, on completion of his apprenticeship, the HBC's London Committee gave him a three-year contract as a writer at an annual salary of £15,[72] and the following year sent him mathematical instruments "at the Company's Expence & for his Sole use & Benefit."[73] Thompson was clearly being groomed as a surveyor, and in September 1792 he began to participate in the HBC's Athabasca project, on which Turnor had been engaged. This endeavour encountered a number of obstacles, the most serious of which was the tension between Joseph Colen, master at York Factory, who strongly promoted this project of exploration, and William Tomison, master of the inland posts, who wished to focus instead on the development of trade. Thompson was thus diverted from exploration, spending much of his energies in establishing and running trading posts in the region north of Lake Winnipeg. On 20 May 1794 his contract was renewed for a further three years, now as "Surveyor to the Northward," and his annual salary quadrupled to £60.[74]

The years 1790–96 have a shadowy presence in the *Travels*. Only one event is specifically dated to this period, an astonishing account of a caribou migration in May 1792 (iv.54–7, 112–14), but many events in the section on the "Musk Rat Country," centred at Reed Lake, also belong to these years (iv.61–81, 117–33). It is not until June 1796, when Thompson was finally able to press northward, making the journey from the Churchill River to the east end of Lake Athabasca, that the *Travels* regains a strongly chronological orientation (iv.85–101, 137–50). This journey, which ultimately failed to yield a practicable route, was followed by a lean winter at Bedford House on Reindeer Lake with Malcolm Ross. Then, on 21 May 1797, his latest three-year contract having just expired, Thompson abruptly informed Ross of his intention to leave the HBC's employ; he then departed from Bedford House, made his way about 60 miles (100 kilometres) south to Alexander Fraser's NWC post, and offered his services to the traders from Montreal.

This pivotal act provoked recriminations in the HBC in its immediate aftermath. Several of Thompson's HBC colleagues suspected collusion; on 2 August 1797, when Colen received the news of Thompson's departure, he wrote in the York Post Journal, "He has I fear been in treaty with them for

72 London Correspondence Book Outwards, H.B.C. Official, 1787–1791, A.6/14: 135v, HBCA.

73 London Correspondence Book Outwards, H.B.C. Official, 1792–1795, A.6/15: 26v, HBCA.

74 York Factory, List of Servants, 1783–1795, B.239/f/1: 64r, HBCA.

the last two years."[75] Thompson's presentation of the episode in the *Travels* is spare – he simply states, "my time was up" (iv.114, 169) – and his act has prompted a great deal of discussion among historians and biographers, who have judged it with attitudes ranging from harshness to sympathy. The collusion scenario has been most fully developed by Glover, who suggests that a 6 April 1797 visit by Fraser to Bedford House had the purpose of recruiting Thompson to the NWC.[76] Undoubtedly the NWC partners knew of the advantages that such an employee could bring to their firm, but the case will always remain circumstantial, for Fraser's visit could have been innocuous. The HBC and NWC shadowed one another throughout the West during this period of intense competition, and although they were rivals, the relationship between the two companies' employees in the field was marked not only by opposition but frequently by cooperation and mutual visits. However, Thompson's critics are on firmer ground in accusing him of treating the HBC unfairly in the manner of his leaving. His departure from Bedford House on the very day after his contract's expiration, having given his employers no notice of his intentions, clearly breaches the spirit if not the letter of his terms of employment. It is hard to characterize Thompson's brief *Travels* account of his actions (iv.114, 169–70) as other than disingenuous.

What attracted Thompson to the NWC? In the *Travels* he professes admiration for "the liberal and public spirit of this North West Company of Merchants of Canada" (iv.115, 171), calling chief partners William McGillivray and Alexander Mackenzie "gentlemen of enlarged views" (iv.114, 170). Thompson may have hoped that a more liberal and enlarged prospect would come to him too. In the short term he received ample opportunity to conduct surveys, and in the long term he may have anticipated greater financial reward should he attain a partnership.

His first task with the NWC was to attend its annual rendezvous at Grand Portage in the summer of 1797. The only surviving record of the mission assigned the new employee is that provided in the *Travels*:

> to learn the true positions of their Trading Houses in respect to each other; and how situated with regard to the parallel of the forty ninth degree of Latitude North ... [to] mark the line of the 49th parallel of Latitude ... especially on the Red River ... to extend my Surveys to the

75 York Factory, Post Journal, 8 September 1796 to 13 September 1797, B.239/a/100: 28r, HBCA.

76 Glover, introduction, xxxvi.

Missisourie River; visit the Villages of the ancient agricultural Natives who dwelt there: enquire for fossil bones of large animals; and any monuments if any, that might throw light on the ancient state of the unknown countries I had to travel over and examine.

(iv.114–15, 170–1)

These instructions (assuming that they are generally accurate) combine the hard-nosed business sense of McGillivray and Alexander Mackenzie, and an intellectual curiosity that may have emanated from Alexander's cousin Roderick, an NWC partner since 1795 and an ardent collector of material about the fur trade, Native peoples, and natural history. Knowing the relative locations of NWC posts had the obvious advantage of allowing for more efficient organization, while the search for remains of prehistoric animals and monuments of antiquity had high currency in the intellectual world of the late eighteenth century. Thompson's mission also reveals the influence of wider geopolitical developments. In 1797 the political map of the West remained ill defined. The 1783 Treaty of Paris that ended the American Revolution delineated a vague boundary between British possessions and the new United States of America, passing through the Great Lakes and west to Lake of the Woods; meanwhile, the Missouri basin formed part of Louisiana, which was nominally ruled by Spain from the end of the Seven Years War in 1763 until its reacquisition by France in 1800. The astute management of the NWC knew that these boundaries would soon have to be fixed, with consequent effects on trading rights. Indeed, Jay's Treaty of 1794 had provided for British evacuation in 1796 of posts located in United States territory. It was thus prudent for the NWC to know the precise location of its establishments in these boundary lands.[77] Finally, a visit to the Mandan villages would extend the NWC's commercial presence to an important trading centre, pose a modest challenge to Spanish sovereignty, and provide a glimpse of an agriculturalist Native group unique among its neighbours.

Thompson left the NWC rendezvous on 9 August 1797 and arrived back at Grand Portage just under ten months later, on 7 June 1798. During this time he rarely stopped travelling and surveying. That fall he made his way from post to post through the Swan River country west of Lake Winnipegosis and down the Assiniboine River, and then ventured in winter across the plains to the Mandan villages, returning back to the Assiniboine and continuing down that river, then up the Red River to make a spring journey through the

77 For Thompson's anachronistic reference to the 49th parallel, see note on 170.

sodden lands of the Upper Mississippi country, before emerging onto Lake Superior as spring turned to summer.[78] The tale of these ten months occupies a central place in the narrative, taking up about one-third of the *1850 Travels* (iv.120–238, 175–266), often in the form of a day-by-day account. The pride Thompson took in this period of his career is nicely encapsulated in his oft-cited record of the comment Alexander Mackenzie made on their meeting at Sault Ste Marie: "Upon my report to him of the surveys I had made, and the number of astronomical Observations for Latitude, Longitude and Variation of the Compass he was pleased to say I had performed more in ten months than he expected could be done in two years" (iv.236, 265).

Thompson spent the next several years travelling and trading on the north-western fringes of the NWC's sphere, working along the upper Athabasca and Saskatchewan Rivers, 1798–1802, and in the Peace River country, 1802–04, before returning to the "Musk Rat Country" north of Lake Winnipeg as a trader, 1804–06. The period from mid-1798 to 1807 leaves fewer palpable traces in the *1850 Travels* than the great circuit of 1797–98, since chronology is largely discontinued for a more thematic approach. Nevertheless, material drawn from the experience of these years includes the account of Natives at Lac La Biche, the story of the migration of Iroquois hunters onto the Plains, and temperature tables kept at Lac La Biche (1798–99), Peace River Forks (1803), and Reed Lake (1805–06).

Two key events in Thompson's life receive no mention at all in his narrative. The first occured on 10 June 1799 at Île-à-la-Crosse, when he married Charlotte Small, the daughter of NWC trader Patrick Small and a Cree woman whose identity is unknown. Despite the fact that this marriage lasted fifty-eight years – until Thompson's death – and yielded thirteen children, very little is known of Charlotte herself. Thompson mentions her sparingly in his journals, occasionally noting her trapping of small game, and only once in the *Travels*, when he states, "my lovely Wife is of the blood of [the Cree], speaking their language, and well educated in the english language; which gives me a great advantage" (iii.34a, Volume II); the passage was later revised and the reference to Charlotte omitted. In the absence of primary sources, Charlotte's identity has, in the words of Jennifer Brown, "undergone various permutations that tell us as much or more about later writers and their contexts, agendas, and priorities as about Charlotte herself."[79] We can safely say

78 See the map "Thompson's North West Company Journeys 1797–1812: Rocky Mountains to Lake Superior," following page 320.

79 Jennifer Brown, "Charlotte Small Thompson Personified: Identities in Motion," paper presented at the American Society for Ethnohistory, November 2006.

that Charlotte's linguistic and survival skills assisted her husband during his fur trade career, and note that, unlike many fur trade alliances, their marriage endured for life.

The second event occurred on 10 July 1804 at the NWC rendezvous at Fort William, when the partners, "having confidence in the Integrity and abilities of David Thompson heretofore one of their Clerks," elected him a wintering partner (that is, a partner based in the field rather than in Montreal) and allotted him two of the company's ninety-two shares, worth more than £4,000.[80] With this act, Thompson leapt in economic and social status, becoming a shareholder and decision maker in a company at the apex of its prosperity and power, and the peer of such men as McGillivray, Roderick Mackenzie, William McKay, Alexander Fraser, and John Gregory, who in years to come would take a prominent place in the business and political life of Lower Canada.

The eventual goal of Thompson's activities in the upper Athabasca and Saskatchewan regions was to push the fur trade west across the Continental Divide, and in June 1801 he had made a first, unsuccessful foray into the Rocky Mountains. On 29 October 1806 he arrived at Rocky Mountain House with the intention of resuming this pursuit and so entered on the final chapter in his fur trade career. The period from 1807 to 1812 was one of great accomplishment for Thompson: he established trading posts among the Kootenai and Flathead, unravelled the mysteries of Plateau geography, and travelled the entire course of the Columbia River. When he reached this point in the *1850 Travels*, though, Thompson had not touched on the events of these final five years of his fur trade career. For these, we must turn to the *1848 Travels*. Thus, a deeper consideration of this period will be reserved for the introduction to Volume II.

5 EAST

In 1812, at the age of forty-two, Thompson decided to retire from active participation in the fur trade. His appearance in Montreal with Charlotte and their five children that September was as much a watershed as his arrival in 1784 at Churchill and in 1797 at Grand Portage. The settled life of the East was a strange and new environment for both David and Charlotte; and at first they stayed close to the NWC world, making their home at Terrebonne,

80 William Stewart Wallace, ed., *Documents Relating to the North West Company* (Toronto: Champlain Society, 1934), 196–202. The two shares had become available after the expulsion of Jean-Baptiste Cadotte *fils*.

the company's depot on the Rivière des Mille-Îles north of Montreal, which was administered by Roderick Mackenzie as seigneur. In the fall of 1812, Thompson bought a house and property there, and he and Charlotte were formally married by the Presbyterian minister James Somerville. Over the next two years, Thompson was modestly involved in the War of 1812–1814. Although he did not see any military action as a member of Roderick Mackenzie's Terrebonne militia, at the request of the Royal Engineers' commander, Ralph Henry Bruyeres, he developed a proposal for a cannon frame.[81]

During these years he drafted his "Map of the North-West Territory of the Province of Canada," which was commissioned by William McGillivray to hang in the Great Hall at Fort William. The so-called Great Map is Thompson's cartographic masterwork. It shows a vast area of western North America, from the shores of Hudson Bay west to the Pacific Ocean and from 45 to 60 degrees North, delineating the great river systems of the Columbia, Peace, Saskatchewan, and Missouri, the great chain of lakes from Superior to Athabasca, and the Rocky and Coast Mountains, as well as the location of seventy-eight NWC posts. The map is both the fruit of twenty-three years of personal travel, observation, and survey, and an assemblage of data from several other figures, including Turnor, Alexander Mackenzie, and John Stuart, and it represents the first cartographic attempt to see the West whole.[82] It is thus a fitting visual counterpart to the *Travels*.

In early 1814 David and Charlotte experienced the loss of two children, five-year-old John and seven-year-old Emma, and the next year the family moved to Williamstown in Upper Canada, where they lived for twenty years amongst many former NWC partners, including John McDonald of Garth, Duncan Cameron, Hugh McGillis, and Simon Fraser.

Although Thompson's involvement in the War of 1812–1814 was minor, he was to play a pivotal role in the settlement of the issues that had led to the hostilities. Under the terms of the December 1814 Treaty of Ghent, the International Boundary Commission (IBC) was established in order to survey and settle the border between the United States and British North America. The IBC began its work in 1816, and from 1817 to 1827 Thompson served as the astronomer and surveyor under articles 6 and 7 of the treaty, dealing with

---

81 J. Mackay Hitsman, "David Thompson and Defence Research," *Canadian Historical Review* 40 (December 1959): 315–18.

82 Two versions of this map have survived, neither of which appears to be the original that hung in the Great Hall. The versions, both entitled "Map of the North West Territory of the Province of Canada," are FO925/4622: 1–10, TNA, and F443–6, AO. See maps.

the boundary from St Regis on the St Lawrence River to the northwest corner of Lake of the Woods. Eight summers were filled with rigorous travel in this area, as the IBC teams conducted field surveys, and the intervening seasons were devoted to the preparation of maps and charts, correspondence with officials, and several conferences in New York City and Albany.[83] Thompson considered this work to be of such significance that in later life he habitually signed himself "Astronomer and Surveyor Under the 6th and 7th Articles of the Treaty of Ghent." With this role, which came with an annual salary of $2,000, and with his continued stake in the North West Company, Thompson enjoyed high social status and material prosperity at Williamstown, and he was able to purchase several properties, including four large parcels of farmland in Glengarry County, two potash works, and an island in the St Lawrence River.

But this prosperity did not last. Reflecting on his post-IBC years, Thompson later wrote to British Secretary of State Lord Stanley, "[H]aving a large family, I endeavoured to increase what I had, but unfortunately lost all I had."[84] Like many retired fur traders, Thompson had invested heavily in McGillivray, Thain and Company, one of the successors of the NWC and since 1821 the Montreal agent of the HBC. In December 1825 the firm failed, and Thompson's loss of £400 marked the beginning of a decline in economic and social status. Bad loans and ill-fated ventures followed – in the most damaging episode, Thompson suffered heavy losses in 1830 when carrying out the terms of a contract to supply the British garrison at Montreal with firewood – and the global recession of the early 1830s compounded his financial problems. In December 1833, faced with mounting debts, Thompson found his properties in Glengarry County transferred to creditors, who auctioned them off three years later.[85] Then, in 1835, Thompson sold his Williamstown house to a local entrepreneur and moved his family to Montreal.[86]

The 1830s and 1840s were decades of rapid growth and change in Montreal. The population almost tripled, a combination of the natural increase of the French Canadian population and heavy immigration from England, Scotland, and Ireland. On his 1842 visit, Charles Dickens observed newcomers "grouped in hundreds on the public wharfs about their chests and

83 See Volume III for a selection of Thompson's IBC letters.
84 David Thompson to Lord Stanley, 27 December 1842, CO42/502: 468–9, TNA.
85 "Auction Sale of Real Estate ... Belonging to the Est. of Mr. D. Thompson" (Montreal: Starke and Company, 2 September 1836), McGillivray Papers, MG24 I3, vol. 2, fo. 694, LAC.
86 The Williamstown house still stands, as the "Bethune-Thompson House."

boxes,"[87] and eight years later Henry David Thoreau commented that the city "appeared to be growing fast like a small New York."[88] During these years Montreal emerged as the commercial capital of the Canadas, as timber and grain became dominant commodities and the colony's networks of railroads and canals channelled these goods to the city.[89] At the same time, Montreal was often in crisis; it suffered major epidemics – of typhus in 1847 and cholera in 1852 – while political and social tensions led to the Rebellions of 1837 and 1838, and to riots over the Rebellion Losses Bill in 1849.

For several years after his move to Montreal, Thompson continued to find occasional work, including canal surveys for the Canadian government's Board of Works, municipal street and lot surveys for the Corporation of Montreal, and small private jobs.[90] Although he had undertaken a rigorous survey of a potential canal route through Muskoka in 1837, by the early 1840s he was losing his ability to carry out fieldwork and to draw up charts promptly. In 1843 Governor Charles Bagot advised against the awarding of a public service post to Thompson, in terms that reveal clearly how the old man was regarded: "The Board of Works ... have, in consideration of Mr Thompson's long professional career, availed themselves of his services, on several occasions, when they considered that his very advanced age and feeble state of body, did not prevent his being moderately efficient ... Mr Thompson has [no] particular claim for permanent public employment."[91]

Thompson's situation became ever more dire through the first half of the 1840s. He sought relief by several means, asking for pensions, offering maps for sale, selling off personal possessions, including his collection of geological specimens, and continuing to canvas for public employment. Within one four-month period, he applied to be director of a registry office, surveyor to the North-East Boundary Commission, clerk with the HBC, and Montreal city surveyor. Although he received some financial assistance in 1844 from Montreal mayor Peter McGill and the prominent merchant George Moffatt

87 Charles Dickens, *American Notes for General Circulation* (London: Chapman and Hall, 1842), 2:203.

88 Henry David Thoreau, *A Yankee in Canada* (Boston: Ticknor and Fields, 1866), 14.

89 Montreal's commercial prosperity slowed between 1846, when the British parliament repealed the preferential Canadian Corn Act, and 1854, when the Reciprocity Treaty was signed with the United States.

90 He often performed other odd jobs. In 1840 he was hired to sell off the salvaged contents of a sunken schooner at Sorel (AO. 76.40–1), and in 1844 he was asked to arbitrate in a dispute between a brickmaker and his dissatisfied customer by calculating the number of bricks in a large pile (AO. 83.23).

91 Charles Bagot to Lord Stanley, 21 March 1843, CO42/504, no. 44, TNA.

(both former fur traders), this respite was temporary. By 1845 he was in need again and, funded by a £10 donation from Governor Metcalfe, in September Thompson travelled to New York City intending to sell his maps and drawings. Booksellers there expressed no interest, claiming that the market was already flooded with material. The scene was set for Thompson's great act of writing.

6 THE WRITING OF THE *TRAVELS*

As much as his second, less triumphant coming down to Montreal proved to be a defeat, it carried within it the seeds of Thompson's greatest work, for it was in the city that he at last turned to writing his narrative. The *Travels* did not appear from a void but is the work of a man who had spent a life concerned with words – as a writer, reader, storyteller, and thinker. Thompson's immense written output has been discussed above, and in the early 1840s this writing consisted of daily journals, draft prose sketches, personal and professional correspondence, and contributions to newspapers.

Thompson continued to read widely, as he had done throughout his life. His childhood reading had consisted of the fantastic fiction typical of his time, and as an HBC employee in his early twenties he had participated in a fur trade culture that had a key literary dimension.[92] To cite one example among several of its kind, when Thompson and George Charles opposed one another at Musquawegan Lake during the winter of 1804–05, they exchanged several volumes, including Oliver Goldsmith's *Essays* and six volumes by the French political writer the Abbé Raynal.[93] The texts that Thompson ordered from his HBC employers were drawn from a range of disciplines, including poetry (John Milton's *Paradise Lost*), philosophy (John Locke's *Essay Concerning Human Understanding*), essays (Samuel Johnson's *Rambler*), and rhetoric (Hugh Blair's *Lectures on Rhetoric and Belles Lettres*), in addition to grammars, dictionaries, and devotional works.[94] His wide-ranging tastes endured after he moved east, and he became a regular reader of the Montreal *Gazette* and *Montreal Herald*. He also obtained a run of the influential English periodical the *Quarterly Review*, in whose pages he could read the ideas

92 See Laura J. Murray, "The Uses of Literacy in the Northwest," in *History of the Book in Canada*, vol. 1: *Beginnings to 1840*, ed. Patricia Fleming et al. (Toronto: University of Toronto Press, 2004), 187–93.

93 AO. 16.30, 37.

94 Officers' and Servants' Account Book: Servants' Commissions, 1787–1802, A.16/111: 18r, 20v, 23r, 26v, HBCA.

of the foremost thinkers of his time.[95] On Sundays, Thompson read religious and devotional works, as reflected in the journal entry for Sunday, 7 July 1850: "the day, as usual, passed in reading the Prayers and the Scriptures."[96]

During the 1840s, Thompson's reading was drawn predominantly from the travel genre, which had become immensely popular. Newspaper advertisements for books of travel were common, and of the more than two thousand English-language titles in the 1842 catalogue of the Montreal Library, more than one-eighth fall into the category "Voyages and Travels."[97] In both the *Travels* and his daily journals he refers to several works that intersect with his own experience, including William Parry's *Journal of a Voyage for the Discovery of a Northwest Passage ... in 1819–20* (1821), John Franklin's *Narrative of a Journey to the Shores of the Polar Sea* (1824), John McIntosh's *The Origin of the North American Indians* (1843), and R.M. Ballantyne's *Hudson's Bay* (1848), as well as works set farther afield, such as John Lloyd Stephens's *Incidents of Travel in Central America, Chiapas, and Yucatan* (1841), and William Francis Lynch's *Narrative of the United States Expedition to the River Jordan and the Dead Sea* (1849).[98]

Thompson's writing and reading found their complement in his renown as a storyteller. In *The Shoe and Canoe*, the IBC assistant secretary and medical officer John Jeremiah Bigsby recalled Thompson's performance at an 1820 dinner party at William McGillivray's house in Montreal: "[H]e has a very powerful mind, and a singular faculty of picture-making. He can create a wilderness and people it with warring savages, or climb the Rocky Mountains with you in a snow-storm, so clearly and palpably, that only shut your eyes and you hear the crack of the rifle, or feel the snow-flakes melt on your cheeks as he talks."[99] Indeed, he preserved some stories orally and in

95 While the dates of Thompson's run of the *Quarterly Review* are not known, the *Travels* contains extracts from and references to articles in several issues of the early 1820s.

96 AO. 61b.11.

97 *Catalogue of Books in the Montreal Library* [Montreal: J. Starke, 1842].

98 In doing so, Thompson was participating in the early nineteenth century's growing culture of reading. As education became more widespread and means of communication improved, literacy rates rose dramatically, leading to the burgeoning publication of books, pamphlets, and periodicals, and the formation of libraries and reading rooms. So in January 1813 the freshly retired fur trader became a subscriber to the Montreal Library (AO. 30.14), and in November 1824 he and eight other Glengarry residents formed a society to promote the establishment of a reading room (AO. 59a.30).

99 Bigsby, *The Shoe and Canoe*, 1:114.

his memory for several decades before committing them to paper. As he concludes his account of the encounter with the devil, he writes that "it is now upwards of sixty three years since" the episode (27l, 57). In an 1889 letter to Tyrrell, the Thompsons' daughter Charlotte reminisces about life with her aged father: "In the latter part of his life, when at the age of seventy-five, he seemed to live his life over in talking to himself aloud over some anecdotes and jokes they played on each other in his travels with his companions. We would hear him laugh heartily over them with tears streaming down his cheeks. He enjoyed sitting in his office thinking over his travels."[100] Even when alone, Thompson had a deep need to narrate.

The *Travels* had an episodic beginning. In August 1840, Thompson noted in his journal that he had solicited the patronage of Charles Poulett Thomson, the newly named Lord Sydenham, governor of Canada, for the writing of a narrative; the proposal has not survived, but Thompson was refused within the week.[101] Then, in 1843, he produced a short "Travels" in his notebooks, consisting largely of a broad geographical description of the West (see Volume II).

Thompson turned again to the writing of a narrative in 1845, and this work formed the germ of the text presented in this volume.[102] This time, he attempted to establish a subscription scheme. His "Prospectus" first appeared in the Montreal *Gazette* of 6 October 1846. And it was full of promise: "This will not be a dry detail. Many curious facts will, for the first time, be given to the public, which will interest the reader. The Work will be published in two crown 8vo, or three duodecimo volumes, and the cost not to exceed Fifteen Shillings ... [I]f sufficient encouragement is received, the First Volume will be issued about the early part of February next."[103] Response must have been lukewarm, for no volume appeared in February 1847, and the propectus was discontinued in late March. Then, in August 1847, Thompson requested the patronage of the Hudson's Bay Company's governor, Sir George Simpson:

> I have drawn up my travels from Latitude 42° to 60 degrees north,
> about 1250 miles, and in Longitude to the Pacific Ocean ... [T]hey are
> simply a wild life in wild countries, without a trait of civilized life, but

100 Charlotte Thompson Scott to J.B. Tyrrell, 13 February 1889, J.B. Tyrrell Papers, MS26, box 90, Thomas Fisher Rare Book Library, University of Toronto.
101 Register of Provincial Secretary's Correspondence, vol. 749, no. 6090, RG4 C1, LAC.
102 For fuller details of the compositional process, see "Textual Introduction."
103 "Prospectus," Montreal *Gazette*, 6 October 1846, 4.

treating of every thing as in my time, taking a view of the formation of the country, it's Rivers Lakes, animals and the Natives, from Hudson's Bay to the Pacific Ocean, it could form perhaps a small Octavo of about 300 pages at five, or six shillings a volume, a humble performance. I am now correcting for the press to get it published by subscription, in hopes it may relieve our distresses, which are such that all the paper, pens and ink are the gift of charity. My hope, and request is, that you will be so good as patronise the work, of which I shall make honorable mention and that by your influence, a small subscription may be made for me P^r month, till I have got it corrected for the press, which may yet take me near three months, but not more.[104]

Simpson denied Thompson's request, although he did offer him a position at the HBC posts below Quebec City, which Thompson declined.

The three-month period anticipated in the appeal to Simpson proved to be overly optimistic. However, at this time, Thompson must have decided that writing was to be his sole occupation, because he gave up his search for other employment and enjoyed a time of great productivity, so that by October 1847 he was arranging the pages of his manuscript "to be fit for publication."[105] But the text was not completed to Thompson's satisfaction. In the winter he became ill and his writing slowed, and then in February 1848 temporary blindness interrupted it entirely. Thompson took up the pen again in May 1848 and enjoyed another prolific period, during which he also wrote several pieces for the Montreal *Gazette*. In May 1849 Thompson finally ceased to be a householder when he and Charlotte moved in with their son Joshua, and in July composition on the *Travels* was suspended for another extended period, because Thompson was afflicted by a nearly fatal case of cholera. The following spring writing resumed, though hesitantly, and in a final confident letter to Simpson, dated 18 April 1850, the author stated, "My travels are ready for publication, but I have not yet determined whether in New York, or London."[106] But Thompson no longer had the means to place his work in either of these metropolitan centres, and Montreal was a barren field for a work such as the *Travels*, since local publishers concerned themselves almost exclusively with textbooks, pamphlets, government publications, and cheap reprints.[107]

---

104 David Thompson to George Simpson, 17 August 1847, D.5/20: fos. 116–17, HBCA.
105 AO. 75.25.
106 David Thompson to George Simpson, 18 April 1850, D.5/28: fos 94–5, HBCA.
107 So when Thoreau visited the city in September 1850 (just as Thompson was concluding his writing) and visited a bookshop to examine works published locally, he was

In any case, Thompson was, by late summer 1850, hampered again by deteriorating eyesight. He last recorded looking at the *Travels* on 1 October and in subsequent journal entries reflected on the growing darkness of his world. On 27 February 1851 he wrote that he "could hardly read large print,"[108] and the next day he left off his journal definitively. In their last years, David and Charlotte lived alternately with their daughter Charlotte and her husband W.R. Scott, and their daughter Eliza and her husband Dalhousie Landell. In 1850 they moved across to Longueuil on the South Shore, and in 1852 they were living with the Scotts in Melbourne Township in the County of Sherbrooke.[109] By 1857 they had returned to Longueuil with the Landells, where Thompson died in February of that year, survived by Charlotte by less than three months.

7 PERSONAE

How is the *Travels* best understood? As we have seen, literary critics of the work have focused attention on questions of style, structure, and genre, seeking to identify the narrative's unifying principle. In the introduction to his edition of the work, Hopwood wrote that it is united by several themes, including adventure, the exposition of the West, and the revelation of the narrator, while in his edition he sought to accentuate the narrative aspects of the text, excising the most purely descriptive and thematic passages, in which historians and geographers are most interested. As we have seen, T.D. MacLulich argued that these thematic passages are more important than the chronological narratives they adjoin, and he claimed that the work possesses a "unity of vision"[110] that brings together all apparent disjunctions and digressions. Warkentin responded cautiously to the problem of unity by simply stating that it is the "passionate activity of Thompson's mind that shapes his narrative."[111]

The story of the *Travels*' composition, related above, and the state of the manuscript itself, described in the "Textual Introduction" below, help to explain much of the work's apparent disjointedness. But the central features

---

told that "there were none but schoolbooks and the like [and that] they got their books from the states" (*A Yankee in Canada*, 14).

108 AO. 61b.32.
109 1852 Census: Canada East, Subdistrict 430, Melbourne Township, Brompton Gore: 10a, LAC. Thanks to Mark Gallop and D'Arcy Jenish for this information.
110 MacLulich, "The Explorer as Sage," 98.
111 Warkentin, "David Thompson," 5.

of the narrative are due to more than historical and material circumstances; the *Travels* is a complex work because, as we have seen, its author was a complex figure. The work reflects all aspects of a man of diverse interests and aptitudes, who sought to educate and entertain, to tell the story of his own experiences, and to understand the land and people of the West. In his life, Thompson took on the roles of storyteller, interpreter, scholar, and philosopher; at the deepest level, he was a mediator, who placed disparate voices into dialogue with one another and who attempted to form syntheses. It is in these several roles that the key to the *Travels*' heterogeneity is to be found.

The Storyteller

In his account of the sojourn at Stromness during his 1784 outbound journey, Thompson describes the Reverend John Falconer, minister of the local kirk, as "a gentleman remarkable for a fine powerful voice and using plain language adapted to the education of his flock" (iv.6, 8), thus introducing the theme of speech even before setting foot in the New World. The *Travels* is the work of a master storyteller who could keep audiences in rapt attention, whether in a fur trade post, at the Beaver Club, or in the family home. Fittingly, many parts of the work can only be truly appreciated when read aloud.

Hopwood, the most literary minded of Thompson's editors, wrote of the "precision, speed, colloquial ease, character, and genuine humour" of the *Travels*' language,[112] and the pages fairly bristle with vivid anecdotes, in which Thompson sets the scene with economy, introduces complicating action, builds quickly to a crisis, resolves the situation, and ends with a reflection. Consider Thompson's account of his reception by William Tomison on his return to Manchester House in 1788, after wintering with the Piegan:

> On our arrival we received a hearty welcome. Mr Tomison was glad
> to see me, but did not like my appearance, he viewed me all round,
> and muttered "ragged, very ragged, can't be mended, must have a new
> jacket," which the tailor made for me. He had a scarlet vest which he
> put on on his arrival at York Factory took off when he left it, and care-
> fully folded and laid by for the next occasion, this was it's third year,
> and on looking at it, he thought it's color somewhat faded, one of the
> men said a little lye will freshen it; he gave it to the man to do so, he
> made the lye too strong and took most of the color out; when brought

112 Hopwood, introduction, 19.

to him the lower part of his favourite vest was nearly white, the rest spotted red and white a ghost could not have changed his color more; he turned it every way to be sure it was his very vest. As he had no more cloth of that color, he had one of blue cloth made.

(27x, 69)

Thompson's confidence, candour, and irony are clearly audible.

Perhaps the finest aspect of Thompson's storytelling art is his deft characterization, spare but incisive, as in the simple description of the mannerisms of the French Canadian trader Nicolas Montour, who visits Manchester House: "[E]very sentence he spoke or answer he made, was attended by a smile and a slight bow" (27g, 54); and he memorably evokes idiosyncratic speech patterns, as when Tomison looks over Thompson's worn jacket muttering, "ragged, very ragged, can't be mended, must have a new jacket" (27x, 69). This aspect of the work is not confined to humans; two of the most colourfully drawn individuals are Bruin, the barely tamed polar bear at Churchill (iv.11–iii.5b, 14–15) and the ermine that Thompson's experiments provoke to a "fighting humour" (iv.33f, 88).

Thompson populates the *Travels* with several other storytellers, so much of the work is related in the first-person voice of the people of the West. There are five extended first-person discourses: two aged Cree tell of the natural history of the beaver (iv.142–5, 194–5); the Ojibway chief Sheshepaskut and the Nor'wester Jean-Baptiste Cadotte *fils* speak of warfare with the Cheyenne and the Sioux (iv.198–203, 236–9); the Hudson's Bay Company trader Mitchell Oman relates tales of inland history and the smallpox epidemic of 1781–82 (iv.257–9, 284–5); and a young Piegan describes a war party against the Snake (iv.280–1, 300–1). The fifth narrative, that of Saukamappee, is the finest of all; personal and intimate, it continues for some fifteen manuscript pages and extends recorded Piegan history back to 1730 (iv.264–78, 289–98). The characteristics of these first-person discourses are the individuality and distinctiveness of the speakers, a clearly defined setting in time and place, and the unobtrusive presence of Thompson as listener.

The Interpreter

Thompson's second authorial guise, that of interpreter, appears on the outward journey when the boatswain of the *Prince Rupert* informs the young HBC apprentice that the Scottish fishermen who ask for old rope to make "fettels for their creels" are fashioning handles for their baskets and buckets (iv.2, 6). The fur trade world he entered was linguistically diverse, as English,

French, Scots Gaelic, and a myriad of Native languages coexisted, with Cree as the fur trade's *lingua franca*. Thompson habitually had to communicate in French and Cree, and it is telling that the HBC called upon him to learn Piegan.

Thompson's notebooks contain the vocabularies of several Native languages, and while these are not integrated into the *Travels*, Thompson frequently acts as interpreter for his reader, explaining the significance of scores of Native, especially Cree, words. To cite one simple example, he states of the polar bear that "he is, what the Indians call Seepnak (strong of life)" (iii.5b, 16). But Thompson sometimes goes beyond mere translation, to compare and even integrate linguistic expressions. Upon hearing some Cree at Rocky Mountain House call the rainbow "*Pee mah tis oo nanoo Che gun*," or the mark of life, Thompson reflects that it is described in similar terms in European discourse (iv.46–7, 104), and in referring to midges as "*midgeuks*," he grafts a Cree plural suffix to an English noun (iii.9, 26).

And Thompson is attentive to the subtleties of pronunciation, stress, rhythm; put simply, he has an ear. As he enumerates the various names in use for Saskatoon berries and pemmican, he comments, in an aside, that "the French ... murder every foreign word" (iii.228b, Volume II). He is attuned to the play of meanings. Among the Wawthlarlar of the lower Columbia, a certain species of salmon is named *quinze sous*; Thompson notes that this amuses his French Canadian companions, for whom *quinze sous* is a small coin (iii.274, Volume II).

But spoken language is not the interpreter's only concern. He also wants to read and explain the features of the land, the nature and behaviour of its organisms, and the customs of its Native inhabitants. He is attuned to all forms of discourse, from the symbolism of Piegan handshakes to the significance of colours used in post-battle face painting. So while travelling in the region of the Lake of the Woods, he notes that bundles of arrows left by Sioux warriors in the crevices of the rocks speak a threat of death to the Ojibwa (iv.121, 176). Thompson is especially interested in the meaning bound up in the minutiae of the environment:

> I had always admired the tact of the Indian in being able to guide himself through the darkest pine forests to exactly the place he intended to go, his keen, constant attention on everything; the removal of the smallest stone, the bent, or broken twig; a slight mark on the ground all spoke plain language to him. I was anxious to acquire this knowledge, and often being in company with them, sometimes for several

months, I paid attention to what they pointed out to me, and became almost equal to some of them; which became of great use to me.

(iv.59–60, 116)

This passage emphasizes the most important activity of Thompson the interpreter: his effort to incorporate into his own discourse a Native perspective. Thompson was a careful and attentive collector of aboriginal tradition and lore, and in describing what we would today term his ethnographic method, he stressed the need for long and intimate contact with Native people: "[M]y knowledge ... I collected from being present at their various ceremonies, living and travelling with them ... it was only in danger and distress that I heard much of their belief" (iii.34a, Volume II).

The Scientist

Writing to George Simpson in 1850, Thompson asserted that he would render his narrative "as interesting as possible not only to the general reader, but also to the scientific."[113] The figure of the scientist is Thompson's third role, for he was an enthusiastic participant in the grand project of his time – the collection and ordering of the world's geological, botanical, zoological, anthropological, and meteorological data. As science came of age, a number of concerns, particularly teleological questions, were dominant: the origins and nature of the earth itself; myriad natural phenomena, from meteor showers to magnetic variation; the classification of plant and animal species; the origins of peoples, particularly North American Natives; and the relationship between physical and geographical circumstances and human societies. A rigorous practitioner of the scientific methods of acute observation and controlled experimentation, Thompson brought an empirical approach and a rationalistic mind to all that came under his consideration. So after having carefully calculated the elevation of the Mississippi's source, Thompson states what could be the guiding principle of his time: "[T]he age of guessing is passed away, and the traveller is expected to give his reasons for what he asserts" (iv.226, 256).

Thompson's empirical observations pervade his work, and his statement that "curiosity chained me to the spot," made while watching a meteor speed towards earth (iv.72, 126), could serve as his motto. The passage on the mosquito is emblematic in this regard:

113 Thompson to Simpson, 18 April 1850, D.5/28: fos 94–5, HBCA.

The Musketoe Bill, when viewed through a good Microscope, is of a
curious formation; composed of two distinct pieces; the upper is three
sided, of a black color, and sharp pointed, under which is a round
white tube, like clear glass, the mouth inverted inwards; with the upper
part the skin is perforated, it is then drawn back, and the clear tube
applied to the wound, and the blood sucked through it into the body.
till it is full.

(iii.8, 25)

Even when being bitten, Thompson remained captivated. To his observations, Thompson added experimentation. Having fed a live mouse to a tamed
horned owl, he noted that the bird would not eat its prey until it had stopped
moving; as the following observation suggests, he then attempted to confirm
the pattern of cause and effect:

[O]ften while the Owl was watching the cessation of motion, with the
end of a small willow, I have touched the head of the Mouse, which
instantly received another crush in it's beak, and thus continued, 'till it
was weary, when loosening it's claws, it seized the Mouse by the head;
by giving motion to the body, it crushed it, and [I] have thus vexed it
until the body was in a pulp, yet the skin whole; by leaving the Mouse
quiet for about half a minute, it was swallowed; from seve[ral] experiments, I concluded, that to carnivorous birds, the death of it's prey is
only known by the cessation of motion

(iv.33a–b, 84)

The flowering of modern science could only happen with the spread of networks for the dissemination of data, and Thompson was particularly anxious
to participate in these learned networks. He corresponded with the Montreal
Natural History Society and the Smithsonian Institution, contributed several
pieces on natural history to the Montreal *Gazette*, and since his youth had
been in the business of sharing geographical knowledge through his maps. In
the late 1840s, the *Travels* became his prime means of integrating what he
had observed into developing systems of knowledge and sharing those findings with fellow men of science. At several points, the text reveals its author's
intellectual engagement with other thinkers, many of whom were his contemporaries and wrote, like him, of North America. As has been noted, the
Travels contains references to Parry, Franklin, and Ballantyne. But topics
much broader than travel engaged Thompson's interest. He consulted the
Moravian missionary John Gottlieb Heckewelder on the Native peoples of

Pennsylvania and the Swiss geologist Horace-Bénédict Saussure on the geology of the Auvergne region. His citations reach back into history, to Herodotus on the wars between the Persians and Egyptians, and to Roman historians on Gaul.

The Philosopher

Thompson went beyond observation and experimentation to reflection, and at these moments took on a fourth guise. He was a philosopher, if we understand philosophy in its general sense, as defined by Noah Webster in the year of Thompson's death as "an explanation of the reasons of things; or an investigation of the causes of all phenomena both of mind and of matter."[114]

This impulse to seek root causes pervades the *Travels*, as in, for example, Thompson's meditation on the ptarmigan:

> No dove is more meek than the white grouse, I have often taken them
> from under the net, and provoked them all I could without injuring
> them, but all was submissive meekness. Rough beings as we were,
> sometimes of an evening we could not help enquiring, why such an
> angelic bird should be doomed to be the prey of carnivorous animals
> and birds, the ways of Providence are unknown to us.
>
> (iv.22, 42)

Thompson's fundamental attitude, here and throughout his work, is a sense of wonder that ventures into the metaphysical realm, and he restlessly sought the principle that lay behind the pattern.

The *Travels'* many reflective passages on human nature, society, and politics also express this philosophical aspect. The story of Tapahpahtum, a Cree hunter who had begged Thompson to raise a wind for him, concludes with the thought, "It seems a natural weakness of the human mind when in distress, to hope from others, equally helpless, when we have lost confidence in ourselves" (iv.79, 131–2). In reflecting on the Piegan, Thompson notes that "almost every character in civilized society can be traced among them, from the gravity of a judge to a merry jester and from open hearted generosity, to the avaricious miser" (iv.293, 309). A limited environmental determinism underlies much of the *Travels*, as Thompson admitted in his 1850 letter to George Simpson: "As I have always held Mankind to be the Creatures of cir-

---

114 Noah Webster, *An American Dictionary of the English Language* (Philadelphia: J.B. Lippincott, 1857), 739.

cumstances, which he may modify, but cannot do away with I make this the foundation of the Life and manners of the Inhabitants."[115]

This aspect of Thompson includes his religious sense. As much as he employed personal observation, experimental method, and rational analysis of evidence, he did so within the context of a deep belief in Christian Revelation. The fourteen-year-old Thompson was scandalized by Samuel Hearne's profession of belief in Enlightenment rationalism, encapsulated in Voltaire's *Dictionnaire*, and retained throughout his life a personal providential faith akin to that expressed by Robinson Crusoe. Thompson is of the generation of Canadian men of science for whom, as Carl Berger puts it, "nature was the handiwork of God and its patterns and operations disclosed His wisdom, power and goodness."[116] Thompson's religious, reverential attitude provides the context for his sympathetic appreciation of Native religious beliefs, almost unique among his contemporaries.

The Mediator

The storyteller, interpreter, scientist, and philosopher cohere in the figure of the mediator. The *Travels* brings several sources into conversation with one another, and Thompson's greatest legacy is this juxtaposition of ways of understanding the world. Empirical observation, oral testimony, the scholarly record, philosophical tenets, and Christian Revelation are kept in a creative tension as Thompson's mind ranges over his experience of the West.

Thompson's writings on geology provide a good example of the way in which he attempted to integrate his sources. The empirical scientist in him employs the methodology of the foremost geologist of the day, Charles Lyell, who posited his mission in his 1833 *Principles of Geology*: "To reconcile the former indications of change with the evidence of gradual mutations now in progress."[117] Thompson's description of the shores of Hudson Bay, combining personal observation with local oral history, reveals how much the spirit of Lyell animated him:

[I]t's formation seems to have been the work of ages past, as well as of the time present, caused by the flux, and reflux of the tides ... within the memory of old men, in many places the land has gained from ¼

---

115 Thompson to Simpson, 18 April 1850, D.5/28: fos 94–5, HBCA.

116 Carl Berger, *Science, God, and Nature in Victorian Canada* (Toronto: University of Toronto Press, 1983), xiii.

117 Charles Lyell, *Principles of Geology* (London: John Murray, 1833), 3:3.

to ½ a mile on the sea; for more than two miles inland of the present shore, drift wood is found in tolerable preservation, showing the line of shore was once there.

(i.2, Volume II)

But he also includes Christian Revelation in his conversation. For him, the Creation and the Flood were historically recent events (in one of his later notebooks Thompson recorded the time elapsed between the Creation and the birth of Christ as between 4,004 and 5,872 years), and this leads to a difficulty in reconciling an emerging geological timeline with the revealed chronology. Thompson expresses the dilemma well, while asserting the power of the human intellect, when he states, "The Great Architect said 'Let them be, and they were' but he has given to his creatures the power to examine his works on our globe; and perhaps learn the order in which he has placed them" (iv,231, 261).

The *Travels*' passages on fossils nicely encapsulate Thompson's methods. First, he cites the published record on fossils east of the Mississippi: the Big Bone Lick site in Kentucky, where several discoveries were made during the eighteenth century, the Osage fossil deposits, found in 1838–40 by the German American amateur paleontologist Albrecht Koch, and a "fable" of the Ohio River, based on a passage in Thomas Jefferson's *Notes on the State of Virginia* (1785), where it is attributed to a delegation of Lenape warriors.[118] Thompson then provides negative evidence relating to the lands west of the Mississippi, stating that Sir John Franklin had found no fossils and that in his own travels, "not a vestige that these great Animals once existed in those parts could be found" (iv.133, 187). He concludes the conversation by bringing in Revelation, writing that ancient animals "were all destroyed by the Deluge, which also put an end to other races of animals, and thus the great Creator made the Earth more habitable for his favourite creature Man" (iv.133, 187).

Dialogue in the *Travels* often takes the form of a comparison between Native and European traditions and belief systems, an exercise that usually concludes with an implied or explicit criticism of Thompson's own culture. He writes, for example, that the Natives regard the aurora borealis as the dancing of their ancestors to the music of the world beyond, while the dark mind of the northern European sees the phenomenon as an omen of war, famine, and pestilence (iv.104f, 157). Or consider his comparison of

---

118 Thomas Jefferson, *Notes on the State of Virginia*, ed. David Waldstreicher (New York: Palgrave, 2002), 107–8.

Native and European ways of walking: "I have often admired the steady cautious step of the Indian in the Forests, he seems to be walking in a careless manner, yet very rarely breaks any branch, or parts of it lying on the ground. while we are breaking every thing that comes in our way" (iii.143, Volume II). This comparison between European and Native ways is sometimes expressed as an encounter between rationalism and supernaturalism. For example, a Cree hunter asks Thompson to conjure his gun so that he would have more success:

> I concluded that he had too slightly wadded the Ball with the moss of the Trees. it had fallen out; to reason with him was of no use, I therefore took his gun, and on each side of the middle of the butt of the gun, put some red sealing wax, and sealed it, taking care to give him several bits of coarse paper with which to wad the Ball; now confident of his gun, he went off, next day went a hunting, and was successful which he attributed to the sealed wax, of which he was careful.
>
> (iii.144–5, Volume II)

And yet Native figures are not always assigned the role of supernaturalists. When an axe goes missing from a work camp near York Factory, it is the Scottish HBC labourers who suspect the intervention of fairy-folk, while their Cree hunter discerns the work of a thieving wolverine and retrieves the missing tool (iv.33k–l, 92).

In many of these episodes of dialogue, the rational and empirical voice prevails. But there are areas in which the limits of the rational are reached, interpretation is confounded, and different voices must be held in tension. Such is the question of instinct and the Manito, which surfaces in relation to the topic of goose migration. Thompson, considering the accuracy with which the birds reach their destination, concludes that "the wise, and learned, civilized Man answers [that this is accomplished], by Instinct, but what is Instinct, a property of Mind that has never been defined; The Indian says the Geese are directed by the Manito, who has the care of them. Which of the two is right" (iv.15 paste-on, 35). The question reappears, with greater insistence, when Thompson recounts his encounter with a herd of migrating caribou in May 1792, about twenty miles up the Nelson River from York Factory. The herd takes two full days to pass, and Thompson the empiricist estimates the number of animals at more than three-and-a-half million. Upon his return to the factory, Thompson recounts his experience and attributes the migration to instinct. The Cree there reply with derision:

Oh Oh. then you think this herd of Deer rushed forward over deep
swamps, in which some perished ... down steep banks to break their
necks; swam across large Rivers, where the strong drowned the weak;
went a long way through woods where they had nothing to eat, merely
to take care of themselves. You white people, you look like wise men
and talk like fools. The Deer feeds quietly and lays down when left to
itself. Do you not perceive this great herd was under the direct orders of
their Manito and that he was with them, he had gathered them together
... and drove them on to where they are to go.

(iv.56–7, 114)

Thompson does not reply; he cannot, for he realizes that the appeal to instinct
really explains nothing, that it is used, as he puts it, in order to "shut up" the
reasoning powers. While Manito and instinct may be integrated into different systems of interpretation, in themselves neither is rational.

The same man who strove to convince his Native and French Canadian
companions that his astronomy involved no occult powers was at a loss to
explain the Ojibwa rite of the shaking tent, and he who described the mosquito so minutely also related the story of a waking encounter with the devil.
On occasion, he must simply admit incomprehension, and he ends his treatment of the Windigo phenomenon among the Ojibwa with the words "I must
confess, the more I studied these deep, sad, aberrations of the human mind,
the more I was involved in perplexity" (iii.91, Volume II).

The conversation between ways of understanding is perhaps at its most
intense on the topic of the Athabasca Beast. When the creature is first mentioned, it is January 1811, and Thompson and his men are ascending the
Athabasca River. Thompson's first reaction to the firm belief of his men in
the existence of an enormous beast is denial: "[A]ll I could say did not shake
their belief in his existence" (iii.230, Volume II). The men can provide no evidence beyond local Native legend, and the episode seems to conclude as just
another rational-supernatural dialogue, in which the former prevails. But the
following day Thompson sees something that confounds him: "[C]ontinuing
our journey in the afternoon we came on the track of a large animal, the
snow about six inches deep on the ice; I measured it; four large toes each
of four inches in length to each a short claw: the ball of the foot sunk three
inches lower than the toes, the hinder part of the foot did not mark well, the
length fourteen inches, by eight inches in breadth" (iii.231, Volume II). Still,
he would not work outside established categories: "I held it to be the track
of a large old grizled Bear; yet the shortness of the nails, the ball of the foot,

and it's great size was not that of a Bear, otherwise that of a very large old
Bear, his claws work away; this the Indians would not allow" (ibid.).

Thompson returns to the subject a third time during the narration of his
activities of October 1811 when he is headed back east. His men point out
a certain mountain and claim that a lake on its summit is the abode of the
beast. Thompson is plunged again into his state of perplexity and muses on
human nature: "I had known these men for years, and could always depend
on their word, they had no interest to deceive themselves, or other persons"
(iii.307, Volume II). And after having heard all of the voices, Thompson can
only conclude, "If put on my oath, I could neither assert, nor deny, it's existence" (iii.307, Volume II). The episode of the Athabasca Beast thus brings
together many of the elements of the *Travels'* polyphony: empirical observation, scholarly systems of classification, Native oral tradition, the question of
reliability of informants, diverse peoples, and humankind's "fondness for the
marvellous." The figures of storyteller, interpreter, scientist, philiospher, and
mediator likewise come together.

The *Travels* is alive with these voices – the storyteller keeping an audience rapt in deep attention, the interpreter guiding a reader through a diverse
land, the scientist engaged in an evolving learned discourse, and the philosopher reflecting on metaphysical questions. It is the figure of the mediator, who brings ways of finding meaning and understanding phenomena into
conversation with one another, who is the soul of Thompson's work and who
ensures that it will always remain fresh.

TEXTUAL INTRODUCTION

THE *TRAVELS* MANUSCRIPT

David Thompson created the narrative of his *Travels* in Montreal between October 1845 and September 1850. His surveying career had come to an end, and he sold many of his possessions to remain solvent while he and his wife Charlotte lived in a succession of humble rented quarters before finally accepting lodging with their children. Already troubled by chronic rheumatism, Thompson found his writing interrupted by a number of health crises, most seriously the temporary loss of eyesight and a severe bout of cholera. And yet as Thompson's vigour and standing diminished, he produced a manuscript of astounding life and power. Although written against a background of financial insecurity and physical frailty, the manuscript testifies to Thompson's enduring vitality of mind and determination of spirit, even as he entered his eighty-first year.[1]

The manuscript of the *Travels* consists of 702 handwritten pages. The Thomas Fisher Rare Book Library at the University of Toronto holds 673 of these pages (MS21),[2] while the Archives of Ontario holds twenty-nine (F443).[3] The Fisher manuscript is kept in file folders in two large manuscript boxes and is made up of 274 folded, intact bifolia sheets, 116 single sheets (some foolscap and some separated bifolia), and nine paste-ons of varying size. The Archives of Ontario manuscript is kept in a file folder in a manuscript box with other items by Thompson and consists of thirteen separated bifolia sheets (yielding twenty-six leaves) and three single foolscap sheets. Save for one paste-on,[4] the narrative is written on the rectos only. All manuscripts are in Thompson's hand, although several sheets contain interlinear notations by Joseph Burr Tyrrell, the editor of the first published edition of the *Travels*.

The manuscript of the *Travels* testifies to the life of its author, not merely through the events it recounts but in its physical nature. First trained as a

1 The story of these years is told in greater detail in "Historical Introduction," above.
2 This collection is hereafter referred to as Fisher MS21.
3 This collection is hereafter referred to as AO. The Archives of Ontario also holds 110 notebooks and field books by Thompson, which include his daily journals.
4 Page iii.9 paste-on.

clerk, Thompson wrote with care; in straitened circumstances, he exercised frugal stewardship of paper and ink; stricken with failing eyesight, his letters grew larger and more loosely formed. And like its author, the manuscript takes effort to interpret. Pages have been clipped, numbered and renumbered, sewn into gatherings and taken apart again; passages have been excised and paste-ons affixed, and some pages identified in indices are no longer extant.

But with the help of three material witnesses, the story of the writing of this work emerges. First and most informative is Thompson's daily journal, which contains hundreds of references to the writing of the *Travels* and, save for a gap from 25 April 1846 to 14 April 1847, is extant to 28 February 1851.[5] Second are three indices prepared by Thompson, which reveal how pages were arranged at distinct moments during the course of composition.[6] The third is the manuscript itself; its physical characteristics and cross-references often reveal the order in which pages were written and the manner in which they were arranged.

The testimony of these witnesses helps us to understand the *Travels* as a continually evolving work, in which drafts moved fluidly into one another, and which was frozen in an incomplete state when Thompson had to abandon his writing. Still, we can identify moments when the text reached a state of cohesion in Thompson's mind, before he turned to revise, rearrange, and compose anew.

The manuscript material shows evidence of four stages of development. By November 1845, Thompson had written twelve pages, which consisted of a description of Hudson Bay and an account of the author's activities from 1784 to 1786, including his arrival at Churchill and his work at York. I call this stub the "1845 Opening."

On 7 August 1847, Thompson completed a draft of 272 pages. This work includes writings on the Canadian Shield, a history of the fur trade and Native peoples of the West, and detailed accounts of several episodes in Thompson's career, including his travels of 1796–98 and his work west of the Rocky Mountains in 1807–12. All but the final thirty pages of this draft were taken over to the next. I call these thirty pages the "1847 Conclusion."

On 17 June 1848, Thompson brought a draft of 374 pages to a conclusion. Consisting mainly of pages drawn from the draft completed in August 1847, it includes a new twelve-page introduction on life at Churchill Factory

---

5 AO. 84.2–28; 75.9–141; 61b.1–32.
6 The first index is found with Fisher MS21 and was compiled in June 1848; the second is in AO. 78.73–84 and dates from late 1849 or early 1850; the third is in AO. 78.69–72 and was made in early October 1850.

and a new ninety-four page conclusion concerning Thompson's activities in 1811–12. I call this work the 1848 version of the *Travels*.

On 29 June 1849, a draft of 344 pages was suspended when Thompson fell ill with cholera. Sixty-six of these pages had been transferred from the 1848 version, and 278 are new composition. This draft contains a new account of Thompson's activities in 1796–98 and extensive geographical and ethnographical material, including such subjects as the Great Plains, Lake Superior, the Ojibwa, and the Piegan (including the renowned narrative of the elder Saukamappee). Then, between 26 May and 16 September 1850, Thompson wrote thirty-five pages designed to be integrated into the draft he had completed the previous June. These include a new opening, dealing with Thompson's childhood and his 1784 voyage to Churchill, and an account of his inland activities in 1786–90. I call this entire work, of 379 pages, the 1850 version of the *Travels*.

Four essays have remained with the Thomas Fisher manuscript, although never formally integrated into the work. Two were clearly intended for inclusion: a nineteen-page manuscript on rivers and lakes of North America, composed in May 1847 and entered on the first *Travels* index as an appendix, and a ten-page essay on Native origins, which Thompson promised to "reserve to the end of my travels."[7] Whether the two other manuscripts, a four-page essay on water and a ten-page piece on mountains, were meant to be included is unclear.

PROVENANCE

Upon the deaths of Thompson and his wife Charlotte in 1857, their eldest surviving son, Joshua Thompson, assumed ownership of his father's papers. Joshua sold Thompson's 110 notebooks, along with the twenty-nine AO pages, to the Canadian Crown Lands Department in 1859 for £600;[8] they appear to have been transferred to the Ontario Crown Lands Department at Confederation in 1867 and were placed in the Archives of Ontario in 1905.[9] Joshua sold the Fisher portion in about 1868 to the Toronto newspaper editor and reformer Charles Lindsey,[10] who in May 1895 sold the papers to the emi-

---

7 Page iv.256, during a discussion of the Natives inhabiting the Boreal Plains.

8 Minutes of Executive Council Meeting of 22 July 1859, State Book U, RG1 E1: 264–5, LAC.

9 AO F443, Finding Aid.

10 Charles Lindsey to J.B. Tyrrell, 13 January 1888, J.B. Tyrrell Papers, MG30 D49, LAC.

nent geologist and explorer J.B. Tyrrell for $400.[11] In 1939 Tyrrell passed the manuscript on to the University of Toronto, and in 1973 it was deposited in the Thomas Fisher Library.[12]

PUBLICATION HISTORY

Charles Lindsey had made an abortive attempt at editing Thompson for publication before selling the manuscript to J.B. Tyrrell. Tyrrell in turn canvassed a number of publishers in the United States in 1895 and undertook extensive revisions to Thompson's text before setting the work aside to concentrate on his geological and mining activities.

Tyrrell turned his attention to the manuscript again in 1911, when he submitted his revised manuscript of the *Travels* to the Champlain Society, an organization founded in 1905 to support the publication of scholarly editions of primary sources of Canadian history. With the help of University of Toronto history professor William Stewart Wallace, Tyrrell prepared the manuscript for publication, which occurred in 1916 as *David Thompson's Narrative of His Explorations in Western America, 1784–1812*. It includes the contents of 484 manuscript pages: 341 pages of the 1850 version of the *Travels*, published as Part I, and the latter 143 pages of the 1848 version of the *Travels*, published as Part II. Thus, 189 pages were omitted, including the "1845 Opening," the "1847 Conclusion," and earlier portions of the 1848 version. While much of the omitted 1848 material had been rewritten for the 1850 version, some pages left out by Tyrrell contain unique material on such topics as the Métis, the collection of maple sugar, and the construction of bison pounds. Nine pages of the 1850 version, concerning the igloo and the aurora borealis, also were omitted. In presenting the text, Tyrrell and Wallace made light changes to Thompson's captalization and punctuation, added paragraph breaks, and divided the work into chapters. Several errors of transcription were committed. Tyrrell provided a preface, introduction, and itinerary, and notes were written by Tyrrell, naturalist Edward A. Preble, and historian Thompson Coit Elliott.

In 1957 Victor Hopwood, a professor of English at the University of British Columbia, identified the twenty-nine Archives of Ontario pages as belonging to the *Travels*, and shortly thereafter the Champlain Society decided to publish a new edition of Thompson containing the recently found material. This

---

11 J.B. Tyrrell Papers, MS26, box 90, files 2, 9, Thomas Fisher Rare Book Library, University of Toronto.

12 Fisher MS21, Finding Aid.

work, edited by University of Manitoba history professor Richard Glover, appeared in 1962 as *David Thompson's Narrative 1784–1812*. In this edition the Archives of Ontario pages are published as Chapter IIA of Part I; aside from the addition of these pages, the contents are identical to those of the 1916 Tyrrell edition. No changes were made to the presentation of the text (other than a reduction in type size), and no corrections were made to errors of transcription. Glover retained Tyrrell's itinerary but provided a new preface and introduction; he condensed or eliminated many of the notes from Tyrrell's edition while contributing many of his own.

Victor Hopwood had planned a popular commercial edition of the *Travels* since the late 1950s, and this work was published in 1971 by Macmillan of Canada as *Travels in Western North America, 1784–1812*. Hopwood's is a highly selective text; his aim was to accentuate the chronological and narrative thrust of Thompson's work, so he excised most of its descriptive elements, including most of Thompson's geographical and ethnographic writings. The text of this edition is drawn from all parts of the *Travels* manuscript, and Hopwood was the first editor to include material from outside the corpus of the *Travels*, employing extracts from Thompson's notebooks and an account of his 1801 attempt to cross the Rocky Mountains. Hopwood altered Thompson's spelling and punctuation in conformity with modern conventions, and introduced paragraph and chapter divisions.

THE CURRENT VOLUME

This edition is divided into three volumes. Volume I contains the complete text of the 1850 version of the *Travels*. Volume II contains the "1845 Opening," the "1847 Conclusion," those parts of the 1848 version that were not reused later in the compositional process, the four Thomas Fisher essays, and an 1843 essay entitled "Travels of David Thompson." Volume III contains a selection of other writings by Thompson, including letters, reports, contributions to newspapers, and essays and prose sketches from his notebooks.

The sequence of pages in Volume I follows Thompson's last intended arrangement of the 1850 version of the *Travels*; appendix A, below, presents the contents of the 1850 version by date of composition. This edition presents Thompson's text as it stood when he stopped writing on 16 September 1850; his interlinear and marginal additions have been silently inserted, and any portions he cancelled have been silently removed. In the few cases where Thompson's cancellations shed light on the development of the text, these portions of excised text are included in braces { }. These include what had once been the opening lines of the work (iv.7, 9), the conclusion of a no longer extant account of the 1785 journey from Churchill to York (iv.13, 32), and the latter part of a sentence about Cree women (iv.38, 97).

Where what is written differs from what must clearly have been intended, readings are suggested in square brackets [ ]. Where pages are damaged, missing words are suggested in angle brackets < >. Readings derived from other sources – for example, where the passage is repeated elsewhere in the *Travels*, in a notebook, or in a newspaper contribution – are given in Roman type; readings that are purely hypothetical are in italic type. Paste-ons are indicated and are presented in a separate paragraph. Inadvertently doubled words have been silently removed. Manuscript page numbers are indicated in square brackets [ ] within the text.

Thompson's spelling has been preserved. While his orthography is usually regular, there are inconsistencies in the spelling of several non-English words, such as "pemmican" and "Wischejak." Obvious errors and spellings that deviate from Thompson's constant practice elsewhere have been corrected, with the corrections placed in square brackets [ ] where a letter or letters have been added, or included in the list of emendations (appendix B, below) where letters have been removed. All abbreviations other than "Mr," "Dr," and "St" have been silently expanded, and superscript letters have been lowered to the line (for example, "p^r" is expanded to "per," "do" to "ditto," "W^m" to "William," "Long^{de}" to "Longitude," and "geo" to "geographical," while "M^r" has been altered to "Mr").

More liberty has been taken with Thompson's often idiosyncratic punctuation. Where sense demands, periods and initial capitals have been inserted, and commas have been replaced by periods. An exception to this practice is the "continuous thought" sentence – a series of phrases that develops an idea from one phrase to the next without the use of periods.[13] There is a grey area between Thompson's period and his comma, and in cases of doubt, the one that best conveys his meaning is employed. Duplicated punctuation marks have been silently removed. The sometimes inconsistent use of

13 For example, on iv.207, 243, Thompson writes of the Common Loon: "The large spotted Loons were in every Pond that was open; this wiley Bird as soon as he saw us set up his cry, and was at a loss whether to fly or dive, for the latter the Ponds were too shoal and full of rice stalks; and before he could raise his flight he had to beat the water with Wings and Feet before he could raise himself, this exposed them to our shots, and we killed several of them, their beautiful spotted skins make favorite Caps for the Natives, and two Canoes of Chippaways being in company were thankful to get them."

spaces between the syllables of Native names and terms has been preserved.[14] Thompson's use of quotation marks is inconsistent. Direct speech may be framed by both opening and closing marks, introduced by only an opening mark, or may lack any marks whatsoever. I have silently regularized the use of quotation marks, supplying opening and closing quotation marks for all direct speech.

Thompson uses paragraph breaks sparingly, sometimes continuing for several manuscript pages without indenting a line. In addition to the breaks that do exist, I have begun a new paragraph where Thompson leaves a long space before a new sentence that begins on the same line, or where there is a long space left at the bottom of the preceding manuscript page. Further paragraph breaks have been added where the content suggests; these are indicated by the ¶ sign. The headings to each section of the text are taken from Thompson's description of his manuscript's contents in his three indices. They are italicized and placed in square brackets [ ]. In order to aid the reader in navigating Thompson's text, I have divided it into four chronological sections.

The annotations have been prepared with the needs of the educated general reader in mind. Footnotes explain historical contexts, identify animal and plant species and geographical features, define specialized terms, and indicate source materials used by Thompson. A few aspects of the annotations are worthy of particular mention. Where Thompson's text is chronologically based, footnotes provide volume and page references to the original journal sequences for the same time period, as found in the Archives of Ontario notebooks. Footnotes are included for all named individuals; for those who appear in passing, biographical information is provided in the note, while recurrent figures are given an entry in appendix 2: "Brief Biographies" (pp. 323–31). When referring to Native groups, where there remains great diversity of nomenclature, I employ names currently in most common use. Phonemic versions of Thompson's Cree words are transcribed using the methodology of Jennifer Brown and Robert Brightman in their edition of George Nelson's *"The Orders of the Dreamed."*[15] The scientific names of organisms are provided only once, at their first mention in the text. Finally, many footnotes contain references to parallel writings by Thompson,

---

14 For example, on iv.43, Thompson writes "Kee che Gah me," while on iv.45, he writes "Keeche gahme."

15 *"The Orders of the Dreamed": George Nelson on Cree and Northern Ojibwa Religion and Myth, 1823,* ed. Jennifer S.H. Brown and Robert Brightman (Winnipeg: University of Manitoba Press, 1988), 25–6.

whether elsewhere in the *Travels*, or in his notebooks, letters, or newspaper contributions; where these writings are included in the current edition, the appropriate volume number is given.

APPENDIX A: CONTENTS OF THE 1850 VERSION OF THE *TRAVELS* BY DATE OF COMPOSITION

The following table indicates the dates of composition of the 379 pages of the 1850 version of the *Travels*. Thompson finished his 1848 version on 17 June 1848 and immediately began to revise the work. The revision soon developed into the writing of the draft that would become the 1850 work, and the first thirty-one pages of the 1850 version, iv.1–iii.12, constitute the most bibliographically complex area of the manuscript, with pages dating from all periods of the work's composition. Thompson continued to alternate between adopting pages from previous drafts and writing new pages, up to manuscript page iv.106. From that point forward, all pages represent fresh compositions. Pages that have been cut during the compositional process are indicated after the date of composition.

iv.1–4	June 1850; prefixed to iv.5
iv.5–6	1849; prefixed to iv.7
	Top two-thirds of iv.5 cut away in 1850
iv.7–10	9–10 August 1847
iv.11–12 to iii.6c	21 June 1848
iii.5b–iii.6c	21–22 June 1848
iii.6d	10 August 1847
iii.6e	23 June 1848
iii.6f–h	1845–46?; originally numbered 25–27
iii.7–9	10–11 August 1847
	Top third of iii.7 cut away in June 1848
	Page iii.9 cut in 1850 when iii.9a–b inserted
	Bottom half of iii.9 became iii.9c
iii.9 paste-on; recto	1845–46?
iii.9 paste-on; verso	1850
iii.9a–b	28 June – 2 July 1850
iii.9c–12	11–14 August 1847
iv.13–24	1846–47
iv.14 paste-on	1849
iv.15 paste-on	1846–47
iv.25	1847–48

iv.26–7	1845?; originally numbered 29–30
	Bottom half of iv.27 cut away
27a–zd	6 July – 16 September 1850
iv.28–33k	1846–47; to iv.33k, "... and makes a good roast"
iv.33k–37	July 1848; from iv.33k, "His fine, large, lustrous ..."
iv.38	1846–47
iv.39–47	Early July 1848
iv.47a–b	1849
iv.48	1847
iv.49	1846–47
iv.50–96	Mid-July to early August 1848
iv.97–104	Late 1846
iv.104a–f; iv.104e paste-on	24–27 January 1849
iv.105–6; iv.105 paste-on	Late 1846
iv.107–241; iv.241 paste-on	Late 1848 – early 1849
	Eight and a half lines cut from foot of iv.124
	Three lines cut from foot of iv.195
iv.242–iv.313	7 March – 29 June 1849

APPENDIX B: EMENDATIONS

Manuscript page	Edition	Manuscript
27a	iron ware	iron wore
27a	necessarys	necessiarys
27c	winding	win, ding
27d	had on trowsers	had on trowsers on
27f	features	feadtures
27g	debts	dedts
27n	carefully led	carefully fed
27t	had not given	did not given
iv.62	on their origin	or their origin
iv.105	pierced	pierched
iv.209	nineteen	ninenteen
iv.223	small low steps	small low steeps
iv.231	happened in his time	happended in his time
iv.235	Peninsula	Peninsular

iv.246	feud	fued
iv.248	Villages	Villagers
iv.263	manly	mainly
iv.265	he showed	his showed
iv.272	arrows shod	arrow shods
iv.301	lives	lifeves
iv.301	country	countryr
iv.302	whom shall the	whom shall they
iv.303	not thinking this	not this thinking
iv.311	children	childrene

The Writings of David Thompson

VOLUME I

The *Travels*, 1850 Version

Page 1.

In the month of May 1784 at the Port of
I embarked
London in the Ship Prince Rupert belonging to the
Hudsons Bay Company, as Apprentice and Clerk to
the said company bound for Churchill Factory, on
the west side of the bay. None of the Officers or
men had their stock of liquor on board from the high
price of those articles. On the third morning at dawn of
day we perceived a dutch lugger about half a mile
from us a boat was directly lowered, and the gunner
a tall handsome young man, stept into her with four
men. They were soon on board of the lugger case of gin
was produced a glass tasted: approved the dutchman
was in a hurry, as he said a Revenue Cutter was cruising near hand, and he must luff off, a Guinea was paid
the case locked, put into the boat and was soon placed in
the steerage cabin of our ship. The case was of half inch
fir deal tacked together, and daubed red, on opening
it, there were nine square bottles of common glass, each
was full with the corks out close to the neck of the bottle, except one with a long cork, the one which the
gunner had tasted, it was taken out a glass handed
round and each praised it, but the Carpenter who
was an old cruiser wished to taste some of the other
bottles a cork was drawn, a glass filled, the colour had
a fine look, it was tasted, spit out and declared to be
sea water, all the others were found to be the same.

The gunner who had thus paid a guinea for three
half pints of gin the contents of the bottle, got into a
fretting humour, but to no purpose the dutchman was
luffing off in fine style. The next morning about
                                                        Ten.
                                                        and

[1784 *Embark at London for Hudson Bay and meet a dutch Lugger with Gin &c A Boat from the deep sea fishery &c. Arrive at Stromness. lay 3 weeks. my school and Westminster Abbey. Books read [at] school. Kelp Kilns &c, burning Kelp*]

[iv.1][1] In the month of May 1784 at the Port of London I embarked in the Ship Prince Rupert belonging to the Hudsons Bay Company, as App[r]entice and Clerk to the said company, bound for Churchill Factory, on the west side of the bay.[2] None of the Officers or Men had their stock of liquor on board from the high price of those Articles. On the third morning at dawn of day, we perceived a dutch lugger[3] about half a mile from us, a boat was directly lowered, and the gunner a tall handsome young man, stept into her with four men, they were soon on board of the lugger, a case of Gin was produced, a glass tasted; approved, the dutchman was in a hurry, as he said a Revenue Cutter was cruising near hand, and he must luff off;[4] a Guinea was paid the case locked, put into the boat, and was soon placed in the steerage cabin of our ship. The case was of half inch boards tacked together, and daubed red, on opening it, there were nine square bottles of common glass, each was full with the corks cut close to the neck of the bottle, except one with a long cork, the one which the gunner had tasted, it was taken out a glass handed round and each praised it: but the Carpenter who was an old cruiser, wished to taste some of the other bottles, a cork was drawn, a glass filled, the colour had a fine look, it was tasted, spit out and declared to [be] sea water, all the others were found to be the same.

The gunner who had thus paid a guinea for three half pints of gin, the contents of the bottle, got into a fighting humour, but to no purpose, the dutchman was luffling off in fine style. The next morning about [iv.2] sun rise, the hills of Scotland lying blue in the western horizon, to the east of us about two miles, we saw a boat with six men coming from the deep sea fishing, the wind was light, and they soon came along side, they were fine manly, hardy looking men, they were sitting up to their knees in fish, for the boat

1 For the conventions of page numbering of the *Travels* manuscript, see note on ix.
2 The *Prince Rupert* sailed from Gravesend on 29 May under the command of Captain Joshua Tunstall, travelling in consort with the *Sea Horse* and *King George*. Ship's Log, *Prince Rupert*, C.1/906: 1v, Hudson's Bay Company Archives (hereafter HBCA).
3 A small vessel with two or three masts, each carrying a four-cornered sail.
4 To bring the head of a vessel nearer to the wind.

was full of the various kinds they had caught. Our Captain bought some fine halibitt and skate fish from them for which they would not take money, but old rope in exchange to mak[e] fettels for their creels, these words I did not understand until the Boatswain, who was a Scotchman told me it was to make rope handles to their baskets and buckets. Our captain pleased with his bargain told me to give them a hat full of biscuit, umbrella's were not in those days, but our broad brimmed hats served for both purposes. Pleased with the ruddy looks of them, I filled my hat as full as it could hold, and had to carry it by the edges of the brim, as I passed by the Captain I heard him give me a hearty curse, and saying I'll never send him for biscuit again; but the boats crew were so pleased they told me to hand down a bucket, which they filled with fresh caught herrings, a great relief from salt meat.

On the sixth day about 9 PM we anchored in the harbour of Stromness, where the three ships bound for Hudsons Bay had to wait for final instructions and sailing orders. As there were no telegraphs in those [days] we were delayed three weeks.[5]

Until this Voyage I had passed my life near to Westminster Abbey the last seven year in the grey coat s[c]hool on royal foundation. This school [iv.3] was formerly something of a Monastery and belonged to Westminster Abbey from which it was taken at the suppression of the monastic order but not finally settled until the reign of Queen Anne. It is still held of the Dean and Chapter of the Abbey by the Tenure of paying a peper corn to the said Dean and Chapter on a certain day, which the Governors annually pay.[6]

During the year, our holidays at different times were about eighteen to twenty days, the greatest part of which I spent in this venerable Abbey and it's cloisters, reading the monumental inscriptions and often as possible Henry the seventh chapel. My strolls were to London Bridge Chelsea and Vauxhal and S'James's Park. Books in those days were scarce and dear and most of the scholars got the loan of such books as his parents could lend him, those which pleased us most were the Tales of the Genii, the Persian, and Arabian

---

5 The ships dropped anchor at Stromness on 6 June and resumed their voyage on 3 July. C.1/906: 5v, 8r, HBCA.

6 The Grey Coat School was founded in 1698 and received a royal charter in 1706. Thompson was presented for admission on 29 April 1777 by Abraham Acworth of Westminster and on 30 December 1783 was selected by the school's governors for HBC employ. Fair Minute Book of Meetings of the Board of Governors 1775–1791, Grey Coat School Records, 1648/11, Westminster Archives; Ruggles, "Hospital Boys of the Bay."

Tales, with Robinson Cruscoe and Gullivers Travels:[7] these gave us many subjects for discussion and how each would behave on various occasions.[8]

With such an account of the several regions of the Earth and on such credible authority, I conceived myself to have knowledge to say something of any place I might come to, and the blue hills of Scotland were so distant as to leave to imagination to paint them as she pleased.

When I awoke in the morning and went upon deck, I could not help staring to see if [what] was before me was reality for I had never read of such a place, and at length exclaimed, I see no trees, to which a Sailor answered "No no. people here do not spoil their clothes by [iv.4] climbing up trees."

One of the first objects that drew my attention were several Kelp kilns for burning sea weed into a kind of pot ash.[9] The sea weeds were collected by a number of Men and Women their legs appeared red and swelled. The sea weeds were collected into baskets, the rope handles of which passed round their breasts, each helped up the load for one another, and as they carried it over rough rocky shore left by the ebb tide to the kilns, the sea water streamed down their backs.

The smoke of the fires of these kilns was as black as that of a coal fire. One day our Captain had invited the other captains and some gentlemen from the Island to dine with him, a little before the time, the wind changed, and the smoke of the fire of the kilns, came direct on our ship turning day into night. The Boatswain was ordered to go and make them put out their kilns, which they refused to do: upon which he threatened to send cannon balls among them to smash their kilns, but the sturdy fellows replied, "you may as well take our lives as our means, we will not put them out." Finding threats would not do, he enquired how much they gained a day; they said, when the

7 The first English edition of *Arabian Nights Entertainments* was published in 1706, translated from the French of Antoine Galland. *The Thousand and One Days: Persian Tales*, translated by Ambrose Philips, appeared in 1714, Daniel Defoe's *Robinson Crusoe* in 1719 and Jonathan Swift's *Gulliver's Travels* in 1726. *The Tales of the Genii*, an original English collection in the style of *Arabian Nights*, was written by James Ridley (under the pseudonym Charles Morell) and published in 1764. All five works were frequently reprinted.

8 For another account of his childhood, see David Thompson to Sir James Alexander, 9 May 1845, FO5/441: 101r–102v, The National Archives of the United Kingdom (hereafter TNA). See Volume III.

9 The Orkney kelp industry supplied British glass and soap factories with alkali-rich slag; kelp production was at its peak from 1770 to 1830. W.P.L. Thomson, *History of Orkney* (Edinburgh: Mercat Press, 1987), 207–11.

kilns burn well they gained ten pence; upon which he gave to each one shil-
ling. The kilns were then soon put out, the smoke cleared away and we again
saw day light. I could not help comparing this hard, wet labor for ten pence a
day, where not even a whistle was heard, with the merry songs of the plough
boys in England.

[*Orkney Isl[an]ds. its natives comfortable, Kind to each other. here the
Crews took stock of Gin for the Voyage. The Ships in the Bay separate for
different Factories, arrive at Churchill Factory*]

[iv.5] This place was to me a new world, nothing reminded me of Westminster Abbey, and my strolls to Vauxhall, Spring Gardens and other places,
where all was beauty to the eye, and verdure for the feet; here all was rock,
with very little soil, every where loose stones that hurt my feet; not a tree to
be seen, I sadly missed the old Oaks, under whose shade I sat, and played. I
could not conceive by what means the people lived; they appeared comfortable, and their low dark houses, with a peat fire, the smoke of which escaped
by a small hole, contained all they required.

They carried on a considerable contraband trade with Holland; which
from the very high duties on Liquors and other articles gave them a profitable
trade. None of the officers, and crews of the three Ships had provided them
selves [iv.6] with liquors for the voyage, as they knew these things could be
procured here, cheaper and better than in London. One afternoon, taking a
walk with one of the petty officers, we entered a low dark house, it was three
or four minutes before we could perceive the gude man, who in his home
spun blue coat was sitting alone by his turf fire; my companion enquired
how times went, and if he had an anker keg of comfort for a cold voyage;[1] he
said of late the Revenue Cutters had been very active, and stocks low; but he
could accomodate him, the price was soon settled; and the Gin found a place
in the ship, and thus it will always be with high duties,

¶ The Kirk was on the shore of the Harbor, the Minister was the Reverend Mr Falkner, a gentleman remarkable for a fine powerful voice and using
plain language adapted to the education of his flock, he appeared to be much
respected.[2] Altho' many of his congregation came several miles over a rough

1 An anker equals 8½ gallons or 32 litres.
2 John Falconer (1742–92), a native of Moray, was educated at King's College, Aber-
   deen, and served as Church of Scotland minister for Sandwick and Stromness from
   1779 until his death. Hew Scott et al., *Fasti Ecclesiae Scoticanae* (Edinburgh: Oliver
   and Boyd, 1928), 7:253.

country, yet his Kirk of a sunday was filled; every man woman and child came with their blue stockings and thick soled shoes neatly folded, under their arms, sitting down on the stones near the church, they were put on their feet, and thus entered the Kirk; on coming out the shoes and stockings were taken off, folded and placed under the arms and thus returned home; their behaviour remarkably good grave yet cheerfull with respect for each other, and kind attention to the women and children. In those days there was no Telegraph; it took three weeks to send Letters to London and receive an answer for sailing orders. We now held our course over the western ocean; and near the islands of America saw several ice bergs, and Hudson's Straits were so full of ice, as to require the time of near a month to pass them; this being effected the three ships separated, one for Albany and Moose Factories, another for York Factory, and the third for Churchill Factory at which last place we arrived in the beginning of September 1784.[3]

[*Description of Hudson's Bay and the manner of the Rivers that fall into it*]

[iv.7] {The travels of David Thompson in Hudsons Bay, and the interior Countries to the Pacific Ocean 1784 a 1812 being twenty eight consecutive Years, during which for the last twenty two years regular Journals of every day were kept: and are now in his possession}[1] Hudson's Bay including Jame's Bay, may be said to be an inland sea, connected to the Atlantic Ocean, by Hudson's Straits: it is in the form of a Horse Shoe; and in Latitude extends from 52 degrees to 60 degrees north; and from 70 degrees to 90 degrees west of Greenwich in the northern part; and covers an area of about 192.770 square statute miles. On it's west side it receives Seal, Churchill; the Kissiskatchewan[2] Hayes, Severn, Albany, and Moose Rivers; On the east side, Ruperts and several other Rivers, the names of which are unknown as they come from barren, desolate, countries. From Seal River leading south to Churchill River, about thirty six miles, the country is of granite rock,

3 The *Prince Rupert* arrived off Churchill Factory on 2 September and weighed anchor for England on the thirteenth. C.1/906: 39v, 41r, HBCA. Thompson had written of his arrival at Churchill in the "1845 Opening" (see Volume II).

1 When Thompson prefixed iv.5–6 to his narrative, he cut these words from the head of iv.7. Thompson had begun the "1845 Opening" with a similar description of Hudson Bay (see Volume II).

2 Here and elsewhere Thompson has altered "Nelson" to "Kissiskatchewan." He regarded the Nelson as the continuation of the Saskatchewan; the latter feeds Lake Winnipeg through Cedar Lake, while the former drains Lake Winnipeg, exiting the lake near Norway House.

along the Bay shore of which is a narrow stripe of marsh land, apparently the alluvial of Seal River. The granite rocks which bounds the sea coast from far to the north ward have their southern termination at Churchill River; in Latitude 58°.47' North Longitude 94°.3' West, then forms a retiring line from the sea shore; for 150 miles to the Kissiskatchewan River, up which the first Granite is found at the distance of one hundred and thirty five miles, being the borders of the most eastern Lakes: and this distance appears to be wholly alluvial; and to be of much the same width all along the Bay side; these alluvials especially of the Kissiskatchewan and Hayes's Rivers have high steep banks of earth and gravel intermixed, from ten to forty feet; the gravel and small stones are all rounded by the action of the water; the Rivers passing through this alluvial have a very rapid current with several Falls.

Churchill River where it enters the Sea, is a noble stream of about one and a half mile in width; on the south side it is bounded by a low point, of rock and sand; on the north side by a low neck of sand, with rock appearing through it; at the extremity of which the Point is about an acre in width, on which was erected about the year 1745 a regular, well constructed Fort of Granite: having about thirty cannon of six to eighteen pound shot. There was no approach to it but by the narrow isthmus of sand. The water was too shoal for three fourths of a mile to the middle [iv.8] of the River, for the Ships; and this was the only place a ship could come to. (It was at this Fort that Mr Wales, the Astronomer observed the Transit of Venus over the Sun in 1769)[3]

[*The taking of Churchill Fort. Cowardice of Mr Hearne*]

¶ In the War with the United States; and with France; in the year 1782 the celebrated Navigator (De la Peyrouse was sent from France, with one Ship of seventy four Guns, and two Frigates to take and destroy the Forts of the Hudson's Bay Company; In the month of August these Vessels anchored in

3 William Wales (1734–98) was one of the foremost English astronomers of the eighteenth century. Sponsored by the Royal Society and accompanied by Joseph Dymond, in 1768 he travelled to Prince of Wales's Fort, where he observed Venus pass between the Earth and the Sun on 3 June 1769. Scientists spanned the globe in order to view this event; while it was hoped that the data collected would enable a more accurate measurement of the distance between the Earth and the Sun, results were poor. David Sellers, *The Transit of Venus: The Quest to Find the True Distance of the Sun* (Leeds: Magavelda Press, 2001).

the Bay, about four miles north of the Fort: and the next day sent a Boat, well manned, to sound the River; at this time the Fort was under the command of the well known traveller Mr Samuel Hearne;[1] who had been in the naval service, he allowed the french Boat to sound the River to their satisfaction; without firing a single shot at them; from this conduct Admiral De la Peyrouse judged what kind of a Commander of the Fort he had to contend with; accordingly next day, on the narrow isthmus of sand and rock of a full mile in length which leads to the Fort, he landed four hundred men, who marched direct on the Fort, with only small arms, the Men in the Fort begged of Mr Hearne to allow them to mow down the French Troops with the heavy guns loaded with grape shot, which he absolutely refused; and as they approached, he ordered the gates to be opened, and went out to meet them, and surrendered at discretion; all the goods, stores, with a large quantity of valuable Furrs fell into their hands, the Fort was destroyed and burnt, but the stone walls of the Fort were of such solid masonry, the fire scarcely injured them. The french Commander declared, that had his sounding Boat been fired at, he would not have thought of attacking such a strong Fort, so late in the season, when there was not time for a regular siege. Mr Hearne was received with cold politeness, and looked upon with contempt by the french Officers.[2]

¶ (Note ... Mr Samuel Hearne was a handsome man of six feet in height, of a ruddy complexion and remarkably well made, enjoying good health; as soon as the Hudson's Bay Company could do without his services they dismissed him for cowardice; Under him I served my first year; It was customary of a Sunday for a Sermon to be read to the Men, which was done in his room, the only comfortable one in the Factory; one Sunday, after the sermon, Mr Jefferson[3] the reader and myself staid a few minutes on orders, he then took Voltaire's Dictionary, and said to us, here is my belief, [iv.9] and I have

---

1 For the French naval officer Jean-François de Galaup, Comte de la Pérouse, and the Churchill factor and renowned traveller Samuel Hearne, see appendix 2.

2 A French force of 400 men under the command of La Pérouse captured Prince of Wales's Fort on 9 August 1782. As Thompson reports, Hearne surrendered without a fight. Edward Umfreville, who in 1782 was at York Factory, exculpates Hearne for this defeat, laying blame on the HBC's negligence in assigning the post a garrison of only thirty-nine men. Edward Umfreville, *The Present State of Hudson's Bay* (London: Charles Stalker, 1790), 136–42. For a meticulous defence of Hearne's conduct during this episode, see Glover, "The Witness of David Thompson."

3 For Hearne's deputy and successor William Jefferson, see appendix 2.

no other;[4] In the autumn of 1785, he returned to England became a member
of the Buck's Club;[5] and in two years was buried);)

[*The seasons, freezing of the River. Salmon &c*]

¶ The present Factory is about five miles above the Fort, in a small Bay
formed by a ledge of rocks which closes on the River about five hundred
yards below the Factory, above which for seven miles is an extensive marsh
to the lower rapids of the River. The Factory is supplied once a year with
goods and provisions, by a Ship which arrives on the last days of August, or
early in September, and in about ten days is ready for her homeward voyage;
the severity of the climate requiring all possible dispatch. The cold weather
now came rapidly on, but as there was no Thermometer, we could only judge
of the intensity of the cold by our sensations, and it's actions on the land
and water. On the fifteenth day of November this great and deep River was
frozen over from side to side, and although the Spring tides of New and full
Moon rose ten to twelve feet above the ordinary level, no impression was
made on the ice, it kept firm, and it was in the middle of June the following
year when the ice broke up, and gave us the pleasant sight of water. About
the middle of October the Marshes and Swamps are frozen over, and the
Snow lies on the Ground; for about two months the Factory yard, inclosed
by stockades of twelve feet in height, was kept clear of snow, but in the latter
end of December, a north east snow storm of three days continuance drifted
the snow to the height of the stockades and over them, and filled the whole
yard to the depth of six to ten feet, which could not be cleared, and through
which avenues had to be cut and cleared of about four feet in width, and thus
remained to late in April, when a gradual thaw cleared the snow away. From
the end of October to the end of April every step we walk is in Snow Shoes.
The Natives walk with ease and activity, and also many of us; but some find
them a sad encumbrance, their feet become sore and their ankles sprained;

4 Voltaire (1694–1778) published his *Dictionnaire philosophique, portatif* in 1764.
  It is a key Enlightenment text, consisting of a collection of short essays on an array
  of philosophical and religious topics. Frequently marked by an ironic tone, the text
  rejects institutional religion.
5 The Noble Order of Bucks, a pseudomasonic organization, was founded in London
  in the 1730s. By the 1770s there were over a dozen Bucks lodges in London and at
  least six elsewhere, including one in Calcutta. Peter Clark, *British Clubs and Societies 1580–1800: The Origins of an Associational World* (Oxford: Clarendon, 2000),
  76.

with many a tumble in the snow from which it is sometimes difficult to rise. In the open season in the months of July and August, Salmon from two to five pounds weight are plentiful; two nets each of thirty fathoms in length by five feet in height maintain the Factory for three to four days in the week, this fish is not found south of [iv.10] Churchill River.

[*Large species of Hare. dress for winter. splitting of Rocks, rolled Gravel*]

¶ Peculiar to Churchill is a large species of Hare[1] it dwells among the rocks, it's meat is better than other Hares, it's skin stronger, the furr long and very soft, of a beautiful white; twenty two were caught, their skins sent to London and readily bought by the Barbers.

The country, soil, and climate in which we live, have always a powerful effect upon the state of society, and the movements and comforts of every individual, he must conform himself to the circumstances under which he is placed, and as such we lived and conducted ourselves in this extreme cold climate, all our movements more, or less, were for self preservation; All the wood that could be collected for fuel, gave us only one fire in the morning, and another in the evening, the rest of the day, if bad weather, we had to walk in the guard room, with our heavy coats of dressed Beaver, but when the weather was tolerable we passed the day in shooting Grouse.[2]

The interior of the walls of the House were covered with rime to the thickness of four inches, pieces of which often broke off, to prevent which, we wetted the whole extent, and made it a coat of ice, after which it remained firm, and added to the warmth of the House, for the cold is so intense, that every thing in a manner is shivered by it, continually the Rocks are split with a sound like the report of a gun. Every where the rocks are fractured from the well known effects of freezing water, this is very well for winter, but in the summer season the Rocks are also fractured; although more than half of their surface is covered with Ponds and rills of water, I could not believe that water thawing could produce this effect; but in the month of July I was sitting on a rock to shoot Curlews as they passed, when a large rock not ten yards from me, split, I went to it, the fracture was about an inch in width, in looking down it, about ten feet from the surface, was a bed of solid ice, the surface of which appeared damp, as if beginning to thaw; a few days after another large Rock split close to me, by the fracture, at the depth of about

1 Arctic hare (*Lepus arcticus*).
2 Willow ptarmigan (*Lagopus lagopus*) and rock ptarmigan (*Lagopus motus*). For a description of these species, see iv.20 (39–40).

twenty feet was a bed of ice in the same state; these Rocks are not isolated, they are part of an immense extent to the westward and northward, every where with innumerable fractures; among these Rocks are narrow vallies of rolled granite pebbles, now twenty to fifty feet above the level of the sea; which was once the beach of the sea; has the land [iv.11] been elevated, or the sea retired; who can tell what has passed in ancient times.[3]

[*October begins winter. Polar Bear and Grouse hunter. Bears killed, one tamed. fond of Molasses. his tricks. Polar Bear gives much oil. rarely killed by one shot*]

¶ By the early part of October all the birds of passage have left us for milder climes, and winter commences. The pools of water are frozen over, and ice on the river side. The polar Bear[1] now makes his appearance, and prowls about until the ice of the sea shore is extended to a considerable distance; when he leaves us to prey on the Seal, his favourite food: during his stay he is for plunder and every kind of mischief, but not willing to fight for it. Only one accident happened, it was in November the snow about eighteen inches deep. A she Bear prowling about came near to one of the grouse hunters his gun snaped, an[d] in turning about to get away he fell, fortunately on his back, the Bear now came and hooked one of her fore paws in one of his snow shoes, and dragged him along for her cubs; sadly frightened, after a short distance he recovered himself, pricked and primed his gun, and sent the load of shot like a ball, into her belly; she fell with a growl, and left him he lost no time in getting up, and running away as fast as snow shoes would permit him.

¶ The polar, or white, Bear, when taken young is easily tamed; In the early part of July the whaling boat in chase of the Beluga[2] came up with a she bear and her two cubs; the bear and one of her cubs were killed the other, a male, was kept, brought to the factory and tamed, at first he had to be carefully protected from the dogs, but he soon increased in size and strength to be a full match for them, and the blows of his [iv.12] fore feet kept them at

---

3 The phenomenon that Thompson observes is isostatic, or postglacial, rebound. Since the weight of continental ice sheets was removed at the end of the last Ice Age, some 11,000 years ago, the western shores of Hudson Bay have risen; the current rate of rebound is approximately one metre per century.

1 *Ursus maritimus*. An earlier version of this passage on the polar bear is on i.4–5 in Volume II.

2 Also known as the white whale (*Delphinapterus leucas*).

a distance. Thus Bruin continued to grow, and his many tricks made him a favourite, especially with the sailors, who often wrestled with him, and his growing strength gave them a cornish hug.[3] In the severity of winter when spruce beer[4] could not be kept from freezing, each mess of four men got a quart of molasses instead of beer, of which Bruin was fond as well as grog, and every Saturday used to accompany the men to the steward's shed when the rations were served to them, the steward always gave him some on one of his fore paws, which he licked into his mouth. On one of these days the steward and Bruin had quareled and as punishment he got no molasses; he sat very quietly while the steward was putting all to rights, but seeing him ready to shut the door, made a dash at the hogshead of molasses, and thrusting his head and neck to the shoulders, into it, to the utter dismay of the steward, he carried off a large gallon on his shaggy hair; he walked to the middle of the yard, sat down, and then first with one paw, then the other, brought the molasses into his mouth, until he had cleaned all that part of his coat, all the time deliciously smacking his lips. Whatever quarrels the steward and the bear had afterwards, the latter always got his ration of Molasses. On Saturday the sailors had an allowance of rum, and frequently bought some for the week, and on that night Bruin was sure to find his way into the guard room. One night having tasted some grog, he came to a sailor with whom he was accustomed to wrestle, and who was drinking too freely, and was treated by him so liberally that he got drunk, knocked the Sailor down and took [iii.5b] possession of his bed; at fisty cuffs he knew the bear would beat him, and being determined to have his bed, he shot the bear. This is the fate of almost every Bear that is tamed when grown to their strength.[5]

¶ This animal affects a northern climate and is found only on the sea side, and the mouths of large rivers but not beyond the ascent of the tide, and keeping the line of the sea coasts, appear more numerous than they really are. Some of the males grow to a large size, I have measured a skin when stretched to a frame to dry, ten and a half feet in length. The fore paw of one of them kil<led> at Churchill, weighed in the scales thirty two pou<unds> a decent paw to shake hands with, the claws are but only about three inches in length, the flesh is so fat and oily that a considerable quantity is collect<ed> for the lamps, and other purposes. The skin is loose, <and>

---

3 *Brewer's Dictionary of Phrase and Fable* defines this as "a hug to overthrow you."
4 Spruce beer may be prepared by boiling spruce twigs in water, adding molasses and yeast, then allowing the mixture to ferment.
5 This anecdote is related in almost identical form in Thompson's Montreal *Gazette* contribution of 24 January 1848; see Volume III.

when taken off appears capable of covering a much lar<ger> animal; he swims with ease and swiftness, and require<s> a good boat with four men to come up with him. Although the white bear is found along the coasts inhabited by the Esquimaux yet very few of the skins of this animal are traded from, or seen with, them, for the white bear tho' seldom he attacks a man, yet when attacked will fight hard for his life, and as he is, what the Indians call Seepnak (strong of life)[6] he is very rarely killed by a sing<le> ball; much less with an arrow that cannot break <a> bone; hence they must be unwilling to attack hi<m.>

The Nahathaway Indians[7] are all armed with guns, and are good shots, but they only attack this species of Bear when they are two together, and one after the other keep a steady fire on him, but a ball in th<e> brain, or heart is directly fatal.

[*Esquimaux their Coasts. their Houses of Snow. the dome, also the domes of the Mandans &c*]

¶ [iii.6] The Esquimaux[1] are a people with whom we are very little acquainted, although in a manner surrounding us, they live wholly on the sea coasts, which they possess from the gulph of the St Lawrence, round the shores of Labrador to Hudsons Straits, these Straits and adjacent Islands, to Hudson's Bay, part of it's east shores; but on the west side of this Bay, only north of Churchill River, thence northward and westward to the Coppermine River; thence to the McKenzie, and westward to Icy Cape, the east side of Behring's Strait. Along this immense line of sea coast they appear to have restricted themselves to the sea shores, their Canoes give them free

---

6 Cree *se'pinao*, "He is tenacious of life, he is long-lived; he is hard to kill (speaking of game which takes several shots)." Edwin Arthur Watkins and Richard Faries, *A Dictionary of the Cree Language as Spoken by the Indians in the Provinces of Quebec, Ontario, Manitoba, Saskatchewan, and Alberta* (Toronto: General Synod of the Church of England in Canada, 1938), 453.

7 Thompson always uses this designation for the Cree. See note on iv.36 (95).

1 Thompson would have encountered the Caribou Inuit. The Caribou were regular visitors to Churchill in the 1780s, somewhat supplanting the Chipewyan, who had been devastated by smallpox. The HBC employed the Caribou to hunt seals and beluga. Ernest Burch, "The Caribou Inuit," in *Native Peoples: The Canadian Experience*, ed. R. Bruce Morrison and C. Roderick Wilson (Toronto: McClelland & Stewart, 1986), 113. For the Inuit, see also Thompson's 2 February 1848 contribution to the Montreal *Gazette*, in Volume III.

access to ascend the Rivers, yet they never do, every part they frequent is wholly destitute of growing Trees, their whole dependence for fuel and other purposes is on drift wood, of which, fortunately there is plenty. The whole is a dreary, monotonous coast of Rock and Moss, without Hills or Mountains to the McKenzie River, thence westward the Mountains are near the shore. This state of the country obliges the Esquimaux to make their habitations in the winter of snow; as I have never seen one made, I shall give Captain Franklin's[2] description of one which he saw built by an Esquimaux whom he named Augustus, for himself and companion.

¶ "Having selected a spot on the River where the snow was about two feet deep, and sufficiently compact, he commenced by tracing out a circle twelve feet in diameter; the snow in the interior of the circle was next divided with a broad knife having a long handle into slabs three feet long, six inches thick, and two feet deep, being the thickness of the layer of snow. These slabs were tenacious enough to bear moving about without breaking, or even losing the sharpness of their angles, and they had a slight degree of curvature corresponding with that of the circle from which they were cut. They were piled upon each other like courses of hewn stone around the circle which was traced out, and care was taken to smooth the beds of the different courses with the knife and to cut them so as to give the wall a slight inclination inwards, [iii.6a] by which contrivance the building acquired the properties of a dome. The dome was closed somewhat suddenly and flatly by cutting the upper slabs in a wedge form, instead of the more rectangular shape of those below. The roof was about eight feet high, and the last aperture was shut by a small conical piece. The whole was built from within, and each slab wa[s] cut so that it retained it's position without requiring support until another was placed beside it, the lightness of the slabs greatly facilitating the operation. When the building was covered in, a little loose snow was thrown over it to close up every chink, and a low door was cut thro' the walls with the knife. A bed place was next formed and neatly faced up with slabs of snow which was then covered with a thin layer of pine branches to prevent them melting by the heat of the body. At each end of the bed a pillar of snow was erected to place a lamp upon, and lastly a porch was built before the door, and a piece of clear ice was placed in an aperture cut in the wall for a window. The purity of the material of which the house was framed the elegance of it's construction, and the translucency of the walls which transmitted a very pleasant light, gave it an appearance far superior to a marble building, and one might survey it with feelings somewhat akin to those produced by the

2 For Arctic explorer Sir John Franklin, see appendix 2.

contemplation of a Grecian temple reared by Phidias, both are temples of art, inimitable in their kinds" PP 265_266. 1820.[3]

¶ Thus the Esquimaux who live in the regions of ice and snow build perfect domes for their habitations, as well and neatly as the Mandane and Pawnee Indians on the pleasant, fertile, banks of the Missisourie River;[4] each of them with the materials the countries afford. While controversies among the learned in Europe have produced many volumes on the invention of the arch, and left it undecided, these Savages as we are pleased to call them, from time beyond tradition have builded and lived in domes, the most complete of all arches. Did this knowledge come from the East.

[*Dr Richardson account of a Esquimaux Village*]

¶ [iii.6b] From the Coppermine to the McKenzie River, a distance of five hundred miles in a straight line, Dr Richardson[1] found the Esquimaux numerous all along the sea coasts, and thus describes them,

¶ "Their winter huts are of a superior kind; they are met with in whole villages, constructed of drift wood trees, planted generally in the sand with their roots uppermost.

These Villages when seen thro' a hazy atmosphere, frequently resembled a crowd of people, and sometimes we fancied they were not unlike the spires of a town appearing above the horizon. The size and quantity of this timber is quite surprising; one straight log of spruce fir measured thirty feet, seven feet in circumference at the small end, and twelve a short distance above the root. There is such an abundance of drift timber on almost every part of the coast that a sufficient supply for a ship might be easily collected. In one Village was a large building for an assembly room, it was in the interior a square of twenty seven feet, having the log roof supported on two strong ridge poles,

---

3 The passage beginning "Having selected a spot ..." and concluding "... inimitable in their kinds" is taken from John Barrow, review of *Narrative of a Journey to the Shores of the Polar Sea in the Years 1819, 20, 21, and 22*, by John Franklin, in *Quarterly Review* 28 (January 1823): 386–7. Augustus (d.1833), whose Inuit name is given by Franklin as Tattannoeuck, belonged to the Caribou; he was well known at Churchill and served Franklin as an interpreter, guide, and hunter. Susan Rowley, "Augustus" in *Dictionary of Canadian Biography* (Toronto: University of Toronto Press, 1987), 6:753–5. This work is hereafter abbreviated as DCB. The igloo described here was built at Fort Enterprise in February 1821. The Greek architect Phidias flourished in the fifth century BCE.

4 For the Mandan and Pawnee, see notes on iv.164 (209, 210).

1 For the physician and naturalist Sir John Richardson, see appendix 2.

two feet apart, and resting on four upright posts. The floor in the centre, formed of split logs dressed and laid with great care was surrounded by a raised border about three feet wide which was no doubt meant for seats. The walls three feet high were inclined outwards, for the convenience of leaning the back against them, and the ascent to the door, which was on the south side, was formed of logs, the outside covered with earth, had nearly a hemispherical form, and round it's base were ranged the skulls of twenty one whales. There was a square hole in the roof and the central log of the floor had a basin shaped cavity one foot in diameter which was, perhaps, intended for a lamp. The general attention to comfort in the construction of the Village, and the erection of a building of such magnitude requiring an union of purpose in a considerable number of people, are evidences of no small progress towards civilization. Whale skulls were confined to the large building, and to one of the dwelling houses, which had three, or four, placed round it. wooden trays, and hand barrows were lying on the ground."[2]

[iii.6c] By the above description of a building we perceive the Esquimaux fashions his building according to the material he has to make use of, to the stiff, weighty, logs of wood he gives a square form; to the light, moveable pieces of snow the round form; it may be said all those people who frequently remove from place to place adopt this form of dwelling as most convenient, it is the form of all their tents, with the fire in the centre, every one sits round it partaking equally of the warmth of the fire; when a dwelling is required more permanent than a Tent, it naturally takes the form of a dome, not only for convenience, but it's form is also the best adapted to that equality of rank which they maintain among themselves.

[Seals at Churchill. their ice hole. the manner the Esquimaux kills them]

In the latter end of February and the months of March and April, from the mouth of the River seaward for several miles, the Seals[1] are numerous, and have many holes in the ice through which they come up: how these holes are made in the apparent solid ice, I never could divine. To look into them, they

2 This passage by Richardson, beginning "Their winter huts ..." and concluding "... lying on the ground," is drawn directly from a review of *Narrative of a Second Expedition to the Shores of the Polar Sea, in the Years 1825–26–27*, by John Franklin, in *Quarterly Review* 38 (October 1828): 349–50. The assembly room described here was found at Nuvurak, an Inuvialuit village at Atkinson Point on the Tuktoyaktuk Peninsula, which Richardson's party visited on 13–14 July 1826.

1 The western shores of Hudson Bay are home to the harbour seal (*Phoca vitulina*), ringed seal (*Phoca hispida*), and bearded seal (*Erignathus barbatus*).

appear like so many wells of a round form, with sides of smooth solid ice and their size seldom large enough to admit two seals to pass together.

[iii.6d] The Seals do not come up on the ice before nine or ten in the morning as the weather may be, and go down between two and three in the afternoon; they are always on the watch, scarce a minute passes without some one lifting his head, to see if any danger is near from the Bear or Man, apparently their only enemies. Three of us several times made an attempt to kill one, or more; but to no purpose, however wounded they had always life enough to fall into the ice hole and we lost them; and I have not heard of any Seal being killed on the spot by a Ball.

The Esquimaux who live to the northward of us, kill these animals for food and clothing in a quiet and sure manner: the Hunter is armed with a Lance headed with Bone or Iron. The latter always preferred: the handle of which, sometimes is the length of twenty yards (measured) made of pieces of drift larch wood, neatly fitted to each other, bound together with sinew, the handle is shortened, or lengthened, as occasion may require.

The Esquimaux Hunter in the evening, when the Seals are gone to the sea, examines their holes, the places where they lie, and having selected the hole, best adapted to his purpose; early in the morning before the Seals come up, goes to the ice hole he has selected, on the south side of which he places his Lance, the handle directed northward, the point of the Lance close to the hole, for the seals lie on the north side of the ice hole, and directing his Lance to the spot the Seals have been lying, having firmly laid the helve of his Lance, he retires to the end of it, and there hides himself behind some broken ice, which if he does not find to his purpose he brings pieces of ice to make the shelter he requires, lying flat on his belly. He awaits with patience the coming up of the Seals; the first Seal takes his place at the north edge of the hole, this is also the direction in which the Lance is laid; the other Seals, two, or three more, are close on each side, or behind; if the Seal is not in the direct line of the Lance, which is some times the case, he gently twists the handle of the lance until it is directly opposite to the heart of the Seal; still he waits with patience until the Seal appears asleep; when with all his skill and strength he drives the Lance across the hole (near three feet) into the body of the Seal, which, finding [iii.6e] itself wounded, and trying to throw itself into the ice hole, which the handle of the lance prevents, only aids the wound; the hunter keeps the handle firm, and goes on hands and knees to near the hole, where he quietly waits the death of the seal; he then drags the seal from the hole, takes out his lance and carefully washes the blood from it. When the hunter shows himself all the seals, for some distance around dive into the ice holes, and do not come up for several minutes. This gives time to the Esquimaux to place his lance at another hole, and wait the seals return, and thus he sometimes kills two of them in one day, but this is not often, as the weather is frequently stormy and cloudy.

[*Esquimaux, their persons. Tents &c. Weapons. dress. boots &c. their Kettles. Cookery Canoes. Bows and Arrows. manner of living &c temper &c*]

¶ The Esquimaux's are of a square, plump make, few of them exceed five feet eight inches in height, the general stature is below this size, and the women are in proportion to the men. Their features though broad, are not unpleasing, with a tendency to ruddy, they appear cheerful and contented, they are supple active and strong; from the land, in the open season, they have berries, and a few rein deer, but it is to the sea they look for their subsistence; the sea birds, the seal, morse,[1] beluga and the whale; living on these oily foods, they are supposed not to be clean, but the fact is, they are as cleanly as people living as they do, and without soap can be expected. All their cooking utensils are in good order. In summer part of them dwell in tents made of the dressed skins of rein deer, these are pitched on the gravel banks, and kept very neat, they make no fire in them to prevent being soiled with smoke, which is made near the tent. The salmon and meat of the rein deer they cure by smoke of drift wood of which they have plenty. They are very industrious and ingenious. Being for eight months of the year exposed to the glare of the snow, their eyes become weak [iii.6f] at the age of forty years almost every man has an impaired sight. The eye sight of the women is less injured at this age. They make neat goggles of wood with a narrow slit, which are placed on the eyes, to lessen the light.

¶ They all use Darts, Lances, Bows and Arrows, as weapons of defence, and for hunting; their Darts, and Lances are made of drift Larch wood, headed with bone of the leg of the Rein Deer, or a piece of iron, the latter preferred, and the length of the Dart is proportioned to it's intended use – for Birds, the Seal, the Beluga Whale, or the Morse: to the Dart, or Lance for the three latter, a large bladder made of seal skins, and blown full of air is attached by a strong line of neatly twisted sinew, this not only shows the place of the wounded animal, but soon tires him, that he becomes an easy prey, tho' sometimes with risque to the Hunter and Canoe. The Morse is the animal most dreaded, and he is allowed to worry himself to death before they approach him. Whale Bone is part of their trade, but whether they procure it by attacking the Whale, as they do the Morse or it is the spoils of

1 Thompson always uses this term to refer to the walrus (*Odobenus rosmarus*).

those thrown ashore, is somewhat uncertain. They are dextrous in throwing the dart, although their Canoes allow only the motion of the upper part of their bodies, and [they] seldom miss a sea bird at thirty yards distance. Their Bows and Arrows are employed on the Rein Deer, Wolf and Fox. They draw the Arrow well and sure, whatever they make displays a neatness and ingenuity that would do honor to a first rate european workman, if he had no other tools than these poor people have.

¶ All along the sea coast where the Esquimaux are found, there are no standing woods of any kind, the whole country is of Rock and Moss. The drift wood is what they wholly depend on for every purpose for which wood is required, and fortunately it is plentiful; brought down by the rivers from the interior countries, and thrown ashore by the waves and tides of the sea; their country every where exhibits Rocks, Ponds and Moss, a hundred miles has not ground for a garden, even if the climate allowed it: their cloathing is much the same every where, made of Rein Deer leather, and Seal skins. Both men and women wear boots, which come to the knee, the foot is made of Morse skin the upper part of seal skin with the hair off, the whole; so neatly sewed together as to be perfectly water tight: these boots are much sought after by the people of the Factories, to walk with in the marshes, where our boots cannot stand the water. They are worth six shillings per pair (at Quebec three dollars) and with care last two years, of open seasons.

Their Kettles are made of black, or dark grey marble, of various sizes, [iii.6g] some will hold four to six gallons, they are of an oblong form, shallow in proportion to their size, this shape serves for fish as well as flesh, they do not put them on the fire, the victuals in them is cooked by means of hot stones to make the water boil, to keep it boiling by the same means requires very little trouble; the kettles are kept clean, and in good order, polished both in the inside and outside; they set a high value on them, but prefer a brass kettle, as lighter and more useful.

¶ Their canoes are made of seal skins sewed together, and held to a proper shape by gunwales, and ribs made of drift Larch, and some times whale bone is added; they are very sharp at both ends and no wider in the middle than to admit a man; their length from twelve to sixteen feet, they are decked with seal skins so as to prevent any water getting into the canoe, the place to admit the man is strengthened by a broad hoop of wood, to the upper part of which is sewed a seal skin made to draw round the man like a purse, this the Esquimaux tightens round his waist, so that only the upper part of the body is exposed to the waves and weather; they urge along their canoes with great swiftness, by a paddle having a blade at both ends; the handle is in the middle, early habit has rendered him expert in balancing himself on the waves of the sea in these sharp canoes called Kaijack.[2] I never saw a european who could balance himself in these canoes for three minutes. Their weapons for killing sea birds, seals & are placed on the deck of the canoe, quite at hand, secured by small cords of sinew. For the removal of their families, they have canoes of about thirty feet in length by six feet in breadth called Oomiaks, made of seal skin, the gunwales and ribs of Larch wood, and whale bone; these are paddled by the women, and steered by an old man.

¶ Their Bows are made of the Larch found on the beach, they are from 3½ to five feet in length, made of three pieces of wood of equal lengths, and morticed into each other. At the back of each joint, or mortice, is a piece of Morse tooth, neatly made to fit the Bow, of nine inches long, a quarter of an inch thick, on each side thinned to an edge: the back of the Bow is a groove of half an inch in depth, leaving the sides 1/8 of an inch thick along the groove; this is filled with twisted, or plaited sinew, running alternately from end to end of the Bow, each layer secured by cross sinews. In undoing a large Bow, about four hundred fathoms of this sinew line was mea= [iii.6h][3] headed with bone, or iron, but being made of Larch, for want of better wood, which occasions them to be too large in proportion to their weight, and lessens their velocity; yet such is the strength of their Bows, they pierce a Rein Deer at one hundred and twenty yards: almost all their weapons are barbed.

When the winter moderates sufficiently to allow them to travel, they use a large sledge made of two runners of Larch, each runner six to seven feet long, six to eight inches deep, and four inches wide, each turning up at the fore part. The runners are fastened together by bars of wood let into the upper side of each runner, on these they lay, and with cords, secure all their baggage, utensils, and provisions; the men to the number of six, or eight, harness themselves to the sledge and march from campment to campment in quest of animals for food and clothing. The women carry the children, and light things, and sometimes assist the men. As soon as mild weather comes on, that they can dwell in tents, they willingly leave their earthy, or snow huts, and live in tents made of the dressed leather of the Rein Deer, which are pitched on clean gravel: they rarely allow a fire to be made in them, as it would soil the leather, but for all purposes make a fire without. When they lie down at night, they have their particular blankets made of Rein Deer or

2 The terms *kaijack* and *oomiak* are added in the margin of iii.6g.
3 The catchword "mea=" appears at the foot of iii.6g, seeming to indicate that the first word on iii.6h was to have been "measured." That Thompson continued instead with a discussion of the point of the bow may indicate a rupture in the flow of composition.

Seal skins, beside which, a large coverlet made of the same materials extends all round each half of the tent and covers every one. Generally there are two families to each tent.

In their conduct to each other, they are sociable, friendly, and of a cheerful temper, but we are not sufficiently acquainted with their language to say much more; in their traffic with us, they are honest and friendly. They are not of the race of the north american Indians, but of european descent.[4] Nothing can oblige an Indian to work at any thing but stern necessity; whereas the Esquimaux is naturally industrious, very ingenious, fond of the comforts of life so far as they can attain them, always cheerful, and even gay; it is true that in the morning, when he is about to embark in his shell of a Canoe, to face the waves of the sea, and the powerful animals he has to contend with, for food and clothing for himself and family, he is for many minutes very serious, because he is a man of reflection, knows the dangers to which he is exposed, but steps into his Canoe and bravely goes through the toil and dangers of the day.

[iii.7] The steady enemy of the Seal is the Polar Bear. How this awkward animal catches the watchful Seal, I could not imagine. The Esquimaux say, he prowls about examining the ice holes of the Seals, and finding one close to high broken ice there hides himself, and when the Seals are basking in the Sun and half asleep, he springs upon them, seizes one, which he hugs to death, and as fast as possible, with his teeth cuts the back sinews of the neck. The Seal is then powerless and Bruin feasts on him at his leisure.

[*The Beluga, or small white Whale. Boats. pursuit &c*]

Few Porpoises[1] are seen, but the Beluga, a small species of white Whale, are very numerous from the latter end of May to the beginning of September, their average length is about fifteen feet, and are covered with fat from three to five inches in thickness, which yields an oil superior to that of the black Whale.

This Summer the Company had a Boat and six Men employed for the taking of the Beluga. The Boat was of light construction and painted white, which is the color of this fish, and as experience has proved the color best adapted to them, as they often, in a manner, touch the Boat; while they avoid

4 The question of the origin of North American Natives was of abiding interest to Thompson. For his theory, see his essay "The Natives of North America" in Volume II.

1 *Phocaena phocaena.*

Boats of any other color. Those taken were all struck with the Harpoon, and often held the Boat in play from three to five miles before they were killed by the Lance, towing the Boat at the rate of five miles an hour; when struck they dive to the bottom with such force as sometimes to strike the harpoon out of them, and thus many escape; in some of those killed I have seen the harpoon much bent. Their young are of a blueish color, and in the month [iii.8] of July weigh about one hundred and twenty pounds, they are struck with a strong boat hook. The Beluga in chase of the Salmon sometimes runs himself ashore, especially up large Brooks, and Creeks. If it is ebb tide he stands every chance of remaining and becoming the prey of Gulls and the Polar Bear. The produce of this summers fishing, was three tuns of oil, which could not pay the expences. There is scarce a doubt but strong Nets well anchored would take very many, and be profitable to the Company.

[No *Spring. Musketoes. sad torments*]

After passing a long gloomy, and most severe winter, it will naturally be thought with what delight we enjoy the Spring, and Summer; of the former we know nothing but the melting of the snow, and the ice becoming dangerous: Summer such as it is, comes at once, and with it myriads of tormenting Musketoes;[1] the air is thick with them, there is no cessation day nor night of suffering from them. Smoke is no relief, they can stand more smoke than we can, and smoke cannot be carried about with us. The narrow windows were so crowded with them, they trod each other to death, in such numbers, we had to sweep them out twice a day; a chance cold north east gale of wind was a grateful relief, and we were thankful for the cold weather that put an end to our sufferings.

¶ The Musketoe Bill, when viewed through a good Microscope, is of a curious formation; composed of two distinct pieces; the upper is three sided, of a black color, and sharp pointed, under which is a round white tube, like clear glass, the mouth inverted inwards; with the upper part the skin is perforated, it is then drawn back, and the clear tube applied to the wound, and the blood sucked through it into the body, till it is full; thus their bite are two distinct operations, but so quickly done as to feel as only one; different Persons feel them in a different manner; some are swelled, even bloated,

1 This passage on the mosquito is celebrated as an emblem of Thompson's inquisitive mind, as it ranges from the minute examination of the insect's bite, to the effect of this bite on humans and animals, to the place of the mosquito in the wider environment.

with intolerable itching; others feel only the smart of the minute wounds; Oil is the only remedy, and that frequently applied; the Natives rub themselves with Sturgeon Oil, which is found to be far more effective than any other oil. All animals suffer from them, almost to madness; even the well feathered Birds suffer about the eyes and neck. The cold nights of September are the first, and most steady relief. A question [iii.9] has often been asked to which no satisfactory answer has ever been given, where, and how, do they pass the winter, for on their very first appearance they are all full grown, and the young brood does not come forward until July. The opinion of the Natives, as well as many of ourselves, is, that they pass the winter at the bottom of ponds, of water, for when these ponds are free of ice, they appear covered with gnats in a weak state; and two, or three days after the Musketoes are on us in full force:

[iii.9 paste-on; recto] This theory may do very well for the low countries, where except the bare rock, the whole surface may be said to be wet and more, or less covered with water, but will not do for the extensive high and dry Plains, where, when the warm season comes on, they start up in myriads a veritable, full grown, plague. We must conclude, that where ever they find themselves when the frost sets in, there they shelter themselves from the winter, be the country wet or dry; and this theory appears probable, for all those countries where they were in myriads, and are now under cultivation by the plough, are in a manner clear of them, and also the Cities and Towns of Canada.

[iii.9 paste-on; verso] But in America there always has been, and will be Woods, Swamps, and rough ground, not fit for the plough, but admirably adapted to produce Musketoes, and the Cows turned out to graze, when they return to be milked bring with them more than enough to plague the farmer.

[iii.9] In September the Sand Fly, and Midgeuks,[2] are numerous, the latter insinuates itself all over the body; the skin becomes heated; with itching; these cease at Sun set, but remain until the season becomes cold. October puts an end to all these plagues. It is a curious fact the farther to the northward, the more, and more, numerous are all these flies, but their time is short.

[iii.9a][3] While these insects are so numerous they are a terrour to every creature on dry lands if swamps may be so called, the dogs howl, roll them-

2 Sandflies and midges are small biting insects of the order *Diptera*; sandflies belong to the family *Psychodidae*, and midges to the family *Chironomidae*. In his use of the term "midgeuks," Thompson adds a Cree animate plural suffix to the English word.
3 Pages iii.9a–b are a bifolium written 28 June to 2 July 1850 and share many affinities with iv.1–4 and 27a–zd, written during the same summer. They are highly personal

selves on the ground, or hide themselves in the water. The Fox seems always in a fighting humour; he barks, snaps on all sides and however hungry and ready to go a birds nesting, of which he is fond, is fairly driven to seek shelter in his hole. A sailor finding swearing of no use, tried what Tar could do, and covered his face with it, but the Musketoes stuck to it in such numbers as to blind him, and the tickling of their wings, were worse than their bites, in fact Oil is the only remedy.

[*Churchill Factory, nothing to do. Mr John Charles*]

I was fortunate in passing my time in the company of three gentlemen the officers of the factory, Mr Jefferson the deputy governor, Mr Prince the captain of the Sloop,[1] that annually traded with the Esquimaux to the northward, and Mr Hodges the Surgeon.[2] They had books, which they freely lent to me, among them were several on history and on animated Nature, these were what I paid most attention to as the most instructive. Writing paper there was none but what was in the hands of the Governor, and a few sheets among the officers. On my complaining that I should lose my writing for want of practice, Mr Hearne employed me a few days on his manuscript, entitled "A Journey to the North." and at another time I copied an Invoice.[3]

It had been the custom for many years, when the governors of the factory required a clerk to send to the school in which I was educated to procure a Scholar that had a mathematical education to send out as Clerk, and to save

(Thompson uses nineteen personal pronouns in these two pages, whereas he had used only twelve in the preceding seventeen pages), and they bear a strong chronological orientation.

1 Thomas Prince (d. 1788), from Aislaby, Yorkshire, was hired by the HBC in 1783 to be master of the sloop *Churchill*. In 1788 he and a companion drowned in the Churchill River; on this occasion William Jefferson referred to him as an "aimiable, and Capable Servant." London Inward Correspondence from HBC Posts, Churchill, 1774–1791, A.11/15: 138v, HBCA.

2 John Toogood Hodges (fl. 1780–87), of Yeovil, Somerset, entered HBC service in 1780 as a surgeon, for which he earned £40 per year. With Hearne and Jefferson, he was seized by La Pérouse in 1782, returning to Hudson Bay in 1783. In that year, with Churchill lacking a writer, Hodges wrote to the HBC's London Committee with an offer to serve in this capacity; the post was assigned to Thompson upon his arrival a year later. Hodges returned to England in 1787.

3 Hearne's manuscript was published in London in 1795 as *A Journey from Prince of Wales's Fort, in Hudson's Bay, to the Northern Ocean*. Entries in Hearne's Churchill post journal indicate that Thompson was employed at writing during May and June 1785. Churchill, Post Journal, 1784–1785, B.42/a/104: 22r–26v, HBCA.

expences he was bound apprentice to them for seven years. To learn what; for all I had seen on their service [iii.9b] neither writing, nor reading wer[e] required, and my only business was to amuse myself, in winter growling at the cold; and in the open season shooting Gulls Ducks, Plover and Curlews, and quarelling with Musketoes and Sand flies.

The Hudsons Bay Company annually send out three Ships to their Factories, which generally arrive at their respective ports in the latter end of August or the early part of September, and this year (1785) the Ship arrived as usual.[4] When the Captain landed, I was surprised to see with him Mr John Charles,[5] a school fellow and of the same age as myself, whom I had left to be bound out to a trade. I enquired of him, what had made him change his mind, he informed me that shortly after my departure, from what he could learn some maps drawn by the furr traders of Canada had been seen by Mr Dalrymple,[6] which showed the Rivers and Lakes for many hundred miles to the westward of Hudsons Bay, that he applied to the Company to send out a gentleman well qualified to survey the interior country, all which they promised to do, and have gentleman fit for that purpose to go out with their ships next year; they accordingly sent to the School to have one ready. As he was the only one of age, he was placed in the mathematical school, run quickly over his studies, for which he had no wish to learn, for three days, for a few minutes each day, taught to handle Hadley's quadrant,[7] and bring down the Sun to a chalk mark on the wall his education was compleat, and pronounced fit for the duties he had to perform; he was very much disappointed at all he saw, but he could not return. Hudson's Bay is certainly a country that Sinbad the Sailor never saw, as he make no mention of Musketoes.[8]

4 In 1785 the *Prince Rupert* arrived on 21 August. Churchill, Post Journal, 1784–1785, B.42/a/104: 35r, HBCA

5 George Charles is intended. See appendix 2.

6 Alexander Dalrymple (1737–1808), a Scottish traveller and geographer, was by 1784 hydrographer of both the East India Company and the Admiralty. The map that Dalrymple saw was drawn by Peter Pond and was submitted in 1785 to Lord Sydney, the home secretary, in support of an NWC petition for trading rights. Thompson again writes of Dalrymple's examination of Pond's map and the sending out of George Charles, on iv.116–17 (172). A direct link between these two events appears to be attested only in Thompson's narrative.

7 John Hadley (1682–1744) invented the reflecting quadrant in 1730. Consisting of two mirrors and an arc measuring one-eighth of a circle, it facilitated the measurement of lunar distances by allowing a celestial object and the horizon to be seen simultaneously.

8 With the last sentence on iii.9b, Thompson links this section to *Arabian Nights* and to the catalogue of his childhood reading on iv.3 (6–7).

[*Leave Churchill for York Factory. 1st day journey. Journey along the Bay. Polar Bears sleeping. Arrive at the Kisiskatchewan, Superstition on Bears. Bear killed. Arrive at York Factory*]

[iii.9c][1] Early in September the annual Ship arrived, and orders were sent for me to proceed directly to York Factory, a distance of one hundred and fifty miles to the south ward.[2] The Hudsons Bay Company had established a very useful line of communication between their several Factories, by means of what were called, Packet Indians.[3] These were each of two Indian men, who left each Factory with letters to arrive at the next Factory about the expected time of the arrival of the Ship at such Factory, and thus the safe arrival of these annual Ships, and the state of the Factories became known to each other, and assistance given where required. The Boat from Churchill Factory crossed the River with the two Packet Indians and myself to Cape Churchill, and landed us without any Provisions, and only one blanket to cover me at night; for we had to carry every thing: it was a very fine day; but unfortunately a gallon of strong Grog was given to these Indians, who as usual as soon as they landed, began drinking, and were soon drunk and the day lost; we slept on the ground each in his single blanket, the dew was heavy; Early in the morning we set off and continued our march to sun set, without breakfast or dinner, the Indians now shot one Goose and three stock Ducks.[4] We came to something like a dry spot, and stopped for the night with plenty of drift wood for fuel; the three Ducks were soon picked, stuck on a stick to roast at the [iii.10] fire; mean time the Goose was picked, and put to roast. Each of us had a Duck, and the Goose among us three. Our march all day had been on the marshy beach of the Bay, which made it fatigueing; and

1 This is Thompson's third attempt at writing the story of his journey from Churchill to York Factory. The first account is on i.5–8 in Volume II, while a second has not survived.

2 On 4 September 1785, Hearne wrote in the Churchill post journal: "Wind and Weather Variable. Early in the Morning sent the York Indians off with a Packet for that Factory. With these Indians I also sent David Thompson agreeable to the Companys Order, and Mr. Martens Request." Churchill, Post Journal, 1785–1786, B.42/a/106: 1r–v, HBCA. On 14 September, Humphrey Marten recorded in the York post journal: "in the Afternoon the two Indians I sent to Churchill on the 28 Instant [sic] returned with David Thompson." York, Post Journal, 1785–1786, B.239/a/86: 1v, HBCA.

3 These men were members of the so-called Homeguard Indians. See note on iv.27 (47).

4 Mallard duck (*Anas platyrhynchos*).

directly after supper, each wrapped himself in his blanket and slept soundly on the ground: the banks of the Brooks were the only kind of dry ground:

¶ The incidents of every day were so much the same, that I shall make one story of the whole; on the evening of the sixth day we arrived at Kisiskatchewan River, a bold, deep, stream of two miles in width; we put up on the bank of a Brook, where my companions had laid up a Canoe, but the wind blowing fresh we could not proceed. Our line of march has constantly been along the Bay side, at high water mark, always wet, and muddy, tiresome walking and very dull; on the left hand was the sea, which when the tide was in appeared deep, but the Ebb retired to such a distance, that the Sea was not visible, and showed an immense surface of Mud, with innumerable boulders of rock, from one to five or seven tons weight. The greatest part were lodged at about half tide, where the greatest part of the drift ice remains on the shores; as Seal River, north of Churchill River, is the most southern place where the shore is of Rock; the whole of these boulders must have come with the ice from the northward of that River, for south of it, and of Churchill River all is alluvial; this evidently shows a strong set of the north sea into Hudson's Bay on it's west side, returning by the east side into Hudson's Straits; for these boulders are found on the west side shores to the most southern part of the Bay. On our right hand was an immense extent of alluvial in marsh, morass, and numerous ponds of water, which furnished water to many small Brooks; the woods, such as they are, were out of sight.

¶ Every day we passed from twelve to fifteen Polar Bears, lying on the marsh, a short distance from the shore, they were from three to five together, their heads close to each other, and their bodies lying as radii from a centre. I enquired of the Indians if the Polar Bears always lay in that form, they said, it was the common manner in which they lie. As we passed them, one, or two would lift up their heads, and look at <us, but> never rose [iii.11] to molest us. The indian rule is, to walk past them with a steady step without seeming to notice them. On the sixth day we had a deep Brook to cross, and on the opposite side of the ford was a large Polar Bear feasting on a Beluga, we boldly took the ford thinking the Bear would go away, but when about half way across, he lifted his head, placed his fore paws on the Beluga, and uttering a loud growl, showed to us such a sett of teeth as made us turn up the stream, and for fifty yards wade up to our middle before we could cross; during this time the Bear eyed us, growling like a Mastiff Dog.

¶ During this time we were waiting the wind to calm, I had an opportunity of seeing the Indian superstition on the Polar Bear; on one of these days we noticed a Polar Bear prowling about in the ebb tide, the Indians set off to kill it as the skin could be taken to the Factory in the Canoe; when the

Bear was shot, before they could skin him and cut off his head, the tide was coming in, which put them in danger, they left the skin to float ashore, and seizing the head, each man having hold of an ear, with their utmost speed in the mud brought the head to land, the tide was up to their knees, when they reached the shore; on the first grass they laid down the head, with the nose to the sea, which they made red with ochre; then made a speech to the Manito of the Bears, that he would be kind to them as they had performed all his orders,[5] had brought the head of the Bear ashore, and placed it with it's nose to the sea, begging him to make the skin float ashore, which; at the Factory would sell for three pints of Brandy; the Manito had no intention they should get drunk, the skin did not float ashore and was lost. In the afternoon of the third day the wind calmed, the Indians told me at Noon, that we had staid there too long, that they would now sing and calm the wind, for their song had great power; they sung for about half an hour; and then said to me, you see the wind is calming, such is the powers of our song. I was hurt at their pretensions, and replied; you see the Ducks, the Plover and other Birds, follow the ebb tide, they know the wind is calming without your song: if you possess such power, why did you not sing on the first day of our being here, they gave no answer, it is a sad weakness of the human [iii.12] character, and which is constantly found, more, or less, in the lower orders of thinly populated countries; they all possess, if we may credit them; some superhuman power.[6] The Ebb tide had now retired about one and a half mile from us. Near sun set, each of us cut a bundle of small willows, and with the Canoe and paddles, carried them about a mile, when we laid the Canoe down, spread the willows on the mud, and laid down to wait the return of the tide; as soon as it reached us, we got into the Canoe, and proceeded up the Kisiskatchewan River for several miles, then crossed to the south shore, and landed at a path of four miles in length through woods of small pines, on low, wet, marsh ground to York Factory, thank good Providence.

[*Description of the great Marsh. Goose Stands &c Goose shooting &c &c arrival and departure*]

---

5 In traditional Cree belief, each particular species of animal is obedient to a *manito*, a spiritual being who maintains human-animal relations. For Thompson's discussion of this belief, see iv.40 (99).

6 The interplay between the rational and the supernatural is another favourite theme of Thompson's, and it animates several stories in the *Travels*. Thompson is not always as dismissive of "superhuman power" as he is here.

[iv.13] {to the south shore, and landed at a path of four miles in length through small pines of very wet marsh ground to York Factory.}[1] I now return to the great marsh along which we travelled.

The aquatic fowl, in the seasons of spring and autumn are very numerous. They seem to confine themselves to a belt of these great marshes of about two miles in width from the sea shore, and this belt is mostly covered with small ponds and the intervals have much short tender grass, which serves for food, the interior of the marsh has too much moss. Of these fowls the wild geese are the most numerous and the most valuable, and of these the grey geese,[2] of which there are four species, and the brent geese a lesser species of the grey goose, it's feathers are darker and it's cry different. Of the Snow Geese,[3] there are three varieties, the least of which is of a blueish color, they are all somewhat less than the grey geese, but of richer meat. It may be remarked, that of wild fowl, the darker the feather, the lighter the color of the meat; and the whiter the feather, the darker the meat, as the Snow Goose and the Swan &c.

¶ The shooting of the wild Goose, (or as it is called the hunt) is of great importance to the Factories, not only for present fresh meat, but also forms a supply of Provisions for a great part of the winter. The grey geese are, the first to arrive in the early part of May, the Snow geese arrive about ten days after. About ten of the best shots of the men of the Factory with several Indians are now sent to the marshes to shoot them. For this purpose each man has always two guns, each makes what is called a Stand, this is composed of drift wood and pine branches, about three feet high, six feet in diameter, and half round in form, to shelter him from the weather and the view of the geese, each stand is about 120 yards from the other, and form a line on the usual passage of the geese, always near the sea shore; two, or three, parties are formed as circumstances may direct, each hunter has about ten mock geese, which are sticks made and painted to resemble the head and neck of the grey goose; to which is added a piece of canvass for a body, they are placed about twenty [iv.14] yards from the Stand, with their beaks to windward; the position in which the geese feed.

¶ When the geese first arrive they readily answer to the call of the Hunter, the Indians imitate them so well, that they would alight among the mock

---

1   These words had concluded a version of the journey from Churchill to York Factory that is no longer extant. An earlier version of the material that follows is on i.8–12, in Volume II.

2   Canada goose (*Branta canadensis*).

3   *Anser coerulescens*.

geese, if the shots of the hunter did not prevent them. The geese are all shot on the wing, they are too shy, and the marsh too level, to be approached. Some good shots, in the spring hunt, kill from 70 to 90 geese, but the general average is from 40 to 50 geese per man, as the season may be. The Snow Goose is very unsteady on the wing; now high, now low, they are hard to hit, they seldom answer to our call, but the Indians imitate them well; for the spring, they answer the call, but do not notice it in autumn, for the table, the Snow Goose is the richest bird that flies. The feathers of the geese are taken care of and sent to London, where they command a ready sale.[4] The feathers of four grey geese, or of five Snow geese weigh one pound. The duration of their stay depends much on the weather; a month at the most, and seldom less than three weeks. The flight of the geese is from daylight to about 8 AM, and from 5 PM to dusk. By the end of May, or the first week in June, the geese have all left us for their breeding places much farther to the northward.

[iv.14 paste-on]: In the spring of the year several of the Geese are found with grain in their crops, some of it as if just eaten, and supposed to be taken from cultivated fields but the grain is that of the wild rice,[5] which grows in abundance to the south westward, the nearest place to York Factory are the small Lakes at the mouth of the River Winipeg, distant about 420 miles. When Mr Wales was at Fort Churchill in 1769, to observe the Transit of Venus over the Sun, from curiosity he several times took angles of the swiftnes of the wild geese, and found that in a steady gale of wind, their flight before it was 60 miles an hour.[6] When shooting at them going before a gale of wind at the distance of 40 to 50 yards, the aim is taken two or three inches before his beak. When going against the wind, at the insertion of the neck.

[iv.14] In the middle of July several flocks of a very large species of grey goose arrive from the southward, they have a deep harsh note, and are therefore called Gronkers, by others Barren Geese;[7] from it being supposed they never lay eggs, if so, how is this species perpetuated, they very seldom alight in our marshes, but as they fly low, a few of them are shot, their meat is like

---

4 In the pre-1782 period, an average of almost 500 pounds (227 kilograms) of goose feathers was traded annually at York Factory; ten pounds of feathers were valued at one made beaver. Victor Lytwyn. *Muskekowuck Athinuwick: Original People of the Great Swampy Land* (Winnipeg: University of Manitoba Press, 2002), 147. According to long-standing HBC policy, company employees were permitted to engage in private trade in bird feathers.

5 *Zizania aquatica*.

6 For Wales, see note on iv.8 (10).

7 The identity of this species is unclear.

that of the common grey goose. I do not remember seeing these geese in autumn.

¶ In the Spring all the geese ducks and other fowls come from the southward; and in autumn, they all come from the northward, their first arrival is the early part of September, and their stay about three weeks. They keep arriving night and day, and our solitary marshes, become covered with noisy animated life, the same mode of shooting them, is now as in the [iv.15] spring, but they do not answer the call so well, and the average number each man may kill is from 25 to 30 geese for the season. The geese salted for the spring hunt, are better than those of autumn, they are fatter, and more firm, those salted in Autumn are only beginning to be fat, which, with young geese, in this state, make poor salted food.

¶ In autumn the last three days of the geese appear to be wholly given in cleaning and adjusting every feather of every part, instead of feeding at pleasure every where. The Manito of the geese, ducks &c has given his orders, they collect and form flocks of from 40 to 60 or more; and seem to have leaders, the Manito of the aquatic fowl has now given his orders for their departure to milder climates, his presience sees the setting in of winter, and the freezing of the ponds &c the leaders of the flock have now a deep note, the order is given, and flock after flock in innumerable numbers rise.[8] Their flight is of a regular form, making an angle of about 25 degrees, the two sides are unequal, the side next to the sea being more than twice the length of the side next to the land; where I have counted 30 geese on one side, the short side had only ten to twelve, and so in proportion. The point of the angle is a single goose, which leads the flock; when tired of opening the air it falls into the rear of the short line, and the goose next on the long, or sea line takes his place, and thus in succession. Thus in two, or three days, these extensive marshes swarming with noisy life become silent, and wholly deserted, except when wounded, no instance has ever been known of geese, or ducks, being found in frozen ponds, or Lakes.

[iv.15 paste-on] The different species of Geese on the east side of the Mountains pass the winter in the mild climate of the Floridas, the mouths of the Mississippe, and around the Gulph of Mexico. From these Shores the wild Geese and Swans proceed to the northward as far as the Latitude of 67 to 69 north; where they have the benefit of the Sun's light and heat for the twenty four hours for incubation, and rarely breed under twenty hours of Sun light. Thus the wild birds proceed from where they winter to where they breed through the pathless air, a distance of about two thousand seven hundred

8 See note on the *manito* on iii.11 (31).

miles in a straight line; and from the place of breeding to the mouths of the Mississippe, and adjacent shores the same distance. The question arises, by what means do the wild geese make such long journeys with such precision of place; the wise, and learned, civilized Man answers, by Instinct, but what is Instinct, a property of Mind that has never been defined; The Indian says the Geese are directed by the Manito, who has the care of them. Which of the two is right;[9]

[iv.15] The Swan is sometimes frozen in, and loses his life.

The Frogs now cease to croak, for they must also prepare for winter. A few Cranes[10] frequent these marshes, as also a few Bitterns,[11] they are in pairs, and thus pass the whole of the open season, yet their eggs are never, or very rarely found, they are so well hid in the rushes of quagmires, which cannot be approached. The Bittern arrive and depart in pairs mostly in the night, it is a bird of slow wing, easy to be killed. [iv.16] The Cranes arrive, and depart, in flocks of thirty to fifty, their flight is an angle of full thirty degrees, both sides are nearly equal, I have never seen the leader quit his place, they are good eating fleshy, but not fat, they make the best of broth. The ducks and lesser birds arrive and depart in flocks, but in no regular order.

[*York Factory, Ship arrives. Winter arrangements. Winter Tents*]

The society and occupations of the Factories along the shores of Hudson's Bay are so much alike, that the description of one Factory may serve for all the others. I shall describe York Factory, being the principal Factory, and in point of commerce worth all the other Factories. The establishment was composed of a Resident, an Assistant, with one, or two clerks, a Steward and about forty men, over whom there was a foreman. The Ship for the Factory arrives generally about the latter end of August, sometimes later, this depends on their passage through Hudson's Straits, which in some years is sadly blocked up with ice; the Ship anchors in the mouth of the River about five miles below the Factory, the whole attention of all hands is turned to the unloading, and reloading of the Ship; the time of doing which, depends on

9 This is another instance in which Thompson compares European and Native modes of understanding natural phenomena. Whereas the European appeals to an abstract, inanimate concept, the Native invokes a personalized agent, and the reference to the "wise, and learned, civilized Man" is clearly sarcastic.

10 Either the sandhill crane (*Grus canadensis*) or the whooping crane (*Grus americana*).

11 American bittern (*Botaurus lentiginosis*).

the weather, and takes from ten to fifteen days. The ship having sailed for London, this may be called the beginning of our year.

¶ The regular occupations of the Factory now commence, eight or ten of the best shots among us, among which are sure to be the clerks, with the few indians that may be near, are sent off to the marshes to shoot geese, ducks, cranes &c for the present supply of the Factory, and to be salted for the winter. Axes are put in order, Boats got ready with Provisions, and about twenty men sent up the River to the nearest forests to cut down pine trees, branch them, lop off the heads, and carry them on their shoulders to the great wood pile, near the river bank; the trees are so small, that a man generally carries two, or three, to the woodpile. When the quantity required for fuel, is thus cut and piled, the wood is taken by a large sledge drawn by the men to a bay of the River, where rafts can be made and floated to the Factory, which is completed in April, but not floated to the Factory until June and July. Accounts, Books, grouse shooting &c employ the time of those at the Factory. Winter soon sets in; the geese hunters return, and out of them are formed two parties of three, or four men, each for grouse shooting snareing hares &c. Each party has a canvas tent, like a soldiers [iv.17] bell tent with the top cut off to let the smoke out,[1a] fowling pieces, ammunition, fish hooks and lines, steel traps and three weeks of salted provisions, with our bedding of blankets &c completes our equipment. The shore ice of the River is now frozen to the width of half a mile, or more; the current of the River has much drift ice, it is time for the hunters to be off, the boats are ready, and we are placed on the ice, with four flat sleds, and a fine large Newfoundland Dog; the Boats return and we are left to our own exertions.

[*Go to French Creek. Camp there. Polar Bear. William Budge. Battle with Bruin. he is killed. One in a Steel Trap*]

¶ Our party consisted of four men and an indian woman,[1b] we loaded the sleds with the tent, our baggage and some provisions, leaving the rest for another trip, each of us hauled about seventy pounds, and the fine dog

1a Thompson compares this structure, a kind of small tipi, to the conical tent in which the British army stored muskets.

1b Marten records in the York post journal for 26 October 1785: "At nine A.M. had a boat launched and set Mr John Ballanden. Robert Tennant. David Thompson and an Indian lad over to hunt and fish at the French Creek, the boat returned." B.239/a/86: 8r, HBCA. Ballenden was to be officer in charge of York Factory 1798–1802, succeeding Joseph Colen. Tennant appears again at page iv.331 (92).

100 pounds weight. We proceeded to a large Brook called French Creek[2] up which we went about a mile to where the Pines of the forest were of some size and clean growth; the tent poles were now cut, and placed to form a circular area of about 12 to 14 feet diameter, and 12 feet in height, the door poles are the strongest, about these poles we wrapped our tent, the fire place is in the centre, and our beds of pine branches, with a Log next to the fire, our furniture a three gallon brass kettle, with a lesser one for water, two, or three tin dishes, spoons &c. A Hoard is next made of Logs well notched into each other, of about eight feet in length, six feet wide at the bottom, five feet in height, and the top narrowed to two feet covered with Logs to secure our provisions and game from the carnivorous animals. Our occupations were angling of Trout, snareing of Hares, shooting white Grouse, trapping of Martens,[3] Foxes, and Wolverines.

Our enemy the Polar Bear, was prowling about, the sea not being sufficiently frozen to allow him to catch Seals.

By the latter end of November we had procured sufficient game to load three flat sleds, for the Factory, hauled by two of us, and our Dog, to arrive at the Factory took us the whole of the day.[4] The same evening William Budge,[5] a fine handsome man, John Mellam,[6] and the indian woman were frying pork and grouse for supper, the smell attracted a Polar Bear, who marched to the Tent, and around it, his heavy tread was heard, and no more cooking

2 French Creek is located opposite York Factory, draining into the Hayes River from the south.

3 *Martes americana.*

4 Marten reports that on 22 November "Robert Tennant and David Thompson came from Mr Ballanden with 15 Rabbets 60lbs of Fish and 30 Partridges with 2 Red and one good Grizzled Fox," and on 30 November that "David Thompson brought from Mr Ballanden 35 lbs of Venison." B.239/a/86: 11v, 12v, HBCA.

5 At least two HBC employees shared this name. One, a sailor, appears to have left the Company's employ in about 1782, while a second began service in 1790. As the York Factory journals for 1785–86 do not indicate the presence of either man at the post, Thompson may have misidentified this figure. Anne Morton, "William Budge," HBCA, http://www.gov.mb.ca/chc/archives/hbca/biographical/b/budge_william.pdf.

6 John Mellam served as York Factory's armourer from 1783 until his return to England in 1792. In the winter of 1785–86 he was employed at various tasks about the factory and accompanied Thompson on grouse-hunting expeditions during January and February. B.239/a/86: 69v, 72v, HBCA. The identity of the Native woman in this anecdote is unclear; undoubtedly Cree, she seems to have been Mellam's companion. Her presence and activity emphasize the role played by Native women in fur trade life, not only as conjugal partners but as contributors to subsistence and survival.

thought of. As usual in the evening, the fowling pieces were being washed and cleaned, and were then not fit for use, but there was a loaded Musquet. At length [iv.18] Bruin found the door, and thrust in his head and neck, the Tent Poles prevented further entrance. Budge climbed up the tent poles, and left Mellam and his indian woman to fight the Bear, the former snatched up the Musket, it snapped; seizing it by the muzzle, he broke off the stock on the head of the Bear, and then with hearty blows applied the barrel and lock to his head; the indian woman caught up her axe, on the other side of the door, and in like manner struck Bruin on the head, such an incessant storm of blows, made him withdraw him self; he went to the Hoard and began to tear it in pieces; for the game a fowling piece was quickly dried, loaded with two balls, and fired into him, the wound was mortal, he went a few paces and fell, with a dreadful growl. Budge now wanted to descend from the smoky top of the Tent, but the Woman with her axe in her hand (2½ lbs) heaped wood on the fire, and threatened to brain him if he came down, he begged hard for his life, she was determined, fortunately Mellam snatched the axe from her, but she never forgave him, for the indian woman pardons Man for every thing but want of courage, this is her sole support and protection, there are no laws to defend her. The next morning on examining the head of the Bear, the skin was much bruised and cut, but the Bone had not a mark on it.

We had two steel traps of double springs, with strong iron teeth, weighing each seventy pounds, and five feet in length, for wolves and Wolverines; one of these was baited with a Grouse, and placed on the ice at the mouth of the brook; a Polar Bear took the bait, the iron teeth closed on his head, he went about half mile and then laid down; the next morning we traced the Bear, he rose up, a curious looking figure with a trap of five feet across his nose, he went directly for the sea, and we respectfully followed; our guns had only small shot; when arrived at the edge of the ice, Bruin made a halt; and no doubt thought such a trap across his nose would be an impediment to swimming, and catching Seals, wisely determined to get rid of it, turning round and looking at us, he bent his head and the trap on the ice, and placing his heavy fore paws on each of the springs, he loosened himself from the trap, and looking at us with an air of contempt, dashed into the sea, [iv.19] and swam away, we got the trap, but his heavy paws had broken one of the springs and rendered the trap useless. The other hunting party about three miles to the eastward of us had also the visit of a Polar Bear one evening from the smell of fried pork and grouse, he came to the tent, marched round, and round it, but found no entrance, his heavy tread warned the inmates to be on their guard. The Bear reared himself up, on the tent, he placed the claws of his fore paws through the canvas tent, the man opposite ready with his gun, guided by his paws, fired, and mortally wounded him; but in falling the Bear brought down the tent and tent poles, under which, with the Bear were three men and one woman, whom, the Bear in the agonies of death, sadly kicked about, until relieved by the man who had shot the Bear, the tent was drawn over his head and he was free;

[*Winter work. Hares &c. Grouse shooting. netting them. White Grouse, change colour*]

¶ I must return to our occupations; of the speckled Trout[1] we caught about ten dozen of two to three pounds weight through holes in the ice of the brook, they were readily caught with a common hook and line, baited with the heart of a Grouse; as the cold increased and the thickness of the ice, the Trout went to deeper water, where we could not find them. The Hares, when they go to feed whic[h] is mostly in the night time, keep a regular path in the snow, across which, a hedge is thrown of pine trees of close branches, but cut away at the path; a long pole is tied to a tree, in such a manner that the butt end shall overbalance the upper end; and the weight of a hare. To this end a snare of brass wire is tied by a piece of strong twine, this end of the pole is tied to the tree laid across the path, by a slip knot, and the snare suspended at four inches above the snow. The Hare comes bounding along, enters the snare, the slip knot is undone, the top of the pole is free, the butt end by it's weight descends, and Puss is suspended by the snare about six to eight feet above the surface of the snow, this height is required to prevent them being taken by Foxes and Martens. The other Hares that follow this path; have, for the night a free passage; but the next day the snare is reset, until no more can be caught; where the Hares are plenty, hedges of pine trees, with their branches extend 200 yards, or more, in length; on a fine Moon light night [iv.20] the Hares move about freely, and from eighteen to twenty caught in a night, but in bad weather, three, or four, or none; the average may be six to eight per night: of all furrs, the furr of the hare is the warmest, we place pieces of it in our mittens, the skin is too thin for any other purpose: When the cold becomes very severe, we leave off snareing until February or March, as the Hares lie still.

There are two species of white Grouse, the Rock and the Willow,[2] the former is a lesser species with a black stripe round the upper eye lid, and feeds among the rocks. The willow Grouse has a red stripe round the upper

1 Brook trout (*Salvelinus fontinalis*).
2 For species of grouse, see note to iv.10 (13).

eye lid, is a finer bird than the rock grouse, and one fifth larger: they are both well feathered to the very toe nails; all their feathers are double, lie close on each other, two in one quill, or socket, and appear as one feather; the under side of the foot, have hard, rough, elastic feathers like bristles. The white Grouse in the very early part of winter, arrive in small flocks of ten to twenty, but as the winter advances and the cold increases, they become more plentiful, and form flocks of fifty to one hundred; they live on the buds of the willows, which cover the ground between the sea shore and the pine forests; on the south side of the Hayes's River, there is a stripe of alluvial formed by a few bold Brooks of half, to one mile in width, and about ten miles in length, next to impassable in summer for marsh and water, where they feed; they are shot on the ground (the Snow) as they feed; at first each man may average ten Grouse per day; but by the beginning of December they become numerous, and the average of each man may be about twenty per day. Each Grouse weighs two pounds, forming a good load to walk with in snow shoes; and at length carry to the tent; where the feathers are taken off, the bowels taken out, and in this state put into the hoard to freeze, and thus taken to the Factory; they now average one pound each, and the feathers of twenty grouse weigh one pound. At night the Grouse, each singly, burrows in the snow, and when the cold is intense, do the same in the middle of the day. However intense the cold, even to 85 degrees below the freezing point, I never knew any to perish with cold, when not wounded; the same of all other birds, kind Providence has admirably adapted them to the climate.

After the bitter cold of December and January is passed, they congregate in large flocks, each man now bags thirty to forty grouse per day, but as this is a Load too heavy to hunt with, part is buried in the Snow and only taken up when going to the Tent. The weather now allowing us to load our guns; for in the intense cold, the shot is no [iv.21] sooner fired, than our hands are in our large mittens; we walk and pick up the bird, then get the powder in, and walk again, at length the shot, and the gun is loaded; it is needless to say, exposed to such bitter cold, with no shelter, we cannot fire many shots in a short day. Gloves are found to be worse than useless.

¶ In the latter end of February, the month of March, and to the end of the season; the Grouse are netted, during which not a shot is fired, except at Hawks:[3] They are a great plague to us, as the flocks were going before us, by short flights a Hawk appearing, they dived down under the Snow and for some time staid there. For this purpose a large snow drift is chosen, level on the top, or made so, on which is placed a square net of strong twine of twenty

---

3 For hawk species, see note on iv.33a (83).

feet each side, well tied to four strong poles, the front side is supported by two uprights, four feet in height; to which is tied a strong line of about fifty feet in length, conducted to a bush of willows, the side poles being about four feet longer than the other, the back of the net is also lifted up about two feet above the snow, so as to leave room for the grouse to pass: two, or three bags of fine gravel are brought, and laid under the centre of the net, mixed with willow buds taken out of the crops of the Grouse we have shot, these are gently dried over the fire to make them look like fresh buds: at first we have no great difficulty in starting, and guiding the flocks towards the net, and so soon as we can bring them within view of the gravel and buds, they eagerly run to them, and crowd one another, the man at the end of the line, pulls away the two uprights, the net falls, we directly run and throw ourselves on the net, as the strong efforts of forty or fifty of these active birds might make an opening in the net. We have now to take the neck of each Grouse between our teeth, and crack the neck bone, without breaking the skin, and drawing blood, which if done, the foxes destroy the part of the net on which is blood and around it, which sometimes happens to our vexation, and we have to mend the net.[4]

¶ Although for the first few days we may net 120 Grouse per day, yet in about a fortnight they become so tame, they no longer form a large flock, and at length we are obliged to drive them before us, like barn door fowls, by eight or ten at a time, for every haul of the net, and thus in the course of a long day, we do not net more than forty to sixty grouse.[5] In these months they have a pleasing, cheerful call, in the early and latter [iv.22][6] part of the day of Ka bow, Ka bow, Kow á é. The Hens have the same call, but in a low note. In bad weather the willow grouse shelters itself under the snow, but the Rock grouse run about, as if enjoying the Storm. During the winter whatever may be the number of the flock, and however near to each other, each burrows singly in the snow. Their feathers are of a brilliant white, if possible whiter than the snow. In the months of March and April, part of the feathers, particularly about the neck, and the fore part of the body, change

4 Hearne provides a description of this procedure, noting that HBC men learned the technique from local Natives. Samuel Hearne, *A Journey from Prince of Wales's Fort, in Hudson's Bay, to the Northern Ocean* (London: A. Strahan and T. Cadell, 1795), 413–15.

5 The York post journal records that Thompson and his companions brought in several loads of between 200 and 400 ptarmigan between mid-December 1785 and early February 1786. B.239/a/86: 14v, 15r, 18v, 20v, HBCA.

6 An earlier version of iv.22 survives. See appendix 1.

color to a glossy brown, or deep chocolate, upon a ground of brilliant white, very beautiful, and in this state, are often stuffed and sent to London.[7] No dove is more meek than the white grouse, I have often taken them from under the net, and provoked them all I could without injuring them, but all was submissive meekness. Rough beings as we were, sometimes of an evening we could not help enquiring, why such an angelic bird should be doomed to be the prey of carnivorous animals and birds, the ways of Providence are unknown to us. They pair in May, and retire to the Pine Forests, make their nests on the ground, unde[r] the low spreading branches of the dwarf Pine. They lay from eleven to thirteen eggs, the young, from the shell, are very active and follow their dam.

¶ There is a third species called the Pine, or Swamp, grouse,[8] of dark brown feathers, it feeds on the leaves of the white pine, and it's flesh tastes of the pine, on which it feeds; it is found sitting on the branches of the tree, ten, or twelve, feet above the snow, or ground; it is a stupid bird. A snare is tied to the end of a stick put round it's neck and pulled to the ground. It is only eaten for want of better: they are not numerous, solitary, and never in flocks.

[*Wood & Tom tit. Pheasant. Crossbeak Butcher Bird. Raven*]

¶ A few Pheasants[1] are shot, they are something larger than the white grouse, of fine dark plumage, but not to be compared to the English Pheasant: Their habits are much the same as the white grouse, except when they are started, they fly to, and settle on, the Trees, and not on the snow, or ground. Late in Autumn and early in the Spring the delicate Snow Bunting[2] appear in small flocks, they are shot, and also taken by small nets, they are a delicacy for the table, they fly from place to place, feed on the seeds of grass, but do not stay more than three weeks each time: The Tomtits[3] stay all winter, [iv.23] and feed on grass seeds. The handsome, little curious bird,

7 This detail reflects a service that the HBC regularly performed for British natural historians, particularly those of the Royal Society. The society's *Philosophical Transactions* frequently published articles describing specimens received from Hudson Bay. For the ptarmigan, see J.R. Forster, "An Account of the Birds Sent from Hudson's Bay," *Philosophical Transactions* 62 (1772): 382–433, and Daines Barrington, "Observations on the Lagopus, or Ptarmigan," *Philosophical Transactions* 63 (1773–74): 224–30.

8 Spruce grouse (*Canachites canadensis*).

1 Sharp-tailed grouse (*Pedioecetes phasianellus*).

2 *Plectrophenax nivalis*.

3 Tomtit may refer to a number of species of small birds. In his *Arctic Zoology* of 1785, Thomas Pennant calls the Hudsonian chickadee (*Penthestes hudsonicus*) the

the Cross Beak,[4] leave us late in Autumn and arrive early in March. They are always in small flocks, and their whole employment seems to be, cutting off the cones of the Pines, which their cross beaks perform as with a pair of scissors, the flock takes to one tree, if large, at a time, and shower down the Cones like hail. I never saw them feed on them: they remain and breed in the summer.

¶ At all seasons the Butcher bird is with us, and called Whisky jack, from the Indian name "Wees kar john,"[5] it is a noisy, familiar bird, always close about the tents, and will alight at the very doors, to pick up what is thrown out; he lives by plunder, and on berries, and what he cannot eat, he hides; it is easily taken by a snare, and brought into the room, seems directly quite at home; when spirits is offered, it directly drinks, is soon drunk and fastens itself anywhere till sober. A Hunter marching through the forest may see a chance one, but if an animal is killed, in a few minutes there are twenty of them, they are a nuisance picking and dirtying the meat, and nothing frightens them which the hunter can hang up. When the cold is intense, the feathers are ruffled out to twice it's size; all carnivorous birds appear; as it were, to loosen their feathers, where as the Grouse seem to tighten their feathers around them. The Raven[6] is the same bird here, as over all the world, stealing and plundering whatever he can, early and late on the wing, and sometimes taken in the traps not intended for him, in winter, when taking to shelter, he ruffles his feathers, and chooses a snug place in the pines exposed to the sun. The Indians do not like the Raven, as in hunting he often follows them, and by cawing noise, startles the animals, so as to make them look about, and be on their guard; when in their power he is sure to die.

[*White Foxes. Marten Traps. Guns &c*]

¶ Other Birds and Animals I shall notice when writing on the interior countries,[1] except the White Fox[2] which is found only along the sea shore,

---

"Hudson's Bay Titmouse," and it is probably this bird that Thompson writes of here. Thomas Pennant, *Arctic Zoology* (London: Henry Hughs, 1785), 2:425.

4 Probably the red crossbill (*Loxia curvirostra*).

5 Canada or gray jay (*Perisoreus canadensis*). This species is called the "butcher bird" because of its fondness for carrion. "Whiskyjack" is derived from the Cree *wiskacānis*.

6 The range of the common raven (*Corvus corax*) includes most of North America, Europe, and Asia.

1 Thompson does this on iv.32–5, below (81–94).

2 Arctic fox (*Alopex lagopus*).

(and not in the interior) and the mouths of Rivers; he is the least in size of all the Foxes, and the least in value; it's skin is worth [iv.24] only, about six to ten shillings; like all his species by nature a thief, following the Hunters to pick up wounded birds, they are readily caught in traps, and killed by set guns. By a well laid line of traps and guns, the produce of the early part of winter is about six of these Foxes per night. With all their cunning they are a stupid animal. On meeting one of them on the ice, I have often made a trap of pieces of ice, baited it, while he was looking at me, then retire some forty yards, he would then run to the trap, look at me, as if asking permission to take the bait, run his head into the trap and be caught; in this respect he differs very much from all the other species.

¶ Speaking so often of traps and set guns, I may as well describe them: For a Marten, a throat log, of about four feet in length, of a small pine is first laid on the snow, frequently some branches under it to keep it from sinking in the snow, two stakes are then driven, one on each side into the snow and moss near the middle; about eight inches from these, other two are driven, to form a door way, the sides and back are also of small stakes; the neck log is about six feet in length, and passes thro' and between the four stakes a few inches, the other end rests on some branches on the snow, a small stick of about six inches, on one end baited with the head of a grouse, the other end is half round, and rests on the throat log, on which a post of four inches in height is placed and supports the neck log, to give free entrance to the animal, the top of the trap, and above the neck log is well covered with pine branches to prevent any access to the bait; other logs are laid on the neck log for weight to detain the animal, which commonly is soon dead. These traps are made large, and strong, in proportion to the animal they are intended for. Set Guns and steel traps are well known to the civilized world.[3]

[*Return to the Factory. Summer dull. Flies. Winter. Fox and Hawk*]

[iv.25] The month of April, from the thawing of the snow, and the grouse leaving to make their nests, obliges us to give up the winter hunting, and we return to the Factory to pass a dull time until the arrival of the geese, for which we get ready. In our Tents we had a comfortable fire, and the chances of the day in shooting, trapping and neting, with a few hearty curses on the hawks and foxes for the grouse they took from us, at which they were very clever, frequently keeping near to us, though out of shot, and as soon as we

---

3 A set gun, also known as a spring gun, is designed to fire a charge when a triggering device is tripped by an animal.

killed a bird, before we could load the gun, one, or the other, would pounce on a grouse and carry it off: We had sometimes the satisfaction of seeing these two rogues worry each other; the Hawks were mostly of the short wing and could not carry much, and a grouse weighing about two pounds, at about two or three hundred yards they had to alight and tear out the bowels, their favorite food, the fox was upon them, and made them take another flight. Sometimes the fox seized the bird, in this case the hawk was continually attacking him with blows of her claws on his neck, near to his head, the fox, sprang at the hawk, to no purpose, and the moment he put down his head, to seize the bird the hawk again struck him, and thus the fox made his meal. The long winged hawks carry a grouse with ease to the Trees, where they are secure from the foxes. The summer months pass away without regret, the myriads of tormenting flies allow no respite, and we see the cold months advance with something like pleasure, for we can now enjoy a book, or a walk. October and November produce their ice and snow, the Rivers freeze over and form a solid bridge to cross where we please, our winter clothing is ready, and gloomy December is on us.

[*Seasons of the months. Rime. Snow blindness. Snow water*]

¶ [iv.26] The cold increases continually, with very little relaxation, the snow is now as dry as dust, about two feet in depth, it adheres to nothing, we may throw a gun into it and take it up as free of snow, as if in the air, and no snow adheres to our Snow Shoes. MM[1] No experiments have been made to know the weight of a cubic foot of Snow in this light state. 4 Gallons of this Snow gives only 2 Inches of Water if so much, even when pressed in the Kettle. The Aurora Borealis is seen only to the northward, sometimes with a tremulous motion, but seldom bright; halo's of the sun also appear. The month of January comes, and continues with intense cold; from the density of the air, the halo's, or mock suns, at times appear as bright as the real Sun; but when in this state, betokens bad weather, the halo's of the Moon are also very pleasing.

A curious formation now takes place called Rime, of extreme thiness, adhering to the trees, willows, and every thing it can fasten on, it's beautiful, clear, spangles forming flowers of every shape, of a most brilliant appearance, and the Sun shining on them, makes them too dazzling to the sight. The lower the ground, the larger is the leaf, and the flower; this brilliant

1 By this abbreviation Thompson indicates the insertion of an explanatory note, which culminates with the word "Kettle."

Rime can only be formed in calm clear weather, and a gale of wind sweeps away all this magic scenery; to be reformed on calm days. It appears to be formed of frozen dew.[2] The actual quantity of snow on the ground is not more than 2½ feet in depth in the woods, clear of drift, very light and dry: almost every fall of snow is attended with a gale of NE wind. The falling snow with the moveable snow on the ground, causes a drift and darkness, in which the traveller is bewildered, and sometimes perishes.

¶ The months of February and March have many pleasant clear days, the gaudy, spangled Rime is most brilliant, and requires a strong eye to look upon it,[3] in months of March and April, the Snow too often causes snow blindness, of a most painful nature, as I never had it.[4] I can only describe the sensations of my companions, the blue eye is the first affected, and suffers the most, the grey eye next, and the black eye the least; but none are exempt from snow blindness; though the black eye is the least affected, the sensations of my companions, and others, were all the same; they all complained of their eyes, being, as it were, full of burning sand; I have seen hardy men crying like children. After a hard march of four months in winter, three men and myself made for a trading post, in the latter part of March, they all became snow blind, and for the last four days I had to lead them with a string tied to my belt, and were so completely blind, that when they wished to drink of the little pools of melted snow, I had to put their hands in the water. They could not sleep at night. On arriving at the trading Post, they were soon relieved by the application of the steam of boiling [iv.27] water as hot as they could bear it, this is the indian mode of cure, and the only efficient cure yet known, but all complained of weakness of sight for several months after. Black crape is sometimes used to protect the eyes from the dazzling light of the snow, but the Hunter cannot long make use of it. The chase demands the whole power of his eye sight.

When thirsty a mouthful of snow, wets the mouth but does not relieve thirst, the water of snow melted by the sun has a good taste, but snow melted in a kettle over a fire, has a smoky taste, and snow being put in, makes good water.

2 Thompson is correct; rime is ice that is deposited on hard surfaces by supercooled water droplets.
3 Here Thompson inserted, then removed: "<the> climate <now> moderates and the snow lowers, but does not thaw."
4 Here Thompson inserted, then removed: "for Accustomed to Ast. Obs[ervatio]ns I had acquired the habit of allowing no more light to enter my eye than I required. I had a complete command of my eye lids."

Of the native Indians along the shores of Hudson's Bay I wish to say as little as possible.[5] The Company has the Bay in full possession, and can enforce the strictest temperance of spirituos liquors, by their orders to their chief Factors, the Ships at the same time bringing out several hundred gallons of a vile Spirit, called English, Brandy.[6] But no such morality is thought of, no matter what service the Indian performs, or does he come to trade his furrs, strong grog is given to him, and sometimes for two, or three days Men and Women are all drunk; and become the most degraded of human beings; <...> inebriated <...> now <...>

[*The furr trade.* HB. *only 2 inland Houses*]

[27a][1] The furr traders from Canada[2] for several years past had so far extended their trading posts through the interior country as almost to cut off the trade from the Factories. The whole of the Furrs collected at Churchill barely loaded the ship's long boat. The Hudson's Bay therefore found it necessary to make trading houses in a few different places, and as the Kisiskatch-

5 The Cree who lived in the vicinity of the bayside posts were referred to as the Home-guard Indians in HBC discourse. Their ancestors had inhabited the Hudson Bay Lowlands for up to four thousand years. Beginning in the late seventeenth century, their economic life became closely tied to that of the HBC, and individuals were often employed as messengers, hunters, and labourers. These Cree numbered 500–700 before the smallpox epidemic of 1782–83, which reduced this population by half. See Lytwyn, *Muskekowuck Athinuwick*. They were often regarded as a separate people from the inland Cree, for whom see the note on page iv.36 (95).

6 English brandy was made from proof malt or molasses spirits that were rectified with products such as raisins, prunes, quicklime, and cutch, the tannin-rich bark of an East Indian tree. The intention was to mimic the authentic French product, made from distilled wine. John A. Chartres, University of Leeds, personal communication with editor, 27 June 2003. Thompson mentions the vileness of English brandy again on page 27h (55).

1 Pages 27a–zd are housed in the David Thompson Fonds, F443, Archives of Ontario, Toronto (hereafter AO), and were numbered by Thompson. Composed in 1850, this part of the narrative is structured chronologically and tells the tale of Thompson's career from 1786 to 1790. From a literary perspective, these pages are the finest in the *Travels*, often attaining the qualities of spiritual autobiography. Some remarkable features include the prominence of the senses and careful description of clothing.

2 Thompson refers to those traders based in Montreal who had assumed the fur-trading routes abandoned after the British conquest of New France in 1759 and who would coalesce into the North West Company.

ewan is the great leading river of the country, these houses were situated on it's [banks] or the branches which flow into it.[3]

This inland trade was still in it's infancy the Company had only two houses. Cumberland House built by Mr Samuel Hearne, and Hudson House about 300 miles above it.[4] The inland trade was carried by twelve large indian canoes, each carrying three men, and six packages of goods, iron ware &c. each package of the weight of 90 pounds, conducted by an elderly native, called the Black Indian,[5] all under the command of Mr William Tomison a gentleman from the Isle of Orkney.[6] This year (1786) they came down to the Factory in the beginning of July, each Canoe brought six packages of fine furrs, each of 90 pounds, besides maintaining all the Men, and pay[ing] their winter expences. The men on this service had eight Pounds sterling each year, out of which they had to furnish their clothing and their other necessarys. The goods sent inland being wholly for the furr trade and provisions they had to buy all they wanted at the Factory, where every article was plain and good, and at a moderate price. That furnished by the Company, were a leather coat (instead of Beaver) Cap and Mittens and Snow Shoes.

[*Embark as clerk to Mr Mitchell Oman. Tracking. description of route to the great Rapid & C[arrying] Place. to Cumberland House. to the Houses for winter. Red Deer &c*]

¶ It was now thought proper to make a trading house about 200 miles higher up the River, leave Hudson House for the present, and instead [27b] to build a House about 40 miles to the southward, on the right bank of the Bow River, the great South Branch of the Kisiskatchewan; the latter to be under the charge of Mr Mitchel Oman, a native of the Isle of Orkney. He had no education, but [was] a fine looking manly, powerful man of a tenacious memory and high moral qualities, and much respected by the Indians,

---

3 For the economic and political background of these events, see "Historical Introduction" (xxv–xxvi).
4 The HBC established Cumberland House in 1774 and Hudson House in 1779.
5 The Black Indian appears in several HBC documents of this period. After conducting the inland brigades in 1786, he and his family spent the winter in the vicinity of South Branch House, hunting and building canoes; the following autumn, the Black Indian and his sons hunted for William Tomison at Manchester House. South Branch House, Post Journal, 1786–1787, B.205/a/1, HBCA; Manchester House, Post Journal, 1787–1788, B.121/a/2, HBCA.
6 For HBC Inland Master William Tomison, see appendix 2.

and whose language he had acquired. I was appointed to be his Clerk, and embarked with him.[1]

¶ York Factory is situated on the left bank of Hayes's River, five miles from the sea, where it joins the Kis is katchewan; the natural route to the inland would be by this great River but it's immense volume of water, heavy Falls and waves make it dangerous for small canoes, and the route by Hayes's River is preferred as being more safe. Every thing being ready: our provisions for the Voyage was given to each canoe, being 60 lbs of Oat meal, 20 lbs of Flour, and about 30 lbs of Bacon. The salt pork and beef, called junk were of too low a quality to bear carriage. In the latter end of July we set off with the tide which took us four miles, and there left us to contend with a strong current of 300 yards in width but somewhat shoal. The current could not be stemmed by paddles, and two men from each canoe went ashore and took the tracking line[2] leaving one man to steer the canoe. Although the whole weight of cargo and baggage did not exceed 800 lbs, yet it required a strong, steady pull to advance two miles an hour. This was performed on the left side of the River which has generally the best beach, and the deepest water near the shore. The labor is not more than common, but rendered almost dreadful by the heat and torment of Musketoes. To alleviate [27c] this latter, the men make for themselves wide, loose caps of coarse cotton with a piece of green bunting in the front; but the sweat from toil and heat makes it unbearable in the day time, but [it] serves well at night.

On the evening of the seventh day we came to the first [falls]; a few over a ledge of rocks which crossed the River, the carrying place was short, our tracking lines were dried and put by for future use. The River now formed Lakes and small streams with several carrying places over which we passed to a low winding ridge of land which separates the waters that flow eastward into Hudsons Bay, and those that run westward into Lake Winepeg. This ridge continues all along the east side of this Lake to the River Winipeg, which it crosses, and form one of it's falls. On the short carrying place by which we crossed this ridge the Indians, time out of mind had placed a manito stone in shape like a coblers lap stone, but of three times it's size, painted red with ochree to which they make some trifling offerings: but the Stone and offerings were all kicked about by our tolerant people.[3] A day

---

1 For HBC trader Mitchell Oman, see appendix 2.
2 Ropes attached to the bow and stern of the canoe, which enable the vessel to be hauled upstream.
3 This Native spiritual site is still marked by the name Painted Stone Portage, which connects the Hayes and the Echimamish Rivers. Similar markers, sometimes known

march more brought us to the Kisiskatchewan by a carrying place, and up it to Lake Winepeg (Sea Lake)[4] along the north shore of which lay our route for about 100 miles.

About the middle of this distance, a bold high point with steep banks juts out into the Lake for several miles. It is considered dangerous to small canoes, and takes nearly a day to go round it.[5] On the south west[6] end of this Lake we again entered the great river and came to a long and heavy fall with strong rapids over lime stone rocks: on it's left bank, is a good carrying place of two miles in length which takes two or three days labor.

[27d] A few miles above this carrying place and falls, is the Cross Lake,[7] a sheet of water of about 20 miles from North to South, but only three miles wide, about the middle of the Lake the River crosses it, which gives this name to the Lake. Two years before an homeguard Indian, as those are called that are in the service of the Factory with Magnus Twatt[8] were proceeding on their voyage with four pieces of goods in their small canoe. They came to this Cross Lake, and nearly got half way over it, when a small gale of north wind came on, which made awkward waves in the current of the River where they were, the Indian saw the danger, and as the waves permitted, threw off his belt and his loose coat and got ready to swim, calling out to Magnes "Strip strip man, not be long in the canoe now man, or you will be drowned,

as "our grandfathers' rocks," were common on river routes. A. Irving Hallowell, *The Ojibwa of Berens River, Manitoba: Ethnography into History* (Fort Worth: Harcourt Brace Jovanovich, 1992), 58. A lapstone was used by cobblers for beating shoe leather.

4 "Winnipeg" is derived from the Cree *wīnipēk*, "dirty water." Thompson's translation is accurate in that the same Cree term referred to Hudson Bay, which was considered "dirty" because its saltwater is undrinkable. Louis Bird, *Telling Our Stories: Omushkego Legends and Histories from Hudson Bay*, ed. Jennifer S.H. Brown, Paul W. DePasquale, and Mark F. Ruml (Peterborough: Broadview, 2005), 77–8.

5 Limestone Point.

6 "North west" is intended.

7 Now known as Cross Bay; its dimensions have been altered by a dam at Grand Rapids, Manitoba.

8 Magnus Twatt (c. 1751–1801) was from Orphir in the Orkneys. He joined the HBC in 1771 as a labourer, serving first at York Factory and then inland. He rose steadily in Company ranks, serving at various times as carpenter, steersman, and inland trader, and was frequently assigned the task of transporting trade goods directly to Native camps. Paul C. Thistle, "The Twatt Family, 1780–1840: Amerindian, Ethnic Category, or Ethnic Group Identity?" *Prairie Forum* 22 (Fall 1997): 193–212.

drowned man." Magnes was fast buttoned up in a tight jacket and had on trowsers and could neither strip, nor swim. As the Indian every moment expected the waves would upset the canoe, he was continually urging his canoe mate to strip, or be drowned, at length they gained a large patch of tall rushes, where they found shelter until the wind moderated. Such are the scenes in these small canoes in a gale of wind.

A few miles brings us to the Cedar Lake of an irregular form and large extent. Its eastern shores are low steep banks of limestone on which grow the white Cedar, the most northern place in which it is found. It is here a dwarf tree with spreading branches to the ground, it's smell is agreeable and makes good beds.[9] The west side is formed of the immense alluvials of the Kis is katchewan, which passes through this Lake. These alluvials have many channels of the River, one of which in about three days brought us to Cumberland Lake, so named from the House on it's [27e] southeast bank. It was in charge of Mr George Hudson,[10] who had been brought up in the same school in which I had received my education, but had left it several years before I entered. The canoes stopped a few minutes to take in dried provisions and proceeded, and gave no time for conversation.

¶ Passing this Lake we continued for three days to proceed with the paddle up the alluvials channels to their end, where the River is one stream. Here the current is strong and we had to bend the tracking line to the canoes and as Clerk take my share of the labor, but every thing was now very different from the wretched labor from York Factory, we were here in a high and dry country, the beach was wide and dry the season the latter end of August the Musketoes were not numerous, the weather fine, and as we advanced the Red Deer[11] became in plenty, and the call of the Stag made the forest resound and be answered by other Stags. Each day we marched fourteen hours averaging 25 miles a day. On the evening of the fourth day we camped at the entrance of the Bow River the next morning four canoes under the charge of Mr Mitchell Oman crossed to, and proceeded up this River, the other canoes with Mr Tomison went up the main River to their wintering Houses. With the tracking line we followed up the left side of the River, every hour appeared to bring us, to a better country, instead of the dark pine forests, the

9 The northern white cedar (*Thuja occidentalis*), common in the Great Lakes region.

10 George Hudson (c. 1762–90) left the Grey Coat School in 1775 to become an HBC apprentice. In 1779 he was recommended for inland service and from 1781 was frequently in charge of Cumberland House.

11 Wapiti (*Cervus elaphus*).

woods were of well grown Poplar,[12] Aspin[13] and white Birch,[14] and for the first time saplings of Ash.[15] The whistling and calls of the Red Deer echoed through the woods, and we often heard the butting of the Staghorns, battling which should be lord of the herd of Does, for these Stags are all Turks. On the evening of the third day up this River we came opposite to where houses were building for the furr trade and the next morning crossed over and placed ourselves about [27f] eighty yards above them.

[*Cleared ground and builded a house. the Indians. Characters of our neighbours and Canadians. Advantages of the Canada furr traders*]

¶ These houses were on account of two furr companies from Canada; one of them of the firm of McTavish and company: under the charge of a scotch gentleman of the name of Thorburn. The other was of the firm of Gregory and company, under the care of a french gentleman.[1] The men were all french canadians, with long red or blue caps, half of which hung down the head; they wore grey capots, or blanket coats belted round their waist,[2] their trowsers of grey cloth or dressed leather, and their shoes of the same. Our

---

12 Balsam poplar (*Populus balsamifera*).
13 Quaking aspen (*Populus tremuloides*).
14 Paper birch (*Betula papyrifera*).
15 Green ash (*Fraxinus pennsylvanica*).
 1 McTavish and Company was headed by Simon McTavish, who became the guiding force behind the NWC, holding three shares in the sixteen-share NWC agreement of 1783–84. Gregory, McLeod and Company was the NWC's main Montreal competitor from 1783 until 1787, when the two concerns were united in a new twenty-share agreement. Thompson seems to have reversed the identities of the post masters. According to the South Branch post journal, the McTavish and Company post was directed by Nicholas Montour, while the Gregory, McLeod and Company post was under the care of Peter Pangman. While William Thorburn is not mentioned in the journal, it is possible that he relieved Pangman when the latter left the Gregory, McLeod post in late December 1786. B.205/a/1, HBCA. For Montour, Pangman, and Thorburn, see appendix 2.
 2 The capote was the stereotypical garment of the fur trade and was cut according to the dimensions of a trade blanket. First developed by Native peoples, it was later adopted by traders from Montreal and became standard HBC attire in 1821. Michael Payne, *The Most Respectable Place in the Territory: Everyday Life in Hudson's Bay Company Service, York Factory, 1788 to 1870* (Ottawa: Minister of Supply and Services Canada, 1989), 121; Dorothy K. Burnham, *Cut My Cote* (Toronto: Royal Ontario Museum, 1973), 21.

dresses were a coarse hat; tight blue jacket with leather trowsers and shoes, to which in winter was added a leather coat.

¶ We now cleared the ground to build a log house of thirty six feet in length by twenty in breadth; which when carried up to seven feet in height, was roofed with split logs. The ridge pole was placed on two upright Logs of twelve feet and gave to each side a slope of five feet. The whole was mudded and covered with earth. The two chimneys were built of mud, mixed with chopped coarse grass, the floors were of split logs: the house divided into three by walls of logs, with doors cut in them, one of twelve feet by twenty for the goods, furrs and provisions, ten feet for a hall for business and trading with the Indians; the other fourteen feet for the men called the guard room. The indian hall was occupied by Mr Oman and myself. Under such able architec's as we were, we had raised a doric building, which might suit a painter of rustic scenery.³ The Indians who traded at these houses were of the tribes of Nahathaways,⁴ and Stone Indians, called Assine poetwak, or people of stony lands.⁵ They appeared to be equally numerous. They were all moder-

3 The party arrived on 25 September 1786, began clearing the site on 2 October, and completed the house on 21 December. B.205/a/1: 3r–8v, HBCA. South Branch House was located on the right bank of the South Saskatchewan, just downstream from modern-day Batoche, Saskatchewan. On 24 July 1794 the post was attacked by a party of Gros Ventres, the inhabitants were killed and the house left in ruins, never to be rebuilt. Doric was the simplest and sturdiest of the three classical Greek architectural orders, the others being Ionic and Corinthian.

4 For the Cree, see note on iv.36 (95).

5 Thompson's term represents the Cree asini·pwa·tak, derived in turn from the Ojibwa assini·-pwa·n, "stone enemy." According to tradition, the Assiniboine became a distinct group after a split within the Yanktonai; they first appear in the historical record in 1640. The Assiniboine migrated west from the woodlands of the Upper Mississippi and by the time Thompson encountered them had become Plains warriors and bison hunters, closely allied with the Plains Cree. Raymond J. DeMallie and David Reed Miller, "Assiniboine," in Handbook of North American Indians, vol. 13: Plains, ed. Raymond J. DeMallie (Washington: Smithsonian Institution, 2001), 1:572–92. This work is hereafter abbreviated as HNAI. The Assiniboine appear at several junctures in the Travels: as visitors to South Branch House in this account of the winter of 1786–87 (27f–h, 53–5); as inhabitants of land south of Assiniboine River trading at Assiniboine House, in the narration of the events of 1797–98 (iv.147–51, 197–201; iv.153–62, 202–8; iv.178–80, 220–1); as the Swampy Ground Assiniboine, trading at Lac La Biche in 1798–99 (iv.245, 274–5); as confederates of the Cree warriors in Saukamappee's narrative (iv.267–71, 291–4); and as horse thieves who launch a raid on Rocky Mountain House (iv.307–9, 317–19). A general description appears on iv.263 (288).

ately tall, manly looking men, with promenent features, well dressed in much the same manner, they were friendly to us, and by [no] means troublesome; our axes and tools lying about, yet nothing was stolen and we builded and finished every thing with as much ease and safety as if we had been alone.

[27g] The french gentleman paid us a visit, he was well dressed, his behaviour easy, mild and polite, he understood english and spoke sufficient for common business; every sentence he spoke, or answer he made, was attended by a smile and a slight bow, our men grave and stiff as pokers; on leaving us he gave us his best smile, and a low bow, in compliment to which our men nodded their heads, which was all they could do. Our other neighbour Mr Thorburn, had been some time in the naval service, and had the frank manners of an english gentleman. He was about 35 years of age, and had seen much of the world, he was glad to see us, and have the pleasure of speaking english.[6]

¶ From him, during winter we obtained information on the fur trade of Canada He remarked to us, that at the cession of Canada to England,[7] the furr trade, with all its influence over the Indians were wholly in the hands of the French. The British merchants soon acquired a share of it, and at length the whole of it; but by means of french traders to whom they furnished the goods for the trade. Some of these were of good characters, men of integrity, where this was the case, the furr trade gave a decent profit to both the Indian trader and the Merchant, but it was too frequently otherwise, with a slight education, if any, and no books, when in their wintering houses, they passed their time in card playing gambling and dancing; which brought on disputes, quarrels and all respect was lost. Goods beyond the extent of their wages were taken by the men to pay their gambling debts, and every festival of the church of Rome was an excuse to get drunk; the fisheries on which they depended for provisions for their support were neglected, and starvation stared them in the face, there was little left to trade furrs, and they returned to the Merchant in beggary, and distress, and [27h] instead of a cargo of furrs, recounted their miseries and sufferings brought on themselves by their own folly and dissipation. To remedy this sad state of the trade, the Merchants had formed two companies, which this winter would unite and form only one company, and as fast as could conveniently be done, place at the

6 Thompson would meet Thorburn again when he visited his Qu'Appelle River post in November 1797 (iv.147, 197).
7 At the 1763 Treaty of Paris, concluding the Seven Years War, France ceded its North American colonies east of the Mississippi to Britain, retaining only St Pierre and Miquelon.

head of each trading house, men of British origen of sober, and steady habits on whom they could rely, and this system was now in operation.

¶ We soon found our neighbours had greatly the advantage of us in carrying on the furr trade, five Men in their large canoes brought twenty four pieces of goods, of which, full one fourth was high wines (strong whisky) to which four times the quantity of water was added to make grog for the Indians. With us three men brought six pieces of goods, of which one fourth was english brandy, a vile spirit to which only two waters could be added, a pint of which, was reckoned of the value of a beaver skin whether in furrs, or in provisions, all expences were thus paid, yet nearly half of it was given away.

[*Dogs &c Bow River trade in furrs & provisions. Country &c*]

The Indians are fond of long clothing, one of our men was a tailor and made a great part of the cloth into coats that came to the knee.[1] The natives had but few horses, which were kept for hunting and bringing the meat to their tents: The Nahathaway women, placed their goods in a kind of saddle bags, which they tied on the dogs. The Stone Indians made a kind of sled of two pieces of short poles[2] which they fasten'd to the dogs, on which they laid their baggage, and thus they marched when the tents were moved from place to place, the tents being of dressed leather were carried on horses, being too heavy for dogs. As the pitching track[3] often passed near ponds of water the dogs made a rush to drink, and lie down to cool themselves, the women ran to prevent their wetting their baggage; and with a big stick drove some back, but more than half got in the pond, and when the women came to avoid a beating, tried to swim out, and would have been drowned if the women had not taken them out, the old men laughing [27i] at the sport. When the tents remove, the able men are all a hunting.

¶ The furrs traded were about one third in beaver skins the rest were mostly and foxes, those red, as well as the wolf skins, each passed as a beaver.[4] Lynxes and Wolverenes the same, but the grey foxes and badgers passed two for one skin. At the trading houses, a tolerable good knowledge of the coun-

1 The South Branch tailor was Peter Sebbeston (b. c. 1763), a native of Sandwick, Orkney. He was employed by the HBC in 1785-95 and also served as a labourer, boatman, and canoe builder.
2 A travois, also used by other Plains Natives. The poles were set to form an isoceles triangle, with the pointed end forward.
3 I.e., the trail along which the sleds travelled.
4 I.e., one fox or wolf skin was accounted to be worth the equivalent of one beaver pelt.

try around for 50 miles is gained by the people going to the hunters tent for the meat of the Bison[5] and Red Deer, as the hunters often shift their ground in search of these animals. By the beginning of April the trade with the Indians was over, and they pitched away[6] for the plains to hunt the Bison and Deer to make dried provisions and dressed leather for tents and clothing. As we expected the ice of the River soon to break up from the mildness of the weather, and rising from the melting of the snow the furrs were assorted, and made into packs of 90 pounds, under a wedge press[7] the provisions examined, and the beat meat mixed with the rendered grease of the Bison made into pimmecan,[8] and placed in bags of well dried parchment skin, each bag weighing ninety pounds. Of this strong and wholesome food an english man requires little more than a pound each day, but a Canadian eats nearly two pounds a day.

[*Mr Hudson his character. No employment. Cumberland Lake. Sturgeon &c*]

¶ About the tenth of April the ice gave way and we prepared to embark, but our neighbours told us, the latter end of the month would be soon enough, as the ice below would not break up before the beginning of May. Each party appeared satisfied with the returns of the trade, and early in May we all left for our several destinations, our neighbours for the Great carrying place on Lake Superior;[1] and our party for York Factory.[2] When arrived at Cumberland House, Mr Tomison left three men and myself to pass the summer under the command of Mr Hudson, who, had been educated in the same mathematical school in which I was, and [27k] like myself bound apprentice to the Hudson Bay Company. He had been here about thirteen years; had lost all his education, except reading and writing, and the little of this, for the accounts of the trade, appeared labor to him; he appeared in a state

5 *Bison bison.*
6 I.e., set forth (towards a place).
7 This kind of fur press, in which the insertion of a wedge provides the force of compression, was favoured at interior posts because it could be built quickly.
8 Pemmican is dried meat (usually of the bison), pounded and mixed with melted fat; in this state it both keeps well and combines a maximum of nourishment in a minimum of space. In his writings, Thompson spells the word, derived from Cree *pimekan*, variously as pemmican, pemican, pemmecan, pimmecan, and pem-me-carn.
1 Grand Portage, at the mouth of the Pigeon River. See note on iv.114 (169).
2 The party left South Branch House on 30 May 1787.

of apathy, always smoking tobacco mixed with weed,[3] had no conversation with any person, the little business he had was done with few words and took no exercise. I was sadly disappointed in him. When we left school a Hadleys quadrant and Robertson elements of navigation in two volumes[4] were presented to each scholar. These I had brought out with me, but when I left Churchill Factory, my blankets, gun and ammunition was a load enough for me to carry one hundred and fifty miles of mud and marsh to York Factory, and they were left to be forwarded by the first opport[un]ity, which never happened: they would have been invalueable to me, I enquired if he had his, he said they had vanished long ago; here again no book, not even a bible.

¶ During the winter, at times we had much leisure, and we employed it in playing at Draughts, for which we had two chequer boards, one with twelve, the other with twenty four men on each side; it is a game of skill and I became expert at it. Having nothing to do, it was my constant employment; and for want of a companion frequently played by myself. A strange incident now happened to me, and which some[times] happens to mankind, which brings with it a strong influence on their conduct for the rest of their lives. I was sitting at a small table with the chequerboard before me, when the devil sat down opposite to me, his features and color were those of a Spaniard, he had two short black horns on his forehead, which pointed forwards, his head [27l] and body down to the waist, (I saw no more) was covered, with glossy, black, curling hair, his countenance mild and grave, we began playing played several games and he lost every game, kept his temper, but looked more grave; at length he got up, or rather disappeared; My eyes were open, it was broad day light, I looked around all was silence and solitude: Was it a dream, or was it a reality. I could not decide. Young and thoughtless as I was, it made a deep impression on my mind. I made no vow, but took a resolution from that very hour never to play a game of chance, or skill, or any thing that had the appearance of them and I have kept it. It is now upwards of sixty three years, since, and yet the whole of this strange incident is plain before me.[5]

¶ I now assisted the men in their labors, learned to make and mend Nets and set them, for our livelihoods depended on our success in fishing. Cumberland Lake is somewhat extensive, near it's middle is a narrow, the northern

---

3   Possibly bearberry (*Arctostaphylos uva-ursi*); see page iv.33e, below (87).

4   John Robertson (1712–76) published *The Elements of Navigation* in 1754. This book was the standard eighteenth-century guide to practical navigation and included tables for determining latitude and longitude at sea. For Hadley's quadrant, see iii.9b above (28).

5   For a discussion of this religious experience, see "Historical Introduction" (xxix).

part has clear water, from a clear stream that flows into it. A branch of the Kisiskatchewan enters the southern part, and makes the water turbid and the Sturgeon[6] caught in this part are fatter and of a fine[r] flavor to those caught in clear water. We had three nets, each of fifty fathoms in length by one fathom in depth with seven to eight inches mesh. The sturgeon were from fifteen to fifty pounds tho' more frequently of the former than the latter weight. The oil collected was sufficient for two lamps at night the year round.

[*up the River to Buckinghame House. Outfit to trade. Barter trade useful to Natives. My outfit*]

¶ Thus summer passed and Autumn came when Mr Tomison arrived from York Factory, with the Canoes and Goods for the trade of the upland country: The men now left here, were those in bad health, or lame from the journey hereto. We embarked and proceeded up the River in the usual routine manner, and nothing happened worth notice until we came to where the River holds it's [27m] course through the great plains where tracking the canoes ended, and the advance of the canoes, against the steady currents of the river was by the paddle. As usual an Indian hunter accompanied us to furnish fresh provisions, which was an easy task. Every day several herds of Bison crossed from the right, to the left, bank of the river. These animals do not appear fond of water, they delight in dry ground and when oppressed by heat and flies do not, like the Deer, seek for refuge under the water of ponds and rivers, but roll themselves on the ground and cover themselves with dust and earth. When they cross the great rivers it is in search of pasturage. They are a head strong animal, and once a herd has taken it's course are not easily driven from it and if this is done, soon return to it. They often came against our file of canoes, and to prevent them from coming on the canoes we had to shove them off with the paddle, for they swim low and are not active in the water their heads only are above it, whereas a Deer when urged springs along, with one fourth of it above the surface. An old Bull will rather fight, than turn aside.

¶ At length we arrived at the trading house lately built, which was named Buckinghame House.[1] After staying a few days: a trading party was formed of six men, of which I was one, under the care of James Gady, who had passed two years with the Pee a gan Indians and had acquired their lan-

6 Lake sturgeon (*Acipenser fulvescens*).
1 Manchester House is intended. Buckingham House was established in 1792.

guage.[2] Each man procured two horses at his own expence for himself and baggage, each man on his own adventure[3] was advanced goods to the amount of about sixty or eighty skins at what was called the standard value, which is about two thirds of what the Indians pay, but to this the Indians always, expect, and get, a present in goods, in proportion of the furrs [27n] they have traded. The goods taken were of small value in money, but of great utility to the Indians. Every thing is carried on by barter profitable to both parties but more so to the Indians than to us. We took from them furrs of no use to them; and which had to pass through an immense distance of freight, and risques before they could be sold in the market of London. See the wife of an Indian sewing their leather clothing with a pointed, brittle bone, or a sharp thorn and the time and trouble it takes; Show them an awl, or a strong needle, and they will gladly give the finest Beaver or Wolf skin they have to purchase it. When the tents remove, a steady careful old man, or two of them are entrusted with the fire, which is carried in a rough wooden bowl with earth in it, and carefully led to the place of the camp. A fire is then made, and as the tents are pitched and ready, one from each tent comes for some fire. A flint and steel saves all this anxiety and trouble. Iron heads for their arrows are in great request, but above all, Guns and ammunition. A war party reckons it's chance of victory to depend more on the number of guns they have, than on the number of men.

¶ My outfit was soon made. Mr Tomison on examening the clothes I had on which was a cotton shirt a blue cloth jacket, and leather trowsers, thought they ought to last seven months, the time to my return, and added another shirt, a leather coat, a blanket and Bison Robe, forty rounds of ammunition, two long knives six flints a few awls, needles &c. with a few pounds of tobacco, and a horse to carry myself and baggage, which obliged me to walk the greatest part of the journey.

2   The HBC's policy of sending envoys to winter with the Siksika, Blood, and Piegan had been instituted in 1784; it was hoped that the links thus formed would facilitate the development of direct trade with these groups. On 9 October 1787, Tomison recorded in the Manchester House journal: "putting the men across to go to the barren ground. 14 in Number. 6 of which are to tent with the Blood Indians. and James Gaddy. with the rest to go to the Pekenow Indians. have sent David Thompson to endeavour to learn the language." B.121/a/2: 15r, HBCA. James Gaddy had wintered with the Piegan in 1785–86 and 1786–87, and would return in 1789–90. He acted as summer master of several of the HBC's inland posts during the 1790s.

3   I.e., each man trading on his own behalf.

[*Eagle catching on conical knowlls &c. Journey on to the One Pine. Cut down for one third. March on. Animals very scarce. Arrive at the Bow River, cross it*]

¶ All things being ready, we set off in the last days of September and crossed to the right bank of the river, and under the guidance of James Gady proceeded in the [270] direction of about WSW for the upper part, of the Bow River near the east foot of the Rocky Mountains, where we expected to find some of the Peeagan Indians camped: a distance of about, — [1] miles, over extensive plains, with patches of wood in places. The trading house from which we, started, was, near the east side of the plains and we passed on the west side of the Eagle Hills; from the river they rise about four hundred feet, in undulating grassy ascents, with very little wood. They are thus named from their west side having several isolated conical knowls, on the tops of which the natives made shallow pits which they covered with slender willows and grass under which they lay, with a large piece of fresh meat opposite their breasts; thus arranged they patiently await the flight of the eagle, which is first seen very high, scaling in rude circles, but gradually lowering, till at length he seems determined to pounce upon the meat, his descent is then very swift with his claws extended, the moment he touches the meat the Indians grasp his two legs in his hands, and dashes him, through the slender willows to the bottom of the pit and strikes his head until he is dead.

Lying in this position, and frequently somewhat benumbed, it requires an active man to pull down an Eagle with his wings expanded, and dash him to the ground.

As the Eagle never loses his courage, the whole must be quickly done, or the Eagle will dart his beak in the mans face, and thus get away, which some-times happens.

Hawks also are frequently taken in the same manner.

The greatest plague to the Eagle catcher, are the grey Foxes of the plains. They are almost as tame as dogs, and while the Indian is lying patiently look-ing at the sky, watching the Eagle, one, or two, of these Foxes, suddenly jump on his breast and seize the piece of meat. A battle ensues in which his cover-ing of willows and grass is destroyed. As the Foxes will be sure to return, the Indian is obliged to shift his place to some other knoll, several miles off and there [27p] try his chance.

¶ I shall not at present attempt to describe the great plains, having had opportunities for the space of twenty years after this to traverse them in

---

1 Here Thompson wrote, then erased, the words "four hundred and fifty."

many directions and confine myself to what did not come under my future notice. As we marched day, after day, we came to the One Pine, so named from a fine tree of white pine, which stood alone, in a patch of aspins.[2] There were no other Pines within sixty, or seventy miles around it, and not the least trace of any pine near it. Such singular kinds of objects are regarded by the native with with superstitious respect. In the dreadful visitation of the small pox[3] some tents of Peeagans were camping near it. One poor fellow as the dreadful malady entered his tent, went and made a speech to it to save himself and family at the same time offered a horse which he hobled and left at the root of the tree.

The next day he did the same, and also the third day. He had now no more horses. The malady increased in his tent, none escaped, and all died but himself. As soon as he gathered strength, he sharpened his axe, went to the pine tree, reproached it with ingratitude, and loving to see dead people, that it was planted by the evil spirit, that as all his family were dead, it should also die. He then took away the horses went up the tree and cut down about one third of it, from the top. It was in this state when we passed. It was about eight years since, and in a state of decay. During the winter I saw this Indian he was a good looking little person, with a deep settled melancholy on his countenance. The old man with whom I lodged, told me, that after the loss of his family, he had taken no wife, lived alone, in the tent of one of his brothers; that he had been several times with the war [27q] parties, never took a shield with him, always placed himself in the front of the battle, as if he wished to die, and yet none of the enemies arrows ever struck him.

2   In November 1792 this tree was observed by Peter Fidler, who gave its name as "Nee tuck kis." "Journal of a Journey over Land from Buckingham House to the Rocky Mountains in 1792 – a 3 by Peter Fidler," E.3/2: 7v, HBCA.

3   Smallpox is a virus, *Variola major*, that is passed from human to human. The epidemic that affected the West between 1780 and 1782 caused severe social and economic dislocation and is mentioned at several points in the *Travels*. In addition to the episode of the Piegan man who made a sacrifice to the One Pine (27p–q, 61; iv.261–2, 286–7), Thompson writes of Native reports of the decline in the number of animals during the epidemic (iv.63–4, 119–20; iii.161, Volume II), the effects of the epidemic on Sioux-Assiniboine relations (iv.154, 203; iii.73–4, Volume II), the experiences of the HBC trader Mitchell Oman in the fall of 1781 (iv.258–62, 284–7), and Saukamappee's account of the infection of the Piegan by the Shoshone (27u, 65–6; iv.273–4, 295–6). Fenn, *Pox Americana*; Paul Hackett, *A Very Remarkable Sickness: Epidemics in the Petit Nord, 1670 to 1846* (Winnipeg: University of Manitoba Press, 2002), 95–100. See also the discussion in "Historical Introduction."

At length the Rocky Mountains came in sight like shining white clouds in the horizon, but we doubted what our guide said; but as we proceeded, they rose in height their immense masses of snow appeared above the clouds, and formed an impassable barrier, even to the Eagle. Our guide also told us, that as we approached these mountains of snow we should find the weather become milder. This we could not believe, but it was so, and the month of November was full as mild as the month of October at the trading house we left to the eastward. For the cold of these countries decreases as much by going westward, as by going to the south.[4] About thirty miles from the mountains we crossed the Bow River running in several channels between gravel shoals, near four feet in depth and two hundred yards wide. During a full months march at about fifteen miles a day, (for we had to keep our horses in good order) over a fine country we found the Bison and Deer very scarce and of course all other animals: we did not meet a single herd; only a chance bull Bison or Red Deer, and they seemed to be wandering, and looking for others of their species. We were all good shots and each had a gun &c, but not one of us was a hunter and could trace an animal on the short grass and hard ground or we should have fared better. Our guide was utterly at a loss to account for the des[t]itute state of the country where he had been so often in danger of being run over by herds of Bisons. Of the few we saw we now and then [27r] contrived to kill a Bull, who would rather fight, than run away, but their flesh, when boiled is so very tough that although our teeth were in good order, and well inclined to do their duty from having had twenty four hours rest, had we masticated the meat by medical rules it would have taken three hours to make our supper.

As it was, we gave each mouthful two, or three hearty nips, and swallowed it down. The flesh of the Bulls in their best state is only fit to be dried and made into beat meat[5] which is frequently done.

[*Meet Peagans. Lodge with an old Man. Bisons &c return northward. Old Sahk a mappe and his native country*][1]

¶ A few miles beyond the Bow River about a dozen Peeagans met us some of their scouts had seen us, but could not say who we were: They were well

---

4 This moderation of the climate is largely due to the effects of warm chinook winds.

5 I.e., pemmican.

1 This is Thompson's first encounter with the Piegan in the 1850 version of the *Travels*. The Piegan were closely allied with the Blood and the Siksika, with whom they shared the northwestern Plains and a traditional bison-based economy. The Piegans'

mounted, and armed with Bows and quivers of arrows. They gave us a hearty welcome, told us to camp where they met us, and would soon bring us some good cow meat; and next morning show us to the camp. Awhile after sun set they brought us two horse loads of fat cow meat, we were hungry, and sat up part of the night roasting and eating; as it was a long month since we had a good meal. Two of them passed the night with us, and were as anxious for news as any people could be; it was on affairs that more, or less, concerned the tribe to which they belonged, the situation and numbers of the tribes of other Indians; whether at peace, or war, or any malady among them. Early the next morning the rest of the party came, and conducted us to their camp, where we arrived about noon. All the elderly men came and gave us their left hand and said they were thankful we had come, as they were in want of ammunition and tobacco.[2] We separated ourselves, two by two to three different tents, where the most respectable men lived. William Flett[3] and myself [27s] were lodged in the tent of an old man, whose hair was grey with age;

position as the tribe nearest the Rocky Mountains brought them into frequent contact with the Shoshone, Kootenai, and Flathead, and by the early eighteenth century, they were at a disadvantage to the mounted Shoshone. This balance of power shifted, however, when the Piegan acquired both horses and firearms, and from the 1740s they exercised military dominance over their neighbours to the south and west. See Binnema, *Common and Contested Ground*; Hugh A. Dempsey, "Blackfoot," *HNAI*, vol. 13, 1:604–28. Thompson had extensive contact with the Piegan; as an HBC apprentice he spent the winter of 1787–88 in a Piegan camp near the Bow River, and as an NWC trader he encountered the Piegan regularly in the years 1799–1802 and 1806–12. During the latter period the Piegan attempted to prevent direct trade with transmontane tribes. Thompson was visited by a Piegan scouting party at Kootanae House in September 1807, and he had to evade the Piegan when crossing the mountains in the fall of 1810. Thompson knew several prominent Piegan figures personally, particularly the military leader Kootanae Appee, the civil chief Sakatow, and the revered elder Saukamappee. The Piegan are a frequent presence in the *Travels*. The 1850 text includes accounts of the winter of 1787–88 (27r–x, 62–8, and iv.261–4, 286–9), the narrative of Saukamappee (iv.264–78, 289–98), and information on Piegan military and political organization and social customs (iv.282–312, 301–20). In the 1848 text, the Piegan appear at several junctures during Thompson's account of the years 1807–12 (Volume II).

2 The Piegan custom of offering the left hand is explained on 27w, below (67).

3 William Flett (1762–1823) was from Firth, Orkney. He entered HBC service as a labourer in 1782, was employed inland beginning in 1785, and in 1810 was made "occasional master" in the Saskatchewan District. At least two other HBC employees shared his name.

his countenance grave, but mild and open; he was full six feet in height, erect, and of a frame that shewed strength and activity.[4]

¶ When we related the scarcity of the Bison and Deer; they were pleased at it, and said it would be to them a plentiful winter. Their argument was; the Bison and Deer, have passed the latter part of the summer, and the fall of the leaves on the Missisourie, and have made the ground bare of grass, and can no longer live there, they must come to us for grass to live on, in our country (the Bow River) and to the northward, to the Kisiskatchewan, wher[e] the snow is beginning to lie on the ground. The winter proved that they reasoned right, for by the beginning of December, the herds of Bulls, which always precedes the herds of Cows began to pass us for the northward; and shortly after the Stags and small herds of Doe red Deer; followed by Wolves and Foxes. After a few days the old man spoke to me in the Nahathaway language, and asked me if I understood it, and how long since I had left my own country. I answered "this is my fourth winter and the Nahathaways are the people we trade with, and I speak their tongue sufficient for common purposes," upon which, with a smile, he said, "I am not a Pee a gan of these plains I am a Nahathaway of the Pasquiaw River" (a River that joins the Kissiskatchewan about fifty miles below Cumberland House.) "that is my native country, and of my fathers for many, many winters. I should have forgotten my mother's tongue were it not that some of my fathers people come among us to buy horses and aid us in War."

I told him I knew the country, had wintered near it, and hunted, Geese and Ducks on the River he mentioned. He said "it is many winters since I last saw the ground where my parents lie. [27t] I came here a young man, and my name is still the same I then received (Sark a map pee. Young man) as you know my country you can name the old men that now live there." I named three old men, but he knew nothing of them. I enquired if the Nahathaways had not given him news of his native country; he replied, they knew nothing of it, and enquired, what people were now hunting there. I informed him that the sons of those he left there, with their families hunted on the north bank of the River, many days march above it that the lowest of them were on the west side of the Eagle Hills, and that his country was now hunted upon by the Indians whom in his time were eastward of Lake Winepeg. He remained silent for some time, and then said, "What a stranger I now find myself in the land of my father's." Although erect and somewhat active, and in full possession of his faculties, yet from the events he related, and comparing them with

4 For the Piegan elder Saukamappee, see appendix 2.

accounts of the french writers on the furr trade of Canada[5] he must have been near ninety years of age, or more for his relation of affairs went back to near the year one thousand seven hundred; and this was now the commencement of the year 1789.[6] (Note. Between three and four years after this he died of old age).[7] He was fond of conversing in his native tongue, and recounting the events of his life, the number and positions of the different tribes of Indians, how they were allied, and the battles they had fought to gain the country of the Bow River (a distance in a direct line of about 800 miles in the direction of s 54 w).

Almost every evening for the time of four months I sat and listened to the old man, without being in the least tired, they were blended with the habits customs, and manners, politics and religion such as it was, Anecdotes of the Indian Chiefs and the means of their gaining influence in war and peace, that I always found [27u] something to interest me. Upon that dreadful malady, the Small Pox, whose ravages had ceased only a few years he did not wish to speak, he said it was brought by a war party of their people, who had attacked a small camp of Snake Indians[8] that had it, and that it spread from

5   Thompson is likely referring to the Jesuit historian Pierre-François-Xavier de Char-levoix (1682–1761). The fruit of his extensive research, which included two visits to Canada, is contained in his authoritative *Histoire et description générale de la Nouvelle France: avec le Journal historique d'un voyage fait par ordre du Roi dans l'Amérique septentrionnale* (1744). The *Histoire*, published in an English translation in 1761, was a standard historical source in the nineteenth century. It is possible that Thompson also consulted some less historically reliable works: Louis Hennepin's *Nouvelle découverte d'un tres grand pays situé dans l'Amérique* (1697, Eng. trans. 1698) or Louis-Armand de Lom d'Arce, Baron de Lahontan's *Nouveaux Voyages* (1703, Eng. trans. 1703).

6   1788 is intended.

7   For the death of Saukamappee, see the entry in appendix 2.

8   The Shoshone. Speakers of a Numic language, the Shoshone migrated to the north-western plains from the south during the late seventeenth century. The first people in the region to obtain horses and use them in battle, by 1730 they had, with their Crow allies, driven the Blackfoot peoples north towards the North Saskatchewan River. During the next fifty years the balance of power shifted as the Blackfoot obtained both horses and a more steady supply of European firearms, allowing them to regain much of their former territory. After the smallpox epidemic (which, as Thompson notes here, had passed from the Shoshone to the Piegan), the Shoshone abandoned the Bow River and by 1805 had retreated south towards the mountainous fringes of the plains for most of the year, subsisting on fish, roots, and berries. See Binnema, *Common and Contested Ground*; Robert F. Murphy and Yolanda Murphy, "North-

tent to tent and camp to camp. He appeared to have no Idea of contagion, and expressed himself that his belief was, the good Spirit had forsaken them for a time, during which, the evil spirit destroyed them and this appeared the prevalent opinion amongst these people. Of the information the old man gave me, it will be found where I give an account of the Indians of the plains.[9]

[*Horses and Mules arrive, Kootanae Appee. War chief his conduct in war. Right and left hands. Su[b]sistence*]

One afternoon, early in January, there was a stir in the camp, and soon after we had the war song of victory sung by the young men, one of whom entered the tent and spoke to the old man for a few minutes. After he went out the old man informed me that a large war party which had been absent for more than two moons had arrived at the frontier camp, and part of them would be here the morrow that they had seen no enemy but the Black People (the name they give to the Spaniards) from whom they had taken a great many Horses and Mules. I enquired if any battle had been fought; he smiled, and said "No, they never fight, they always run away." I was at a loss what to think on so brave a people as the Spaniards running away, and when some of the Horses and Mules were brought to us, I examined them, but not the least trace of blood, or any injury from weapons could be seen.[1] A few days after

ern Shoshone and Bannock," *HNAI*, vol. 11: *Great Basin*, ed. Warren L. D'Azevedo (Washington: Smithsonian Institution, 1986), 284–307; Demitri B. Shimkin, "Eastern Shoshone," *HNAI*, vol. 11, 308–35. Although he did not have direct contact with the Shoshone himself, Thompson writes of them at several points in the *Travels*, particularly in the context of their relationship with the Piegan. In addition to the accounts of Piegan-Shoshone warfare of the 1730s and the transmission of smallpox and its aftermath in the early 1780s, contained in Saukamappee's narrative, Thompson describes Piegan attacks on the Shoshone made in 1788 (iv.279–82, 299–301) and 1811 (iii.173–4, Volume II), and a raid on the Shoshone involving the Piegan war chief Kootanae Appee's son Poonokow (iv.291–3, 307–9).

9   Saukamappee's narrative is on iv.264–78 (289–98).

1   This incident is also recorded on iv.311–12 (320) and iii.167–8 (in Volume II). The most regular and prolific raiders of Spanish convoys in New Mexico were the Comanche and Apache, but these stories reveal that the Piegan also participated periodically. Jack Nisbet suggests that the Spanish party was attacked in what is now southern Colorado, while Theodore Binnema believes that the Piegan did not encounter the Spanish directly but are more likely to have stolen the goods from a party of Utes, who were known as "Black People" to several Plains groups (Nisbet, *Sources*, 26; Binnema, *Common and Contested Ground*, 217n31).

Koo ta nae Ap pee the war chief[2] paid a visit to the old man, on entering the
tent he gave me his left hand, and I gave him my right hand, upon which he
looked at me, and smiled as much to say a contest would not be equal; at his
going away the same took place. He passed about half an hour, conversing
on the late campaign and went away. [27v] No ceremony took place between
them, their behaviour was, as if they had always lived in the same tent.

The old Man recommen[d]ed me to his protection which he promised. He
was apparently about forty years of age, and his height between six feet two
to four inches, more formed for activity than strength, yet well formed for
either; his face a fine oval, high forehead and nose somewhat aquiline; his
large black eyes, and countenance were open, frank, but somewhat stern; he
was a noble specimen of the Indian Warrior of the great plains. The old man
told me he first gained his now high reputation by conducting the retreats of
the war parties of his people; when pressed on by superior numbers. Before he
became the head warrior, when obliged to retreat, each Chief with his party
shifted for themselves and great distress often happened, this he had prevented by his speeches and conduct. His plan were to keep together around
him a band of bold and resolute men with which he guarded the rear; and
on perceiving the enemy becoming confident and not sufficiently cautious to
lay an ambuscade, let some of the foremost pass, attack them in the rear; it
was an onset of a very few minutes and in the confusion and dismay march
of[f] and join his people who stood ready to protect them. This checked the
advance of the enemy and gave safety to the retreating party, and has thus
gained the confidence of his people. On meeting the enemy he placed his
people according to the number of guns they have separating them along
his front so that between each gun, there should be the same number of
Archers.

[27w] The great plains on which these encounters take place are too open
for an ambuscade, except by lying down in undulating grounds. The old man
now remarked to me that as we proceed on, we should see a great many Indians who had never seen a white man, as very few of them went to the trading
houses. "If one of our people offers you his left give him your left hand, for
the right hand is no mark of friendship. This hand wields the spear, draws
the Bow, and the trigger of the gun; it is the hand of death. The left hand is
next to the heart, and speaks truth and friendship, it holds the shield of protection, and is the hand of life." Kootanae Appee made a present to him of
a spanish Mule, with saddle and bridle as when taken. The saddle was well
made of well tanned leather of a chocolate color the bridle was the same, but

---

2 For Piegan military chief Kootanae Appee, see appendix 2.

the bit of the bridle and the stirrups were heavy and made by an awkward blacksmith, these he discarded for those of their own make. The Mule was a fine animal of a dark brown color.

When the tents pitched from place to place[3] he always walked on foot, carrying his pipe stems and medicine bag, he now rode his Mule of which he appeared to be proud. Our subsistence was on the flesh of the Bison, hunted and killed on horseback to the middle of January, when the herds were driven into Pounds to the middle of March. During this time the Women are busily employed in splitting the flesh into thin pieces and hanging it over the smoke to dry, and when dried is a favourite food to all people. Their Pimmecan is too often mixed with choak cherries,[4] braised with the stone of the cherry and dried of which they make large quantities, and which requires the powers of an Ostrich to digest. If the belly has no ears to listen to reason, neither has it a tongue to complain of hard work.[5] The time was approaching for us to return to the trading House from which we set out.

My little outfit was expended, for my subsistence as intended.[6]

[*Trade. Return to the trading house. Mr Tomison. Hudson house and horses*]

My companion and the other men, for their adventures[1] had each made a handsome collection of furrs in Beaver, Wolf and Fox [27x] skins, the article that paid best, was blue Beads. The young men purchased them, to make presents to the women, Guns and amm[un]ition were first, traded, and all the iron work we had then the bagatelles of rings, thimbles, hawks bells, &c, but Tobacco was the great luxury, and like money commanded all things.

The party that came to trade was rather larger than usual and consisted of about thirty men out of upwards of five hundred able men of this people. To these were given all the furrs they had to trade and bring back the articles they wanted, so that those who had not twenty skins of their own, brought to

3 I.e., when the tents were dismantled and transferred to a new location.
4 *Prunus virginiana*.
5 Plutarch attributes the proverb that the belly lacks ears to Cato the Elder. Plutarch, "Marcus Cato," in *Parallel Lives*, ed. Bernadotte Perrin (Cambridge: Harvard University Press, 1914), viii.1, 2:322. That the belly lacks a tongue seems to be Thompson's own invention.
6 I.e., Thompson had traded the goods with which he had left Manchester House the previous October.
1 The private trading that the men had undertaken over the winter.

trade sixty to eighty skins in furrs, and received a present from the Trader in proportion to the furrs he traded, which was his own.

¶ On our arrival we received a hearty welcome. Mr Tomison was glad to see me, but did not like my appearance, he viewed me all round, and muttered "ragged, very ragged, can't be mended, must have a new jacket," which the tailor made for me. He had a scarlet vest which he put on on his arrival at York Factory took off when he left it, and carefully folded and laid by for the next occasion, this was it's third year, and on looking at it, he thought it's color somewhat faded, one of the men said a little lye will freshen it; he gave it to the man to do so, he made the lye too strong and took most of the color out; when brought to him the lower part of his favourite vest was nearly white, the rest spotted red and white a ghost could not have changed his color more; he turned it every way to be sure it was his very vest. As he had no more cloth of that color, he had one of blue cloth made.

¶ As soon as the River was clear of ice, the canoes were got ready and the furrs embarked for York Factory, as very little goods remained he determined that myself with one other man should take care of them at Hudson House, a trading post lower down which had been left vacant and near which no Indians were expected [27y] to come to trade.[2] It was situated about four miles in the immense forest, that extends from Hudson's Bay and the Atlantic Ocean to the great plains. An account of the goods left being taken, Mr Tomison descended the stairs to the lower room where I was writing, and perceiving a single duck shot, took it up, went up stairs untied the bag, and put it in with the other shot. This parsimony was habitual to him, brought up in a barren rocky Island, (one of the Orkneys) where every thing is husbanded with care, he placed too high a value on things beneath his notice and never could conform himself to the customs of these wild countries and these Natives, who despise such habits of parsimony, as the effects of a sordid, mind. He was a truly, honest, kind hearted man would have made a first rate steward, but was not adapted to be at head of affairs. Two years after, in an altercation with an Indian, who thought himself not liberally dealt with in trade, he was slightly stabbed in the thigh, and returned to his native country.[3]

2 Thompson was at Hudson House 24 May to 19 September 1788 and kept the post journal for the master, James Tate. Hudson House, Post Journal, 1788–1789, B.121/a/3, HBCA. The others present were Nicholas Allen, Peter Brown, William Rich, and Andrew Flett.

3 Thompson was not alone in his criticism of Tomison's excessive parsimony. While Tomison did take leave in Britain in 1789, he returned to the inland trade the following year and did not retire definitively until 1810. Tomison was stabbed through the

¶ The Horses belonging to the company and the Men (about forty) were brought and placed about five miles back in the forest among some small meadows with two men to take care of them and make smoky fires of green wood to give some relief to the horses from Musketoes and other flies. We had at least four months to pass with barely a months dried provisions, and for the rest we had to hunt the Bison and Deer, which we thought rather an honor than a hardship. We made arrangements with the horse keepers to meet us at the edge of the forest with two good horses, with which we hunted, and loaded with meat; which lasted a few days and then returned again to hunt. For this we had ample space, as the plains [27z] on the left bank of the River extend in length 450 miles along it's banks, by about forty in breadth through which passes several brooks, at a distance from each other, with many small ponds of a saline, mild purgative quality, but the general features are those of a dry country, every where covered with short tender grass, nourished by the dews and rains which are here more copious than to the southward, probably from the north side of these plains being the southern bounda[r]y of the great forests that stretch from Latitude 53 degrees, to 70 degrees north.

[*How to clear and cool river water. thirst. Thirst taken away by bathing. Red Deer. Antelope*]

¶ The heats of summer often made us wish for cold water which the river could not give us. When at the house we used to take a four gallon kettle full of river water, and place it in the cellar. The river water is so turbid, that the hand cannot be seen a few inches below the surface yet after standing two nights there was very little deposit in the Kettle, and the water did not cool; but upon bringing the kettle full of water to a smart boil for about two minutes and then placing it in the cellar, in a few hours the water became clear, and as cold as we could wish it and remained so, and deposited a very clay of a whitish color to the depth of full one inch and som[e]times to near two inches. We generally hunted within ten or fifteen miles of the river that when oppressed by thirst we might there find relief which too often happened; After hard riding all day, exposed to the action of the sun, sadly thirsty, we put up at night without a drop of water. We had a fine roast from a small fire of the dried dung of the Bison, hungry as we were [27za] we could not eat. When the dew fell, we sometimes licked the grass, but it gave us no relief, and made our tongues sore. After passing a feverish night, at dawn of day we

knee at Edmonton House on 15 April 1799; this is likely the incident to which Thompson refers. Edmonton House, Post Journal, 1798–1799, B.60/a/4: 31v, HBCA.

saddled our horses, and rode for the river, our horses as eager as ourselves. On coming near to it, without stopping, the speed of the horses, we dropped our guns, powder horns and shot bags, and by one of the numerous Bison paths rode full speed into the river, both horse and man went under, rose, and swam to shore. The cooling sensation was delicious and entirely took away all thirst, so that we had not the least wish to drink. After enjoying ourselves in this wet state for some time, we took a slight drink, and resumed our look out for Deer &c.

¶ Until August the Red Deer furnished [us] with meat. Our mode of hunting the Deer while feeding; one crawled on knees, and then, when near did the same keeping flat on the grass, while the other kept steady on horseback if the shot was fatal, so much the better, but frequently the deer was only wounded, and started of, in this case the other of us gave chase, and as a Deer is a tender animal seldom, went above five miles before it was over taken and shot. Red Deer, is not a favourite meat, it's fat hardens when cold. We sometimes got an Antelope,[1] but that by chance. These beautiful deer, that run with the swiftness of a Hawk on the wing, on seeing them, we stopped our horses and throwing the reins to the ground for them to stand quiet we separated ourselves, and laid down about thirty yards from the horses, and there waited them, when within about 200 yards they would stop and look at the horses, then step gently forward to satisfy their curiosity, which brought them within shot of one of us, and a Ball is fatal to such a delicate animal. At times we had rough customers to deal with, we now and then met a black Bear,[2] but they were not worth killing their furr were out of season and they were lean, a she bear, with her cubs came to steal our meat, she was [27zb] hungry and determined to have the meat, or fight for it a ball in the head laid her quiet and sent the cubs away.

[*The plains. Ponds of salts. The Bisons cross over farther. Bisons*]

¶ These fine plains will, in time, to come be the abode of Mankind, probably semicivilized leading a pastoral life, tending Cattle and Sheep. The Farmer requires a considerable quantity of wood for buildings, fences, and fuel and it is only in chance places, even along the river side, where such can be found. The farmer must place himself on the north side of these plains where he will have abundance of wood, and extend his farm into the plains as far as he pleases, say two miles, all the rest of these plains of 350 miles in

1 Pronghorn (*Antilocapra americana*).
2 *Ursus americanus.*

length, by about 38 miles in breadth will be pastoral, and inhabited by herds-men and shepherds dwelling in round leather tents; moving from place to place as circumstances require, and finding in hollows and banks of brooks the little wood they want.

¶ There are also many Ponds of medicineal water, the salts of which lie dried on the shore for several feet around them. One sultry afternoon in August as we rode we came to a fine clear pond which looked very tempting we were both very thirsty, but I perceived dried salts lying in a little bay and pointed them out to my companion, he said he would alight, and only wash his mouth which was parched up; this was a forbearance I did not dare to venture, but instead of only washing his mouth, he took a hearty draught; and found the water cool and agreeable; it had it's effect as a mild purgative. In the early part of August the Bison came from the southward, and crossed the River to the north side herd after herd, day and night, until these solitary plains where a chance deer was all that was to be seen, soon became, literally a moving mass of black cattle; they appeared very hungry and devoured the tender grass, even when started they [27zc] ran only a short distance, then stopped and grazed.

The Cows were fat and excellent meat. The younger Bulls kept near the Cows in small herds, and were in tolerable order, but the old Bulls fed sepa-rate, poor and ferocious.

[*Break my right Leg. Cumberland House. Mr Turnor arrives. Practical astronomy. Arrive at York Factory*]

¶ In the early part of September Mr Tomison arrived with the Canoes and goods from York Factory, every thing was packed up and they proceeded up the river to Buckinghame House, the winter station for the furr trade.[1] The three horsekeepers, with Andrew[2] and myself were ordered to bring up the horses to the same place, with all which we safely arrived. Winter came on, and affairs went on as usual. The next year in the early part of March on coming down a rude steep bank I fell and broke the large bone of my right leg and had to be hauled home; which, by the mercy of God turned out to be

1 The men left Hudson House on 19 September 1788 and arrived at Manchester House on 3 October.
2 Andrew Flett (c. 1762–after 1795), from Orphir, Orkney, was hired by the HBC as a labourer in 1786. He spent most of his fur trade career working in the York Inland Department. Described variously as "good" and "steady" in servants' ledgers, Flett became a canoeman in 1793 and bowsman in 1794. He returned to Britain in 1795.

the best thing that ever happened to me.[3] Mr Tomison behaved with the tenderness of a father to me and alleviated my sufferings all he could. As soon as the mild weather came on, and the river clear of ice, the furrs and canoes were got ready to proceed to York Factory and I descended the river to Cumberland House[4] which, at that time (1789) was not a depot, and where I was left, with two men to pass the summer, and fish for our livelihood; the fish caught were Sturgeon of an excellent quality, but too rich for my low state of health, and I became emaciated till the berries became ripe, when the kind hearted indian women brought me plenty of berries for my support; this was pure charity, for I had nothing to give them and I was much relieved.

In the latter end of August Mr Tomison with the canoes [27zd] and goods for the furr trade, and left three men and myself with goods to trade and pass the winter, for at that time this house had a valuable trade of about twenty packs of fine furrs, each of ninety pounds weight. In the begining of October two canoes arrived from York Factory bringing Messrs Philip Turnor,[5] Hudson, and Isham,[6] The former to survey the country to the west end of the Athabasca Lake, with Mr Hudson for his assistant, The latter to take his station as a furr trader. This was a fortunate arrival for me, as Mr Turnor was well versed in mathematics, was one of the compilers of the nautical Almanacs and a practical astronomer; Under him I regained my mathematical education, and during the winter became his only assistant and thus learned practical astronomy under an excellent master of the science. Mr Hudson unf[ort]unately for himself, was too fond of an idle life, became dropsical, and soon died.[7]

3 For a discussion of this accident, which occurred on 23 December 1788, see "Historical Introduction" (xxx).
4 Thompson was at Cumberland House from 26 May 1789 to 9 June 1790. Malchom Ross ran the post during the summer of 1789, and then Tomison took charge, 7 October 1789 to 21 April 1790, after which Ross resumed command.
5 For HBC surveyor Philip Turnor, see appendix 2. He arrived at Cumberland House on 7 October 1789 and during the winter taught astronomy, first to Thompson and then to Peter Fidler. Turnor's survey of Athabasca (which Thompson mentions on iv.97, 146 and iv.117–18, 173) lasted from September 1790 to July 1792.
6 Charles Thomas Isham (1754/55–1814), the son of Chief Factor James Isham and a Cree woman, became an HBC apprentice in 1766 and went inland as a labourer in 1774. He became an inland trader in May 1789, a few months before Thompson encountered him at Cumberland House. Jennifer S.H. Brown, "Charles Thomas Isham," DCB, 5:450–1.
7 Hudson died at Cumberland House on 19 April 1790.

By too much attention to calculations in the night, with no other light than a small candle my right eye became so much inflamed that I lost its sight,[8] and in the early part of May when the rivers and lakes became navigable, my health and strength were thought too weak to accompany Mr Turnor as his assistant and a Mr Peter Fidler took my place.[9] With the canoes and furrs I descended the Rivers and crossed the lakes &c to York Factory, then under the charge of Mr Humphrey Martin[10] and took my station as clerk and accountant of the Factory. A few days sufficed for all the writing and accounts. The rest of the year was spent in shooting Geese, Ducks and white Grouse.[11]

8 On 10 May 1790 Ross recorded in the post journal that Thompson was taken ill, and on 19 May that his right eye was "very bad." Cumberland House, Post Journal, 1789–1790, B.49/a/21: 50r–51r, HBCA. When in February 1848 Thompson lost the sight in his left eye, he recalled "the right eye has been blind now 58 years, with a cataract in the Eye." AO. 75.35. He was treated by Dr Henry Howard of Montreal, who recorded that Thompson had a cicatrix, or scar, in the centre of his right cornea. Henry Howard, *The Anatomy, Physiology, and Pathology of the Eye* (Montreal: Armour and Ramsay, 1850), 357–8.

9 For HBC trader and surveyor Peter Fidler, see appendix 2.

10 As Humphrey Marten had retired in 1786, Joseph Colen is intended. For Colen, see appendix 2.

11 Thompson arrived at York on 7 July 1790, having been in the interior for just under four years, and he remained there until 5 September 1792. When he arrived he would have met his younger brother, John, who had been engaged the previous year as an HBC servant. John was made a middleman on a canoe team and was sent inland on 27 July.

Page
30.

On our return about halfway up the black river, we came to one of the falls, with a steep rapid both above and below it, we had a carrying place of 200 yards, we then attempted the strong current above the fall, they were to track the canoe up by a line, walking on shore, while I steered it, when they had proceeded about eighty yards, they came to a Birch Tree, growing at the edge of the water, and there stood and disputed between themselves on which side of the tree the tracking line should pass, I called to them to go on, they could not hear me for the noise of the fall, I then waived my hand for them to proceed, meanwhile the current was drifting me out, and having only one hand to guide the canoe, the Indians standing still, the canoe took a sheer across the current, to prevent the canoe upsetting I waved my hands to them to let go the line and leave me to my fate, which they obeyed, I sprung to the bow of the canoe took out my clasp knife, cut the line from the canoe and put the knife in my pocket, by this time I was on the brow of the fall, all I could do was to place the canoe to go down bow foremost, in an instant the canoe was precipitated down the fall twelve feet, and buried under the waves, I was struck out of the canoe, and when I arose among the waves, the canoe came on me and buried beneath it, to raise myself I struck my feet against the rough bottom and came up close to the canoe which I grasped, and being now on shoal water, I was able to conduct the canoe to the shore, my two companions ran down along the beach to my assistance, nothing remained in the canoe but an axe, a small tent of grey cotton and very green, when the canoe was hauled on shore I had to lay down on the rocks, wearied and bruised, and exhausted by my exertions, the Indians went down along the shore, and in half an hour time returned with my oil tea, lined with cork containing my sextant and a few instruments, and our three paddles, we had no time to lose, my all was my shirt and a blue linen vest, my companions were in the same condition, we divided the small tent into three pieces to wrap ourselves, as a defence against the flies

¶ [iv.28] Having described what is peculiar to the wild shores of Hudson's Bay, I now turn to the interior country, and include a space from Hudson's Bay of about three hundred miles in width, known to the furr traders by the name of the Musk Rat country.[1] The geology of this country is quite distinct from the countries westward, it is composed of granite, and other silicious Rocks. From the parallel of 50 a 55 degrees north this rocky region extends northward to the extremity of the continent, and is about 400 miles in width; to the southward of the above line, this region extends southward to the coasts of Labrador; every where it's character is much the same, almost every where rock covered with moss, the spots of tolerable soil are neither large, nor frequent, containing very many Lakes, the Streams from which find their way to the large Rivers. This region is bounded on the west by the great chain of Lakes, the principal of which are Lake Superior, the Rainy Lake, the Lake of the Woods, Winepeg, the Cedar, and chain of Lakes northward to the Athabasca and great Slave Lakes. The northern parts are either destitute of Woods, or they are low and small; especially about Hudson's Bay where the ground is always frozen; even in the month of August, in the woods, on taking away the moss, the ground is thawed at most, for two inches in depth: Mr Joseph Colen, the Resident at York Factory, on having a Cellar dug for a new building, found the earth frozen to the depth of five and a half feet, below which it was not frozen. All the Trees on this frozen soil have no tap roots, their roots spread on the ground, the fibres of the roots interlace with each other for mutual support; and although around Hudson's Bay there is a wide belt of earth of about one hundred miles in width, apparently of ancient alluvial from the rounded gravel in the banks of the Rivers, yet it is mostly all a cold wet soil, the surface covered with wet moss, ponds, marsh, and dwarf trees. The only dry places are the banks of the Brooks, Rivulets, and Lakes.

[*Woods of the interior – their use and situation. White and grey Birch. Pines. The Berries. Pipe Stems of a shrub. Arrow Wood. Weed berry &c*]

1 Here the Musk Rat Country appears to be coterminous with the Canadian Shield, which Thompson generally calls the "Stony Region." Elsewhere, the term Musk Rat Country refers to a smaller area within the Canadian Shield, north of Lake Winnipeg. On iv.61 (118) Thompson gives the area of the Musk Rat Country as 22,360 square miles. In 1806 he wrote a long essay on the "Rat Country" in his notebooks. AO. 17.210–189; see Volume III.

¶ The rocky region close westward of this coarse alluvial already noticed, in very many places, especially around it's Lakes, and their intervals, have fine Forests of Pines, Firs, [iv.29] Aspins, Poplars, White and grey Birch,[1] Alder[2] and Willow;[3] all these grow in abundance, which makes all this region of rock and Lake appear a dense forest, but the surface of the Lakes cover full two fifths, or more, of the whole extent. The most usefull trees are the White Birch, the Larch, and the Aspin. The White Birch, besides it's bark, which is good for tanning leather; has also a Rind which covers the bark, of which Canoes are made; this Rind is thick in proportion to the intense cold of winter where the tree grows, in high Latitudes, it is one fourth of an inch thick, and wherever the winter is very cold; On the west side of the Mountains where the winters are very mild, the Rind is too thin to be of any use; it thus appears to be a protection to the tree against the frost. The Wood of the Birch tree is used for making Sledges and Sleds, Axe helves and whatever requires strength and neatness, as the frames of Snow Shoes, but does not bear exposure to wet weather. The Rind is very useful to the Natives and Traders; for making Canoes, Dishes, coverings for canoes, and for Tents and Lodges in the open seasons. The White Birch is seldom more than four feet in circumference, but to the branches of which the head is formed, carries this girth with little dimunition; it can be raised from the bark only in mild weather, in hot weather it freely comes away, and a well grown tree will give from fifteen to thirty feet of Birch Rind; it requires a practised Man to raise it without injuring it. The Rind is never renewed, and the bark not having the shelter of the rinds becomes full of cracks, and the tree decays.[4] In the spring of the year incisions in the tree yield a sap, which is boiled to a well tasted syrup.

¶ The grey birch[5] grows among the Rocks, it [is] a dwarf tree, crooked, knotty, and full of branches, it's wood is stronger than the white birch; it's rind too thin to be of use, it has many tatters hanging to it, which are much used for quickly lighting a fire. The Larch[6] is well known, a strong elastic wood, and make the best of Sleds. The poplar and aspin, make the best of fire wood for a tent, the wood does not sparkle, and the smoke is mild; the smoke

---

1 Probably the dwarf birch (*Betula pumila*); see below.
2 Speckled alder (*Alnus rugosa*).
3 Several species exist (*Salix spp.*).
4 With his use of the term "rind," Thompson distinguishes between the tree's smooth, white, papery outer bark and its orange inner bark. Thompson elaborates on this distinction and on the uses of the paper birch on iv.68–70, below (123–5).
5 Possibly a variety of swamp birch (*Betula spp.*).
6 Tamarack (*Larix laricina*).

of no other woods ought to be used for drying meat and fish. The smoke of these woods preserves [iv.30] both, and gives an agreeable taste; in places, there are fine forests of Aspins of six inches to one foot diameter, and thirty to forty feet without branches. The White and Red Firs grow on a sandy soil, they are of dwarf growth, and full of knots and branches. There are four species of the Pine, besides the Cypress;[7] the white Spruce[8] is noted for it's fine spreading branches, which form the beds of the traveller and the hunter; In the frozen clime of Hudson's Bay, only half of this tree can be used, the north east side being very brittle and can hardly be called wood. The other Pines[9] are mostly found in the interior, they thrive most near Lakes and Rivers, and in favorable places are of six feet girth, and forty to fifty feet in height. By the Natives the saplings of these serve for tent poles, laths and timbers for canoes, by the traders, the same purposes, and building of Houses.

¶ Of Berries there are twenty species all known in europe, but one. They are, the dry[10] and swamp Cranberry,[11] the Crow[12] and Black Berries,[13] two kinds of Raspberries;[14] the Strawberry;[15] two kinds of Cherry's,[16] both are small, White[17] and red Currants:[18] the black Currant,[19] a mild purgative; two kinds of Gooseberries,[20] two of Hip berries;[21] the Juniperberry;[22] the Eye berry:[23] the Bear Berry;[24] this has a low spreading plant which lies flat on

7 Probably the common juniper (*Juniperus communis*).

8 *Picea glauca.*

9 The three other members of the pine family are likely the jack pine (*Pinus banksiana*), balsam fir (*Abies balsamea*), and black spruce (*Picea mariana*).

10 Northern mountain cranberry (*Vaccinium vitisidaea*).

11 Small cranberry (*Vaccinium oxycoccus*).

12 *Empetrum nigrum.*

13 Possibly the allegheny blackberry (*Rubus allegheniensis*) or the bristly blackberry (*Rubus setosus).*

14 Red raspberry (*Rubus idaeus*) and possibly cloudberry (*Rubus chamaemorus*).

15 *Fragaria virginiana.*

16 Chokecherry (*Prunus virginiana*) and pin cherry (*Prunus pennsylvanica*).

17 The identity of the "White Currant" is unclear.

18 Northern red currant (*Ribes rubrum*).

19 Northern black currant (*Ribes hudsonianum*).

20 Probably two subspecies of the northern gooseberry (*Ribes oxyacanthoides*).

21 Probably two subspecies of the wild rose (*Rosa acicularis*).

22 Common juniper (*Juniperus communis*).

23 Dwarf raspberry (*Rubus arcticus*).

24 *Arctostaphylos uva-ursi.* Thompson refers to the Cree and Ojibwa smoking mixture *kinnikinik,* "that which is mixed." Charlotte Erichsen-Brown, *Use of Plants for the Past 500 Years* (Aurora, ON: Breezy Creeks Press, 1979), 126.

the ground, it has it's use in medicine; the Natives collect and dry the leaves, where ever it can be procured; it is mixed with tobacco for smoking, giving to the smoke a mild, agreeable flavour. A berry of an agreeable acid called the Summer Berry,[25] it ripens late in Autumn, the Shrub of this berry has a large pith, takes a good polish and is used for Pipe Stems; and the Mis ars kut um berry,[26] perhaps peculiar to north america; the berry grows abundantly on willow like shrubs, is of the color of deep blue, or black; the size, of a full grown green pea, very sweet and nourishing, the favorite food of small birds, and the Bears. They are very wholesome, and may safely be eaten as long as the appetite continues; this berry is much sought after by the Natives, they collect and dry them in quantities for future use; and mixed [iv.31] with Pim me can, becomes a rich and agreeable food. The wood is of a fine size for arrows, and where this can be got, no other is employed; it is weighty, pliant and non elastic; As this berry is preceded by a beautiful flower, and the berry is as rich as any currant from Smyrna,[27] and keeps as well it ought to be cultivated in Canada, and in England.

[*Fish. Pike. Trout and White Fish. Nets &c. Carp Red & White*]

The Rivers and Lakes, have Pike,[1] (the water wolf,) he preys on every fish he can master, even on his own species; he seises his prey by the middle of the back, and keeps his hold until it is dead; when he swallows it. It catches readily at any bait, even a bit of red rag. It is a bold native fish, and in summer is often found with a mouse in it's stomach. It's jaws are strong, set with sharp teeth, somewhat curved, it is of all sizes from one to fifteen pounds; it is seldom found in company with the Trout,[2] which last appears to be the master fish; for where they are found in the same Lake, the Pike are confined to the shallow bays. The Trout to attain to a large size, they require to be in extensive deep Lakes. In this region they are from one to twenty pounds, they are as rich as meat. The white fish[3] are well known, their quality and size depends much on the depths of the Lakes. In shoal Lakes they are generally poor and in deep Lakes fat and large, they are almost the sole subsistence

---

25 High-bush cranberry (*Viburnum opulus*).
26 Saskatoon service berry (*Amelanchier alnifolia*).
27 Modern-day Izmir, Turkey, renowned for its dried fruit; there is also a variety of dried grape called the Smyrna raisin.
 1 Northern pike (*Esox lucius*).
 2 Lake trout (*Salvelinus namaycush*).
 3 Lake whitefish (*Coregonus clupeaformis*).

of the Traders and their men in the winter, and part of the summer; they are caught in Nets of five to six inches mesh, fifty fathoms in length, and five to six feet in depth; which are set and anchored by stones in three to five fathoms water, if possible on a sandy, or fine gravel, bottom. They weigh from two to ten pounds. They are a delicate fish, the net ought not to stand more than two nights then taken up and washed in hot water, dried and mended; Some of the Lakes have only a fall fishery and another in the spring, in this case the fish are frozen, and lose part of their good taste. Fish do not bear keeping, the maxim is; "from the hook or the net, directly into the kettle of boiling water." Those who live wholly on fish, without any sauce, frequently without salt, know how to cook fish in their best state for sauces make a fish taste well, which otherwise [iv.32] would not be eatable. There are two species of Carp, the red[4] and grey;[5] the former is a tolerable fish; the latter is so full of small bones, only the head and shoulders are eaten. They spawn in the spring, on the small Rapids, are in shoals, the prey of the Eagle, the Bear, and other animals. The Sturgeon to be good must be caught in muddy Lakes, he is the fresh water hog, fond of being in shoal alluvials; in such lakes it is a rich fish; but in clear water not so good, they weigh from ten to fifty pounds. The Pickerel,[6] the Perch[7] and Methy[8] are common; these are all the varieties of fish found in this region worth notice.

[*Birds. Whip poor will. Rook. Eagle brown. Eagle striking wild geese, it's swiftness. White Eagle. it's fishing*]

With the Spring a variety of small birds arrive, they breed and remain during the summer, and depart to the southward in Autumn, they are all known to Europe. The Whip poor will, arrives in the month of March, in the afternoon and evening, as well as the morning he flits from tree to tree, about ten feet from the snow, with it's head downwards, repeats it's cry of Whip poor will for two, or three minutes, and then flies to another tree, only one species is known. The Natives regard it as a peculiar bird and never hurt it.[1] In some summers the flocks of Pigeons[2] are numerous, and make sad

---

4 Longnose sucker (*Catostomus catostomus*).
5 A variety of redhorse (genus *Moxostoma*)
6 Walleye (*Stizostedion vitreum*).
7 Yellow perch (*Perca flavescens*).
8 Burbot (*Lota lota*).
1 It is unclear which species Thompson intends, but the behaviour he describes is not indicative of the whip-poor-will (*Caprimulgus vociferus*).
2 Passenger pigeon (*Ectopistes migratorius*); now extinct.

havoc of the Straw and Raspberries, in other summers they are very few. The Rooks[3] arrive in the latter end of April, the Natives regard the time of their arrival as the sure sign that winter has passed away, and the mild weather set in. The British population in Canada call them Crows, which latter bird is not known in North America. Two species of Eagle visit us, the large brown Eagle[4] is seen in March, and gives it's name to the Moon of this month;[5] it is merely a visitor, soars high, seldom alights, and then shows itself a most majestic bird; it is sometimes shot, as the Natives set a high value on it's plumage, and respect it as the master of all other birds; from the tip of one wing to the tip of the other wing, it has been measured nine feet. It's talons are long, very curved and strong, and it strikes with great force. [iv.33] It is supposed capable of carrying off a bird equal to it's own weight, which is ten to twelve pounds, some have weighed fourteen pounds; yet the great Eagle of the Plains is larger than these.

¶ The Grey Goose is accounted a very swift bird on the wing. At a distance we perceived a flock of these geese pursued by an Eagle, the latter did not seem to gain much on the former, they passed about one hundred yards from us (out of shot) the Eagle was then close to them, and going a short distance further, it came up to the third goose from the rear, and with one of it's claws, drove it's talons thro' the back of the goose close behind the wings, it fell as if shot, the Eagle stooped to take it, we ran and frightened it away: and it kept on it's flight after the other geese; we picked up the goose, quite dead, the claws had perforated through the back bone over the heart. As they passed us, we remarked, the Eagle gained fast on the geese. The Hawks in like manner strike the birds they prey on; the Natives say the Eagle readily carries off Duck, and Hares, but the grey goose is too heavy for him, but he soon tears it to pieces with his sharp, crooked beak; the Fox will contend with the Hawks for the birds they kill in the great marshes, and plains but never with the Eagle, the Wolf tries for the prey of the latter, and is sure to be beaten.

¶ The other species of Eagle is the White Headed,[6] from the head and upper part of the neck being covered with white feathers which lie close on

---

3 Common crow (*Corvus brachyrhynchos*).
4 Golden eagle (*Aquila chrysaetos*).
5 Thompson refers to a Cree cycle of moons; in the 1848 version of the *Travels*, he notes the eagle moon of March is called "Meek e shoo Peeshim" (iii.147; see Volume II).
6 Bald eagle (*Haliaeetus leucocephalus*). In December 1847 Thompson contributed two pieces about this bird to the Montreal *Gazette*, containing much of the same information included here (see Volume III). On iv.100-1, below (148-9), Thompson

each other, it is called the bald headed Eagle, I believe it peculiar to North America, the color of the rest of the neck, and of the body, is all the shades of a deep brown, with tinges of dark yellow. It lives mostly on fish, without any objection to a chance hare, or duck. They are generally found in pairs, and build their nest in the branches of a poplar, close on the banks of a Lake, or River: like the other species they lay only two, or three eggs; and rears it's young with great care; as it is, comparatively, slow of flight,[7] although it's wings extend seven to eight [iv.33a] feet, it hovers over the surface of the water; for some fish, of a weight it can take out of the water, and carry off to it's nest. That it is successful the old, and young eagles, attest by their fatness; the inside fat is purgative, and when they feed on trout, highly so; their flesh is eaten by the Natives, as being more fat and juicy, and prefer them to Grouse. They seize their prey by the back, between the fins, and if weighty, make for the shore; and there with their beak, cut off the head, of the fish; and thus take it to the nest. It sometimes strikes a fish too weighty for it, in this case the fish carries the Eagle under water, where it loosens it's claws, and comes to the surface, it's feathers all wet, it floats well, but as it cannot swim, is drifted to the shore by the wind or current, and must wait it's feathers to dry, before it can take flight.

[*Owls &c. Horned Owl. Owls & Mice. ejects hair &c. Swans shooting them in the night. Enticing and shooting Swans, Cranes. Bittern, Ducks*]

There are five species of the Hawk, three pass the winter, they prey on every thing they can master.[1] There are four species of the Owl, one of them is very small,[2] two of the others are large, one of these is called the great White Owl;[3] it weighs ten to twelve pounds; the other is the noted Horned Owl,[4] so named from it's having on each side of the head, stiff, erect, feathers

---

describes his unhappy experience of eating the "inside fat" of a bald eagle during his 1796 journey to Lake Athabasca.

7 In the margin Thompson wrote the words "6 lbs weighed 16 lbs."

1 The northern goshawk (*Accipiter gentilis*) and gyrfalcon (*Falco rusticolus*) can be found in the Canadian Shield during the winter. Other hawk and hawklike birds to which Thompson refers here may include the osprey (*Pandion haliaetus*), sharp-shinned hawk (*Accipiter striatus*), and peregrine falcon (*Falco peregrinus*).

2 Probably the boreal owl (*Aegolius funereus*).

3 Snowy owl (*Nyctea scandaica*).

4 *Bubo virginianus*. The fourth owl may be the northern hawk owl (*Surnia ulula*) or the great gray owl (*Strix nebulosa*).

in shape and size, like the ears of the White Fox; it is a fine looking, grave bird, with large lustrous eyes, and in the dark sees remarkably well, and preys wholly in the night. They are easily tamed, I have often kept one during the winter; it lives chiefly on mice, which it never attempts to swallow until it is sure it is dead, of this it judges by the animal ceasing to move; perched on it's stand, and a live mouse presented to it, with it's formidable talons, it seized the mouse by the loins, and instantly carried it to it's mouth, and crushed the head of the mouse; still holding it in one of it's claws, it watched till all motion ceased and then, head foremost, swallowed the mouse; often while the Owl was watching the cessation of motion, with the end of a small willow, I have touched the head of the Mouse, which instantly received another crush in it's beak, and thus continued, 'till it was weary, when loosening [iv.33b] it's claws, it seized the Mouse by the head; by giving motion to the body, it crushed it, and [I] have thus vexed it until the body was in a pulp, yet the skin whole; by leaving the Mouse quiet for about half a minute, it was swallowed; from seve[ral] experiments, I concluded, that to carnivorous birds, the death of it's prey is only known by the cessation of motion; like all other birds that swallow their prey whole, the hair, if an animal, or the feathers if a bird, are by some process in the stomach, rolled into hard, small, round, balls; and ejected from the mouth with a slight force. The meat of the Owls is good and well tasted to hunters.

¶ The aquatic birds are more numerous, and in great variety; but they pass to the southward as the cold weather comes on. They arrive in the month of May, and leave us by the middle, or latter end of October, as the season may be. There are two species of the Swan, the largest[5] weighs about twenty four pounds, the lesser[6] about fifteen; when fat, they lay from seven to nine eggs, when shot, twelve eggs have been counted in them; but nine is the greatest number I have found in a nest, and also of the number they rear; when fat they are good eating, but when poor the flesh is hard and dry, they are a shy bird, and their nests not often found: they frequent the lesser Lakes; and seldom approach the shores. The Natives often shoot them in the night; for this purpose, fir wood, split into laths, to burn freely, is made into small parcels, one of which is placed in an old kettle, or one made of wood, placed on a strong, short, stick, to keep it two, or three feet above the Canoe. When it is quite dark, two Indians embark, one steers the Canoe quietly, and steadily, towards the Swans, (they keep near each other;) the other is in the bow of the

5 Trumpeter swan (*Cygnus buccinator*).
6 Tundra swan (*Cygnus columbianus*).

Canoe, with his gun, and the torch wood; which is lighted and soon in full blaze, and is kept in this state by the man in the bow; as soon as the Swans perceive the fire, they commence, and continue, their call of Koke Koke, they appear aware of danger, but are fascinated by the fire, they keeping calling and swiming half round, and back in the same place, gazing on the fire; until the Canoe is [iv.33c] within about thirty yards, when the bow man, by the light of the fire, levels his gun, and shoots the Swan, nearest to him; if he has two guns the other Swan is shot as he rises on his flight. Another mode by which the Swan is enticed within shot, is, the Indian lies down in some long grass, rushes, or willows near the water edge of the Lake, with a piece of very white birch rind in his hand, or fastened to a short stick; this is made to show like a Swan, and the call made; then drawn back; then again shown; thus it attracts the Swans who gently approach, to within shot, this requires great patience, perhaps three, or four hours. It is more successful with a single Swan, than with a pair, or more. The several species of Geese I have already noticed;[7] but very few breed in this region, and those only of the Grey Geese, they lay from eleven to thirteen Eggs; which they will defend against the Fox and the Mink[8] to no purpose, the Eggs are sure to be eaten and perhaps one of the geese.

There are a great variety of Ducks, some of them lay fifteen eggs, the young are reared with great care, in a heavy shower of rain the young are all under their parents wings; one variety builds in hollow trees, which it enters by a hole in the side of the tree; and is named the Wood Duck.[9] Two species of Crane[10] pass the open season, they make their nests among quagmire rushes, which cannot be approached; they have about nine young, which are hidden until they are fully half grown. The Bittern is found among the rushes, reeds, and tall grass of the marshes, it does not weigh more than three, or four, pounds, and holding it's long neck and bill erect it gives a hollow note, as loud almost as an Ox, and keeping itself hid, those not acquainted with it, are at a loss to know what animal it can be; it takes it's name from having on each breast a narrow stripe about two inches in length, of rough, raised, yellow skin, which is very bitter, and must be taken off, otherwise, this well tasted bird is too bitter to be eaten. Like the Crane, it lives on Roots, frogs

---

7 See iv.13 (32).

8 *Mustela vison.*

9 Probably the common goldeneye (*Bucephala clangula*), rather than the wood duck (*Aix sponsa*).

10 Sandhill crane (*Grus canadensis*) and whooping crane (*Grus americana*).

and small Lizards. Of the Plover, there are a few species,[11] they are not plenty, the Boys kill them with their arrows.

[*The Loon his mode of life. frightens us. Pelicans. Cormorants Merganser & Gulls. Eggs*]

[iv.33d] The water is the element of the Loon,[1] on the land he is unable to walk, his legs being placed too far backwards, nor from the ground can he raise his flight, and is quite helpless; but in the water, of all birds he is the most completely at home. He swims swiftly and dives well, going under water apparently with the same ease, as on the surface; he has the power of placing his body at any depth, and when harassed in a small lake, places his body under water, to be secure from the shot, leaving only his neck and head exposed and this he sinks to the head; in any of these positions he remains at pleasure; he prefers acting thus on the defensive, than flying away: for being very short winged, he has to go some thirty yards near the surface before he can raise his flight, and is so steady on the wing, that he is accounted a dead shot;[2] the Loon is very destructive among the small fish, yet seldom fat: it lays only three eggs, when boiled, the inside appears streaked black and yellow, and are so ill tasted they cannot be eaten; it's flesh is also bad. When on discovery to the northward, one evening on camping we found a Loons nest; the eggs were taken, but were found not to be eatable: two Lads lay down near the nest, in the night the pair of Loons came, and missing their eggs, fell upon the Lads, screeching and screaming, and beating them with their wings; the Lads thought themselves attacked by enemies, and roared out for help; two of us threw off our blankets, and seized our guns, the Loons seeing this returned to the Lake, we were at a loss what to think or do, the Lads were frightened out of their wits, in a few minutes we heard the wild call of the Loons; the Indian said it was the Loons, in revenge for the loss of their eggs; and giving them his hearty curse of "death be to you," told us there was no danger, and the Loons left us quiet for the rest of the night.

¶ The Pelican[3] is represented as a solitary bird, it may be so in other countries; but not in this region. They are always in pairs, or flocks of five to

11 The semipalmated plover (*Charadrius semipalmatus*), killdeer (*Charadrius vociferus*), and possibly the American golden plover (*Pluvialis dominica*).
1 *Gavia immer*.
2 I.e., makes an easy target for the hunter.
3 White pelican (*Pelecanus erythrorhynchos*).

twenty, [iv.33e] this is the largest fishing bird in this country, it is occasionally shot, or knocked on the head for it's feathers and pouch; the color is a dirty white, the wings extend about seven and a half feet, it's height is about thirty to thirty four inches, of which the bill, which is straight, measures about fourteen inches. It is capacious, and under the bill and upper part of the throat is a pouch that will hold a full quart of water. This bird when measured from the end of the tail to the point of the beak is about five feet in length; it's tail feathers are used for arrows, and the pouch, when cleaned and dried, is used to keep tobacco and Bear's weed for smoking; The Pelican is very destructive among small fish to a pound in weight.[4] It has a wide throat, and after filling it's stomach, also fills it's pouch, which becomes much distended, and half putrid, is, fish by fish, emptied into the throat. Such is it's fishing habits in the morning, and the same in the afternoon; they frequent the Rapids of small Streams, and when thus gorged sit close to each in a line. In this state they are unable to fly, and when our voyage in canoes leads us among them before they can rise, they have to disgorge the putrid fish in their pouches, the smell of which is so very bad, that we hurry past as fast as possible; the Black Bears who frequent the same Rapids, never injure them; these birds are so impure, they are the bye word of the Natives and the Traders.

¶ There are two species of Cormorant,[5] both of them very expert in fishing, their flesh and Eggs are almost as bad as those of the Loon; There are also several species of the Merganser,[6] or fishing Ducks, altho' they live on fish, yet both their flesh and eggs are eatable, when no better can be got; The three species of Gulls[7] conclude the list of birds that live on fish; they are all good to eat, their eggs as good as those of a Duck, especially the largest kind which is the size of a teal duck; their young cannot fly until they are full grown, and as all the species are too light to dive; become an easy prey to the Eagle, the Hawk, and to Man: On some of the Islets in the Lakes, they breed in such numbers that the Native Women, collect, as many as their blankets can hold.

---

4 I.e., of up to one pound in weight.
5 Only the double-crested cormorant (*Phalacrocorax auritus*) is native to the Canadian Shield.
6 These are the common merganser (*Mergus merganser*), red-breasted merganser (*Mergus serrator*), and hooded merganser (*Lophodytes cucullatus*).
7 Herring gull (*Larus argentatus*), ring-billed gull (*Larus delawarensis*), and common tern (*Sterna hirundo*).

[*Mice and Ermine, tricks of the last*]

[iv.33f] All the Animals of this Region are known to the civilized world, I shall therefore only give those traits of them, which naturalists do not, or have not noticed in their descriptions. There are two species of the Mouse, the common,[1] and the field Mouse with a short tail;[2] they appear to be numerous, and build a House where we will, as soon as it is inhabited, they make their appearance; but the country is clear of the plague of the Norway Rat,[3] which, although he comes from England part owner of the cargo, as yet, has not travelled beyond the Factories at the sea side.

¶ The Ermine,[4] this active little animal is an Ermine only in winter, in summer of a light brown color, he is most indefatagable after mice and small birds, and in the season, a plunderer of eggs; wherever we build, some of them soon make their burrows, and sometimes become too familiar. Having in June purchased from a Native about three dozen of Gull eggs, I put them up in a room, the stairs, a plain flight of about eight feet. The Ermine soon found them, and having made a meal of one egg, was determined to carry the rest to his burrow for his young; I watched to see how he would take the eggs down stairs; holding an egg between his throat and two fore paws, he came to the head of the stairs, there he made a long stop, at a loss how to get the egg down without breaking it, his resolution was taken, and holding fast the egg, dropped down to the next stair on his neck and back; and thus to the floor, and carried it to his nest: he returned and brought two more eggs in the same manner; while he was gone for the fourth, I took the three eggs away; laying down the egg he brought, he looked all around for the others, standing on his hind legs and chattering, he was evidently in a fighting humour; at length he set off and brought another, these two I took away, and he arrived with the sixth egg, which I allowed him to keep; he was too fatigued to go for another. The next morning he returned, but the eggs were in a basket out of his reach, he knew where they were, but could not get at them, and after chattering awhile, had to look for other prey. In winter we take the Ermine in small traps for the skin, which is valued to ornament dresses.

1 Deer mouse (*Peromyscus maniculatus*).
2 Meadow vole (*Microtus pennsylvanicus*).
3 *Rattus norvegicus*.
4 *Mustela erminea*. In his comment, Thompson refers to the use of "ermine" to indicate the colour white.

[*Squirrels. Martens. Trapper and his traps. The Trapper cuts his foot badly and marches 120 Miles. Suffers pain for a Month. Marten, his habits. Hare & Lynxes. Fox*]

[iv.33g] There are two species of Squirrel, the common[1] and the flying Squirrel[2] the former burrows under the roots of large Pines, from which he has several outlets, that when the Marten, or the Fox dig for him, he has a safe egress, and escapes up the tree with surprising agility, where he is safe. The flying Squirrel is about, one fifth larger, and of the same color, it's name arises from a hairy membrane, which on each side extends from the fore to the hind leg: and which it extends when leaping from tree to tree; this latter builds it's nest in the trees; they both feed on the cones of the Pine, using only those in a dry state; they are numerous; their elegant forms, agile movements, and chatterings, very much relieve the silence of the Pine Forests.

¶ The haunts of the Marten are confined to the extensive forests of Pine, especially the thickest parts, they are of the size of a large cat, but of a more compact and stronger make; the color brown, the deeper color the more valuable, some few approach to a black color; two he, or three she, Martens, in trade are of the value of one Beaver. They are always on the hunt of mice, squirrels and birds; They are caught in traps, already described; and as their skins are valuable, and their flesh good; they are trapped by the Natives and the Men of the Factories: the best bait for them is the head of a Grouse with the feathers on; or the head of a hare; even the leg of a hare is preferred to a bait of frozen meat, which he seldom takes. Among the Natives the snareing of hares, and trapping of Martens are the business of the Women and become their property for trade. The White Men sometimes make ranges of Marten Traps for the length of forty or fifty miles, at about six to eight traps Per Mile: in this case the Trapper makes a hut of Pine Branches about every ten miles, which length of traps is as much as he can manage in a day; the trapping is most successful in the month of November and early part of December: and the months of February and March, after which the skin soon becomes out of season. At each hut the Trapper ought to leave a stock of fire wood sufficient for the next night he passes there, as he frequently does not arrive until the day light is gone, and cutting wood in the night is dangerous.

¶ An old acquaintance who had a long range of traps, had neglected to leave fire wood at the hut at the end of the range, arriving late in the evening

1 Red or spruce squirrel (*Tamiasciurus hudsonicus*).
2 Northern flying squirrel (*Glaucomys sabrinus*).

had to cut fire wood for the night. With all his caution a twig [iv.33h] caught the axe and made the blow descend on his foot, which was cut from the little toe, to near the instep; he felt the blood gushing, but finished cutting the fuel required; having put every thing in order, he took off his shoe and the two blanket socks; tore up a spare shirt, and bound up the wound, using for salve a piece of tallow; he was six days journey from the Factory and alone; the next morning, having mended his shoe and socks, he got them on, but how to march forward was the difficulty; a hut with fire wood at the end of every ten miles along the range of traps was some encouragement; having tied his blankets and little baggage on the flat sled which every Trapper has; with pain he tied his foot to the snow shoe, then tied a string to the bar of the snow shoe, the other end in his hand, thus set off alone, to perform in winter a journey of about one hundred and twenty miles, hauling a sled, and with one hand lifting his wounded foot. The Snow Shoe was steady and soft on the snow; the first mile made him stop several times, and shook his resolution; but continuing his foot became less painful and could easily be borne; he had so much of the spirit of the Trapper in him, that he could not pass a trap in which a Marten was caught without taking it out, although it added to the weight he was hauling: In the evening he arrived at the first hut, put every thing in order, lighted his fire, and sat down, and as he told me, more proud of the fortitude of the day, than of any day in his life; he slept well his foot did not swell; and the next morning, with some pain renewed his journey to the second hut, and thus to the fifth hut. During these days he had the trapping path to walk on, which was soft and steady; he had now about sixty miles to go without a path; he had now to hang up the Martens and every thing he could do without, boil the bark of the Larch Tree, which lies close to the wood, beat it to a soft poultice and lay it on the wound; his sled was now light and his hand regular in lifting his foot and snow shoe; in five days he arrived at the factory having suffered much each evening in getting fire wood: during all this time of travelling his foot was not in the least swelled; when at the Factory he thought he would be at his ease, but this was not the case, his foot became swollen, with considerable pain [iv.33i] and for a month he had to make use of a crutch.

¶ I have often tried to tame the Marten, but never could trust him beyond the length of his chain: to one which I kept some time, I brought a small hawk slightly wounded, and placed it near him, he seemed willing to get away; and did not like it; two days after I winged a middle sized Owl, and brought it to him, he appeared afraid of it, and would willingly have run away but did not dare to cease watching it. Shortly after I found a Hare in one of snares just taken, I brought it alive to near the Marten, he became much agitated, the skin of his head strangely distorted to a ferocious aspect, he chattered, sprung to the Hare, as if with mortal hatred; this appeared to me strangely unaccountable, all this state of excitement against a weak animal it's common prey. Walking quietly through the Forest to visit the snares and traps, I have several times been amused with the Marten trying to steal the hare, suspended by a snare from a pole; the Marten is very active, but the soft snow does not allow him to spring more than his own height above the surface, the Hare is suspended full five feet above the surface; determined to get the Hare, he finds the pole to which the Hare is hanging, and running along the pole, when near the small end, his weight overbalances the other end, and the Marten is precipitated into the snow with the hare, before he recovers, the Pole has risen with the Hare out of his reach; he would stand on his hind feet, chatter at the hare with vexation; return to the Pole, to try to get the hare, to be again plunged in the snow; how long he would have continued, I do not know, the cold did not allow me to remain long; seeing me, he ran away.

¶ The Lynx[3] may be regarded as a very large cat, readily climbs trees, and preys on Mice, Hares, Squirrels and Birds, it's habits are those of a Cat: it is a shy animal; it's skin is not worth much, the skin being thin and weak; the Natives take this animal in a trap, in which is a wisp of grass rolled round some Castorum and the oil stones of the Beaver,[4] against this he [iv.33k] rubs his head, displaces the stick which suspends the trap, and he is caught; by the same means he is caught in a snare; while rubbing his head he purrs like a Cat, the flesh is white and good, and makes a good roast.

His fine, large, lustrous, eyes have been noticed by naturalists, and other writers. They are certainly beautiful, but better adapted to the twilight, than the glare of sun shine. I am inclined to think that the habits of the Fox[5] are better known in Europe than to us, for in populous countries it requires all his arts and wiles to preserve his life.

[*Wolverene. his tricks &c. steals six Axes. Wolverene, feather bag torn. Traps &c for him*]

The Wolverene,[1] is an animal unknown to other parts of the world, and we would willingly dispense with his being found here. It is a strong, well made,

3 *Felis lynx.*
4 *Castor canadensis.* For castoreum, see note on iv.141 (193).
5 Red fox (*Vulpes vulpes*).
1 *Gulo gulo.*

powerful animal his legs short, armed with long sharp claws, he climbs trees with ease, and nothing is safe that he can get at; by nature a plunderer, and mischievous, he is the plague of the country. A party of six men were sent to square timber for the Factory,[2] and as usual left their heavy axes where they were working, when they went to the tent for the night. One morning the six axes were not to be found; and as they knew there was no person within many miles of them, they were utterly at a loss what to think, or do. They were all from the very north of Scotland, and staunch believers in ghosts, fairies, and such like folk, except one; at length one of them, who thought himself wiser than the rest, addressed his unbelieving companion, "Now Jamie, you infidel, this comes of your laughing at ghosts and fairies, I told you they would make us suffer for it, here now all our axes are gone, and if a ghost has not taken them, what has." Jamie was sadly puzzled what to say, for the axes were gone; fortunately the Indian lad who was tenting with them, to supply them with grouse came to them; they told him all their axes were taken away, upon looking about [iv.33l] he perceived the foot marks of a Wolverene, and told them who the thief was, which they could not believe until by tracking the Wolverene, he found one of the Axes hid under the snow: in like manner three more axes were found. The others were carried to some distance and took two hours to find them, they were all hidden separately, and to secure their axes they had to shoulder them every evening to their tent.

¶ During the winter haul, the feathers of the birds are the property of the hunters; and those of the white Grouse sell for sixpence a pound to the Officers of the ship, we gave our share to Robert Tennant, whom we called Old Scot.[3] He had collected the feathers of about 300 grouse in a canvas bag, and to take it to the Factory, tied it on the Dog's sled, but some snow having fallen in the night the hauling was heavy; and after going a short distance the bag of feathers had to be left, which was suspended to the branch of a tree: On our return we were surprized to see feathers on the snow, on coming to the tree on which we had hung the bag, we found a Wolverene had cut it down, torn the bag to pieces, and scattered the feathers so as hardly to leave two together. He was too knowing for a trap but killed by a set Gun. In trapping of Martens, ranges of traps sometimes extend forty miles, or more. An old trapper always begins with a Wolverene trap, and at the end of every twenty traps makes one for the Wolverene, this is a work of some labor, as the trap

2 York Factory.
3 Robert Tennant (c. 1728–93) of Glasgow entered HBC service in 1767 and spent most of his career as a sailor at York Factory. He was one of Thompson's hunting companions in 1785–86 (Biography File, HBCA).

must be strongly made and well loaded, for this strong animal his weight is about that of an english Mastiff, but more firmly made; his skin is thick, the hair coarse, of a dark brown color, value about ten shillings but to encourage the Natives to kill it; is valued at two beavers being four times it's real value.

[*Three species of Wolf. Wood Wolf. size. attack Deer. Wolves mode of killing deer. Paucity of Animals*]

[iv.34] Of the three species of Wolf,[1] only one is found in this stony region that I have described, and this species appears peculiar to this region; it is the largest of them, and by way of eminence is called the Wood, or Forest Wolf, as it is not found elsewhere; it's form and color much the same as the others, of a dark grey, the hair, though not coarse, cannot be called soft and, fine, it is in plenty, and with the skin makes warm clothing. It is a solitary animal. Two are seldom seen together except when in chase of some animal of the Deer species, fortunately they are not numerous, they are very rarely caught in a trap; but re[a]dily take the bait of a set Gun, and killed. The cased skin of one of these Wolves, came with ease over a man of six feet, two inches in height dressed in his winter clothing, and was ten inches above his head, yet powerful and active as he is, he is not known to attack man kind, except in a rare case of something like canine madness, and his bite does not produce hydrophobia.[2] At least, it never has been so among the Natives and the dogs bitten by him, only suffer the pain of the bite. Foxes have sometimes, this canine madness or some thing like it, but hydrophobia is wholly unknown.

¶ Two of these Wolves are a full match of either the Moose,[3] or Rein Deer,[4] the only two species found in this region. When they start one of these Deer, they are left far behind, but the Deer must stop to feed, they then come up to, and again start the Deer, and thus continue until the animal, harassed for want of food and rest becomes weak and turns to bay. In this state ready to defend itself with it's powerful feet, the Wolves cautiously approach, one going close in front to threaten an attack, yet keeping out of the reach of it's fore feet [iv.35] the other Wolf, goes behind, keeping a little on one side to be out of the direct stroke of the hind feet; and watching, gives a sharp bite to cut the back sinew of one of the hind legs, this brings on a smart stroke of the

1 Grey wolf (*Canis lupus*). Only one species proper is recognized.
2 Rabies.
3 *Alces alces.*
4 Caribou (*Rangifer tarandus*). The caribou of North America and the reindeer of Eurasia are now considered to be the same species, as Thompson suspected.

hind legs of the Deer, but the Wolf is on one side, and repeats his bites until the back sinew is cut, the Deer can now no longer defend itself, the back sinew of the other hind leg is soon cut, the Deer falls down and becomes the easy prey of the Wolves; the tongue and the bowels are the first to be devoured. From the teeth of the old Wolves being sharp pointed, it does not appear they gnaw the bones, but only clean them of the flesh, and in this state we find the bones. The Deer in summer sometimes takes to the water, but this only prolongs his life for a few hours. They are very destructive to the young deer; and their loud howlings in the night make the Deer start from their beds and run to a greater distance. When wounded, he will defend himself, but tries to get away, and dies as hard as he lived. There is something in the erect form of man, while he shows no fear, that awes every animal.

¶ The animals described as found on this Stony Region are few in proportion to the extent of the country, the Natives with all their address can only collect furrs sufficient to purchase the necessaries of life; and part of their clothing is yet of leather in summer, very disagreeable in rainy weather, and the avidity with which the furr bearing animals is sought, almost threatens their extinction; the birds of passage may be as numerous as ever, comparatively only a very few can be killed as they pass, and the Natives acknowledge, that with all their endeavours they can barely subsist by the chase, even when making use of all the animals they catch for food.

[*The Natives. "Dinnae." Nahathaways & Language in dialects. Indians their form and features, active, fatigue*][1]

[iv.36] Having passed six years in different parts of this Region, exploring and surveying it, I may be allowed to know something of the natives, as well as the productions of the country.[2] It's inhabitants are two distinct

---

1 Thompson made significant revisions to his writings on the Cree at least five times during the composition of the *Travels*, and iv.36–50 represents his final selection of material. Earlier drafts, iii.34a–b and iii.136–50 in Volume II, contain much of the infomation found here, as well as unique writings on Cree games and weapons, the sweat lodge, and the emergence of the Métis as a distinct people. The Cree presence also permeates other parts of the *Travels*: Cree belief and lore appear incidentally in writings of the flora and fauna of the Canadian Shield (iv.28–35, 77–94), Cree hunting techniques are described in writings about large game (iv.50–8, 108–15), and the Cree appear in accounts of Thompson's activities in the region north of Lake Winnipeg (iv.61–81, 117–33) and in the Boreal Plains (iv.243–56, 273–83).

2 Thompson passed six winters at posts in the Canadian Shield. With the HBC he spent 1792–93 at Seepaywisk House on Sipiwesk Lake (a broadening of the Nelson River),

races of Indians; North of the latitude of fifty six degrees, the country is occupied by a people who call themselves "Dinnie" by the Hudson Bay Traders "Northern Indians" and by their southern neighbours "Chee pa wy ans" whom I shall notice hereafter.[3] Southward of the above latitude the country is in possession of the Na hath a way Indians their native name[4] (Note. these people by the french canadians, who are all without the least education, in their jargon call them "Krees" a name which none of the Indians can pronounce; this name appears to be taken from "Kee this te no" so called by one of their tribes and which the french pronounce "Kris te no," and by contraction "Krees"[5] R, rough, cannot be pronounced by any Native). These people are separated into many tribes or extended families, under different names, but all speaking dialects of the same language, which extends over this stony region, and along the Atlantic coasts southward to the Delaware River in the United States, (the language of the Delaware Indians being a dialect of the parent Na hath a way) and by the Saskatchewan River westward, to the Rocky Mountains.[6] The Na hath a way, as it [is] spoken by the

1794–95 at Reed Lake House northwest of Lake Winnipeg, 1795–96 at Duck Portage on the Churchill River, and 1796–97 at Bedford House on Reindeer Lake. With the NWC he spent 1804–05 at Musquawegan on the Churchill River and 1805–06 at Reed Lake House. Thompson traded with Cree at all of these posts and traversed the region several times.

3 Thompson writes about the Chipewyan on iv.82–5 (133–6) and iv.107–14 (161–5), and on iii.133–6 in Volume II. For the various names employed to refer to this group, see note on iv.82 (134).

4 Thompson's term represents the Woods Cree ne·hithawe, meaning "those who speak the same language." David H. Pentland, "Synonymy," in James G.E. Smith, "Western Woods Cree," HNAI, vol. 6: Subarctic, ed. June Helm (Washington: Smithsonian Institution, 1981), 267–8. At the time of first contact with Europeans, the Cree appear to have inhabited the lands around James Bay and the western shores of Hudson Bay, west to Lake Winnipeg and south to Lake Nipigon. Participation in the fur trade permitted the Cree to extend their lands west and south. Thompson was involved with Cree-speaking groups for almost his entire career in the West, and he seems to have had great personal affinity for them; it was only the Homeguard Indians of the bayside whom he considered degraded. Thompson's wife Charlotte Small was the daughter of a Cree woman.

5 "Cree" derives from the Ojibwa kirištino, originally referring to a particular band south of James Bay; French traders adopted the word for all Cree speakers. David H. Pentland, "Synonymy," in John J. Honigmann, "West Main Cree," HNAI, vol. 6, 227.

6 Thompson is referring to the Algonquian language family; in addition to Cree proper, it includes Ojibwa, Micmac, Malecite, Montagnais-Naskapi, and Blackfoot. The

southern tribes is softened and made more sonorous the frequent th of the parent tongue is changed to the letter y as Nee ther (me) into Nee yer, Kee ther (thou) into Kee yer, Wee ther (him) into Wee yer, and as it proceeds southward becomes almost a different language.[7] It is easy of pronunciation, and is readily acquired by the white people for the purposes of trade, and [iv.37] common conversation.

¶ The appearance of these people depends much on the climate and ease of subsistence. Around Hudson's Bay and near the sea coasts, where the climate is very severe, and game scarce, they are seldom above the middle size, of spare make, the features round, or slightly oval, hair black, strong and lank; eyes black and of full size, cheek bones rather high, mouth and teeth good, the chin round; the countenance grave yet with a tendency to cheerful, and the mild countenances of the women make many, while young, appear lovely; but like the labouring classes, the softness of youth soon passes away. In the interior where the climate is not so severe, and hunting more successful, the Men attain to the stature of six feet; well proportioned, the face more oval, and the features good, giving them a manly appearance; the complexion is of a light olive, and their colour much the same as a native of the south of Spain; the skin soft and smooth. They bear cold and exposure to the weather better than we do and the natural heat of their bodies is greater than ours, probably from living wholly on animal food,[8] for they have no vegetables during winter, and only berries during the open season, yet suffer no inconvenience for want of vegetable food. They can bear great fatigue but not hard labor, they would rather walk six hours over rough ground, than work one hour with the pick axe and spade, and the labor they perform, is mostly in an erect posture as working with the ice chissel piercing holes through the ice, or through a beaver house, and naturally, they are not industrious, they do not work from choice, but necessity; yet the industrious of both sexes are praised and admired; the civilized man has many things to tempt him to an active life, the Indian has none, and is happy sitting still, and smoking his pipe.

Delaware Indians, or Lenape, were living in the region of the Delaware River at the time of European contact.

7 Today, these two Cree dialects are known as the "th" dialect, spoken by Woods Cree, and the "y" dialect, spoken by Plains Cree. Richard A. Rhodes and Evelyn M. Todd, "Subarctic Algonquian Languages," *HNAI*, vol. 6, 55. See also iv.203 (239), where Thompson compares the Cree and Ojibwa languages.

8 The body's metabolism of protein produces heat at a rate five times greater than it does in the metabolism of carbohydrates and fat. Barbara R. Landau, *Essential Human Anatomy and Physiology*, 2nd edn. (Glenview, IL: Scott, Foresman and Company, 1980), 629.

[*Natives. Dress. Manners. kindness and affection. care to death*]

[iv.38] {the women make many of them lovely.}[1] The dress of the Men is simply of one or two loose coats of coarse broad cloth, or molton, a piece of the same served to form a rude kind of stockings to half way up the thigh, a blanket by way of a cloak. The shoes are of well dressed Moose, or Rein Deer skin, and from it's pliancy enables them to run with safety, they have no covering for the hood in summer, except the skin of the spotted northern Diver;[2] but in winter, they wrap a piece of Otter, or Beaver skin with the furr on, round their heads, still leaving the crown of the head bare, from which they suffer no inconvenience. The dress of the women is of 1½ yards of broad cloth sewed like a sack, open at both ends, one end is tied over the shoulders, the middle belted round the waist, the lower part like a petticoat, covers to the ankles, and gives them a decent appearance, the sleeves covers the arms and shoulders, and are separate from the body dress. The rest is much the same as the men, for a head dress they have a foot of broad cloth, sewed at one end, ornamented with beads and gartering, this end is on the head, the loose parts are over the shoulders, and is well adapted to defend the head and neck from the cold and snow. The women seldom disfigure their faces with paint, and are not over fond of ornaments. Most of the Men are <tat>toed, on some <p>art of their bodies Arms &c. Some of the Women have a small circle on each cheek.

The natives in their manners are mild and decent, treat each other with kindness and respect, and very rarely interrupt each other in conversation; after a long separation, the nearest relations meet each other, with the same seeming indifference, as if they had constantly lived in the same tent, but have not the less affection for each other, for they hold all show of joy, or sorrow to be unmanly; on the death of a relation, or friend, the women accompany their tears for the dead with piercing shrieks, but the men sorrow in silence, and when the sad pang of recollection becomes too strong to be borne retire in to the forest to give free vent to their grief.

Those acts that pass between man and man for generous charity, and kind compassion in civilized society, are no more than what is every day practised by these Savages; as acts of common duty; is any one unsuccessful in the chase, has he lost his little all by some accident, he is sure to be relieved by the others to the utmost of their power; in sickness they carefully attend each other <to the> latest breath and then decently <secure> the dead from <...>

1 Thompson excised these opening words, carried over from a page that is no longer extant, when iv.38 was integrated into this section in July 1848.
2 The common loon.

[*Nahathaways superior in Religion tradition &c. my endeavours to learn their religion. their religious belief. Great Spirit. Manito's their duty &c &c. Ghosts. Pah kok. Sun. Moon & Earth. the Soul. The falls. Stones. Evil Spirit. Soul*]

[iv.39][1] Of all the several distinct Tribes of Natives on the east side of the mountains, the Na hath a way Indians appear to deserve the most consideration; under different names the great families of this race occupy a great extent of country, and however separated and unknown to each other they have the same opinions on religion, on morals, and their customs and manners differ very little. They are the only Natives that have some remains of ancient times from tradition. In the following account I have carefully avoided as their national opinions all they have learned from white men, and my knowledge was collected from old men, whom with my own age extend backwards to upwards of one hundred years ago, and I must remark, that what other people may write as the creed of these natives, I have always found it very difficult to learn their real opinion on what may be termed religious subjects. Asking them questions on this head, is to no purpose, they will give the answer best adapted to avoid other questions, and please the enquirer. My knowledge has been gained when living and travelling with them and in times of distress and danger in their prayers to invisible powers, and their view of a future state of themselves and others, and like most of mankind those in youth, and in the prime of life think only of the present but declining manhood, and escapes from danger turn their thoughts on futurity.[2]

After a weary day's march we sat by a log fire, the bright Moon, with thousands of sparkling stars passing before us, we could not help enquiring who lived in those bright mansions; for I frequently conversed with them as one of themselves; the brilliancy of the planets always attracted their attention and when their nature was explained to them, they concluded them to

1 Pages iv.39–47 bring together Thompson's writings on Cree cosmology. Although Thompson viewed Cree belief and ritual through the lens of his own Christianity, this account is nonetheless remarkable for the detail and sympathy with which these topics are treated. In 1823, HBC trader George Nelson recorded information even more comprehensive than Thompson's. See Nelson, *"The Orders of the Dreamed,"* ed. Brown and Brightman. The fullest modern treatment of the components of Cree cosmology may be found in "Northern Algonquian Religious and Mythic Themes and Personages: Contexts and Comparisons," part 3 of Brown and Brightman's edition, 119–85, from which transcriptions of Cree terms in the notes are taken.
2 In an earlier version of this passage, iii.34a (see Volume II), Thompson also acknowledges the help of his wife, Charlotte Small, as translator.

be the abodes of the spirits of those that had led a good life. A Missionary has never been among them, and my [iv.40] knowledge of their language has not enabled me to do more than teach the unity of God, and a future state of rewards and punishments; hell fire they do not believe, for they do not think it possible that any thing can resist the continued action of fire. It is doubtful if their language in it's present simple state can clearly express the doctrines of Christianity in their full force.

¶ They believe in the self existence of the Kee che Kee che Manito (the Great, Great Spirit).[3] They appear to derive their belief from tradition, and that the visible world, with all it's inhabitants must have been made by some powerful being: but have not the same idea of his constant omnipresence, omniscience and omnipotence that we have, but that he is so when he pleases, he is the master of life, and all things are at his disposal; he is always kind to the human race, and hates to see the blood of mankind on the ground, and sends heavy rain to wash it away. He leaves the human race to their own conduct, but has placed all other living creatures under the care of the Manitos (or inferior Angels) all of whom are responsible to Him; but all this belief is obscure and confused, especially on the Manitos, the guardians and guides of every genus of Birds and Beasts; each Manito has a separate command and care, as one has the Bison another the Deer; and thus the whole animal creation is divided amongst them. On this account the Indians, as much as possible, neither say, nor do any thing to offend them, and the religious hunter, at the death of each animal, says, or does, something, as thanks to the Manito of the species for being permitted to kill it. At the death of a Moose Deer, the hunter in a low voice, cries "wut, wut, wut;" cuts a narrow stripe of skin from off the throat, and hangs it up to the Manito. The bones of the head of a Bear are to be thrown into the water, and thus of other animals; if this acknowledgement was not [iv.41] made the Manito would drive away the animals from the hunter, although the Indians often doubt their power or existence, yet like other invisible beings they are more feared than loved.

¶ They believe in ghosts, but as very rarely seen, and those only of wicked men, or women; when this belief takes place, their opinion is, that the spirit of the wicked person being in a miserable state comes back to the body and round where he used to hunt; to get rid of so hateful a visitor, they burn the body to ashes, and the ghost then no longer haunts them. The dark Pine Forests have spirits, but there is only one of them which they dread, it is Pah

---

3 *Kisemanitōw* is the superior deity in Cree and Ojibwa cosmology. As Thompson notes, he is benevolent and is considered the "master of life."

Kok,[4] a tall hateful spirit, he frequents the depths of the Forest, his howlings
are heard in the storm, he delights to add to it's terrors, it is a misfortune to
hear him something ill will happen to the person, but when he approaches a
Tent and howls, he announces the death of one of the inmates; of all beings
he is the most hateful and most dreaded.

¶ The Sun and Moon are accounted Divinities and though they do not
worship them, always speak of them with great reverence; they appear to
think the Stars only as a great number of luminous points perhaps also divinities; and mention them with respect, they have names for the brightest stars,
as Sirius, Orion and others, and by them learn the change of the seasons as
the rising of Orion for winter and the setting of the Pleiades for summer.
The Earth is also a divinity, and is alive, but [they] cannot define what kind
of life it is, but say, if it was not alive it could not give and continue life to
other things and to animated creatures. The Forests, the ledges and hills of
Rock, the Lakes and Rivers have all something of the Manito about them,
[iv.42] especially the Falls in the Rivers, and those to which the fish come to
spawn, the Indians when the season is over frequently place their Spears at
the Manito stone of the Fall as an offering to the Spirit of the Fall, for the fish
they have caught. These stones are rare, and sought after by the natives to
place at the edge of a water fall; they are of the shape of a Cobler's lap stone,
but much larger, and polished by the wash of the water.[5]

The "Met chee Manito," or Evil Spirit,[6] they believe to be evil, delighting
in making them miserable, and bringing misfortune and sickness on them,
and if he had the power would wholly destroy them; he is not the tempter,
his whole power is for mischief to, and harassing of, them, to avert all which
they use many ceremonies, and offer sacrifices, which consists of such things
as they can spare, and sometimes a dog is painted and killed; whatever is
given to him is laid on the ground, frequently at the foot of a pine tree. They
believe in the immortality of the soul, and that death is only a change of
existence which takes place directly after death. The good find themselves
in a happy country, where they rejoin their friends and relations, the Sun
is always bright, and the animals plenty; and most of them carry this belief
so far, that they believe whatever creatures the great Spirit has made must
continue to exist some where, and under some form; But this fine belief is

4 The attributes of the forest spirit *Pāhahk* are variable; it is commonly envisioned as a
   skeletal being and is associated with starvation and death.
5 As, for example, the manito stone at Painted Stone Portage, mentioned on 27c (49).
6 *Macimanitōw* is the primary evil deity in Cree cosmology, opposed to and less powerful than *Kisemanitōw*.

dark and uncertain; when danger was certain, and it was doubtful if we saw the day, or if we saw it, whether we should live through it, and a future state appeared close to them, their minds wavered, they wished to believe what they [iv.43] felt to be uncertain, all that I could do was to show the immortality of the soul, as necessary to the reward of the good, and punishment of the wicked but all this was the talk of man with man, it wanted the sure and sacred promise of the heavenly Redeemer of mankind, who brought life and immortality to light.

[*Weesarkejauk. Deluge. Otter and Beaver. Musk Rat. Great Spirit renovates*]

There is an important being, with whom the Natives appear better acquainted with than the other, whom they call "Wee sark e jork" (the Flatterer)[1] he is the hero of all their stories always promising them some good, or inciting them to some pleasure, and always deceiving them. They have some tradition of the Deluge, as may be seen from the following account related by the old men.[2]

¶ After the Great Spirit made mankind, and all the animals, he told Wee sark e jauk to take care of them and teach them how to live, and not to eat of bad roots; that would hurt and kill them; but he did not mind the Great Spirit; became careless and incited them to pleasure, mankind and the animals all did as they pleased; quarelled and shed much blood, with which the Great Spirit was displeased; he threatened Wee sark e jauk that if he did not keep the ground clean he would take every thing from him and make him miserable but he did not believe the Great Spirit and in a short time became more careless; and the quarrels of Men, and the animals made the ground red with blood, and so far from taking care of them, he incited them to do, and live, badly; this made the Great Spirit very angry and he told, Wee sark e jauk that he would take every thing from him, and wash the ground clean; but still he did not believe; until the Rivers and Lakes rose very high and

1 *Wīsahkēcāhk* is the Cree version of the trickster figure common to many Native groups. Like Coyote and Raven, he is mischievous, pathetic, and morally ambiguous.
2 Thompson recorded at least two other accounts of the Cree flood myth: on iii.34bb–bbb of the 1848 version of the *Travels* (Volume II) and in his notebooks, at AO. 47.88–79 (Volume III). Elements that Thompson's account shares with most recorded versions of the myth are an Earth diving contest, the success of the musk-rat, and *Wīsahkēcāhk*'s remaking of the world. Unique or less common aspects are *Kisemanitōw*'s unleashing of the flood as a punishment and his refashioning of human beings. Nelson, "*The Orders of the Dreamed*," 128–36.

overflowed the ground, for it was always raining; and the Kee che Gah me
(the Sea) came on the land, and every man and animal were drowned except
one Otter, one Beaver and one Musk Rat. We sark e jauk tried, to stop the
sea, but it was too strong for him, and [iv.44] he sat on the water crying for
his loss, the Otter, the Beaver and the Musk Rat rested their heads on one of
his thighs.

When the Rain ceased, and the Sea went away, he took courage, but did
not dare to speak to the Great Spirit.

After musing a long time upon his sad condition he thought if he could get
a bit of the old ground he could make a little island of it, for he has the power
of extending, but not of creating any thing; and as he had not the power of
diving under the water, and did not know the depth to the old ground he was
at a loss what to do. Some say the Great Spirit took pity on him, and gave
him the power to renovate every thing, provided he made use of the old materials, all of which lay buried under water to an unknown depth. In this sad
state, as he sat floating on the water, he told the three animals that they must
starve unless he could get a bit of the old ground from under the water of
which he would make a fine Island for them. Then addressing himself to the
Otter, and praising him for his courage, strength and activity and promising
him plenty of fish to eat, he perswaded the Otter to dive, and bring up a bit
of earth; the Otter came up without having reached the ground; by praises,
he got the Otter to make two more attempts, but without success, and was so
much exhausted, he could do no more. Wee sark e jauk called him a coward
of a weak heart, and that the Beaver would put him to shame; then speaking
to the Beaver praised his strength and wisdom and promised to make him a
good house for winter, and telling him to dive straight down the Beaver made
two attempts without success, and came up so tired that Wee sark e jauk had
to let him repose a long time, then promising him a wife if he brought up a
bit of earth, told him to try a third time; to obtain a wife, he boldly [iv.45]
went down, and staid so long, that he came up almost lifeless.

¶ Wee sark e jauk was now very sad, for what the active Otter, and strong
Beaver could not do, he had little hopes the Musk Rat could do; but this was
his only rescource: He now praised the Musk Rat and promised him plenty
of roots to eat, with rushes and earth to make himself a house; the Otter
and the Beaver he said were fools, and lost themselves, and he would find
the ground, if he went straight down. Thus encouraged he dived, and came
up, but brought nothing; after reposing, he went down a second time, and
staid a long time, on coming up, Wee sark e jauk, examined his fore paws
and found they had the smell of earth, and showing this to the Musk Rat,
promised to make him a Wife, who should give him a great many children,

and become more numerous than any other animal, and telling him to have a strong heart; and go direct down. The Musk Rat went down the third time, and staid so long, that Wee sark e jauk feared he was drowned. At length seeing some bubbles come up, he put down his long arm and brought up the Musk Rat, almost dead, but to his great joy with a bit of earth between his fore paws and breast; this he seized, and in a short time extended it to a little island, on which they all reposed.

¶ Some say, Wee sark e jauk procured a bit of wood, from which he made the Trees, and from bones, he made the animals; but the greater number deny this, and say, the Great Spirit made the rivers take the water to the Keeche gahma of bad water (the salt sea)[3] and then renovated Mankind, the Animals, and the Trees; in proof of which, the Great Spirit [iv.46] deprived him of all authority over Man kind and the animals, and that he has since had only the power to flatter and deceive. It has been already noticed that this visionary being is the hero of many stories, which the Women relate to amuse away the evenings, they are all founded upon the tricks he plays upon, and the mischiefs he leads, the animals into, by flattering and deceiving them, especially the Wolf and the Fox, but the recital of the best of these stories would be tameness itself to the splendid Language, and gorgeous scenery of the tales of the oriental nations.[4]

[*the Rainbow. Worship of the evil Spirit. Character*]

The Nahathaway Indians have also another tradition relative to the Deluge to which no fable is attached. In the latter end of May 1806, at the Rocky Mountain House, (where I passed the summer)[1] the Rain continued the very unusual space of full three weeks, the Brooks and the River became swollen, and could not be forded, each stream became a torrent, and much water on the ground: A band of these Indians were at the house, waiting the Rain to cease and the streams to lower, before they could proceed to hunting; all was anxiety, they smoked and made speeches to the Great Spirit for the Rain to

---

3 From a Cree perspective, Hudson Bay.
4 The *Arabian Nights* and *Persian Tales*.
1 In May 1806 Thompson was at Reed Lake. The year 1801 is probably intended. Thompson writes in his "Account of an Attempt to Cross the Rocky Mountains," which covers 6–30 June 1801, that the region of Rocky Mountain House had suffered "late heavy Rains, which have ... soaked and overflowed the Ground" (26v–27r; see Volume III).

cease, and at length became alarmed at the quantity of water on the ground; at length the rain ceased, I was standing at the door watching the breaking up of the clouds, when of a sudden the Indians gave a loud shout, and called out "Oh, there is the mark of life, we shall yet live." On looking to the eastward; there was one of the widest and most splendid Rain bows I ever beheld; and joy was now in every face.

¶ The name of the Rainbow is Peeshim Eap pe ah (Sun lines). I had now been twenty two years among them and never before heard the name of the mark of life given to the Rain bow (Pee mah tis oo nanoo Che gun) nor have I ever heard it since; upon enquiring of the old Men, why [iv.47] they kept this name secret from me, they gave me the usual reply, "You white men always laugh, and treat with contempt what we have heard and learned from our fathers, and why should we expose ourselves to be laughed at"; I replied "I have never done so, our books also call the Rainbow the mark of life;[2] what the white [men] sometimes despise you for is your one day, making prayers to the Good Spirit for all you want; and another shutting yourselves up, making speeches, with ceremonies and offerings to the Evil Spirit; it is for this worship of the Evil Spirit that we despise you, you fear him because he is wicked, and the more you worship him, the more power he will have over you; worship the Good Spirit only; and the bad Spirit will have no power over you." "Ah," said they; "he is strong, we fear for ourselves, our wives and children."

¶ Christianity alone, can eradicate these sad superstitions, and who will teach them. Where the Natives are in villages, or even where they occasionally assemble together for two, or three months; a Missionary may do some good, but the Natives who, in a hard country live by hunting, scattered by three, or four, families over a wide extent of forest, are beyond the labors of a Missionary, yet the influence of the white people have done much to lessen the worship and offerings to the evil Spirit. From the french Canadians they cannot add to their morality, and the dreadful Oaths and curses they make use of, shocks an Indian. The Indian, altho' naturally grave, is fond of cheerful amusements, and listening to stories, especially of a wonderful cast; and fond of news, which he listens to with attention and his common discourse is easy and cheerful. Like the rest of mankind, he is anxious to know something of futurity, and [where] he shall take up his wintering ground.

2 In the Book of Genesis the rainbow symbolizes God's covenant with the Earth's inhabitants and is a pledge that the Earth will never again be destroyed by a flood (Genesis 9:13–16).

[*Conjuring Box &c*]¹

[iv.47a] For to acquire this important knowledge, they have recourse to Dreams and other superstitions; and a few of their best conjurers sometimes take a bold method of imposing upon themselves and others. One of my best acquaintances, named "Ise pe sa wan," was the most relied on by the Natives to enquire into futurity by conjuring; he was a good hunter, fluent in speech, had a fine manly voice; and very early every morning, took his rattle, and beating time with it, made a fluent speech of about twenty minutes to the Great Spirit and the Spirits of the forests, for health to all of them and success in hunting; and to give to his Poo wog gin,² where to find the Deer, and to be always kind to them, and give them straight Dreams, that they may live straight.

¶ The time chosen was a fine afternoon, in the open season; "Ise pe sa wan" was the actor. After taking the sweating bath; he had four long slender poles brought of about sixteen feet in length. These were fixed in the ground to form a square of full three feet; At five feet above the ground four cross pieces were tied firmly; and about full three feet above these, other four pieces were strongly tied across the upright poles; all this, at the bottom and top, with the sides were closely covered with the dressed leather skins of Deer; leaving one side loose for a door. This being done, fine sinew line was brought; with this, the thumb was tied to the fore finger in two places, the fingers to each other in the same manner; both hands being thus tied, they were brought together palm to palm, and tied together at the waist; then the arms tied close above the elbows. The Legs were tied together close above the ancles, and above the knees; sometimes the toes are tied together in the same manner as the hands; A few [iv.47b] yards of leather line is tied round his body and arms; a strong line is passed under the knees, and round the back of the neck, which draws the knees to a sitting posture. A large Moose leather skin, or a Bison Robe, is wrapped round him, and several yards of leather line bind the Robe or leather skin close around him; in this helpless state two men lift and place him in the conjuring box in a sitting posture, with his rattle on his right side.

1 More properly known as the shaking lodge, this ceremony is of central importance in Cree and Ojibwa religious life. As Thompson states, its purpose is to probe into future or distant events, and the rite includes such elements as the binding and release of the diviner, the summoning of spirits, and the communication of a message to the gathered observers.

2 See note on iv.48, below (107).

All is now suspense, the Men, Women, and Children keep strict silence; In about fifteen, or twenty minutes; the whole of the cords, wrapped together are thrown out, and instantly the Rattle and the Song are heard, the conjuring box violently shaken, as if the conjuror was actually possessed; sometimes the Song ceases, and a speech is heard of ambiguous predictions of what is to happen. In half an hours time, he appears exhausted, leaves the leather box and retires to his tent, the perspiration running down him, smokes his pipe and goes to sleep.

The above is acted on a piece of clear ground; I sometimes thought there must be some collusion, and the apparent fast knots, were really slip knots; but the more I examined, the more I became convinced the whole was a neat piece of jugglery.[3] On one of these occasions, five Scotchmen were with me on some business we had with the Natives; we found the above Indian preparing his conjuring box; of course no business could be done until this was over. When my men perceived the conjuror about being tied, they said, if they had the tying of him, he would never get loose. This I told to the Indians, who readily agreed the Scotchmen should tie him: which they did in the usual way, and they placed him in the conjuring box; quite sure he could not get loose; In about fifteen minutes, to their utter astonishment, all the cords were thrown out in a bundle, the Rattle, and the Song in full force, and the conjuring box shaken, as if going to pieces; my men were at a loss what to think or say. The Natives smiled at their incredulity; at length they consoled themselves by, saying the Devil in person had untied him, and set him loose.[4]

[*Dances. Poowogan. Dreams*]

¶ [iv.48] I found many of the Men especially those who had been much in company with white Men, to be all half infidels, but the Women kept them in order, for they fear the Manito's; All their dances have a religious tendency. They are not, as with us, dances of mere pleasure, of the joyous countenance; they are grave, each dancer considers it a religious rite for some purpose;

3 Pretended magic; sleight of hand.
4 The association of the shaking lodge with demonic forces was a common European reaction. Nelson, *"The Orders of the Dreamed,"* 158. This episode likely dates from the period 1790–97; Thompson seems to have been in charge of the labourers, whose Scottish nationality indicates the HBC. While Thompson expresses skepticism at the practice of divining, significantly he does not attempt to provide a rationalistic explanation of the phenomenon.

their motions are slow and graceful; yet I have sometimes seen occasional dances of a gay character; I was at their Tents on business, when the Women came and told me they wanted Beads and Ribbons, to which I replied, I wanted Marten Skins; early the next morning five young women set off to make Marten Traps; and did not return until the evening, they were rallyed by their husbands and brothers; who proposed they should dance to the Manito of the Martens, to this they willingly consented, it was a fine, calm, moon light night, the young men came with the Rattle and Tambour, about nine women formed the dance, to which they sung with their fine voices, and lively they danced hand in hand in a half circle, for a long hour; it is now many years ago, yet I remember this gay hour.[1]

Every man believes, or wishes to believe, he has a familiar being, who takes care of him, and warns him of danger, and other matters which otherwise he could not know; this imaginary being he calls his Poo wog gan;[2] upon conversing with them on this Being on whom they relied; it appeared to me to be no other than the powers of his own mind when somewhat excited by danger or difficulty, especially as they suppose their dreams to be caused by him, "Ne poo war tin." (I have dreamed;) too often a troubled dream from a heavy supper; but at times they know how to dream for their own interest or convenience; and when one of them told me he had been dreaming it was for what he wished to have, or to do, for some favor, or as some excuse for not performing his promises. For so far as their interests are concerned they do not want policy.

[Character. Marriage & Children]

¶ [iv.49] When injurid, they are resentful, but not more than the lower class of europeans. They frequently pass over injuries, and are always appeased with a present, unless blood has been shed, in this case however they may seem to forgive, they defer revenge to a more convenient opportunity; courage is not accounted an essential to the men, any more than chastity to the women, tho' both are sometimes found in a high degree. The greatest praise one Indian gives to another, is, that he is a man of a steady humane disposi-

---

1 Here Thompson excised the words: "Of the beings whom they believe to inhabit the Forests, Pah kok the dreadful Ghost of the Pine Forests is most feared," adding the note "done."

2 Thompson's dismissive treatment of the *pawākan* belies its central importance in Cree cosmology. The *pawākan* is the dream visitor who appears during the puberty vision fast and is regarded as a lifelong personal guardian, guide, and counsellor.

tion, and a fortunate hunter; and the praise of the women is to be active and good humoured: their marriages are without noise or ceremony, nothing is requisite but the consent of the parties, and Parents: the riches of the man consists solely in his abilities as a Hunter; and the portion of the woman is good health, and a willingness to relieve her husband from all domestic duties. Although the young men appear not to be passionate lovers, they seldom fail of being good husbands, and when contrariety of disposition prevails, so that they cannot live peaceably together, they separate with as little ceremony as they came together, and both parties are free to attach themselves to whom they will, without any claim on their characters; but if they have lived so long together as to have children, one, or both, are severely blamed.

Polygamy is allowed, and each man may have as many wives as he can maintain, but few indulge themselves in this liberty, yet some have even three. This is seldom a matter of choice, it is frequently from the death of a friend who has left his wife, sister, or daughter to him, for every woman must have a husband. The children are brought up with great care and tenderness, they are very seldom corrected, the constant company and admonition of the old people is their only education, whom they soon learn to imitate in gravity as far as youth will permit; they very early and readily betake themselves to fishing and hunting, from both men and women impressing on their minds, that the man truly miserable is he, who is dependent on another for his subsistence.

They have no genius for mechanics, their domestic utensils are all rude, their snow shoes and canoes show ingenuity which necessity has forced on them, the state of every thing with them rises no higher than absolute necessity, and in all probability their ancestors some hundred years ago, were equal to the present generation in the arts of life. {They have a slight knowledge of the revolution}[1]

[*Hunting &c Moose Deer. feeding and qualities*]

[iv.50] The Natives of this Stoney Region subsist wholly by the chase and by fishing, the country produces no vegetables but berries on which they can live. The term "hunting" they apply only to the Moose and Rein Deer, and the

---

1   While the page that originally followed iv.49 has not survived, Thompson's writings on the Cree in his 1806 Rat Country essay contain the following passage: "They have a slight Knowledge of the Revolution of the Stars which helps them to know the coming change of the Seasons as the setting of the Pleiades with the Sun is a sure Mark that the Birds of passage will quickly arrive & the rising of Orion, that

Bear; they look for, and find the Beaver, they kill with the Gun, and by traps the Otter[1] and other animals. Hunting is divided into what may be termed "tracking" and "tracing." Tracking an animal is by following it's footsteps, as the Rein Deer and the Bear and other beasts; tracing, is following the marks of feeding, rubbing itself on the ground, and against trees; and lying down; which is for the Moose Deer, and for other animals on rocks and hard grounds. My remarks are from the Natives who are intimately acquainted with them, and make them their peculiar study.

¶ The first in order is the Moose Deer, the pride of the forest, and the largest of all the Deer, is too well known to need a description. It is not numerous in proportion to the extent of country, but may even be said to be scarce. It is of a most watchful nature it's long, large, capacious ears enables it to catch and discriminate, every sound; his sagacity for self preservation is almost incredible; it feeds in wide circles one within the other, and then lies down to ruminate near the centre; so that in tracking of it, the unwary, or unskillful, hunter is sure to come to windward of, and start it; when, in about two hours, by his long trot, he is at the distance of thirty or forty miles, from where it started; when chased it can trot, (it's favorite pace) about twenty five to thirty miles an hour; and when forced to a gallop, rather loses, than gains ground. In calm weather it feeds among the Pines, Aspins and Willows; the buds, and tender branches of the two latter [iv.51] are it's food: but in a gale of wind he retires amongst the close growth of Aspins, Alders and Willows on low ground still observing the same circular manner of feeding and lying down. If not molested it travels no farther than to find it's food, and is strongly attached to it's first haunts, and after being harrassed, it frequently returns to it's usual feeding places.

¶ The flesh of a Moose in good condition, contains more nourishment than that of any other Deer, five pounds of this meat being held to be equal in nourishment to seven pounds of any other meat even of the Bison but for this, it must be killed where it is quietly feeding; when run by Men, Dogs, or Wolves for any distance, it's flesh is alltogether changed, becomes weak and watery and when boiled; the juices separates from the meat like small globules of blood, and does not make broth; the change is so great, one can hardly be perswaded it is the meat of a Moose Deer. The nose of the Moose, which is very large and soft, is accounted a great delicacy. It is very rich meat, the bones of it's legs are very hard and several things are made of them, his

the Cold weather has set in & the Snow will continue on the Ground." AO. 17.205; Volume III.

1 *Lutra canadensis.*

skin makes the best of leather. It is the noblest animal of the Forest, and the richest prize the Hunter can take. In the rutting season the Bucks become very fierce, and in their encounters sometimes interlock their large palmated horns so strongly that they cannot extricate them; and both die on the spot, and which happens too often. Three of us tried to unlock the horns of two Moose which had died in this manner, but could not do it, although they had been a year in this state, and we had to use the axe.

¶ In the latter end of September we had to build a trading house at Musqua e gun Lake,² an Indian named Hug ge mowe quan came to hunt for us, and on looking about thought the ground good for Moose, and told us to make no noise; he was told no noise would be made [iv.52] except the falling of the trees, this he said the Moose did not mind; when he returned, he told us he had seen the place where a Doe Moose had been feeding in the beginning of May; in two days more he had unravelled her feeding places to the beginning of September, one evening he remarked to us, that he had been so near to her, that he could proceed no nearer, unless it blew a gale of wind, when this took place, he set off early and shot the Moose Deer, this took place in the very early part of October;³ This piece of hunting the Indians regarded as the work of a matchless hunter beyond all praise.

¶ The Natives are very dextrous in cutting up, and separating the joints, of a Deer, which in the open season, has to be carried by them to the tent or if near the water to a canoe; this is heavy work; but if the distance is too great, the meat is split and dried by smoke, in which no resinous wood must be used; this reduces the meat to less than one third of its weight. In winter this is not required, as the flat Sleds are brought to the Deer, and the meat with all that is useful is hauled on the Snow to the tent. The Moose Deer, have rarely more than one Fawn at a birth, it's numbers are decreasing for, from it's settled habits a skillful hunter is sure to find, and wound, or kill this Deer, and it is much sought for, for food, for clothing and for Tents. The bones of the head of a Moose must be put into the Water or covered with earth or snow.⁴

2 Thompson was at Musquawegan Lake on the Churchill River from 6 October 1804 to 1 June 1805. His journal for the period is AO. 16.18–60.

3 While Huggemowequan is not mentioned by name, Thompson records that two young Cree hunters brought a doe moose to the Musquawegan post on 19 October 1804. AO. 16.22. A parallel version of this incident is on iii.46 (see Volume II).

4 Here Thompson alludes to Cree ritual. In his study *Grateful Prey*, Robert Brightman notes that Cree hunters typically suspend the skulls of game animals, especially bears, beaver, caribou, and moose, from trees, a practice believed to influence the regeneration of the animal. When time does not permit, the skulls may be disposed

[*Rein Deer. the great herd. method of Natives. doctrine of Instinct &*
Manito]

¶ I have already described the Stony Region, as extending from the most
northern part of this continent, bounded on the east by the sea, southward
to Labrador and Novascotia, on the west by the chain of great Lakes.[1] This
great extent may properly be called the country of the Rein Deer, an animal
too well known to need description; and this Region is peculiar to the Rein
Deer, on this continent it is found no where else. The Natives have [iv.53] well
named it, "Marthee Teek" the "ugly deer," and from it's migratory habits,
the Wandering Deer. It's form and way of life, though admirably adapted to
the rude countries and severe climates it inhabits, yet when compared with
the graceful Antelope, it may be called not handsome. Their sight appears
not good, and the eye dull, and has nothing of the brilliancy of the eyes of
other deer, when examining any thing that appears doubtful, it extends it's
neck and head in an awkward manner, and cautiously approaches until it is
sure what the object is.

It's large, broad, hard, hoofs make it very sure footed, and quite safe, and
swift on swamps, rocks, or smooth ice.

It's meat is good, but has something of a peculiar taste. The fat is somewhat like that of mutton, the Tongue in richness and delicacy far exceeds any
other deer, and is even superior to the tongue of the Bison. It's strong form
and broad hoofs enables it to swim with ease and swiftness; they boldly cross
the largest Rivers and even Bays and Straits of the sea; but in doing this, their
want of clear eye sight leads them too far from land, and are lost. When few
in number, and scattered, they are cautious and timid; but when in large
herds, quite the reverse and are ready to trample down all before them.

At York Factory, in the early part of the open season, the Rein Deer are
sometimes numerous; when they are so, commencing about four miles above
the Factory, strong hedges of small pine trees, clear of their branches, are
made, near to, and running parallel with, the bank of the River; at intervals of about fifteen yards door ways are made in which is placed a snare of
strong line, in which, the Deer in attempting to pass, entangles itself; when
thus caught, it is sometimes strangled, but more frequently found alive; and

of as Thompson describes, by being placed in water or buried. Robert Brightman,
Grateful Prey: Rock Cree Human-Animal Relationships (Regina: Canadian Plains
Research Centre, 2002), 117, 199.

1 On iv.28, above (77).

ready to defend itself. [iv.54] The men, who every morning visit the hedge, are each armed with a spear of ten to twelve feet; and must take care that the Deer is at the length of his line and carefully avoid the stroke of his fore feet, with which he is very active, and defends itself.[2] The meat at this season is always poor and what is salted is barely eatable; it is only in Autumn and the early part of the winter that they are in good condition.

In the latter end of the month of May 1792, the ice had broken up. Mr Cooke and myself in a canoe proceeded about twenty miles up the River to shoot the Rein Deer, as they crossed the River;[3] we passed two days in which time we had killed ten deer. On the third morning the weather cold and uncomfortable, we were sitting by our fire, when we heard a noise as of distant thunder, and somewhat alarmed, put our four guns, and blankets into the canoe, and sat quickly in it; waiting what it could be; with surprise we heard the sound increasing and rushing towards us, but we were not long in suspense, about forty yards below us, a vast herd of Rein Deer, of about one hundred yards of front, rushing through the woods, headlong descended the steep bank and swam across the river; in the same manner ascended the opposite bank, and continued full speed through the woods; we waited to see this vast herd pass, expecting to see it followed by a number of wolves; but not one appeared, and in this manner the herd continued to pass the whole day to near sunset; when a cessation took place. On each hand were small herds of ten to twenty deer, all rushing forward with the same speed. The great herd were so closely packed [iv.55] together, that not one more, if dropped among them, could find a place. The next day, a while after sun rise, the same sound and rushing noise was heard, and a dense herd of the same front, with the same headlong haste came down the bank and crossed the river, and continued to about two in the afternoon, attended by small herds

---

2   While the caribou hedge described here appears to be operated by HBC men, the device was Native in origin. Most caribou hedges, both Native and European, were located between 3 and 15 miles (5 to 25 kilometres) up the Nelson River from York Factory. Lytwyn, *Muskekowuck Athinuwick*, 86–7.

3   In May 1792 Thompson was stationed at York Factory. In the York post journal entry for 11 June 1792, Joseph Colen records that "Messrs Thomas, Cook and Thompson set off in a Canoe up the River to look for Deer." York, Post Journal, 1791–92, B.239/a/92: 33v, HBCA. William Hemmings Cook (1768–1846) began his HBC career in 1786 as a writer; after several years as an inland trader, he served as chief factor at York, 1810–13. In the winter of 1792–93, Thompson and Cook were stationed at the neighbouring posts of Seepaywisk and Chatham Houses. Irene M. Spry, "William Hemmings Cook," *DCB*, 7:206–7.

on either side after which small herds passed, but not with the same speed, and by sun set finally ceased.

¶ When we returned to the Factory and related what we had seen, they could hardly believe us and had we not by chance been up the river, nothing would have been known of the passage of this great herd: for the weather, for a long fortnight after the breaking up of the ice is very precarious and uncomfortable. Some time after, conversing with some of the Natives on this herd of Rein Deer, they said that large herds do sometimes pass in the spring, they [had] often seen their roads, but had seldom seen the herds. The Factory next southward, the direction of the Deer was that of Severn River, about 250 miles distant,[4] they knew nothing of this herd and through the summer had no more than usual. At York Factory it was otherwise, the Deer were more numerous than usual, but only near the sea side.

¶ We attempted to estimate the number of Deer that passed in this great herd but the Natives pointed out their method, which we thought the best; this was to allow the Deer a full hour and a half (by the Sun) in the morning to feed and the same before sun set; this would give ten full hours of running, at what we thought twenty miles an hour, which they reduced to twelve miles, observing that large herds appear to run faster than they really do. By this means they extended the herd of the [iv.56] first day to one hundred and twenty miles in length and the herd of the second day to half as much more making the whole length of the herd to be one hundred and eighty miles in length by one hundred yards in breadth. The Natives do not understand high numbers, but they readily comprehend space, though they cannot define it by miles and acres; and their Clock is the path of the Sun. By the above space, allowing to each deer, ten feet by eight feet; an area of eighty square feet; the number of Rein Deer that passed, was 3,564,000,[5] an immense number; without including the many small herds. Thus what we learn by numbers, they learn by space.

¶ Then applying themselves to me, they said, "You that look at the Stars tell us the cause of the regular march of this herd of Deer," I replied. "Instinct," "What do you mean by that word." "It's meaning is 'the free and voluntary

---

4   The HBC established this post, at the mouth of the Severn River on Hudson Bay, in 1685. As the bird flies, Severn is approximately 200 miles (322 kilometres) southeast of York.

5   Thompson calculates the area of the herd to be 180 miles (290 kilometres) by 100 yards (91 metres), or 950,400 feet by 300 feet. This yields a product of 285,120,000 square feet, which divided by the 80 square feet estimated to be occupied by a single caribou gives 3,564,000 animals.

actions of an animal for it's self preservation.'" "Oh Oh, then you think this herd of Deer rushed forward over deep swamps, in which some perished, the others ran over them; down steep banks to break their necks; swam across large Rivers, where the strong drowned the weak; went a long way through woods where they had nothing to eat, merely to take care of themselves. You white people, you look like wise men and talk like fools. The Deer feeds quietly and lays down when left to itself. Do you not perceive this great herd was under the direct orders of their Manito and that he was with them, he had gathered them [iv.57] together, made them take a regular line, and drove them on to where they are to go:" "And where is that place." "We don't know, but when he gets them there, they will disperse, none of them will ever come back." And I had to give up my doctrine of Instinct, to that of their Manito. I have sometimes thought Instinct, to be a word invented by the learned to cover their ignorance of the ways and doings of Animals for their self preservation; it is a learned word and shuts up all the reasoning powers.[6]

[*Mah thee Moose*]

¶ On this stony region, there is another species of Deer, which I take to be a non descript;[1] by the Nahathaway Indians it is called "Mah thee Mooswak," (the ugly Moose) it is found only on a small extent of country mostly about the Hatchet Lake; in Latitude [*space*] and Longitude [*space*].[2] This deer seems to be a link between the Moose and the Rein Deer; it is about twice the weight of the latter; and has the habits of the former; it's horns are palmated somewhat like those of a Moose, and it's colour is much the same; it feeds on buds and the tender branches of Willows and Aspins, and also on moss. In all my wanderings I have seen only two alive, and but a glimpse of them, they bounded off with the trot of the Moose; and two that were killed by the Hunters; one of them was entirely cut up; the other had only the bowels taken out; this I wished to measure but I saw the Hunters eyed with

---

6 Again, Thompson places European and Native modes of understanding into dialogue in a way that is unflattering to the former.

1 I.e., not theretofore described by zoologists.

2 Hatchet Lake is on the Fond du Lac River, northwest of Wollaston Lake, through which Thompson travelled on his 1796 expedition to Lake Athabasca. The "Mah thee Mooswak" is likely the woodland caribou (*Rangifer tarandus-caribou*), known for its rarity and retiring habits. On iv.96–7, below (145), Thompson states that Black Lake, northwest of Hatchet Lake, is the "principal haunts" of this animal, and relates a Chipewyan account of the creature.

superstition what I wished to do, and desisted, and turned the matter off by enquiring how many of their skins make a comfortable Tent, they told me ten to twelve. They keep their haunts like the Moose, and when started return [iv.58] to them, but [I] could not learn whether they fed in rude circles, like the Moose; Their meat is almost as good as that of the Moose, and far better than that of the Rein Deer; When each of us was roasting a small piece at the fire, one of the Hunters said to me, "We did not like to see you measure the Deer, for fear their Manito would be angry, he is soon displeased, and does not like his Deer to be killed, and has not many of them."

The reason that this species of Deer is so very little known is, it's haunts is on the verge of the barren lands, far to the eastward of the route of the Traders, and the country produces but very few furrs.

[*my character. Indian tact. predict seeing the Brigade before us &c. Canadian character*]

It may now [do to] say something of myself, and of the character the Natives and the french Canadians entertained of me, they were almost my only companions.

My Instruments for practical astronomy, were a brass Sextant of ten inches radius an achromatic Telescope of high power for observing the Satellites of Jupiter and other phenomana one of the same construction for common use, Parallel glasses and quicksilver horizon for double Altitudes; Compass, Thermometer, and other requisite instruments,[1] which I was in the constant practise of using in clear weather for observations on the Sun, Moon, Planets and Stars; to determine the positions of the Rivers, Lakes, Mountains and other parts of the countries I surveyed from Hudson Bay to the Pacific Ocean. Both Canadians and Indians often enquired of me why I observed the Sun, and sometimes the Moon, in the day time; and passed whole nights with my instruments looking at the Moon and Stars. I told them it was to determine the distance and direction from the place I observed to other places.

1 The sextant measures angles, usually the altitude of a celestial body above the horizon; the achromatic telescope, as Thompson notes, is used for observing Jupiter's moons and other bodies; the quicksilver horizon is a substitute for the natural horizon, and parallel glasses shield this horizon from the wind; the compass is used to take bearings and calculate variation between true and magnetic north; the thermometer is used to correct for refraction of bodies due to air density. David Smyth, "David Thompson's Surveying Instruments and Methods in the Northwest, 1790–1812," *Cartographica* 18, no. 4 (1981): 1–17.

Neither the Canadians nor the Indians believed me; for both argued that if what I said was truth, I [iv.59] ought to look to the ground, and over it; and not to the Stars. Their opinions were, that I was looking into futurity and seeing every body, and what they were doing; how to raise the wind; but did not believe I could calm it, this they argued from seeing me obliged to wait the calming of the wind on the great Lakes, to which the Indians added, that I knew where the Deer were, and other superstitious opinions.

¶ During my life I have always been careful not to pretend to any knowledge of futurity, and that I knew nothing beyond the present hour; neither argument, nor ridicule had any effect, and I had to leave them to their own opinions[2] and yet inadvertingly on my part, several things happened to confirm their opinions. One fine evening in February two Indians came to the house to trade; the Moon rose bright and clear with the planet Jupiter a few degrees on it's east side; and the Canadians as usual predicted that Indians would come to trade in the direction of this star. To show them the folly of such predictions, I told them the same bright star, the next night, would be as far from the Moon on it's west side, this of course took place from the Moon's motion in her orbit; and is the common occurence of almost every month, yet all parties were perswaded I had done it by some occult power to falsify the prediction of the canadians. Mankind are fond of the marvelous, it seems to heighten their character by relating their hav[ing] seen such things. I had always admired the tact of the Indian in being able to guide himself through the darkest pine forests to exactly the place he intended to go, his keen, constant attention on everything; the removal of the smallest stone, the bent, or broken twig; a slight mark on the ground [iv.60] all spoke plain language to him. I was anxious to acquire this knowledge, and often being in company with them, sometimes for several months, I paid attention to what they pointed out to me, and became almost equal to some of them; which became of great use to me.

The North West Company of Furr Traders, from their Depot in Lake Superior sent off Brigades of Canoes loaded with about three Tons weight of Merchandise, Provisions and Baggage; those for the more distant tradings Posts are sent off first; with an allowance of two days time between each Brigade to prevent incumbrance on the Carrying Places; I was in my first year in the

2 For example, while Thompson was making astronomical observations when encamped with four lodges of Ojibwa on the Red River on 12 March 1798, his guide boasted to the Natives that Thompson had "supernatural Knowledge," upon which the men came en masse to beg him for their lives. Thompson wrote in his journal that, unable to persuade them that he was mortal, he advised them that they would live if they worshipped the "Supreme Being." AO. 7.15.

third Brigade of six Canoes each and having nothing to do, but sketch off my survey and make Observations, I was noticing how far we gained, or lost ground on the Brigade before us, by the fires they made, and other marks, as we were equally manned with five men to each canoe; In order to prevent the winter coming on us before we reached our distant winter quarters the Men had to work very hard from day light to sun set, or later, and at night slept on the ground, constantly worried by Musketoes; and had no time to look about them; I found we gained very little on them; at the end of fifteen days we had to arrive at Lake Winipeg (that is the Sea Lake from it's size) and for more than two days it had been blowing a north west gale, which did not allow the Brigade before us to proceed; and I told the Guide, that early the next morning we should see them; these Guides have charge of conducting the march, and are all proud of coming up to the canoes ahead of them; and by dawn of day we entered the Lake now calm, and as the day came on us saw the Brigade that were before us, only one Mile ahead of us, the Guide and the men shouted with joy, and when we came up to them told them of my wonderful predictions, and [iv.61] that I had pointed out every place they had slept at, and all by looking at the Stars; one party seemed delighted in being credulous, the other in exageration;[3] such are ignorant men, who never give themselves a moments reflection. The fact is Jean Baptiste[4] will not think, he is not paid for it; when he has a minute's respite, he smokes his pipe, his constant companion and all goes well; he will go through great hardships, but requires a belly full, at least once a day, good Tobacco to smoke a warm Blanket, and a kind Master who will take his share of hard times, and be the first in danger. Naval and Military Men are not fit to command them in distant countries; neither do they place confidence in one of themselves as leader; they always prefer an Englishman, but they ought always to be kept in constant employment however light it may be.

[*Musk Rat Country. Reed Lake. Natives and Animals few. Natives and Animals formerly numerous*]

Having passed eight winters in different parts of this Stony Region,[1] and as many open Seasons in discovering part of it's many Rivers and Lakes and

3 This probably occurred in 1798, when Thompson was on his way to Lac La Biche. In that year Thompson left Grand Portage on 14 July with the English (Churchill) River brigade. Upon entering Lake Winnipeg on 30 July he records: "in the Morng. above the Grand Rapid, we met the Slave Lake Canoes 6 in No." AO. 10.133.
4 Here used as collective nickname for French Canadians.
1 I.e., the Canadian Shield.

surveying them; and as the productions, the mode and manner of subsistence is every where the same; to prevent repetitions I shall confine myself to a central position, for the phenomena of the climate, and every thing else worth attention; This place is the Reed Lake [called] (Pee pee .quo oo musk, oo Sak a ha gan) by the Natives.[2] It is a sheet of water of about forty miles in length, by three to five miles in width; the land all around it, sometimes showing cliffs, but in most places, rising gently to the height of about one hundred feet, every where having fine forests of Birch Aspins, and several kinds of Pine; the Trading House in Latitude 54°··40' N Longitude 101°··30' West of Greenwich. The Thermometer was made by Dollond[3] and divided to 102 degrees below Zero. This section of the Stony Region is called the Musk Rat Country and contains an area of about 22,360 square miles; of which, full two fifths of this [iv.62] surface is Rivers and Lakes, having phenomena distinct from the dry, elevated, distant, interior countries.

¶ The Natives are Na hath a way Indians, whose fathers from time beyond any tr[a]dition, have hunted on these Lands; in conversing with them on their origin, they appear never to have turned their minds to this subject; and that mankind and the animals are in a constant state of succession; and the time of their great grandfathers is the extent of their actual knowledge of times past; their tradition of the Deluge and of the Rainbow I have already mentioned;[4] yet their stories all refer to times when Men were much taller and stronger than at present, the animals more numerous, and many could converse with mankind particularly the Bear, Beaver Lynx and Fox.

¶ Writers on the North American Indians always write as comparing them, with themselves who are all Men of education, and of course [the Natives] lose by comparison. The Indian has the disadvantage in not having the light of Christianity, of course his moral character has not the firmness of christian morality, but in practice he is fully equal to those of his class in Europe; living without law they are a law to themselves, the Indian is said to be a

2 Reed Lake is part of the Grass River system, which flows into the Nelson. Thompson served the HBC under Malchom Ross at Reed Lake from 2 September 1794 to 16 June 1795, and returned as an NWC trader from 4 August 1805 to 10 June 1806. Thompson refers mainly to the latter period here, the journals for which are AO. 16.1–78; 17.95–131.

3 Peter Dollond (1730–1820) entered the London opticians trade in 1750; his firm supplied the HBC from 1779 and was renowned for the precision and quality of its surveying, navigational, and optical instruments. It is still extant in Great Britain as Dollond and Aitchison, Opticians.

4 On iv.43–6 (101–3) and iv.46–7 (104), respectively.

creature of apathy, when he appears to be so, he is in an assumed character to conceal what is passing in his mind: as he has nothing of the almost infinite diversity of things which interest and amuse the civilized man, his passions, desires and affections are strong; however appear subdued, and engage the whole man; the law of retaliation, which is fully allowed, makes the life of man be respected; and in general he abhors the sheding of blood, and should sad necessity compel him to it, which is sometimes the case, he is held to be an unfortunate man, but he who has committed wilful murder, is held in abhorrence, as one with whom the life of no person [iv.63] is in safety, and possessed with an evil spirit. When Hudson's Bay was discovered, and the first trading settlements made, the Natives were far more numerous than at present.

In the year 1782, the small Pox from Canada extended to them, and more than one half of them died; since which although they have no enemies, their country very healthy yet their numbers increase very slowly. The Musk Rat country, of which I have given the area, may have ninety two families, each of seven souls, giving to each family an area of two hundred and forty eight square miles of hunting ground; or thirty five square miles to each soul, a very thin population. A recent writer (Ballantyne)[5] talks of myriads of wild animals; such writers talk at random, they have never counted, nor calculated; the animals are by no means numerous, and only in sufficient numbers to give a tolerable subsistence to the Natives, who are too often obliged to live on very little food, and sometimes all but perish with hunger.

Very few Beaver are to be found, the Bears are not many and all the furr bearing animals an Indian can kill can scarcely furnish himself and family with the bare necessaries of life. A strange Idea prevails among these Natives, and also of all the Indians to the Rocky Mountains, though unknown to each other, that when they were numerous, before they were destroyed by the Small Pox all the animals of every species were also very numerous and more so in comparison of the number of Natives than at present; and this was confirmed to me by old Scotchmen in the service of the Hudson's Bay Company and by the Canadians from Canada the knowledge of the latter extended over all the interior countries, yet no disorder was known among the animals; the fact was certain, and nothing they knew off could account

5 Robert Michael Ballantyne (1825–94) worked as an HBC clerk 1841–47. In his work *Hudson's Bay; or, Life in the Wilds of North America* (Edinburgh: W. Blackwood, 1848), he writes that Rupert's Land is "undefaced by the axe of civilized man, and untenanted by aught save a few roving hordes of Red Indians, and myriads of wild animals" (28). Thompson derides Ballantyne again on iv.237 (265).

for it; it might justly be supposed the destruction of Mankind would allow
the animals to increase, even to become formidable to the few [iv.64] Natives
who survived, but neither the Bison, the Deer nor the carnivorous animals
increased, and as I have already remarked, are no more than sufficient for the
subsistence of the Natives and Traders.[6] The trading Houses over the whole
country are situated on the banks of large Lakes, of at least twenty miles in
length by two or three miles in width; and as much larger as may be, as it is
only large and deep Lakes that have Fish sufficient to maintain the Trader
and his Men; for the Indians can at best only afford a Deer now and then.

[*Lakes. White & Pike. Nets. fish. Carp. Winter food*]

Some Lakes give only what is called a Fall Fishery this fishery commences
in October and lasts to about Christmas; the fish caught are white fish and
pike, whatever is not required for the day is frozen and laid by in a hoard;
and with all care is seldom more than enough for the winter and a fish once
frozen loses it's good taste unless kept in that state until it is thrown into the
Kettle of boiling water. Fish thawed and then boiled are never good; We who
pass the winter on fish, and sometimes also the summer, are the best judges,
for we have nothing with them, neither butter nor sauces; and too often not a
grain of salt. The best Lakes are those that have a steady fishery; and according to the number and length of the Nets give a certain number of white Fish;
throughout the winter. The deep Lakes that have sandy, pebbly beaches, with
bottoms of the same may be depended on for a steady fishery. The Fish on
which the Traders place their dependance are the White Fish, in such Lakes
as I have last described. It is a rich well tasted, norishing food; but in shoal
muddy Lakes it is poor and not well tasted; and when a new trading House is
built which is almost every year, every one is anxious to know the quality of
the fish it contains for whatever it is they have no other for the winter. These
fish vary [iv.65] very much in size and weight, from two to thirteen pounds
and each great Lake appears to have a sort peculiar to itself, it is preyed upon
by the Pike and Trout; and also the white headed, or bald, Eagle.

¶ The seine is rarely used, it is too heavy and expensive, and useless in
winter. The set Net is that which is in constant use.[1] Those best made are

---

6 On iv.260, below (285), Thompson quotes Mitchell Oman's statement that the number of animals in fact decreased during the smallpox epidemic.

1 The seine net is used to surround and herd fish, and must be manoeuvred either from
   a boat or from shore. The set (or gill) net is hung vertically in the water, entangling
   fish as they attempt to pass through its mesh.

of holland twine, with a five and a half inch mesh but this mesh must be adapted to the size of the fish and ranges from three to seven inches; the best length is fifty fathoms, the back lines, on which the net is extended and fastened are of small cord; every thing must be neat and fine: Instead of Corks and Leads; small stones are tied to the bottom line with twine at every two fathoms, opposite to each on the upper line a float of light pine, or cedar wood is tied which keeps the net distended; both in summer and winter the best depth for nets, is three to five fathom water; in shoal water the fish are not so good. In winter the nets being sheltered by the ice, the fishery is more steady, not being disturbed by gales of wind. In some Lakes, in Spring and Autumn there are an abundance of grey and red Carp; the former have so very many small bones, that only the head and a piece behind it are eaten; but the red Carp are a good fish though weak food. The daily allowance of a Man is eight pounds of fish, which is held to be equal to five pounds of meat; almost the only change through the year are hares and grouse, very dry eating; a few Martens, a chance Beaver, Lynx, and Porcupine.[2] Vegetables would be acceptable but not worth the trouble and risk of raising; and almost every small trading house is deserted during the summer, or only two men left to take care of the place;[3] every person with very few exceptions, enjoys good health, and we [iv.66] neither had, nor required a medical Man.

¶ Formerly the Beavers were very numerous, the many Lakes and Rivers gave them ample space; and the poor Indian had then only a pointed stick shaped and hardened in the fire, a stone Hatchet, Spear and Arrow heads of the same; thus armed he was weak against the sagacious Beaver, who, on the banks of a Lake made itself a house of a foot thick, or more; composed of earth, and small flat stones, crossed and bound together with pieces of wood; upon which no impression could be made but by fire. But when the arrival of the White People had changed all their weapons from stone to iron and steel, and added the fatal Gun, every animal fell before the Indian; the Bear was no longer dreaded, and the Beaver became a desirable animal for food and clothing, and the furr a valuable article of trade; and as the Beaver is a

---

2 *Erethizon dorsatum.*

3 Kitchen gardens were a feature of most large and permanent trading posts, such as Fort Chipewyan and Cumberland House. Produce such as potatoes, turnips, and barley supplemented the diet of fish and game, and reduced the need for imported provisions. James Parker, *Emporium of the North: Fort Chipewyan and the Fur Trade to 1835* (Regina: Alberta Culture and Multiculturalism/Canadian Plains Research Centre, 1987), 50–1. Gardens were planted at many smaller posts in the Plains but were rarer in the Canadian Shield.

stationary animal, it could be attacked at any convenient time in all seasons, and thus their numbers soon became reduced.[4]

[*State of Natives, former & present Value of Skins in barter. Black Bear food. fishing. Meat. Den &c Bear, speech*]

The old Indians when speaking of their ancestors, wonder how they could live, as the Beaver was wiser, and the Bear stronger, than them, and confess, that if they were deprived of the Gun, they could not live by the Bow and Arrow, and must soon perish. The Beaver skin is the standard by which other Furrs are traded; and London prices have very little influence on this value of barter, which is more a matter of expedience and convenience to the Trader and Native than of real value.

¶ The only Bears of this country, are the small black Bear, with a chance yellow Bear, this latter has a fine furr and trades for three Beavers in barter, when full grown.[1] The Black Bear is common and according to size passes for one or two Beavers, [iv.67] the young are often tamed by the Natives, and are harmless and playful, until near full grown, when they become troublesome, and are killed, or sent into the woods; while they can procure roots and berries, they look for nothing else, but in the Spring, when they leave their winter dens, they can get neither the one, nor the other, prowl about and go the Rapids where the Carp are spawning; here Bruin lives in plenty; but not content with what it can eat, amuses itself with tossing ashore ten times more than it can devour, each stroke of it's fore paw sending a fish eight or ten yards, according to it's size. The fish thus thrown ashore attract the Eagle and Raven; the sight of these Birds flying about, leads the Indian to the place, and Bruin loses his life and his skin.

¶ The meat of the Bear feeding on roots and berries becomes very fat and good, and in this condition it enters it's den for the winter; at the end of which the meat is still good and has some fat, but the very first meal of fish the taste of the meat is changed for the worse, and soon becomes disagree-

4 Thompson's comments indicate how Native adoption of European technology made hunting more efficient and enabled the pursuit of larger and more elusive prey. Bird, *Telling Our Stories*, 189–208. Robert Brightman suggests that many Cree believed that European technology had inverted human-animal power relationships, so that humans assumed a dominance formerly enjoyed by animals. Brightman, *Grateful Prey*, 194.

1 There is only one species, the black bear (*Ursus americanus*); colour phases of this species include black, brown, and blond.

able. When a Mah mees Dog,[2] in the winter season has discovered a den and the Natives go to kill the Bear, on uncovering the top of the den, Bruin is found roused out of it's dormant state, and sitting ready to defend itself; the eldest man now makes a speech to it; reproaching the Bear and all it's race with being the old enemies of Man, killing the children and women, when it was large and strong; but now, since the Manito has made him, small and weak to what he was before, he has all the will, though not the power to be as bad as ever, that he is treacherous and cannot be trusted, that although he has sense he makes a bad use of it, and must therefore be killed; parts of the speech have many repetitions to impress it's truth on the Bear; who all the while is grin[n]ing and growling, willing to fight, but more [iv.68] willing to escape, until the axe descends on it's head, or is shot; the latter more frequently, as the den is often under the roots of fallen trees, and protected by the branches of the roots.

When a Bear thus killed was hauled out of it's den; I enquired of the Indian who made the speech, whether he really thought the Bear understood him, he replied, "how can you doubt it, did you not see how ashamed I made him, and how he held down his head;" "He might well hold down his head when you was flourishing a heavy axe over it, with which you killed him."[3] On this animal they have several superstitions, and he acts a prominent part in many of their tales. All the other furr bearing animals have been already noticed.[4]

[*Birch Tree. Rind &c. for Tents*]

¶ On the western parts of this region the Forests have trees of a finer and larger growth, and now contain two kinds of Birch, the white and the red; one of Poplar and one of Aspin, one kind of Larch, two of Fir; four of Pine; with Alders and Willows. Of these the White Birch is the most valuable, and contributes more than all the others to the necessaries and comforts of life.

---

2 The meaning of this Cree word is obscure. It appears to contain the diminutive suffix *is*, while the root *mahm* may represent the verb *meya'māo*, "to smell," making the dog's name "little smeller." Watkins and Faries, *Cree Language*, 175; Stewart Hill, Fox Lake Cree Nation, personal communication with editor, 16 November 2006. The Mahmees dog is mentioned again on iv.140–1 (192–3).

3 On iii.185–6 (see Volume II), Thompson recounts two stories in which animals appear to understand human speech. He states there that "whatever kind of intelligence an animal collects for his safety is from the eye of Man, which is powerful on all animals, and which in such cases, must have a peculiar expression."

4 On iv.33f–35 (88–94).

Of the Birch their Bows, Axe helves and Spear handles are made, and several other things; in the Spring the sap, when boiled down, yields a weak molasses; but the most useful part is the Rind, which is peculiar to this tree; the bark is of a redish color, and good for tanning; this bark is covered with a Rind, it's growth in a horizontal, or longitudinal, direction; while that of the Tree, and it's bark are vertical; in my travels I have noticed, that the thickness of the Rind depends on the climate; the colder the climate the thicker the Birch Rind; on the west side of the Mountains where the winter is very mild, the White Birch is a noble large Tree, but the Rind too thin to be useful for Canoes.[1] In this region few white Birch exceed thirty inches in girth; but in general the Rind is excellent for all purposes and is from two eight, to three eights in thickness; it is all marked [iv.69] with what is called cores on the outside of the rind, of about an inch in, length; and narrow, when these go through the rind, it makes it useless for canoes. When the Natives see a Birch Tree with deep cores, they say it has been severely flogged by Wee sauk e jauk (the Flatterer) for by their tradition, when the Trees were renovated after the deluge, Wee sauk e jauk commanded them all to appear before him, which order they all obeyed but the Birch Tree; which for disobedience he flogged, of which the cores are the marks.[2]

¶ The best time for raising the rind off the Birch Tree is the early part of summer, the tree being smooth is difficult to ascend, and for this purpose the Native ties a strong leather cord to the great toes of his feet, leaving a space between them of about one foot, and having a strong square headed knife, very sharp at the point, in his belt, he ascends the tree to as high as the Rind is good, then raising a small strip from around the tree, in a straight line downwards cuts quite through the rind, which readily leaves the bark and while the sap is rising comes off so freely that two persons with light poles keep it to the tree until it can be carefully taken down; it is then warmed and it's circular form made flat, laid on the ground, and kept so, by light logs of wood; and thus becomes fit for use. The common length from one tree is from nine to fifteen feet, with a breadth of twenty four to thirty inches, very few trees yield a greater breadth, in this climate.

¶ As the Birch Rind is impervious to water; Canoes are made of it of all sizes to thirty feet in length, by four to five feet in breadth on the middle bar; this large size is made use of by the Traders, for the conveyance of furrs and

1 When Thompson crossed the mountains in March 1811, he was unable to find birchbark of sufficient thickness to construct a canoe, and instead built a vessel of cedar boards, an experience related in the 1848 version of the *Travels* on iii.237, Volume II.
2 For another account of this legend, see iii.34bbb (in Volume II).

goods, and is so light, it is carried by two men, when turned up, on shore, is affords good shelter to the Men, against [iv.70] rain, and the night. The canoes of the Natives are from ten to sixteen feet in length, and breadth in proportion, during the open season, they are almost constantly in them; hunting; removing from place to place, the Rivers, and numerous Lakes giving free access through the whole country. Their dishes and domestic utensils are mostly of Birch Rind, which are made of various sizes, and pack up within each other, and being light, with a smooth, firm, surface are easily kept clean.

This Rind is inflamable, and makes bright torches. For coverings to their tents and lodges, the Rind is sewed together so as to take the form required; and being water proof, make[s] a light comfortable tent in all weathers, and when the rain is over, the Natives can directly remove; whereas a leather tent, when soaked with rain, requires a day's time and fire to dry it. Unfortunately the cold of winter renders it brittle and liable to accidents; and it must be warmed before it can be rolled up for removal; and the same to unroll it. The red Birch[3] has a tougher wood, and in this respect is preferred to the White, but it's rind is thin, and as it grows among rocks, very often is small, crooked and knotty. The Fir is resinous and makes good flambeaux's[4] for spearing fish at night. The Larch is in request for making the flat Sleds, used by the Natives for the removal of their goods and provisions in winter, it sparkles too much to be used for firewood, and all the Pine woods are more, or less, the same for fuel. The Firs and resinous Pines when wholly decayed, become fine sand, without any vegetable mould, but all the trees and willows, not of the pine genus, enrich the soil by the decay of the leaves and the wood; The Larch is leafless all winter, the other Pines shed their leaves in summer, yet they also become sand, and do not [iv.71] profit the soil.

[Meteors]

The great expanse of Lake surface in this region, causes phenomena, that are peculiar to such a surface; In the winter season, every fine clear, calm, night, especially in the early part; there are innumerable very small luminous, meteoric points, which are visible for the twinkling of an eye, and disappear, when they are more numerous and brighter than usual they fortell a gale of wind. On one occasion, five of us had to leave our new built winter house, as the fishery could not maintain us, and try to get to another trading

---

3 Possibly the water birch (*Betula occidentalis*).
4 Torches.

house where the fish were more plentifull; On coming to the Sus quage mow Lake, of about thirty miles in length, by three to five miles in width; it was so slightly frozen over we did not think proper to cross it, but wait until the ice became stronger.[1]

¶ This was in November, roaming about for hares and grouse; I found a fine River of about thirty yards in width that entered the Lake through a marsh; about half a mile up which, was a Beaver House, with a few yards of open water, kept from freezing over by the Beaver. The Moon was full and rose beautifully over the east end of the Lake; While the water can be kept open, in the early part of the night the Beaver swim about; and Andrew Davy[2] a tall young scotchman and myself took our guns and lay down near the Beaver House to shoot the Beaver as they swam about; a Beaver came near to Andrew, his gun snapped, the Beaver gave a smart stroke on the water with his broad tail, as if to bid us good night, and plunged into his house; although there were no more hope for that night, being hungry, we continued to watch until about eleven o'clock; – As we were about to rise, a brilliant light over the east end of [iv.72] the Lake, it's greatest length; it was a Meteor of a globular form, and appeared larger than the Moon, which was then high; it seemed to come direct towards us, lowering as it came, when within three hundred yards of us, it struck the River ice, with a sound like a mass of jelly, was dashed into innumerable luminous pi[e]ces and instantly expired. Andrew would have run away but he had no time to do so; curiosity chained me to the spot. We got up, went to our fire, found nothing to eat, and lay down. As the ice of the River was covered with about one sixth of an inch of frozen snow, just enough to show our foot steps the next morning we went to see what marks this meteor had made on the ice, but could not discern that a single particle was marked, or removed; it's form appeared globular, and from it's size must have had some weight it had no tail, and no luminous

1 This body of water, now known as Landing Lake, is just northeast of Seepaywisk House, where Thompson spent the winter of 1792–93. In November 1792 he and four companions travelled from this post to Chatham House for supplies and were waylaid at Landing Lake from 9 to 18 November as they awaited its freezeup. AO. 1.29.
2 Andrew Davey (c. 1764 – after 1799), of the Parish of Firth, Orkney, joined the HBC as a labourer in 1782; after only two months' service he was taken prisoner by La Pérouse at the fall of Prince of Wales's Fort. Upon his return to Hudson Bay, Davy was assigned to the York Department, where he spent most of his career, becoming a canoeman in 1788 and steersman in 1792. His character was consistently described as "very good" in servants' ledgers.

sparks came from it until dashed to pieces. The Meteors that have been seen in Europe have all appeared to be of a fiery nature, some have exploded with a loud noise, and stones have descended from them.

¶ Two, or three nights afterwards, I was, as usual roaming about to find some game, about six in the evening, from the east end of the Lake, coming in the same direction, I saw a Meteor, which appeared larger, but not so bright as the first. I was near the Beaver house, but walking in a large grove of fine Aspins, the Meteor entered the wood about eight feet above the ground, as it struck the trees, pieces flew from it, and went out; as it passed close by me striking the trees with the sound of a mass of jelly I noticed them; although it must have lost much of it's size from the many trees it struck, it went out of my sight, a large mass. The Aspins have on their bark a [iv.73] whitish substance like flour, after dry weather, the next day I examined the Aspins struck by the Meteor, but even this fine flour on the bark was not marked; I was at a loss what to think of it, it's stroke gave sound, and therefore must have substance. These two Meteors were, perhaps, compressed bodies of phosphoric air; but without the least heat, for had there been any the second Meteor passed so near to me I must have felt it.[3]

[*Rime. Ice flowers. evaporation. Mirage. Reed Lake. Climate. Ice*]

¶ I have already described the brilliant Rime which covers the Willows and Shrubs along the shores of Hudson's Bay,[1] this is readily accounted for, by the evaporation from the sea; but the inland Lake shores have it equally brilliant, though not in such abundance; and also proceeds from the evaporation from the Lakes though frozen over, and the open rapids, and half frozen swamps have it in abundance, the Lake shores less, until swept away by a gale of wind, to be reformed in calm weather. It is well known that water frozen into ice, the latter has a greater bulk than the quantity of water frozen; and however solid the ice appears, it is actually porous; When the Lakes are frozen over, and the ice is from three to five inches in thickness, the vapours through it, form plots of ice flowers, which are composed of thin shining leaves of ice; round a centre, and have a brilliant appearance; they are of all sizes, some so small as to be called snow pearl, the clearest ice have the plots of small flowers, that which is opaque has the largest flowers; when the Sun shines, the leaves are lightly tinged with the colours of the Rainbow, have fine gaudy

3 Thompson and his companions had likely witnessed the Leonid meteor shower, which occurs annually in November.

1 On iv.26 (45–6).

appearance, but too bright for the eye to bear any time; the first fall of snow covers them to be seen no more.

¶ What is called Mirage is common on all these Lakes, but frequently simply an elevation of the woods and shores that bound the horizon; yet at times draw attention from the changes of scenery it exhibits, and on these Lakes has often kept me watching it for [iv.74] many minutes; and would have staid longer if the cold had permitted; The finest, and most changeable Mirage is seen in the latter part of February and the month of March, the weather clear, the wind calm, or light; the Thermometer from ten above, to twelve degrees below zero, the time about ten in the morning. On one occasion, going to an Isle where I had two traps for Foxes, when about one mile distant, the ice between me and the Isle appeared of a concave form, which, if I entered I should slide into it's hollow, sensible of the illusion, it had the power to perplex me. I found my snow shoes, on a level, and advanced slowly, as afraid to slide into it; in about ten minutes this mirage ceased, the ice became and showed a level surface, and with confidence I walked to my traps, in one of which I found a red Fox; this sort of Mirage is not frequent. That most common elevates and depresses objects, and sometimes makes them appear to change places;

¶ In the latter end of February at the Reed Lake,[2] at it's west end, a Mirage took place in one of it's boldest forms; About three miles from me was the extreme shore of the Bay; the Lake was near three miles in width, in which was a steep Isle of rock, and another of tall Pines; on the other side a bold Point of steep rock. The Mirage began slowly to elevate all objects, then gently to lower them, until the Isles, and the Point appeared like blacks spots on the ice, and no higher than it's surface; the above bold Bay Shore, was a dark black curved line on the ice; in the time of three minutes they all arose to their former height, and became elevated to twice their height, beyond the Bay, the rising grounds, distant eight miles, with all their woods appeared, and remained some what steady for a few minutes; the Isles and Point again disappeared; the Bay Shore, with the distant Forests, came rolling forward, with an undulating motion, as if in a dance, the distant Forests became so near to me I could see their branches, [iv.75] then with the same motion retired to half distance; the Bay shore could not be distinguished, it was

---

2 In his journals, Thompson carefully describes the appearance of several mirages at Reed Lake between 28 February and 14 April 1806. He notes that "the higher the Eye the more reflection disappeared & the lower the Eye, the higher the Reflection róse." AO. 17.119.

blended with the distant land; thus advancing and retiring, with different elevations for about fifteen minutes, when the distant Forests vanished, the Isles took their place and the Lake shores their form; the whole wild scenery was a powerful illusion, too fleeting and changeful for any pencil. This was one of the clearest and most distinct Mirages I had ever seen. There can be no doubt it is the effect of a cause which, perhaps, was, waves of the atmosphere loaded with vapours, though not perceptible to the eye, between the beholder and the objects on which the mirage acts, with the Sun in a certain position, when the objects were seen on the ridge of the wave, it gave them their elevation; when in the hollow of the wave, their greatest depression; and viewed obliquely to the direction of the wave, the objects appeared to change places. There may be a better theory to account for the Mirage.[3]

While the Mirage is in full action, the scenery is so clear and vivid, the illusion so strong, as to perplex the Hunter and the Traveller; it appears more like the power of magic, than the play of nature.

When enquiring of the Natives what they thought of it, they said it was Manito korso; the work of a Manito; and with this argument they account for every thing that is uncommon.

Although the climate and country of which I am writing is far better than that of Hudson's Bay yet the climate is severe in Winter the Thermometer often from thirty to forty degrees below Zero. The month of December is the coldest; the long absence of the Sun gives full effect to the action of the cold; the Snow increases in depth, it may be said to fall as dry as dust; the ice rapidly increases in thickness, and the steady cold of the rest of winter adds but little to that of the end of this [iv.76] month; but it's contraction by intense cold, causes the ice to rend in many places with a loud rumbling noise and through these rents, water is often thrown out, and flows over part of the ice, making bad walking. This month has very variable weather, sometimes a calm of several days, then Gales of wind with light snow, which from it's lightness is driven about like dust. This dull month of long nights we wish to pass away, the country affords no tallow for candles; nor fish oil for lamps; the light of the fire is what we have to work and read by. Christmas when it comes finds us glad to see it and pass. We have nothing to welcome it with.

3 Mirages are caused by the refraction of light as it travels from hotter to cooler air and vice versa. An inferior mirage occurs when ground temperature is higher than air temperature, causing an image of the sky to appear on the ground (as in an apparent pool of water in the desert). A superior mirage, like that witnessed by Thompson, occurs when the temperature of air below the line of sight (such as the trees and cliffs on the opposite side of a lake) is lower than that above.

[*Ta pah pah tum. wind. Canadians &c. his defence*]

¶ In one of the calms of this month Ta pah pah tum,[1] a good hunter came to us for some provisions and fish hooks, he said his three wives and his children had had very little to eat for nearly a whole Moon adding you may be sure that we suffer hunger when I come to beg fish, and get hooks for my women to angle with. He took away about thirty pounds of fish, which he had to carry about twenty miles to his tent. I felt for him, for nothing but sad necessity can compel a Na hath a way hunter to carry away fish, and angle for them, this is too mean for a hunter; meat he carries with pleasure; but fish is degradation.

¶ The calm still continued; and two days after Ta pa pah tum came in the evening; he looked somewhat wild; he was a powerful man of strong passions; as usual I gave him a bit of Tobacco, he sat down and smoked, inhaling the smoke as if he would have drawn the tobacco through the pipe stem; then saying, "now I have smoked, I may speak; I do not come to you for fish, I hope never to disgrace myself again; I now come for a wind which [iv.77] you must give me"; in the mood he was in, to argue with him was of no use, and I said, "why did you not bring one of your women with you, she would have taken some fish to the tent"; "My women are too weak, they snare a hare, or two every day, barely enough to keep them alive. I am come for a wind which you must give me"; "You know as well as I do, that the Great Spirit alone is master of the Winds; you must apply to him, and not to me"; "Ah, that is always your way of talking to us, when you will not hear us, then you talk to us of the Great Spirit I want a Wind, I must have it; now think on it, and dream how I am to get it." I lent him an old Bison Robe to sleep on; which was all we could spare.

¶ The next day was calm; he sat on the floor in a despondent mood, at times smoking his pipe; and saying to me, "Be kind to me, be kind to me, give me a wind that we may live"; I told him the Great Spirit alone could cause the wind to blow; and my french canadians were as foolish as the poor Indian; saying to one another, "it would be a good thing, and well done, if he got a wind; we should get meat to eat." The night was very fine and clear, I passed most of it observing the Moon and Stars as usual; the small meteors were very numerous, which indicated a Gale of Wind; the morning rose fine;

1 Thompson had made contact with the Cree hunter Tapahpahtum at Reed Lake in August 1805 but mentions him rarely in his journal of the winter. For another account of this incident, and a second mention of Tapahpahtum, see iii.46 and iii.92, in Volume II.

and before the appearance of the Sun, tho' calm with us, the tops of the tall Pines were waving, all foretelling a heavy gale, which usually follows a long calm; all this was plain to every one; Very early Ta pah pah tum said; "Be kind and give me a strong wind"; vexed with him; I told him to go, and take care the trees did not fall upon him; he shouted "I have got it"; sprang from the floor, snatched his gun, whipt on his Snow Shoes, and dashed away at five [iv.78] miles an hour; the gale from North East came on, as usual with snow and high drift, and lasted three days; for the two first days we could not visit the nets, which sometimes happens; the third day the drift ceased, but the nets had been too long in the water without being washed, and we had to take them up.

¶ On this gale of wind, a common occurrence I learnt my men were more strangely foolish than the Indians; some thing better than two months after this gale, I sent three of the men with letters to another trading house and to bring some articles I wanted; here these Men related how I had raised a storm of wind for the Indian, but had made it so strong that for two days they got no fish from the nets, adding, they thought I would take better care another time. In these distant solitudes, Men's minds, seem to partake of the wildness of the country they live in.

¶ Four days after Ta pah pah tum with one of his women came, he had killed three Moose Deer, of which he gave us one, for which I paid him; He was now in his calm senses: and I reasoned with him on the folly of looking to any one, to get what the Great Spirit alone could give; and that it made us all liable to his anger. He said "I believe it, I know it, I spent the autumn and the early part of winter in working on Beaver Houses, it is hard work, and only gives meat while we are working; When the Snow was well on the ground I left off to hunt Moose Deer, but the winds were weak, and unsteady; my women had to snare hares, my little boy, with his Bow killed a few grouse, which kept us alive until the long Calm came. I waited a little, then in the evening I took my Rattle [iv.79] and tambour and sung to the Great Spirit and the Manito of the Winds; the next evening I did the same, and took out of my medicine bag, sweet smelling herbs and laid them on a small fire to the Manito I smoked and sung to him for a wind, but he shut his ears, and would not listen to me; for three days I did the same; but he kept his ears shut I became afraid that he was angry with me; I left my tent and came to you, my head was not right, what you gave me was a relief for my women and children, I again sung, but the wind did not blow, he would not hear me, my heart was sore, and I came to you, in hopes you had power over the winds; for we all believe the Great Spirit speaks to you in the night, when you are looking at the Moon and Stars, and tells you of what we know nothing." It seems a natural weakness of the human mind when in distress, to hope from others, equally helpless, when we have lost confidence in ourselves.

[*Wisk a hoo. sad fate*]

¶ Wisk a hoo, was naturally a cheerful, good natured, careless man, but hard times had changed him, he was a good Beaver worker, and trapper, but an indifferent Moose Hunter, now, and then killed one by chance. He had twice been so reduced by hunger, as to be twice on the point of eating one of his children to save the others, when he was fortunately found and relieved by the other Natives; these sufferings had, at times, unhinged his mind, and made him dread being alone, he had for about a month, been working Beaver, and had now joined Ta pap pah tum; and their Tents, were together; he came to trade, and brought some meat the [iv.80] other had sent. It is usual when the Natives come to trade to give them a pint of grog; a liquor which I always used very sparingly; it was a bad custom but could not be broken off; Wisk a hoo as soon as he got it, and while drinking of it; used to say in a thoughtful mood "Nee weet to go, I must be a Man eater." This word seem[s] to imply "I am possessed of an evil Spirit to eat human flesh": "Wee tee go" is the evil Spirit, that devours humankind.[1] When he had said this a few times, one of the Men used to tie him slightly; and he soon became quiet; these sad thoughts, at times came upon him, from the dreadful distress he had suffered; and at times took him in his tent, when he always allowed himself to be tied during this sad mood, which did not last long.

Three years afterwards, this sad mood came upon him so often, that the Natives got alarmed, they shot him, and burnt his body to ashes; to prevent his ghost remaining in this world.

[*Apis ta wah shish. Reflections*]

A pist a wah shish (the Dwarf) was of low stature, but strongly made and very active, a good Beaver worker, and a second rate hunter of Moose deer; he was careful and industrious; When the leaves of the trees had fallen, and winter was coming on he had parted from the others to work Beaver; at first he was successful; but the third house he attacked the Beaver had worked many stones into it, that he broke his ice chissel and blunted one of his axes useless; the other was all they had to cut firewood; the edges of the Lakes

---

1 Thompson treats the Windigo phenomenon at length on iii.90–2 in Volume II and on iv.196–8, below (234–6).

were frozen [iv.81] over, and canoes could not be used. Distressing times came, and they were reduced to use as food, the youngest child to save the others, they were so weak they could barely get a little wood for the fire; sitting in sorrow and despair looking at the child next to lose it's life, a Rein Deer came, and stood a few yards from the tent door, he shot it and became the means of saving them, and recovering their strength; and for the winter he was a fortunate hunter. Both himself, his family, and the Natives believed that this Deer was sent by the Manito in pity to himself and family; he kept the skin, which I saw.

The Indians did not hold him culpable, they felt they were all liable to the same sad affliction; and the Manito sending him a Deer, showed a mark of favor.[1] As the strong affections of an Indian is centred in his children, for they may be said to be all he has to depend upon, they believe the dreadful distressed state of mind which necessity forces on them to take the life of one [of] their children to preserve the others, leaves such sad indelible impressions that the parents are never again the same they were before, and are liable to aberrations of mind. It is only on this Region and the Lakes westward to near the great plains, where there are Horses, that the Natives are subject to this distress of hunger, their Dogs are starved and do them very little good. If the country contained but half the Deer and other animals some writers speak of, the Natives would not suffer as they do. Notwithstanding the hardships the Natives sometimes suffer, they are strongly attached to their country of Rivers, Lakes, and Forests.

[*Che pa wy ans. character. Women. futurity*]

[iv.82] Hitherto my remarks have been on that portion of the great Stoney Region hunted on by the Nahathaway Indians; the northern portion of this region, interior and north of Hudson's Bay to far westward is hunted upon, and claimed by a distinct race of Indians, whom, however dispersed, claim their origen, and country to be, from Churchill River at it's sortie into the

---

1 In his notebooks, Thompson recorded a more elaborate and slightly different account of Apistawahshish's sacrifice. AO. 28.8–10; see Volume III. In this version, the hunter and his wife have seven children, of whom three are sacrificed before the family is saved by the fortuitous appearance of a doe moose. Thompson writes that Apistawahshish and his wife went on to have three more children, whom their fellow Cree regarded as gifts to replace those who had been lost. Elsewhere in his notebooks, Thompson writes of the struggle between an "Aphistawish" and a bear, but it is unclear whether this is the same man. AO. 47.80.

sea; and since the building of the Stone Fort;[1] they call the place by the name of the Stone House. Their native name, by which they distinguish themselves is "Din nae" to some hunting on a particular tract of country, an adjective is added "Tza Din nae," Beaver Dinnae. Their southern neighbours, the Nahathaway's call them "Che pa wy ans" (pointed skins) from the form in which they dry the Beaver skins, by the Hudson's Bay traders "Northern Indians."[2]

¶ Their physiognomy is of an oval form, the skull convex, the chin pointed the cheek bones raised, the nose prominent and sharp, the eyes black and small, fore head high, mouth and teeth good, hair black, long and lank, and of the men coarse the countenance, though not handsome is manly, tall in stature, of spare make, but capable of great fatigue; they are a peaceable people, abhoring blood shed; The Nahathaways look on them with a sort of contempt, being themselves too much inclined to war, they consider the Hunter to be naturally a Warrior; The Din nae themselves give some occasion for this, in imitating what ceremonies they learn from them; yet treating their women like slaves, a conduct which the Nahathaways detest;[3] When quarreling the Dinnae never resort to Arms but settle the affair by wrestling, pulling hair, and twisting each other's necks. Although to their neighbours they are open to ridicule, yet not so to the white people, who encourage their peaceable habits, and themselves justly remark [iv.83] that a fine country, and plenty to eat may encourage people to go to war on each other; but the fatigues they go through in hunting makes them glad to rest at night.

¶ Although they often suffer hunger, yet the steady frugality they strictly observe, never allows distress to come on their families; Their country has very large, and many lesser Lakes, when the land is scarce of Deer, or long calms come on, they take to the Lakes to angle Trout or Pike at which they

1 Prince of Wales's Fort.
2 Chipewyan is from the Cree *či·pwaya·n*, "(those who have) pointed skins." Like other Athapaskan peoples, the Chipewyan refer to themselves as *dene*, "the people." The HBC designation, "Northern Indians," was used in contradistinction to the "Southern Indians," or Cree. The Chipewyan comprise the most southeasterly subgroup of the Northern Athapaskan language family, concentrated in the Western Subarctic. Traditional Chipewyan economy is based on the caribou; herds were followed north into the tundra in summer and south to the boreal forests in winter. James G.E. Smith, "Chipewyan," *HNAI*, vol. 6, 271–84. Thompson travelled and traded in the southern margins of Chipewyan lands intermittently between 1793–99 and 1802–05.
3 For Thompson's discussion of the relations between the sexes in Cree culture, see iv.49 (108).

are very expert, and although they use our hooks; for large fish prefer their own, which are of bone, and a fish caught with their bone hook, does not get loose as sometimes happens to our hooks: Whether fish, or meat, whatever is not required is carefully put by for next meal. They carefully collect every article that can be of use to them; and when they remove, which they very often do, from place to place the women are very heavily loaded; the men with little else than their gun, and fishing tackle, even a girl of eight years will have her share to carry; while the Boys have some trifle, or only their Bows and Arrows.

¶ This hard usage makes women scarce among them, and by the time a girl is twelve years of age, she is given as a Wife to a Man of twice her age, for the young men cannot readily obtain a wife, and on this account Polygamy is rare among them. The hardships the Women suffer, induces them, too often to let the female infants die, as soon as born; and look upon it as an act of kindness to them, and when any of us spoke to a woman who had thus acted; the common answer was; "She wished her mother had done the same to herself." Upon reasoning with the Men, on the severe laborious life of the women, and the early deaths it occasioned; and that it was a disgrace to them; and how very different the Na hath a ways treated their women; they always intimated, they were an inferior order of [iv.84] mankind, made for the use and service of the Men; the Nahathaways were a different people from, and they were not guided by, them; and I found they were too often regarded as the property of the strongest Man; until they have one or more children; I have been alone with them for months, and always found them a kind good people, but their treatment of the Women always made me regard them as an unmanly race of Men.

¶ Whether in distress, or in plenty, or in whatever state they may be I never saw any act of a religious tendency; they make no feasts, have no dances, nor thanksgivings; they appear to think every thing depends on their own abilities and industry, and have no belief in the greater part of the religious opinions of the Nahathaways; from the regular migrations of the water fowl and rein deer, they infer something of a Manito takes care of them, but neither does, nor can, prevent their killing them; they believe in a future state, and that it is much the same as in this life; they appear to have no high ideas of it; but somewhat better than the present; they dread death as a great evil, but meet it with calmness and fortitude; the wife of the deceased must mourn his loss for a year, her hair which is cut off and placed beside him, when dead, is now allowed to grow and she may become a Wife; but there is no restraint on the Men at the death of their wives; they take a wife as soon as they can, and seldom allow a Widow woman to pass a year of mourning: They do not bury their dead, but leave them to be devoured; this they might easily prevent by covering them with wood, or stones: which is sometimes done, and sometimes the dead is placed on a scaffold, but these instances are very rare; Some of them have an ancient tradition that a Great Spirit descended on a rock, took a Dog, tore it to small pieces, and scattered it, that these pieces, each [iv.85] became a Man, or a Woman, and that these Men and Women, are their original parents, from whom they have all come; and thus the Dog is their common origin;[4] On this account they have very few dogs; frequently several tents have not a Dog among them; and they abhor the Dog Feasts of the Nahathaway's and of the French Canadians; the latter regard a fat Dog as a luxury, equal to a fat pig;

Their morals are as good as can be expected; they exact chastity from their wives and seem to practise it themselves; they are strictly honest; and detest a thief; and are as charitable and humane to those in want as circumstances will allow them. When the martial Tribes[5] by right of conquest over the Snake Indians, took possession of the Great Plains the Nahathaways occupied the lands thus left; and from the rigorous clime of sixty one degrees north, went southward to fifty six degrees north, the Dinnae, or Che pawyans, in like manner occupied the country down to the last named Latitude; and westward by the Peace River to the Rocky Mountains; and have thus quietly extended themselves from the arctic regions to their present boundary, and will continue to press to the southward as far as the Nahathaways will permit.[6]

4   Samuel Hearne recorded a more elaborate and somewhat different account of the Chipewyan origin myth. In this version, the first person on earth was a woman, who became pregnant by a doglike animal which transformed itself into a young man at night. A giant arrived and tore the dog to pieces, the scattered parts becoming the lakes, rivers, fish, animals, and birds. The woman and her offspring, the ancestors of the Chipewyan, were then given dominion over this creation. Hearne, *A Journey*, 342–3. See also John Franklin, *Narrative of a Journey to the Shores of the Polar Sea, in the Years 1819–20–21–22* (London: J. Murray, 1824), 1:249–50.
5   The Blackfoot.
6   Here Thompson describes a general southwesterly movement of Native peoples. Groups of Cree and Assiniboine moved from the Eastern Woodlands onto the Plains throughout the eighteenth century. Simultaneously, the Blackfoot migrated from the North Saskatchewan River south and west towards their former lands, where they came into conflict with the Shoshone. At the urging of the HBC and NWC, in the late eighteenth century many Chipewyan bands moved south into the boreal forests.

[country. H B Co hard to get Men &c. Koz daw & Paddy. Missinippe. Outfit]

Having now given a sketch of the people among whom I am about to travel; I have to return back a few years from my wintering place in Reed Lake, where I brought together that part of the Great Stony Region,[1] and now enter on the northern part of this Region hunted on by the Natives I have described. Having requested permission of Mr Joseph Colen, the Resident at York Factory, to explore the country north westward from the junction of the Rein Deer's River with the Missinippe (Great Waters)[2] to the east end of the Athabasca Lake a country then wholly unknown,[3] I proceeded to Fairford House,[4] for we must give titles to our Log Huts, where Mr [iv.86] Malcolm Ross[5] had wintered, but not a single man could be spared from the trade in furrs to accompany me, and with great difficulty the Hudson's Bay Company then procured Men to keep up the few interior Trading Houses they then had; for the War which raged between England and France[6] drained the Orkney Islands of all the Men, that were fit for the Navy, or the Army; and only those refused were obtained for the furr trade: There is always a Canoe with three steady men and a native woman waiting the arrival of the annual Ship from England to carry the Letters and Instructions of the Company to the interior country trading houses; but very few men came out with her for the trade, and those few were only five feet five inches and under; a Mr James Spence[7]

1 Pages iv.61–81, where Thompson describes the region of the Canadian Shield in which Reed Lake is found (117–33).

2 The Churchill River.

3 The advance of Montreal traders into the Athabasca region in the late 1770s both revealed its vast fur-bearing potential and threatened the livelihood of the HBC's bayside posts. In order to assert itself in the region, the HBC began to establish posts in the Churchill River system and sent Philip Turnor on his 1790–92 expedition. Colen hoped that a more direct passage from the Churchill to Lake Athabasca could be found, bypassing the westerly route through Lac Île-à-la-Crosse and over the Methye Portage.

4 Fairford House, on the Churchill River just below the mouth of the Reindeer River, was established by Malchom Ross in September 1795 and seems to have operated for only one winter. Thompson was at the post 27 May to 10 June and 21 July to 30 August 1796.

5 For HBC trader Malchom Ross, see appendix 2.

6 The war between Great Britain and the French Republic began in 1793.

7 Of the several HBC employees who shared this name, two are possible subjects of this passage. James Spence "Junior" (c. 1758–97) of Kirkwall, Orkney, joined the HBC

was in charge of the Canoe, and his indian wife looking steadily at the Men, and then at her husband; at length said, "James have you not always told me, that the people in your country are as numerous as the leaves on the trees, how can you speak such a falsehood, do not we all see plainly that the very last of them is come, if there were any more would these dwarfs have come here." This appeared a home truth, and James Spence had to be silent.

¶ Finding that I could have no white man to accompany me somewhat damped my ardor, but my curiosity to see unknown countries prevailed, and a few Chepawyans happening to be there; and had traded their few furrs I engaged two young men of them to accompany me; both of them had hunted for two winters over the country we were to explore, but had never been on the Rivers and Lakes in summer. Their only practice in canoes had been, on a calm day to watch for the Deer taking refuge in the Lakes from the flies, and for Otters and Fowls, which gave them no experience of the currents and rapids of Rivers; yet such [iv.87] as they were, I was obliged to take them; they were both unmarried young men; One of them named Koz daw, was of a powerful, active, make; gay, thoughtless, and ready for every kind of service: would climb the trees, and have the Eagles in their nests; yet under all this wildness was a kind and faithful heart. The other from his hard name, which I could not pronounce, I named Paddy,[8] he was of a slender form, thoughtful, of a mild disposition; As nothing whatever was ready for us, we had to go into the Forests for all the materials to make a Canoe; of sevente[e]n feet in length by thirty inches on the middle bar.

¶ This House though well situated for trade; had but a poor fishery with three Nets, each of fifty fathoms in length, we could barely maintain our-selves, the fish caught were White Fish, Pike and Carp, with a few Pickerel, none of them very good. Fairford House is in Latitude 55° · 33'-28" North,

in 1775, served as a labourer, canoeman, and steersman, and retired in 1795. James Spence "Senior" (c. 1753–95) of Birsay, Orkney, joined the HBC in 1773, served as a steersman, and managed Buckingham House from 1793 to 1795. He was married to a Cree woman named Nestichio, with whom he had four children. Alice M. Johnson, ed., *Saskatchewan Journals and Correspondence, 1795–1802* (London: Hudson's Bay Record Society, 1967), 17n.

8 Although Thompson states that he named Paddy, a man of this name belonged to the Chipewyan band with whom Peter Fidler spent the winter of 1791–92 and may be the same figure. Peter Fidler, "Journal of a Journey with the Chepawyans or North-ern Indians ..." in J.B. Tyrrell, ed., *Journals of Samuel Hearne and Philip Turnor between the Years 1774 and 1792* (Toronto: Champlain Society, 1934), 526. Kozdaw has not been identified.

and Longitude 103°- 9'··52" West of Greenwich, on the banks of the Missinippe (Great Waters) so called from the spreading of it's waters. It's southern
head is the Beaver River from the Beaver Lake not far from the east foot of
the Mountains, which, on entering the chain of Lakes, and the land of Rocks,
spreads into very irregular forms of Lakes, which at distances are crossed by
Dams of rock, and by channels falls into the same rude Lakes, to within one
hundred miles of Churchill Factory, having for this last distance, the regular
form of a River with many Rapids and Falls to within about ten miles of the
sea where it meets the tide waters. The whole of the above distance from the
valley of the chain of Lakes to the sea, is a poor country for Deer and the furr
bearing animals; and also for fish; There are some [iv.88] very good fisheries,
but they are in the deep Lakes of this Region wholly independent of the Missinippe, though the Streams from them are discharged into it.

[*Set off. Rein Deer's Lake. 50 Miles of Ponds & C Places to Manito Lake*]

¶ Early on the tenth day of June 1795[1] we were ready, our outfit consisted of
one fowling gun; forty balls, five pounds of shot, three flints and five pounds
of powder, one Net of thirty fathoms; one small Axe, a small Tent of grey
cotton; with a few trifles to trade provisions as beads, brass rings, and awls,
of which we had little hopes; our chief dependence next to good Providence,
was on our Net and Gun. The sortie[2] of the Rein Deer's River; which is the
great northern branch of Churchill River is about one mile above Fairford
House; and up this Stream we proceeded in a north direction for sixty four
miles to the Rein Deers Lake; Latitude 56·20·22 Longitude 103·18·47. The
River is a fine deep stream, of about three hundred yards in width, having
five falls and the same number of Carrying Places; the Falls have a descent of
four to fourteen feet; with only one rapid. It's current is moderate from one
to two miles Per hour, and forms several small Lakes. The banks are of sloping high rocks, with several sandy bays; the Woods of small Birch, Aspin,
and Pines, growing on the rocks with very little soil; in many places none
whatever; the Trees supported each other by the roots being interlaced in the
same manner as the Trees are supported on the frozen lands of Hudson's Bay
which never thaw; and both are kept moist in summer by being covered with
wet moss.

1 1796 is intended. Thompson, Kozdaw, and Paddy left on 10 June, reached the east
   end of Lake Athabasca on 2 July, and returned to Reindeer Lake on 21 July. For the
   journals of this expedition, see AO. 4.110–16; 5.245–238; 6.290–98.
2 Mouth (literally, "exit").

The Natives are frequently very careless in putting out the fires they make, and a high wind kindles it among the Pines always ready to catch fire; and burn until stopped by some large swamp or lake; which makes many miles of the country appear very unsightly, and destroys many animals and birds especially the grouse, who do not appear to know how to save themselves, but all this devastation is nothing to the Indian, his country is large.[3] [iv.89] We proceeded along the west side of the Lake, in a direction of due North, for one hundred and eight miles to a Point of tolerable good Pines, the best we had seen, and on which, late in Autumn we built a trading House[4] Latitude 57·23·N· Longitude 102·59 W:

The whole distance we have passed has a rocky barren appearance; the woods small and stunted; in several places the fire had passed. In the above distance the Paint River falls in, a considerable stream from the westward; and also a few Brooks. The water is clear and deep, and the Lake is studded with Islands of rock, and dwarf Pines cover them. We proceeded up the Rivulet which we found shoal, with many rapids, and soon led us to Ponds and Brooks, with several Carrying Places, which connect them together for fifty miles, the last of which placed us on the banks of the Manito Lake.[5] Latitude 57·47·38 N Longitude 103·17·12 W

[*Manito Lake. it's woods &c country*]

¶ The whole of this route can be passed in the open season only by small Canoes; the country as usual poor and rocky; Hitherto we had not met with a single Native, and our Gun and Net gave us but short Allowance; This Route is practised by the Natives to avoid the great length of the Rein Deer's and Manito Lakes, and the crossing of the great Bays of these Lakes, which would be dangerous to their small Canoes. This great Lake is called Manito (super natural) from it's sending out two Rivers, each in a different direction; from it's east side a bold Stream runs southward and enters the Rein Deers Lake on it's east side; and from the west side of the Manito Lake, it sends out the Black River,[1] which runs westward into the east end of the Athabasca

---

Native peoples frequently used fire as a deliberate means of managing vegetation and game. Burning increases fresh browse for animals, promotes berry propagation, and increases ease of travel and sighting of game. Henry T. Lewis, *A Time for Burning* (Edmonton: Boreal Institute for Northern Studies/University of Alberta, 1982).

4 For the construction of Bedford House, see iv.101, below (150).

5 Wollaston Lake.

1 The Fond du Lac River.

Lake; which is perhaps without a parallel in the world.[2] Some have [iv.90] argued that such a Lake must soon be drained of its water; they forget that it is the quantity of water that runs off, that drains a Lake; and were the two Rivers that now flow in opposite directions made to be one River in a single direction, the effect on the Lake would be the same. Add to this, the head of a River flowing out of a Lake is a kind of a Dam, and can only operate on the Lake in proportion to the depth to the bottom; which in general is several hundred feet below this bottom of the head of the River; and were the River to drain the Lake to this level, the River would cease to flow but the Lake would still contain a great body of water.

¶ The last fifty miles had been over a low rocky, swampy country and tormented with myriads of Musketoes; we were now on the banks of the Manito Lake, all around which, as far as the eye could see, were bold shores, the land rising several hundred feet in bold swells, all crowned with Forests of Pines; in the Lake were several fine Isles of a rude conical form, equally well clothed with Woods; I was highly pleased with this grand scenery; but soon found the apparent fine forests to be an illusion, they were only dwarf Pines growing on the rocks; and held together by their roots being twisted with each other. On our route, seeing a fine Isle, which appeared a perfect cone of about sixty feet in height, apparently remarkably well wooded to the very top of the cone; I went to it, my companions saying it was lost time; on landing, we walked through this apparent fine forest, with our heads clear above all the trees, the tallest only came to our chins; While we were thus amusing ourselves, the Wind arose and detained us until near sun set. [iv.91] To while away the time, we amused ourselves with undoing the roots of these shrub Pines for about twenty feet on each side; when the whole slid down the steep rock into the Lake, making a floating Isle of an area of four hundred feet; and so well the fibres of the roots were bound together, that when it came to where the waves were running high, it held together, not a piece separated and thus drifted out of our sight. We set loose a second islet of about the same area; then a third, and a fourth islet, all floated away in the same manner: On the Isle, the roots of these small pines were covered with a compact moss of a yellow color about two inches thick. The mould on the rock under these pines, was very black and rich, but so scant, that had the area of four hundred feet been clean swept, it would not have filled a bushel

2 Wollaston Lake straddles the watersheds of the Arctic Ocean and Hudson Bay. The waters of the Fond du Lac River flow to the Arctic via Lake Athabasca and the Mackenzie River, while those of the Cochrane River flow to Hudson Bay by way of Reindeer Lake and the Churchill River.

measure, perhaps the produce of centuries.[3] This Isle was a steep cone, the sixteen hundred square feet we uncovered, showed the rock to be as smooth as a file, and nowhere rougher than a rasp; and had it been bare it would have been difficult of ascent; it was about two miles from other land; then how came these pines to grow upon it; they bare no cones, nor seeds and no birds feed on them; these wild northern countries produce questions, difficult to answer.

¶ After coasting the west side of this Lake for Eighty miles we put up on the evening of the twenty third of June at the head of the Black River; which flows out of this Lake and finally discharges itself into the east end of the Athabasca Lake, which I found to be in Latitude 58°·27'·55" North; and in Longitude 103°·27'·1" West of Greenwich Variation 15° East. What I after wards learned of the Indians on the geography of the Manito Lake confirmed my opinions of it; By their information this Lake is of very great extent; the eighty miles we coasted [iv.92] they counted as nothing; they say, that none of them has seen it's northern extent, and of the east side, except the southern part. The deep, long rolling waves in a gale of wind, equal to any I have seen in Lake Superior, showed a very deep Lake and that the roll of the waves came from a great distance.

[*Moss lands of the above Lake &c. Areas of ditto belong to the Red Man and the Deer*]

It was always my intention to have fully surveyed this and the Rein Deer's Lake, but the sad misfortune which happened in the lower part of the Black River, made me thankfull to save our lives. That these countries are unknown, even to the Natives, can excite no surprise; their canoes are small and when loaded with their Wives, Children, and Baggage, are only fit for calm water, which is seldom seen on these Lakes; The east sides of these two Lakes, have a range of full six hundred miles, on which there are no Woods; all is

---

3 This episode has affinities with the "Voyage to Lilliput" section of *Gulliver's Travels*, in which the narrator is cast ashore in a land of miniature proportions, remarking "the tallest Trees, as I could judge, appeared to be seven Foot high." Jonathan Swift, *Gulliver's Travels*, ed. Claude Rawson (New York: Oxford University Press, 2005), 24. D.M.R. Bentley describes this incident as an early Canadian example of Joseph Addison's "*new* or *uncanny*." D.M.R. Bentley, "UnCannyda," *Canadian Poetry* 37 (Fall/Winter 1995): 1–16.

Rock and Moss; on these barren lands, in the open season the Rein Deer are numerous; they have food in abundance, and the constant cold nights puts down the flies.

The Natives, when they hunt on the North East parts of the Rein Deer's Lake, cannot stay long: the Moss, when dry, makes a tolerable fire; but in wet weather, which often happens it holds the rain like a sponge, and cannot be made to burn: this want of fire often obliges them to eat the meat raw, and also the fish; the latter I have seen them [do] by choice; especially the pike, and a Trout is no sooner caught than the eyes are scooped out and swallowed whole, as most delicious morsels.

Whatever Deer they may kill, they cannot dry the meat; and as soon as they have eaten plentifully and procured as many skins as they can carry, they leave these lands of Moss, for those of Woods where they can have a comfortable fire, and get poles of pine wood to pitch their Tents for shelter.

The Natives told me, when enquiring of the [iv.93] country to the eastward of the Manito Lake; that two of them had been two day's journey direct eastward of the Lake, and saw nothing of woods, but every where rock and moss, with small Lakes, in which the Ducks were taking care of their young and no other animal than a few herds of Rein Deer, and Musk Oxen; and it seems such is all the country between these great Lakes and Churchill River Factory and far to the northward.

¶ The Rein Deers Lake contains an area of 18,400 square miles; and the Manito Lake has an are[a] of not less than about 30,000 square miles. From the head of the Black River to Churchill Factory is 339 statute miles, including the width of the Manito Lake, which may be reckoned at eighty miles, or more. It is a pity the Hudsons Bay Company do not have these countries explored; by their charter they hold these extensive countries to the exclusion of all other persons. By civilised men, especially those of the United States, who have a mortal antipathy to the North American Indian; or, as he is now called the, "Red Man"; it is confidently predicted, that the Red Man, must soon cease to exist, and give place to the White Man; this is true of all the lands formerly possessed by the Red Man, that the White Man has thought it worth his while to seize by fraud or force, but the Stony Region is an immense tract of country which the Supreme Being, the Lord of the whole Earth, has given to the Deer, and other wild Animals; and to the Red Man for ever, here, [iv.94] as his fathers of many centuries past have done, he may roam, free as the wind; but this wandering life, and the poverty of the country, prevents the labors of the Missionary to teach them the sacred truths of christianity.

[*Black River. Lakes &c. it's Manito Fall. Black Lake barren country*]

On the 25th day of June we descended the Black River for nine miles to
the Hatchet Lake. The River flows between two hills, in a valley with coarse
grass on each side; it is about twenty yards in width, and five feet in depth,
and moderate current. The Hatchet Lake, has an area of about three hundred square miles, the banks rise to about three hundred feet apparently well
wooded with Pines, but very few are above twenty feet in height, and full of
branches. The whole is a wretched country of solitude, which is broken only
by the large Gull and the Loons. The first twelve miles of the River have several strong rapids and two carrying places, one of 204, the other of 298 yards.
By observations the Latitude was 58°··44'··35" Longitude 103°··56'··28" West
near the north end of the Black Lake, which is a small Lake.

The River had now increased it's water by the addition of the Porcupine
and Trout Rivers, and several Brooks, it has also a greater descent; In it's
course of one hundred and fifty three miles from the above place by observation in the Black Lake, it meets with, and forms, many small Lakes; and
collects their waters to form a Stream of about one, to two, hundred yards
in width: it's bottom is sand and pebbles, or rude stones and small rocks,
smoothed by the water; on a bed of Limestone, which is the rock of the country; it's course [iv.95] is sinuous, from the many hills it meets, and runs round
in it's passage; it's current is strong, with many rapids, some of them one mile
in length; it has four falls, three of them are about half way down the River;
the fourth fall is the end of a series of rapids, cutting through a high hill; at
length the banks become perpendicular, and the river falls eight feet, the carrying place is six hundred yards in length. For half a mile further the current
is very swift; it is then for one hundred and eighteen yards, compressed in a
narrow channel of rock of only twelve yards in width at the end of this channel a bold perpendicular sided point of limestone rock projects at right angles
to the course of the river, against which the rapid current rushes and appears
driven back with such force that the whole river seems as if turned up from
it's bottom it boils, foams and every drop is white; part of the water is driven
down a precipice of twenty feet descent, the greater part rushes through the
point of rock and disappears for two hundred yards; then issues out in boiling whirlpools.

The dashing of the water against the rocks, the deep roar of the torrent, the
hollow sound of the fall, with the surrounding high, dark frowning hills form
a scenery grand and awful, and it is well named the Manito Fall. While the
Na hath a ways possessed the country, they made offerings to it, and thought
it the residence of a Manito; they have retired to milder climates; and the

Chepawyans have taken their place who make no offerings to any thing; but my companions were so awe struck, that the one gave a ring, and the other a bit of tobacco. They had heard of this Fall, but never saw it before.[1]

The second Black Lake is a fine sheet of water it's length about thirty miles in a west direction, it's breadth [iv.96] one to six miles; in the east end there are five small isles and a large Island near the north shore. The north side of the Lake is a high hill, in some places abrupt cliffs of rock, the south side is more pleasing, it's fine sandy beaches, the banks with small Aspins and Birch in full leaf; the ground firm and dry, covered with Bear's Berries, the leaf of which is mixed with tobacco for smoking, the interior rising by easy ascents, and apparently well wooded formed a pleasing landscape to us, who had so long been accustomed to rude scenery; it is the only place which had an appearance of being fit for cultivation; but it was appearance only the woods were small, even the Pines rarely rose to the height of twenty feet; and the soil was too sandy The area of this Lake may be about one hundred and twenty miles.

¶ This Lake appears to be the principal haunts of the species of Deer which I have already described;[2] and which I believe to be yet a non descript. The Na hath a ways, who pay great attention to distinguish every species of Beast and Bird from each, do not class them with the Rein Deer, and call them Mah the Moose wah (the Ugly Moose). This is the only Lake in which I have seen them, and the Natives say they are not numerous, and are confined to this Lake and it's environs. A civilized man may never travel this way again; there is nothing to tempt him a rude barren country that has neither provisions nor furrs, and there are no woods of which he could build a warm hut; and at best his fuel, of which a large quantity is required, could be only of small poles, which would burn away, almost as fast as he could cut them. In the winter the Natives do not frequent these countries but hunt to the west ward.

[Black River. hardships. 3 Tents of Chepawyans]

¶ [iv.97] On the North side, the Black River rushes through a low mountain in a long cataract, on the south side is a carrying place of 5560 yards of open woods, the ground level and sandy. From hence we went three miles to a heavy Fall in several precipices of full forty feet, the carrying place is

1 Still known as Manitou Falls, this feature is found on the Fond du Lac just below the Thompson Rapids.
2 On iv.57 (114–15).

one mile in length, the banks high and steep, and the path bad from much fallen wood, and rocky ground, at the end of which we had to descend a high steep bank of loose earth and gravel: one fourth of a mile lower was another fall, and carrying place of half a mile, we then proceeded eight miles to a long heavy rapid, six miles farther the Black River enters the east end of the Athabasca Lake, the end of our journey in Latitude 59°··16'·22" N Longitude 105°··26' West on the 2d of July: This great Lake had been surveyed by Mr Philip Turnor in 1791. He had marked and lopped a pine tree at which we passed the night.[1]

¶ From the Manito to the Athabasca Lake, by the course of the Black River, and it's Lakes is 162 Miles, of varied country, but the further westward the better, and the bold, high, sloping, woody hills of the Athabasca Lake had something soft and pleasing. This journey was attended with much danger, toil and suffering, for my guide knew nothing of the river, it's rapids and falls, haveing merely crossed it in places in hunting. We were always naked below the belt, on account of the rapids, from the rocks, shoals, and other obstructions we had to hand them, that is, we were in the water, with our hands grasping the canoe, and leading it down the rapids. The bed of the river is of rough or round loose stones, and gravel, our bare feet became so sore that we descended several rough rapids at great risque of our lives. On the 25th June we came to three tents of Che pa wy an Indians of five families; they were clean, comfortable, and every thing in good order, as usual, they received us in a hospitable manner, we put up for the night, and staid next day until past Noon to refresh ourselves and I obtained an observation for Latitude. They were hunting and living on the large species of Deer, the Mahthe Moose the meat was fat and good, they told me the habits of this species are utterly different from the common wandering Rein Deer, it's meat far superior, and in size nearly twice that of the common Deer, their eye sight much better, and the hunting of them almost as different as that of the Moose Deer, of which there are none in these parts.

[*Black River. wrecked on a Fall on the return. my knife. Gulls*]

[iv.98] On our return, about halfway up the black river, we came to one of the falls, with a strong rapid both above and below it, we had a carrying place

---

1 Turnor made his survey of Lake Athabasca on 15–31 August 1791. He reached the east end of the lake on 20 August and ascended the Fond du Lac River for about three miles. Stripped trees, or lopsticks, were common features on fur trade routes, serving either as landmarks or as monuments honouring travellers of high social rank. Podruchny, *Making the Voyageur World*, 134–5.

of 200 yards, we then attempted the strong current above the fall, they were to track the canoe up by a line, walking on shore, while I steered it, when they had proceeded about eighty yards, they came to a Birch Tree, growing at the edge of the water, and there stood and disputed between themselves on which side of the tree the tracking Line should pass. I called to them to go on, they could not hear me for the noise of the fall, I then waved my hand for them to proceed, meanwhile the current was drifting me out, and having only one hand to guide the canoe, the Indians standing still, the canoe took a sheer across the current, to prevent the canoe upsetting, I waved my hand to them to let go the line and leave me to my fate, which they obeyed.

¶ I sprung to the bow of the canoe took out my clasp knife, cut the line from the canoe and put the knife in my pocket, by this time I was on the head of the fall, all I could do was to place the canoe to go down bow foremost, in an instant the canoe was precipitated down the fall (twelve feet), and buried under the waves, I was struck out of the canoe, and when I arose among the waves, the canoe came on me and buried beneath it, to raise myself I struck my feet against the rough bottom and came up close to the canoe which I grasped, and being now on shoal water, I was able to conduct the canoe to the shore, my two companions ran down along the beach to my assistance; nothing remained in the canoe but an axe, a small tent of grey cotton, and my gun; also a pewter basin. When the canoe was hauled on shore I had to lay down on the rocks, wounded bruised, and exhausted by my exertions. The Indians went down along the shore, and in half an hours time returned with My box, lined with cork, containing my Sextant and a few instruments, and papers of the survey Maps &c and our three paddles, we had no time to lose, my all was my shirt and a thin linen vest, my companions were in the same condition, we divided the small tent into three pieces to wrap round ourselves, as a defence against the flies [iv.99] in the day, and something to keep us from the cold at night, for the nights are always cold.

¶ On rising from my rock bed, I perceived much blood at my left foot, on looking at it, I found the flesh of my foot, from the heel to near the toes torn away, this was done when I struck my feet against the rough bottom to rise above the waves of the fall of water. A bit of my share of the tent bound the wound, and thus bare footed I had to walk over the carrying places with their rude stones and banks. The Indians went to the woods and procured Gum of the Pines to repair the canoe, when they returned, the question was how to make a fire, we had neither steel, nor flint, I pointed to the gun from which we took the flint, I then produced my pocket knife with it's steel blade, if I had drawn a ghost out of my pocket it would not more have surprized them, they whispered to each other, how avaricious a white man must be, who rushing on death takes care of his little knife, this was often related to other

Indians who all made the same remark, I said to them if I had not saved my little knife how could we make a fire, you fools go to the Birch Trees and get some touchwood, which they soon brought, a fire was made, we repaired our canoe, and carried all above the Fall and the rapid, they carried the canoe, my share was the gun, axe, and pewter basin; and Sextant Box.

¶ Late in the evening we made a fire and warmed our selves. It was now our destitute condition stared us in the face, a long journey through a barren country, without provisions, or the means of obtaining any, almost naked, and suffering from the weather, all before us was very dark. But I had hopes that the Supreme Being through our great Redeemer to whom I made my short prayers morning and evening would find some way to preserve us; on the second day, in the afternoon we came on a small lake of the river, and in a grassy bay we saw two large Gulls hovering, this led us to think they were taking care of their young, we went, and found three young gulls, which we put in the canoe, it may here be remarked, the Gull cannot dive, he is too light; these gulls gave us but a little meal, they had not four ounces of meat on them, it appeared to sharpen hunger;

[*Eagles fat effects. very weak. Return to Fairford Ho*]

¶ The next day as we proceeded, I remembered an Eagles Nest on the banks of a small Lake before us, I enquired of my companions if the young eagles could fly, they said, "they are now large but cannot yet fly, why do you enquire," I said, "do you not remember the Eagle's Nest on a Lake before us, we shall be there by mid day, and [iv.100] get the young eagles for supper," accordingly we came on the Lake and went to the Eagles nest, it was about sixteen feet from the ground, in the spreading branches of a Birch tree, the old ones were absent, but Kozdaw was barely at the nest before they arrived, and Paddy and myself, with shouts and pelting them with stones, with difficulty prevented the Eagles from attacking Kozdaw, he soon threw the two young eagles down to us, they placed themselves on their backs, and with beak and claws fought for their lives, when apparently dead, Kozdaw incautiously laid hold of one of them, who immediately struck the claws of one foot deep into his arm above the wrist so firm were the claws, in his arm, I had to cut off the leg at the first joint above the claws, even then when we took out a claw, it closed in again, and we had to put bits of wood under each claw until we got the whole out.

¶ We continued our journey to the evening, when as usual we put ashore, and made a fire. On opening the young eagles, their insides appeared a mass of yellow fat, which we collected, and with the meat, divided into three equal portions; Paddy and myself eat only the inside fat, reserving the meat for next day, but we noticed Kozdaw, roasting the meat; and oiling himself with the fat; in the night we were both awakened by a violent dysentry from the effects of the eagles fat, Kozdaw now told us that such was always the effects of the inside fat of the fishing Eagle (the bald headed) and also of most birds of prey that live on fish, Paddy bitterly reproached him for allowing us to eat it, we had to march all day in this state, in the evening, I filled the pewter basin with Labrador Tea,[1] and by means of hot stones made a strong infusion, drank it as hot as I could, which very much relieved me. Paddy did the same, with like effect.

¶ We continued our voyage day after day, subsisting on berries, mostly the crow berry, which grows on the ground; and is not nutritious. The sixteenth of July; both Paddy and myself were now like skeletons, the Effects of hunger, and dysentry from cold nights and so weak, that we thought it useless to go any further but die where we were. Kozdaw now burst out into tears, upon which we told him that he was yet strong, as he had not suffered from disease. He replied, "if both of you die, I am sure to be killed, for every one will believe that I have killed you both, the white men will revenge your death on me, and the Indians will do the same for him;" I told him to get some thin white birch rind, and I would give him a writing, which he did, with charcoal I wrote a short account of [iv.101] our situation, which I gave him, upon which he said "now I am safe." However we got into the canoe, and proceeded slowly, we were very weak, when thank God, in the afternoon we came to two tents of Chepawyans, who pitied our wretched condition; they gave us broth, but would allow us no meat until the next day: I procured some provisions, a flint and nine rounds of ammunition, and a pair of shoes for each of us on credit, to be paid for when they came to trade, also an old kettle; we now proceeded on our journey with thanks to God, and cheerful hearts. We killed two Swans, and without any accident on the 21st July arrived at Fairford House from whence we commenced our Journey.

¶ From this time to the 26th August, our time was spent in fishing and hunting, and with all our exertions we could barely maintain ourselves. During this time seventeen Loons got entangled in the Nets, a few were drowned, but the greater part alive; the Loon is at all times a fierce bird, and all these with beak and claws fought to the last gasp. I have often taken one, out of the Net, alive and placed it in the yard, and set the dogs on it, but it fought so fiercely, screaming all the time, the dogs would not attack it. They

---

1 *Ledum palustre*. An evergreen shrub with a sweet, spicy aroma, it is the most popular Native tea.

live wholly on fish; which gives their flesh so strong a taste that few can eat
them, especially if they feed on trout, those that live on Carp, White Fish,
Pickerel and Pike have a better taste, but always bad; they lay only two, or
three eggs, which when boiled are of a yellowish color, veined with black,
and are not eatable, they are most expert fishers, though seldom fat; and
often gorge themselves, that they cannot fly; but they are expert divers, and
have the power of sinking their body so that only their head is above water,
and at will maintaining it; their dive is generally forty to fifty yards, and but
a little below the surface. On the land he is helpless, can neither walk, nor fly,
but quite at home in the water.

[go to *Deer's Lake. Rein Deer's Lake. the cold. the freezing of the Lake.
great cold. Aur Bor*]

¶ On the 26th August Mr Malcolm Ross, with four small Canoes loaded
with Goods arrived from York Factory, each carrying about six hundred
pounds weight. We left this house and proceeded up the Rein Deer's River to
the Lake, and to near the head of the Rivulet, where was a point of tolerable
Pines, near the middle of the Lake, on the west bank, which by numerous
observations I found to be in Latitude 57°··23' N Longitude 102°··58'··35"
West of Greenwich Variation 15 degrees east. We builded Log Huts to pass
the winter,[1] the chimneys were of mud and coarse grass, but some how did
not carry off the smoke, and the Huts were wretched with smoke, so that
however bad the weather, we were glad to leave the Huts. Our whole dependence for food was on our set nets, and what little Deer's meat the Che pa wy
ans might bring us. The fishery during the short open season was somewhat
successful for white fish, but [iv.102] they were not of the best quality; but
when the Lake became frozen over as usual the Fish shifted their ground, and
all we could procure was a bare subsistence.

---

1   The story of this time is more complicated than Thompson suggests. Having met at
    Fairford House on 26 August, Ross and Thompson decided to proceed along Thomp-
    son's route towards Lake Athabasca. On 5 September they passed the future site of
    Bedford House and continued north, but on 11 September they were prevented from
    proceeding because of low water levels. The men returned south and erected Bedford
    House. Glover suggests that Thompson, hoping to have solved the HBC's problem of
    access to the Athabasca region, had wilfully deluded himself about the practicability
    of the route he had explored during the summer. Glover, introduction, xxxii–xxxv.
    Whether this is the case or not, Thompson's actions did leave Ross and himself in the
    precarious position of wintering in an inhospitable country.

¶ Winter soon set in, the most severe I ever experienced; I had for some years been accustomed to keep Meteorological Journals, my Thermometers were from Dollond one of Spirits, and one Quicksilver; each divided to forty two degrees below Zero, being seventy four degrees below the freezing point; I had long suspected that in extreme cold, as the Spirits approached the bulb, it required two or three degrees of cold, to make the Thermometer descend one degree, I therefore wrote to Mr Dollond, to make me a large Thermometer divided to upwards of one hundred degrees below zero, he sent a Thermometer of red colored spirits of wine[2] divided to 110 degrees below zero, or 142 degrees below the freezing point, (zero is 32 degrees below the freezing point). The month of October was many degrees below the freezing point, and on the 17th day the snow remained on the ground. On November the 10th, the Thermometer was 10° below zero; on the 11th day 27° below Zero, the 12th day 12°, the 13th day 15°; on the 14th day 25° degrees, on the 15th day 28 degrees below zero, and this great deep Lake of 230 miles in length, by 80 to 100 miles in width was entirely frozen over. In the course of the winter, the ice of the Lake became five to six feet thick, on the following year, the first water seen along shore was on the 5th day of July, on the 7th day, a gale of wind shook the ice to pieces, and the whole disappeared, scarce a fragment on the shore after being frozen over for 7¾ months.

¶ I may here remark that my hard life, obliging me to cut holes in the ice for angling for fish, at all seasons while the Lake was frozen over, has led me to notice a curious operation of nature, the ice of these great Lakes, without any current in them, is very little thawed on the surface by the action of mild weather, the little that is softened in the day, the night makes solid ice, it is the water beneath the ice, that makes it decay; when the mild season comes, the ice is gradually worn away by the water; often in making holes for angling, while the surface appeared solid as winter, my ice chissel soon went through; on taking up a piece of about one square foot, the solid ice may be four inches thick. The rest was what we call candles, that is, icicles of fifteen to eighteen inches, or more in length, each distinct from the other, it is thus that nature prepares the ice to be broken up by a strong gale of wind; In the morning of the 7th July the Lake had the appearance of winter, in the afternoon as clear of ice, as if it had never been frozen over. A Gale of Wind had left nothing but icicles on the shore.

[iv.103] Although during November the cold was intense, yet not so much so as to prove the Thermometers, 1795[3] on the 15th December the large

---

2 Rectified ethyl alcohol.
3 1796 is intended.

Thermometer fell to 42 below zero, but the other showed only 40 degrees, and that of Quicksilver fell into the bulb, which was only four fifths full. On the morning of the 18th December, by the large Thermometer it was 56 degrees below zero, the small spirit Thermometer stood at 48° degrees, and it appeared no degree of cold could make it descend into the bulb: it may be remarked that for four days previous to this great degree of cold, the Thermometer was at 35 degrees, 37, 44 and 46 degrees below zero. On the 18th December at 8 AM the Thermometer was −56; at Noon −44; and at 9 PM −48 degrees below zero. It was a day of most intense cold, the ice on the Lake was splitting in all directions, the smoke from the chimneys fell in lumps to the ground. These intense colds gave me frequent opportunities of freezing quicksilver; I often attempted to beat it out into thin plates like lead, but however cautiously I proceeded, the edges were all fractured, and a few quick blows with the hammer, however light, would liquefy it.

Hitherto I have said little on the Aurora Borealis of the northern countries; at Hudson's Bay they are north westward and only occasionally brilliant. I have passed four winters between the Bay and the Rein Deer's Lake,[4] the more to the westward the higher and brighter is this electric fluid,[5] but always westward; but at this, the Rein Deer's Lake, as the winter came on, especially in the months of February and March, the whole heavens were in a bright glow. We seemed to be in the centre of it's action, from the horizon in every direction from north to south, from east to west, the Aurora was equally bright, sometimes, indeed often, with a tremulous motion in immense sheets, slightly tinged with the colors of the Rainbow, would roll, from horizon to horizon, sometimes there would be a stillness of two minutes; the Dogs howled with fear, and their brightness was often such, that with only their light I could see to shoot an owl at twenty yards; in the rapid motions of the Aurora, we were all perswaded we heard them, reason told me I did not, but it was cool reason against sense. My men were positive they did hear the rapid motions of the Aurora, this was the eye deceiving the ear; I had my men blindfolded by turns, and then enquired of them, if they heard the rapid motions of the Aurora. They soon became sensible they did not, and yet so [iv.104] powerful was the Illusion of the eye on the ear, that they still believed they heard the Aurora. What is the cause that this place seems to be in the centre of the most vivid brightness and extension of the Aurora; from whence this immense extent of electric fluid, how is it formed whither does it

---

4 The winters were five: 1792–93 (Seepaywisk House), 1794–95 (Reed Lake), 1795–96 (Duck Portage), 1804–05 (Musquawegan House), and 1805–06 (Reed Lake).
5 This term, common in the nineteenth century, expresses an understanding of electricity as a kind of substance lacking mass.

go. Questions without an answer. I am well acquainted with all the countries to the westward, the farther west the less is this Aurora, at the Mountains it is not seen.

[*Aurora Borealis*][1]

[iv.104a] On the Aurora Borealis of North America, particularly of the Rein Deer's Lake and Fort Enterprise,[2] the latter by Captain John Franklin, assisted by Dr Richardson an[d] Lieut[enant] Hood.[3] No 2 and 3 of the Appendix of the first Journey to the Polar Sea. Qu[a]rt[er]ly Review No 56.[4]

On several hundred Appearances of the Aurora Borealis. This meteor[5] it would seem, is stronger and most frequent about the Arctic Circle, or between that and the parallel of 64 degrees. The multitude of facts observed separately by these gentlemen, and sometimes in different places, lead to conclusions some what different from those usually entertained with regard to this meteorological phenomenon. They have determined for instance beyond all doubt, that the height of the Aurora instead of being, as supposed by Mr Dalton,[6] and others, beyond the region of the atmosphere, is, in fact, rarely above six, or seven miles. This was satisfactorily proved by angles taken in

---

1 Pages iv.104a–f were written between 24 and 27 January 1849 and inserted into this draft of the *Travels*. The cause of the aurora borealis was of abiding interest to Thompson and a persistent puzzle to his contemporaries (we now know that the phenomenon is produced by the collision of charged particles from the solar wind with atoms and molecules in Earth's upper atmosphere). Thompson's notebooks contain an account of the aurora of 17 November 1848 (AO. 28.18), a theory that large lakes cause the aurora (AO. 77.12), and a discussion of the regions in which the aurora appears (AO. F4a/3–4). In December 1848 two pieces by Thompson on the aurora borealis appeared in the Montreal *Gazette*, which closely parallel his writings here (see Volume III).

2 Located on Winter Lake, northeast from Great Slave Lake on the Yellowknife River, Fort Enterprise served as quarters for the first Franklin expedition during the winter of 1820–21.

3 For Robert Hood, see appendix 2.

4 [John Barrow], Review of *Narrative of a Journey to the Shores of the Polar Sea ...* The subsequent two paragraphs are taken almost verbatim from the review, 404–5.

5 In its original usage, "meteor" could refer to any atmospheric phenomenon, the aurora borealis being classified as a "luminous meteor." *Oxford English Dictionary*, 2nd edn., 9:684, s.v. "meteor."

6 John Dalton (1766–1844), a chemist and natural philosopher, pioneered the atomic theory of matter. His *Meteorological Observations and Essays* (1793) contains a section on the aurora borealis.

the same moment at two distant places, always exceedingly small at one, or both stations – by the extreme rapidity a beam darts from one side of the horizon to it's opposite side, which could not happen if 100 miles high, or upwards. – by it's frequently darting it's beams beneath the clouds, and at very short distances from the earth's surface and by it's being acted upon by the wind.

¶ Mr Hood was told by one of the North West Partners,[7] that he once saw the coruscations of the Aurora Borealis so vivid and low that the Canadians fell on their faces and began praying [iv.104b] and crying, fearing they should be killed – that he threw away his gun and knife that they might not attract the flashes, for they were within two feet of the earth, flitting along with incredible swiftness and moving parallel to the surface – he added they made a loud rustling noise like the waving of a flag in a strong breeze. This rustling noise which is universally asserted by the servants of the North West Company was not however heard by any of the Officers of the expedition, but, says Captain Franklin, it would be an absurd degre[e] of scepticism to doubt the fact any longer, for our observations have rather increased than diminished the probability of it.

Fort Enterprise was situated on a rising ground on the bank of a river and near a lake, in Latitude 64-28 N longitude 113-6 W. While Captain Franklin was on the expedition to the arctic ocean in 1819, 20 and 21, Captain Parry[8] with two Vessels was on the expedition of discovery of a North West passage to the Pacific Ocean, and wintered at Melville Island in latitude 75 degrees north, being 700 statute miles north of Fort Enterprise, yet in this high latitude the Aurora Borealis was faint and extremely weak compared with it's appearance at Fort Enterprise.

¶ It has hitherto been supposed, that the magnetic needle was not affected by the Aurora, but a vast number of experiments prove, that in certain positions of the beams and arches the needle was considerably drawn aside and mostly so when the flashes were between the clouds and [iv.104c] the earth, or when their actions were quick, their light vivid, and the atmosphere hazy.

---

7 Although he was not an NWC partner, this figure may be the clerk Willard Ferdinand Wentzel (c. 1777–1832); he was seconded to the Franklin expedition in 1820–21 and is mentioned as a source of information in the appendices on the aurora in Franklin, *Narrative of a Journey*. This anecdote is repeated on the paste-on to iv.104e, below (156).

8 For the Arctic explorer Sir William Edward Parry, see appendix 2. For the information recorded here, Thompson may have relied on an article about Parry's narrative in the *Quarterly Review* 25 (April 1821): 175–216; see 200–1.

At the same time it was observed that the needle was partially affected when the air was hazy, snow falling, or when the clouds in the day time assumed the form of the aurora. It was not however a trembling or vibration, but a deviation from it's natural direction, which if constant might have been nothing more than the diurnal variation with which the magnet is known to be affected. Though there is no reason to doubt this phenomenon being occasioned by a diluted, or attenuated electricity, yet a pith ball electrom- eter[9] elevated on a pole never indicated an atmosphere charged with it. This was precisely the same at Melville Island where, however the Aurora was extremely weak compared with it's appearance at Fort Enterprise.

Captain Parry in Latitude 75 N, lowest point of the Thermometer –55. Captain Franklin in 64··20 N lowest point –57 and myself in latitude 57··23 N lowest –56. Both these Captains were in the years 1819–20 and 21. The winter of 1796 a 7, was passed by me at Bedford House, on the banks of the Rein Deer's Lake in latitude 57··23 N Longitude 102·38·35 W, it's course and distance to Fort Enterprize N31W 666 statute miles. Intense cold soon came on, the month of October was below the freezing point in mean temperature, the 13th November at 7 AM –15. 14th – 7 AM –25 the 15th – 7 AM –28 and this great and deep Lake of about 250 miles in length by 100 miles in width was frozen over on the 15th November, and did not break up until the 5th day of July in the following year.

¶ At this place every clear night the Aurora was visible and sometimes [iv.104d] brilliant, In the early part of November, and as the cold increased, became more extensive until it covered the whole vault of heaven. During the month of October the Aurora occupied the northern part of the sky, but more to the east than to the west of north. The severe cold of November extended it to the south of east and west; and in December it was over the whole hemi- sphere, but fainter in the south than elsewhere. Around the horizon it formed arches, they were seldom above thirty degrees above the horizon, from the points of the arches beams issued sometimes to the opposite horizon, but frequently lost in the zenith, in an undulating motion, the apparent curves keeping their lines, they were compared to sheets of linnen a mile in length, by a great breadth, shaken by a gale of wind. They sometimes appeared to come near to us, and the men involuntarily bowed their heads though evi- dently a good distance above us. The colour of these sheets of Aurora was less red than the rest. Their motions were not always equally rapid, but when

---

9 A pith ball electrometer measures the quality and quantity of electricity in an elec- trified body, such as the atmosphere, by the repulsion of the pith ball from a fixed stem.

least so, from horizon to horizon never exceeded three seconds in time, in this case, they seemed to linger in the Zenith. When the weather was hazy, or lightly cloudy, the Aurora beneath the clouds were of a deeper red than usual. On a fine moon light night they were not visible, though present in the atmosphere; this we knew from their usual appearance until the rising of the Moon, and also when the Moon set in the night, the Aurora appeared in all it's varied forms. The beautiful halos, seen round the Moon, with tinges of the colours of the rainbow we attributed to the presence of the Aurora.

The ever changeing motions of the Aurora often engaged [iv.104e] our attention until the severe cold drove us into the house. While viewing the ever varying aurora, the men were all very sure they heard the sound of their motions but when blind folded they became sensible they did not hear them; and yet when the handkerchief was off their eyes, the illusion directly returned, and they were sure they did hear them. These men were all from the north of Scotland. It was the Eye deceiving the Ear. The Aurora has a line of locality, and on this line it is seen in the zenith and on both the east and west horizons. The Rein Deers Lake appears to be in this line, and from this place Bedford House the direction of the line is about N35W. Fort Enterprize was four degrees on the east side of this line and Captain Parry at Melville Island in latitude 75°N, so far to the eastward of this line that the Aurora was seen with a faint light. The account of the NW Partner.

[iv.104e paste-on] A Partner of the North West Company informed Lieutenant Hood, that he had seen the Aurora so splendid in light and near to the earth, that the flashes ran along the surface of the ground, he became alarmed and threw away his knife and gun; the Canadians became so terrified, thinking they would be killed that they fell on their knees, crying and praying for their lives.

The splendid Aurora which in Canada in the month of November 1848, in the observatory at Toronto drew the North 2½ degrees out of it's usual direction.[10]

It thus appears that a splendid Aurora embodied on the east horizon or on the west has an influence on the magnetic needle, and the reason why the Aurora did not affect the Compasses at Fort Enterprise and the Rein Deer's

10 The aurora borealis was observed on the night of 17 November 1848. One newspaper account described "flitting bars of molten silver ... flung round the sky in rapid coruscations." Montreal *Gazette*, 27 November 1848. In his notebooks Thompson writes that the aurora was also observed at Genesee, in upstate New York, and at Madrid, Spain, on the same evening. AO. 28.18.

Lake, was, that it extended over all the northern hemisphere from east to west and thus acted equally on every part of the compass.

Whatever the Aurora may be it does not appear to have any affinity to the electric fluid of Lightning.

¶ [iv.104e] This Meteor seems to affect the great bodies of fresh water, over which they are seen more or less splendid every winter and during the summer seasons every clear night they are visible in the north eastern part of the sky, even as low as the latitude of 52 degrees north, as in Lake Winepeg. In the north of Europe, and perhaps of Asia they appear only from time to time, but in the above regions the Aurora is constantly seen, as sure as the winter returns, so sure is their appearance with less or greater splendor as the winter may be.

On travelling to the westward of the line I have described, they become less and less visible, and when about 50 or 60 miles eastward of the Rocky Mountains are no longer visible and on the west side of the Mountains to the Pacific Ocean the Aurora is not seen. Is the constant appearance of the Aurora peculiar to North America and on this part of the continent limited to a certain space of length and breadth, and if so what can [iv.104f] be the cause of this limitation. The learned think themselves obliged to define the appearances of nature, and the Officers on the polar expedition, defined the Aurora Borealis to be diluted, or attenuated electricity perhaps the best that could be given: yet in its greatest splendor, and vivid motions, none of the experiments showed electricity, or that it partook of the properties of electric fluid as seen in Lightning. In the heats of summer, in the evenings and early parts of the nights, flashes of lightning are very frequent, but they instantly disappear, and show nothing of the continuance of the Aurora, which appears to have a constant duration, although the light of the Sun in the day, and at times the Moon in the night prevents its being visible.

In northern Europe the appearance of the Aurora and it's varying, changes of place and position gave to the gloomy minds of the people the evolutions of armies in battle, and they predicted tumults and wars, famines and pestilence. The Indians of North America have a very different opinion and call them the "Dead" by the name of "Jee pe ak" (the souls of the dead) and when the Aurora is bright in vivid graceful motion, they exclaim, "See how happy our fathers are tonight, they are dancing to the enlivening songs of the other world."

1st The Aurora Borealis in North America has a locality where it is constantly seen in clear weather at night.

2nd This locality appears to be a line of about N35W from Bedford House, West bank of the Rein Deer's Lake.

3rd It's splendid Appearance passes over the great northern Lakes Manito, Athabasca, Slave and Great Bear.

4th This line of N35W is over a region of intense cold in winter. From Albany to Churchill, the west side of Hudson's Bay the course N47W 672SM and extended northward may be taken as the eastern limit of the Aurora in it's splendor. Eastward of this line it is faint.

5th That in clear nights of intense cold the Aurora approaches near to the surface of the Earth, the flashes low, and frequent, so as to terrify men.

6th That neither the pith ball electrometer, nor any other experiments which acts on the electric fluid of lightning, has ever, in the least, acted on the Aurora.

7th That the electric fluid is no sooner seen, than it disappears as ligh[t]ning, and it's flashes in summer evenings.

8th That the Aurora Borealis is constantly visible over a certain region, except in cloudy weather, or during the light of the Sun or Moon.

9thly That from all the above the Aurora Borealis is a fluid unknown to us, and for which we have no name but that of Aurora Borealis.

[*Trout angling*]

[iv.104] I have said our livelihood depended on fishing and hunting. Part of the fishery was angling for large trout, they are not to be taken but in deep water, from 20 to 40 fathoms, or more, for this fish, hooks are not used; but the Che pa wy an method adopted; the first thing done is making, one, or more holes in the ice with the ice chissel, which is a small bar of iron of two pounds weight, at one end flat, at the other end a chissel of an inch in width, the greater part of this is inserted in a groove of a strong pole of birch of full Six feet in length, the chissel end projecting about five inches; with this, a hole is quickly made in the ice of any dimensions, with out the person in the least wetting himself, the axe is never used. A sounding line is now used to ascertain the depth of water, which must not be less than twenty fathoms, as large trout are found only in deep water, the set line is now carefully measured, with a coil of five fathoms neatly made up with a slip knot is attached to. The bait, is the half of a white fish, the head part only, as the trout always takes the white fish head foremost, a small round stick of birch, well dried and hardened by the fire, but not burnt, is slightly attached to the under part of the bait, about six inches in length, the line is fixed about one third below the head of the bait, this is placed as near as possible about six feet above the bottom. The trout takes the bait, the slip knot of five fathoms of line gives way, which enables him to swallow the bait, at the end of which he is brought up with a jerk, which causes the piece of wood, to become vertical in his mouth, his jaws are extended, and we often find him drowned, a strange death for a fish.

¶ In angling for trout, every thing is the same, the fish caught alive are better than those drowned, whether by a set line, or in a net; the weight of the trout was from twenty five to forty five pounds. I have heard of trout fifty five pounds; they are a very rich fish, make a nutritious broth, and pound for pound are equal to good beef. One day as usual I had pierced the ice with new holes, or cleaned out the old holes with an ice racket,[1] an old Che pa wy an Indian came to me, I told him I had five holes in the ice, and for these [iv.105] two days had caught nothing, he shook his head, left me, and went about one hundred yards westward of me, we were about five miles from land, he then looked at all the land with in sight, shifted his place, until all his marks coincided he then pierced a hole thro' the ice, put down his angling tackle, and in about an hours time brought up a fine trout of full thirty pounds, by one PM he caught another, rather larger, soon after which he gave over, put up his tackle and came to me, I had caught nothing; he asked to see my bait, which I showed to him, it was like his, he noticed that it was not greased, he showed his bait, which was well greased and taking out of a little bag, a piece of grease with which he greased the bait twice a day; he told me I must do the same, he remarked to me that I came too soon, and staid too late; that the trout took bait only from a while after sun rise to near sun set, but that about noon was the best time; it has always appeared strange to me that a Trout in forty fathoms water, with a covering of full five feet thickness of ice, on a dark cloudy day should know when the sun rises and sets, but so it is. I followed the Che pa wy an's advice, and was more successful.

[*Rein Deer, hot blood &c. it's Paunch; Snow & Ice insects*]

In hunting, we had but little success, and killed only a few Rein Deer, on fine days small herds would go out on the Lake some four miles from land, and lie down for a few hours on the ice as if to cool themselves; one fine day Mr Ross and myself killed a Doe, our hands were freezing, we opened her, and put our hands in the blood to warm them, but the heat of the blood was like scalding water which we could not bear, both of us were accustomed to hunting and knew the heat of the blood of many animals, we were surprised,

---

1 More commonly known as an ice scoop. The form of this instrument resembles that of a snowshoe, French *raquette*.

we examin[e]d the stomach, it was full of a white moss.[1] I tasted it, and swallowed a little, it was warm in my stomach. I then traced the Deer to where they had been feeding, it was on a white crisp moss in a circular form, of about ten inches diameter each division distinct, yet close together. I took a small piece about the size of a nutmeg, chewed it, it had a mild taste, I swallowed it, and it became like a coal of fire in my stomach, I took care never to repeat the experiment:

¶ [iv.105 paste-on] It is by food of this warm nature, that the Animals and Birds of the cold regions are not only enabled to bear the intense cold, but find it warm. What is the heat imparted to the blood, by each kind of food; from the water melon, and wild rice, to the Rein Deer Moss.

¶ [iv.105] This solved to me the excessive heat of the blood of the Rein Deer, on this Lake only I have found this Moss. I have tasted all the mosses of Lake Superior, and many other [iv.106] Lakes, but have found nothing of the same, is this moss then peculiar to the northern barren countries of rock and moss that the food of the Rein Deer, and Musk Oxen shall make the temperature of fifty to seventy degrees below the freezing point as the month of April is to our cattle; it appears so. Mr Ross, and myself several times, when we went a hunting, took a Thermometer with us, to ascertain the heat of the blood of the Rein Deer, but it so happened, when we had a Thermometer with us we killed no Deer, and therefore could not know the heat of the blood. The Stomach, or Paunch, of the Rein Deer is taken out of the animal, the orifice tied up, and then for three days hung in the smoke, but not near the fire, it is now sour, bits of meat and fat are mixed with the contents, it is then boiled, and all those who have eaten of it, say it is an agreeable, hearty food.

¶ In the spring of the year, as the snow begins occasionally to thaw, myriads of small black insect[s][2] make their appearance, so numerous, that the surface of the snow is black with them, they are about one twentieth of an inch in length of a compact make, they cover the sides of Lakes, and Rivers; snow shoe paths, and other places; they come with the first thawing of the snow, and disappear with the snow. The question is, from whence are these myriads of insects which are seen on the snow, they cannot come from the ground, penetrate three feet of hard snow, they are never found below the surface of the snow. How do they live, upon what do they live. Upon examining the edges of the ice, as it began to thaw I saw a great number of insects

1 Reindeer moss (*Cladina rangiferina*), the bitter taste of which is due to the presence of fumarprotocetraric acid.
2 Snow fleas (*Achorutes*).

some thing like those in the snow, they were rather larger, the head had two feelers, the body increased in size to the end, where it was round. They had two legs, some were dead, others dormant, those that were fully alive and active, upon my touching them with my finger, made a leap of about one inch into an almost invisible crevice of the ice, and there remained. The native name is Oo pin ar nar tar we week jumping insects. From whence come so suddenly these myriads of insects [iv.107] on the surface of the snow, and edges of the ice; and in such myriads; and only on the snow and ice, and each has a distinct insect.

[*Chepawyan Women, their hardships. Wrestling for a Woman*]

¶ My residence on the Rein Deer's Lake which has become the country of the Che pa wy ans; gave me an insight into the morals and manners of these people which I had not before. I have already noticed the treatment of the Women and every thing that passed this Winter confirmed it; during this season many of them came in to trade; the bank of the Lake to the House, was a low regular slope; seeing a Woman carrying a heavy child, and hauling a long, loaded sled; as she came to the bank, I desired one of the Men, who was remarkable for his great strength, to assist her, she gave the trace to him; thinking a Woman could not haul any weight worth notice, he carelessly put two fingers to the trace of the Sled, but could not move it; he had at length to employ all his strength to start the Sled, and haul it to the House; the Sled and load weighed about one hundred and sixty pounds; among them was a little girl of about six years of age. She had her sled and hauled on it, a brass Kettle that held four gallons; The Boys had a light Sled, or carried a few pounds weight, the Men had little else than their Guns; such is the order when removing from place to place during the winter; Those who make use of Canoes during the summer, and they are now almost in general use, place the women in far more easy circumstances, and the Men take their share of paddling the canoes; loading and unloading them; but in fact the Women are considered as the drudges of the Men.

[iv.108] The Women, until they have children, appear to be the property of the strongest Man, that has no woman; One day in the latter end of February, a Chepawyan called the Crane and his Wife came to the House, he was well named, tall, thin, and active, he at times hunted for us. His Wife was a good looking young Woman, they appeared to love each other, but had no children. Six, or seven of us were sitting in the guard room talking of the weather, the Crane was smoking his pipe, and his Wife sitting beside him. When suddenly a Chepawyan entered, equally tall, but powerfully made, he went directly to the Crane and told him, "I am come for your woman, and I must have her, my woman is dead, and I must have this woman to do my work and carry my things;" and suiting the deed to the word, he twisted his hand in the hair of her head to drag her away; on this, the Crane started up and seized him by the waist, he let go the Woman, and in like manner seized the Crane; and a wrestling match took place, which was well maintained by the Crane for some time; but his adversary was too powerful, and at length his strength failed, and he was thrown on the floor, his opponent placing his knee on his breast, with both hands seized his head and twisted his neck so much, that his face was almost on his back, and we expected to see it break; in an instant we made him let go, kicked him out of the house, with an assurance, that if he came back to do the same, we would send a ball through him; he seemed to think he had done [no] wrong; upon which we told him that he was welcome at any time to come and smoke, or trade, but not to quarrel. After standing a few minutes, he called to the Crane; "You are now under the protection of the White Men, in the summer I shall see you, on our lands and then I shall twist your neck, and take your woman from you;" he went away and we saw [iv.109] no more of him;

[*The Chepawyan that shot another, his story. Ground red with blood*]

¶ Their lands, which they claim as their own country; and to which no other people have a right, are those eastward of the Rein Deer's and Manito Lakes to Churchill Factory and northward along the interior of the sea coast, all other lands they hunt on belonged to the Nahathaways who have retired to the southwestward.

¶ Early in the month of December, past midnight, a Che pawyan of middle stature of about twenty five years of age, came to the house alone, he brought a bundle of Beaver and Marten skins; he looked about with suspicion; and enquired if any of the Natives were near the house, we told him, there had been none for several days; he then traded his furrs for necessaries, except a few Martens for Beads and Rings. He told me he had a Wife and two children; and enquired if I knew a certain Indian, I said I did; "Then when you see him, tell him we are all well; he is my uncle, and the only man that is kind to me." After smoking, I offered him a Bison Robe to sleep on; but he told me he must set off directly; which he did, having staid only about an hour. There was something strange about him, which excited my curiosity.

¶ About a month afterwards his Uncle came to the House; I told him I had seen his Nephew, and that he came alone in the night to trade, and desired me to say they were all well; and then enquired the reason of his hasty leaving the house after trading; he smoked for some time; and then said "My Nephew is a man, but he has not been wise he is not strong, about five winters ago, a young woman was given to him; and after a few moons, we camped with some other tents of Chepawyans where [iv.110] there was a tall young strong man who had no woman. He went to my nephew and demanded him to give up his wife, which he refused to do, upon which the other took hold of him, threw him on the ground, and began twisting his neck, we told him to let him alone and take the woman; She was unwilling to go with him; upon which he laid hold of her hair to drag her away; my nephew sprung up, took his gun and shot him dead, and made the ground red with man's blood, which he ought not to have done; We all pitched away and left the place, since which he lives alone; and is afraid to meet any tents, for they take every thing from them, and leave them nothing but the clothes they have on; he has been twice stripped of all he had, and therefore keeps away by himself." I told them, that if I had a Wife,[1] and any one came to take her away, I would surely shoot him; "Ah that is the way you white Men, and our Neighbours the Na hath a ways always talk and do, a Woman cannot be touched but you get hold of guns and long knives; What is a woman good for, she cannot hunt, she is only fit to work and carry our things, and on no account whatever ought the ground to be made red with man's blood." "Then the strong Men take Women when they want them"; "Certainly the strong Men have a right to the Women. And if the Woman has children. That is as the strong man pleases." So far as Women are concerned, they are a sett of Brutes.

¶ The expression "The ground red with Man's blood" is used by all the Natives of North America as very hateful to see, but by the southern Indians accustomed to War, it is lim[i]ted to that of their relations and tribe; yet it has a meaning I never could comprehend in the same sense as the Natives [iv.111] use it, for they seem to attach a mysterious meaning to the expression. In the latter end of March this forlorn Native again came to the House alone, he had made a good hunt of furrs, and traded them in clothing for himself and family, ammunition and tobacco, not forgetting beads and other articles for his wife. I enquired of him if what his Uncle told me was true, he said it was; that he had been twice pillaged, and that the Women were worse than the Men; "you see I have again come to you in the night and before I came into the house I made sure there were no Chepawyans, for if I had met any they would have taken the whole of my hunt from me, and left me with nothing."

1 Thompson married Charlotte Small on 10 June 1799, about two and a half years after this incident.

I enquired why he did not tent with the Nahathaways who think much of their women, and love brave men. He was at a loss what to say, or do.

[*The forlorn Chepawyan Woman on the other World*]

With regard to the immortality of the soul; and the nature of the other world; the best evidence of their belief I learned from a woman; her husband had traded with me two winters, they had a fine boy of about six years of age, their only child; he became ill and died; and according to their custom she had to mourn for him twelve moons; crying in a low voice "She azza, She azza." (my little son) never ceasing while awake, and often bursting into tears.

About three months after I saw her again, the same cry, the same sorrowful woman, her husband was kind to her; About six months after this I saw her again, she no longer cried "She azza," and was no longer a sorrowing woman; I enquired of her the cause of this change, she replied, "When my little son went to the other world there was none to receive him, even his Grandfather is yet alive; he was friendless, he wandered alone in the pitching track of the tents," (here she shed tears) "there was none to take care of him no one to give [iv.112] him a bit of meat. More than two Moons ago his father died, I sorrowed for him and still sadly regret him, but he is gone to my son, his father will take great care of him he will no longer wander alone, his father will be always with him, and when I die I shall go to them."

Such was the belief that comforted this poor childless Widow, and in which I encouraged her, and telling her that to be happy in the other world, and go to our relations, we must lead good lives here.

[*Angling. Baits W[hite] Fish &c. Claim of country. Archery*]

These people though subject to great vicissitudes yet suffer less from extreme hunger than the Nahathaways the latter pride themselves with living by hunting animals, look on fish as an inferior food, and the catching of them beneath a Hunter. The former pride themselves on being expert anglers, and have made it their study; the great Lakes of their country yield the finest fish, and when the Deer fail they readily take to angling, altho' it affords them no clothing. They are in possession of many secrets of making baits for taking the different kinds of fish; which they would not impart to me, but being in their company some thing was seen, the bait for the Trout the largest fish of the Lakes, was the head half of a White Fish, well rubbed with Eagles fat, for want of it, other raw fat, but not grease that had been melted at the fire: The

Pike and Pickerel take almost any thing, even a red rag; but the pride of these people is to angle the White Fish an art known to only a few of the Men; they would not inform me of it's composition, the few baits I examined appeared to be all the same; and the castorum of the Beaver worked into a thick paste was the principal item; around were the fine red feathers of the Woodpecker, a grain of Eagles fat was on the top of the bait, and the hook was well [iv.113] hid in it; the bait had a neat appearance. The art of angling White Fish is to them of importance, a young man offered a gun for the secret and was refused.

¶ These people, the "Dinnae" their native name, though better known to us by the name of Chepawyans; extend in different tribes, speaking dialects of the same language, to near the Pacific Ocean, by the way of Fraser's River; I have already mentioned, they claim as their own rightful country, from Churchill Factory, and northward to the arctic sea, their origin by this account of themselves must have been from Greenland by what means they came to the north eastern part of this conti[nent] is better a subject of discussion in the Appendix than here; If we knew the state of Archery in Greenland, or Iceland it might lead us to something certain on these people; All the Natives of North America, except the "Dinnae" in drawing the Arrow, hold the Bow in a vertical, or upright position which gives to the arms their full action and force; but the Dinnae, or Chepawyans, hold the Bow in a contrary, or horizontal position, the Arrow is held on the string, by two fingers below and the thumb above and with the Bow string thus drawn to the breast which does not allow to the Bow two thirds of it's force, practice has made them good marksmen, but the arrows are feeble in effect. Do any of the [iv.114] people of Greenland, Iceland, or the northern nations of Europe, or Siberia, handle the Bow in this manner if so, some inference may be drawn from it.[1] Of the state of the Thermometer, and other peculiarities of the climate they will be found in the Appendix.[2]

1 In his essay "The Natives of North America" (see Volume II), Thompson attempts to answer the question "From what other part of our world has this continent been peopled?" Marshalling evidence such as the manner of holding the bow, language families, and population movements within the historical period, he concludes that North American Natives are of European origin. He mentions this essay again on iv.256 (282–3).

2 If this meteorological appendix was prepared, it has not survived.

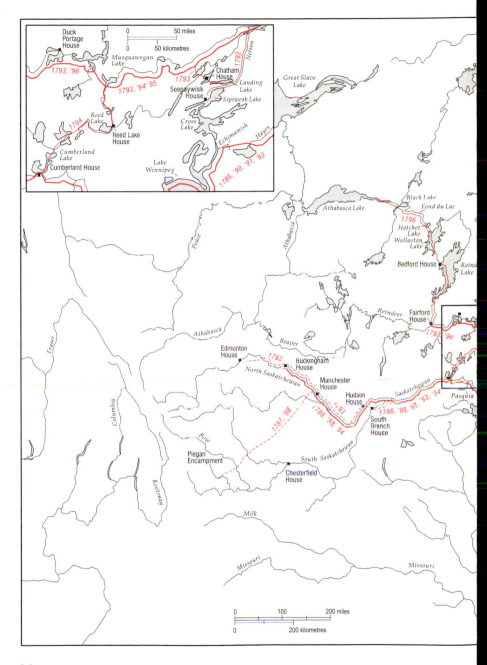

Map 3

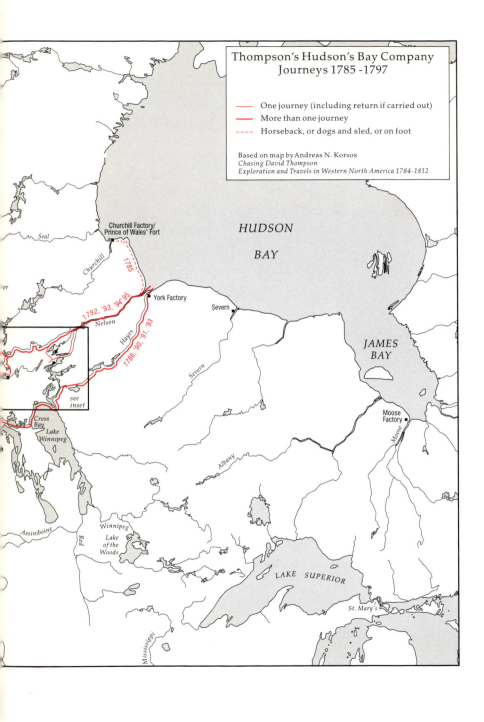

Thompson's Hudson's Bay Company
Journeys 1785 -1797

——— One journey (including return if carried out)
——— More than one journey
- - - - Horseback, or dogs and sled, or on foot

Based on map by Andreas N. Korsos
Chasing David Thompson
Exploration and Travels in Western North America 1784-1812

HUDSON

BAY

JAMES
BAY

Churchill Factory/
Prince of Wales' Fort

Seal

Churchill

1785

York Factory

Severn

1792, '93, '94 '95

Nelson

Hayes

1786, '90, '91, '93

Severn

Moose
Factory

Moose

see
inset

Cross
Bay

Lake
Winnipeg

Albany

Assiniboine

Winnipeg

Red

Lake
of the
Woods

LAKE   SUPERIOR

Mississippi

St. Mary's

FIRST YEAR WITH THE NORTH WEST COMPANY: 1797–1798

Page 170.

in. and get a portion of maize: which keeps them in good condition. but in proportion to the population the Horses are few. the chief with about ten Lodges had only three.

They do not require so many horses as the Indians of the Plains who frequently move from place to place. yet even for the sole purpose of hunting their Horses are too few. we paid a visit to Wanoch, a french canadian. who had resided many years with these people. he was a handsome man, with a native woman, fair and graceful for his wife. they had no children. he was in every respect as a native. He was an intelligent man, but completely a Frenchman. brave, gay and boastful. with his gun in one hand and his spade in the other, he stood venturous recounter to the Indians about us all his warlike actions and the battles in which he had borne a part. to all of which, as a matter of course, they assented. From my knowledge of the Indian character it appeared to me he could not live long, for they utterly dislike a boastful man. I learned that a few years after. coming from a Skirmish. he praised his own courage and conduct and spoke with some contempt of the courage of those with him, which they did not in the least deserve. and for which he was shot. As Wanoch was as a native with them I enquired if they had any traditions of ancient times. he said he knew of none beyond the days of their great. great Grand fathers. who formerly possessed all the Streams of the Red River. and head of the Mississippi. where the Wild Rice and the Deer were plenty. but then the Bison and the Horse were not known to them. on all these Streams they had Villages and cultivated the ground as now. they lived many years this way how many they do not know. at length the Indians of the Woods armed with guns which killed and frightened them. and iron weapons. frequently attacked them. and against these they had no defence. but obliged to quit their

The countries I had explored was under the sanction of Mr Joseph Colen, the Resident at York Factory the most enlightened Gentleman who had filled that situation; by a Letter from him; I was informed, that however extensive the countries yet unknown yet he could not sanction any further surveys.[1] My time was up, and I determined to seek that employment from the Company Merchants of Canada, carrying on the Furr Trade, under the name of the North West Company.[2] With two Natives I proceeded to their nearest trading House, under the charge of Mr Alexander Fraser;[3] and by the usual route of the Canoes arrived at the Great Carrying Place on the north shore of Lake Superior, then the depot of the merchandise from Montreal; and of the Furrs from the interior countries.[4] The Agents who acted for the Company

1 Such a letter has not been located.

2 On 21 May 1797, Malchom Ross wrote the following entry in the Bedford House journal: "21st Sunday ... this morning Mr David Thompson aquainted Me, with his time being out, with your Honours, and thought himself a free born Subject, and at liberty to choose any service, he thought to be moust to his advantage and is to Quit your honours Service and Enter the Canadian Co[m]pany's Employ." Bedford House, Post Journal, 1796–1797, B.14/a/1: 32v, HBCA. Thompson's date of indenture to the HBC was 20 May 1784. Upon the expiration of this seven-year apprenticeship in May 1791, the governor and council of the HBC offered him a three-year contract at £15 per year, which in May 1794 was renewed for another three years at £60 per year. Thompson evidently considered that as of 21 May 1797 he was free to offer his services to any employer. For a discussion of Thompson's departure from the HBC to the NWC, see "Historical Introduction" (xxxi–xxxii).

3 On 23 May 1797 Thompson wrote in his journal: "This day left the Service of the Hudsons Bay Co and entered that of the Company of Merchants from Canada May God Almighty prosper me." AO. 5.164. For NWC trader Alexander Fraser, see appendix 2. In the spring of 1797 Fraser had established his post at the head of the Reindeer River and on 6 April had visited Ross and Thompson at Bedford House. B.14/a/1: 29r, HBCA.

4 Also known as Grand Portage, this was the site of the NWC's annual rendezvous. Thompson remained here from 22 July to 9 August 1797. Over the following few years, the NWC abandoned both the post and the portage with which it was associated, as the terms of the 1783 Treaty of Paris had placed them in the territory of the United States, and Jay's Treaty of 1794 had mandated the British evacuation of posts on American soil by 1 July 1796. In its stead, the NWC constructed Fort William at the mouth of the Kaministiquia River. Thompson again traversed the region of Grand Portage in 1822–25 during his work for the International Boundary Commission.

and were also Partners of the firm, were the Honorable William McGillivray[5] and Sir Alexander McKenzie,[6] gentlemen of enlarged views; the latter had crossed the Rocky Mountains by the Peace River and was far advanced by Frasers River towards the Pacific Ocean, when want of Provisions and the hostility of the Natives obliged him to return. From the Great Slave he had explored the great River which flowed from it into the Arctic Sea, and which is justly named McKenzies River.[7]

My arrival enabled these Gentlemen and the other Partners who were present to learn the true [iv.115] positions of their Trading Houses in respect to each other; and how situated with regard to the parallel of the forty ninth degree of Latitude North, as since the year 1792 this parallel of Latitude from the north west corner of the Lake of the Woods to the east foot of the Rocky Mountains, had become the boundary Line between the British Dominions and the Territories of the United States: instead of a line due west from the north west corner of the Lake of the Woods to the head of the Mississippe, as designated by the Treaty of 1783.[8] The scource, or head of the Mississippe was then unknown except to the Natives and a very few Furrs Traders; and by them, from it's very sinuous course, supposed to be farther north, than the northern banks of the Lake of the Woods. And wherever I could mark

5 For NWC director William McGillivray, see appendix 2.
6 For explorer Alexander Mackenzie, see appendix 2.
7 The Mackenzie River already bore a Dene name, which it retains today: *Dehcho*, meaning "Great River."
8 Although not adopted, the 49th parallel had been proposed as a boundary line between British and French possessions in North America during the negotiations that led to the signing of the Treaty of Utrecht in 1713, ending the War of the Spanish Succession. Since the 49th parallel had not been formally designated as the boundary in 1792, as Thompson asserts here, it is implausible that in 1797 he was asked to determine the position of NWC posts in relation to it. According to article 2 of the Treaty of Paris, 1783, the boundary was to run "through Lake Superior northward of the Isles Royal and Phelipeaux to the Long Lake; thence through the middle of said Long Lake and the water communication between it and the Lake of the Woods, to the said Lake of the Woods; thence through the said lake to the most northwestern-most point thereof, and from thence on a due west course to the river Mississippi." The NWC (and HBC) were obliged to abandon several posts, as article 2 of Jay's Treaty of 1794 provided that "His Majesty will withdraw all his troops and garrisons from all posts and places within the boundary lines assigned by the treaty of peace to the United States." It was not until the Convention of 1818 was signed that the 49th parallel became the boundary between Lake of the Woods and the Rocky Mountains.

the line of the 49th parallel of Latitude to do so, especially on the Red River. Also, if possible to extend my Surveys to the Missisourie River; visit the Villages of the ancient agricultural Natives who dwelt there: enquire for fossil bones of large animals; and any monuments if any, that might throw light on the ancient state of the unknown countries I had to travel over and examine. The Agents and Partners all agreed to give orders to all their Trading Posts, to send Men with me, and every necessary I required to be at my order.[9]

[*The furr Traders. Mr Peter Pond's Map. The HBCo. mean behaviour. Mr Philip Turnor. Mr Pond's boundary line. The Boundary Line*]

How very different the liberal and public spirit of this North West Company of Merchants of Canada; from the mean selfish policy of the Hudson's Bay Company styled Honorable; and whom, at little expence, might have had the northern part of this Continent surveyed to the Pacific Ocean, and greatly extended their Trading Posts; whatever they have done, the British Government [iv.116] has obliged them to do. A short account of the transactions of this Company will prove to the public the truth of what I assert, and will throw some light on the discoveries that from time to time have been made. The furr trade was then open to every Person in Canada who could obtain credit for a canoe load of coarse Merchandise; and several different Persons engaged in this trade, besides those Merchants from Scotland, who formed the North West Company;[1] Among the Clerks of this last Company was a Mr Peter Pond,[2] a native of the city of Boston, United States. He was a person of industrious habits, a good common education, but of a violent

9 The components of Thompson's mission from the NWC are covered in the narrative that follows: (i) delineating the 49th parallel on the Red River (iv.186, 226); (ii) extending surveys to the Missouri River and visiting the Mandan-Hidatsa villages (iv.148–79, 198–221); (iii) inquiring for fossil bones of large animals and any ancient monuments (iv.131–3, 186–7). David Malaher argues that the NWC's recruitment of Thompson was motivated primarily by their desire for an accurate survey of the region between Lake of the Woods and Lake Superior, in the face of the looming settlement of sovereignty issues between Great Britain, the United States, and Spain, which held nominal title to the Missouri. David Malaher, "David Thompson's Surveys of the Missouri/Mississippi Territory in 1797–98," paper presented at the 9th North American Fur Trade Conference and Rupert's Land Colloquium, 25 May 2006.

1 For the formation of the NWC, see "Historical Introduction" (xxvi).

2 For pioneering fur trader Peter Pond, see appendix 2. For the murders in which he was implicated, see note below.

temper and unprincipled character; his place was at Fort Chepawyan[3] on the north side of the Athabasca Lake, where he wintered three years.

At Lake Superior he procured a Compass, took the courses by the compass through the whole route to his wintering place; and for the distances adopted those of the canadian canoe men in Leagues, and parts of the same, and sketching off the Lake shores the best he could. In the winters, taking the Depot of Lake Superior as his point of departure, the Latitude and Longitude was known as determined by the French Engineers. He constructed a Map of the route followed by the Canoes. It's features were tolerably correct; but by taking the League of the Canoe Men for three geographical miles (I found they averaged only two miles) he increased his Longitude so much as to place the Athabasca Lake, at it's west end near the Pacific Ocean. A copy of this Map was given to the Agents of the North West Company; whom, in London laid it befor[e] Sir Hugh Dalrymple,[4] then in office, whose character stood high as a gentleman of science, and great geographical knowledge; and who comparing the Longitude of the west end of the Athabasca Lake by Mr Pond's map with the Charts of Captain Cook found the distance to [iv.117] be only one hundred miles; or less, directly conceived that it offered a short route to the coasts of Asia for dispatches and other purposes. To verify this Map, the Colonial Secretary applied to the Hudson's Bay Company to send out a Person duly qualified to ascertain the Latitude and Longitude of the west end of the Athabasca Lake with this request the Company were obliged to appear to comply.[5]

For this purpose in 1785 they sent out a Mr George Charles aged fifteen years, whom they had made their Apprentice for seven years; when he landed at Churchill Factory I saw him, and enquired how he came to undertake this business, he told me he had been about one year in the mathematical school, had three times with a quadrant brought down the Sun to a chalk line on the

3 Pond's post, founded in 1778, was located on the Athabasca River about 35 miles (56 kilometres) south of Lake Athabasca. It was replaced in the fall of 1788 when the NWC's Roderick Mackenzie established Fort Chipewyan on the south shore of Lake Athabasca; this post was moved to the northwest shore of the lake in 1796 or 1797. Fort Chipewyan served as the headquarters of the NWC's lucrative Athabasca Department and was opposed by an XY Company post (1799–1804) and by the HBC's Nottingham House (1802–06) and Ford Wedderburn (1815–21). After the union of the fur companies, operations were centralized at the NWC post.

4 Alexander Dalrymple is intended. See note to iii.9b (28).

5 The words "appear to" were inserted during revision of this page. Thompson's account has been neither confirmed nor disproved by other sources.

wall, was declared fully competent, and sent out to go on discovery of course nothing could be done.[6] Had this honorable Company intended the position of the west end of the Lake should be known, there were then many Naval Officers on half pay; who would gladly have undertaken the expedition to the Athabasca Lake and settled it's position. What the views of the Company could be for preventing the knowledge required, though often a subject of conversation, none could divine, their Charter gave them the Country, and the furr traders of Canada had had Houses there for several years.

Whatever the views of the Company may have been, this trick of sending out a Lad, prevented the Colonial Office from obtaining the desired information for five years. The pressing demands of this Office then obliged the Hudson's Bay Company to engage a Gentleman fully competent, a Mr Philip Turnor; one of the compilers of the Nautical Almanac [iv.118] who, in the year 1790 proceeded to Fort Chepawyan at the west end of the Athabasca Lake, and head of the great Slave River, where he wintered, and by Observations found the place to be in Latitude [space] Longitude [space] and from this place, the following year returned to England; After this great exertion of the Hudson's Bay Company, they again became dormant to the time of Captain Franklin's survey of the Arctic Coast, from the Copper Mine River.

¶Mr Peter Pond, I have mentioned as an unprincipled man of a violent charac[ter] he became implicated in the death of a Mr Ross, a furr trader, and afterwards a principal in the murder off a Mr Wadden, another furr trader. For this latter crime he was brought from the Athabasca Lake to Canada, and sent to Quebec to be tried for the murder he had committed; but the Law authorities did not consider the jurisdiction of the Court of Quebec to extend into the territories of the Hudsons Bay Company, and therefore they could not take cognizance of the crime, and he was set at liberty; he went to his native city Boston this was in 1782.[7]

¶ The following year peace was made; the Commissioners on the part of Great Britain were two honest well meaning gentlemen, but who knew noth-

---

6 For HBC employee George Charles, see appendix 2.

7 Thompson's chronology of these events is erroneous. Jean-Étienne Waddens (1738–82), an independent Swiss trader, was with Peter Pond at Lac La Ronge, where he was fatally shot in March 1782. Waddens's widow petitioned for Pond's arrest, but the case does not appear to have gone to trial. J.I. Cooper, "Jean-Étienne Waddens," DCB, 4:757. John Ross, of the firm of Gregory, McLeod and Company, was shot and killed in the Athabasca country in the winter of 1786–87. Two of Pond's men were arrested for this crime but were acquitted when tried at Quebec. Barry M. Gough, "Peter Pond," DCB, 5:681–6.

ing of the geography of the countries interior of Lake Ontario, and the Maps they had to guide them were wretched compilations, one of them, of which I had a fellow Map, was Farren's dated 1773, which went as far as Lake Ontario, and to the middle of this Lake, beyond which, the [iv.119] interior countries were represented composed of Rocks and Swamps and laid down as uninhabitable.[8] Mitchell's Map was the best.[9] Such Maps gave Mr Peter Pond who was personally acquainted with those countries every advantage. A boundary line through the middle of Lake Champlain, and thence due west would have been accepted at that time by the United [States] for it was more than they could justly claim, had a gentleman of ability been selected on the part of Great Britain, but at that time North America was held in contempt. To the United States Commissioners Mr Pond designated a Boundary Line passing through the middle of the St Lawrence to Lake Superior, through that Lake and the interior countries to the north west corner of the Lake of the Woods; and thence westward to the head of the Missisourie[10] being twice the area of the Territory the States could justly claim; This exorbitant demand the British Commissioners accepted; and was confirmed by both Nations. Such was the hand that designated the Boundary Line between the Dominions of Great Britain and the Territories of the United States. The celebrated Edmund Burke, said, and has left on record, "There is a fatality attending all the measures of the British Ministry on the North American Colonies."[11]

8 William Faden (1749–1836) came to prominence as a mapmaker during the American Revolutionary War and in 1783 was appointed "Geographer in Ordinary" to George III. Laurence Worms, "William Faden," *Oxford Dictionary of National Biography* (Oxford: Oxford University Press, 2004), 18:882. This work is hereafter abbreviated as *ODNB*. In 1777 Faden published a map entitled *The British Colonies in North America*. See *British Museum Catalogue of Printed Maps, Charts, and Plans* (London: Trustees of the British Museum, 1967), 5:873.

9 John Mitchell (1711–68) gained a reputation as a botanist in Virginia before moving in 1745 to London, where he increasingly turned his attention to cartography. In 1755 Mitchell produced *A Map of the British and French Dominions in North America with the Roads, Distances, Limits, and Extent of the Settlements*, expressly commissioned to assert British territorial claims against France. George III's "Red-lined" version of this map was used during the Treaty of Paris negotiations. Elizabeth Baigent, "John Mitchell," *ODNB*, 38:409–10.

10 Mississippi is intended.

11 This exact formulation is not found in Burke's published works, but its sentiments echo his 1775 "Speech on Conciliation with America." Thompson's source may be Sir James Prior's 1826 biography of Burke, in which Prior quotes the original manuscript notes of this speech. Of the British government's response to the complaints of

This sad, but just remark has been exemplified in every transaction we have had with the United States on Territory; and in this respect Lord Ashburton was outwitted by Mr Daniel Webster at the Treaty of Washington, both in New Brunswick, and the interior of Canada. It may be said, the country thus acquired by the United States is off no importance to England; be it so; then let England make a free gift to the States of what the latter require; History will place all these transactions in their proper light, and the blockhead treaty of Lord Ashburton will be a subject of ridicule.[12]

[Load of Canoes. My Instruments. Sieux Arrows in the Rocks and country to Height of Land. Massacre by the Sieux. Isles of the dead. Height of Land to Winepeg House. Lake Winepeg]

[iv.120] The south east end of the Great Carrying [Place], was in a small Bay of Lake Superior in Latitude 47-58·1 N Longitude 89.44-20 W of Greenwich. It was then, and had been for several years, the Depot of the Furr Traders; to this place the Canoes from Montreal came, each carrying forty, to forty five pieces of merchandize, including spiritous liquors; each piece of the weight of ninety to one hundred pounds; these Canoes then were loaded with the packs of furrs, the produce of the winter trade of the interior countries, and returned to Montreal; The Merchandise for the winter trade of the distant trading Posts was here assorted, and made up in pieces each weighing ninety pounds; the Canoes were of a less size, and the load was twenty five pieces, besides the the provisions for the voyage and the baggage of the Men: being a weight of about 2900 pounds, to which add five Men, the weight a canoe carries will be 3700 pounds.

These Canoes are formed into what are called Brigades of four to eight Canoes for the different sections of the interior countries. On board of one

American colonists, Burke states, "[The Minister] hath been driven to the necessity of making concession, but hath been forced, by some secret force or fatality, to load and clog his measures with principles and conditions, such as must render it impossible for the Americans to accept it, and which must therefore in the end prove a plan to render them still more obnoxious to Parliament and Government here." Sir James Prior, *Memoir of the Life and Character of the Right Hon. Edmund Burke* (London: Baldwin, Cradock and Joy, 1826), 1:302–3. Coincidentally, the five-year-old Thompson was a scant distance from the Palace of Westminster when Burke's speech was delivered.

12 The Webster-Ashburton Treaty of 1842 settled several outstanding boundary claims, including the eastern Canadian and New Brunswick border with Maine, and the boundary line between Lake Superior and Lake of the Woods.

of these canoes, of a Brigade of four under the charge of Mr Hugh McGillis,[1] I embarked on the ninth day of August, in the year 1796,[2] for the survey of the southern sections.

My instruments were, a Sextant of ten inches radius, with Quicksilver and parallel glasses, an excellent Achromatic Telescope; a lesser for common use; drawing instruments, and two Thermometers; all made by Dollond.[3] We proceeded over the Great Carrying Place, the length of which is eight miles and twenty yards in a North West direction to the Pigeon River, which is about three hundred feet above Lake Superior: this was carried over by the Men in five day's hard labor. From this to the Height of Land the distance is thirty eight miles [iv.121] including twelve carrying places, of five and a half miles of carriage, which makes severe labor for the canoe men: A short distance south eastward of the Height of Land in the crevices of a steep rock, about twenty feet above the water of a small Lake, are a number of Arrows which the Sieux Indians shot from their Bows; the Arrows are small and short.

The Chippaways,[4] the Natives say; these Arrows are the voice of the Sieux and tell us. "We have come to war on you and not finding you, we leave these in the rocks in your country, with which we hoped to have pierced your bodies." This was about the year 1730. These Indians the Sieux Nation are

---

1 For NWC clerk and partner Hugh McGillis, see appendix 2.
2 1797 is intended. For the journals of Thompson's journey from Grand Portage to Bas-de-la-Rivière, lasting from 9 August to 1 September, see AO. 5.180–90.
3 This list of instruments is almost identical to that on iv.58 (115); only the compass is lacking here.
4 This is Thompson's first reference to the Ojibwa in the 1850 version of the *Travels*. While the Algonquian-speaking Ojibwa originally occupied the lands north of Lake Superior and Lake Huron, their participation in the fur trade was accompanied by movement west and north into and beyond the areas of Lake of the Woods, Lake Winnipeg, and the Upper Mississippi. The designations employed by Thompson, "Chippaway" here and "Oojibaways" and "Oochepoys" below (iv.183, 224; iv.213, 247), all represent the Ojibwa self-designation *očipwe*, the etymology of which is obscure. Ives Goddard, "Synonymy," in E.S. Rogers, "Southeastern Ojibwa," *HNAI*, vol. 15: *Northeast*, ed. Bruce Trigger (Washington: Smithsonian Institution, 1978), 768–70. Thompson frequently mentions the Ojibwa in passing during the narration of his travels in these areas from September 1797 to May 1798 (iv.120–234, 175–263). While recounting his stay at the NWC post of Jean-Baptiste Cadotte in March–April 1798, Thompson writes in detail of Ojibwa religious beliefs and practices and of hostilities between the Ojibwa and Cheyenne (iv.192–203, 231–40). The 1848 version (in Volume II) contains passages on Ojibwa-Cheyenne warfare (iii.67–9), the Wahbino movement (iii.87–9), and the windigo phenomenon (iii.90–2).

yet a powerful nation, and their present hunting grounds are between the Mississippe and Missisourie Rivers and now make use of Horses instead of Canoes.[5]

The Height of Land is in Latitude 48-6··43 N Longitude 90-34-38 W and Variation six degrees East, and is the dividing ridge of land from which the Streams run south eastward into Lake Superior and north eastward[6] into Lake Winepeg, and from thence into Hudson's Bay.

The country so far, is at present, of no value to the farmer, time may do some thing for it as a grazing country from it's many Brooks and small Lakes of clear water.

The country now declines to the North eastward with many small Streams, which form a fine River. The first place worth notice is the Rainy Lake, a fine body of water of nineteen miles in length; out of which falls the Rainy River by a descent of about ten feet; close below which is a trading House of the North [West] Company in Latitude 48-36·58 N Longitude 93-19·30 W.[7]

5 The Sioux (a name that derives from the Ottawa *na-towe-ssiwak*, "speakers of a foreign language") are divided into three main groups: the eastern Santee, central Yankton-Yanktonai, and western Teton. At the beginning of the historical period, the Sioux occupied the lands west and south of Lake Superior, and their economy centred around wild rice and maple sugar. During the seventeenth century, the Sioux encountered French traders. In the early eighteenth century, hostilities developed between the Teton and the Cree, during which the former were often joined by the Santee and the Ojibwa and the latter by the Assiniboine. During this time, all Native groups in the region began to migrate to the west and south, and by the time Thompson traversed the lands west of Lake Superior, the Sioux had left the woodlands for the Prairies and Plains, adopting an economy based on bison and maize. Thompson's placement of the Sioux between the Mississippi and Missouri is largely accurate, although the Teton had by 1850 migrated as far west as the Black Hills. As Thompson's work indicates, strong enmity had arisen between the Sioux and the Ojibwa who occupied their ancestral lands. Raymond J. DeMallie, "Sioux Until 1850," *HNAI*, vol. 13, 718–60; Guy Gibbon, *The Sioux: The Dakota and Lakota Nations* (Malden, MA: Blackwell, 2003). The Sioux appear in the *Travels* in Thompson's account of the 1736 Lake of the Woods massacre (iv.122, 178), the narration of the journey to the Mandan-Hidatsa villages in 1797–98 (iv.151–69 *passim*, 200–13; iv.178–80, 220–1; iii.71–82 *passim*, Volume II), and travels between Red River and Lake Superior in 1798 (iv.202–19 *passim*, 238–52).

6 Westward is intended.

7 The NWC's Rainy River House was founded in 1785 and served as the NWC's depot for the more distant Athabasca and Columbia regions; it was this post to which Thompson returned in 1808 (iii.207, Volume II) and 1810 (iii.171; iii.228d, Volume II).

The distance from the Height of Land is one hundred and seventeen miles the country improving, and in several places good Farms can be made. The Rainy River is a fine stream of water of about 200 yards in breadth, with only one Rapid, at which in the season, many fine Sturgeon are speared by the Natives. The length of the River to the Lake of [iv.122] the Woods is 50½ miles. This is the finest River in this country. The banks present the appearance of a country that can be cultivated but those acquainted with it, think the rock too near the surface. The Lake of the Woods is in length 32½ miles with many bays, its area may be about 800 square miles, with many islets. The north eastern shores are of granite; it's western of lime stone; and touches on the great western alluvials.

¶ It seems that when the French from Canada first entered these fur countries, every summer a Priest came to instruct the Traders and their men in their religious duties, and preach to them and the Natives in Latin it being the only language the Devil does not understand and cannot learn; He had collected about twenty Men with a few of the Natives upon a small Island, of rock; and while instructing them a large war party of Sieux Indians came on them and began the work of death; not one escaped; whilst this was going on the Priest kept walking backwards and forwards on a level rock of about fifty yards in length, with his eyes fixed on his book, without seeming to notice them; at length as he turned about, one of them sent an arrow through him, and he fell dead. At this deed the rocky isle trembled and shook; the Sieux Indians became afraid, and they retired without stripping the dead, or taking their scalps. These Isles, of which there are three, are to this day called "The isles of the dead" (Les isles aux Morts). Such was the relation an old Canadian gave me, and which he said he had learned of the Furr Traders who then resided among those Indians.[8]

---

8 This massacre occurred on 6 June 1736. The attackers were a mixed group of Teton, Santee, and Ojibwa; the French party numbered twenty-one and included the Jesuit priest Jean-Pierre Aulneau and Jean-Baptiste de la Vérendrye, son of the renowned explorer Pierre Gaultier de Varennes, Sieur de la Vérendrye. The attack was a response to the elder La Vérendrye's breaking of kinship ties with the Santee, when in 1734 he had allowed Jean-Baptiste to accompany a Cree war party against them. Gary Clayton Anderson, *Kinsmen of Another Kind: Dakota-White Relations in the Upper Mississippi Valley, 1650–1862* (Lincoln: University of Nebraska Press, 1984), 30, 41–4. There were no survivors; the search party that located the corpses reported that the victims appeared to have been seated at council when they were attacked and that most had been scalped. Thompson's version, heard from an "old Canadian" sixty-one years after these events, illustrates how the incident, in a somewhat embellished form, survived in local folklore. For the contemporary accounts of the finding

¶ The Lake of the Woods is memorable for being by every treaty the north-eastern[9] boundary of the Dominions of Great Britain and the [iv.123] Territories of the United States. This Lake may be said to be the most southern Lake of the Stony Region that has limestone shores at it's west end, the north and eastern parts like the other Lake[s], have the shores and banks of granite, greenstone and clay slate. This Lake, by several Falls sends out the River Winepeg (Sea River) in a north eastern direction into Lake Winepeg, it is a bold deep Stream of about three hundred yards in width. It has many isles and channels, the whole is of granite formation. By the course of the River it's length is 125 miles; In this distance there are thirty two Falls, with as many carrying places, the total length of which is three miles. At it's sortie into Lake Winepeg is a trading House first established by the French; and kept up by the north west Company: in Latitude 50-37··46 N Longitude 95··59·34 W Variation nine degrees east.[10]

¶ The whole extent of country from Lake Superior to this House can support, comparatively, to the extent of country, but few Natives, who are of the Chippeway Tribe; the country never could have been rich in animals; and has long been exhausted: the Deer is almost unknown, and but few furr bearing animals remain; the principal support of the Natives is the fish of the Lakes, of which are Sturgeon, White Fish, Pike, Pickerel and Carp, the quality good. The greatest use of the Winepeg House is for a depot of Provisions which are brought to this place by the canoes and boats from the Bison countries of the Red and Saskatchewan Rivers; and distributed to the canoes and boats for the voyages to the several wintering furr trading Houses.

¶ Lake Winepeg (or the Sea) so called by the Natives from it's size,[11] is of the [iv.124] form of a rude Parallelogram; and it's geological structure is the same at that of all the Lakes northward and westward it's eastern shores and banks are of the granitic order; the north side mostly high banks of earth; the west side is low, the shores, and the isles wholly of limestone; On the west side, in it's southern bay, it receives the Red River distant from the Winepeg

---

of the victims, see Lawrence J. Burpee, ed., *Journals and Letters of Pierre Gaultier de Varennes de la Vérendrye and his Sons* (Toronto: Champlain Society, 1927), 208–31, 262–6. See also Bill Moreau, "The Death of Père Aulneau, 1736: The Development of Myth in the Northwest," in *CCHA Historical Studies* 69 (2003): 52–63.

9   Here and below, northwestern is intended.

10 One of La Vérendrye's sons had erected Fort Maurepas at the mouth of the Winnipeg River in 1734. In 1792 an NWC post called Bas-de-la-Rivière was established close to this site, and the following year the HBC built Fort Alexander.

11 See note on 27c (50).

House forty two miles, northward of the same bay the Dauphine River; at it's north west corner the Saskatchewan River, besides other lesser streams on it's west and east sides; all which enlarge the Saskatchewan, which flows out at the north east corner of the Lake, in Latitude 53.43-45 N Longitude 98°.31-0 West. The length of the west side of this Lake from the Winepeg House to the sortie of the Saskatchewan River into the Lake is 231 Miles, N36W and it's east side is about 217 miles; the north side 45 miles, and the south side about the same; and including it's, Isles has an area of about 10,080 square miles.[12] The woods all around this Lake are small, with many branches, in winter the climate is severe; and there are very few deer, and other animals; but the fish are good, and it's isles in the summer season are covered with the nests of the common Gull, the eggs of which are nearly as good as those of our common Fowls; There are but few Natives about this Lake, and they lead a hard life.

[*The great Plains & Rivers. The three great Rivers. The Hills. The soil of the hills, difficult to find a Market. The Plains. Missisourie. Planters Sawyers & Snags. the Bow River. The earth carried northward. distribution of Rivers. Coal Beds. Smoke River. Fossil Bones. fable of ditto*]

Hitherto the Reader has been confined to the sterile Stony Region and the great Valley of the Lakes. [iv.125] My travels will now extend over countries of a very different formation; these are the Great Plains as a general name, and are supposed to be more ancient than the Stony Region and the great Valley of the Lakes.[1]

By a Plain I mean lands bearing grass, but too short for the Scythe; where the grass is long enough for the Scythe, and of which Hay can be made, I name Meadows. These Great Plains may be said to commence at the north side of the Gulph of Mexico, and extend northward to the latitude of fifty four degrees; where these plains are bounded by the Forests of the north

12 Thompson revised these figures during composition. The original figures were 194 miles for the west side, 180 for the east, 68 for the north and south, and 13,500 square miles for the area.

1 This essay on the Great Plains bears the marks of careful planning and arrangement. Thompson opens with a panoramic survey of the region, then describes each of the Plains' subregions (the eastern boundaries in greatest detail), before reconsidering contemplatively the entire area. Topics considered within the essay include impediments to river navigation, coal, and fossil remains. Thompson had written extensively about the Plains in his 1843 "Travels" (AO 71.55–37; Volume II) and in the 1848 text at iii.120–2 (Volume II).

which extend unbroken to the arctic Sea. On the east they are bounded by the Mississippe River, and northward of which by the valley of the Lakes; and on the west by the Rocky Mountains. The length of these Plains from South to North is 1240 miles; and the breadth from east to west to the foot of the Mountains, from 550 to 800 miles giving an area to the Great Plains of 1,039,500 square miles, in which space the Ozark Hills are included.

¶ The perpetual snows and Glaciers of the Mountains, which every where border the west side of these Plains furnish water to form many Rivers; all these south of the latitude of 49 degrees flow into the Mississippe River, the most northern of which is the Mississourie River. Close northward of the scources of the Mississourie, are the south branches of the Saskatchewan River which descends to Hudson's Bay. The next great Rivers northward are the Athabasca and Peace Rivers, which with other lesser streams form McKenzie's River, which empties itself into the Arctic Sea. It may be remarked among other great differencies between the Stony Region and the Great Plains that all the Rivers of the former Region, or that pass through it, meet with, and also form many Lakes, [iv.126] and Falls; while all the Rivers in their courses through the Great Plains, and the northward forest lands do not form a single Lake. Thus the three great Rivers of North America enter different Seas. The Mississippe from Latitude 47··39··15 N Longitude 95··12··45 running about S by E into the gulph of Mexico in Latitude [*space*] Longitude [*space*]. The Saskatchewan rising in Latitude 51··48··25 N Longitude 116··45··13 W running NE ward into Hudsons Bay in Latitude 57·6 North Longitude 91-20 W and McKenzie's River, it's great southern branch rising in Latitude 52·20 N Longitude 118°··0'-0" W running NNE ward into the sea in Latitude [*space*] Longitude [*space*].

So different are the courses of these Rivers on the same side of the Rocky Mountains from which they take their rise; and on entering the different seas into which they discharge their waters, they all appear of about equal magnitude. The east side of these Great Plains have a fine appearance, the soil is rich, with many extensive Meadows. A range of fine low Hills sufficiently well wooded, with many springs of fine water and Rivulets, which form small Rivers navigable to Canoes and Boats as the Dauphine, Swan, Mouse and Stone Indian Rivers, with several Rivulets all flowing through a rich soil.[2] The Hills are the Turtle Hill, the most southern and not far from the Missisourie River The next northward are the Hair, the Nut, the Touchwood,

---

2 The Mouse River is known today under its French name, the Souris (although it sometimes bears its English name where it flows through North Dakota); the Stone Indian River is the Assiniboine.

the Dauphine, the Eagle, and the Forrest Hills.[3] The west side of these Hills as seen from the Plains have gentle elevations of about two hundred feet; but as seen from the eastward, present an elevation of five to eight hundred feet above the common level, and have very fine Forrests of well grown trees of Birch, several kinds of Pine, Poplar, Aspin, and small Ash and Oaks.[4]

¶ These Hills are the favorite resort of the Moose and Red Deer, with two, or three species of the Antelope.[5] The Black, Brown and Yellow Bears feed on the [iv.127] Berries, the Nuts and any thing else they can catch; one of them was shot that was guarding part of an Antelope, which he had killed and partly eaten; how this clumsy brute could have caught so fleet an animal as the Antelope was a matter of wonder. The Bears lay up nothing for their subsistence in winter, and are the[n] mostly dormant. As we travelled through the fine forests, we were often amused with the activity of the Squirrels collecting hazel nuts[6] for their supply in winter and of which each collects more than a bushel, whereas the Squirrels of the Pine Forests of the north seem to lay up nothing, but are out every day feeding on the cones of the White Pine. The Field Mice are also equally active in laying in store provisions for the winter.

¶ The climate is good, the winters about five months, the summers are warm, and autumn has many fine days. The soil is rich and deep, and much vegetable mould from the annual decay of the leaves of the Forest Trees, and

3 Several of these ranges, along the northeastern edge of the Plains, are today known under different names. The Turtle Hills are Turtle Mountain (see iv.151, 201); the Hair Hills are possibly the Hairy Hill, identified by John Palliser, in southwestern Manitoba; the Nut Hills are Nut Mountain in east-central Saskatchewan (although on iv.141, 193, the term appears to refer to Duck Mountain); the Touchwood Hills are in east-central Saskatchewan; the Dauphine Hills are Duck and Riding Mountains west of Dauphin Lake (although this identification ruptures Thompson's spatial sequencing); the Eagle Hills are on the south bank of the Battle River in west-central Saskatchewan; the Forrest Hills are likely the Thickwood Hills, north of the North Saskatchewan River. John Palliser, *A General Map of the Routes in British North America Explored by the Expedition under Captain Palliser* (London: Stanford's, 1865); J. Howard Richards, *Atlas of Saskatchewan* (Regina: University of Saskatchewan, 1969), 42–3.

4 Bur oak (*Quercus macrocarpa*).

5 In referring to two or three species, Thompson may include deer, such as the wapiti (*Cervus elaphus*), mule deer (*Odocoileus hemionus*), and white-tailed deer (*Odocoileus virginianus*), in addition to the pronghorn (*Antilocapra americana*).

6 American hazelnut (*Corylus americana*) and beaked hazelnut (*Corylus cornuta*) are found on the Plains.

the grass of the Meadows; Civilization will no doubt extend over these low hills; they are well adapted for raising of cattle; and when the wolves are destroyed, also for sheep; and agriculture will succeed to a pastoral life, so far as Markets can be formed in the country, but no further; for Canada is too distant and difficult of access. The only Port open to them is York Factory on the dismal shores of Hudson's Bay, open four months in the year, and to go to York Factory and return will require all that part of the summer which cannot be spared: but when a civilized population shall cover these countries, means will be found to make it's produce find a Market.

From the gulph of Mexico to the Latitude of 44 degrees north, these Great Plains may be said to be barren for great spaces, even of coarse grass, but the cactus grows in abundance on a soil of sand [iv.128] and rolled gravel; even the several Rivers that flow thro' these Plains do not seem to fertilise the grounds adjacent to them; These Rivers are too broad in proportion to their depth and in autumn very shallow, the Mountains are comparatively low, and therefore sooner exhausted of their winter snows, and travellers often suffer for want of water, but as one advances northward the soil becomes better and the Missisourie River through it's whole length to it's confluence with the Mississippe carries with it lands of deep soil, on which are many Villages of the Natives, who subsist partly by agriculture, and partly by hunting.

¶ The course of the Missisourie is through an elevated part of these Plains, and it's great body of water has a swift current of about four miles an hour, which makes the ascent of this River in boats very laborious, although there are neither rapids, nor falls: Although the heads of this River give several passages across the Mountains yet from the labor being so great; and also exposed to attacks from hostile Indians, that Steam Vessels are the only proper craft for this River; and even to these, it's many shoals and sands offer serious impediments, for it's waters are very turbid. From these there arises more vexation than danger; this latter is incurred every day by what are called Sawyers, Planters and Snags, names which have been ridiculed, without offering better in their stead,[7] but however these things may be laughed at,

---

7   The usage of these words developed in North America in the late eighteenth century. Thompson likely has in mind an 1823 *Quarterly Review* article about three books of North American travel in which the reviewers, John Barrow and William Gifford, write that "danger arises from the roots and stems of sunken trees, or those which are floating level with the surface of the water, known, by nice distinctions, under the sonourous and classical names of *snags, mags, sawyers,* and *planters.*" John Barrow and William Gifford, review of *Account of an Expedition from Pittsburgh to the Rocky Mountains, Narrative Journey of Travels from Detroit Northwest,* and *A*

they are very serious obstacles to the navigation of this River, and also of the Mississippe. They all proceed from Trees torn up by the roots, by the freshets from heavy rains, or the melting of the Snow. The Planter is a tree that has it's head and branches broken, it's roots frequently loaded with earth, and sometimes stones; drags the bottom until something stops it, and the roots become firmly fixed in the bottom; when the water is high and covers them, they are [iv.129] dangerous, but in low water can be seen; The Sawyer is generally a Tree of large dimensions broken about the middle of its length, it's roots are in the mud of the bottom of the River, sufficiently to retain them there; but not so firmly as to keep the broken tree steady, the strong current bends the tree under as much as the play of the roots will permit, the strain on which causes a reaction, and the tree rises with a spring upwards to several feet above the water, and with such force as will damage, or destroy any vessel; but as the rising of these Sawyers are often seen at some distance they are avoided; though I have seen some that being by the current immersed many feet under water have taken fifteen to twenty minutes between each appearance. The smaller the Tree the quicker they work. A Bison Bull in swiming across the River got on a small one, and remained swiming with all his might, though still in the same place. When the water becomes low, many of these Sawyers have very little water and we see the whole machinery. The Snag is the same as the Planter, only always under water, so that it is not seen, and cannot be avoided. Several boats have been sunk by them: the water is so turbid, nothing can be seen under it's surface. The River next northward of the Missisourie is the Bow River, so named from a species of Yew Tree on it's banks, of which good Bows are made.[8] This is the most southern River of the British Dominions and the South Branch of the Saskatchewan.[9]

The Bow River flows through the most pleasant of the Plains, and is the great resort of the Bison and Red Deer, and also of the Natives. The soil appears good along it's whole extent, but for the most part is bare, of Woods, and those that remain [iv.130] are fast diminishing by fire. The soil of the Plains appears to continue increasing in depth, and the same through the Forests. In Latitude 56 degrees north, is the Smoke River, the great south branch of the Peace River; by the Gullies and Ravines the earth appears to

Journal of Travels into the Arkansa Territory, in *Quarterly Review* 29 (April 1823): 5.

8 Rocky Mountain Douglas fir (*Pseudotsuga menziesii glauca*). Bow River is a translation of the Cree *manachaban sipi*. Thompson, *David Thompson's Narrative*, ed. Tyrrell, 188n1.

9 Thompson applies the name Bow to both that river proper and the South Saskatchewan.

have a depth of about 300 feet; Those who wish to find a material cause for this apparent increasing depth of soil from south to north; are led to suppose a great flood of water from the gulph of Mexico rushed northwards along the Mountains, denuded all the south parts of it's earth, leaving sand and rounded gravel for a soil; and carried the earth northward where it has settled in great depth; here is a grand cause with a great effect. But how came the Rivers not to be defaced.[10] The Rivers that roll through this immense unbroken body of land of Plains and Forests, are so beautifully distributed; all their banks so admirably adjusted to the volumes of water that flow between them that neither the heaviest rains, nor the melting of the Snows of the Mountains inundate the adjacent country. In all seasons, the Indians the Bisons and Deer repose on their banks in perfect security. Who ever calmly views the admirable formation, and distribution of the Rivers so wonderfully conducted to their several seas; must confess the whole to have been traced by the finger of the Great Supreme Artificer for the most benevolent purposes, both to his creature Man and the numerous Animals he has made none of whom can exist without water. Water may be said to be one of the principal elements of [iv.131] life.

¶ Coal appears to be sparingly found in North America; and the beds very far between each other. The only beds of coal that have come to my knowledge are those which lie near the foot of the Rocky Mountains; the Missisourie is said to have Coal, but of this I am not sure. The branches of the Saskatchewan River in the freshets lodge Coal on the sands of the Rivers. On the main River when the water lowers, several bushels of very good Coal can be collected on the Sands and at the Rocky Mountain House where I passed two winters and one summer,[11] we found the bank about 100 yards below the House to be of pure coal and of an excellent quality. My Blacksmith tried this coal; and at the first trial it melted the rod of iron, and from the great heat it gave he had to use half charcoal; and thought the quality of the Coal superior to any brought from England. This bed of Coal extends to as far 56 degrees of north Latitude and Longitude [space] West, for the Smoke River is

10 Thompson's writings on geology are best understood in the context of early-nineteenth-century debates about the antiquity of the earth, and particularly the difficulty of reconciling the emerging geological timeline with biblical chronologies. They have a close affinity to the natural theology of William Buckland, who in works such as *Reliquiae Diluvianae* (1823) attempted to harmonize the account of creation in Genesis with the findings of geology.

11 Thompson was at or near Rocky Mountain House between December 1800 and May 1802, and wintered there in 1806–07. He spent November 1802 to March 1804 near the junction of the Peace and Smoke Rivers.

so named from the volumes of dark smoke sent from the Coal Mines there on fire, and which have been burning beyond the memory of the oldest Indian of that River. From the very numerous remains in Siberia and parts of Europe of the Elephant, Rhinocerous, and other large Animals, especially near the Rivers, and in their banks, of those countries, I was led to expect to find the remains of those Animals in the Great Plains, and the Rivers that flow through them; but all my steady researches, and all my enquiries led to nothing. Over a great extent of these Plains not a vestige could be found, [iv.132] nor in the banks of the many Rivers I have examined.[12]

The fossil bones of the large animals[13] that have been found on this Continent appear to be limited to the United States east of the Alleghany Mountains (Hills) and on the west side to the Ohio River,[14] and the countries southward on the east side of the Mississippe and to South America. On the west side of the Mississippe only one large bone has been found, which the Natives reverenced and has given a name to two Tribes, the great, and the little, Osage Indians.[15] This large bone, several years ago was purchased from the Natives and placed in the museum of Washington City.[16] The Natives when questioned on the fossil bones of the Ohio River, made a fable for an answer. That in old times these Mammoths were numerous they devoured all other Animals, and did not allow Man to live; at length the Great Spirit became angry, he descended with the Thunder in his hands, and destroyed them all; except the big Bull, the Thunder struck him on the forehead but did not kill him, he bounded away, sprang over the Mississippe River, and ran to the west, where he yet lives[17] (Note. When on the head waters of the

12 Thompson was unaware of the abundant remains of dinosaurs along the Red Deer River, which were discovered in June 1884 by his future editor, J.B. Tyrrell.

13 Fossils were of enduring interest to Thompson, and in August 1848 he contributed a piece to the Montreal *Gazette* in which he recounted the discovery of the frozen remains of a mammoth in northern Siberia in 1799 (Volume III).

14 At Big Bone Lick, where several discoveries were made during the eighteenth century.

15 This is a folk etymology, derived from similarity to the Latin *os* (bone). Osage comes from the Siouan group's self-designation as *wazhazhe*. Garrick A. Bailey, "Osage," *HNAI*, vol. 13, 1:493. The fossil deposits to which Thompson refers were found in 1838–40 by the German American amateur paleontologist Albrecht Koch, who promoted his finds in pamphlets, books, and exhibitions during the 1840s.

16 In fact, Koch sold several of his specimens to the British Museum in 1844; they are now housed at the Museum of Natural History in London.

17 This story is based on a passage in Thomas Jefferson's *Notes on the State of Virginia* (1785), where it is attributed (107–8) to a delegation of Lenape warriors then living on the Ohio River.

Athabasca River and Mountain defiles to the Columbia River; the Natives, but especially the White and Iroquois Hunters all declared these places to be the haunt of an enormous Animal who lived on grass, moss, and the tender shoots of the willows; nor could all my arguments when there make a single convert to the contrary).[18]

Not a single fossil bone of an Elephant, Rhinocerous, or Mammoth has been found in all Canada nor about any of the Great Lakes and valley of the Lawrence and northward to the Arctic Circle, although almost [iv.133] all these countries are sufficiently known; nor has the travels of Captain Franklin in the Arctic Regions been attended with any success on this subject. On the west side of the Rocky Mountains I passed six years of discovery,[19] yet not a vestige that these great Animals once existed in those parts could be found. We may therefore conclude, that the great animals of North America were limited to the east and west sides of the Allegany Hills, and the east side of the valley of the Mississippe, and no farther to the northward and westward on this Continent: and that these were all destroyed by the Deluge, which also put an end to other races of animals, and thus the great Creator made the Earth more habitable for his favourite creature Man.[20]

[*River Dauphine to Lake Winepegoos. Lake Winepegoos & Swan River. Mr. Grants. Billeau & Hugh McGillis. No Mineral Springs*]

I hope I have now given such a general view of the formation of the Great Plains and their eastern borders as will enable the reader readily to follow me in my travels. One of the principal objects of the North West Company was to ascertain the Courses of the Rivers, the situation of the Lakes, and of their several Trading Houses, which in some parts appeared to be too near each other, and in other places, too distant. From the Winepeg House[1] we coasted the Lake with it's shores of limestone, mostly low, but at times forming cliffs to the height of fifty feet to the mouth of the Dauphine River. To this place our straight course has been N43W 127 miles. We now proceeded up the

---

18 Thompson encountered tales of this creature while travelling in the upper Athabasca region in 1811. See references at iii.230–1 and iii.305–7 (Volume II).

19 Thompson's "six years of discovery" are 1807–12.

20 This reflection illustrates Thompson's attempt to integrate his understanding of the Earth's history with the biblical narrative.

1 Bas-de-la-Rivière, where the Winnipeg River enters Lake Winnipeg. For the journal of Thompson's travels from 1 September 1797, when he left this post, to 9 November, see AO. 5.190–201; a second journal, covering 23–6 September and 14–18 October, is AO. 7.1r–2v.

Dauphine River, a fine stream of about thirty yards in width, and an average of three feet in depth, as we advanced the country improved in soil, and also the Forests through which it runs, but the Deer and the Beaver are few; Having proceeded eighty eight miles in a straight course of s74w, the River has many turnings in this distance we came to the Meadow Carrying Place [iv.134] of 2760 yards, which leads from the River to Lake Winepegoos (the little Sea).² The Dauphine comes out of this Lake, but it's course is now so circuitous, with shoal Rapids, that the Carrying Place is preferred. We went over this Lake for fifty nine miles, to the entrance of the Swan River, a small stream of about fifteen to twenty yards in width, with a depth of about three feet and gentle current, through a fine country, for we are now among the fine low Hills I have already mentioned; the Beaver are now plenty; but the Deer are only beginning to leave the heights of the Hills where they pass the summer. Having proceeded twelve miles we came to the Swan River House of the North West Company in Latitude 52-24-5 N Longitude 100-36··52 W Variation 13° East.³ There were but two families of the Natives, Nahathaway Indians to whom these countries belong: but several Chippewas have lately come from the southward where their own countries are exhausted of the Beaver and Deer. These two families having procured Ammunition and Tobacco went off to inform the others of the arrival of the Canoes.

¶ From the Swan River on the 26th September 1796⁴ we proceeded with Horses across the country to the Stone Indian River, (on which the North West Company have several trading Houses.) to the upper House in charge of Mr Cuthbert Grant.⁵ N 40°½ W 90 miles; this distance was mostly through fine Forests through which our Horses found the ground every where good, except a few wet meadows, in which they did not go ancle deep. My Indian Guide had learned that the Pawnee Indians had been defeated, and altho' by Indians of whom he knew nothing, yet kept bawling the whole day, "We

2 Lake Winnipegosis, which Thompson entered on 14 September 1797.
3 Swan River House was located about 12 miles (20 kilometres) from the river's mouth. For Thompson's stay there on 21–23 September 1797, see AO. 5.196.
4 1797 is intended.
5 Thompson's itinerary is more complicated than he indicates. On 23 September he and Cuthbert Grant left Swan River House on horseback and proceeded to Pierre Belleau's post on Snake Creek, where they spent the night of 24 September. The next day they continued to Aspen House, Grant's post on the Assiniboine, where Thompson remained from 25 September to 14 October; he was again at this post from 2 to 9 November. For the events of this time, see AO. 5.196–201; 7.1r–2v. For NWC clerk and partner Cuthbert Grant, see appendix 2.

have fought with the Pawnee's and have conquered them."[6] He was a Chippaway. In the evening when we camped; I told him, he was the only Warrior [iv.135] I ever knew that boasted of conquering a people, whom he never saw, nor was likely to see, and that no one would believe him. He replied, "We young men, at present, have no opportunities of distinguishing ourselves, the enemies that our fathers warred on, are driven across the Missisourie River, far beyond our reach, but I will sing no more."

We now turned to the trading House in charge of Mr Billeau,[7] situated between the Swan and Stone Indian Rivers, and as usual observed for Latitude and Longitude, which gave it 51°-51'-9" N 102°-3-0" W the course N 12 W 30 miles. In this distance. the country had much wet ground from the many ponds kept full by Beaver Dams. We returned to Mr Grants, and from thence journeyed to the upper House on the Red Deer's River in charge of Mr Hugh McGillis,[8] in Latitude 52-59·7 N Longitude 101··32-27 W the course N 10 E 111 Miles, but the Ponds formed by the Beaver, and their Dams which we had to cross lengthened our Road to 150 miles; these sagacious animals were in full possession of the country; but their destruction had already began, and was now in full operation.

¶ All the above Trading Houses of the North West Company from Canada were on the south west sides of the range of low Hills which border the east side of the Great Plains and hitherto all my journeys were those of pleasure; the Moose Deer of these Hills, although always a very wary animal, yet from their being more numerous, and also from the Forests being more open, were not the same cautious, timid, animal that it is in the close, dark, Pine Forests of the north; aided perhaps, by being accustomed to see other species of Deer and Horses; but the Stag with his half a dozen [iv.136] of Does, which he as carefully guards, and is as ready to fight for, as any Turkish Pacha[9] for his Harem, that is the pride of these forests and meadows. But when the season

6   For the Pawnee, see note on iv.164 (210).
7   Having overnighted at this post on 24–25 September, Thompson returned on 15–18 October; for the record of this stay, see AO. 5.200; 7.2r–2v. Pierre Belleau (fl. 1785–1805) worked as a trader for the NWC, 1789–1802, and during his career ran posts on the Swan, Assiniboine, and South Saskatchewan Rivers. In 1804 he was given the responsibility of taking the news of the amalgamation of the NWC and XYC from Montreal to Fond du Lac on Lake Superior.
8   Thompson likely arrived at the Upper House on the Red Deer River around 22–23 October and departed on 29 October (AO. 8.8, 32). For Hugh McGillis, see appendix 2.
9   A pasha was a high-ranking officer of the Ottoman Empire.

of love is over, as now, his Does leave him, his head droops, and is no longer
the lordly animal that appeared as light on the ground as a Bird on the wing.
On such a variety of Hill and Plain, of Forests and Meadows I expected to
have found several mineral Springs, which are so frequent in other countries;
but neither my attention to this object, nor my enquiries could find one single
Spring; all my information led only to the saline Brooks of the Red River,
from some of which Salt is made by boiling the saline water. All these fine
countries are the hunting grounds of the Nahathaway Indians.

[*Ancient state of Man & the Beaver. Beaver Dams. Beaver houses and burrows. Dog. Mah meese*]

Previous to the discovery of Canada (about 320 years ago,) this Continent
from the Latitude of forty degrees north to the Arctic Circle, and from the
Atlantic to the Pacific Ocean, may be said to have been in the possession of
two distinct races of Beings, Man and the Beaver.[1] Man was naked and had
to procure clothing from the skins of animals; his only arms were a Stake,
pointed and hardened in the fire. A Bow with Arrows, the points hardened
with fire, or headed with stone, or bone of the legs of the Deer. A Spear
headed in the same manner, and a club of heavy wood, or made of a round
stone of four, or five pounds weight, inclosed in raw hide, and by the same
bound round a handle of wood of about two feet in length; bound firm to
the Stone. Such were the weapons Man had for self defence and with which
to procure his food and clothing. Against the bones of an Animal his Arrows
and Spear had little effect; the flank of every animal is open, and thither, into
the bowels, the Indian directed his fatal and unerring Arrows. (Note. Every
[iv.137] Hunter is acquainted with the effects of wounds in the different parts
of an animal; with an arrow in or a ball, through, the bowels, an animal if
pursued will go a long way: but if let alone, soon becomes as it were sick, lies
down on it's belly and, there dies). Besides his weapons, the Snare was much
in use, and the Spear to assist it for large animals, and by all accounts the
Deer, and furr bearing animals were very numerous, and thus Man was Lord
of the dry Land and all that was on it.

1 The essay on Man and the Beaver, like Thompson's writings on the mosquito and
the Plains, reflects the author's contemplative and inquisitive mind. In November–
December 1848, at about the time that this section was composed, Thompson pub-
lished three pieces in the Montreal *Gazette* that closely parallel its contents (Volume
III). For an earlier version of this section, see iii.105–8 in the 1848 version of the
Travels (Volume II).

¶ The other race was the Beaver, they were safe from every animal but Man, and the Wolverene. Every year each pair having from five to seven young, which they carefully reared, they became innumerable, and except the Great Lakes, the waves of which are too turbulent, occupied all the waters of the northern part of the Continent. Every River where the current was moderate and sufficiently deep, the banks at the water edge were occupied by their houses. To every small Lake, and all the Ponds they builded Dams, and enlarged and deepened them to the height of the dams. Even to grounds occasionally overflowed, by heavy rains, they also made dams and made them permanent Ponds, and as they heightened the dams increased the extent and added to the depth of water; Thus all the low lands were in possession of the Beaver, and all the hollows of the higher grounds. Small Streams were dammed across and Ponds formed; the dry land with the dominions of Man contracted, every where he was hemmed in by water without the power of preventing it; he could not diminish their numbers half so fast as they multiplied; and their houses were proof against his pointed stake, and his arrows could seldom [iv.138] pierce their skins. (Note. In my travels several thousands of the Natives were not half so well armed). In this state Man and the Beaver had been for many centuries, but the discovery of Canada by the French and their settlements up the St Lawrence soon placed the Natives far superior to the Beaver.

Without Iron, Man is weak, very weak, but armed with Iron, he becomes the Lord of the Earth, no other metal can take it's place. For the furrs which the Natives traded, they procured from the French Axes, Chissels, Knives, Spears and other articles of iron, with which they made good hunts of the furr bearing animals, and procured woollen clothing. Thus armed the houses of the Beavers were pierced through, the Dams cut through, and the water of the Ponds lowered, or wholly run off, and the houses of the Beaver and their B[u]rrows laid dry, by which means they became an easy prey to the Hunter.

The Beaver is an animal well known; the average weight of a full grown male is about fifty five pounds. His meat is agreeable to most although the fat is oily; the tail is a delicacy. They are always in pairs, and work together. Their first business is to insure a sufficient depth and extent of water for the winter, and if nature has not done this for them they make dams to obtain it. If there are more families than one in a piece of water, they all work together, each appearing to labor on a particular part.

The Dam is made of Earth, pieces of wood laid oblique to the direction of the dam. The wood employed is always of Aspin, Poplar or large Willow and Alders; if Pine is used it is through necessity, not by choice: the bottom is well laid, and if small stones are at hand, they make use of them for the bottom of the Dam, the earth is brought between their fore [iv.139] paws and throat, laid down, and by several strokes of the tail made compact; the pieces of wood, are with their teeth, which are very sharp, and formed like small chissels, cut into the lengths they want, brought to the dam and worked in- and thus the Dam is raised to the height required. It is a remark of many, that Dams erected by the art of Man, are frequently damaged, or wholly carried away by violent freshets, but no power of water has ever carried away a Beaver Dam. Having secured a sufficient depth of water each family builds a separate house, this is in the form of a low dome; from the door way which is a little way in the water, gradually rising to about thirty inches in height and about six feet in diameter, the materials are the same as those of the Dam, and worked in the same manner, only the pieces of wood are much shorter, and if at hand small flat stones are worked in, and the coating of the first year may be about four to five inches thick and every year an additional coat is added, until it is a foot, or more, in thickness. Grass then grows upon it, and it looks like a little knowl. The next work is to make Burrows of retreat; the first year seldom more than one, or two can be made, and sometimes none; these are carried on from a few inches below the surface of the water, direct from it, gradually rising, of about a foot in height by twenty inches in breadth, so that a Beaver can turn in them; their length depends of the easiness of digging the groun[d] the general length is about ten feet, but in good earth they often are of twenty feet, or more. The second and third year the number of Burrows are augmented [iv.140] to five or six, and where the Beaver have been a long time the Ponds, and small Lakes have numerous burrows.

The Indians think the Male and Female are faithful to each other, they bring up their young for the first year with care and protection, until the next spring when the female is about to litter she drives them all away, and some of them before they can be made to stay away, receive severe cuts on the back from the teeth of the old ones. The young Beavers are very playful and whimper like children. The Beaver is supposed to attain to the age of fifteen years, some think to twenty years. The Beaver hunter is often at a loss what to do, and sometimes passes a whole day without coming to a determination; his shortest and surest way, is to stake up the door way of the house, the stakes he carries with him ready for the purpose, but the Beaver are so watchful that his approach is heard and they retire to their burrows. Some prefer, first finding the burrows and closing them up with stakes and cutting off all retreat from the house; which ever method he takes, difficulties and hard labor attends him. To determine the place of the Beavers, for the whole family of seven, or nine, are seldom all found in the house, the

Indian is greatly assisted by a peculiar species of small Dog, of a light make, about three feet in height, muzzle sharp and brown full black eyes, with a round brown spot above each eye, the body black, the belly of a fawn color it's scent very keen, and almost unerring.[2] This Dog points out by smelling and scratching, the weakest part of the Beaver House, and the part where they lie. The same in the burrows, which is then doubly staked; the Indian with his Axe and Ice Chissel makes a hole over the place shown by [iv.141] the Dog, the Beaver has changed it's place, to find to which end of the burrow it is gone, a crooked stick is employed until it touches the Beaver; another hole is made, and the Beaver is killed with the Ice chissel, which has a heavy handle of about seven feet in length. When the dog smells and scratches at two, or three places on the Beaver House, it is a mark that there are several in it, the door way being doubly staked, the Indian proceeds to make a hole near the centre of it, to give full range to his ice chissel, and not one escapes, but all with hard labor; such was the manner of killing the Beaver until the introduction of Steel Traps, which baited with Castorum[3] soon brought on the almost total destruction of these numerous and sagacious animals.

[*fall of the leaves. Long Dam. 52 houses. two old Men. antiquity. punishment. tradition of infatuation. Steel Traps. Steel Traps and Castorum. result of their destruction*]

¶ From this long digression I return to my travels in the Nut Hill; on a fine afternoon in October,[1] the leaves beginning to fall with every breeze, a season to one of pleasing, melancholy, from the reflections it brings to the mind; my guide informed me, that we would have to pass over a long beaver Dam; I naturally expected we should be obliged to lead our horses carefully over it; when we came to it, we found it a narrow stripe of apparently old solid ground, with short grass, and wide enough for two horses to walk abreast; we passed on, the lower side showed a descent of seven feet, and steep, with a rill of water from beneath it. The side of the dam next to the water was a gentle slope. To the southward was a sheet of water of about one

---

2 For this breed, see note on iv.67 (123).

3 Castoreum is the orange-brown secretion of glands located in the beaver's perineum. On iv.145 (195–6), below, Thompson describes the effect of steel traps and castoreum on beaver trapping.

1 Probably 14 October 1797. On that day Thompson left Aspen House on the Assiniboine for Belleau's post on Snake Creek, a route that would have taken him across Duck Mountain. In his journal he records that he travelled "to the Rivulet, which we crossed with our Horses on a Beaver Dam." AO. 7.2r.

mile and a half square of area, surrounded by moderate, low, [iv.142] grassy banks, the Forests mostly of Aspin and Poplar but, very numerous stumps of the trees cut down and partly carried away by the Beavers. In two places of this Pond were a cluster of Beaver Houses, like miniature villages. When we had proceeded over more than half way of the Dam, which was a full mile in length, we came to an aged Indian, his arms folded across his breast, with a pensive countenance, looking at the Beavers swiming in the water, and carrying their winter's provision to their houses, his form tall and erect, his hair almost white, which was almost the only effect that age appeared to have on him, though we concluded he must be about eighty years of age, and in this opinion we were afterwards confirmed by the ease and readiness with which he spoke of times long past. I enquired of him, how many beaver houses there were in the Pond before us, he said, "there are now fifty two, we have taken several of their houses; they are difficult to take, and those we have taken were by means of the noise of the water on their houses from a strong wind which enabled us to stake them in, otherwise they would have retired to their burrows, which are very many." He invited us to pass the night at his tent which was close by, the Sun was low, and we accepted the offer.

In the Tent was an old, man, almost his equal in age, with women and children; we preferred the open air, and made a good fire, to which both of the old men came, and after smoking awhile conversation came on. As I had always conversed with the Natives as one Indian with another, and been attentive to learn their traditions on the animals on Mankind, and on other matter in ancient [iv.143] times, and the present occasion appeared favorable for this purpose. Setting aside questions and answers which would be tiresome; they said by ancient tradition of which they did not know the origen the Beavers had been an ancient people, and then lived on the dry land; they were always Beavers, not Men, they were wise and powerful, and neither Man, nor any animal made war on them.

"They were well clothed as at present, and as they did not eat meat, they made no use of fire, and did not want it. How long they lived this way we cannot tell, but we must suppose they did not live well, for the Great Spirit became angry with them, and ordered We sauk e jauk to drive them all into the water and there let them live, still to be wise, but without power; to be food and clothing for man, and the prey of other animals, against all which his defence shall be his dams, his house and his burrows:[2] You see

2 Some Algonquian myths assert that beavers had human origins, while others, like that Thompson heard, insist that beavers and humans had always been different species. The fur traders Alexander Henry the Elder and George Nelson both recorded

how strong he makes his dams, those that we make for fishing wiers are often destroyed by the water, but his always stands. His House is not made of sand, or loose stones, but of strong earth, with wood, and sometimes small stones, and he makes burrows to escape from his enemies, and he always has his winter stock of provisions secured in good time. When he cuts down a tree, you see how he watches it, and takes care that it shall not fall on him." "But if so wise, for what purpose does the Beaver cut down large trees of which he makes no use whatever." "We do not know, perhaps an itching of his teeth and gums."

Here the old Indian paused, became silent, and then [iv.144] in a low tone talked with each other. After which he continued his discourse. "I have told you that we believe in years long passed away, the Great Spirit was angry with the Beaver, and ordered Wee sauk e jauk (the Flatterer) to drive them all from the dry land into the water; and they became and continue very numerous: but the Great Spirit has been, and now is, very angry with them and they are now all to be destroyed; about two winters ago, Wee sauk e jauk showed to our brethren, the Nepissings and Algo[n]quins the secret of their destruction; that all of them were infatuated with the love of the Castorum of their own species; and more fond of it than we are of fire water: We are now killing the Beaver without any labor, we are now rich, but shall soon be poor, for when the Beaver are destroyed we have nothing to depend on to purchase what we want for our families, strangers now overrun our country with their iron traps, and we, and they will soon be poor:" The Indian is not a materialist, nor does he believe in Instinct, a word of civilized Man, which accounts for great part of the actions of Mankind, and of all those of animated nature; the Indian believes that every animal has a soul which directs all it's motions, and governs all it's actions; even a tree, he conceives must some how be animated, though it cannot stir from it's place.

¶ Some three years ago (1797)[3] the Indians of Canada and New Brunswick, on seeing the Steel Traps so successful in catching Foxes and other animals, thought of applying it to the Beaver instead of the awkward wooden traps they made, which often [iv.145] failed; At first they were set in the

Ojibwa versions of this myth. In the 1760s, Henry was told that beavers, having grown more intelligent than humans, had been deprived of the power of speech by the trickster Nenabozo, and in 1811 Nelson wrote down an account describing how a Native family had been transformed into the first beavers. For discussions of the beaver origin myth, see Nelson, *The Orders of the Dreamed*," ed. Brown and Brightman, 128–36; Brightman, *Grateful Prey*, 193.

3 I.e., in 1794.

landing paths of the Beaver, with about four inches of water on them, and a piece of green aspin for a bait, and in this manner more were caught than by the common way; but the beaver paths made their use too limited, and their ingenuity was employed to find a bait that would allure the Beaver to the place of the trap; various things and mixtures of ingredients were tried without success: but chance made some try if the male could not be caught by adding the Castorum of the female; a mixture of this Castorum beat up with the green buds of the Aspin, was made a piece of dry willow of about eight inches in length beat and bruised fine, was dipped in this mixture, it was placed at the water edge about a foot from the steel trap, so that the Beaver should pass direct over it and be caught; this bait proved successful; but to the surprise of the Indians, the females were caught as well as the males; The secret of this bait was soon spread; every Indian procured from the Traders four to six steel traps, the weight of one was about six to eight pounds; all labor was now at an end, the Hunter moved about at pleasure with his traps and infallible bait of Castorum.

¶ Of the infatuation of this animal for Castorum I saw several instances. A trap was negligently fastened by its small chain to the stake to prevent the Beaver taking away the trap when caught; it slipped, and the Beaver swam away with the trap, and it was looked upon as lost. Two nights after he was taken in a trap with the other trap fast to his thigh. Another time a Beaver passing over a Trap to get the Castorum, had his hind leg broke, with his teeth he cut his broken leg off, and went away, we concluded he would not come again [iv.146] but two nights afterwards, he was found fast in a trap. In every case the Castorum is taken away. The stick with this, was always licked, or sucked clean, and seemed to act as a suporific, as they remained more than a day, without coming out of their houses. The Nepissings, the Algonqui[n]s and Iroquois Indians having exhausted their own countries, now spread themselves over these countries, and as they destroyed the Beaver, moved forwards to the northward and westward; the Natives, the Nahathaways, did not in the least molest them;[4] the Chippaways and other tribes made use of Traps of Steel; and of the Castorum.

¶ For several years all these Indians were rich, the Women and Children, as well as the Men, were covered with silver brooches, Ear Rings, Wampum, Beads, and other trinkets. Their mantles were of fine scarlet cloth, and all was finery and dress. The Canoes of the Furr Traders were loaded with packs of Beaver, the abundance of the article lowered the London prices. Every

4 For the emigration of Iroquois and other eastern Natives to the West, see note on iv.250 (278).

intelligent Man saw the poverty that would follow the destruction of the Beaver, but there were no Chiefs to controul it; all was perfect liberty and equality. Four years after (1797)[5] almost the whole of these extensive countries were denuded of Beaver, the Natives became poor, and with difficulty procured the first necessaries of life, and in this state they remain, and probably for ever.[6] A worn out field may be manured, and again made fertile; but the Beaver, once destroyed cannot be replaced; they were the gold coin of the country, with which the necessaries of life were purchased.

It would be worth while for some Gentleman who has nothing to do; to look at the sales by auction; the number of skins by private sale; and otherwise disposed of, to count the number of Beavers that have been killed. [iv.147] and procured from the northern part of this Continent.

[*Stone Indian River, very sinuous &c*]

We now journeyed to a trading House in charge of Mr Thorburn,[1] in Latitude 50··28··58 N and Longitude 101-45·45 West, in a course S 7 E 68 Miles. Having settled the position of this place we proceeded down the Stone Indian River to the House in charge of Mr John McDonell,[2] in Latitude 49-40·56 N Longitude 99-27-15 West, on a course S 69 E 131 miles. These distances in a straight line are along the banks of the Stone Indian River, of about thirty

5 I.e., by 1801.
6 The sharp decline in beaver populations throughout subarctic North America in the last few years of the eighteenth century is well attested in contemporary sources. There is some disagreement about the cause; some writers, like Thompson, blame overintensive trapping, others the effects of an infectious disease. In May 1797, Cree hunters told George Sutherland at Edmonton House that there was a "distemper Among the Beaver of which great numbers have died." Edmonton House, Post Journal, 1796–1797, B.60/a/2: 24, HBCA. Peter Fidler reported that about 1800 "some disorder occasioned by the Change of Air ... suddenly reduced [the beaver]." Manetoba District Report, 1820, B.51/e/1: 6, HBCA. Calvin Martin suggests that the beaver may have fallen victim to a bacterial infection, such as tularemia. Calvin Martin, "Wildlife Diseases as a Factor in the Depopulation of the North American Indian," *Western Historical Quarterly* 7 (January 1976): 56–61.
1 This post on the Qu'Appelle River was built about 1787. Thompson left Grant's House for this post on 9 November and stayed here until 19 November. For NWC trader William Thorburn, see appendix 2.
2 Called either John Macdonnell's House or Assiniboine House, this post was on the north bank of the Assiniboine River. Thompson was there 23–28 November 1797. For NWC trader John Macdonnell, see appendix 2.

yards in breadth, but deriving it's water from rains and Snows, is of various depths; according to the seasons, in autumn always shoal. Its course is on the east side of the great Plains, and the south west side of the low Hills, from whence it receives several Brooks, and from the Plains the Calling River, and a few Brooks. Its course is very sinuous, this, and with it's shoals, detains the Canoes for the upper trading Houses to late in the season; From Mr Grant's to Mr John McDonell the distance is in a direct line near two hundred miles, which the windings of the River increases to near six hundred miles. This River every where flows thro' a pleasant country of good soil, and in time to come will no doubt, be covered with an agricultural population;

¶ The Bison, the Moose and Red Deer with two species of the Antelope, give to the Nahathaway Indians, an easy subsistence; but in a short time the only furrs they will have to buy the necessaries they want, and cannot now do without, are the Wolf Fox, Badger and Musk Rat, with the dried meat of the Bison and Deer. The Stone Indians, a numerous tribe of the Sieux Nation possess the country southward and [iv.148] westward of this River, to the Missisurie River, but this latter in common with several other Tribes, they are friendly to the white people, a fine looking race of Men and Women, but most noted Horse thieves of the Horses of other Tribes. It is said of a York-shire man "Give him a bridle, and he will find a horse;"[3] but these will find both the bridles and the Horses. We remained with Mr John McDonell twelve days; in which time I put my journal, su[r]veys and sketches of the countries that were in black lead into ink, and having sealed them up, directed them to the Agents of the North West Company.

[*set off for the Mandane Villages. Journey to the Missisourie. Men. Dogs. the cold weather & Gales. kill 4 or 5 Bisons. Tent smoky. Stone Ind. Lost in the Plains. severe Weather &c. send back two Horses. Stone Indians. hostility and advice. 15 Tents destroyed*]

¶ Having made our preparations for a journey to the Mandane Villages on the banks of the Missisourie River; on the 28th November 1797[1] we set off.

---

3 A stronger form of this proverb, originating in Lancashire, states, "Shake a bridle over a Yorkshireman's grave, and he will rise and steal a horse." Insults.net, "Historical Insults," Insults.net, http://www.insults.net/html/historical/curses_2.html.

1 For the journey to the Mandan-Hidatsa villages, which lasted from 28 November to 30 December 1797, see AO. 7.2b–8r; 9.124–118; W. Raymond Wood and Thomas D. Thiessen, ed., *Early Fur Trade on the Northern Plains: Canadian Traders among the Mandan and Hidatsa Indians, 1738–1818* (Norman: University of Oklahoma Press, 1985), 96–112. For an earlier *Travels* version of the journey, see iii.70–4 (Volume II).

Our guide and interpreter, who had resided eight years in their Villages was a Monsieur René Jussomme[2] who fluently spoke the Mandane Language. Mr Hugh McCrachan,[3] a good hearted, Irishman, who had been often to the Villages, and resided there for weeks and months; and seven french Canadians,[4] a fine, hardy, good humoured sett of Men, fond of full feeding, willing to hunt for it, but more willing to enjoy it. When I have sometimes reproved them, for what I thought Gluttony; eating full eight pounds of fresh meat per day, they have told me, that, their greatest enjoyment of life was Eating. They are all extremely ignorant, and without the least education, and appear to set no value on it. All these, except my servant man, A Brosseau who had been a soldier, were free traders on their own account for this journey; each of them, on credit from Mr McDonell, took a venture in goods and trinkets to the amount of forty to sixty skins to be paid in furrs, by [iv.149] trading with the natives of the Villages. I was readily supplied with every thing I required which was chiefly ammunition, tobacco, and a few trinkets for expenses. For my service I had two Horses. Monsieur Jussomme had one, and the men thirty dogs their own property, each two hauled a flat sled upon which their venture was lashed; these Dogs had all been traded from the Stone Indians, who make great use of them in their encampments. They were all like half dog, half wolf, and always on the watch to devour every thing they could get their teeth on; they did not willing work, and most of them had never hauled a flat sled, but the Canadians soon, break them in, by constant flogging, in which they seem to take great delight; when on the march the noise was intolerable, and made me keep two or three miles ahead.

¶ As my journey to the Missisourie is over part of the Great Plains, I shall give it in the form of a journal, this form, however dull, is the only method in my opinion, that can give the reader a clear idea of them. With our three Horses and thirty Dogs with their Sleds, we crossed the Stone River on the ice; the Snow on the ground was three inches in depth. We went about six miles and put up in the woods of the Mouse River, which joins the Stone Indian River about two miles below, the House. The dogs unused to hauling going any where, and every where from the Men, who employed themselves all the way, in swearing at, and flogging them; until we put up, when the Dogs were unharnessed, a piece of line tied round the neck of each, and one, or both fore feet were brought through it, to keep them quiet and from

2 For free trader René Jusseaume, see appendix 2.
3 For trader Hugh McCrachan, see appendix 2.
4 In his journal, Thompson names these French Canadian companions as Joseph Boisseau, Alexis Vivier, Pierre Gilbert, François Perrault, Toussaint Vaudril, Louis-Joseph Houl, and Jean-Baptiste Minie. AO. 9.125.

straying away. At 8 PM the Thermometer –20 degrees below zero. November 29th. A Westerly breeze at 7 AM –27 below zero, the Men thought it too cold to proceed. November 30th. 7 AM –32 being 64 degrees below [iv.150] the freezing point 9 PM –30 too cold to proceed over the open plains: and certainly an intensity of cold not known on the same parallel of Latitude near the Mountains. Necessity obliged us to hunt the Bison, we killed two Bulls, we could bring only half the meat to the Tent, which satisfied ourselves and the Dogs. December 1st. A WSW Gale. Thermometer –37. below Zero. We could not proceed but had the good fortune to kill a good Bison Cow which kept us in good humour. The severe cold and high wind made the Tent very smoky, so that, notwithstanding the bad weather, we walked about in the woods the greatest part of the day, and when in the Tent we had to lie down. December 2nd. At 8 AM Thermometer –36 at 8 PM –15 the wind WSW. We killed a Bison Cow, which kept the Dogs quiet. December 3rd – At 8 AM –3 at 8 PM –3 the weather was now mild but a WNW Gale came on with snow and high drift that we could not see a fourth of a mile from us, and our journey is over open plains from one patch of Wood to another patch; for the Mouse River, on which we are camped, has Woods only in places, and many miles distant from each other, and these patches of Wood must be kept in sight to guide over the plains and none of the Men knew the use of the Compass, and did not like to trust to it. We could not proceed and the Tent was disagreeable with smoke.

¶ December 4th. 7 AM +4 above Zero. WSW gale of Wind. At 9 AM we set off, and went eleven miles to a grove of Oaks, Ash, Elm,[5] Nut Trees, and other hard Woods; which are always the Woods of this River; At this place we [iv.151] came to five Tents of Stone Indians, whom as usual, received us with kindness; they did not approve of our journey to the Missisourie; and informed us, that some skirmishes had taken place between the Mandane and Sieux Indians in which the latter lost several Men; which they attributed to the Ammunition furnished to the former by the trading parties from the Stone Indian River, such as ours were; and that they had determined to way lay us, and plunder us of all we had, and also take all our scalps, and warned us to be on our guard; I did not like this news, but the Men paid no attention to it, thinking it proceeded from hatred to the Mandanes. We then followed the River banks for seven miles, and camped at 4 PM. The River is about twenty yards wide, at present the water very low. December 5th. 7 AM Thermometer –13 below zero, became mild, in the afternoon a WSW Gale came on and increased to a Storm by 6 PM. Monsieur Jussomme our Guide,

---

5 American elm (*Ulmus americana*).

informed us, that he would now take the great traverse to the Turtle Hill;[6] we were early up, and by 7½ AM set off; he led us about South four miles to a small grove of Aspins on the banks of a brook thence about six miles to the Turtle Brook from the Hill; thence S by W seven miles; we now came on a rising ground at 1 PM, but the Turtle Hill was not in sight; and all before, and around us, a boundless plain: and Monsieur Jussomme could not say where we were; the weather appeared threatening and preparing for a Storm; our situation was alarming: and anxiety in the face of every man, for we did not know to which hand to turn ourselves for shelter: I mounted my Horse and went to the highest ground near us, and with my telescope viewed the horizon all around, but [iv.152] not the least vestige of woods appeared; but at due North West from us, where there appeared the tops of a few Trees, like Oaks. They anxiously enquired if I saw Woods. I told them what I had seen, and that with my old Soldier[7] I should guide myself by the Compass, and directly proceed as the Woods were far off; McCrachan and a Canadian joined us; the other six conferred among themselves what to do, they had no faith in the Compass on land, and thought best to march in some direction until they could see woods with their own eyes: but we had not proceeded half a mile before all followed us, thinking there would be a better chance of safety by being all together. The Gale of Wind came on, and kept increasing the Snow was four to six inches in depth with a slight crust on it. We held on almost in despair of reaching the Woods, fortunately the Dogs were well broke in and gave us no trouble. Night came upon us, and we had carefully to keep in file, at times calling to each other to learn that none were missing. At length at 7 PM, thank good Providence, we arrived at the Woods, very much fatigued, walking against the Storm was as laborious as walking knee deep in water. We got up our tent and placed ourselves under shelter. Although we had taken six hours on this last course, yet I found by my Observations we had come only thirteen miles.

¶ December 6th. A heavy westerly gale of wind with mild weather. The Horses and Dogs as well as ourselves were too much fatigued to proceed. Two Bison Bulls were killed, though very tough, kept away hunger and fed the Dogs. December 7th. At 7 AM Thermometer +25, only five degrees below the freezing point, a fine mild day. We proceeded five miles up the Mouse River to an old trading House, called "Ash House" from the plenty of these fine Trees; it had to be given up, from it's being too [iv.153] open to the incur-

6 Turtle Mountain, on what is now the Canada–United States border.
7 I.e., Boisseau.

sions of the Sieux Indians.[8] Two Stone Indians came to us, they said their camp was not far off. Monsieur Jussomme's Mare and my yellow Horse had both become lame of each one foot, and could proceed no further through the Plains, each of these Horses had one white foot and three black feet. The white foot of each was lame in the same manner, the hair of the white foot was worn away by the hard snow, and a small hole in the flesh close above the hoof, the three black feet had not a hair off them, my other Horse was dark brown with four black feet. As the Horses of this country have no shoes, the colour of the hoof is much regarded; the yellow hoof with white hair is a brittle hoof and soon wears away; for this reason, as much as possible the Natives take only black hoofed Horses on their War expeditions. As the camp of Stone Indians were going to the House of Mr John McDonell to trade we delivered the Horses to the care of an old Indian to be taken to the House. Monsieur Jussomme was now without a Horse and had to purchase Dogs. December 8th. 7 AM Thermometer –18 below Zero, a cold day, which was employed in hunting, without success. I observed for Latitude and Longitude. December 9th. 7 AM Thermometer –26 below zero. We went up the River SWd 7½ miles to eight tents of Stone Indians; who treated us with hospitality, and each of [us] got a good meal. Learning that we were going to the Missisourie, they warned us to beware of the Sieux Indians, whom they thought would lie in wait for us at the Dog Tent Hills,[9] and keep on our guard against a surprise. We offered a high reward to a young man to guide us to the Mandane Villages, but however tempting the offer, neither himself, nor any other would accept the offer, they plainly told us, that we might expect to find the Sieux [iv.154] Indians on our road; and they were not on good terms with the Mandanes. We went about three miles and put up, in view of the Turtle Hill. We are near the place, where in 1794, fifteen Tents of Stone Indians were destroyed by a large War Party of Sieux Indians, although of the same Nation.

From their own accounts, some forty or fifty years ago a feud broke out, and several were killed and wounded on both sides; about five hundred Tents separated from the main body, and took up their hunting grounds on the Red River and the Plains stretching north westward along the right bank of the Saskatchewan River to within 300 miles of the Mountains, and being in

8 The North West Company established Ash House, or Fort du Frêne, in 1795 on the north bank of the Souris. As Thompson reports, the post was abandoned the following year. G.A. McMorran, "Souris River Posts in the Hartney District," in Manitoba Historical Society, *Transactions*, series 3, 5 (1948–49): 46–62.

9 Now known as Dog Den Butte. Thompson passed this feature on 24–25 December.

alliance, and strict confederacy with the Nahathaways, who accompanied them to war they were powerful, and with their allies, made their brethren, the Sieux Nation, feel the Weight of their resentment for several years, until the small pox of 1782 came, which involved them all in one common calamity, and very much reduced the numbers of all parties. The Sieux had lost several of their Men, who went to hunt but did not return, and suspicion fell on the Stone Indians and their allies. They determined on revenge, and the destruction of these fifteen Tents was the result. The Sieux afterwards found the loss of their Men was by the Chippeways, their never ceasing enemies, and deeply regretted what they had done, the old Men made an apology, and proffered peace which was accepted in 1802, and a reunion took place; and in this Peace, their allies and [iv.155] confederates were included; and which continues to this day.[10]

[*cross to the Turtle Hill. heavy Storm. One Man missing, recovered. 2 dogs and Sled lost. along the Turtle Hill. to the Mouse River. Indian advice. Stormy Region. No Deer nor Birds. hunting. Elbow of Mouse River. cross to the Dog Tent Hill. Sieux seen. Dog Tent Hills, prepare to cross the Plains. arrive at the Missisourie*]

¶ December 10th. 7 AM Thermometer –20 below Zero; The hummock of Woods on the Turtle Hill, which was our mark, gave our course by the compass S 30° E. As we had to cross a plain of twenty two miles, and having felt the severe changes of weather, I desired the Men to follow close in file, for they now had faith in the Compass. At 7½ AM our bit of a caravan set off; as the Dogs were fresh, we walked at a good pace for some time, a gentle south wind arose; and kept increasing; by 10 AM it was a heavy Gale, with high drift and dark weather, so much so, that I had to keep the Compass in my hand, for I could not trust to the Wind, by Noon, it was a perfect Storm, we had no alternative but to proceed, which we did slowly and with great labor, for the Storm was ahead, and the snow drift in our faces. Night came on, I could no longer see the Compass and had to trust to the Wind; the weather became mild with small rain, but the Storm continued with darkness; some

10 Thompson's is one of many accounts of the formation of the Assiniboine as a distinct group. While clear historical evidence is scant, it is now believed that the split between the Assiniboine and the Yanktonai took place before the seventeenth century. Raymond J. DeMallie and David Reed Miller, "Assiniboine," HNAI, vol. 13, 1:572–93; Binnema, *Common and Contested Ground*, 155. Hostilities between the Assiniboine and the Sioux were frequent during the eighteenth century.

of the foremost called to lie down where we were, but as it was evident we were ascending a gentle rising ground, we continued, and soon, thank good Providence, my face struck against some Oak saplings, and I passed the word that we were in the Woods, a fire was quickly made, and as it was on an elevated place it was seen afar off; as yet the only one with me was my servant who led the Horse, and we anxiously waited the others; they came hardly able to move, one, and then another, and in something more than half an hour, nine had arrived; each with Dogs and Sleds, but one Man, and a Sled with the Dogs were missing; to search for the latter was useless; but how to find the former we [iv.156] were at a loss; and remained so for another half an hour, when we thought we heard his voice, the Storm was still rageing, we extended ourselves within call of each other, the most distant man heard him plainly, went to him, raised him up, and with assistance brought him to the fire, and we all thanked the Almighty for our preservation. He told us he became weak, fell several times and at length he could not get up, and, resigned himself to perish in the storm, when by chance, lifting up his head he saw the fire, this gave him courage; stand he could not but shuffled away on hands and knees through the snow, bawling with all his might, until we fortunately heard him. We threw the Tent over some Oak saplings and got under shelter from showers of rain, hail and sleet. At 7½ PM Thermometer +36, being four degrees above the freezing point; by a south wind making, in little more than twelve hours a difference of temperature of fifty six degrees. I had weathered many a hard gale, but this was the most, distressing day I had yet seen.

December 11th. At 8 AM Thermometer +37, being five degrees above the freezing point. A south gale with showers of snow. A mild day, but we were all too tired to proceed. A fine grove of Aspins was within thirty yards, which the the darkness prevented us seeing; we removed our Tent to it. The Dogs and Sled missing belonged to Francis Hoole and the value of sixty skins in goods, with all his things were on it; but none would accompany him to look for it, although he offered the half of all that was on it; so much was the chance of the similar distress of yesterday dreaded. December 12th Thermometer +30 two degrees below the freezing point, Wind a SSW gale. We went eight miles along the north side of the [iv.157] Turtle Hill and put up. We were all very hungry, and the Dogs getting weak; we had seriously to attend to hunting; a small herd of Bulls were not far off, and three of us went off to them, the two that were with me were to approach by crawling to them, and if they missed, I was to give chase on horseback, for which I was ready; after an hour spent in approaching them, they both fired, but without effect, the herd started, I gave chase, came up with them, and shot a tolerable good Bull; This is the usual manner of hunting the Bison by the Indians of the Plains: This gave us provisions for the present and the Dogs feasted on the offall.

December 13th. At 7 AM Thermometer –15 below zero, clear weather with a north gale and high drift, we could not proceed, but as usual in clear weather I observed for Latitude, Longitude and the Variation of the Compass. We took the case of Francois Hoole into consideration who had lost his Dogs and all his venture; and each of us agreed to give him goods to the value of two beavers, and haul it for him, which gave him a venture of eighteen skins, and the Irishman McCrachan, and myself, doubled it, for it was out of his power to return alone. December 14th. At 7 AM Thermometer –18 below zero. At 8 AM set off, and kept along the Hill to shorten as much as possible the wide Plain we have to cross to the Mouse River; we proceeded in a SE course about seventeen miles; and put up, the day fine, though cold; As this was the last place where Poles to pitch the Tent could be got, we cut the number required of dry Aspin to take with us.

December 15th. At 7 AM Thermometer –21 below zero. Having no provisions, part of the Men went a hunting, and managed to kill an old Bull, who preferred fighting to running away; after boiling a piece of it for three hours, it was still too tough to be eaten, but by those who have sharp [iv.158] teeth, the tripe of a Bull is the best part of the animal.

December 16th. at 7 AM Thermometer –19 below zero. We could go no further along the Turtle Hill, and had to cross a wide Plain to a grove of Oaks on the Mouse River, the wind blowing a North Gale with drift, the Men were unwilling to proceed having suffered so much, but as wind was on our backs, I perswaded them to follow me, and at 8-20 AM we set, and safely arrived at the Grove: our course S by W nineteen miles. On our way we fortunately killed a fat Cow Bison, which was a blessing, for we had not tasted a bit of good meat for many days, and we had nothing else to subsist on. In the evening our conversation turned upon the Sieux way laying us; for we were approaching the Dog Tent Hills, where we were to expect them; and our situation with so many Dogs and loaded Sleds to take care of, was in a manner defenceless; but we had proceeded too far to return, my hopes lay in the lateness of the season, and the effects the stormy weather must have on a War Party, who frequently take no Tents with them: The last camp of Stone Indians advised us to leave the usual road; cut wood, and haul it with us to make a fire for two nights, and boldly cross to the Missisourie, which could be done in three days but this was too much dreded to be followed. In the evening a very heavy gale came on from the NWd we were thankful that we had crossed the Plain, and were well sheltered in a grove of tall Oaks. December 17th. At 7 AM Thermometer –22 below zero, at 9 AM Thermometer –23 [iv.159] below zero. NW Gale with snow drift, too cold to proceed.

December 18th. At 7 AM Thermometer –32 below zero. 2 PM –7 below zero, too cold to proceed although a fine clear day. We saw a herd of Cows about a mile from the tent, we crawled to them, and killed three, then went to the Tent, harnessed the Dogs to bring the meat, while we were busy, a dreadful Storm came on, fortunately an aft wind, had it been a head wind, we could not have reached the Tent. December 19th At 7 AM Thermometer –17 below zero. 9 PM –24 below zero. All day a dreadful Storm from the westward, with high drift, the Sky was as obscure as night, the roaring of the wind was like the waves of the stormy sea on the rocks. It was a terrible day, in the evening the Storm abated. My Men attribute these heavy gales of wind, and their frequency to the lateness of the season; but this cannot be the cause, for no such stormy winds are known to the westward; here are no hills worth notice, all is open to the free passage of the winds from every quarter, for my part I am utterly at a loss, to account for such violent winds on this part of the Plains and this may account for the few Bisons we have seen, and the smallness of the herds, which rarely exceed twenty; whereas to the westward, and near the Mountains the ground is covered with them, and hitherto we have not seen the track of a Deer, and even a Wolf is a rare animal as for Birds we have seen none: even the long, strong winged Hawks are not known. What can be the cause of these Storms, and the severe cold of this country. Our Latitude is now 48··9··16 North, Longitude 100°··34'··12" West, which ought to have a milder climate.

December 20th. At 7 AM –41 below zero. NNW breeze, though very cold, yet a fine day. At 9½ AM we set off, and went up along the Mouse River, about South, thirteen miles [iv.160] and at 3½ PM put up close to the River. The Woods are of Oak, Ash, Elm, and some other hard woods, mixed with Poplar and Aspin but no Pines: When the grass is set on fire in the summer, which is too often the case, all the above woods, except the Aspin, have a thick coat of Bark around them, to which the grass does little, or no injury; but the thin bark of the Aspin however slightly scorched, prevents the growth of the Tree, and it becomes dry, and makes the best of fuel, having very little smoke. December 21st. A stormy morning with snow to 11 AM then clear and fine. We could not proceed as Hugh McCrachan was taken ill. An old Bull was killed for the Dogs. At 7 PM Thermometer –26 below zero. December 22nd. At 7 AM Thermometer –32 below zero, NW breeze and clear, keen cold day. At 8½ AM we set off, still following up the River, SSwd for fifteen miles and put up. Where there are Woods along this River; they are in narrow ledges of forty, to one hundred yards in width, all the rest are the boundless Plains. December 23rd. A cloudy, cold day, with snow until noon, when it became fine and clear. We set off up along the River SW twelve miles and camped; Three Men went ahead to hunt, they killed four Bulls, no Cows in sight. We have now plenty to eat, but very tough meat, so much so, we get fairly tired with eating before we can get a belly full. We are now at the Elbow of the Mouse River and can follow it no farther; as the River now comes from the north westward and is mostly bare of Woods.[1] Although now a small Stream of fifteen yards in breadth, it has every where, like all the Rivers of the Plains, double banks; the first bank is that which confines the Stream of water, and generally about ten to twenty feet in height; then on [iv.161] each side is a level of irregular breadth; generally called, Bottom, of thirty to six hundred yards in breadth, from which rises steep, grassy sloping banks to the heights of sixty to one hundred feet which is the common level of the Plain, large Rivers have often three banks to the level of the Plain. It is in these Bottoms that the Trees grow, and are sheltered from the Storms: for on the level of the Plain, it is not possible a tree can grow but where the Bottoms are wide enough, the Trees come to perfection. Here I measured Oaks of eighteen feet girth, tall and clean grown, the Elm, Ash, Beech, and Bass Wood, with Nut Trees were in full proportion, for these Bottoms have a rich soil from the overflowing of the River.

December 24th. Wind south, a steady breeze, with low drift, fine mild weather. At 8½ AM we set off, and – went ESE ½ a mile to the heights of the River; and in sight of the Dog Tent Hill; our course to a Ravine was S 48 W 19 miles; across a plain, the ground was undulating in form, without any regular vallies; but has many knowls; as we approached the Hill, we anxiously kept our eyes on it's being the place the Sieux Indians were to way lay us: About 2 PM, I perceived something moving on the ridge of the hill, and by my Telescope, saw a number of Horseman riding to the southward; I made signs to the men to lie down which they did, after watching their motions for about ten minutes; I saw plainly they did not see us, and rode descending the west side of the Hill, and were soon out of sight; thus [iv.162] kind Providence, by the Storms, and lateness of the season saved our lives and property. About a Month after, the Stone Indians informed Mr McDonell, that the above with the want of provisions were the occasion of their leaving the Hill; and they would return. From the eastward the Dog Tent Hill (by the Stone Indians Sungur Teebe) has the appearance of an irregular bank of about 200 feet above the level of the east Plains, in steep slopes of hard gravelly soil;

1 The "Elbow" is the southwest meander of the Souris River.

with nine or ten gullies, or ravines, each has a small spring of water, with a few Oak and Elm Trees in their bottoms; we put up at 4½ PM at the western spring and it's few trees of Oak and Elm. At 7 PM Thermometer –15 below zero.

December 26th. 7 AM Thermometer –16 below zero. Noon Thermometer –2. at 8 PM +2 above zero. Early a terrible Storm arose from SSWd and raged all day; the sound of the wind was like the waves of the sea on a shoal shore. Joseph Houle, killed a good Cow but could only bring some of the meat on his back. December 27th. At 7 AM Thermometer +5 at Noon +20 at 9 PM +25 above zero. The day was clear with a heavy gale from WSW. We could not proceed and had no success in hunting. We cut firewood to take with us; for we had learned the Mandanes and Pawnees, were hostile to each [other], and a large Village of the latter, was but a short distance below the former, and it was to this Village we were journeying; and having very frequently conversed with Messrs Jussomme and McCrachan, on the Roads, the customs and manners of the several Tribes of Indians of these countries I became acquainted with what we had to expect; in our defence less state I was determined to avoid any collision with the Natives [iv.163] that were hostile to us, and with the consent of all the Men, took the resolution to come on the Missisourie River several miles above the lower Mandane Village, and to do this we had a march of two days across the open Plains. December 28th. At 7 AM Thermometer +20 above zero. A fine clear mild day, thank God. At 7½ AM we set off taking firewood and Tent poles with us, and proceeded S 40 W 22 miles and at 4½ PM, pitched our Tent to pass the night. The ground, we passed over is far from being level, and with six inches of snow, made tiresome walking; we saw but few Bisons; and about an hour before we put up, saw ten or twelve Horsemen far on our left. The night was fine.

December 29th. A very fine mild day. At 7··20' AM we set off, and seeing the heights of the Missisourie, changed our course to S 25 W 15 miles, to, and down, the heights of the River; and at 3½ PM put up close to the Stream in a fine bottom of hard wood. The country hilly and tiresome walking; we lost much time, partly in viewing the country, but more so in bringing back the Dogs from running after the Bisons, of which there were many herds; An old Bull disdained to run away, but fortunately attacked the Sled, instead of the Dogs, and would soon have had it in pieces had not the Men made him move off, run he would not. About two miles from the River two Fall Indians[2] came to us, and killed a good Bull for us; The River is frozen over, it's width 290 yards but the water is low. The woods the same as those on

2 Thompson's term for the Hidatsa.

the Mouse River, with Poplar, Aspin and Birch all of good growth. December 30th. A northerly gale with cloudy weather. At 7-40' AM we set off and walked partly on the River ice, and partly on the Bottoms S b E 6 miles to the upper Village of the [iv.164] Fall Indians:[3] S 27 E 7 Miles to the principal Village of these people.[4] SE 1½ mile to another Village,[5] thence S 11 E 2 miles to the fourth Village[6] and S 55 E one mile to the principal Village of the Mandanes.[7]

[*Villages and Neighbours. Mandanes & Fall Indians. Houses. population. Weapons & defence. Domestic habits. Horses few*][1]

Thus from bad weather, we have taken thirty three days, to perform a journey of ten days in good weather. The distance we have gone is 238 miles but has given me the opportunity of determining the Latitude of six different places; and the Longitude of three, on the Road, to the River. Three of the

3 The name of this Hidatsa winter village is not known.
4 Big Hidatsa.
5 Sakakawea Village.
6 Black Cat.
7 Deapolis. The ancestors of the Siouan-speaking Mandan and Hidatsa had founded agricultural villages along the Missouri by about 1100. These villages became a focal point for Plains trade, drawing commerce from several Native groups, as well as from fur trade posts to the north and east and Spanish settlements to the southwest. During the eighteenth century, European interest in the Mandan was magnified by intense speculation about their cultural origins. It was suggested that their agrarian way of life and reputed fair complexion indicated descent from a lost medieval European colony (often identified as Norse or Welsh). Mandan settlements on the Heart River were visited by La Vérendrye and his sons between 1738 and 1743. The smallpox epidemic of the early 1780s led the Mandan to abandon the Heart River villages and take up residence at the confluence of the Knife and Missouri Rivers, where they settled among the Hidatsa. European visitors became frequent during the 1790s, and the Mandan and Hidatsa hosted the expedition of Lewis and Clark during the winter of 1804–05. Roy W. Meyer, *The Village Indians of the Upper Missouri: The Mandans, Hidatsas, and Arikaras* (Lincoln, NE: University of Nebraska Press, 1977); W. Raymond Wood and Lee Irwin, "Mandan," *HNAI*, vol. 13, 1:349–64; Binnema, *Common and Contested Ground*, 66.
1 Thompson stayed at the Mandan-Hidatsa villages from 30 December 1797 to 10 January 1798. For Thompson's journals of this time, see AO. 7.8r–9v; 9.118–116; Wood and Thiessen, *Early Fur Trade*, 112–18. For an earlier *Travels* version of the stay, see iii.75–81 (Volume II).

Men staid at the Fall Indian Villages; one with Manoah a frenchman who has long resided with these people;[2] the rest of us came to the great Village; and at different Houses took up our quarters. The inhabitants of these Villages, have not been many years on the banks of the Missisourie River, their former residence was on the head waters of the southern branches of the Red River; and also along it's banks; where the soil is fertile and easy worked with their simple tools, southward of them were the Villages of the Pawnees,[3] with whom they were at peace, except occasional quarrels; south eastward of them were the Sieux Indians, although numerous, their stone headed arrows could do little injury; on the north east were the Chippeways in possession of the Forests; but equally weak until armed with Guns, iron headed arrows and spears; The Chippaways silently collected in the Forests; and made war on the nearest Village, destroying it with fire, when the greater part of the Men were hunting at some distance, or attacking the Men when hunting, and thus haressing them whenever they thought proper, the mischief done, they retreated into the forests, where it was too [iv.165] dangerous to search for them. The Chippaways had the policy to harrass and destroy the Village nearest to them, leaving the others in security; The people of this Village removed westward from them, and from stream to Stream, the Villages in succession, until they gained the banks of the Missisourie; where they have built their Villages and remain in peace from the Chippaways, the open Plains being their defence.

¶ Monsieur Jussome introduced me to a Chief called the "Big White Man"; which well designated him;[4] and told him I was one of the chiefs of the white men, and did not concern myself with trade, which somewhat surprised

2 This man, surnamed Ménard, arrived at the Mandan-Hidatsa villages some time between 1778 and 1783. For Thompson's visit to Ménard, see iv.170, below (214). Contrary to what Thompson writes there, Ménard was murdered by an Assiniboine party as he was returning from the Assiniboine River to the Mandan-Hidatsa villages in the fall of 1804. Wood and Thiessen, *Early Fur Trade*, 43–5.

3 The traditional home of the Pawnee was the valleys of the Platte, Loup, and Republican Rivers. Primarily an agricultural people like the Mandans, they supplemented their economy with the bison hunt. In 1806 there were approximately 6,000 Pawnee. Douglas R. Parks, "Pawnee," *HNAI*, vol. 13, 1:515–47.

4 Shahaka (c. 1765–c. 1815) was the chief at Deapolis. In 1804 he welcomed the Lewis and Clark expedition, and in 1806 he went east with the explorers, visited Washington and Philadelphia, and had an audience with President Thomas Jefferson at Monticello. He returned to his people in 1809. Carl Waldman, ed., *Biographical Dictionary of American Indian History to 1900*, rev. edn. (New York: Checkmark, 2001), 346, s.v. "Shahaka."

him, until told that my business, was to see the countries, converse with the Natives, and see how they could be more regularly supplied with Arms; Ammunition and other articles they much wanted; this he said would be very good; as some times they were many days without ammunition. Our things were taken in, and to myself and my servant Joseph Boisseau, was shown a bed for each of us. My curiosity was excited by the sight of these Villages containing a native agricultural population; the first I had seen and I hoped to obtain much curious information of the past times of these people; and for this purpose, and to get a ready knowledge of their manners and customs Messieurs Jussomme and McCrachen accompanied me to every Village but the information I obtained fell far short of what I expected; both of those who accompanied me were illiterat, without any education, and either did not understand my questions, or the Natives had no answers to give.

¶ I shall put [iv.166] together what I saw, and what I learned. In company with those I have mentioned; we examined the Villages and counted the houses. The upper Village has thirty one Houses and seven Tents of Fall Indians. The Village next below is called the great Village of the above people, it contains eighty two Houses, is situated on the Turtle River,[5] a short distance above it's confluence with the Missisourie. The next Village has fifty two Houses, and is also on the Turtle River; This Village was the residence of Manoah, a few houses were of Fall Indians, the other Houses were of Mandanes. The fourth Village was on the right bank of the Missisourie, of forty houses of Mandanes. The fifth and last Village contained One hundred and thirteen houses of Mandanes. Except the upper Village of the Fall Indians they were all strongly stockaded with Posts of Wood often to twelve inches diameter; about two feet in the ground and ten feet above it, with numerous holes to fire through; they went round the Village, in some places close to the houses; there were two door ways to each of the Stockades, on opposite sides; wide enough to admit a Man on Horseback, I saw no doors, or gates, they are shut up when required, with Logs of wood.

The houses were all of the same architecture; the form of each, and every one was that of a dome, regularly built, the house in which I resided; was one of the largest; the form a circle, probably drawn on the ground, and about six feet above it, all inclining inwards; bound together on the top by circular pieces of wood, on the outside of about five inches, and [iv.167] on the inside about three inches, in width; and in these were also inserted the lower end of another sett of boards of about five feet in length; and bound together on their tops in the same manner, but inclining inwards at a greater angle than

5 The Knife River.

the lower tier; and thus in succession, each tier the boards were shorter, and more inclined inwards, until they were met at the top, by a strong circular piece of wood of about three feet diameter; to which they were fastened; and which served to admit the light and let out the smoke; The house in which I lodged was about forty feet in diameter; and the height of the dome about eighteen feet. On the outside, it was covered with earth in a dry state to the depth of four or five inches, and made firm and compact. Every house was covered in the same manner. Between each house was a vacant space of fifteen to thirty feet. They appeared to have no order, otherwise than, each house occupying a diameter of thirty to forty feet; and a free space round it of an average of twenty feet. On looking down on them from the upper bank of the River, they appeared like so many large hives clustered together; From what I saw, and the best information I could get, the average population of each house was about ten souls. The houses of the Mandanes had not many children; but it was otherwise with the Fall Indians: the former may be taken at eight soul[s], and the latter, at ten, to each House. This will give to the Mandanes for 190 houses, a population of 1520 souls; of which they may muster about 220 warriors. The Fall Indians of 128 houses, and seven tents have a population of 1330 souls, of which 190 are warriors: the whole military force of these Villages may be about 400 men fit for war. I have heard their force estimated at 1000 men, but this was for [iv.168] want of calculation.

¶ The native Arms, were much the same as those that do not know the use of Iron, Spears and Arrows headed with flint; which they gladly lay aside for iron; they appear to have adopted the Spear as a favorite weapon, it is a handle of about eight feet in length, headed with a flat iron bayonet; of nine to ten inches in length, sharp pointed, from the point regularly enlarging to four inches in width, both sides sharp edged; the broad end had a handle of iron of about four inches in length, which is inserted in the handle, and bound with small cords; it is a formidable weapon in the hands of a resolute man. Their Guns were few in proportion to the number of Men for they have no supplies, but what are brought to them by small parties of Men, trading on their own account, such as the party with me; we had ten guns, of which the Men traded seven; and parties of Men of the Hudson's Bay Company in the same manner. They had Shields of Bulls hide a safe defence against arrows and the spear, but of no use against balls.

¶ They enquired how we built our houses, as they saw me attentively examining the structure of theirs; when informed; and drawing a rough plan of our Villages, with Streets parallel to each other, and cross Streets at right angles; after looking at it for some time; they shook their heads, and said, "In these straight Streets we see no advantage the inhabitants have over their enemies, the whole of their bodies are exposed, and the houses can be set on fire; which our houses cannot be, for the earth cannot burn; our houses being round shelter us except when we fire down on them, and we are high above them; the enemies have never been able to hurt us when we are in our Villages; and it is [iv.169] only when we are absent on large hunting parties that we have suffered; and which we shall not do again."[6] The Sieux Indians have several times on a dark stormy night, set fire to the Stockades; but this had no effect on the houses. Their manner of building and disposition of the houses, is probably the best, for they build for security, not for convenience.

¶ The floor of the house is of earth, level and compact; there is only one door to each house, this is a frame of wood, covered with a parchment Bison skin; of six feet by four feet; so as to admit a horse. To each door was a covered porch of about six feet, made and covered like the door: On entering the door, on the left sit's the master of the house and his wife; on a rude kind of sofa: covered with Bison Robes; and before is the fire, in a hollow of a foot in depth; and at one side of the fire is a Vase of their pottery, or two, containing pounded maize, which is frequently stirred with a stick, and now, and then about a small spoonful of fine ashes put in, to act as salt; and makes good pottage;[7] when they boil meat it is with only water; and the broth is drank; we saw no dried meat of any kind; and their houses are not adapted for curing meat by smoke for although the fire is on one side of the house, and not under the aperture, yet there is not the least appearance of smoke, and the light from the aperture of the dome gave sufficient light within the house. Around the walls, frame bed places were fastened, the bottom three feet from the ground; covered with parchment skins of the Bison, with the hair on, except the front, which was open, for a bed, was a Bison robe, soft and comfortable. On the right hand side of the door, were separate Stalls for Horses; every morning the young men take the Horses to grass, and watch over them to the evening, when they are brought [iv.170] in, and get a portion of maize: which keeps them in good condition; but in proportion to the population the Horses are few; the Chief with whom I lodged had only three.

6 This discussion of town design continues the *Travels'* theme of juxtaposition of Native and European culture. Ironically, when Shahaka returned to Deapolis in 1809, his descriptions of life in the cities of the East were not believed; discredited, he lost his former status. Waldman, ed., "Shahaka."

7 Soup or stew.

They do not require so many horses as the Indians of the Plains who frequently move from place to place, yet even for the sole purpose of hunting their Horses are too few.

[*Manoah. tradition. Agriculture. Rooks &c. Domestic habits. murder, law of. dress and dancing. Mandane dances & ceremony*]

¶ We paid a visit to Manoah, a french canadian, who had resided many years with these people; he was a handsome man, with a native woman, fair and graceful, for his wife, they had no children; he was in every respect as a Native. He was an intelligent man, but completely a Frenchman, brave, gay and boastfull; with his gun in one hand and his spear in the other, he stood erect, and recounted to the Indians about us all his warlike actions, and the battles in which he had borne a part, to all of which, as a matter of course, they assented. From my knowledge of the Indian character, it appeared, to me he could not live long, for they utterly dislike a boastful man. I learned, that a few years after, coming from a Skirmish, he praised his own courage and conduct and spoke with some contempt of the courage of those with him, which they did not in the least deserve, and for which he was shot.

¶ As Manoah was as a Native with them I enquired if they had any traditions of ancient times; he said, he knew of none beyond the days of their great, great Grandfathers, who formerly possessed, all the Streams of the Red River, and head of the Mississippe, where the Wild Rice and the Deer were plenty, but then the Bison and the Horse were not known to them; On all these Streams they had Villages and cultivated the ground as now; they lived many years this way how many they do not know, at length the Indians of the Woods, armed with guns which killed and frightened them, and iron weapons, frequently attacked them, and against these they had no defence; but were obliged to quit [iv.171] their villages; and remove from place to place until they came to the Missisourie River, where our fathers made Villages,[1] and the Indians of the Woods no longer attacked us: but the lands here are not so good, as the lands our fathers left, we have no wild rice, except in a few Ponds, not worth attention. Beyond this tradition, such as it is I could learn nothing. They at present, as perhaps they have always done, subsist mostly on the produce of their agriculture; and hunt the Bison and Deer, when these animals are near them, they have no other flesh meat; and

---

1 Here Thompson slips from third-person to first-person narration. The speaker is presumably Ménard, although he cannot have been referring literally to his own ancestors.

the skins of these animals serves for clothing; The grounds they cultivate are the alluvials of the River, called Bottoms. The portion to each family is allotted by a council of old Men, and is always more than they can cultivate, for which they have but few implements; The Hoe and the pointed Stick hardened in the fire are the principal.

They have but few Hoes of iron; and the Hoe in general use is made of the shoulder blade bone of the Bison, or Deer, the latter are preferred; they are neatly fitted to a handle, and do tolerable well in soft ground.

The produce they raise is mostly Maize (Indian Corn) of the small red kind, with other varieties all of which come to perfection, with Pumpkins and a variety of small Beans. Melons have been raised to their full size and flavor, every article seen in their villages were in clean good order, but the want of iron implements limits their industry; yet they raise, not only enough for themselves, but also for trade with their neighbours. We brought away upwards of 300 pounds weight. In sowing their seeds they have to guard against the flocks of Rooks, which would pick up every grain, and until the grain sprouts, parties of Boys and girls during the day are employed to drive them away. During the day they appear to have no [iv.172] regular meals; but after day set the evening meal is served with meat; at this meal, several are invited by a tally of wood, which they return, each brings his bowl and rude spoon and knife; the meat is boiled; roasting of it would give a disagreeable smell; which they are carefull to prevent, allowing nothing to be thrown into the fire and keeping the fire place very clean. The parties invited were generally from seven to ten men; women are never of the party, except the Wife of the master of the house, who sometimes joined in their grave, yet cheerful conversation. Loud laughter is seldom heard.

Both sexes have the character of being courteous and kind in their intercourse with each other; in our rambles through the villages every thing was orderly, no scolding, nor loud talking: They look upon stealing as the meanest of vices, and think a Robber a far better man than a Thief.[2] They have no laws for the punishment of crime, every thing is left to the injured party, the law of retaliation being in full force. It is this law which makes Murder so much dreaded by them, for vengeance is as likely to fall on the near relations of the murderer, as on himself, and the family of the Relation who may have thus suffered, have now their vengeance to take; Thus an endless feud arises; to prevent such blood shed, the murderer, if his life cannot be taken,

---

2 The distinction is that robbery is committed against a victim who is present, and theft against one who is absent or unaware.

for he frequently absconds; the old men attempt to compound for the crime[3] by presents to the injured party, which are always refused, except they know themselves to be too weak to obtain any other redress. If the presents are accepted the price of blood is paid, and the injured party has no longer any right to take the life of the criminal. This law of Retaliation, and compounding by presents for the life of the murderer, when accepted, appears to be [iv.173] universal laws with all the Natives of North America.

The dress of the Men is of leather, soft and white. The covering for the body is like a large shirt with sleeves, some wear the Bison leather with the hair on, for winter dress; with a leather belt; the leggins of soft white leather, so long as to pass over the belt; their shoes are made of Bison, with the hair on; and always a Bison Robe. The Women's dress is a shirt of Antelope or Deer leather, which ties over each shoulder, and comes down to the feet, with a belt round the waist short leggins to the knee, and Bison Robe shoes the sleeves separate, in which they looked well. Both Men and Women are of a stature fully equal to Europeans; and as fair as our french canadians; their eyes of a dark hazel, or light black, the hair of dark brown, or black, but not coarse; prominent nose, cheek bones moderate, teeth mouth and chin good; well limbed; the features good the countenance mild and intelligent; they are a handsome people. Their amusements are gambling after the manner of the Indians of the Plains. They have also their Musicians and dancing Women; In the house of the Chief, in which I staid, every evening, about two or three hours after sun set; about forty or fifty men assembled, they all stood; five or six of them were Musicians with a drum, tambour, rattle, and rude flutes; The dancing women were twenty four young women of the age of sixteen to twenty five years. They all came in their common dress; and went into a place set apart for them to dress; and changed to a fine white dress of thin Deer skins, with ornamented belts, which showed their shapes almost as clearly as a silk dress.

They formed two rows of twelve each, about three feet apart; The Musicians were in front of the Men, and about fourteen feet from the front row of the Women. When the music [iv.174] struck up, part of the Men sung, and the Women keeping a straight line and respective distance, danced with a light step, and slow, graceful motion towards the Musicians, until near to them, when the music and singing ceased, the Women retired in regular line, keeping their faces towards the Musicians. A pause of three or four minutes ensued, the music struck up, and the dance renewed in the same manner: and thus in succession for the time of about an hour, each dance lasted about ten

3 I.e., make material compensation for the offence.

minutes. There was no talking, the utmost decorum was kept; the Men all silently went away; the dancing Women retired to change their dress, they were all courtesans; a sett of handsome, tempting women. The Mandanes have many ceremonies, in all which the women bear a part but my interpreter treated them with contempt; which perhaps they merited. The curse of the Mandanes is an almost total want of chastity: this, the men with me knew, and I found it was almost their sole motive for their journey hereto: The goods they brought, they sold at 50 to 60 Percent above what they cost; and reserving enough to pay their debts, and buy some corn; spent the rest on Women, therefore we could not preach chastity to them, and by experience they informed me that siphylis was common, and mild.

¶ These people annually, at least once in every summer, have the following detestable ceremony, which lasts three days. The first day both sexes go about within and without the Village, but mostly on the outside, as if in great distress, seeking for persons they cannot find, for a few hours, then sit down and cry, as if for sorrow, then retire to their houses. The next day the same is repeated, with apparent greater distress accompanied with low singing. The third day begins with both sexes crying (no tears) and eagerly searching for those they wish to find, but cannot; at length tired with this folly: the sexes separate, the Men sit down [iv.175] on the ground in one line, with their elbows resting on their knees, and their heads resting on their hands as in sorrow; The Women, standing, and crying heartily, with dry eyes, form a line opposite the Men; in a few minutes, several women advance to the Men, each of them takes the Man she chooses by the hand, he rises and goes with her to where she pleases, and they lie down together and thus until none remain, which finishes this abominable ceremony. No woman can choose her husband; but the women who love their husbands lead away aged Men.[4] Messieurs Jussomme and McCrachan, said they had often partaken of the latter part of the third day: and other men said the same. Manoah strongly denied that either himself, or his Wife had ever taken part in these rites of the devil.

The white men who have hitherto visited these Villages have not been examples of chastity; and of course religion is out of the question: and as to the white Men who have no education, and who therefore cannot read the little religion they ever had is soon forgotten where there is no Church to remind them of it.

4 In traditional Mandan culture, an elder could transfer power to a younger man by means of ritual intercourse with the younger man's wife. This custom may animate the rite that Thompson describes here. Wood and Irwin, *Early Fur Trade*, 357, 360.

[*Fall Indians. Villages. Women to be faithful. Latitude & Longitude. the River*]

¶ Fall Indians who also have Villages, are strictly confederate with the Mandanes, they speak a distinct language; and it is thought no other tribe of Natives speak it; very few of the Mandanes learn it; the former learn the language of the latter, which is a dialect of the Pawnee language.[1] The Fall Indians are now removed far from their original country, which was the Rapids of the Saskatchewan River, northward of the Eagle Hill; A feud arose between them, and their then neighbours, the Nahathaway and Stone Indians confederates, and too powerful for them, they then lived wholly in tents, and removed across the Plains to the Missisourie; became confederate with the Mandanes [iv.176] and from them have learned to build houses, form villages and cultivate the ground; The architecture of their houses is in every respect that of the Mandanes, and their cultivation the same; some of them continue to live in tents and are in friendship with the Chyenne Indians, whose village was lately destroyed;[2] and now live in tents to the westward of them; Another band of these people now dwell in tents near the head of this River in alliance with the Pee a guns and their allies; The whole tribe of these people may be estimated at 2200 to 2500 souls.[3] They are not so fair as the Mandanes: but somewhat taller. Their features, like, those of the plains have

1 The Mandan and Hidatsa languages are related, belonging to different branches of the Siouan language family; Hidatsa has its closest affinity with Crow. Contrary to what Thompson writes, Mandan is not related to Pawnee, which belongs to the Caddoan language family.

2 Members of the Algonquian language family, the Cheyenne migrated from the western Great Lakes onto the northern Plains under pressure from the Sioux and Ojibwa. By the late eighteenth century they were living along the Cheyenne River and westward into the Black Hills, where they built villages and practised agriculture. For the Ojibwa chief Sheshepaskut's account of Ojibwa-Cheyenne warfare and the destruction of the Cheyenne village of Biesterfeldt, see iv.198–203, below (236–9), and iii.67–9 in Volume II. John H. Moore, *The Cheyenne* (Cambridge, MA: Blackwell, 1996).

3 Two Native groups were known as the Fall: the Algonquian-speaking Gros Ventres, identified with the area around the rapids of the Saskatchewan, and the Siouan-speaking Hidatsa, neighbours of the Mandan. The historical relationship between the two groups remains unclear. Based largely on Thompson's account, Mary Malainey suggests that a considerable number of Gros Ventres settled among the Hidatsa at the Knife River villages. Mary E. Malainey, "The Gros Ventre/Fall Indians in Historical and Archaeological Interpretation," *Canadian Journal of Native Studies* 25, no. 1 (2005): 155–83.

a cast of sterness, yet they are cheerful, very hospitable; and friendly to each other, and to strangers. What has been said of the Mandanes may be said of them; except in regard to Women. The Fall Indians exact the strict chastity of their wives; adultry is punishable with death to both parties; though the Woman escapes this penalty more often [than] the man; who can only save his life by absconding which, if the woman does not do, she suffers a severe beating, and becomes the drudge of the family. But those living in the Villages I was given to understand have relaxed this law to the man, in favor of the present of a Horse, and whatever else can be got from him. As they do not suffer the hardships of the Indians of the Plains the Men are nearly equal to the Women in number, and few have more than two wives, more frequently only one. It always appeared to me that the Indians of the Plains did not regard the chas[t]ity of their wives as a moral law, but as an unalienable right of property to be their wives and the mothers of their own children; and not to be interfered with by another Man The morality of the Indians, may be said to be founded on it's necessity [iv.177] to the peace and safety of each other, and although they profess to believe in a Spirit of great power, and that the wicked are badly treated after death; yet this seems to have no effect on their passions and desires the crimes they hold to be avoided are, theft, treachery, and murder.

Christianity alone by it's holy doctrines and precepts, by it's promises of a happy immortality, and dreadful punishments to the wicked, can give force to morality. It alone can restrain the passions and desires and guide them to fulfill the intentions of a wise, and benevolent Providence. As the Missisourie River with all it's Villages and population are within the United States, it is to be hoped Missionaries will soon find their way to these Villages, and give them a knowledge of christianity, which they will gladly accept.[4]

Having made the necessary astronomical observations we prepared to depart; the latitude of the Upper Village (Fall Indians) was found to be 47-25·11 North Longitude 101··21-5 West of Greenwich. The lower Village (Mandanes), Latitude 47-17··22 North Longitude 101··14··24 W Variation of the Compass ten degrees east. In the language of the natives, Missisourie, means, "the great troubled, or muddy, River," from the great quantity of sediment it contains.[5] Every where this River has bold banks, often steep,

4 The Knife River villages had been abandoned in 1837 when the Mandan and Hidatsa were nearly destroyed by a smallpox epidemic. In 1845 the survivors had resettled at the Like-a-Fishhook village farther up the Missouri.

5 The river was named after the Missouri, a Siouan-speaking people. The Illinois word *ouemessourita*, meaning "one who has a wood boat," refers to the group's use of

and mostly of earth. Above the banks the soil appears hard and dry the bottoms rich and well wooded. From the Mountains to it's confluence with the Mississippe, following it's courses is 3506 miles. The whole distance is a continuous River, without meeting, or forming, a single Lake; with very strong current. This River drains an area of 442,239 square miles.

[*Return. perswade a Chief to return. Arrive February 3, 1798. Another party sets off. Two Men & 1 Mandane killed. the country described. Stay 3 Weeks. Observations*]

We now set off,[1] our caravan consisted of thirty one Dogs, loaded with furrs of Wolves and Foxes, with [iv.178] meal and corn; and two Sieux Indian Women, which the Mandanes had taken prisoners, and sold to the Men, who, when arrived at the Trading House would sell them to some other Canadians. My Horse I left with my Host, and bought two stout Dogs to haul our luggage, and provisions. Our march, as usual, commenced with flogging the Dogs, and swearing at them in the intervals; my old soldier, who on going out had only Horses to take [care] of, and used to reprove them, now he had Dogs could swear and flog as well as any of them. A council had been held; as the Articles brought to them, was by no means sufficient to supply their wants, to send a small party to the Trading House, get a knowledge of the Road, make sure friends of the Stone Indians, and see the stock of Goods in the Trading Houses; Accordingly a Chief in the prime of life, called the White Man, with four young men were selected, and came with us, and also an old man and his old wife, each of the latter carrying a bag of meal for their provisions they said they were anxious to see the Houses of the White Men before they died; and when told they were both too weak to perform the journey, they said their hearts were strong, but by the time they had ascended the heights of the river, they were convinced they were too weak and returned.

¶ Monsieur Jussomme and myself spoke to the Chief of the extreme hazard of such a small party escaping their enemies; and that if they wished to have a direct trade with us, they must form a party of at least forty men with

dugout canoes. Michael McCafferty, "Correction: Etymology of *Missouri*," *American Speech* 79 (Spring 2004): 32.

1 The return journey from the Mandan-Hidatsa villages to John Macdonnell's House lasted from 10 January to 3 February 1798; for the journal for this time, see AO. 7.9v–12r; 9.116–112; Wood and Thiessen, *Early Fur Trade*, 118–28. For an earlier *Travels* version of the journey, see iii.81–2 (Volume II).

Horses, and come when the Snow was not on the ground; that even among the Stone [iv.179] Indians, who are friendly, there were bad men enough, on seeing such a small party, that would plunder them: and they had all better return, he said, "we do not know the country; we are too few, and I will return, the young men belong to another Village, and they will do as they please." After fourteen days on our return and suffering excessive bad weather, two of the Mandane young men returned; the other two continued with us. On the first day of February we came to eight Tents of Stone Indians, in the same place as we went; they treated the two Mandanes with great kindness. We told them we had returned by the usual route; as the Mandanes assured us there was no danger; they said we had not acted wisely, for the good weather will bring the Sieux to the Dog Tent Hill, you have narrowly escaped, for we are sure they are now there. We killed very few Bisons, and lived as much on Corn as on Meal.

We continued our Journey and on the third day of February (1798) we arrived at the Trading House of the North West Company, from whence we set out, thankfull to the Almighty for our merciful preservation. We have been absent sixty eight days.[2] The next day Mr Hugh McCrachan and four men with an assortment of goods for trade set off for the Mandane Villages and the two Mandane young men, to whom Mr M'Donell made several presents, which highly pleased them.

I strongly advised them all not to follow the usual route, carefully to avoid the Dog Tent Hill, and follow the route by which we went to the Missisourie, and which the Stone Indians also strongly advised; This they all promised to do, and set off; The weather being fine, Canadian like, who believe there is no danger until they are involved in it; they took the usual route, and at the campment of the Dog Tent Hills [iv.180] found the Sieux lying in wait for them; they fell on them killed two of the Canadians and one of the Mandanes, and the others would have shared the same fate, had they not begun quarreling about the plunder of the goods. The Mandane got safe to his Village, and Hugh McCrachan and the two men returned to the House, in a sad worn out condition, the humanity of some Stone Indians saved their lives, or they must have perished with hunger. In the following summer as Mr Hugh [Mc]Crachan was on his usual trading journeys to the Mandanes he was killed by the Sieux Indians. Our road from the Village of the Mandanes to the Stone Indian River House, following from Woods to Woods for fuel and shelter are To the Dog Tent Hill is N 28 E 50 Miles; thence to the Elbow of

2 Thompson remained at John Macdonnell's House from 3 to 26 February 1798. For the journals of this stay, see AO. 7.12r–12v; 9.112–111.

the Mouse River N 49 E 20 miles; thence to Turtle Hill south end N 18 E 56 miles, thence along the Hill N 9 W 24 miles; thence to the Ash House on the Mouse River N 3 W 24 miles; thence to the House of Mr McDonell N 69 E 45 miles, but a straight line between the two extreme points is N 26 E 188 miles.

The whole of this country may be pastoral, but except in a few places, cannot become agricultural even the fine Turtle Hill, gently rising, for several miles, with it's Springs and Brooks of fine Water has very little wood fit for the Farmer. The principal is Aspin which soon decays; with small Oaks and Ash. The grass of these plains is so often on fire, by accident, or design, and the bark of the Trees so often scorched, that their growth is constr[i]cted, or they become dry; and the whole of the great Plains are subject to these fires during the Summer and Autumn before the Snow lies on the ground. These great Plains appear to be given by Providence to the Red Men for ever, as the wilds and sands of Africa are given to the Arabians. It may be enquired, what [iv.181] can be [the] cause of the violent Storms, like Hurricanes which, in a manner desolate this country, when such Storms are not known to the westward. No assignable cause is known; there are no Hills to impede it's course, or confine it's action, what are called Hills, are gentle rising grounds, over which the Winds sweep in full freedom, and the same question may be asked of certain parts of the Ocean.

My time for full three weeks was employed in calculating the astronomical observations made to, and from, the Missisourie River; and making a Map of my survey, which, with my journal was sealed up, and directed to the Agents of the North West Company. By a series of observations this Trading House is in Latitude 49··40··56 North, and Longitude 99-27-15 West, Variation 11 degrees E.

[*set off to Survey. Stone Ind River. Snow Water. The Country to Red River. Woods &c. Woods open at Red River. Chippaway Character. Lodges. Noses bit off*]

On the 26th day of February (1798) I took leave of my hospitable friend Mr John McDonell, who furnished me with every thing necessary for my Journey of survey.[1]

---

1 Thompson left John Macdonnell's house on 26 February 1798 and arrived at the junction of the Assiniboine and Red Rivers on 7 March. For the journals of this journey, see AO. 7.12v–13r; 9.112–109. An earlier *Travels* version is iii.82–3 (Volume II).

With me were three canadians and an Indian to guide us, and six dogs hauling three Sleds loaded with Provisions and our baggage. Our Journey was down the Stone Indian River, sometimes on the Ice of the Stream, but on account of it's windings, mostly on the North Side; cutting off the windings as much as possible; In the afternoon we came to the Manito Hills,[2] they are a low long ridge of sand Knowls, steep on the west side, but less so on the east side; they have a very little grass in a few places, no snow lies on them all winter, which is the reason the Natives call them Manito; or preternatural. Except the Sand Ridge, the country we have come over is very fine, especially the junction of the Mouse River which is about 1½ [iv.182] mile below the House; the woods were of Oak, Ash, Elm Bass Wood, Poplar, Aspin and a few Pines having small Plains and Meadows. (short and long grass) In the evening we put up: and as usual had to melt snow to make water to drink and cook our supper. To melt Snow into well tasted water requires some tact. The Kettle is filled with Snow packed hard, it is then hung over the fire, and as it melts, it is with a small stick bored full of holes to the bottom to lessen the smoky taste. When it becomes water the taste is disagreeable with smoke, but in this state it readily quenches thirst, and for such is often drank; to clear it of smoke the water is made to boil for a few minutes which clears it of the smoke. Snow is then put in, until it is cold, and the water is well tasted and fit for use. We continued our journey day after day, the Snow increasing every day in depth; and to beat the path for the Dogs and Sleds became very tiresome work; the Snow Shoes sunk six inches every step of the foremost man, our Guide every day became so fatigued I had to relieve him for two or three hours.

On the seventh of March we arrived at it's junction with the Red River in Latitude 49··53.1 N. Longitude 97··0·0 West Variation 9 degrees East. The straight course is N 82 E 112 statute miles; to perform which we walked 169 miles, but the windings of the River is treble the former distance, and more. An Indian compared the devious course of the River to a Spy, who went here and there, and every where, to see what was going on in the country. The whole of this country appeared fit for cultivation and for raising Cattle, the climate is as mild as Montreal in Canada, which [is] 4½ degrees south of this River; The Woods as we descended the River were less in size and height, especially the [iv.183] Oak. We saw but few animals, a few Red Deer, and a chance small herd of Bisons, for these animals avoid deep snow.

---

2   These sand dunes, south of present-day Carberry, Manitoba, have also been known as the Bad Woods, Bald Head Hills, Devil Hills, Spirit Hills, and Manitoba Desert.

¶ Hitherto we have been on the hunting grounds of the Nahathaway Indians; who possess this River, and all to the eastward, and to the northward as far as the latitude of 56 degrees north. The Red River, and all the country south ward and the Upper Mississippe, and countries eastward to, and all, Canada, are the hunting grounds of the Chippaways (or Oo jib a ways).[3] Part is already occupied by civilized men, and the greatest part of their territories will in time be in the hands of those that cultivate the soil. They are a large, scattered tribe of the primitive Nahathaways, and speak a close dialect of their language, which they have softened. As they live, comparatively, in a mild climate, their country is different in soil and it's productions which renders them less dependent on hunting; The dark extensive forests of the north, give food, shelter, and comparative security to the Moose, the Rein Deer, and other wild animals, and exercise the sagacity and industry of the Hunter. On the contrary, the open Woods of these give the Deer no such advantages, and a Moose is a rare animal. Of all the Natives, these people are the most superstitious, they may be accounted the religionists of the North.[4] As they have no Horses, and only Dogs for winter use and not many of these to haul their things in winter, they have very few tents of leather they are mostly of rush mats neatly made, sometimes of Birch Rind, or Pine Branches, always low, and seldom confortable. As soon as mild weather comes on, they live in Lodges, which are long, in proportion to the number of families. Strong poles are placed on triangles for the length required, about six [iv.184] or seven feet high, the front looks to the south, and is open, the back part is formed of poles about three feet apart, in a sloping position, resting on the ground, and on the ridge pole, covered with Birch Rind, sometimes rush mats, and pine branches. In summer they all use Canoes and in winter the flat Sled; in this season the women, haul, or carry heavy loads and the men also take their Share. They are well made for hunting and fatigue, they are more fleshy than their neighbours, and their skin darker. These are the people of whom writers tell so many anecdotes,[5] as they are better known to the Whites than any other tribe; they are naturally brave, but too much given to revenge; and

3   For the Ojibwa, see note to iv.121, above (176).
4   A religionist is one "addicted or attached to religion." *Oxford English Dictionary*, 2nd edn., 13:569, s.v. "religionist."
5   By the time Thompson wrote this passage in 1848, the Ojibwa had been described in many published works. Thompson may have in mind such texts as Jonathan Carver's *Travels through the Interior Parts of North-America* (1778), Alexander Henry the Elder's *Travels and Adventures in Canada and the Indian Territories between the Years 1760 and 1776* (1809), and Henry Rowe Schoolcraft's *Narrative of an Expedition through the Upper Mississippi to Itasca Lake* (1834).

although they exact fidelity from their wives, rarely punish with death, the woman is sometimes punished by the husband biting off the fleshy part of the nose; the Women declare it to be worse than death, as it is the loss of their beauty, and for the rest of life a visible mark of crime and punishment, but this barbarous act is very rarely inflicted but when the man is drunk.

[*bad travelling. bad walking. Change of Pines to Aspins &c. Mr Chaboillez. Population &c. Woods. Soil &c. Racoon. Red River. No Market. thawing of Snow*]

On the 7th day of March we began the survey of the Red River,[1] and continued to the 14th of March, when we arrived at the Trading House of the North West Company, under the charge of Monsieur Charles Chaboiller,[2] who gave us a kind reception. Our journey for the last eight days has been most wretched traveling; the Snow was full three feet deep; the ice of the River had much water on it, from the mild weather, with small showers of rain, or wet snow.

On the River, the mixture of snow and water which stuck to the Sleds, made it impossible for the Dogs to haul them, and it often required two of us to extricate a Sled, with the assistance of the Dogs, and every thing had to be dried in bad weather. To beat the Road was a most laborious work, the ankles and knees were sprained with the weight of wet snow on each Snow Shoe, for [iv.185] the Snow was not on firm ground, but supported by long grass, I had to take his place,[3] and tying a string to the fore bar of each snow shoe, and the other end in my hand, with my gun slung on my back, and thus lifting my snow shoes, marched on; We journeyed on the west side of the River; the whole distance was meadow land, and no other Woods than saplings of Oak, Ash, and Alder.

1 Thompson left the junction of the Assiniboine and Red Rivers (the site of modern-day Winnipeg) on 7 March 1798, arrived at Charles Chaboillez's House on 14 March, and stayed there until 21 March. For the journals of these days, see AO. 7.13v–16r; 9.109–105. Here Thompson states that he spent his time "writing Letters. Observations &c with drawing a little." AO. 9.106. An earlier *Travels* account is iii.83–6 (Volume II).

2 For NWC trader Charles Chaboillez, see appendix 2. Chaboillez's Pembina post operated only in 1797–98; a new post was established by Alexander Henry the Younger in 1801, becoming for a short time the locus of an Ojibwa residential settlement. Harold Hickerson, "The Genesis of a Trading Post Band: The Pembina Chippewa," *Ethnohistory* 3 (Fall 1956): 289–345.

3 I.e., take the place of the sled dog.

¶ From the many charred stumps of Pines it was evident this side of the River was once a Pine Forest. In the more northern parts, where Pine Woods have been destroyed by fire, Aspins, Poplars and Alders have sprung up, and taken the place of the Pines; but along this, the Red River, from the mildness of the climate, and goodness of the soil, Oak, Ash, Alder, and Nut Woods have succeeded the Pines. This change appears to depend on soil and climate; for in the high northern latitudes, where in many places there is no soil, and the Pines spread their roots over the rocks, Pine grounds, when burned, are succeeded by Pines; for Aspins Poplars and Alders require some soil. Along the Great Plains, there are very many places where large groves of Aspins have been burnt, the charred stumps remaining: and no further production of Trees have taken place, the grass of the Plains covers them; and from this cause the Great Plains are constantly increasing in length and breadth, and the Deer give place to the Bison. But the mercy of Providence has given a productive power to the roots of the grass of the Plains and of the Meadows, on which the fire has no effect; The fire passes in flame and smoke, what was a lovely green is now a deep black; the Rains descend, and this [iv.186] odious colour disappears, and is replaced by a still brighter green; if these grasses had not this wonderful productive power, on which fire has no effects, these Great Plains would, many centuries ago, have been without Man, Bird, or Beast. We crossed several Brooks of salt water, which come from ponds of salt water on the west side of the River, one, or two of these are so strongly impregnated, that good salt is made of the water by boiling; the meat salted with it, is well preserved, but somewhat corroded. On the 12th, we came to four Lodges of Chip pa ways, they had killed two poor Bulls, of which we were glad to get a part, and the next day two of them came with us, which relieved us from the fatigue of beating the road.

¶ At this trading Post I staid six days, making astronomical observations which determined this place to be in Latitude 48°··58'·24' north Longitude 97°··16'··40" W of Greenwich Variation 8½ degrees East. This house is therefore one minute and thirty six seconds, in the United States; the Boundary Line between the British Dominions and the Territories of the United States being the forty ninth parallel of north Latitude from the Lake of the Woods to the east foot of the Rocky Mountains. I pointed out the Boundary Line to which they must remove; and which Line, several years after was confirmed by Major Long of the Corps of Engineers, on the part of the United States.[4] From the junction of the Stone Indian, with this, the Red River, the

4 Nowhere in his journals does Thompson state that his observations taken at Chaboillez's House were made in reference to the 49th parallel. For the 49th parallel

course is S 11¼ W 65½ statute miles, but to the Boundary Line 64 miles. The number of Men that now trade at this House are 95, which at seven souls for each man, (rather a low average), gives 665 Souls. And at the Rainy River House which lies in Latitude 48-36·58 N Longitude [iv.187] 93··19··30 W. in a course S 82 E 184 miles. The Chippaways who trade at this House are 60 men, giving an average of 420 souls; By the extent of their hunting grounds, each family of seven souls, has 150 to 180 square miles of hunting ground, and yet have very little provisions to spare; this above is sufficient to show the ground does not abound in wild animals. The Beaver has become a very scarce animal; the soil and climate not requiring the same materials for his House become a more easy prey. During the Summer these Natives subsist on fish, and in Autumn, part of them on wild rice.

The Woods about this House are Oak, Ash, Elm and Nut Woods, the Oaks of fine growth, tall and straight the largest of these measured ten feet girth at six feet above the ground. In the hollows of the decayed Trees, the Racoons[5] take shelter, they are not found to the northward: they are a fat animal, and like all other animals that feed on Nuts, their fat is oily; without the skin and bowels, the weight of one is about fifteen pounds. They lay up nothing for the winter, and are dormant during the cold weather. The Red River is here 120 yards in width. Eleven miles below this the Reed River from the eastward falls in, it's width is about the same, but not so deep.[6] This part of the River is called Pembina from a small Stream that comes in.

¶ As this River has a rich deep soil and every where fit for cultivation it must become a pastoral and agricultural country, but for want of woods, for buildings and other purposes, must be limited to near the River, the open Plains have no Woods and afford no shelter. Note. (Twenty years after this (1798)[7] Several Canadians who had married native women with their families

as an international boundary, see the note on iv.115 (170). Stephen Harriman Long (1784–1864), a United States Army engineer and inveterate explorer, led an 1823 expedition to the Upper Mississippi and Red Rivers. Long's party was at Pembina in 5–9 August 1823, and the engineer determined that the entire settlement, save for one house, lay south of the 49th parallel. William H. Keating, *Narrative of an expedition to the source of St. Peter's River, Lake Winnepeek, Lake of the Woods, &c., performed in the year 1823* (Minneapolis: Ross and Haines, 1959); Lucile M. Kane et al., eds., *The Northern Expeditions of Stephen H. Long: The Journals of 1817 and 1823 and Related Documents* (St Paul: Minnesota Historical Society Press, 1978).

5 *Procyon lotor.*
6 The Roseau River (of which "Reed" is a translation).
7 I.e., in 1818.

first settled, and they were soon joined by the Servants of the Hudson's Bay Company, who had done [iv.188] the same, with their families. This Settlement rapidly increased it's population, and now (1848) numbers about 5000 souls.[8] The great draw back on this fine Settlement is the want of a Market; York Factory in Hudson's Bay, is apparently their Market, but the distance is too great, being N 24° E 616 miles on a straight line; and the devious route they would have to follow cannot be less than 900 miles. In this distance there are many Carrying Place[s], over which every thing must be carried; such a journey with their produce would require the greater part of the short summer of those countries; and leave the Farmer no time for the cultivation of his ground. It would be a journey of toil, hard labor and suffering, and night and day devoured by Musketoes and other flies. Hence York Factory cannot be a market for the Red River. The extra pr[o]duce of this River cannot find a Market at Montreal, the distance is too great and the obstacles too many, and too laborious to be overcome. Nor can a Market be found on the Mississippe, to get to the head of this River is a tedious route with many Carrying Places. In time civilisation will advance to them by this River, but until then the Red River must remain an isolated Settlement.

¶ Here in the Latitude of 49 degrees, the Snow, clear of drift, is three to three and a half feet in depth; and in the Latitude of 58 degrees north the Snow has the same depth; but falls dry as dust, it adheres to nothing, and a cubic foot of well packed Snow yields, when melted, from four to five inches of water. Hence the northern Rivers, on the melting of the Snow, are not much affected, the Snow yields but little water, and the frosts of every night check it's quantity. But to the southward, the Rivers overflow from the quantity of [iv.189] water contained in the Snow, and the thaw being more steady, with greater warmth.

[*Mr Cadotte. Language &c &c. the weather of Spring. Old Chief. Sugar. Snow thawed, return to Mr Cadotte*]

¶ On the 21st March we proceeded on our Journey,[1] and on the 25th arrived at the trading House of the North West Company under the charge

8 Thompson refers here to the entire district of Assiniboia, rather than Pembina in particular. Settlement of Assiniboia began in 1812, after the Red River Colony was established (1811) under the patronage of Thomas Douglas, Fifth Earl of Selkirk. According to the census of 1846, the population of Assiniboia was 4,871.
1 Thompson left Chaboillez's House on 21 March 1798, stopped at an NWC post operated by Vincent Roy on 22–23 March, and arrived at Cadotte's House on 25 March;

of Monsieur Baptiste Cadotte.[2] The weather was fine, and at night the frost made the Snow firm for several hours of the day. Our journey was up along the Red River; in some places there were fine Ledges of Woods along the River, of moderate width, from thirty to three hundred yards; they were of Oak, Ash, Elm, Bass and other woods. As we ascended, the Aspin became more frequent. the whole a fine rich deep soil. About fifteen to twenty miles westward are the Hair Hills;[3] of gentle rising grounds, with groves of Wood in places. At the east foot of these Hills are the low grounds with Ponds of salt water; and from which several Brooks come into the Red River. The Deer and Bisons are very fond of the grass of these places which appears to keep them in all seasons in good condition.

¶ Mr Baptiste Cadotte was about thirty five years of age. He was the son of a french gentleman by a native woman, and married to a very handsome native woman, also the daughter of a Frenchman: He had been well educated in Lower Canada, and spoke fluently, his native Language with Latin, French and English. I had long wished to meet a well educated native, from whom I could derive sound information for I was well aware that neither myself, nor any other Person I had met with, who was not a Native, were sufficiently masters of the Indian Languages.

¶ As the season was advancing to break up the Rivers, and thaw the Snow from off the ground, I enquired if he would advise me to proceed any further with Dogs and Sleds: he said the season was too far advanced, and my further advance must be in Canoes; my last wintering ground was the Rein Deers Lake in Latitude 57··23 North which Lake was frozen over to the 5th day of July, when it [iv.190] broke up by a gale of wind,[4] and having hitherto been confined to northern climes, I was anxious to see the workings of the climate of 48 degrees north, aided by the influence of the great, and warm Valley of the Mississippe, which was near to us. I shall therefore give a few days in the form of a journal. March 27th. A fine morning, At 6½ AM we set off and went up along the River thirteen Miles, through Willows, small Birch and Aspins; with a few Oak and Ash in places to 2 PM when we came

he set off again on 27 March but returned to the post on 31 March. For the events of these days, see AO. 7.16r–18r; 9.106–102, and an earlier *Travels* text, iii.86–90 (Volume II).

2 For NWC trader Jean-Baptiste Cadotte, see appendix 2. Cadotte's post was located on the banks of the Red Lake River, where it joins the Clearwater.

3 Now known as the Pembina Hills or Pembina Mountains.

4 For this event, see iv.102 (151).

to seven Tents of Chippeways, and to She she pas kut (Sugar)[5] the principal Chief of the Chippeway Tribe; he appeared to be about sixty years of age, and yet had the activity and animated countenance of forty. His height was five feet, ten inches his features round and regular, and his kind behaviour to all around him, and to strangers concealed the stern, persevering Warrior, under whose conduct the incursions of the Sieux Indians were repressed and the Village Indians driven to the Missisourie: We stopped at his Tent, as usual we were well received; he thought the season to much advanced but would send a Guide with us the morrow.

The Snow was thawing and wet very bad walking. On my Journey to the Missisourie I had two Thermometers; On my return, on a stormy night, one got broke, and the one remaining I had carefully to keep for my astronomical observations, so that I can only give the weather in general terms. March 28th. The night was mild, and the Snow still wet; At 5¼ AM the Guide came, and we advanced about four miles, when our Guide took care to break his Snow Shoes and went back to the Tents, and in the evening the Chief sent me another Guide; but we had to put up and wait all day.

[iv.191] The Chippeways had killed a black Bear, but on coming to our campment, they were so tired with heavy walking, they left the meat with us, until they returned. Three Geese were seen and at 8 PM Lightning, Thunder and Rain came on, the latter during the whole night. March 29th. Rain continued until noon; The Snow was now so mixed with water, that we could not proceed. In the evening Rain came on and continued. Every thing was wet, without a chance of drying our clothes and baggage. March 30th. Showers of Hail and Sleet. With the Guide went to examine the country before us: which appeared like a Lake, with water. I had therefore to return to Mr Cadotte, and wait the Rivers to become clear of ice, which was now too weak to venture upon. Our order of march was each of us carrying on his back every thing the water could injure, every step, from ancle to the knee in snow water; the Dogs dragging the Sleds, floating in the water. Swans, Geese, and Ducks were about: but the Eagles and large Hawks which to the northward are the first to arrive, none were seen: On the 31st, After three hours march, at the rate of one mile an hour; we became too fatigued, laid down our loads, and with one man light, we went to the house to get help, bad as the River was, we ventured on it; like desperate men; my companion fell through three times, and I escaped with only once; the water was only three feet deep, and we carried a long light pole in each hand. At 2 PM thank good Providence,

5 For Ojibwa chief Sheshepaskut, see appendix 2.

we arrived at the house of Mr Cadotte who directly sent off five men to bring every thing to this place. Here a few days has thawed three and a half feet to three feet of heavy snow, which in the Latitude of 57 or 58 degrees [iv.192] north, require five, or six weeks of lingering weather.

[*The Wahbino. campment. despised. Man eating. Wee te go*]

We had now to wait the River becoming clear of ice, and get a Canoe in order for our voyage.[1] In the mean time I collected some information on the Religion and Ceremonies of these people. I learned that of late a superstition had sprung up, and was now the attention of all the Natives. It appeared the old Songs, Dances and Ceremonies[2] by frequent repetition had lost all their charms, and religious attention; and were heard and seen with indifference: some novelty was required and called for; and these people are the leaders of the Tribe in superstition and ceremonies. Accordingly two, or three crafty chiefs, contrived to dream (for all comes by Dreams) after having passed some time in a sweating cabin, and singing to the music of the Rattle. They dreamed they saw a powerful Medicine, to which a Manito voice told them to pay great attention and respect, and saw the tambour with the figures on it, and also the Rattle to be used for music in dancing: They also heard the Songs that were to be sung: They were to call it the Wahbino: It was to have two orders; the first only Wah bino the second Kee che Wah bino; and those initiated to bear the name of their order. (fool, or knave) Every thing belonging to the Wah bino was sacred, nothing of it to touch the ground, nor to be touched by a Woman.

Under the guidance of the Wah bino sages, Tambours were made, the frame circular of eight inches in depth and eighteen inches diameter, covered with fine parchment; the frame covered with strange figures in red and black, and to it were suspended many bits of tin and brass to make a gingling noise; the Rattle had an ornamented handle; and several had Wahbino Sticks, flat, about three feet, or more in length, with [iv.193] rude figures carved and painted: The Mania became so authoritative that every young man had to purchase a Wahbino Tambour; the price was what they could get from him; and figured dances were also sold; the Knaves were in their glory, admired

---

1   Thompson was delayed at Cadotte's House from 31 March to 9 April 1798. For the journal of this period, see AO. 7.18r–v; 9.102–101.

2   By "the old Songs, Dances and Ceremonies," Thompson indicates the rites of the *midewiwin* society, by which the Ojibwa traditionally expressed their religious sense.

and getting rich on the credulity of others, but there were several sensible
Men among them, who looked with contempt on the whole of this mumery;[3]
it was harmless, and since there must be some foolery, this was as harmless
as any other. I asked the old Chief, what he thought of it; he gave me no
answer, but looked me full in the face, as much as to say, how can you ask
me such a question.

¶ I was present at the exhibition of a Wahbino dance; A Kee chee Wah
bino Man arrived, he soon began to make a speech on the great power of the
Wahbino, and to dance to his Song. He seated himself on the ground, on each
hand, a few feet from him, sat two men, somewhat in advance; the Dancers
were five young men naked, and painted, above the waist: I sat down by one
of the two Men: The Wah bino Man began the Song in a bold strong tone of
voice, the Song was pleasing to the ear, the young Men danced, sometimes
slowly, then changed to a quick step with many wild gestures, sometimes
erect, and then, to their bodies being horizontal: shaking their Tambours,
and at times singing a short chorus. They assumed many attitudes with ease,
and showed a perfect command of their limbs. With short intervals, this
lasted for about an hour. I watched the countenance of the Indian next to
me, he seemed to regard the whole with sullen indifference; I enquired of
him, "what was the intent and meaning of what I had seen and heard"; With
a smile of contempt "By what you have seen, and heard; they have made
themselves [iv.194] masters of the Squirels, Musk Rats and Racoons' also of
the Swans. Geese, Cranes and Ducks: their Manito is weak." "Then all these
are to be in abundance." "So they say, but we shall see." "What becomes
of the Bison, the Moose and Red Deer," With a look of contempt; "Their
Manito's are too powerful for the Wah bino." I found that several of the Indians looked on the Wah bino as a jugglery[4] between knaves and fools: yet for
full two years it had a surprising influence over the Indians, and [they] too
frequently neglected hunting for singing and dancing.

About two hours after the exhibition, an Indian arrived with twenty two
Beaver Skins to trade necessaries for himself and family, he was a Man in the
prime of life. The Knave of a Keeche Wahbino made a speech to him on the
powerful effects of the Great Wahbino Song, and which he directly sang to
him.

The Song being ended; the Indian presented him eighteen Beaver Skins,
reserving only four for himself, for these he traded ammunition and tobacco,
and nothing for his Wife and family; and the Knave seemed to think he was

3 Ridiculous or pretentious ceremony.
4 Trickery.

but barely paid for his song and ought to have been paid the twenty two Beaver Skins. I enquired of Mr Cadotte, if he could interpret to me the Song we had just heard: he replied, that although they spoke in the language of his native tongue, he did not understand a single sentence of the Song, only a chance word, which was of no use.

We both had the same opinion, that they have a kind of a mystical language among themselves; understood only by the initiated, and that the Wah bino Songs, were in this mystical language; that novelty had given it a power, which it would soon lose; he remarked that almost all the Wah bino singers, were idle Men and poor hunters. This folly spread to a considerable distance, and the Lake of the Woods became it's central place, several Lodges, containing forty or fifty families, living more [iv.195] by fishing than hunting became enamoured of the Wahbino Song and Dance, and so many dancing together they too often became highly excited and danced too long. One of them made a neat drum for himself; on which he placed strings of particular bones of small animals, as mice, squirrels and frogs, with strings of the bones and claws of small birds; and on beating the drum, as the strings of bones changed positions, pretended to tell what was to happen. These Lodges were now encamped at the sortie of the Rainy River into the Lake of the Woods, on a fine, long sandy Point on the left side of the River: long poles were tied from tree to tree, on which were carefully hung the Wah bino Medicine Bag and Tambour of each Man.

On this Point the North West Canoes camped when a gale of wind was on the Lake. The Lake was in this state in 1799, when we arrived, and we put up about ten AM. At Noon by double Altitude I observed for Latitude

While doing so, an Indian of my acquai[nta]nce, came and sat down. When I was done, looking at the parallel glasses and quicksilver, he said, "My Wah bano is strong." I knew that his meaning was to say, "By what you are doing, you give to yourself great power, my Wahbino can do the same for me." I told him the Great Spirit alone was strong, your Wah bino is like this, taking up a pinch of sand and letting it fall. He then said the Sun is strong; my answer was, the Great Spirit made the Sun, at this he appeared surprised and went away.

[iv.196] The next morning the Gale of Wind continued; the Indian came to me, and said, "yesterday you despised my Wahbino, and I have thrown it away."

In the night the Gale had thrown down the Pole to which the Tambour and Medicine Bag was tied; and the Dogs had wetted them; he was indignant, and took his gun to shoot the Dogs, but his good sense prevented him; and looking at his Tambour and Medicine Bag with contempt, exclaimed "If you, the Wahbino had any power, the Dogs would not have treated you as they have done." Other Tambours were in the same condition, the news of this accident spread, the sensible men took advantage of it; and by the following summer nothing more was heard of the Wah bino Medicine.[5]

¶ I called to Mr Cadotte's attention a sad affair that had taken place a few months past on the shores of the Lake of the Woods. About twenty families were together for hunting and fishing. One morning a young man of about twenty two years of age on getting up, said he felt a strong inclination to eat his Sister; as he was a steady young man and a promising hunter, no notice was taken of this expression; the next morning he said the same, and repeated the same several times in the day for a few days. His Parents attempted to reason him out of this horrid inclination; he was silent and gave them no answer; his Sister and her Husband became alarmed, left the place, and went to another Camp. He became aware of it; and then said he must have human flesh to eat, and would have it; in other respects his behaviour was cool, calm and quiet. His father and relations were much grieved; argument had no effect on him, and he made them no answer to their questions. The Camp became alarmed for it was doubtful who would be his victim.

5   Thompson's account (and its earlier parallel on iii.87–9, found in Volume II) is evidence of the origin and diffusion of the *waabanowiwin*. This rite emerged about 1796, probably in association with the decline in animal populations, and as Thompson notes, was regarded by followers of the *midewiwin* as a false and upstart religion. While at Pembina in 1802, Alexander Henry the Younger noted that Ojibwa there were "making the wabbano," commenting that "it is not so solemn as the grand medicine nor does it require such ceremonious initiation." Elliott Coues, ed., *New Light on the Early History of the Greater Northwest: The Manuscript Journals of Alexander Henry and David Thompson* (Minneapolis: Ross and Haines, 1965), 198–9. John Tanner reported in his 1830 narrative that "the Waw-be-no was fashionable among the Ojibbeways, but ... has ever been considered by the older and more respectable men as a false and dangerous religion." Edwin James, *A Narrative of the Captivity and Adventures of John Tanner* (Minneapolis: Ross and Haines, 1956), 122. Practitioners of the *waabano* (Ojibwa "what is represented by the east") served their followers by making cures and charms, and by attempting to influence the manitos of game animals; they were especially known for handling burning objects. The *waabanowiwin* persisted much longer than Thompson indicates, into the early twentieth century. Christopher Vecsey, *Traditional Ojibwa Religion and Its Historical Changes* (Philadelphia: American Philosophical Society, 1983), 191–2; Maureen Matthews and Roger Roulette, "Fair Wind's Dream: *Naamiwan Obowaajigewin*," in *Reading Beyond Words: Contexts for Native History*, 2nd edn., ed. Jennifer S.H. Brown and Elizabeth Vibert (Peterborough: Broadview Press, 2003), 264n3.

¶ His Father called the Men to a Council, where the state [iv.197] of the young man was discussed; and their decision was, that an evil Spirit had entered into him, and was in full possession of him to make him become a Man Eater (a Wee te go). The father was found fault with for not having called to his assistance a Medicine Man, who by sweating and his Songs to the tambour and rattle might have driven away the evil spirit, before it was too late. Sentence of death was passed on him, which was to be done by his Father. The young man was called, and told to sit down in the middle, there was no fire, which he did, he was then informed of the resolution taken to which he said "I am willing to die"; The unhappy father a[ros]e, and placing a cord about his neck strangled him, to which he was quite passive; after about two hours, the body was carried to a large fire, and burned to Ashes, not the least bit of bone remaining. This was carefully done to prevent his soul and the evil Spirit which possessed him from returning to this world; and appearing at his grave; which they believe the souls of those who are buried can, and may do, as having a claim to the bones of their bodies.

¶ It may be thought the Council acted a cruel part in ordering the father to put his Son to death, when they could have ordered it by the hands of another person. This was done, to prevent the law of retaliation; which had it been done by the hands of any other person, might have been made a pretext of revenge by those who were not the friends of the person who put him to death. Such is a state of society where there are no positive laws to direct mankind.[6] From our comparing notes; it appeared to us that this sad, evil desposition to become Wee te go; or Man Eaters, was wholly [iv.198] confined to the inhabitants of the Forests; no such disposition being known among the Indians of the Plains; and this limited to the Nahathaway and Chippeway Indians, for numerous Natives under the name of Dinnae (Chepawyans) whose hunting grounds are all the Forests north of the latitude of 56 degrees, have no such horrid disposition among them. The word Wee te go, is one of the names of the Evil Spirit and when he gets possession of any Man, (Women are wholly exempt from it) he becomes a Man Eater, and if he succeeds; he no longer keeps company with his relations and friends, but roams all alone through the Forests a powerful wicked Man, preying upon whom he can, and as such is dreaded by the Natives. Tradition says, such evil Men were formerly more frequent than at present, probably from famine. I have known a few instances of this deplorable turn of mind, and not one instance could plead hunger,

6 By positive law, Thompson means law that is formally laid down; it is distinguished from natural law, considered to be inherent.

much less famine as an excuse, or cause of it. There is yet a dark chapter to be written on this aberration of the human mind, on this head.[7]

[*Chyenne War. Prepare for Chyenne War. Chyenne Village burned. Chyenne Woman. her death. Sand Lake massacre*]

The Chief, She she pas kut, with a few men arrived,[1] with a few Beaver Skins and Provisions; I enquired of him, the cause of his making war on the Chyenne Indians and destroying their Village and the following is the substance of our conversation.[2]

¶ "Our people and the Chyenne's for several years had been doubtful friends; but as they had Corn and other Vegetables, which we had not and of which we were fond, and traded with them we passed over and forgot, many things we did not like; until lately; when we missed our Men who went a hunting, we always said they have [iv.199] fallen by the hands of our enemies the Sieux Indians but of late years, we became perswaded the Chyennes were the people, as some missing went to hunt where the Sieux never came; We were at a loss what to do; when some of our people went to trade Corn, and while there, saw a Chyenne Hunter bring in a fresh Scalp, which they knew;

7 This description (and its earlier parallel on iii.90–2, in Volume II) is one of the most important European accounts of the phenomenon of the Windigo (Cree *wīhtikōw*, Ojibwa *wīntikō*). In traditional Cree and Ojibwa belief, the Windigo is figured as an anthropomorphic monster who takes possession of and transforms human beings, disposing them to cannibalism. Thompson's account is notable because he subsumes the figure of the Windigo into that of *Macimanitōw*, whereas many other sources consider the two as distinct. For a thorough discussion of the Windigo phenomenon, see Nelson, "*Orders of the Dreamed*," ed. Brown and Brightman, 158–71.

1 In his journal entry for 2 April, Thompson records, "The old Sucre came in, brought a few Skins & the flesh of part of 2 Bears." AO. 9.102.

2 Sheshepaskut likely described the destruction before 1790 of the Cheyenne village known as the Biesterfeldt site, an event that probably also lies behind Thompson's passing reference on iv.176 (218) to the Cheyenne village "lately destroyed." Located on the banks of the Sheyenne River in modern-day North Dakota, Biesterfeldt had been occupied since at least 1724 and was abandoned after the Ojibwa attack. Excavations at the site have confirmed Sheshepaskut's testimony of the presence of horses, an agricultural economy, and the burning of the village. The chief's account also indicates the existence of Cheyenne-Ojibwa trading relationships, against a background of mutual suspicion and periodic outbreaks of hostility. Moore, *The Cheyenne*; Joseph Jablow, *The Cheyenne in Plains Indian Trade Relations, 1795–1840* (New York: J.J. Augustin, 1950).

they said nothing, but came directly to me, a Council was called, at which all the Men who had never returned from hunting were spoken of by their relations; and it was determined the Chyenne Village must be destroyed; As the Geese were now leaving us, and Winter at hand, we defered to make war on them until the next Summer; and in the mean time we sent word to all the men of our tribe to be ready and meet us here when the berries are in flower. Thus the winter passed; and at the time appointed we counted about one hundred and fifty men. We required two hundred, but some of the best hunters could not come they had to hunt and fish for the families of the Warriors that came. We made our War Tent, and our Medicine Men slept in it; their Dreams forbid us to attack them until the Bulls were fat; the Chyenne's would then leave their Village weak to hunt and make provisions, to which we agreed.

The time soon came, and we marched from one piece of Woods to another, mostly in the night until we came to the last great Grove that was near to the Village. Our Scouts were six young men. Two of them went to a small Grove near [iv.200] the Village, and climbing up the tallest Oaks, saw all that passed in the Village and were relieved every evening and morning by [an]other two.

We thus passed six days, our provisions were nearly done, and we did not dare to hunt. Some of our Men dreamed we were discovered and left us. On the seventh morning as we were in council, one of the young men who were on the watch came to us, and gave us notice, that the Chyenne had collected their Horses and brought them to the Village. We immediately got ourselves ready, and waited for the other young man who was on the Watch; it was near mid day when he came, and informed us that a great many men and women had gone off a hunting, and very few remained in the Village. We now marched leisurely to the small Grove of Oaks, to give the hunting party time to proceed so far as to be beyond the sound of our Guns. At this Grove we ought to have remained all night and attack the next morning; but our Provisions were done, and if they found the Bisons near; part of them might return; From the Grove to the Village was about a mile of open plain; as we ran over, we were perceived, there were several Horses in the Village on which the young people got, and rode off.

We entered the Village and put every one to death, except three Women; after taking every thing we wanted, we quickly set fire to the Village, and with all haste retreated for those that fled at our attack would soon bring back the whole party, and we do not wish to encounter Cavalry in the Plains."

Here the old Chief lighted his pipe and smoked in a thoughtful manner. Mr Cadotte then took up the [iv.201] narrative. "Those left in charge of the

Village were twelve Men of a certain age, and as there was no time to scalp them in the manner they wished, their heads were cut off [and] put into bags; with which, and the prisoners, they marched through the Woods to the camp near the Rainy River. Here they recounted their exploits, and prepared for a grand war dance the next day; which accordingly took place. One of the three Women prisoners was a fine steady looking woman with an infant in her arms of eight months, which they in vain tried to take from her, each time she folded it in her arms with desperate energy, and they allowed her to keep it.

The war circle being made by the Men, their Wives and Children standing behind them, the three prisoners were placed within the war circle; the heads taken were rolled out of the bags on the ground: and preparatory to their being scalped, the whole circle of Men, Women and Children with tambours rattles and flutes, shouted the War whoop, and danced to the song of Victory. The prisoner Woman with her infant in her arms did not dance, but gently moved away to where the head of her husband was lying, and catching it up, kissed it and placed it to the lips of her infant; it was taken from her and thrown on the ground; a second time she seized it, and did the same; it was again taken from her, and thrown on the ground; a third time she pressed the head of her husband to her heart, to the lips of herself and child; it was taken from her with menace of death; holding up her infant to heaven, she drew a sharp pointed knife from her bosom [iv.202] plunged it into her heart, and fell dead on the head of her husband. They buried her, and her infant was taken to, and brought up at, the Rainy River House."

The old Chief still smoking his pipe, said the Great Spirit had made her a Woman, but had given her the heart of a Man.[3] Our discourse then turned on the Sixty Seven, souls, Men Women and Children that two springs ago were destroyed by the Sieux Indians at the Sand Lake of the Mississippe where they were making Sugar;[4] The Chief replied that he did not know what

3 Thompson recorded two other accounts of this gruesome episode: in the *Travels* on iii.67–9 (Volume II) and in his notebooks on AO. 52.92, in the same volume as an 1822 journal. The two *Travels* texts differ only slightly. The notebook version, while unmistakeably a narration of the same event, differs in several particulars; the incident takes place at the NWC's Assiniboine House, the prisoners are Piegan, their captors are Cree and Assiniboine, and the woman takes up the severed head of her husband only once before stabbing herself.

4 Thompson passed Sand Lake, on the Upper Mississippi, on 6 May 1798 (see iv.215, below, 249). In his journal entry for 7 May he writes: "The Chippeways were killed by the Nadowessies on the 19th Febr[uar]y 1797 – ab[ou]t 1¼ day's March Southward of the Sand Lake in the Interiour Country 46 Souls in all." AO. 9.86. In a letter

to say to it; it was a bad affair and they longed to revenge it: but they in a manner brought it on themselves. For several years there had been no regular war between us, they had left the Woods, made very little use of Canoes, and having many Horses were living in the Plains and had we waited would have left the whole of the Woods to us. The Sand Lake was finely wooded with large Maples[5] which had never been tapped; this tempted our people, they went and made a great deal of Sugar; this did for once, and the Sieux took no notice of it; but when they returned the next Spring, this was making that Lake their own, the Sieux did not care for it, but would not allow it to be taken from them. They formed a war party, and so completely surprised our people, that not one escaped, and the enmity that was dying away between us is now as bad as ever. While they keep the Plains with their Horses, we are not a match for them, for we being footmen, they could get to windward of us, and set fire to the grass; When we marched for the Woods, they would be there before us, dismount and under cover fire on us. Until we have Horses like them, we must keep to the Woods, and leave the Plains [iv.203] to them until we have Horses.

[Mr Cadotte. Primitive & Dialects]

¶ On conversing with these Chippaways they all readily understood me, though frequently I did not understand them, and Mr Cadotte had to interpret between us. He also expressed his surprise that they should understand me, which he did not; they replied, we understand him because he speaks the language of our Fathers, which we have much changed and made better. On comparing the Nouns and Verbs of the primitive language of the Nahathaways with the Chippaway dialect; the greatest change appeared in constantly rejecting the "th" of the former for the "y" of the latter, as for Ke ther (you) Ke yer, for Nee ther (me) Nee yer, for Wee ther (thou) Wee yer; and softening a great number of others, rejecting some and substituting others, and giving to the whole a more sonorous sound as best adapted to their oratory. The dialects of the primitive language extend to the Delaware River; and the Delaware Indians speak a dialect of the primitive language.[1] By astronomi-

---

of 9 July 1797, Thomas Duggan, storekeeper at St Joseph Island, reported that forty-five Ojibwa and five Santee were killed in the incident. Thomas Duggan to Joseph Chew, 9 July 1797, RG8, C250: 256, LAC.

5 Sugar maple (*Acer saccharum*).

1 By "primitive language," Thompson means the original language from which the several dialects are derived. Delaware belongs to an eastern branch of Algonquian.

cal observations this House is in Latitude 47··54··21 N. Longitude 96··19 W Variation 10 degrees East. The course of this River is from the south west ward until it is lost in the Plains, the groves are at a considerable distance from each other, by no means sufficient for the regular Farmer, but may become a fine pastoral country, but without a Market, other than the inhabitants of the Red River.

[*Clear Water to Red Lake River. Lake. Chippaways fish spearing. Red Lake and Carrying Place 6M*]

¶ The Rivers becoming clear of ice, a Birch Rind Canoe of eighteen feet in length, by three feet in breadth was made ready; and on the ninth day of April with three Canadians, and a native Woman, the Wife of [iv.204] one of the Men, and twelve day's provisions in dried meat, We set out to survey the country to the scource of the Mississippe River.[1] We had the choice of two Rivers, that direct from the Red Lake; the current moderate, but liable to be encumbered with ice from the Lake, or the Clear Water River of swift current; without any ice; we preferred the latter, and proceeded slowly up it. This River was fifty five yards in width by about eight feet in depth, from the melting of the Snow, but as all these Rivers are fed by Snow and Rains, in the months of August and September this River's depth will not exceed one or two feet. Although the country appears a perfect level the current ran at the rate of full four miles an hour, the River was too deep, to anchor our ticklish[2] Canoe, but seeing a piece of Wood on the middle of the River I left the Canoe and walked as fast as I could, yet the current carried the wood faster than I walked.

On the eleventh we passed the junction of the Wild Rice River from the westward, with a body of water equal to half this River, and we have now less water with more moderate current. On the twelfth we arrived at the Carrying Place which leads to the Red Lake River, having come sixty four miles up this sinuous River. The east side, or right bank had fine Forest's, but as we advanced, the Aspin became the principal growth of the Woods. The West Bank had patches of hard wood trees with much fine meadow which led to the Plains, the whole a rich deep soil.

---

1 Thompson's journey from Cadotte's House to Turtle Lake, lasting from 9 to 27 April 1798, is recorded in his journals on AO. 7.18v–22r; 9.101–93, and in the 1848 version of the *Travels* on iii.93–4 (Volume II).
2 Easily overturned.

The Carrying Place is four miles in length of part marsh and part good ground to the Bank of the Red Lake River, in Latitude 48-0··55 N Longitude 95··54-28' W. Variation 10° East.

[iv.205] Our course was now up this River to the Red Lake, a distance of thirty two miles. Both banks of this River well timbered with Oak, Ash, and other hard Woods, intermixed with much Aspin and Poplar, a rich deep soil, but now from the melting of the Snow every where covered with water, the country so level, that only a chance bit of dry bank was to be seen; At night we cut down Trees and slept upon them. As our provisions were dried meat we did not require fire to cook our supper, and a Canadian never neglects to have touchwood for his pipe. By Observations the head of the River on the banks of the Lake, is in Latitude 47··58··15 N Longitude 95··35··37 W. The straight course and distance from Mr Cadotte's House is, N 82 E 35 Miles, to perform which we have gone over 117 Statute miles and employed seven long days, setting off at 5 AM and putting up at 7 PM. At the Lake the kind old Chief, She she pas kut with six Lodges of Chippaways were camped. He gave us three pickerel and two large pike, a welcome change from dried meat. As they had no Canoe, and therefore could not spear fish in the night, they requested the loan of mine, which was lent to them.

¶ The spearing of fish in the night is a favorite mode with them, and gives to them a considerable part of their livelihood. The Spear handle is a straight pole of ten to twelve feet in length, headed with a barbed iron; A rude narrow basket of iron hoops, is fixed to a pole of about six feet in length. A quantity of birch rind is collected and loosely tied in small parcels. When the night comes, the darker the better, two Men and a Boy embark in a Canoe, the one gently and quietly to give motion to the Canoe, the pole and basket is fixed in the Bow under which the Spearman stands, the Birch Rind is set [iv.206] on fire, and burns with a bright light, but only for a short time, the Boy from behind feeds the light so as to keep a constant blaze. The approach of the flaming light seems to stupify the fish, as they are all speared in a quiesent state. The Lake or River is thus explored for several hours until the Birch Rind is exhausted, and on a calm night a considerable number is thus caught. Those in my Canoe speared three Sturgeon, each weighing about sixty pounds. For a clear water Lake they were very good; for the Sturgeon may be called the Water Hog, and is no where so good and fat as among the alluvials of Rivers.[3]

3 Nocturnal spearfishing by torchlight is practised by Natives in many parts of North America. For a discussion of Ojibwa spearfishing that cites Thompson's description, see Larry Nesper, *The Walleye War: The Struggle for Ojibwe Spearfishing and Treaty*

¶ This, the Red Lake is a fine sheet of Water of about thirty miles in length by eight to 10 miles in breadth; the banks rise about twenty to thirty feet, the soil is somewhat sandy and produces Firs of fine growth, with the other usual woods, and in places the white Cedar but of short growth. This Lake, like several other places, has occasionally a trading House for one Winter only, the country all around being too poor in furrs to be hunted on a second winter. The Lake being covered with ice, and patches of water, at places we paddled the Canoe, and where the ice was firm made a rude Sledge on which we placed the Canoe and Baggage, and hauled it over the ice to a patch of water and thus continued for seventeen miles; a laborious work and always wet, the weather frequent showers of Rain and Sleet; and then clear weather. We now came to a Carrying Place of six miles in length, in a south direction, over which we carried our Canoe and things.

The Road was through Firs and Aspins, with a few Oaks and Ash. Near the middle of the Carrying Place the Ground had many ascents and descents of twenty to forty feet, the first we have seen since we left the Red River. By 9 PM on the 23rd of April we had carried [iv.207] all over, and now had to cross the country to the Turtle Lake, the head of the Mississippe River at which we arrived on the 27th. Our Journey has been very harassing and fatigue-ing; from Pond to Pond and Brook to Brook with many carrying places, the Ponds, or small Lakes were some open, others wholly or partly covered with ice; the Brooks so winding, that after paddling an hour we appeared to have made very little, or no advance.

[*Country to Turtle Lake. Loons. Wild Geese. killed at Churchill. Rice. Experiment of Dr John Hunter. Turtle Lake. The wild Rice. Turtle & Red Cedar Lake. Mr Sayer. Collecting wild rice. Wild Rice & Sugar making. Sugar Groves*]

The country every where appeared low and level, something like an immense swamp. Every where there was much wild rice, upon which the wild fowl fed, and became very fat and well tasted; The Swan was a very rare bird; and of the different species of Geese only two species of the Grey Goose; but the Ducks in all their varieties; the Cranes and Bitterns upon their usual

Rights (Lincoln: University of Nebraska Press, 2002), 56–9. While the Ojibwa fisher-men here use birchbark for their torches, Thompson notes elsewhere that the more resinous fir is preferred as fuel (iv.70, 125 and iv.214, 248). Thompson also writes of daylight spearfishing at Rainy River (iv.121, 178) and Fond du Lac (iv.224, 255), and, in the 1848 version of the *Travels*, in the Columbia Basin (Volume II).

food were equally good; Of the Plover species there were but few, the Ponds having their low banks covered with long grass. In some Ponds there were Pelicans and Cormorants, the former as disgusting as usual. The large spotted Loons were in every Pond that was open; this wiley Bird as soon as he saw us set up his cry, and was at a loss whether to fly or dive, for the latter the Ponds were too shoal and full of rice stalks; and before he could raise his flight he had to beat the water with Wings and Feet before he could raise himself, this exposed them to our shots, and we killed several of them, their beautiful spotted skins make favorite Caps for the Natives, and two Canoes of Chippaways being in company were thankful to get them. It is very well known that at Churchill Factory in Hudsons Bay in Latitude 58··47··32 N Longitude 94.13.48 West, in the spring wild grey geese are killed with wild Rice in their stomachs; on which they must have fed near the Turtle Lake in Latitude 47·39·15 N [iv.208] Longitude 95·12··45 W. The direct distance between the two places is N 3° E 780 statute miles. Wild Rice but not in any quantity: so as to feed numerous flocks of Geese, grow in places near the Latitude of 50 degrees north, but even from these few places the distance to Churchill Fort will be about 660 miles. The wild rice grows in great plenty all around the Turtle Lake, allowing this Lake to be their centre. The Ponds Brooks, Rivulets and small Lakes in which the wild Rice grows in abundance occupies an extent of area of at least six thousand square miles.

It is a weak food, those who live for months on it enjoy good health, are moderately active, but very poor in flesh; The Wild Geese, before a Gale of Wind fly at the rate of sixty miles an hour, which at this rate requires thirteen hours from these rice grounds to take them to Churchill Fort (Note. Conversing with Surgeon Howard of Montreal[1] on the great distance the Wild Geese fly without digesting the rice in their stomachs, he related to me an experiment of the late Dr John Hunter[2] on digestion: He had two grey hounds one morning he fed them both with the same quantity and quality of Meat; the

1 Henry Howard (1815–87) immigrated to Canada from Ireland in 1842 and soon became a prominent specialist in ophthamology. In February 1848 he treated Thompson for a cataract and a cicatrix, a case that he recounted in his 1850 work *The Anatomy, Physiology, and Pathology of the Eye.* See note on 27zd (74); Howard, op. cit., 357–8; Rodrigue Samuel, "Henry Howard," DCB, 9:425–6.

2 John Hunter (1728–93), a surgeon and anatomist, was named Surgeon-Extraordinary to George III in 1776. Particularly skilled in dissection, Hunter presented the results of his investigations in numerous publications. Jacob W. Gruber, "John Hunter," ODNB, 28:898–906. The source of the greyhound digestion experiment has not been located.

one he tied up, and remained quiet all day; and with the other he hunted
all day, about sun set they were both killed. On examining the hound that
was tied up, the Meat was wholly digested; but in the stomach of the hound
that had hunted all day the meat was but little changed, thus it appears that
animals on a rapid march do not digest their food, or very slowly) These
extensive rice grounds are probably the last place where the Wild Fowl that
proceed [iv.209] far to the northward (about 1400 miles) to make their nests,
and bring up their young, feed for a few days, to give them strength for their
journey, for the late springs of the northern climes they pass over cannot give
them much. In the Brooks and small Lakes were several Otters, of which we
killed one; to make the flesh of this animal more palatable, the Natives hang
it in the smoke for a couple of days.

For the first time we saw the small brown Eagle,[3] some days we saw at
least a dozen of them, but always beyond the reach of our Guns. From Mr
Cadotte's House on the Red River to this place, the Turtle Lake we have been
nineteen days, rising early and putting up late, and yet by my astronomical
observations, the course and distance is s 71 Eastward 56 statute miles, in a
direct line not quite three miles a day. These circuituous routes deceive the
traveller, and induce him to think he is at a much greater distance from a
given place than what he actually is. The Turtle Lake which is the very head
of the Mississippe River, is four miles in length, by as many in breadth and
it's small bays give it the rude form of a Turtle;[4] (Note. By the Treaty of 1783
between Great Britain and the United States,[5] the northern boundary of the
latter was designated to be a Line due west from the north corner of the Lake
of the Woods (in Latitude 49·46¾ N) to the head of the Mississippe which
was supposed to be still more to the north; This supposition arose from the
Fur Traders on ascending the Mississippe which is very sinuous, counting
every pipe a League of three miles, at the end of which they claim a right to
rest and smoke a pipe. By my survey I found these pipes to be the average
length of only two miles, and they also threw out of account the windings of

3 Possibly the broad-winged hawk (*Buteo platypterus*).
4 In 1832 Henry Schoolcraft had identified Lake Itasca, some 30 miles (50 kilometres)
   southwest of Turtle Lake, as the source of the Mississippi. Henry Rowe Schoolcraft,
   Narrative of an Expedition through the Upper Mississippi to Itasca Lake (New York:
   Harper and Brothers, 1834). Thompson was likely aware of Schoolcraft's claim and
   probably persisted in regarding Turtle Lake as the source because, from this place,
   waters flow in a consistent southeasterly direction. The drainage from Lake Itasca is
   longer but flows north before turning southeast.
5 For the Treaty of Paris, see note on iv.115 (170).

the River, and thus placing the Turtle Lake 128 geographical [iv.210] miles too far to the north)

¶ Two Canoes of Chippaway Indians came to us on their way to the Red Cedar Lake;[6] As my Canoe from coming too often in contact with the ice was leaky I embarked with them to the Red Cedar Lake. From the SW corner of the Turtle Lake a Brook goes out, by the name of the Turtle Brook of three yards in width by two feet in depth at 2½ miles Per hour, but so very winding, that rather than follow it, we made a Carrying Place of 180 yards, to a small Lake which sends a Brook into it, and which we followed, and then continued the main stream following it's incredible windings and turnings through, apparently an extensive very low country of grass and marsh. There were three falls, along which we made as many carrying Places, and several rapids over a gravel bottom; As we proceeded several Brooks came in from each hand, and we entered the Red Cedar Lake in a fine Stream of fifteen yards in width, by two feet in depth, and three miles an hour. Proceeding five miles over the Lake we came to the trading house of Mr John Sayer, a Partner of the North West Company, and in charge of this Department.[7] By my Observations this House is in Latitude 47··27··56 N Longitude 94··47··52 West Variation 6 degrees East.

¶ From the north bank of Turtle Lake to this trading house the course and distance S 58 E 25 Miles but the windings of the River will more than treble this distance. The Stream has a grassy valley in which it holds it's zigzag course; the land is very low the Woods on each side of the Valley are of Oak, Ash Elm, Larch, Birch, Pines, Aspins, and where a little elevated fine Maple. The soil every where deep and rich with abundance of long grass. The Brooks and Ponds, and the Turtle Rivulet almost from side to side full of the Stalks of the Wild Rice, which makes it very [iv.211] laborious to come against the current, as the Canoe must keep the middle of the stream against the full force of the current. Mr Sayer and his Men had passed the whole winter on wild rice and maple Sugar which keeps them alive, but poor in flesh; Being a good shot on the wing I had killed twenty large Ducks more than we wanted, which I gave to him a most welcome present, as they had not tasted meat

---

6 Now known as Cass Lake.

7 For NWC trader John Sayer, see appendix 2. Thompson arrived at Sayer's Cass Lake post on 29 April 1798 and remained there until 3 May. For the journal of these days, see AO. 7.22r–23r; 9.92. During this time, Thompson and Sayer, finding that their chronology disagreed by a day, made a wager: whoever was correct would receive from the other "half a dozen of Madeira to be drank at the Grand Portage." AO. 9.92.

for a long time. A mess of rice and sugar was equally acceptable to me who had lived wholly on meat; and I tried to live upon it, but the third day was attacked with heart burn and weakness of the stomach, which two meals of meat cured; but the rice makes good soup. From the remarks I have made in the vicissitudes of my life, I have always found that men leading an active life readily change their food from vegetable to animal without in convenience, but not from animal to vegetable, the latter often attended with weakness of the bowels.

The wild Rice is fully ripe in the early part of September. The Natives lay thin birch rind all over the bottom of the Canoe, a Man lightly clothed, or naked places himself in the middle of the Canoe, and with a hand on each side, seizes the stalks and knocks the ears of rice against the inside of the Canoe, into which the rice falls, and thus he continues until the Canoe is full of rice; on coming ashore the Women assist in unloading. A Canoe may hold from ten to twelve bushels. He smokes his pipe, sings a Song; and returns to collect another canoe load;

And so plentifull is the rice, an industrious Man may fill his canoe three times in a day. Scaffolds are prepared about six feet from the ground [iv.212] made of small sticks covered with long grass; on this the rice is laid, and gentle clear fires kept underneath by the women, and turned until the rice is fully dried. The quantity collected is no more than the scaffolds can dry, as the rice is better on the stalk than on the ground. The rice when dried is pounded in a mortar made of a piece of hollow oak with a pestle of the same until the husk comes off. It is then put up in bags made of rushes and secured against animals. The Natives collect not only enough for themselves; but also as much as the furr traders will buy from them; Two or three Ponds of water can furnish enough for all that is collected.

¶ In the Spring the Natives employ themselves in making Sugar from the Maple Trees, the process of doing which is well known. The old trees give a stronger sap than the young trees; The Canadians also make a great quantity, which, when the sap is boiled to a proper consistence, they run into moulds, where it hardens, but the Indians prefer making it like Muscovado sugar,[8] this is done simply by stirring it quickly about with a small paddle. The Plane Tree[9] also makes a good sugar, the sap is abundant, and the sugar whiter, but not so strong. Both sugars have a taste, which soon becomes agreeable, and as fine white loaf sugar can be made from it as from that of the West Indies.

8 Muscovado sugar is obtained from the juice of the sugar cane by means of evaporation and draining.
9 Manitoba maple (*Acer negundo*).

The Natives would make far more than they do, if they could find a Market. The men of family that trade at this House are about Sixty; and Mr Sayer who has been in the Furr Trade many years, is of opinion that seven persons to a family is about a fair average, this will give 420 souls. The Natives here call [iv.213] themselves "Oo che poys,"[10] and for some few years have begun to give something like a right of property to each family on the sugar maple groves, and which right continues in the family to the exclusion of others, but as this appropriated space is small in comparison of the whole extent; any, and every person is free to make sugar on the vacant grounds. The appropriation was made by them in council, in order to give to each family a full extent of ground for making Sugar and to prevent the disputes that would arise where all claim an equal right to the soil and it's productions, and as in the making of sugar, several kettles and many small vessels of wood and birch rind for collecting and boiling the sap are required, which are not wanted for any other purpose, are thus left in safety on their own grounds for future use.

[*Proceed on the Voyage. Mississippe, its turnings. Indian his Nose bit off & stuck on again. Mississippe, it's very sinuous course. descent, it's noble valley. length & discharge*]

¶ Our Canoe being in very bad order from rough usage among the ice Mr Sayer purchased a good canoe for us, for the value of twenty beaver skins in goods and our Canoe. It was my intention to have gone a considerable distance down the River, but Mr Sayer strongly advised to go no further down than to Sand Lake River, as beyond we should be in the power of the Sieux Indians. On the third day of May we took leave of our kind host,[1] our provisions were wild rice and maple sugar; with powder and shot for ducks. One mile beyond the house we entered the River, now augmented to twenty six yards in width by three feet in depth, at two miles an hour: The valley of the Mississippe, lay now clear before me, it's direction South East; it's appearance was that of a meadow of long half dried grass without water of about half a mile in width, or less. On the left side points of wood came to the edge of this valley, but not into it, at a mile, or a mile and a half from each other, the intervals were [iv.214] bays of hay marsh. On the right hand the line of

10 I.e., Ojibwa.
 1 For Thompson's journey from Cass Lake to Fond du Lac House on Lake Superior, lasting 3–10 May 1798, see AO. 7.23r–26v; 9.92–87 and iii.96–8 in the 1848 version of the *Travels* (Volume II).

Woods was more regular; Being well experienced in taking levels,[2] the Valley of the River before us showed a declining plane of full twenty Per Mile for the first three miles; this would give a current which no boat could ascend; but this was completely broken down by the innumerable turnings of the River to every point of the compass. Seeing a Pole before us at less than five hundred yards, the four hands in the canoe paddled smartly for thirty five minutes before a current of 2½ miles an hour to arrive at it, in which time we estimated we had passed over about three miles of the windings of the River. Meeting an Indian in his canoe ascending the River, he smoked with us, and on my remarking to him the crookedness of the River, he shook his head, and said Snake make this River, I thought otherwise, for these windings break the current and make it navigable. I have always admired the formations of the Rivers, as directed by the finger of God for the most benevolent purposes. At 7 PM we put up in Lake Winepegoos[3] formed by the waters of this River it's length is seventeen miles, by about six miles in width, the principal fish is Sturgeon. The woods have all day had much Fir, both red and black, the latter very resinous and much used for torches for night fishing. The soil of the Woods is now sandy; with Points of alluvial, on which are Oaks and other hard woods, and the bays have White Cedar, Birch and Larch. On leaving the Lake the valley of the River appeared more level.

On the 4th at noon put ashore to observe for Latitude and shortly after the River passing over a fine bottom of gravel, I found the River to be 26 yards wide 2½ feet deep by 2¼ miles an hour, nine miles below the Leach River from Leach Lake, southwestward of us comes in, it's size appears equal to this River, which it [iv.215] deepens, but does not add to it's breadth. For this day the valley of the River is from half to one mile in width, on each side well wooded with fine Firs.

May 5th. After proceeding two miles saw the first leaves on the Willows, the Maple and other Trees are in full bud, but have no leaves. We came to a Rapid, and a Fall over a smooth Rock of eight feet desent; the whole is thirteen feet perpendicular, with a Carrying Place of 263 yards. Six miles further the Meadow River[4] from the north eastward joins, it's size and water equal to this, the Mississippe, which is now fifty to sixty yards in breadth. We met a Man wounded in the shoulder, in a quarrel with another Man, his Wife

---

2 The taking of levels is a standard surveying technique. A theodolite is used to measure the vertical angle between points in the landscape, and the height difference between the points is determined through triangulation.

3 Lake Winnibigoshish.

4 Prairie River.

was paddling the Canoe, it appeared jealousy was the cause. On the 6th May we continued our route; in the course of the day we met an Indian and his Wife the Man had a large fresh scar across his nose, and when smoking with us, asked if he was not still handsome; on arriving at Sand Lake we learned that the evening before, while drinking, another Indian had quarreled with him and in a fit of jealousy had bit off his nose and thrown it away, but in the morning finding his nose was missing, he searched for, and found it, the part that remained was still bleeding, on which he stuck the part bitten off, without anything to keep it; it adhered; and taking a looking glass, exclaimed, "as yet I am not ugly." I was after wards informed, the cure became complete, and only the scar remained.[5]

¶ The Swan River from the north eastward fell in with a bold stream of water. In the afternoon at 5 PM we arrived at the mouth of the Sand Lake River a short distance above which I measured the [iv.216] Mississippe River; 62 yards in width; 12 feet in depth; at 4 yards from the shore 10 feet, at two yards 8 feet in depth by full two miles an hour. The mouth of the Sand Lake River is in Latitude 46-49-11 N Longitude 93··45··7 W and from the Red Cedar Lake S 48 E 68 Miles. As the Mississippe is the most magnificent River, and flows through the finest countries, of North America. I shall endeavour to explain the peculiar formation of it's head waters. From the Turtle to the Red Cedar Lake, the passage was too much obstructed by ice to allow me to form a correct idea of it's windings; but from the latter Lake to the mouth of the Sand Lake River there was no ice; From the Red Cedar Lake to the latter river is 68 miles direct distance; to perform which four hands in a light Canoe paddled forty three hours and thirteen minutes. Of this direct distance ten miles were Lake, leaving fifty eight miles of River; and allowing three hours and thirteen minutes for passing the Lake; forty hours remain. Four hands in a light Canoe before a current of two, and at times, two and a half miles an hour, will proceed, at least five miles an hour; and this rate for forty hours will give a distance of two hundred miles of the windings of the river for fifty eight miles in a direct line, being nearly three and a half miles to one mile. Every mile of these sinuousities of the River the current turned to every point of the compass, and it's direct velocity was diminished, yet continuing to have a steady current, measured at two full miles an hour, must have a descent of full twenty inches Per mile to maintain this current; which in two hundred miles gives a descent, or change of level in this [iv.217]

5 In his journal entry for 7 May 1798, Thompson identifies the two combatants as Muskass (who lost his nose) and Namapeth. AO. 9.86.

distance of 333 feet 4 inches, equal to a change of level of 5 3/4 feet for each mile in a direct line.

Thus the descent, from the Turtle to the Red Cedar Lake is 97 3/4 feet, and from this Lake to the Sand Lake River 333 1/3 feet; giving a change of level of 431 feet, apparently through a low country. (Note. Lieutenant Lynch of the US Navy in his survey of the River Jordan from the Sea of Tiberias to the Dead Sea, says the difference of level of the two seas is something more than one thousand feet. The distance between these Seas in the direct line of the River is sixty miles, but the windings of the Jordan increases the distance to two hundred miles which gives a descent of five feet to a mile, they descended it in two boats in safety, passing over twenty seven strong rapids and many lesser to the Dead Sea)[6]

To the intelligent part of mankind, the scources of all the great rivers have always been subjects of curiosity; witness the expeditions undertaken; the sums of money expended, and the sufferings endured to discover the sources of the Nile, the research of ages.[7] Whatever the Nile had been in ancient times in Arts and Arms, the noble valley of the Mississippe bids fair to be, and excluding its pompous, useless, Pyramids and other works; it's anglo saxon population will far exceed the Egyptians in all the arts of civilized life and in a pure religion. Although these are the predictions of a solitary traveller unknown to the world they will surely be verified (1798). The course and length of the River [iv.218] Mississippe from it's scource to it's discharge into the gulph of Mexico in Latitude 29°··0' North Longitude 89·10 West is S 14 E 1344 Miles. This great River including the Missisourie, drains an extent of 981,034 square geographical miles, equal to 1,136,365 square statute miles.[8] In common average of low water this River discharges 82,000

---

6 William Francis Lynch (1801–65) of the United States Navy published his *Narrative of the United States' Expedition to the River Jordan and the Dead Sea* in 1849. Lynch determined the level of Lake Tiberias to be 312 feet, and that of the Dead Sea to be 1,316 feet.

7 Speculation about the source of the Nile dates to antiquity. Interest in the source of the White Nile was particularly high during the 1830s and 1840s, and the three well-publicized expeditions organized by the Ottoman rulers of Egypt in 1839–42 included several European participants. The source of the White Nile was determined by John Hanning Speke and James Grant in 1862. John O. Udal, *The Nile in Darkness: Conquest and Exploration, 1504–1862* (Norfolk: Michael Russell, 1998).

8 A geographical mile, determined by one minute of arc along Earth's equator, is equal to just over 6,087 feet, while a statute mile equals 5,280 feet.

cubic feet of water in a second of time; at this rate it annually places in the gulph of Mexico 17 57/100 cubic miles of fresh water; and including freshets and steady high water, a volume equal to 19 1/3 cubic miles.

[*poor country. Sand Lake. Monsieur Boiske interprets my Observations. Sugar trading. Arrive at the great Morass. Cross the Morass. remarks. Savannah Brook. River St Louis. Carrying Places &c. it's navigation*]

On the 6th day of May we arrived at the Sand Lake River, up which we turn, and bend our course for Lake Superior. Since we left the Red River on the 9th day of April we have not seen the track of a Deer, or the vestige of a Beaver not a single Aspin marked with it's teeth. The Indians we met all appeared very poor from the animals being almost wholly destroyed in this section of the country; their provisions were of wild rice and sugar; we did not see a single duck in their canoes, ammunition being too scarce; nor did we see a Bow and Arrows with them, weapons which are in constant use among the Nahathaways for killing all kinds of fowl; they were bare footed and poorly dressed.

The Sand Lake River, is twenty yards wide, by five feet in depth, at one and a half miles an hour, it's length two miles to the Sand Lake, proceeding more than a mile we came to a trading house of the North West Company under the charge of Monsieur Boiské.[1] Here were the Women and children of about twenty families, the Men were all hunting in the Plains on the west side of the Mississippe [iv.219] to make half dried meat, and procure skins for leather of the Bison but the meat thus split and dried is very coarsely done, and to make it something decent it has to pass through the hands of the Women. These people can only dress the hide of the Bison into leather; but have not the art of dressing it with the hair on, to make Robes of it, so usefull for cloathing and bedding. As the Men were hunting on what is called the War Grounds,

1 The NWC post on the west shore of Big Sandy Lake was established in 1794. Charles Bousquet was employed as a clerk in 1795 by NWC partner John Sayer, and he spent several years trading at Big Sandy Lake before leaving the NWC for the XYC in 1802. After the firms' 1804 union, Bousquet served in the NWC's Lake Winnipeg Department, retiring to the Red River Settlement. Coues, ed., *Early History of the Greater Northwest*, 927; Bruce White, *The Fur Trade in Minnesota: An Introductory Guide to Manuscript Sources* (St Paul: Minnesota Historical Society Press, 1977), 35; Georges Dugas, *The Canadian West* (Montreal: Librarie Beauchemin, 1905), 282. See also iii.96–7 in the 1848 version of the *Travels* (Volume II).

that is, the debateable lands between them and the Sieux Indians, the women were anxiously waiting their arrival.[2] The night being fine, as usual I was observing for the Latitude and Longitude of the place; in the morning an aged Man, no longer able to hunt came to me, and said, I come on the part of the Women, for they want to know where the Men are, are they loaded with meat, and when will they arrive; I requested Monsieur Boiské to tell him, that I knew nothing of the matter, and saw only the Moon and Stars, but he took his own view of the question; and told him to tell the Women; the Men are safe, they will be here tomorrow, each has a load of Meat, but it is poor, there is no fat on it; and they must not get drunk again until the Bisons are fat (August), and who ever bites off another man's nose, would be killed by the Sieux in the first battle, "Umph" said the old man, "while we can get fire water we will drink it." The Women were pleased, and said all the Men were fools that drank fire water. He informed me the Women in general kept themselves sober, and when the Men were about to drink they hid all the Arms, and Knives and left them nothing but their teeth and fists to fight with. This gentleman, was of the same opinion with the other Traders, that ardent Spirits was a curse to the [iv.220] Natives, it not only occasioned quarrels, but also revived old animosities, that had been forgotten. It kept the Indians poor and was of no use as an article of trade.

He showed me his winter hunt, in value fifty beaver skins. The Minks and Martens were inferior the Lynxes appeared good, but the furr not so long as in the north but the Fishers[3] were uncommonly large, the color a rich glossy black brown, and the furr fine: The Beaver's were mostly fall and spring skins, and as such were good in color and furr, but not a single Fox, or Wolf. These animals are almost unknown, there is nothing for them to live on. All his furrs came from the Forests between the Mississippe and Lake Superior.

We had traded 16 Cwt[4] of Maple Sugar from the Natives; this was packed in baskets of birch rind, of 28 to 68 lbs each. The Sugar appeared clean and well made; that of the Plane Trees, looked like the East India Sugars; and much the same in taste: In this article I have already noticed the supply is greater than the demand. The Men of family that trade here are about forty two, which at seven souls to each man, is 294. We had now to cross the country to gain the River St Louis, and by it descend to Lake Superior. Our Provisions were four pieces of dried bison meat; four beaver tails and two quarts

2 For this transitional zone, see Harold Hickerson, *The Chippewa and Their Neighbours*, rev. edn. (Prospect Heights, IL: Waveland, 1988), ch. 6.
3 *Martes pennanti*.
4 Hundredweight; 1 hundredweight equals 112 pounds or 50.8 kilograms.

of swamp cranberries, they were the largest I had ever seen, being about the size of a small hazel nut.

This trading house is in Latitude 46.46..30. N Longitude 93-44-17 West Variation 6 degrees East. On the 7th May went over the Sand Lake of four miles in length, by about one mile in width to Savannah Brook, up which we proceeded eight geographical miles of which 1¼ mile is a large Pond, but the windings lengthen the Brook to thirteen miles, [iv.221] to a great Swamp, of 4½ S Miles across it in a N 81 E direction the latter part of what may be termed bog; over which we passed by means of a few sticks laid length ways, and when we slipped off we sunk to our waists, and with difficulty regained our footing on the sticks. No Woods grow on this great Swamp except scattered pine shrubs of a few feet in height; yet such as it was, we had to carry our Canoe and all our things, and all the furrs, provisions, baggage and Canoes of the Mississippe have to be carried on their way to the Depot on Lake Superior, and likewise all the goods for the winter trade. It is a sad piece of work. The Person in charge of the brigade; crosses it as fast as he can, leaves the Men to take their own time, who flounce along with the packs of furrs, or pieces of goods, and "sacre"[5] as often as they please. Heavy Canoes cannot be carried over but at great risque both to the Men and Canoes, and the Company have Canoes at each end. This great Swamp, extended as far as we could see northward and southward, and I could not learn it's termination either way. It appears to be somewhat like a height of land between the Mississippe and the River St Louis, as from it's west side it sends a brook into the former; and from it's east side a brook into the latter.

With an extra Man to help us, it took us a long day to get all across it. At the east end I observed for Latitude and Longitude which gave 46··52·3 N Longitude 92·28·42 W Variation 6 degrees east. We now entered a Brook of seven feet wide, three feet deep, by two miles an hour and descended it for twelve miles, but it's windings will extend it to twenty miles, in which distance it receives one brook from the southward, and two from the northward which increased it to ten yards wide, seven feet deep by 1¾ miles an hour. We now entered the River St Louis a bold stream of about one hundred yards in width by eight feet in depth, and [iv.222] the current three miles an hour. Having descended the River 4½ Miles we put up at 7¼ PM. We have been all day in the Forests that surround Lake Superior. The Brook of to day had many wind fallen trees across it, which we had to cut away. In several places we saw the marks of beaver for the first time. On examining a Swan we shot, it had thirteen eggs, from the size of a pea to that of a walnut, yet I do not

---

5 I.e., exclaim the French oath *sacré Dieu* ("holy God").

remember ever seeing more than nine young ones with them. The Woods we have passed are a few Oaks of moderate size, some Ash, but the principal part Maple, Plane, White Birch, Poplar and Aspin; on the low grounds Pines and Larch.

¶ Hitherto the width, depth, and rate of current of the Brooks and Rivers are those of high water from the melting of the snow, but as all of them, even the Red River depend on the Snow and Rains for their supply of water; in the months of August, September and October they are all shoal. The Men who have navigated these streams for several years are now with me, and they assure me that this River (St Louis) bold and deep as it now is, in the above months has only eighteen inches of depth, running among stones which they are often obliged to turn aside to make a passage for their canoes. In the night we heard a Beaver playing about us, flapping his broad tail on the water, with a noise as loud as the report of a small pistol, which was a novelty to us. Upon descending the first rapids, and proceeding downwards, the Men were surprised to find the marks on the trees to which they were accustomed to tie the Canoes at their meals, to be from six to eight feet abov[e] the present level of the River. This may be accounted for, by our being on this river about a month more early than usual, and the sharp night frosts, [iv.223] preventing the melting of the snow on the heights and interiour of Lake Superior. This River has many rapids, on one of which the waves filled the Canoe half full of water; These were succeeded by a Cataract of small low steps of a full mile in length round a point of rock, across which we made a carrying place of 1576 yards. Four miles farther, of almost all rapids; we came to the Long Carrying Place of seven miles in length. On our, left the River descends the lower heights by a series of low falls ending with a steep fall, estimated at 120 feet in height, below which the River flows with a moderate current into Lake Superior.

[*Lake Superior. Country poor. The fog on Indians spearing. X of Level to Mississippe. X of Level 1478 feet*]

The surface rock of the country is a slaty sand stone, very good for sharpening knives and Axes. Near the mouth of the River is a trading House of the North West Company under the charge of Monsieur Lemoine;[1] his returns

---

1 The NWC post at Fond du Lac was established about 1793 and was situated on the south side of the St Louis River, about three miles from its mouth. It served as the headquarters for the NWC's trade in the district and stood until at least 1813. In 1817 the American Fur Company took over trade in the region and established a

were 600 lbs of Furrs with the expectation of trading 400 lbs more 9 Kegs of gum from the Pine Trees for the Canoes and 12 Kegs, each of ten gallons, of Sugar. This House is in Latitude 46·44·33 N Longitude 92-9·45 W. Variation 4½ degrees East, I have only set down my observations made at certain places, but they are numerous all over the survey, as every clear day and night no opportunity was ommitted of taking observations for Latitude, Longitude and Variation to correct the courses and distances of the survey. The Canoes that descend the River to the upper end of the Long Carrying Place, are carefully laid up, and there left, in like manner the Canoes that come from the Lake are left at the lower end. We found three large Canoes [iv.224] and a north Canoe, of 28 feet in length, much broken this was too large for us, but we had no choice, we repaired it, and as we had only three men fitted it up with two oars, which have the force of four paddles, as we had now to encounter the Winds and waves of Lake Superior.

¶ The Natives that trade at this House are about thirty Men of family, and are about 210 souls, in Winter, from the poverty of the country they can barely live, and a small stock of sugar is part of their support. Deer are almost unknown, and they are supplied with leather as with other necessaries. In the open season their support is by fishing, for which the spear is much in use. Their Canoes are about fifteen feet in length by three feet in breadth, and flat bottomed; With a Woman or a Lad to paddle and steer the canoe, the Indian with his long spear, stands on the gunwales at the bar behind the bow; and ticklish as the canoe is, and the Lake almost always somewhat agitated, he preserves his upright posture, as standing on a rock. On the Lake, especially in the fore part of the day, a low fog on the surface of the water, caused by the coldness of the water and the higher temperature of the air; which hides the Canoe; and only the Indian Man with his poised spear ready to strike is seen, like a ghost gliding slowly over the water.

new post. Douglas A. Birk, "John Sayer and the Fond du Lac Trade: The North West Company in Minnesota and Wisconsin," in *Rendezvous: Selected Papers of the Fourth North American Fur Trade Conference, 1981,* ed. Thomas C. Buckley (St Paul: North American Fur Trade Conference, 1984), 52. Little is known of Lemoine. He is probably the same man who was in charge of the NWC's Fort Charlotte, at the west end of Grand Portage, in 1793–94, and may be the Jean Baptiste Lemoine who in 1817 led an HBC expedition from Montreal to Norway House. Charles M. Gates, ed., *Five Fur Traders of the Northwest* (Minneapolis: University of Minnesota Press, 1933), 69n7; Arthur S. Morton, ed., *The Journal of Duncan M'Gillivray of the North West Company at Fort George on the Saskatchewan, 1794–5* (Toronto: Macmillan, 1929), lii; E.E. Rich. ed., *Colin Robertson's Correspondence Book, September 1817 to 1822* (Toronto: Champlain Society, 1939), 230.

I have sometimes amused myself for twenty minutes with the various appearances this low fog gives to these fishermen. As the elevation of the Scource of the Mississippe is a subject of curiosity to all [iv.225] intelligent men, especially to those of the United States, to whom this noble River belongs, I shall continue my estimated calculations to determine its level above that of the Sea in the gulph of Mexico.

From the Mississippe River at the mouth of the Sand Lake River; by this River and Savannah Brook there is an ascent of 16 ft 3 Inches, to the great Morass, which may be taken as level. From the east side of this Morass a Brook descends to the River St Louis, by it's windings of twenty miles, at 12 Inches Per mile is 20 feet, giving to the Mississippe an elevation of 3 feet 9 inches above this part of the River St Louis. The descent of this River to Lake Superior is 34 miles of strong current at 20 inches Per mile, gives 56 feet 8 inches, 11 miles of strong Rapids at 5 feet Per mile, equal to 55 feet of descent. One full mile of low Falls having a Carrying Place, and a descent of twenty feet. One Carrying Place of 7 miles; the Falls 20 feet Per mile equal to 140 feet to which add the last Fall of 120 feet in height equal to 260 feet.

Then 21 miles of current at 15 inches Per mile equal to 26 feet 3 inches, giving to the above part of the River St Louis a descent of 417 feet 11 inches to Lake Superior. This Lake by the levels taken to it's east end is 625 feet above the tide waters of the St Lawrence River. Hence we have from the Sea to Lake Superior an ascent of levels of 625 feet: The ascent to the Morass Brook, of the River St Louis 418 feet; and difference of level of the Mississippe 3 feet 9 Inches, giving a total of 1046 feet 9 inches of this last River above the level of the [iv.226] Sea, at the mouth of the Sand Lake River; and from hence to the Turtle Lake, by the calculations already made 431 feet; equal to 1478 feet: the elevation of the Turtle Lake, the scource of the Mississippe, above the Sea.[2]

It is tedious to the reader to attend to these calculations, and yet to the enquiring mind they are necessary that he may know the ground on which they are based, for the age of guessing is passed away, and the traveller is expected to give his reasons for what he asserts. To take the levels of several hundred miles of Rivers is too expensive, unless there is some great object in view, and all that the public can expect, or obtain, in these almost unknown countries, are the estimates of experienced men.

---

2 The actual elevation of Lake Superior is 600 feet (183 metres) and that of Turtle Lake 1,342 feet (409 metres); Thompson overestimated the difference in elevation between the two bodies of water by 111 feet (34 metres).

[*Lake Superior. Survey of 1822 &c. Length. Breadth. depth &c &c. geology &c &c. Basalt. Pye Island. Thunder Point. Copper of On to nog gan River. Number of Rivers &c. alluvial. direction. Auvergne. 900 ft of alluvials*]

On Lake Superior a Volume could be written; I have been twice round it, and six times over a great part, each survey correcting the preceding. The last survey of this Lake was under the orders of the Foreign Office for to determine, and settle the Boundary Line, between the Dominions of Great Britain and the Territories of the United States.[1] The Courses were taken by the Compass, and the Distances by Massey's Patent Log,[2] the latter so exact, as to require very little correction. The many astronomical observations made have settled the exact place of the Shores of this great Lake; the Maps of which, with the Boundary Line are in the Foreign Office in London; and also in the Office of the United States at Washington, and are not published.[3] The River St Louis flows into it's west end; and the discharge of the Lake is at it's south east corner, by the Falls of St Maries, which are in Latitude 46··31··16 north, [iv.227] Longitude 84··13··54 W, giving the straig[h]t course, and distance S 89 E 383 S Miles, it's breadth increases from the west to the east end, to 176 miles. It has two great bays on it's east side, across which are many

1 Here Thompson again interrupts the story of his journey in order to reflect on the area through which he will be travelling. Chronological narration is resumed on iv.232 (261). Thompson first circled Lake Superior in 1798, in a counterclockwise direction, as part of his initial NWC mission. Upon his retirement from the fur trade in 1812, his journey east took him and his family along the north shore of the lake. Thompson's surveying work for the International Boundary Commission took him back to Superior in the early 1820s: in 1822 he again circled the lake, this time in a clockwise direction; in 1823 and 1824 he passed through it on his way to and from Lake of the Woods; and in 1825 he travelled as far as Fort William, before a bout of dysentery forced him back to Sault Ste Marie. An earlier version of the description of Lake Superior is on iii.98–100 (Volume II). For Thompson's work on the boundary survey, see "Historical Introduction" (xxxvi–xxxvii).

2 A patent log is an instrument that measures the rate at which a vessel sails.

3 The International Boundary Commission maps are today housed in the Records of Boundary and Claims Commissions and Arbitrations, Cartographic Records, Record Group 76.10, United States National Archives; and in the Foreign Office Library Maps and Plans, FO925/1916B, TNA. The sixty-one official maps of the International Boundary Commission were first published (almost fifty years after Thompson wrote this passage) in John Basset Moore, *History and Digest of the International Arbitrations to Which the United States Has Been a Party* (Washington: Government Printing Office, 1898), vol. 6.

Islands.[4] The shores of the south side are 671 miles, and those of the north and east sides 946 miles, being a circuit of 1617 miles. It's area is about 28,090 square miles. It's level above the Sea is 625 feet. It's depth is as yet unknown, even near the shores of Pye Island and the head land of Thunder Bay;[5] it has been sounded, with 350 fathoms of Line, and no bottom and this by Men experienced in taking soundings. Supposing it's greatest depth to be only 400 fathoms, equal to 2400 feet it's bottom is 1775 feet below the surface of the Ocean.

Taking it's area at 28,090 square miles and it's average depth at 200 fathoms, this Lake contains 5930 cubic miles of fresh water. All summer the water tastes very cold, and in winter only the bays, and around the Islands are frozen, which the waves of the frequent gales of wind break up, and cause much floating ice. In easterly, or westerly gales of wind the roll of it's waves are like those of the sea.

¶ When surveying this Lake in the year 1822, on the north Side, about fifty miles eastward of St Louis River, about 1 PM we put ashore to dine, the day clear and fine and the Lake perfectly calm; as we were sitting on the Rocks, about a full mile from us direct out in the Lake, suddenly there arose an ebullition of the water; it's appearance was that of a body of water thrown up from some depth it was of about thirty yards in length, by four feet in height, it's breadth we could not see, from within this the water was thrown up about ten feet in very small columns [iv.228] as seen through our glasses. To the eye it appeared like heavy rain; the Lake became agitated, the waves rolled on the shore; and we had to secure the Canoes, this lasted for about half an hour. I took a sketch of it; when it subsided, the waves still continued; and we were for three hours unable to proceed. During this time and the whole day the wind was calm.[6]

¶ On the western part of the south shore, the rock is mostly of Sandstone as are also the Islands; some of the Cliffs are much worn by the waves, and have heaps of debris, the Islands are in the same state, one of them is worn through,[7] and in calm weather a canoe and men can pass with the arch three feet above their heads. Along this shore, proceeding eastward the lime stone appears and continues and seems every where to underlay the sandstone.

---

4 Probably Batchawana Bay and Agawa Bay. Michipicoten Bay contains no islands.
5 Pie Island, at the mouth of Thunder Bay, and the Sibley Peninsula.
6 This incident occurred on 19 July 1822, during the International Boundary Survey of the lake. In his journal, Thompson describes the phenomenon as columns of white vapour, "as if arising out of the Lake." AO. 51.65.
7 Probably one of the Apostle Islands.

Every where the land rises boldly from the Lake shore, and at the distance of about fifteen miles are crowned by the Porcupine hills, lying parallel to the Lake and the elevation of the land appears to be full 2500 feet above the Lake; the whole has the appearance of a continuous Forest, and so far as the eye can judge may be cultivated. The north and east sides of this Lake are very different from the south, side; they rise abruptly in belts of rude rounded shaped rock rolling back to the height of 850 to 2000 feet above the Lake; at a distance they appear to be one Forest but a nearer approach shows many a place of bare rock. The whole extent of the 946 miles of this coast is of the granitic order, in all the varieties that quartz, feltspar, and mica can form with othe[r] [iv.229] materials; and offers a fine field for the geologist and mineralogist: but in all this distance were ten Farmers to search for a place where each could have a lot of 200 acres of good land, alongside of each other I do not think they would find it. In the north east[8] corner of the Lake there is much Basalt, the only place in which I have seen this mineral on the east side of the Mountains. In this corner is Thunder Bay, so named by the Natives from it's frequent occurrence. Off the west point is Pye Island, so named from it's shape; it is of Basalt, part of this Island has perpendicular sides of at least 100 feet in height; close to which, the Lake has been sounded with 350 fathoms of lead line and no bottom; We may conclude the depth of the Lake to be here 400 fathoms, which will give the Basalt walls of the Island 2500 feet in height. The east end of the Bay is Thunder Point, rising 1120 feet above the surface of the water, which has been several times sounded without finding the bottom; giving to the Lake the same depth as at Pye Island, this Basalt Point has a height of 3520 feet; Great part of it is finely fluted, and the edges of their concaves fine and sharp; and the waves of the Lake seem to have no effect on it, though exposed to all their force; indeed the Basalt walls of both places appear as fresh and firm as if Providence had placed them there only a few years ago.

¶ From the west end of the Lake by the north and east sides to the Falls of St Maries are thirty one Rivers, of which the St Louis the Mishipocoton; and the Nee pe go,[9] are about 150 yards in width; the others from thirty to sixty [iv.230] yards wide, and twenty eight Brooks. On the south side there are forty Rivers two of these of 150 yards in width the others from twenty to seventy yards and forty one Brooks. All these Rivers and Brooks are fed by the Rains and snow, and by the evaporation from this great Lake which rests upon the surrounding high Lands, and is not wafted beyond them. From the

8 North west is intended.
9 The Michipicoten and Nipigon Rivers.

heights of these lands all the above Streams rush down in a series of Rapids and Falls, with some intervals of moderate current, as they pass over a table land. On the south side the River On to nog gan (the native name) has from old times been noted for the pieces of pure copper found there, of which the Indians made their weapons before the arrival of the French; and afterwards for the services of the Churches.

¶ Learning from my Men that a short distance up the River there was a large Mass of Copper, we left our canoe and proceeded on foot to it; we found it lying on a beach of limestone at the foot of a high craig of the same; it's shape round, the upper part a low convex, all worn quite smooth by the attrition of water and ice, but now lying dry. We tried to cut a chip from it, but it was too tough for our small axe. (Note. This mass of pure copper has since been taken to Washington at the expence of 5000 dollars; and found to weigh 3000 lbs by information)[10] At the extremity of the great Point called by the Natives Kee we woo nan oo (We return) now shortened to Kee we now, in a small harbour we took pieces of copper ore. I named it Copperass harbour. Both at this place, at the above River and a few other places I learn the people of the United States for these three years (1848)[11] have worked the Copper Mines with considerable profit; and have also found much silver

¶ [iv.231][12] yards, with twenty eight Brooks. On the south side, there are forty Rivers, two of these of 120 yards in breadth with forty one Brooks. It is not easy to conceive the vast quantity of alluvial of all kinds brought down by seventy one Rivers and Sixty nine Brooks rushing down these high lands, that surround the Lake, the accumulation of centuries must be very great yet such is the depth of the Lake, not a single River shows a point of alluvial worth notice. (Note. In the Province of Auvergne in France, there appears to have been a Lake of the size of Lake Superior the barriers of which appear

10 This copper boulder, located on the south fork of the Ontonagon River, was noted by Alexander Henry the Elder in 1766. It was removed in 1843 by Julius Eldred and transported to Detroit, where it was confiscated by the United States War Department. Transferred to the Smithsonian Institution in 1860, it is now in the collections of the National Museum of Natural History. In 1991 a repatriation request by the Keweenaw Bay Indian Community was denied. Alexander Henry the Elder, *Travels and Adventures in Canada, 1760–1776,* ed. James Bain (New York: Burt Franklin, 1969), 196–7. Native American Repatriation Review Committee, "Assessment of a Request for the Repatriation of the Ontonagon Boulder by the Keweenaw Bay Indian Community," Smithsonian National Museum of Natural History, http://anthropology.si.edu/repatriation/reports/regional/northeast/ontonagon.htm.

11 I.e., beginning in 1845.

12 The words at the head of iv.231 pick up from those at the foot of iv.229.

to have been broken down by an earthquake, and the Lake emptied. One alluvial from a River destroyed at the same time, was computed to be nine hundred feet in height from the bottom of the Lake. This catastrophe must have happened previous to the time of Julius Caser, for had it happened in his time, or since, the Roman historians would have noticed such an event. Saussure.)[13]

The northern part of North America is noted for it's numerous and large Lakes far more than other part of the world. The Great Architect said "Let them be, and they were" but he has given to his creature the power to examine his works on our globe; and perhaps learn the order in which he has placed them.[14] If we examine the positions of all these Lakes, their greatest lengths will be found to be about between North and thirty degrees west, and South and thirty degrees east, which are the lines of direction of the east side of the Great Plains, and of the Rocky Mountains; the anomalies to this order are Lakes Michigan [iv.232] Superior and Athabasca. The west sides of the Lakes are of Limestone and the east sides of Granite. Between these two formations are the great wide chasms, or valleys filled with water, which are the Lakes. And the three above Lakes, although lying west and east, have their south sides of Limestone and their north sides of the Granitic order, and their deep waters in the same kind of valley. The few Lakes that lie, as it were within the east side of the Great Plains, as Cumberland and the Cedar Lakes are wholly within the limestone formation, and are comparatively shoal water Lakes.

[*Survey &c. Natives. Montreal River. Carrying Place. Mr Cadotte embarks. Natives few. the Echo Point. Kee we naw. Corn sours. Rice does not. Arrive at St Maries. Agents. Lake Superior. Families. hunting grounds &c few Animals. Arrive at Grand Portage. Falls of St Maries. canal &c*]

¶ Having settled by Observations the Latitude and Longitude of the trading house of St Louis's River, at the west end of Lake Superior; on the 12th of May we proceeded to survey the south side of the Lake.[1] In the afternoon

13 This ancient lake is known as the Limagne. Horace-Bénédict Saussure (1740–99), a Swiss physicist, devoted himself to the study of Alpine geology and is the author of *Voyages dans les Alpes* (1779–96).

14 This passage provides significant insight into Thompson's world view, revealing how his understanding is informed both by faith in Christian revelation and by the use of empirical observation and the faculty of reason.

1 Here the narrative resumes its chronological structure. For Thompson's journey from Fond du Lac House to Sault Ste Marie, lasting from 12–28 May 1798, see AO. 7.23r–28v; 9.83–78.

we came to four Lodges of Chip a ways they had just arrived from the interior, having wintered at the west end of the Porcupine Hills and now pass the summer on the borders of the Lake to maintain themselves by fishing. They are about 28 families, and by the usual rule of seven souls to a family, their number is 196 persons. My Men thought, for the number of Men, there were more old Women than usual. Although the interior rises high, yet near the Lake the shores were low, with many fine sandy beaches, for setting of nets for fishing; yet the Natives make no use of them, although they see the success of the white men: If a Net is given to them, they are too indolent to take care of it, and it soon becomes useless. They prefer the precarious mode of spearing fish which is practible only in calm, or very moderate weather. The woods [iv.233] seen from the Lake were of white and red Birch, Spruce Pines, Larch and Aspins, all of small growth.

¶ The next day we passed an Island of Sand Stone which the Waves had worn into rude arches, with many caves. The next day we came to three Lodges containing fifteen families, being 105 souls. An American of the States was living with them, and had adopted their way of life in preference to hard labor on a farm.[2] In the afternoon we passed Monsieur Michel Cadotte[3] with five Men and several Lodges of the natives from their winter quarters, now to live by fishing. The night and morning of the 15th May was a severe frost. The Land all day very high and bold shores. Having gone eleven miles we came to the Montreal River of 25 yards in width, between banks of rock, near the Lake is a Fall of thirty feet in height. The course of this River is through the Porcupine Hills the lower parts of which are now the coasts of the Lake; Two of my Men had wintered near the head of this River. As the whole length of the River is a series of Falls between steep bank[s] of rock the distance from the Lake to the House was one continued Carrying Place of 130 Rests (a Rest, or Pose,[4] is the distance the cargo of the Canoe is carried from place to place and then rest.) In this hilly country a Rest may be from five to six hundred yards, and the 130 rests about forty miles. The men say the distance takes them thirty seven days of carrying to the House. All the trading Houses on the south side of the Lake require many miles of carrying, with [iv.234] some intervals of current to take the cargo of the canoe to the wintering ground. The Men who winter, and have to traverse the country in

2 In his journal entry for 14 May 1798, Thompson writes that he came to "3 Lodges of Chippeways with an American named Bell who came off to us & returned." AO 9.83.
3 For fur trader Michel Cadotte, see appendix 2.
4 French *pause*, meaning "break."

every direction say the Lakes are few and small, more like beaver ponds than Lakes; and that in very many places sand stone for sharpening knives and axes are to be found.

¶ We came to a Lodge of five families, they had seen no person for eight Moons and had all their winters hunt with them, of about 360 pounds of furrs. Further on was a Lodge of ten families. Early on the 17th May we came to the Fair River, at the east end of the Porcupine Hills. The interior country has now lower land. The Woods hitherto have much white Cedar, with Birch, Aspin and Pines with a few Maple and Plane Trees, all of very common growth. An extensive body of ice lying before us, we had to put ashore and pass the day. We set a Net but caught only six Carp. The wind having drifted the ice from the shore, early on the 18th we set off and soon came to the On to nog gan River, where lay the great mass of Copper I have already mentioned. Here was a Mr Cadotte with four Lodges of Indians. He informed us that last summer (1797) a party of Americans had visited the River and proceeded twenty miles up it to the Forks of the River, they had promised the Indians to come this summer (1798) and build a Fort and work the mines, for which the Chip paways were waiting for them; but this promise they did not perform until the year 1845.[5] Mr Cadotte had a few goods remaining and requested a passage with us for himself and goods which we gave him and he embarked with us. Full twenty five miles North eastward of the On to nog gan River are high steep, rocks [iv.235] of a reddish color, which have the most distinct Echo, I have ever heard. We stopped a short time to amuse ourselves with it; The Rocks were about 200 feet in height, and the place of the Echo appeared about sixty feet above us; The Echo of the words we spoke, seemed more sharp and clear than our voices, and somewhat louder. One of the Men, Francois Babue, who had been many years in the furr trade of the Lake used to abuse the Echo until he worked himself into a violent passion; did the same this time until his expressions becoming too coarse, we moved off, he swearing, that he thought it very hard he never could have the last word.

5 Northern Michigan was the site of a copper rush in the early 1840s. In response to a rapid influx of copper prospectors, in 1844 the United States government established Fort Wilkins, on the tip of the Keweenaw Peninsula, 80 miles (129 kilometres) northeast of the Ontonagon River's mouth. Industrial-scale copper mining began in the Ontonagon area in 1847 with the establishment of the Minesota Mine at Rockland. Bruce Johanson, Ontonagon County Historical Society, personal communication with editor, 1 January 2007.

¶ The greatest part of this day we were in much danger from the Ice, which lay in the Lake a short distance from the shore; had it come in, we could not have saved ourselves as the Rocks were high and steep. At 7½ PM we put up on Kee we naw Carrying Place; This is a remarkable place, being an Isthmus of 2060 yards, in a south course and forms a body of Land in circuit 94 Miles into a Peninsula, known under the name of Point Kee we naw. The bank is about twenty feet in height; the first 1100 yards is good ground, the other 960 yards a perfect swamp. To avoid going round this Peninsular of high land; the people of the States in time to come will cut a Canal through the Isthmus, at a small expence, as a Lock is not required.[6] The night being clear, as usual, I observed for Latitude and Longitude the former 47.14.·27 N. Longitude 88°-38'·36" West From the Carrying Place is a Brook of 1½ mile to a small Lake, and then a kind of Lagoon of 24 miles to Lake. Superior. Part of the Lagoon, on one side the Woods were on fire, the heat and smoke made us lay by for a few hours. On the 22nd and 24th May we had heavy rain with vivid Lightning and loud Thunder.

¶ [iv.236] The provisions we had to live on were hulled Corn, part of a bag of wild rice, with a few pounds of grease to assist the boiling. It is customary after supper, to boil Corn or rice for the meals of next day, and in good weather we set off by 4 AM, the Kettles were taken off the fire in a boiling state and placed in the Canoe, and two hours after we had a warm breakfast; If Lightning and Thunder came in the day the Corn became sour and had to be thrown away; but the rice never soured; the same thing in the night, when the kettle had corn it was soured, but if of rice it kept good: the Men assured me that Lightning and Thunder had no effect on the wild rice; and that in the heats of Summer the Corn soured so frequently, they were half starved; to boil a Kettle of Corn requires three to four hours the rice is cooked in half an hour, but it is very weak food. All the Corn for these voyages has to be steeped in hot lye of wood ashes to take off the rind of the grain. On the 28th May we arrived, Thank God at the Falls of St Maries, the discharge of Lake Superior, and the head of the River St Lawrence,[7] which flows into Lake Huron.

Here I had the pleasure of meeting Sir Alexander McKenzie[8] the celebrated traveller who was the first to follow down the great Stream of water flowing

---

6 The Portage Lake and Lake Superior Ship Canal, linking Keweenaw Bay with Lake Superior, was completed in 1874.

7 St Mary's River is intended.

8 For Alexander Mackenzie, see appendix 2.

northward from the Slave Lake into the Arctic Sea, and which great River bears his name, and made well known to the public by the journeys of Sir John Franklin. Upon my report to him of the surveys I had made, and the number of astronomical Observations for Latitude, Longitude and Variation of the Compass he was pleased to say I had performed more in ten months than he expected could be done in two years. The next day the Honorable William McGillivray[9] arrived. [iv.237] These gentlemen were the Agents, and principal Partners of the North West Company: they requested me to continue the survey of the Lake round the east and north sides to the Grand Portage, then the Depot of the Company.

¶ The survey we had finished was of the south side, from the west, to the east end; following the shores, the distance is 671 miles, but the direct line is only 383 miles. We had met with 110 families and allowing twenty families not seen, will give 130 families. Mr Cadotte, who has been for many years a Trader in these parts, thought 125 families to be nearer the number. Allowing these Natives to have possession of hunting ground only to the distance of 70 miles from the Lake, the extent will be 26810 square miles, and this divided by 130, will give to each family an extent of 206 square miles of hunting ground; yet with this wide area; the annual average hunt of each family of all kind of furrs, from the Bear down to the Musk Rat, will not exceed sixty to seventy skins in trade; allowing a Bear skin to be the value of two beavers; and eight to ten musk Rats to be the value of one beaver. Deer are so scarce that all they kill does not furnish leather for their wants, and when the mild seasons come they all descend to Lake Superior to live by fishing. Calculation is tedious reading, yet without it, we cannot learn the real state of any country. (Note. Mr Ballantyne, of the Hudson's Bay Company has lately published a work, with the title of "Six years residence in Hudson's Bay," in which, speaking of the Bay, he says "the interior has Myriads of wild animals" The Natives will thank him to show them where they are. When he wrote those words he must have been thinking of Musketoes, and in this respect he was right)[10]

The Forests of the Lake are such as has been already [iv.238] described; I could not learn that any of the Forest Trees acquired a growth to merit particular notice, except the white Birch, the Rind of which is very good for canoes, and of a large size.

On the first day of June we left the Falls of St Maries and from thence surveyed the east and part of the north shores of Lake Superior to the 7th day of

9 For William McGillivray, see appendix 2.
10 For Ballantyne, see note on iv.63 (119).

this month,[11] when late we arrived at the Grand Portage, then the Depot of the North West Company, to which the furrs of the interiour country came, and from whence the merchandise was taken for the furr trade to about the same time the following year, as already described.

¶ The Falls of St Maries is a Rapid of about three fourths of a mile in length in which it descends eleven feet, and then by three channels of easy current descends to Lake Huron.[12] The carrying place is about a mile in length of low wet ground, very easy for a canal and locks; and which at length is about to be completed in this year 184[*space*]. The opposite banks of these rapids belong to the United States, it is steep and above twenty feet in height, and a canal could not be made but at an enormous expence. While waiting the Province of Canada to make a canal on the only side in which it can be made, these enterprising people made a deep channel at the foot of their steep bank with a tow path for their Vessels, but the strength of the current makes the passage somewhat dangerous, this the canal will now do away with.[13] The mines of copper ore that have been worked both by the citizens of the United States and the people of this province now demand a canal which otherwise would not have been made, although the fisheries of Lake Superior required a canal many years ago, but as yet, only the people of the States are engaged in these fisheries, although superior to that of any other which is always the case with deep water.[14]

11 For the journey of 1–7 June 1798 from Sault Ste Marie to Grand Portage, see AO. 7.28v–29v; 10.128–9.

12 The three channels are the East, Middle, and West Neebish.

13 The NWC built a rudimentary lock on the north side of the St Mary's River in 1797, which was destroyed in the War of 1812–14. This was followed by several other primitive locks and channels during the first half of the nineteenth century. A canal on the American side of the river was constructed in 1853–55, at a cost of just under $1,000,000.

14 Thus ends a long, largely chronologically structured movement in the 1850 version of the *Travels*, iv.85–iv.238 (137–266), covering Thompson's activities from May 1796 to June 1798. While iv.238–313 contain many dateable episodes, on these pages Thompson arranges his material thematically rather than chronologically.

Page 272.

faces to appear to the best advantage, and were proud of our
-selves. On seeing some of my friends I got away and went to them
and by enquiries learned that my parents had gone to the
low countries of the Lakes, and that before I was three moons
away my wife had given herself to another man, and that
her father could not prevent her, and they were all far to
the northward there to pass the winter. At this unlooked
for news I was quite disheartened; I said nothing, but my
heart was swollen with anger and revenge. and I passed
the night scheming mischief. In the morning my friends
reasoned with me upon my vexation about a worthless
woman, and that it was beneath a warrior anger, there
were no want of women to replace her and a better
wife could be got. Others said, that if I had staid with my wife
instead of running away to kill Snake Indians nothing of this
would have happened. My anger moderated, I gave my Scalp
to one of my friends to give to my father, and renouncing
my people, I left them, and came to the Peeagans who gave
me a hearty welcome; and upon my informing them of
my intention to remain with them the great Chief gave
me his eldest daughter to be my wife she is the sister of
the present Chief, and as you see, now an old woman.
The terror of that battle and of our guns has prevented any
more general battles, and our wars have since been car
-ried by ambuscade and surprize, of small camps in
which we have greatly the advantage, from the Guns.
arrow shods of iron. Long Knives, flat bayonets and now
from the Traders, while we, have these weapons the Snake
Indians have none but what few they sometimes take
from

[Description of the Stony Region. unfit for white men. Temperature of Stony Region. Rein Deers and Reed Lakes]

[iv.239] Hitherto these travels have exten[d]ed over a tract of country on the east parts of north america, which from it's formation I have called the Stoney Region (perhaps rocky, would be more appropriate) already described,[1] it is little else than rocks with innumerable Lakes and Rivers, and south of 58 degrees north has forests of small Pines, which increase in size going southward, with Aspin, Poplar and Birch, but northward of the above latitude the country is covered with various kinds of moss. Northward of 61 degrees this region may be said to extend to the Rocky Mountains. On the latitude of 58-40 north this region from Churchill in Hudsons Bay extend[s] 640 miles to the westward and from Fort Albany in the same bay, on the parallel of 52 degrees, this region is 660 miles in wi[d]th, including the Lakes on it's west side. From Albany southward it's west side embraces the great Lakes Superior and Huron, the north bank of the Ottawa and St Lawrence Rivers to the Gulp[h],[2] and it's east side is every where bounded by the sea. On the whole of this great extent of country containing an area of about [*space*] square miles, the Deer and other wild animals of the forest are thinly scattered for the comparative extent of country; and the native Indians are in the same proportion.

¶ The summer is from five to six months, or more properly the open season, with frequent frosts, and heats, but always [iv.240] tormented with Musketoes and other flies. In the winter the snow is deep and the cold intense, in the months of December, January and February the Thermometer is for many days at fifty to seventy degrees below the freezing point. In the open season the Natives and Traders make use of Canoes, and in winter of flat sleds; for removing from place to place. Such is the country of the north east, or siberian,[3] side of north America.

¶ For Agriculture it offers nothing to the farmer except a few places detached from each other, without a market; nor can it become a grazing country, the torment of the flies is too great to allow cattle to graze until the cool nights of September, the sufferings of the Deer must be seen to be believed; even the timid Moose Deer on some days is so distressed with the flies, as to be careless of life, and the hunters have shot them in this state, and the cloud of flies about them so great, and dense, that they did not dare to

1 On iv.28–35 (77–94) and iv.50–81 (108–33).
2 The Gulf of St Lawrence.
3 Having the same geographical relationship to North America as Siberia has to Asia.

go to the animal for several minutes, such cannot be a grazing country, especially when to this is added, a long cold winter with great depth of snow. We may therefore fully conclude, that as all kind Providence has fitted the Arabians to live, and enjoy his naked hot sandy deserts so the same merciful Being has fitted the Indian to live and enjoy his cold region of forests and deserts of snow. The means for the enjoyments of civilis[e]d life is denied to both, and the white man is unfitted to take the place of the arabian or the indian. Modern geologists would consider this Stoney Region to be a formation that had been uncovered and left by the sea, long after the land to it's westward, on which I shall now describe.

[iv.241] The climate of this region is best explained by the meteorol[o]g[ic]al tables kept. (To be in a note) that at Bedford House, on the west bank of the Rein Deer's Lake, in Latitude 57°··23' N. Longitude 102··59 West.[4]

October	Mean heat +26	greatest +54	least heat +15
November	ditto +1.5	ditto +45	ditto –37
December	ditto –18	ditto +30	ditto –56
January	ditto –19	ditto +25	ditto –50
February	ditto –16.7	ditto +15	ditto –49
March	ditto –5	ditto +44	ditto –43
April	ditto +11.5	ditto +40	ditto –30
May 20 days	ditto +24.5	ditto +50	ditto –7

In summer, the Thermometer for a few days in July, the heat was at +80, making the range of the heat and cold to be 136 degrees. The Ice in this great Lake was firm to the 6th day of July, when a heavy gale of wind broke it up. Where there is soil in the Pine Forests, the heat of summer thaws it only a few inches.

At the Reed Lake[5] in Latitude 54·36' N. 100°··37' West the temperature of the following months was.

October 8 days.	Mean +27	Greatest +38	Least heat +18
November	ditto +18	ditto +34	ditto –15
December	ditto –10	ditto +31	ditto –45
January	ditto –21.3	ditto +11	ditto –47
February	ditto +6	ditto +39	ditto –31
March	ditto +6	ditto +41	ditto –30
April	ditto +31	ditto +63	ditto –7
May 26 days	ditto +43	ditto +73	ditto +19

4 For Thompson's account of his stay at Bedford House, in the winter of 1796–97, see iv.101–14, above (149–65).

5 Thompson spent two winters at Reed Lake: 1794–95 with the HBC and 1805–06 with the NWC. The first set of data is from 1794–95.

In the summer, for a few day in July the heat rises to 88 degrees, and except in some few places of thick pine forests, the ground is thawed during the summer.

[iv.241 paste-on] The temperature of the Reed Lake for the following months in the years 1805 and 1806 were as follows.

1805	September	Mean +47	Greatest +58	Least +38	Range 20°
	October	ditto +29	+50	+12	38°
	November	ditto +11	+28	−12	40
	December	ditto +7	+22	−22	44
1806	January	ditto −13	+20	−38	58
	February	ditto −8	+26	−37	63
	March	ditto +16	+34	−12	46
	April	ditto +25	+53	−14	67
	May	ditto +47	+84	+26	58°

The months of June, July and August were very warm, but the Thermometer not kept as I was absent.

[*description of the dry Region westward. temperature of Red Deers Lake. Animals more plenty. Description of the Beaver & Porcupine*]

[iv.242] Leaving the Stoney region and it's Lakes is a great extent of land of a very different formation; and extending westward to the foot of the Rocky Mountains; it is almost wholly composed of ear[t]h, with few rocks, and only in the northern part has a few Lakes, none of them large; This great body of dry land extends from the gulph of Mexico to beyond the Arctic Circle. From north of the parallel of 52 degrees to the latitude of 72 degrees the whole is a forest of mostly the Pine genus with, in favorable places, Birch, Poplar and Aspin. Southward of the latitude of 52 degrees are the great plains which extend to the Gulp[h] of Mexico.[1] The breadth of this land is from 550 to about 850 miles. This western country of forests and plains have Animals peculiar to itself; and those that are common to both regions are here larger and in better condition from a somewhat milder climate, and more abundance of food.

¶ Of the Natives, there are none sufficiently numerous to be called "a Nation." I have therefore called them "Tribes" though many of them speak languages quite distinct from each other, as the word Tribe may be a small number, speaking the same language, and holding firmly together as one

1 Thompson thus subdivides the Plains into the southern Prairie region, described on iv.125–33, above (180–7), and the northern Boreal Plains, described here.

great family.² Such are the Rapid Indians,³ the Sussee⁴ and Ko ta nae⁵ Indians, each of these have a very different language, and each so rough and difficult to articulate that the neighbouring people rarely attempt to learn them, each of these Tribes may have a population of 500 to 1000 souls, to speak the language of it's Tribe, and this number is all that do speak the language. The intelligent people of the United States who have paid attention to the north American Indians have always been struck with the numerous radical Languages of the Indians, and from [iv.243] whence they could have come, but all lies in obscurity, and the few theories of learned men on the peopling of this continent are in general so contrary to facts, that they can be regarded only as theory.

2 At the time Thompson wrote, both "nation" and "tribe" referred to groups of people bound by a common language and often descent. The term "nation" was generally reserved for larger polities, such as England and France, while a "tribe" might represent a division within a larger group (such as the twelve tribes of Israel); hence Thompson's caveat about the distinctness of Native languages. *Oxford English Dictionary*, 2nd edn., 10:231, s.v. "nation"; 18:503, s.v. "tribe."

3 For the Gros Ventres, see note on iv.176 (218).

4 An Athapaskan group, the Sarcee have their origins in the Lesser Slave Lake region. They became distinct from the Beaver in the early eighteenth century, moving onto the northwest Plains, where they adopted an economy based on the bison hunt and allied themselves with the Blackfoot. They are now officially known as Tsuu T'ina. Because their closest linguistic relatives, the Beaver, Sekani and Chipewyan, still lived in the subarctic, the Sarcee language appeared to be a linguistic isolate. Hugh A. Dempsey, "Sarcee," *HNAI*, vol. 13, 1:629–37. Thompson mentions the Sarcee again on iv.263 (288), notes their husbandry of horses on iv.307–8 (317), and discusses their language at iii.151 (Volume II).

5 Some Kootenai traditions indicate that they were originally a Plains people, but by the end of the eighteenth century they lived almost exclusively west of the Continental Divide along the Kootenay River, to which their lives were oriented. They comprised two main divisions, the Upper and Lower Kootenai. The former crossed the divide for the annual bison hunt and made regular attempts to engage in commerce with European traders. In 1806 Thompson was assigned the mission of extending trade to the Kootenai, and in the summer of 1807 he crossed the Rocky Mountains and established Kootanae House, where he wintered in 1807–08 and 1808–09. The Kootenai are mentioned in passing in the 1850 version of the *Travels* on iv.264 (288), iv.275 (296), and iv.307 (317), but figure prominently in the 1848 version (see Volume II). As Thompson notes, the Kootenai language is a linguistic isolate. Bill B. Brunton, "Kootenai," *HNAI*, vol. 12: *Plateau*, ed. Deward E. Walker, Jr. (Washington: Smithsonian Institution, 1998), 223–37.

¶ On the region of the western forest land, at a fine Lake called the Red Deers Lake,[6] at the head of the small streams which feed the Beaver River the southern branch of the Churchill River in October we erected a trading house and passed the winter.[7] Its Latitude 54°·46'··23" N Longitude 111°··56' W It's climate in (Note,

November	Mean temperature +13.5	Greatest +37	Least −6
December	ditto −6.5	ditto +40	ditto −48
January	ditto −5	ditto +40	ditto −48
February	ditto +9	ditto +43	ditto −26
March to the 14th	ditto +12	ditto +44	ditto −13.

This trading House is 10½ Minutes north, and 11¼ degrees west of the Reed Lake on the Stoney region and so far shows a milder climate, had the thermometer been continued through the rest of the year, the difference would have been very great, and that the temperature of April on this dry region is equal to that of May on the Stoney region from the lesser quantity of Snow, and the Sun exerting it's influence on the bare ground in April, which on the latter it does not do to the middle of May.

¶ The Lake from our set nets gave us fish of Pike, White Fish, Pickerel and Carp for about one third of our support, and the Hunters furnished the rest, which was almost wholly of the Moose Deer; in five months they gave us forty nine Moose all within twenty miles of the House and a few Bull Bisons, whereas on the Stoney Region, it would be a fortunate trading house, that during the winter had the meat of six Moose Deer brought to it, and even that quantity would rarely happen. On this region all the animals attain their [iv.244] full size. (Note. A male Beaver, allowed to be full grown and in good condition, measured from the tip of the nose to the insertion of the tail, three feet and half an inch, the tail thirteen inches in length, by seven inches in breadth. Girth round the breast thirty two inches round the hind quarters thirty six inches. The head five inches in length. It's weight, as alive sixty five pounds.[8] A Porcupine from the tip of the nose to the insertion of the tail twenty six inches, the tail ten inches in length, round and closely armed with

6 Lac La Biche. The Portage La Biche joins this lake, which lies in the Athabasca drainage basin, with the Beaver River, which is part of the Churchill River system.

7 Thompson and his men arrived at Lac La Biche on 4 October 1798. Thompson ran this new NWC post until 9 March 1799, when he delivered its charge to François Decoigne. For the journal of this winter, see AO. 10.157–80.

8 Thompson took these dimensions from his notebooks. They are those of a beaver he measured at Buckingham House, on the North Saskatchewan River, on 26 December 1793. AO. 1.75.

barbed quils; Girth round the breast twenty inches; the hair of a dark grey intermixed with which are his well barbed quills which are very slightly fixed in the skin, the quill is white to the barb, which is black, and are placed from his shoulders to, and on the tail, the sides and belly have none; they are thickest and longest on the rump, they are from one to two and a half [inches] in length; some few about three inches, and near a quarter of an inch in girth; on the larger quills the barbed part is half an inch in length, containing small circular barbs through it's length.

When approached, it places it's head under its breast lies down and presents only it's back and tail, and if an animal attempts to seize him it gives a jerk with it's back, which drives the quills deep into it's mouth, and are held fast by the barbs, and prevents all farther attacks. Confident of their power of defence they pursue their slow walk, careless of the barking of Dogs, the yelping of Foxes, or other animals. A hungry Fox or Fisher will sometimes try to turn it on it's back but gets it's nose and face so full of quills, as to desist.

[*Indians at the Red Deers Lake. Religion. Crimes remain on the soul. religious opinions on debt & worship*]

[iv.245] The natives that traded at this House, were about thirty Nahathaway, and the same number of Swampy Ground Stone Indians[1] who still continue to prefer their ancient mode of life to living in the Plains, where the rest of their Tribes are; The languages of both these people are soft and easy to learn and speak. That of the Stone Indians is so agreeable to the ear, it may be called the Italian Language of North America; and by the Tribes of these people under the name of Sieux extends over the east side of the Plains and down a considerable distance of the upper part of the Mississippe. Their opinions, rites and ceremonies of religion are much the same as the Nahathaways, with whom they are strictly allied. All these people are superior in stature and good looks, to the generality of those on the Stoney Region from a better country and a greater supply of food. They have their Medicine Bags, which is generally well filled with sweet smelling vegetables, and have the bones of some particular part of the Beaver, Otter, Musk Rat, Racoon,

---

1 Thompson's "Swampy Ground Stone Indians" are Assiniboine who had travelled west to the foothills of the Rockies, where they traded at Rocky Mountain House and came into conflict with the Siksika, Blood, and Piegan. In noting that they prefer their "ancient mode of life," Thompson alludes to their Yanktonai origins in the woodlands of the Upper Mississippi. Some Ojibwa also traded at Lac La Biche.

Bear and Porcupine, mostly of the head, or hind parts, to which they attach a superstitious virtue especially to those of their Poo wog gan, the Manito of which they regard as favorably [disposed] to them.[2]

They all hold the doctrine of the immortality of the Soul, or as they call it, "Life after Death" and their Ideas of the other world is much the same as they have of their present existence, only heightened to constant happiness in social life, and success in hunting without fatigue. They all hope to be happy after death, if the Great Spirit finds them to be good; whether he will do so, does not occupy much of their thoughts in the prime [iv.246] of life, but as age advances is frequently the subject of their conversations for they have much time to spare, and few subjects to engross their attention. They all agree that the crimes committed is marked on the soul and thus marked enters the other world; They believed that those who were placed in the happy state had their Souls clean and white, but none could inform me how the stains on the Soul had been eradicated, this is a doctrine too profound for them, and on which they were utterly at a loss. They feel it and have some ceremonies and some sacrifices to obtain it; but in which they place little confidence. A Man who had been guilty of a crime, (I could not learn what it was) enjoined on himself the penance of eating nothing for a whole year, that was not placed in his mouth, and which he steadily kept, he afterwards declared he would never make such another vow as the provisions thus placed in his mouth, was not enough and badly cooked, which the Indians said he deserved for placing himself in the power of other people and in a manner making them his servants.

¶ An Indian named As kee a Waw shish (Son of the Earth)[3] between 40 and 50 years of age, and whom I found a good man and respected by the natives, when a young man unfortunately became heir to a feud between his family, and that of another family, and each had to retaliate the injurys of times past. One spring on the arrival of the wild geese, when the Indians collect together to enjoy the season, these two families met, the young man at the head of the other family [iv.247] had often said, he would on the first occasion have his revenge; and sought it of Askee a Wawshish but fell himself

2 For the *pawākan*, see note on iv.48 (107). A medicine bundle typically contains small natural objects of particular significance to their owner and is used for ritual purposes. Thompson mentions medicine bundles again on iv.304 (315).

3 In his journals, Thompson records that Askeeawawshish visited the Lac La Biche post twice in late February 1799. AO. 10.178–9. The respect and trust that he enjoyed are indicated by the fact that he traded pelts on behalf of two other hunters, in addition to his own.

in the encounter, some twenty five years before the time I am speaking off. The Indians related this to do away with any impression I might have against him; As I understood that he was still continuing his penance for having shed human blood, I was anxious to learn of himself what were his thoughts on this sad subject his relation was,

¶ "After the first excitement was over of myself and the family to which I belonged I became melancholy and disheartened, I no longer enjoyed hunting and as both family were nearly related, the Women said that I ought to go to war and kill a Snake Indian that he might have a slave to attend him in the other world this would please him and make us friends when we met in the other world. Thus the summer passed away, and a very hard winter came on, deep snow heavy gales of wind with long calms between made hunting so difficult that we could hardly maintain ourselves; this made the old people, change my penance for another in which I was not to leave them, and my penance now is, and from that time has been, at the first dawn of day to rise, take my rattle and sing to the Great Spirit to make me good and a skillful hunter, and when I die to blot out the mark of the red blood on my soul; for I feel perfectly perswaded it will remain with me as long as I live, and every crime we commit is in the same state."

¶ Such is the confession of every serious Native, they know of nothing by which the pardon of sins can be obtained and although many of us spoke their language sufficiently fluent for trade and the [iv.248] common business yet we found ourselves very deficient if we attempted to impress on them any doctrine of Christianity beyond the unity of God, his creation and preservation of mankind and of every thing else, to all which they readily assented as consonant to truth and their own ideas. On taking the necessaries which they require for the winter season, and which are mostly on credit, several of them, especially of those advanced in life, have made a bargain with me, that if they should die in the winter I should not demand the debt due to me; in the other world, and to which I always agreed. The life of a Hunter is precarious but a provident family will make dried provisions for hard times, and let things be as hard as is sometimes, the Indian sees none better than himself and knows he is master of every thing he can secure by hunting, or otherwise: Whereas to the constant labor of the lower classes of Europe they live in penury without daring to touch the abundance all around them. The Natives that live in Villages may profit by the labors of a prudent Missionary; but the wandering Indians that live wholly by hunting, and are rarely more than a few days in place, and in this only by families cannot hope for the labors of a Missionary; the little they can learn must come from the Traders, and if they cannot learn morality from them, can teach them to leave of the worship and sacrifi[ci]ng a dog to the Mauchee Manito (the Devil) and leave off prayers to the inferior Manitoes, and direct all their prayers and thanksgiving to the Great Spirit alone, the Master of Life.

[*Temperature of Peace River. Beaver on western forest. Iroquois Algonquins & Nepissings. Women &c. Accidents to them &c. they send 75 to the southward. also of the Algonquins & Nepissings. Iroquois in the plains. 25 killed by the Willow Indians. Councils and their war dance. and the war dance of Spik a nog gan. dirty. separate to hunt*]

[iv.249] On the more northern part of this great western forest, at the Forks of the Peace and Smoke Rivers,[1] (the principal stream which forms the Mackenzie.) in Latitude 56°.8'··17" N Longitude 117°·13'-14" W the temperature for the year[2] were

January	Mean –10	Greatest heat +39	Least –49	Range 88° degrees
February	ditto +7	+41	–38	79
March	ditto +22.5	+57	–32	89
April	ditto +37.6	+71	+16	55
May	ditto 64	+80	+30	50
June	ditto +64.5	+86	+44	42
July	ditto +63	+84	+46	38
August	ditto +60	+85	+38	47
September	ditto +55	+86	+21	65
October	ditto +40	+71	+19	52
November	ditto +14.6	+41	–13	54
December	ditto –4	+19	–38	57
Mean	+35	+86	–38	124°

The trading house at these Forks of the River is about 150 miles east ward of the foot of the Rocky Mountains and it's elevation above the level of the sea about 4,000 feet above the level of the sea.

¶ The whole of the great western Forest had very many Beaver, it had few Lakes, but what was better for the Beaver many small brooks, and streams which they dammed up and made Ponds for their houses, and the Natives had thus an annual supply of furrs to trade all they required, and had the furr trade been placed in the hands of one company under the controul of

1 Thompson was at this forks from November 1802 to March 1804. The post at this site had been built by Alexander Mackenzie in 1792.

2 1803.

govern[ment] might have continued to do so to this time; but from Canada the trade was open to every adventurer, and some of these brought in a great number of Iroquois, Nepissings and [iv.250] Algonqins, who, with their steel traps had destroyed the Beaver on their own lands in Canada and New Brunswick;[3] The two latter, the Men were tall, manly, steady and good hunters, the few women they brought with them were good looking and well behaved and their dress came to the feet and both sexes respected by the Natives.

¶ The Iroquois formed about half the number of these immigrants, they considered themselves superior to all other people, especially the white people of Canada which they carried in their countenances, being accustomed to show themselves off in dances and flourishing their tomahawks before the civilized people of canada and making speeches on every occasion, which were all admired and praised through politeness to them, gave them a high opinion of themselves; The few women they brought with them were any thing but beauty and their dress was careless with the shirt on the outside, and petticoats to only a little below the knees, the toes and feet turned inwards which made them walk like ducks, so different from the slender tall forms of the women of the Plains, their easy, graceful walk and dress touching the ground. Part of these went up the Red River, and about 250 of them came up the Saskatchewan River, in company with the canoes of the Fur Traders to one of the upper Posts called Fort Augustus[4] where the River passes through fine Plains, upon the banks and in the interior country are numerous herds of Bisons and several kinds of Deer, and many Bears of several colours.

3 Migration of Iroquois, Nipissing, and Algonquin hunters to the Plains took place from 1790 to 1815, with the largest numbers going west in 1800–04. Most of these men were from communities near Montreal. While some travelled west independently, the majority signed contracts with the NWC and XYC. In November 1800, Thompson and Duncan McGillivray received permission from the Piegan to introduce Iroquois hunters to the foothills of the Rockies, and in 1802 William Tomison of the HBC reported that the NWC and XYC had recently brought more than 300 Iroquois hunters to the Plains. Johnson, ed., *Saskatchewan Journals and Correspondence*, xci–xcii; Trudy Nicks, "The Iroquois and the Fur Trade in Western Canada," in *Old Trails and New Directions: Papers of the Third North American Fur Trade Conference* (Toronto: University of Toronto Press, 1980), 85–101; Jan Grabowski and Nicole St-Onge, "Montreal Iroquois *engagés* in the Western Fur Trade, 1800–1821," in Binnema, Ens, and Macleod, eds., *From Rupert's Land to Canada* (Edmonton: University of Alberta Press, 2001).

4 This NWC post on the North Saskatchewan was established by Angus Shaw and Duncan McGillivray in 1794.

¶ The Algonquins and Nepissings paid every attention to the advice given to them, and performed the voyage without accident; but the Iroquois treated our warnings with contempt; When advised to be cautious in the hunting of the Bisons, especially when wounded; they would laugh and say they killed an ox with the stroke of an axe, [iv.251] and should do the same to the Bisons. The second day in hunting one of them wounded a Bull which ran at him, and although he avoided the full stroke of the head, yet was so much hurt that it was about two months before he was well. The next day as two of them was crossing a low point of wood near the river, they saw a Bull fired at and wounded him, the Bull rushed on one of them – who to escape ran behind an Old rotten, stump of a tree of about ten feet high, the furious animal came dash against it, threw it down and the man lay beneath it, the Bull also fell on it, and rolled off: The comrade of the poor fellow ran to the river and hailed the canoes; several of the Men came, the Bison was dying, they took the stump away, but the Iroquois was crushed and dead. These two accidents somewhat lowered their pride as they found that even their guns could not always protect them. A few days after, as two of them were hunt-ing (they always went by two) they met a colored Bear, which one of them wounded, the Bear sprung on him, and standing on his hind feet seized the Iroquois hugging him with his fore legs and paws, which broke the bones of both arms above the elbow, and with it's teeth tore the skin of the head from the crown to the forehead, for the poor fellow had drawn his knife to defend himself, but could not use it; fortunately his comrade was near, and putting his gun close to the Bear shot him dead. The poor fellow was a sad figure, none of us were surgeons, but we did the best we could, but for want of proper bandageing his arms were three months in getting well. These acci-dents happening only to the Iroquois made them superstitious and they con-cluded that some of the Algonquins had thrown bad medicine on them, and a quarrel would probably have taken place had we not been with them. These accidents were the fault of their mode of hunting, being accustomed to hunt only timid animals, and keeping about one hundred [iv.252] yards from each other, to cover more ground did very well for Deer; but to hunt the animals of the Upper countries as the Bison and Bear and which are fierce and dan-gerous, requires the two hunters to be close to each other, the one reserving his fire in case of the wounded animal being able to attack them; they were faulty in their hunting, until experience taught them better.

The native hunt mostly alone, and from the preca[u]tions very seldom meet with an accident. On arrival at Fort Augustus all these people had to disperse and go to some place to pass the winter and make their furr hunts. The hills to the southward, at the foot of the mountains were known to have many Beavers, and thither they were disposed to go; but at a kind of council, we pointed out the dangers they would encounter, as it was the country of the powerful tribes of the Plains who had gained the country by war, and held it as a conquered country open to the incursions of their enemies, in which they would probably be destroyed, or at least plundered; by some of the war parties; and advised them to go to the forest lands of the north where there were also many Beaver, the Natives few and peaceable, and where they could hunt in safety; This advice was directly followed by the Algonquins and Nepissings, they separated themselves into small parties, and passed the winter in safety and made good hunts.

This advice had a very different effect on the Iroquois, who determined to send off a large party to examine the country to the southward and see what the disposition of the Natives were to them, whom they appeared to despise. Accordingly part hunted near the Fort while a party of about seventy five Men well armed went off, foolishly taking their self conceit and arrogance with them. They soon came to a small camp of Peeagans the owners of the country and all their enquiry was where the Beaver was most plenty as [iv.253] if they were masters of the country. As they did not understand each other, the whole was by signs, at which the Indians are tolerably expert. The Peeagans did not know what to make of them, but let them pass. In this manner they passed two more small camps to the fourth which was a larger camp of Willow Indians.[5] Having now proceeded about eighty miles, they agreed to go no further spend a few days and return. Although the Natives did not much like their behaviour they treated them hospitably as usual to strangers. After smoking and feasting, they performed a dance; and then sitting down by signs invited the Willow Indians to a gambling match, this soon brought on a quarrel, in which the arrogant gestures of the Iroquois made the other party seize their arms, and with their guns and Arrows lay dead twenty five of them, the others fled, leaving their blankets and a few other things to the Willow Indians, and returned to Fort Augustus in a sad state.

¶ This affair made the Indians of the Plains look on them with contempt for allowing so many to be killed like women, without even firing a shot in their defence, for the Willow Indians were but a few more than the Iroquois, and mostly armed with Bows and Arrows, which, whatever may be thought

---

5 The Gros Ventres. In 1802 Peter Fidler described an incident in which fourteen Iroquois and two Canadians were killed by Gros Ventres near Chesterfield House, likely the same event to which Thompson refers here. Johnson, ed., *Saskatchewan Journals and Correspondence*, 311–17.

by civilized men, is a dreadful weapon in the hands of a good Archer. The defeated Iroquois sent word of their misfortune to the parties that were hunting, and all together collected about 120 men; Councils were held and war parties to be formed for revenge, to which the Nahathaway Indians, (the natives and masters of the country) were invited, in hopes they would join them; but all to no purpose, the Nahathaways told them they would not enter into their quarrel against their old allies and, and pointed out to them, that three times their numbers would make no [iv.254] impression on the Indians, they were numerous, good cavalry and accustomed to war; adding you yourselves may go and take your revenge, but we do not think any of you will return. All this lowered their self conceit and arrogance, they saw plainly the Natives of those countries had no great opinion of them, and giving up all thoughts of revenge, as they were now to separate for the winter agreed to make a feast and perform all their dances, to which the Nahathaways were invited; The next day they all appeared in their best dresses; and the feast took place about noon of the choice pieces of the Bison and Red Deer; at which, as usual, grace was said and responded to by the guests.

The feast being over the dances began by the Iroquois and their comrades; after a few common dances, they commenced their favorite dance of the grand Calumet;[6] which was much admired and praised, and they requested the Nahathaways to dance their grand Calumet, to which they replied, they had no smoking dance; this elated the Iroquois, and they began their War dance from the discovery of the enemy, to the attack and scalping of the dead, and the war hoop of victory. The Nahathaways praised them. The Iroquois being now proud of their national dances, requested of the Nahathaways to see their War dance, and intimating they thought they had none, which was in a manner saying they were not warriors. I felt for my old friends and looking round, saw the smile of contempt on the lips of Spik a nog gan (the Gun Case) a fine, stern warrior of about fifty years of age, with whom I had been long acquainted, and whom I knew excelled [iv.255] in the dance, I asked him if he intended to take up the challenge, he said, he had no wish to show himself off in dancing before these strangers; "You certainly do not wish them to return to their own country and report of you as so many women. You Spik a nog gun, your eye never pitied, nor your hand never spared, an enemy is the

6 The calumet (French "reed") is a ceremonial pipe stem. As the purpose of the calumet dance is the establishment of ritual kinship and alliance, it was a particularly appropriate choice for this occasion. William N. Fenton, *The Iroquois Eagle Dance: An Offshoot of the Calumet Dance* (Syracuse: Syracuse University Press, 1991), 161–2.

fittest man to represent your countrymen in the War dance; and show these strangers what you are,"

¶ Somewhat nettled, he arose, put on a light war dress, and with his large dagger in his right hand, he began the War dance, by the Scout, the Spy, the Discovery, the return to camp, the Council, the silent march to the ambuscade, the war whoop of attack the tumult of the battle, the Yells of doubtful contest and the War whoop of victory; the pursuit, his breath short and quick the perspiration pouring down on him his dagger in the fugitive, and the closing War whoop of the death of his enemy rung through our ears. The varying passions were strongly marked in his face, and the whole was performed with enthusiasm. The perfect silence, and all eyes rivetted on him, showed the admiration of every one, and for which I rewarded him. The Iroquois seemed lost in surprise, and after a few minutes said, our dances please ourselves, and also the white people and Indians where ever we go, but your dance is war itself to victory and to death. It was evident they were much mortified and at length one of them remarked that he did not scalp his enemy to which he replied with contempt, "any old woman can scalp a dead man."

¶ I was much pleased with the effect this dance had on the Iroquois, it seemed to bring them to their senses, and showed them, that the Indians of the interior countries were fully as good Warriors, Hunters and Dancers, as themselves. They lost all their self conceit and arrogance, and became plain well behaved men, left off talking of war, and turned to hunting. Having taken on credit from the Traders their necessaries for the winter, they [iv.256] separated into small parties of two or three, each having about six steel traps for beaver, of light workmanship with strong elastic springs of which the bait is the castroum of the beaver, called the beaver medicine. They chose their hunting grounds to the westward and northward among the forests at the east foot of the Rocky Mountains. None of the Natives formed a favorable opinion of the Iroquois for their whole number they had only about six women with them, each had a husband; and they could not conceive how men could live without women; they also looked on them as a dirty people for sleeping in their clothes; for the dress that an Iroquois put on in November, he will walk and sleep in to the month of April, and longer if it does not wear away, so very contrary to the custom and habits of the Natives.

The learned men of Europe have their theories on the origen of the North American Indians and from whence they came, and from want of information have decided, and set the question at rest, by asserting, they all came direct from the east coast of Asia, a theory so contrary to facts, their own tradition, and all their movements since the furr traders came first among them, particularly of those from Canada. This subject I shall pass over at present, and reserve to the end of my travels.[7] It must now be remembered that what I now relate is of the great body of dry land at the east foot of the Mountains, the northern part of forests, and the southern of Plains through which roll the Missisoure and its tributaries, the Bow and Saskatchewan Rivers with their many branches.

[HB *first settlement. Early part of the furr trade. Mr Cole killed. Indians numerous. the small Pox. the Animals disappear on the death of the Natives. Journey to the One Pine. cut off. Indian reasons of the Animals diminishing*]

The Hudson's Bay Company did not extend their settlements into the interior country for several years after Canada, in 1763, was ceded to England. Their first trading house was made by Mr Samuel Hearne in 17[*space*] at the sortie of the Saskatchewan into the Lakes,[1] and was so well situated that it is continued [iv.257] to this day under the name of Cumberland House, it's situation has been changed two, or three, times from wood for fuel and other purposes, having worn too far from the house.

Previous to this, the Fur Traders from Canada[2] had extended their Houses a hundred miles beyond up the Saskatchewan, and considerable to the northward on the head waters of the Churchill River. About 1776, the Hudson's Bay Company under Mr Tomison, built a trading house about 120 miles up the first named River.[3] At this time the Nahathaway Indians were very numerous and engrossed to themselves all the Goods brought by the Fur Traders, the Animals of every kind were in abundance. Provisions of all kinds of meat so plentiful, and forced upon the Traders, that all that could be done, was to take a little from each, to give him a little Tobacco, Ammunition to those that had Guns, and Beads, Awls &c to the Women, for they claim a right to the dried Provisions, as the Men do to the Furrs.

The great Tribes of the Plains were only known by name to the Traders, and the state of the country as described to me by some old furr traders, and particularly by Mitchell Oman a native of the Orkney Islands, who had been several years in the Hudsons Bay service. He was without education yet of a superior mind to most men, curious and inquisitive, with a very retentive

7 Thompson addresses the question of Native origins in his essay "The Natives of North America," found in Volume II.
1 Samuel Hearne established Cumberland House in 1774.
2 The Montreal-based traders who would coalesce into the NWC.
3 Hudson House, established in 1779.

memory.[4] Of those times he said, "our situation was by no means pleasant, the Indians were very numerous, and although by far the greater part behaved well, and were kindly to us, yet amongst such a number there will always be bad men, and to protect our selves from them we had to get a respectable chief to stay with, and assist us in trading, and prevent as much as possible, the demands of these Men; there were two Houses from Canada, one was under a Mr Cole, who, by not taking this precaution, got into a quarrel and [was] [iv.258] shot;[5] The next year we went up the River about 350 miles above Cumberland House and built a trading house which we named Buckingham house,[6] and which was situated on the left bank of the River, where it passes thro' the northern part of the great Plains, which freed us from being wholly among the Nahatheways and allowed the Indians of the Plains to trade with us, and the houses from Canada, but still our situation was critical and required all our prudence;

¶ The following year, as usual, we went to York Factory with the furrs, and returned with goods for the winter trade; we proceeded about 150 miles up the River to the Eagle Hills, where we saw the first camp and some of the people sitting on the beach to cool themselves, when we came to them, to our surprise they had marks of the small pox,[7] were weak and just recovering, and I could not help saying, thank heaven we shall now get relief, for none of us had the least idea of the desolation this dreadful disease had done, until we went up the bank to the camp and looked into the tents, in many of which they were all dead, and the stench was horrid; Those that remained had pitched their tents about 200 yards from them and were too weak to move away entirely, which they soon intended to do; they were in such a state of despair and despondence that they could hardly converse with us, a few of them had gained strength to hunt which kept them alive. From what we could learn, three fifths had died under this disease; Our Provisions were nearly out, and we had expected to find ten times more than we wanted, instead of which, they had not enough for themselves; They informed us,

4 For HBC trader Mitchell Oman, whom Thompson served as clerk in 1786–87, see appendix 2. See also 27b, above (48–9).

5 The principal post was Fort Montagne D'Aigle. John Cole (d. 1779) was employed by both the HBC and Montreal fur traders during the 1770s. On 22 April 1779, while trading in the Eagle Hills on behalf of Peter Pangman, Cole was shot and killed during an argument over a horse. E.E. Rich, "John Cole," DCB, 4:160.

6 Hudson House is intended. Buckingham House was erected in 1792.

7 For the smallpox epidemic of 1780–82, see note on 27p (61).

that as far as they knew, all [iv.259] the Indians were in the same dreadful state as themselves, and that we had nothing to expect from them.

We proceeded up the River with heavy hearts, the Bisons were crossing the River in herds, which gave us plenty of provisions for the voyage to our wintering ground.

When we arrived at the House instead of a crowd of Indians to welcome us, all was solitary silence, our hearts failed us. There was no Indian to hunt for us, before the Indians fell sick, a quantity of dried provisions had been collected for the next summers voyage, upon which we had to subsist, until at length two Indians with their families came and hunted for us. These informed us, that the Indians of the forest had beaver robes in their tents some of which were spread over the dead bodies, which we might take, and replace them by a new blanket, and that by going to the tents we would render a service to those that were living by furnishing them with tobacco, ammunition, and a few other necessaries and thus the former part of the winter was employed.[8] The bodies lately dead, and not destroyed by the Wolves and Dogs, for both devoured them, we laid logs over to prevent these animals."

¶ From the best information this disease was caught by the Chip a ways (the forest Indians, and the Sieux (of the Plains) about the same time, in the year 1780, by attacking some families of the white people, who had it, and wearing their clothes. They had no idea of the disease and it's dreadful nature; From the Chip a ways it extended over all the Indians of the forest to it's northward extremity; and by the Sieux over the Indians of the Plains and crossed the Rocky Mountains. More Men died in proportion than Women and Children, for unable to bear the heat of the fever they rushed into the Rivers and Lakes to cool themselves, and the greater part thus perished, the countries [iv.260] were in a manner depopulated, the Natives allowed that far more than one half had died, and from the number of tents which remained, it appeared that about three fifths had perished; despair and despondency had to give way to active hunting both for provisions, clothing and all the necessaries of life; for in their sickness, as usual, they had offered almost every thing they had to the Good Spirit and to the Bad, to preserve their lives,

8 By "Indians of the forest" Oman indicates the Cree and Ojibwa. In performing this act, the traders would not only obtain furs, for which the survivors would be paid in goods, but by wrapping the corpses in new blankets they would prepare them in the traditional way for the journey to the afterlife. A. Irving Hallowell, "The Spirits of the Dead in Saulteaux Life and Thought," *Journal of the Royal Anthropological Institute of Great Britain and Ireland* 70, no. 1 (1940): 35.

and were in a manner, destitute of every thing. All the Wolves and Dogs that fed on the bodies of those that died of the Small Pox lost their hair, especially on the sides and belly, and even for six years after many Wolves were found in this condition and their furr useless. The Dogs were mostly killed.

¶ With the death of the Indians a circumstance took place, which never has, and in all probability; never will be accounted for, I have already mentioned that before that dreadful disease appeared among the Indians they were numerous, and the Bison, Moose, Red, and other Deer more so in proportion and Provisions of Meat, both dried and fresh in abundance, of this all the Traders and Indians were fully sensible, and it was noted by the Traders and Natives, that at the death of the latter, and their being thus reduced to a small number, the numerous herds of Bisons and Deer also disappeared both in the Woods and in the Plains, and the Indians about Cumberland House declared the same of the Moose, and the Swans, Geese and Ducks with the Gulls no longer frequented the Lakes in the same number they used to do, and where they had abundance of eggs during the early part of the Summer, they had now to search about to find them.

¶ As I was not in the country at this time I can only give the assertion of the Traders and the Natives, who could have [iv.261] no interest in[9] relating this sad state of the country. In the early part of September in 1786, I entered these countries and from that time can speak from my own personal knowledge. In the following October,[10] six men and myself, were fitted out with a small assortment of goods, to find the Pee a gan Indians and winter with them: to induce them to hunt for furrs, and make dried Provisions; to get as many as possible to come to the houses to trade, and to trade the furrs of those that would not come. Each of us had a Horse, and some had two, furnished by ourselves. Our road lay through a fine country with slight undulations of ground, too low to be called Hills, everywhere clothed with fine short grass and hummocks, or islands of wood, almost wholly of Aspin and small, but straight, growth, About the tenth day we came to the "One Pine."[11] This had been a fine stately tree of two fathoms girth, growing among a patch of Aspins, and being all alone, without any other Pines for more than an hundred miles, had been regarded with superstitious reverence. When the small pox came, a few tents of Pee a gans were camping near it, in

9 I.e., could derive no benefit by.
10 1787. Here Thompson recounts the same journey from Manchester House to the Piegan camp that is described on 27m–s (58–63).
11 For the One Pine, see the note to 27q (61).

the distress of this sickness, the master of one of the tents applied his prayers to it, to save the lives of himself and family, burned sweet grass and offered upon it's roots, three horses to be at it's service, all he had, the next day the furniture of his horses with his Bow and Quiver of Arrows, and the third morning, having nothing more, a Bowl of Water. The disease was now on himself, and he had to lie down. Of his large family, only himself, one of his wives, and a Boy survived.

As soon as he acquired streng[t]h, he took his horses, and all his other offerings from the "Pine Tree," then putting his little Axe in his belt, he ascended the Pine Tree to about two thirds of it's height, and there cut it off, out of revenge for not having [iv.262] saved his family; when we passed, the branches were withered, and the tree going to decay. For three and twenty days we marched over fine grounds looking for the Indians without seeing any other animals than a chance Bull Bison, from the killing of a few we procured our provisions.

We found a Camp on the south side of the Bow River from it's tender grass the favorite haunts of the Bisons yet this camp had only provisions by daily hunting and our frequent removals led us over a large tract of country, on which we rarely found the Bisons to be numerous, and various camps with whom we had intelligence were in the same state with the Camp we lived with. It is justly said, that as Mankind decrease, the Beasts of the earth increase, but in this calamity the Natives saw all decrease but the Bears, and dried provisions of meat before so abundant that they could not be traded, were now sought as much as furrs. The enquiries of intelligent Traders into this state of the Animals from the Natives were to no purpose. They merely answered, that the Great Spirit having brought this calamity on them, had also taken away the Animals in the same proportion as they were not wanted, and intimating the Bisons and Deers were made and preserved solely for their use; and if there were no Men there would be no Animals. The Bisons are vagrant, wandering from place to place over the great Plains, but the Moose and other Deer are supposed to keep within a range of ground, which they do not willingly leave, but all were much lessened in number.

A few years after I passed over nearly the same grounds and found the Bisons far more numerous.[12]

[Country of the Stone. Fall & Sussee country. Pee a gans]

12 Thompson returned to the Bow River in late November 1800.

[iv.263] The Indians of the Plains are of various Tribes and of several languages which have no affinity with each other.[1]

The Stone Indians[2] are a large tribe of the Sieux Nation, and speak a dialect, differing little from the Sieux tongue, the softest and most pleasing to the ear of all the indian languages. They have always been, and are, in strict alliance with the Nahathaways, and their hunting grounds are on the left bank of the Saskatchewan and eastward and southward to the upper part of the Red River, and their number 400 Tents each containing about eight souls, in all 3200.

The Fall Indians,[3] their former residence was on the Rapids of the Saskatchewan, about 100 miles above Cumberland House; they speak a harsh language, which no other tribe attempts to learn; in number about 70 tents at ten souls to each tent. They are a tall well made muscular people, their countenances manly, but not handsome. Their Chief was of a bad character, and brought them into so many quarrels with their allies, they had to leave their country and wander to the right bank of the Missisourie, to near the Mandane Villages. The Sussees,[4] are about ninety tents and may number about 650 souls. They are brave and manly, tall and well limbed, but their faces somewhat flat, and cannot be called handsome. They speak a very guttural tongue which no one attempts to learn.

The next are the three tribes of the Pee a gan, called Pee a gan a koon, the Blood Indians, (Ken ne koon) and the Blackfeets, (Sax ee koon). These all [iv.264] speak the same tongue, and their hunting grounds contiguous to each other; these were formerly on the Bow River, but now southward to the Missisourie.[5]

All these Plains, which are now the hunting grounds of the above Indians, were formerly in full possession of the Kootanaes, northward;[6] the next the

1 Thompson was in contact with Natives of the northwestern Plains for much of his later fur trade career. In addition to his winter with the Piegan in 1787–88, between 1800 and 1812 he travelled along the North Saskatchewan several times, and during 1800–02 and 1806–07 he resided at Rocky Mountain House and Fort Augustus.
2 For the Assiniboine, see note on 27f (53).
3 For the Gros Ventre, see note on iv.176 (218).
4 For the Sarcee, see note on iv.242 (272).
5 With this observation Thompson introduces his treatment of the Piegan, which will continue for fifty manuscript pages to the end of the 1850 version of the *Travels*. For the Piegan, see note on 27r (62–3).
6 For the Kootenai, see note on iv.242 (272).

Saleesh[7] and their allies, and the most southern the Snake Indians and their tribes,[8] now driven across the Mountains.[9]

[*Sark a map pee. An aged Man. Account. Snake Indian battle. again join the Pee a gans. Battle. Gun employed. Order of Battle with the Snake Indians & defeat*]

¶ The Pee a gan in whose tent I passed the winter was an old Man of at least 75 to 80 years of age; his height about six feet; two or three inches, broad shoulders, strong limbed his hair gray, and plentiful, forehead high and nose prominent, his face sligh[t]ly marked with the small pox, and all together his countenance mild, and even, sometimes playfull; although his step was firm and he rode with ease. He no longer hunted, this he left to his sons; his name was Sauk a map pee (Young Man) his account of former times went back to about 1730 and was as follows.[1]

"The Peeagans were always the frontier Tribe, and upon whom the Snake Indians made their attacks, these latter were very numerous, even without

7 The Salishan linguistic family is widespread in the Northwest, both in the interior and along the Pacific coast. In his use of the term "Saleesh," Thompson usually designates the Flathead, an Interior Salish group which had historically lived east of the Continental Divide. He recognized, however, the linguistic relationship between the Flathead and what he terms here their "allies," the Kalispel and Spokane. Carling I. Malouf, "Flathead and Pend d'Oreille," HNAI, vol. 12, 297–312; Jack Nisbet, *The Mapmaker's Eye: David Thompson on the Columbia Plateau* (Pullman, WA: Washington State University Press, 2005), 156–7. In 1809 Thompson established Saleesh House for the purpose of encouraging trade with the Flathead, and all of these groups figure prominently in the account of his activities of 1807–12, found in the 1848 version of the *Travels* (Volume II).

8 For the Shoshone, see note on 27u (65–6).

9 Here Thompson describes the shifting power relationships between Native groups on the northwestern Plains. For much of the eighteenth century, the Kootenai, Flathead, and Shoshone inhabited the western margins of the Plains, with the latter enjoying military dominance in the region. The Piegan acquisition of guns gave them such a military advantage that by the 1780s the other tribes had retreated for most of the year to lands west of the Continental Divide. The smallpox epidemic of 1780–82 accelerated this westward migration. Binnema, *Common and Contested Ground*, 91–3, 100–2, 128.

1 For Saukamappee and his narrative (which continues until p. 298), see "Historical Introduction" (xxix) and appendix 2.

their allies; and the Pee a gans had to send messengers among us to procure help. Two of them came to the camp of my father, and I was then about his age, (pointing to a Lad of about sixteen years) he promised to come and bring some of his people, the Nahathaways with him, for I am myself of that people, and not of these with whom I am. My father brought about twenty warriors with him. [iv.265] There were a few guns amongst us, but very little ammunition and they were left to hunt for the families; Our weapons was a Lance, mostly pointed with iron, some few of stone A Bow and a quiver of Arrows; the Bows were of Larch, the length came to the chin, the quiver had about fifty arrows, of which ten had iron points, the others were headed with stone. He carried his knife on his breast and his axe in his belt. Such was my fathers weapons, and those with him had much the same weapons. I had a Bow and Arrows, and a knife, of which I was very proud.

¶ We came to the Pee a gans and their allies, they were camped in the Plains on the left bank of the River (the north side) and were a great many. We were feasted, a great War Tent was made, and a few days passed in speeches, feasting and dances. A war chief was elected by the chiefs, and we got ready to march.[2] Our spies had been out and seen a large camp of the Snake Indians on the Plains of the Eagle Hill, and we had to cross the River in canoes, and on rafts, which we carefully secured for our retreat. When we had crossed and numbered our men, we were about 350 Warriors (this he showed by counting every finger to be ten, and holding up both hands three times and then one hand) they had their scouts out, and came to meet us, both parties made a great show of their numbers, and I thought that they were more numerous than ourselves. After some singing and dancing, they sat down on the ground, and placed their large shields before them, which covered them: We did the same, but our shields were not so many, and some of our shields had to shelter two men, in [iv.266][3] Theirs were all placed touching each other, their Bows were not so long as ours, but of better wood, and the back covered with the sinews of the Bisons which made them very elastic and their arrows went a long way and whizzed about us as balls do from guns, they were all headed with a sharp, smooth, black stone (flint) which broke when it struck any thing. Our iron headed, arrows did not go thro' the shields, but stuck in them; On both sides several were wounded, but none lay on the ground; and night put an end to the battle, without a scalp being taken on either side, and in those days such was the results, unless one party was more numerous than the other. The great mischief of war then, was as now,

2 Thompson explains the roles of Piegan civil and war chiefs on iv.282–4 (302–3).
3 Thompson does not complete this sentence on the next page.

by attacking and destroying small camps of ten to thirty tents, which are obliged to separate for hunting.

¶ I grew to be a man, became a skilfull and fortunate hunter, and my relations procured me a Wife she was young and handsome and we were fond of each other. We had passed a winter together, when Messengers came from our allies to claim assistance. By this time the affairs of both parties had much changed; we had more guns and iron headed arrows than before; but our enemies the Snake Indians and their allies had Mis stut im (Big Dogs, that is Horses)[4] on which they rode, swift as the Deer, on which they dashed at the Pee a gans and with their stone Puk a mog gan[5] knocked them on the head, and they had thus lost several of their best men. This news we did not well comprehend and it alarmed us, for we had no idea of Horses and could not make out what they were. Only three of us went and I should not have gone, had not my wife's relations frequently intimated, that her father's medicine bag would be [iv.267] much honored by the scalp of a Snake Indian.

¶ When we came to our allies, the great War Tent with speeches, feasting and dances as before; and when the War Chief had viewed us all it was found between us and the Stone Indians we had ten guns and each of us about thirty balls and powder for the war, and we were considered the strength of the battle. After a few days march, our Scouts brought us word that the enemy was near in a large war party, but had no Horses with them for at that time they had very few of them. When we came to meet each other, as usual, each displayed their numbers, weapons and Shiel[d]s, in all which they were superior to us, except our guns which were not shown, but kept in their leathern cases, and if we had shown they, would have taken them for long clubs. For a long time they held us in suspense; a tall Chief was forming a strong party to make an attack on our centre, and the others to enter into combat with those opposite to them; We prepared for the battle the best we could, those of us who had guns stood in the front line, and each of us two balls in his mouth, and a load of powder in his left hand to reload.

4 Cree *mistatim*, formed from the words *misih*, "big," and *atim*, "dog." Horses were introduced to North America in the sixteenth century by the Spanish, and equestrian culture spread across the West through a combination of horse raiding, trade, and breeding. As Saukamappee's narrative shows, the Piegan first encountered the horse during the 1730s. Before a century had elapsed, Piegan culture had become closely identified with its use.

5 Cree *pakamakan*, literally "a manufactured object designed for hitting." This war club, common in the Plateau and Southwest, usually consisted of a stone head affixed to a wooden handle (Roland Bohr, University of Winnipeg, personal communication with editor, 15 January 2007).

We noticed they had a great many short stone clubs for close combat, which is a dangerous weapon, and had they made a bold attack on us, we must have been defeated as they were more numerous and better armed than we were, for we could have fired our guns no more than twice; and we were at a loss what to do on the wide plain, and each Chief encouraged his men to stand firm. Our eyes were all on the tall Chief and his motions, which appeared to be contrary to the advice of several old Chiefs, all this time we were about the strong flight of an arrow from each other. At length the tall Chief retired, and they formed their long usual [iv.268] line by placing their shields on the ground to touch each other, the shield having a breadth of full three feet or more. We sat down opposite to them, and most of us waited for the night to make a hasty retreat. The War Chief was close to us anxious to see the effect of our guns. The lines were too far asunder for us to make a sure shot, and we requested him to close the line to about sixty yards, which was gradually done, and lying flat on the ground behind the shields we watched our opportunity when they drew their Bows to shoot at us, their bodies were then exposed and each of us, as opportunity offered, fired with deadly aim, and either killed, or severely wounded, every one we aimed at.

The War Chief was highly pleased, and the Snake Indians finding so many killed and wounded kept themselves behind their shields; the War Chief then desired we would spread ourselves by two's throughout the line, which we did, and our shots caused consternation and dismay along their whole line. The battle had begun about noon, and the Sun was not yet half down, when we perceived some of them had crawled away from their shields and were taking to flight. The War Chief seeing this went along the line and spoke to every Chief to keep his Men ready for a charge of the whole line of the enemy, of which he would give the signal; this was done by himself stepping in front with his Spear, and calling on them to follow him as he rushed on their line, and in an instant the whole of us followed him, the greater part of the enemy took to flight, but some fought bravely and we lost more than ten killed, and many wounded; Part of us pursued, and killed a few, but the chase had soon to be given over, for at the body of every Snake Indian killed, there were five or six of us trying to get his scalp, or part of his clothing, his [iv.269] weapons, or something as a trophy of the battle, as there were only three of us, and seven of our friends, the Stone Indians, we did not interfere, and got nothing.

[*Scalps & disposal of Souls of the slain. he goes to his tribe. sees a Horse. Arrives at his tribe: his Wife has another Man. leaves his people. becomes a Pe ag an*]

The next morning the War Chief made a speech, praising their bravery, and telling them to make a large War Tent to commemorate their victory, to which they directly set to work and by noon it was finished.

The War Chief now called on all the other Chiefs to assemble their men and come to the Tent. In a short time they came, all those who had lost relations had their faces blackened; those who killed an enemy, or wished to be thought so, had their faces blackened with red streaks on the face, and those who had no pretensions to the one, or the other, had their faces red with ochré. We did not paint our faces until the War Chief told us to paint our foreheads and eyes black, and the rest of the face of dark red ochree, as having carried guns, and to distinguish us from all the rest. Those who had scalps now came forward with the scalps neatly streched on a round willow with a handle to the frame; they appeared to be more than fifty, and excited loud shouts and the war whoop of victory. When this was over, the War Chief told them that if any one had a right to the scalp of an enemy as a war trophy, it ought to be us, who, with our guns had gained the victory, when from the numbers of our enemies we were anxious to leave the field of battle; and that ten scalps must be given to us; this was soon collected, and he gave to each of us a Scalp.

¶ All those whose faces were blackened for the loss of relations, or friends, now came forward to claim the other scalps to be held in their hands for the benefit of their departed relations and friends; this occasioned a long conversation with those who had the scalps; at length [iv.270] they came forward to the War Chief, those who had taken the trophy from the head of the enemy they had killed, said the Souls of the enemy that each of us has slain, belong to us, and we have given them to our relations which are in the other world to be their slaves, and we are contented. Those who held scalps taken from the enemy that were found dead under the shields were at a loss what to say, as not one could declare he had actually slain the enemy whose scalp he held, and yet wanted to send their Souls to be the slaves of their departed relations. This caused much discussion; and the old Chiefs decided it could not be done, and that no one could send the soul of an enemy to be a slave in the other world, except the Warrior who actually killed him; the scalps you hold are trophies of the Battle, but they give you no right to the soul of the enemy from whom it is taken, he alone who kills an enemy has a right to the soul, and to give it to be a slave to whom he pleases. This decision did not please them, but they were obliged to abide by it.

¶ The old Chiefs then turned to us, and praising our conduct in the battle said, each of you have slain two enemies in battle, if not more, you will return to your own people, and as you are young men, consult with the old men to whom you shall give the souls of those you have slain; until which let them wander about the other world. The Chiefs wished us to stay, and promised to each of us a handsome young wife, and [to] adopt us as their sons, but we told them we were anxious to see our relations and people, after which, perhaps we might come back. After all the War ceremonies were over, we pitched away in large camps with the women and children on the frontier of the Snake Indian country, hunting the Bisons and Red [iv.271] Deer, which were numerous, and we were anxious to see a Horse of which we had heard so much. At last, as the leaves were falling, we heard that one was killed by an arrow shot into his belly, but the Snake Indian that rode him, got away; numbers of us went to see him, and we all admired him, he put us in mind of a Stag that had lost his horns, and we did not know what name to give him, but as he was a slave to Man, like the dog, which carried our things; he was named the Big Dog.

¶ We set off for our people, and on the fourth day came to a camp of Stone Indians, the relations of our companions, who received us well and we staid a few day[s]. The Scalps were placed on poles, and the Men and Women danced round them, singing to the sound of Rattles, Tambours and flutes. When night came, one of our party, in a low voice, repeated to the Chief the narrative of the battle, which he in a loud voice, walking about the tents, repeated to the whole camp, after which, the Chiefs called those who followed them to a feast, and the battle was always the subject of the conversation and driving the Snake Indians to a great distance. There were now only three of us to proceed, and upon enquiry, [we] learned a camp of our people, the Nahathaways were a days journey's from us, and in the evening we came to them, and all our news had to be told, with the usual songs and dances, but my mind was wholly bent on making a grand appearance before my Wife and her Parents, and presenting to her father the scalp I had to ornament his Medicine Bag; and before we came to the camp, we had dressed ourselves, and painted each other's [iv.272] faces to appear to the best advantage, and were proud of ourselves.

¶ On seeing some of my friends I got away and went to them, and by enquiries, learned that my parents had gone to the low countries of the Lakes, and that before I was three Moons away my wife had given herself to another man, and that her father could not prevent her, and they were all far to the northward there to pass the winter. At this unlooked for news I was quite disheartened; I said nothing, but my heart was swollen with anger and revenge, and I passed the night scheming mischief. In the morning my friends reasoned with me upon my vexation about a worthless woman, and that it was beneath a warrior anger, there were no want of women to replace her and a better wife could be got. Others said, that if I had staid with my wife instead of running away to kill Snake Indians, nothing of this would have happened. My anger moderated, I gave my Scalp to one of my friends to give to my father, and renouncing my people, I left them, and came to the Pee a gans who gave me a hearty welcome; and upon my informing them of my intention to remain with them, the great Chief gave me his eldest daughter to be my wife, she is the sister of the present Chief, and as you see, now an old woman.

[*Snake Indian camp attack. brings on the Small Pox. dreadful effects. Allies weak. peaceable, till 5 tents were killed. Old Chief's speech. not to destroy Women & Children. Speeches &c. Scouts cannot find the Snake Indians*]

¶ The terror of that battle and of our guns has prevented any more general battles, and our wars have since been carried by ambuscade and surprize, of small camps, in which we have greatly the advantage, from the Guns, arrows shod of iron, long knives, flat bayonets and axes from the Traders. While we have these weapons, the Snake Indians have none, but what few they sometimes take [iv.273] from one of our small camps which they have destroyed, and they have no Traders among them. We thus continued to advance through the fine plains to the Stag River[1] when death came over us all, and swept away more than one half of us by the small pox, of which we knew nothing until it brought death among us. We caught it from the Snake Indians. Our Scouts were out for our security, when some returned and informed us of a considerable camp which was too large to attack and something very suspicious about it; from a high knowl they had a good view of the camp, but saw none of the men hunting, or going about, there were a few Horses, but no one came to them, and a herd of Bisons feeding close to the camp, with other herds near. This somewhat alarmed us as a stratagem of War; and our Warriors thought this camp had a larger not far off; so that if this camp was attacked which was strong enough to offer a desperate resistance, the other would come to their assistance and overpower us as had been once done by them, and in which we lost many of our men.

The council ordered the Scouts to return and go beyond this camp, and be sure there was no other. In the mean time we advanced our camp. The Scouts returned and said no other tents were near, and the camp appeared in the same state as before. Our Scouts had been going too much about their

---

1 The Red Deer River. Saukamappee refers not to a single journey but to the gradual movement of the Piegan south and west.

camp and were seen; they expected what would follow, and all those that could walk, as soon as night came on, went away. Next morning at the dawn of day, we attacked the Tents, and with our sharp flat daggers and knives, cut through the tents and entered for the fight; but our war whoop instantly stopt, our eyes [iv.274] were appalled with terror, there was no one to fight with but the dead and the dying, each a mass of curruption. We did not touch them, but left the tents, and held a council on what was to be done. We all thought the Bad Spirit had made himself master of the camp and destroyed them. It was agreed to take some of the best of the tents, and any other plunder that was clean and good, which we did, and also took away the few Horses they had, and returned to our camp.

¶ The second day after this dreadful disease broke out in our camp, and spread from one tent to another as if the Bad Spirit carried it. We had no belief that one Man could give it to another, any more than a wounded Man could give his wound to another. We did not suffer so much as those that were near the river, into which they rushed and died. We had only a little brook, and about one third of us died, but in some of the other camps, there were tents in which every one died. When at length it left us, and we moved about to find our people, it was no longer with the song and the dance; but with tears, shrieks, and howlings of despair for those who would never return to us. War was no longer thought of, and we had enough to do to hunt and make provisions for our families, for in our sickness we had consumed all our dried provisions; but the Bisons and Red Deer were also gone, we did not see one half of what was before, whither they had gone to we could not tell, we believed the Good Spirit had forsaken us, and allowed the Bad Spirit to become our Master, what little we could spare we offered to the Bad Spirit to let us alone and go to our enemies. To the Good Spirit [iv.275] we offered feathers, branches of trees, flowers and sweet smelling grass. Our hearts were low, and dejected and we shall never be again the same people.

¶ To hunt for our families was our sole occupation and kill Beavers, Wolves, and Foxes to trade our necessaries; and we thought of War no more, and perhaps would have made peace with them, for they had suffered dreadfully as well as us; and had left all this fine country of the Bow River to us. We were quiet for about two or three winters, and although we several times saw their young men on the scout we took no notice of them, as we all require young men to look about the country that our families may sleep in safety and that we may know where to hunt. But the Snake Indians are a bad people, even their allies the Saleesh and Koo ta naes cannot trust them, and do not camp with them, no one believes what they say, and are very treachourous; every one says they are rightly named Snake People, for their tongue is forked like that of a Rattle Snake, from which they have their name.

¶ I think it was about the third falling of the leaves of the trees, that five of our tents pitched away to the valleys in the Rocky Mountains, up a branch of this River (the Bow) to hunt the Big Horn Deer (Mountain Sheep) as their horns make fine large bowls, and are easily cleaned; they were to return on the first snow. All was quiet and we waited for them until the snow lay on the ground, when we got alarmed for their safety; and about thirty Warriors set off to seek them, it was only two days march, and in the evening they came to the camp, it had been destroyed by a large party of Snake Indians, who left their marks, of snakes heads painted black on sticks they had set up. The bodies were all there with the Women and Children but scalped, and partly devoured by the Wolves and Dogs.

[iv.276] The party on their return related the fate of our people; and other camps on hearing the news came and joined us. A War Tent was made and the Chiefs and Warriors assembled; the red pipes were filled with Tobacco,[2] but before being lighted an old Chief arose, and beckoning to the Man who had the fire to keep back, addressed us, saying, 'I am an old man, my hair is white and have seen much: formerly we were healthy and strong and many of us, now we are few to what we were, and the great sickness may come again. We were fond of War, even our Women flattered us to war, and nothing was thought of but Scalps for singing and dancing. Now think of what has happened to us all, by destroying each other and doing the work of the bad spirit; the Great Spirit became angry at our making the ground red with blood; he called to the Bad Spirit to punish and destroy us; but in doing so, not to let one spot of the ground, to be red with blood, and the bad Spirit did it as we all know. Now we must revenge the death of our people and make the Snake Indians feel the effects of our guns, and other weapons; but the young women must all be saved, and if any has a babe at the breast, it must not be taken from her, nor hurt; all the Boys and Lads that have no weapons must not be killed; but brought to our camps, and be adopted amongst us, to be of our people, and make us more numerous and stronger than we are. Thus the Great Spirit will see that when we make war we kill only those who are dangerous to us, and make no more ground red with blood than we can help, and the Bad Spirit will have no more power on us.' Every one signified his assent to the old Chief, and since that time, it has sometimes been

2 Thompson discusses the significance of the red pipe on iv.304 (315).

acted on, but more with the Women than the Boys, and while it weakens our enemies makes us stronger.

¶ A red pipe was now lighted and the same old Chief [iv.277] taking it, gave three whiffs to the Great Spirit praying him to be kind to them and not forsake them, then three whiffs to the Sun, the same to the Sky, the Earth and the four Winds; the Pipe was passed round, and other pipes lighted. The War Chief then arose, and said 'Remember my friends that while we are smoking the bodies of our relations and friends, are being devoured by wolves and Dogs, and their Souls are sent by the Snake Indians to be the slaves of their relations in the other world. We have made no war on them for more than three summers, and we had hoped to live quietly until our young men had grown up, for we are not many as we used to be; but the Snake Indians, that race of liars, whose tongues are like rattle snakes, have already made war on us, and we can no longer be quiet. The country where they now are is but little known to us, and if they did not feel themselves strong they would not have dared to have come so far to destroy our people. We must be courageous and active, but also cautious; and my advice is, that three scout parties, each of about ten warriors with a Chief at their head, take three different directions, and cautiously view the country, and not go too far, for enough of our people are already devoured by wolves and our business is revenge, without losing our people.'

¶ After five days, the scout parties returned without seeing the camp of an enemy, or any fresh traces of them. Our War Chief Koo tanae Appe[3] was now distressed, he had expected some camp would have been seen, and he concluded, the Snake Indians had gone to the southward to their allies, to show the scalps they had taken and make their songs and dances for the victory, and in his speech denounced constant war on them until they were exterminated." Affairs were in this state when we arrived, and the narrative old man having given us the above information, lighted his pipe; and smoking it out said, "the Snake Indians are no match for us; they have no guns, [iv.278] and are no match for us, but they have the power to vex us and make us afraid for the small hunting parties that hunt the small deer for dresses and the Big Horn for the same and for Bowls. They keep us always on our guard."[4]

[*Two Indians killed by a grizled Bear. Bear burnt. War Party of 50 march. Come near a large camp. Plunder 50 horses and return*]

3 For Piegan war chief Kootanae Appee, see appendix 2.
4 Here Saukamappee's account comes to an end, and Thompson resumes his own narrative voice.

¶ A few days after our arrival, the death cry was given, and the Men all started out of the Tents, and our old tent mate with his gun in his hand. The cry was from a young man who held his Bow and Arrows, and showed one of his thighs torn by a grizzled Bear, and which had killed two of his companions. The old Man called for his powder horn and shot bag, and seeing the priming of his gun in good order, he set off with the young man for the Bear, which was at a short distance, they found him devouring one of the dead, the moment he saw them he sat up on his hind legs, showing them his teeth and long clawed paws. In this, his usual position, to defend his prey, his head is a bad mark, but his breast offers a direct mark to the heart, through which the old Man sent his ball, and killed him. The two young men who were destroyed by the Bear, had each, two iron shod Arrows, and the camp being near, they attacked the Bear for his skin and claws, but unfortunately their arrows stuck in the bones of his ribs, and only irritated him; he sprung on the first and with one of his dreadful fore paws tore out his bowels and three of his ribs; the second he seized in his paws, and almost crushed him to death, threw him down, when the third Indian, hearing their cries, came to their assistance and sent an arrow, which only wounded him in the neck, for which the Bear chased him, and sligh[t]ly tore one of [iv.279] his thighs. The first poor fellow was still alive, and knew his parents,[1] in whose arms he expired. The Bear, for the mischief he had done was condemned to be burnt to ashes, the claws of his fore paws, very sharp and long, the young man wanted for a collar but it was not granted those that burned the Bear watched until nothing but ashes remained.

The two young men were each wrapped up separately in Bison robes, laid side by side on the ground, and covered with logs of wood and stones, in which we assisted. By the advice of the Civil Chief, in his speeches in the early part of every night, we pitched southward to about eighty miles beyond the Bow River. We had a few showers of snow, which soon melted, the herds of Bisons were sufficient for daily use, but not enough for dried provisions, however a council was held, and as they did not intend to go farther south, towards the Snake Indians, but after hunting about where they were, for a Moon, return to the northward to trade their furrs, whether it would not be adviseable to know if their enemies were near them or not. After consultation it was agreed to send out a war chief, with about fifty warriors to examine the country for a few day's journey. The Chief soon collected his warriors and having examined their arms, and that every one had two pair of shoes, some dried provisions and other necessaries, in the evening the principal War

---

1 I.e., saw and recognized his parents.

Chief addressed the Chief at the head of the party; reminding him that the warriors now accompanying him, would steadily follow him, that they were sent to destroy their enemies, that he must be wise and cautious and bring back the Warriors entrusted to his care. Among them was the eldest son of the Old Man in whose tent we lived. They all marched off very quietly, as if for hunting. After they [iv.280] were gone; the old man said it was not a war party, but one of those they frequently sent, under guidance of those who had showed courage and conduct in going to war, for we cannot afford to lose our people we are too few, and these expeditions inure our men to long marches and to suffer hunger and thirst.

¶ At the end of about twenty days they returned with about thirty five Horses in tolerable condition, and fifteen fine mules, which they had brought away from a large camp of Snake Indians. The old Man's son gave him a long account of the business. "On the sixth evening the scouts ahead came and informed the Chief, that we must be near a camp as they had seen horses feeding: night came on and we went aside to a wood of cotton and poplar trees on the edge of a brook, in the morning some of us climbed the trees and passed the day but saw nothing. In the night we went higher up the brook, and as it was shoal, we walked in it for some distance, to another wood, and there lay down. Early the next morning, a few of us advanced through the wood, but we had not gone far, before we heard the women with their dogs come for wood for fuel. Some of us returned to the Chief, and the rest watched the women, it was near mid day before they all went away, they had only stone axes and stone clubs to break the wood; they took only what was dry, and cut none down. Their number showed us the camp must be large, and sometimes some of them came so close to us that we were afraid of being discovered.

¶ The Chief now called us round him, and advised us to be very cautious as it was plain we were in the vicinity of a large camp; and manage our little provisions, for we must not expect to get any more until we retreated; if we fire a gun at the Deer it will be heard; and if we put an arrow in a deer, and he gets away, and they see the deer, it will alarm them, and we shall not be able to get away. 'My intention is to have something to show our people, and when we retreat take as many Horses as we can with us, to accomplish which, we must [iv.281] [await] a fair opportunity, and in the mean time be hungry, which we can stand some time as we have plenty of water to drink.' We were getting tired, and our solace was of an evening to look at the horses and mules, at length he said to us to get ready, and pointing to the top of the Mountains, 'see the blue sky is gone and a heavy storm is there, which will soon reach us;' and so it did; About sun set we proceeded thro' the wood, to the horses, and with the lines we carried, each helping the other, we soon had a horse or a mule to ride on. We wanted to drive some with us, but the Chief would not allow it, it was yet day light when we left the wood, and entered the plains, but the Storm of Wind was very strong and on our backs, and at the gallop, or trot, so as not [to] tire our horses, we continued to midnight, when we came to a brook, with plenty of grass and let them get a good feed. After which we held on to sun rising, when seeing a fine low ground, we staid the rest of the day, keeping watch until night, when we continued our journey. The Storm lasted two days and greatly helped us."

¶ The old Man told his son, who, in his relation had intimated he did not think the Chief very brave; that it was very fortunate that he was under such a Chief, who had acted so wisely and cautiously, "for had he acted otherwise not one of you would have returned," and some young men coming into the tent, whom he supposed might have the same opinions as his son; he told them; "that it required no great bravery for a War Party to attack a small camp which they were sure to master; but that it required great courage and conduct, to be for several days in the face of a large camp undiscovered; and each of you [iv.282] to bring away a horse from the enemy, instead of leaving your own scalps."

[*Peagans & Indians of the Plains &c. Characters of the civil and war chief. Koo tan ae App ee's character*]

The Pee a gans, with the tribes of the Blood, and Blackfeet Indians, who all speak the same language, are the most powerful of the western and northern plains, and by right of conquest have their west boundary to the foot of the Rocky Mountains, southward to the north branches of the Missisourie, eastward for about three hundred miles from the Mountains and northward to the upper part of the Saskatchewan. Other tribes of their allies also at times hunt on part of the above, and a great extent of the Plains, and these great Plains place them under different circumstances, and give them peculiar traits of character from those that hunt in the forests. These latter live a peaceable life, with hard labor, to procure provisions and clothing for their families, in summer they make use of canoes, and in winter haul on sleds all they have, in their frequent removals from place to place. On the other hand the Indians of the Plains make no use of canoes, frequently stay many days in a place, and when they remove have horses and dogs, both in summer and winter to carry their baggage and provisions: they have no hard labor, but have powerful enemies which keep them constantly on the watch, and are never secure but in large camps.

¶ The manners and customs of all these tribes of the Plains are much alike, and in giving those of the Pee a gans, it may serve for all the others. Being the frontier tribe, they lead a more precarious and watchful life than the other tribes, and from their boyhood are taught the use of arms, and to be good warriors, they become more martial and more moral than the others, and many of them have a chivalrous bearing, ready for any enterprise. They have a civil and military Chief. The first was called Sak a tow, the orator and appeared hereditary in his family, as his father had been [iv.283] the civil Chief, and his eldest son was to take his place at his death and occasionally acted for him. The present Chief was now about sixty years of age (1800) about five feet ten inches in height, remarkably well made, and in his youth a very handsome man. He was always well dressed, and his insignia of office, was the backs of two fine Otter skins covered with mother of pearl, which from behind his neck hung down his breast to below the belt; When his son acted for him, he always had this ornament on him. In every council he presided, except one of War. He had couriors which went from camp to camp, and brought the news of how things were, of where the great herds of Bisons were feeding, and of the direction they were taking. The news thus collected, about two or three hours after sun set, walking about the Camp, he related in a loud voice, making his comments on it, and giving advice when required. His language was fluent and he was admired for his eloquence, but not for his principles and his advice could not be depended, on, being sometimes too violent and more likely to produce quarrels than allay them yet his influence was great.

The War Chief was Koo ta nae Appé (Kootanae Man.)[1] his stature was six feet six inches, tall and erect, he appeared to be of Bone and Sinew with no more flesh, than absolutely required, his countenance manly, but not stern, his features prominent, nose somewhat aqu[i]line; his manners kind and mild; his word was sacred, he was both loved and respected and his people often wished him to take, a more active part in their affairs but he confined himself to War, and the care of the camp in which he was, which was generally [iv.284] of fifty to one hundred tents, generally a full day's march nearer to the Snake Indians than any other camp. It was supposed he looked on the civil Chief, with indifference as a garrulous old man more fit for talking than any thing else, and they rarely camped together. Kootanae Appé by his five wives had twenty two sons and four daughters. His grown up sons were as tall as himself and others promised the same. He was friendly to the White Men, and in his speeches, reminded his people of the great ben-

---

1 For Piegan war chief Kootanae Appee, see appendix 2.

efit of the Traders were to them, and that it was by their means they had so many useful articles, and guns for hunting, and to conquer their enemies. He had acquired his present station and influence from his conduct in war. He was utterly averse to small parties, except for horse stealing, which too often brought great hardships and loss of life, he seldom took the field with less than two hundred warriors but frequently with many more, his policy was to get as many of the allies to join him as possible, by which all might have a share of the honour and plunder, and thus avoid those jealousies and envy-ings so common amongst the Chiefs. He praised every Chief that in the least deserved it, but never appeared to regard fame as worth his notice yet always took care to deserve it; for all his expedi[ti]ons were successful.

[*features of the plain Indians. Beards. character. Apathy &c. Various char-acters. dandies. ornaments &c. Dress. Walk & White People*]

¶ The Pee a gans and their allies of the Plains, with us, would not be counted handsome, from infancy they are exposed to the weather and have not that softness of expression in their countenances which is so pleasing, but they are a fine race of men, tall and muscular, with manly features, and intel-ligent [iv.285] countenances, the eye large, black and piercing, the nose full, and generally straight, the teeth regular and white, the hair long, straight and black; their beards, apparently would be equal to those of white men, did they not continually attempt to eradicate it; for when grown old and no longer pluck out the hairs they have more beard than could naturally be expected. Their color is something like that of a Spaniard from the south of Spain, and some like that of the French of the south of France, and this com-parison is drawn from seeing them when bathing together.

¶ In questioning them of their origen, and from whence they formerly came, they appear to have no tradition beyond the time of their great grandfathers, that they can depend on, and in their idle time sometimes is the subject of their conversation. They have no tradition that they ever made use of canoes, yet their old men always point out the North East as the place they came from, and their progress has always been to the south west. Since the Trad-ers came to the Saskatchewan River, this has been their course and progress for the distance of four hundred miles from the Eagle Hills, to the Moun-tains near the Missisourie but this rapid advance may be mostly attributed to their being armed with guns and iron weapons. Of their origen, they think themselves and all the animals to be indigenus, and from all times existing as at present. The Indians are noticed for their apathy, this is more assumed than real; in public he wishes it to appear that nothing can affect him, but in private he feels and expresses himself sensible to every thing that happens to him, or to his family. After all his endeavours to attain some object in hunting, or other matters, and cannot do it, he [iv.286] says, the "Great Spirit will have it so," in the same manner as we say "It is the will of Providence." Civilized Men have many things to engage their attention and take up their time, but the Indian is very different, hunting is his business, not his amusement, and even in this he is limited for want of ammunition, hence his whole life is in the enjoyments of his passions desires and affections contracted within a small circle, and in which it is often intense.

The Men are proud of being noticed and praised as good hunters, warriors, or any other masculine accomplishments and many of the young men as fine dandies as they can make themselves. I have known some of them take full an hour to paint their faces, with White, Red, Green, Blue and Yellow, or part of these colors, with their looking glasses, and advising one another, how to lay on the different colors in stripes, circles dots, and other fancies, then stand for part of the day in some place of the camp to be admired by the women. When married all this painting is at end, and if they will paint it only with one color, as red, or yellow ochre. The country affords no ornaments for the men, but collars of the claws of the fore paws of the Bear.

¶ The Women, as usual with all women are fond of ornaments, but the country produces none, except some of the teeth of the deer, which are pierced, strung together, and form bracelets for the wrists and sometimes a fillet of sweet scented grass round the forehead, the rest of their ornaments are from the Traders, as Beads of various colors, Rings Hawks Bells, and Thimbles scarce any has ear rings, and never any in the nose. On the first arrival of a stranger in a camp, who has never seen them, he may not find the young women so handsome as he could [iv.287] wish, for there is a line of beauty in women, which is somewhat different in every people and nation, but where, if the features are regular, we soon get habituated. These Women have in general good features, though hardened by constant exposure to the weather, their dress is of deer skin mostly of the Antelope, white and pliant which is fastened over the shoulders, belled round the waist and descends to their ancles, or to the ground show them to advantage. The dress of the Men is very simple, a pair of long leggins, which come to the ground, and would reach to the breast, are secured by a belt, over which the rest hangs down. Some few wear a shirt of dressed leather, and both sexes wrap a Bison robe round them. Their walk is erect, light and easy, and may be said to be graceful. When on the plains in company with white men, the erect walk of the Indian is shown to great advantage. The Indian with his arms folded in his robe seems to glide over the ground; and the white people seldom in an erect posture, their bodies swayed from right to left, and come with their arms as if to saw a passage through the air. I have often been vexed at the comparison.

[*Marriage. Polygamy &c. sometimes in trust. Account of more Women than Men. run away matches. Poo no kow affair. Poo no kow's run away match. is shot & dies. death of his widow. Various characters. The Man that died of hunger. Disgrace. Suicide of a Wife. The suicide Wife's husband. Children brought up*]

¶ The young men seldom marry before they are fully grown, about the age of 22 years or more, and the women about sixteen to eighteen the elder women who are related to them are generally the match makers, and the parties come together without any ceremony. On the marriage of the young men, two of them form a tent until they have families, in which also reside the widowed Mothers and Aunts. Polygamy is allowed and practised, and the Wife more frequently than her husband the cause of it, for when a family comes a single wife can no longer do the duties and labor required unless she, or her husband; have two widowed relations [iv.288] in their tent, and which frequently is not the case; and a second Wife is necessary for they have to cook, take care of the meat, split and dry it; procure all the wood for fuel; dress the skins into soft leather for robes and clothing; which they have also to make and mend, and other duties which leaves scarce any part of the day to be idle, and in removing from place to place the taking down of the tents and putting them up, are all performed by women. Some of the Chiefs have three to six wives, for until a woman is near fifty years of age, she is sure to find a husband.

¶ A young Indian with whom I was acquainted and who was married often said, he would never have more than one wife, he had a small tent, and one of his aunts to help his wife; Nearly two years afterwards passing by where he was I entered his tent, and his first wife, as usual, sitting beside him, and on the other side three fine women in the prime of life, and as many elderly of the sex, in the back part. When I left the tent, he also came out, and telling me not to laugh at him for what he formerly said of having only one wife and he would explain to me how he had been obliged to take three more. "After I last saw you a friend of mine, whom I regarded and loved as a brother would go to war, he got wounded, returned, and shortly after died, relying on my friendship, when dying he requested his parents to send his two wives to me, where he was sure they would be kindly treated and become my wives. His parents brought them to me, with the dying request of my friend, what could

I do, but grant the claim of my friend and make them my wives, those are the two that sit next the door. The other one was the wife of [iv.289] a cousin who was also a friend of mine, he fell sick and died, and bequeathed his wife to my care, the old women at the back of the tent are their relations. I used to hunt the Antelopes, their skins make the finest leather for clothing, although the meat is not much, yet it is good and was sufficient for us; but now I have given that over, and to maintain seven women and myself, am obliged to confine myself to hunting the Red Deer and the Bison, which give us plenty of meat, tho' the leather is not so good."

¶ The old Indian (Sark a map pee) whom I have already mentioned, pointed out to me, a curious kind of polygamy besides his old wives; on the other side of the tent sat three young women of about sixteen or eighteen years of age, whom about two months before, had been given to him for wives by their parents; I noticed that he treated them as if they were his daughters, he told me they were placed with him on trust. "You must know among us are families far more numerous and powerful, than other families and of which some of the relatives make a bad use of their influence and oppress those that are weak, tho' as brave as themselves. Two of these young women are sisters and the whole three were betrothed to three young men; and would have been given to them, had not three Men of two powerful families who have each already four or five wives, demanded that these young women should be given to them; as their parents are not powerful to prevent this, these three young women have been given to me, and in my tent they will remain until this camp separates, and they go to some distance, when they will be given to the young men for whom they are intended; And thus each of them [iv.290] will regard me as their father." He has always been a friend to the weak, and has thereby gained great influence.

Some time after, I met an old Warrior whom I had known for a long time. I spoke to him of what Sark a map pee had told me of the three young women in his tent, and that I had never known such a custom amongst the Indians of the Woods, and enquired if it was common among those of the plains. He said it is not common, yet it happens too often; "Had one of those Men who wanted those young women came to Sark a map pee tent and demanded them, what would he have done" "If any had been fool enough to have done so he would have shot him, as he would a Bear, and as careless of the consequences." The grown up population of these people appear to be about three men to every five women, and yet the births appear in favour of the boys. The few that are killed in battle will not account for this, and the deficiency may be reckoned to the want of woollen or cotton clothing. Leather does very well in dry weather but in wet weather, or heavy rains it is very uncomfortable, and as is frequently the case on a march, cannot be dried for a few days; it thus injures the constitution and brings on premature decay, of this the Natives appear sensible, for all those that have it in their power, buy woollen clothing.

¶ The Indians of the Plains all punish Adultery with death to both parties. This law does not appear to be founded on either religious, or moral, principles, but upon a high right of property as the best gift that Providence has given to them to be their wives and the mothers of their families, and without whom they cannot live. Every year there are some runaway matches between the young men and [iv.291] women; these are almost wholly from the hatred of the young women to polygamy. When a fine young woman proud of herself, finds that instead of being given to her lover, she is to be the fourth, or fifth wife to some Man advanced in years, where she is to be the slave of the family, and bear all the bondage of a wife, without any of it's rights and priviledges, she readily consents to quit the camp with her lover, and go to some other camp at a distance, where they have friends. In this case the affair is often made up, and the parents of the young woman are more pleased, than otherwise; yet it sometimes ends fatally. But the most of these elopements are with the young women given to be the fourth or fifth wife; in this case the affair is more serious, for it is not the father, but the husband that is wronged, and revenges the injury. If the young couple can escape a few months the affair is sometimes settled by a present of one or two horses; but if the young man is considered a worthless character, which is often the case, his life pays the forfeit of his crime; and if the woman escapes, the same fate, her nose is cut off as a mark of infamy, and some of these unfortunate women have been known to prefer death to this disgrace. Yet some cases are very hard.

Poo no kow (the Stag) was a son of the War Chief, Kootanae Appee. He was betrothed to a young woman, and only waited until the leather for a tent could be dressed to be a tent for them; during which, upon an insult from the Snake Indians, his father collected his Warriors to revenge it, and some of his sons accompanied him, among whom was Poo no kow; the expedition was [iv.292] successful and he proudly returned with two fine horses one of which he intended for his father in law. During the expedition, by present and promises the father of another young man obtained her for his son. A friend went off [to] his fathers camp to inform him of the disposal of his intended bride, and think no more of her, but his love for her was too strong to follow this advice. With his two horses he went near the camp, but did not enter it; here his friend parted with him, whom he requested to send one of his aunts to him; she came, and he explained to her, how he was dealt with and that he was determined to have his bride, tho' he should kill the man that had her, his aunt seeing his resolution, promised to speak to her and see what she would do, the young woman, as soon as she was informed of it, went to him, and they both set off for the Trading House on the Saskatchewan River,[1] a journey of six days.

¶ When near the House he saw a number of horses belonging to it, and not wishing to make his appearance on jaded[2] horses, he unsaddled his own, and was putting the saddles on other two horses, when an Indian who was guarding them perceiving him and thinking he was stealing them, shot him thro' the belly. He knew the wound was mortal, but had strength to reach the House, where he lay down and related what had passed. The next morning finding himself dying he took his sharp dagger in his hand, and held it ready to plunge into the heart of the young woman who had accompanied him and who was sitting beside him, he said to her, "Am I to go alone; do you really love me" she burst into tears [iv.293] held down her head, but said nothing; "I see you do not love me and I must go alone, tell my brothers of what has happened and that I die by my own hand," then with his dagger cut his belly from side to side, and with an hysteric laugh fell dead. The Traders buried him.[3]

¶ The Pee a gan young woman remained two days and as her fate appeared certain she was advised to go to some camp of the Blackfeet, but she refused, saying, he told me to go to his brothers, and to them I must go, and requesting a horse, which was given to her, with provisions, she went to the camp of the brothers of her deceased lover, and to them related the sad story; they pitied her, as they knew the Man to whom she was given would kill her, and told her so, and enquired what she intended to do, she said I know what I ought to have done, but my heart was weak, it is not so now; my life is gone; if I die by the hand of the man to whom I was given, I shall die a bad death, and in the other world wander friendless and no one to take care of me; your brother loved me, he is in the other world, and will be kind to me and love me, have pity on me and send me to him; an arrow thro' her heart laid her dead, for

1 Fort Augustus.
2 Fatigued.
3 Thompson had related the story of Poonokow's death in a notebook of 1822. AO. 52.79–78. In this account, Thompson states that Poonokow, having been wounded by a Cree guard, was found the next day by the NWC trader James Hughes and carried to the post. The actions of the Piegan woman are the same, but Poonokow's final words are slightly different: "tell my Father & Friends that the Nahathaways did not kill me, they shall not have that honor, I will deprive them of it."

her soul to rejoin her lover, and they buried her as the widow of their brother. Whatever may be the ideas of some civilized atheists, the immortality of the soul is the high consolation of all the rude tribes of North America.

¶ The character of all these people appear to be grave, steady and deliberate, but on becoming acquainted with them there is no want of individual character, and almost every character in civilized society can be traced among them, from the gravity of a judge to a merry jester and from open hearted generosity, to the avaricious miser. This last character is more detested by them, than by us, from [iv.294] their precarious manner of life, requiring assistance from each other, and their general character, especially in provisions is great attention to those that are unfortunate in the chace and the tent of a sick man is well supplied (Note. We had been hunting the Bison, and every horse was loaded with meat, even those we rode, on; returning we came to a few Aspins, where every one made a halt, and from the load of every horse a small bit was eat and thrown on a decayed root of a tree, to appease the Spirit of a Man who had died there of hunger many years past; and all the conversation until we came to the camp, turned upon such an uncommon death") They have a haughtiness of character, that let their wants be what they will they will not ask assistance from each other, it must be given voluntarily and disgrace they cannot bear, especially in publick.

¶ Upon some business I was at one of their camp with five men, in the afternoon as we were about going away, and talking with some twenty men, sitting on our horses, about furrs and provisions an Indian passed us on foot, apparently somewhat irritated at something that had happened in hunting, he had let his horse loose, and his little horse whip was at his wrist; his wife was outside the door of her tent as well as many other women listening to us, when he came to her he said something to her, and struck her gently with his whip; she entered the tent, and in an instant came out, and passed about three yards from him, then facing him, she said to him, you have before all these disgraced me, you shall never do it again; and drawing a sharp pointed Knife she plunged it into her heart, and fell dead. The whole camp seemed to regret her death, and blamed him [iv.295] for it; but not a word against her suicide, for a blow especially in public, is a high disgrace. She was carefully buried, and what belonged to her, broken or killed. Her husband was fond of her, he sat quietly in his tent all day, but at night went to some distance, and there call upon and lament her. Before her death he was an active and successful hunter but since then never went a hunting and lived upon any thing that was given to him. After he had passed more than two months this way, his friends became alarmed, and represented to him that he was acting more like a woman than a man, and that he must become again the Warrior and the Hunter, and brought to him two young women, the cousins of his former wife, to be his wives, but he never regained his former cheerfulness. The affections of an Indian are deep, for he has nothing to turn them to other things.

The Natives of all these countries are fond of their Children, they have faults like other children, but are not corrected by being beat. Contempt and ridicule are the correctives employed. These shame them, without breaking their spirit, and as they are all brought up in the open camp, the other children help the punishment. It sometimes happens that Husband's and Wives separate, if they have children the boys are taken by the father and the Mother brings up the girls, but even in this case the father always retains his rights to them until they are married. In every large camp the Chiefs appoint a number of young men to keep peace and order in the camp; in proportion to it's size, these are called Soldiers, they are all young men lately [iv.296] married, or are soon to be married, they have a Chief, and are armed with a small wooden club. They have great power and enforce obedience to the orders of the Chiefs.

[*Soldiers. their duty and acts. Their games. the Arrow & Ring. The Bowl. Gambling. hiding a tooth in one hand. the game & results*]

The Hunters having informed the old Men, that the Bisons were driven to too great a distance for hunting they called the Soldiers to see that no person went a hunting until the herds of Bisons came near of which they would inform them. The same evening a Chief walked through the camp informing them that as the Bisons were too far off for hunting they had given orders to the Soldiers to allow no person to hunt until farther notice. Such an order is sure to find some tents ill provided. While we were there, hunting was forbidden on this account. Two tents which had gambled away their things, even to their dried provisions, had to steal a march on the Soldiers under pretence of looking after their horses; but finding they did not return were watched. In the evening of the second day they approached the camp, with their horses loaded with meat which the Soldiers seized, and the owners quietly gave up; the former distributed the Meat to the tents that had many women and children, and left nothing to the owners, but those that had received the Meat, in the night sent them a portion of it. Not a murmer was heard, every one said they had acted right.

But the great business of the Soldiers is, with the Gamblers, for like all people who have too much time on their hands, they are almost to a man, more or less given to gambling day and night. All these the Soldiers watch with attention, and as soon as they perceive any dispute [iv.297] arise, toss the gambling materials to the right and left, and kick the stakes in the same manner; to which the parties say nothing, but collect every thing and begin again. In the day time the game generally played is with a round ring of about three inches diameter, bound round with cloth or leather, and the game is played by two men, each having an arrow in his right hand: one of them rolls the ring over a smooth piece of prepared ground and when it has rolled a few yards, each following it, gently throw their arrows through it to rest about halfway on the ring, which now lies on the ground and according to the positions of the arrows, one has gained and the other lost; each of these acts for a party who have an interest in the game; and it some times requires two or three hours to decide the game. They have also sometimes horse racing but not in a regular manner, but bets between individuals upon hunting in running down animal[s], as the Red and Jumping Deer,[1] or the killing of so many Cow Bisons at a single race.

¶ Another game is small pieces of wood of different shapes, which are placed in a bowl, and then [thrown] up a little way, and caught in the bowl, and according as they lay the game is won or lost; if the holder of the bowl has gained, he continues until he has completed twenty, or ten, as the number may be agreed on. He then hands the Bowl to his opponent to try his luck, or if during any part he has lost, the Bowl is handed to the other, until the first has gained the number agreed on, who is declared the final winner. All games are played by [iv.298] either individuals for themselves, or as acting for parties and I do not know any games where parties act against parties, it would prove too dangerous altho' this is the case with the Indians of the low countries.

¶ The Game to which all the Indians of the Plains are most addicted, and which they most enjoy is by hiding in one of the hands, some small flat thing generally the flat tooth of a Red Deer, and the other party to tell in which hand it is. It is played by two persons but generally by parties. It takes place in the early part of the night and continues a few hours. It is played in a large tent; the opposite parties sitting on different sides of the tent in the hind part of the tent the Umpire sits with the stakes on each side. Both parties throwing their robes and upper dress off, and sit bare above the belt, and each having chosen it's lucky man; the Umpire shows the Red Deers tooth, which is marked to prevent being changed, he hides it in one of his hands, and the party that guesses the hand in which it is begins the game; it's lucky man showing he has the tooth, begins a song in which his companions join him,

---

1 Mule deer (*Odocoileus hemionus*).

he in the mean time throwing his arms and hands into every position; the other party are quietly watching all his motions, in a few minutes he extends his arms straight forward with both hands closed, and about six inches apart, and thus hold them until the opposite party guess in which hand the tooth is; this is not always immediately done, but frequently after a short consultation; if they guess wrong, the other [iv.299] winning party continue with the same gest[ic]ulations and song as before; until a good guess is made and the tooth handed to the lucky man of the other party, and thus the game is continued until one of them counts ten, which is game. When the guess is made in which hand is the tooth, both hands are thrown open. The Umpire now takes the stakes of the losing party and places them, on the side of the winning party, but keeps them separate. The losing party now hand to the Umpire another stake to regain the one they have lost. Thus the game continues with varied success until they are tired, or one party cannot produce another stake; in this case the losing party either give up the stakes they have lost to the winners, or direct the umpire to keep for the renewal of the game the next night. However simple this game appears, it causes much excitement and deep attention in the players. The singing, the gest[ic]ulations, and the dark flashing eyes as if they would pierce through the body of him that has the tooth, their long hair, and muscular naked bodies, their excited, yet controlled countenances, seen by no other light than a small fire, would form a fine scene for an Artist.

The stakes are Bison Robes, clothing, their tents, horses and Arms, until they have nothing; to cover them but some old robe fit for saddle cloths, yet they have some things which are never gambled, as all that belongs to their wives and children, and in this the tent is frequently included; and always the Kettle, as it cooks the meat of the children and the Axe as it cuts wood to warm them, the Dogs [iv.300] and horses of the women are also exempt.

[*Comparison of languages. Religion. Religion and belief in futurity. Religion and morals on property. Equality, except by influence. Chief's Coat*]

¶ The Languages of this continent on the east and north side of the Mountains as compared with those of Europe may be classed as resembling in utterance,[1] The Sieux and Stone Indian to the Italian, The Nahathaway and Chip a way with their dialects to the French. The Pee a gan with their allies, the Blood and Blackfeet Indians to the English, and the northern people, the Din nae, or Che pawyans to be the German. Of the several Tribes that hunt

1 I.e., in their sound.

on the great Plains none of them have what we call a creed, yet there is a general belief in some things, and to directly question them on their religion is of no use, as those who have lived long with them know very well. Persons who pass through the country often think the answers the Indians give is their real sentiments. The answers are given to please the querist.

The sacred Scriptures to the Christian; the Koran to the Mahometan give a steady belief to the mind, which is not the case with the Indian, his ideas on what passes in this world is tolerably correct so far as his senses and reason can inform him; but after death all is wandering conjecture taken up on tradition, dreams and hopes. The young people seldom trouble themselves beyond the present time, but after thirty, their precarious life of hunting and war, the loss of parents, relations and friends with much spare time, brings on reflection, and turns their thoughts to futurity. They all appear to acknowledge that there is one great power, always invisible, that is the master of life and to whom every thing belongs, that he is kind and beneficent; and pleased to see mankind [iv.301] happy, but how far he is pleased to interfere with the concerns of Mankind, they are not agreed, some think, that his providence is continually exerted, that they can have nothing but what he allows to them, founding their arguments on his power and being the master of every thing; but the greater part believe every man to be the master of his own fortune and that this depends on his own conduct, yet they all allow the Great Spirit to be the master of the seasons, and of the animals with every thing else, that is not under their control, but on all these things their ideas are very vague, and sometimes from their conversation they believe in fatality, which is no part of their, belief as grounded on the ever varying visissitude of their lives. Living in the open wide plains, where every thing is visible and can be brought within the range of their reason, they are free from the superstitions of the natives of the forests,[2] and seldom address the Great Spirit but on public occasions as on going to War; and for the herds of Bisons to continue to feed in their country or any epidemic sickness.

They believe there are inferior Beings to the Great Spirits, under whose orders they act, that have the care of the animals, of the Plains and the Forests, but do not allow them the power, or reverence, which the Natives of the Forests bestow on their Manitoes. All the Natives of north America from Ocean to Ocean, however unknown to each other, and dissimilar in language, all believe in the immortality of the soul, and act on this belief. Although this heavenly belief has not the [iv.302] high sanction of the holy Redeemer of mankind who alone has brought life and immortality to light,

2 I.e., the Cree and Ojibwa.

yet vague and obscure as it is, it is the mercy of the Almighty to them. They have no ideas of a judgement in the other world, with rewards and punishments but think the other world is like this we inhabit only far superiour to it in the fineness of the seasons, and the plenty of all kinds of Provisions, which are readily got, by hunting on fleet horses to catch the Bisons and Deer and which are always fat. The state of society there is vague yet somehow the good will be separated from th[e] bad and be no more troubled by them, that the good will arrive at a happy country of constantly seeing the Sun, and the bad wander into darkness from whence they cannot return, and the darkness will be in proportion to the crimes they have committed.

¶ Their morals appears to proceed from an inherent sense[3] of the rights of individuals to their rights of property, whether given to them, or acquired by industry, or in hunting, all these belong to the person who is in possession of them; and which gives him a right to defend any attempt to take them from him. No man is allowed connexion with his female relations nearer to him than his second cousins, and by many these are held too near. Two sisters frequently become the wives of the same husband, and is supposed to give harmony to their families

Among people who have no laws, injuries will arise, without any authority to redress them, this is felt and acknowledged, and most would willingly see a power that could proportion the punishment to the offence, but to whom shall the [iv.303] power be given, and who would dare to take it, even when offered to him. Not one. The Chiefs that are acknowledged as such, have no power beyond their influence, which would immediately cease by any act of authority and they are all careful not to arrogate any superiority over others.

When out on the Plains one of these Chiefs had rendered me several services, for which I had then nothing to pay him on my return to the house; by the interpreter, I sent him a fine scarlet coat trimmed with orris lace,[4] and a message that as I understood he was going to war, I had sent him this coat as a recompense for his services with some tobacco, but the interpreter, not thinking this homely message sufficiently pompous, on the delivery of the coat, told him I had sent it to him as being a great Chief and to be his dress on going to war as a Chief. He was surprised at such a message; and the next day, by a young man, sent it with the message to the Chief at the next camp, who not liking the tenor of the message, sent both to another camp, and thus it passed to the sixth hand, who being something of a humourist, sent it to a very old chief, who was not expected to live, he kept it, telling the

3 Thompson had first written "conscientiousness," then substituted "inherent sense."
4 Lace of various patterns in gold and silver.

messenger to thank the Trader for sending him such a fine coat to be buried in. Some time after the Chief to whom I had sent the coat came in to trade and enquired if the message sent with the coat came from me; I told him the message I had sent and that the coat was a recompense for his services. He was very angry with the interpreter, and told me not to employ him among his people as he was looked on as a pompous fool, and that his lies would cause his death, (which happened two years after;) he then related how the coat and message had been sent forward, 'till [iv.304] it came to the old dying chief; and that the message as delivered by the interpreter had caused much conversation "as I am, as yet, but a young chief. Had the coat with such a message have been sent to the War or civil chief, they would have taken the coat, and laughed at the message, but for this I am not old enough." The consequence was, that I had to pay him the value of the coat in other goods. Even the War and Civil chiefs have no authority beyond the influence of what their good conduct gives to them.

[*Raised bad tobacco. Tobacco grounds rob[b]ed. Stone pipes-red. Pipe Stems. Dreams*]

The natives of the forest pride themselves on their Medicine bags, which are generally well stocked with a variety of simples which they gather from the woods and banks of the Lakes and Rivers, and with the virtues of which they are somewhat acquainted. The Indians of the Plains, have none of these, and collect only sweet scented grasses, and the gums that exude from the shrubs that bear berries and a part of these is for giving to their horses to make them long winded in the chase. But these people must also have something to which they can attach somewhat of a super natural character for religious purposes, and for this purpose they have adopted the Red Pipe, and Pipe Stem, and which seems to have been such from old times; for until the year 1800 they had always raised tobacco[1] in proportion to their wants. When they became acquainted with the tobacco of the U[nited] States brought by the traders, which they found to be so superior to their own, that they gradually left off cultivating it, and after the above year, raised no more; The tobacco they raised had a very hot taste in smoking, and required a great

1 Likely a cultivar of *Nicotiana quadrivalvis* (Indian tobacco). Native to California, this plant had spread north and east along aboriginal trade routes. Thompson's text is evidence of the waning of tribal cultivation of this plant about the turn of the nineteenth century and of its replacement by trade tobacco. Jack Nisbet, "Smoke," in *Visible Bones: Journeys across Time in the Columbia River Country* (Seattle: Sasquatch, 2003). For more on tobacco, see iii.156 (Volume II).

proportion of bears berry weed to be mixed with it. The white people gave it the name of the devil's tobacco. As very few of them can find furrs to trade the quantity of tobacco they require; I enquired of them, why they did not[2]

[iv.306] also for a medicine pipe there are certain ceremonies to be gone through, and a woman is not allowed to touch a medicine pipe; and their long pipe stems are equally sacred. These are of three to more than four feet in length, and about three to five inches in girth, and well polished. Each respectable man has from, three to four of these pipes stems, which are tied together when not in use and hung on a tree; on removing from place to place the owner slings them over his back and at the campment again hangs them up.

That equality among the Natives however strictly held, does not prevent a great part from wishing to distinguish themselves, in some manner and as there cannot be many remarkable Warriors and Hunters, a few mix with other tribes and learn their languages, and become acquainted with their countries and mode of hunting. Others turn Dreamers and tell what other tribes are doing and intend to do; where the Bisons and Deer are most plenty, and how the weather will be; and the boldest Dreamers point out the place of the camp of their enemies, and what they intend to do. Some shrewd men by their dreams are very useful for making bargains, exchanging and buying horses, making marriages, and giving advice, which in any other manner would not be taken, and dreams also indulges that innate love of mankind for prying into, and predicting futurity. If what they have foretold come to pass they are accounted wise men, and if it fails, it was only a dream. Time often hangs heavy on them, and for this gambling is their greatest relief.

[*Numbers*]

¶ The civilized man from very early youth, is accustomed to hear numbers spoken of from One to One Million; thus fifty, five hundred, or five thousand, &c, are to him as units, his mind gives no [iv.307] individuality to each unit that compose the number be it of what it will, but the Indian forms his numbers from individuals, and appears to have no idea of numbers independent of them. Perhaps formerly the uneducated Shepherds, and Herdsman obtained their ideas of numbers in the same manner, and [I] have frequently been told of Shepherds who could not by numbers count the Sheep in his flock, but by his own way could quickly tell if there was one missing.

2 Page iv.305 is missing.

The Nahathaway Indians count numbers the same manner as we do to the number of 100, which they call the great ten; and a thousand, the great, great ten; beyond which they do not pretend to number, and even of this they make no use, and any things, as of birds and animals that would amount to this number, they would express it by a great many. But the Indians of the plains count only by tens, and what is above two tens, they lay small sticks on the ground to show the number of tens they have to count and in describing the great herds of Bisons or Deer, they express them by a great, great many, and the space they stand on; for numbers is to them an abstract idea, but space of ground to a certain extent they readily comprehend and the animals it may contain; for they do not appear to extend their faculties beyond what is visible, and tangible.

[*Horse stealing from enemies. Stone Indian horse stealing. their tricks. Wasps*]

¶ The Pee a gan Indians and their tribes of Blood and Blackfeet, being next to the Mountains often send out parties under a young Chief to steal Horses from their enemies to the south and west side of their Mountains, known as the Snake the Saleesh and the Kootanae Indians. This is allowed to be an honorable [pursuit], especially as it is attended with danger and requires great caution and activity. But the country of the Stone Indians and Sussees, are full from four to six hundred miles in the plains, eastward of the Mountains, and too [iv.308] far to look for horses, the Sussees content themselves with rearing horses; but the Stone Indians are always in want of horses which appears to be occasioned by hard usage. They are most noted horse stealers and wherever they appear in small parties the horses are immediately guarded.[1] They steal horses from other tribes, but frequently at great risque. Those who are near to the trading settlements too often steal the horses of other tribes when they come to trade; and also those of the Traders, in doing of which they are very expert. When the Traders leave their stations to proceed with their furrs to the different depots to exchange for goods: the horses of the trading House, are sent some few miles under the care of two or three Men well armed, to where there are plenty of good grass, water, and a wood

1 Much of this material on Assiniboine horse theft had been published in the Montreal *Gazette* in two articles of 1848 (see Volume III). In the first, published on 16 February, Thompson tells the story of the Assiniboine who disguised themselves as antelope. In the second, published on 15 August, he recounts the narrative of those who carried off horses by the innovative use of a wasp's nest.

of Poplar and Aspin, the latter to make a smoky fire to relieve the horses from the torment of the Musketoes and horse flies. One summer (I think 1802) a large camp of Stone Indians, had sent some young men to a Blackfoot Camp, who brought away about thirty horses, they were quietly followed to the Stone Indian camp, and about three nights afterwards. The Blackfeet young men took not only the greatest part of the horses stolen from them, but collected as many more and drove them all off to their own camp.

This distressed the Stone Indian camp and as they knew the other camps were guarding their horses, they determined to steal horses from the trading Houses. Accordingly six smart young men were selected and sent to the Upper House on the Saskatchewan River[2] a distance of five or six day's journey.

When within a few miles of the house they came to about fifty horses guarded by three men whose station was on a low bank that overlooked the place where the horses were feeding, all the mares had, as usual, the fore feet tied together with a leather thong to prevent them strolling about and more readily kept together. The Men kept strict watch, only one [iv.309] man slept at a time and in the night two of them walked among the horses well armed. Thus for six days they watched for an opportunity; during which time, with their Arrows they had killed three buck Antelopes. They were now tired of waiting and determined to try their fortune; In the afternoon when they perceived the Men had dined three of them with the skins of the Antelopes and their horns, disguised themselves to appear like deer, the other three also put horns on their heads, of which there were plenty on the plains; the latter went behind the horses and there entered among them and untied the feet of the horses, those with the Antelope skins pretended to feed as deer and got among the horses for the same purpose, the Men were deceived but remarked it was the first time they had seen the Antelopes feeding among horses. As soon as the horses were all untied the Indians gave a signal to each other, with the lines bridled the best horses and jumping on them as they were, horns and all, gave the hunting halloa, and drove the whole of the horses off at a round gallop. The Men were so surprised that they could scarcely believe what they saw, and before they could recover themselves to use their guns, the whole of the horses were far out of shot.

The Stone Indians brought them all to the camp, and were received with the praises of the men, and the dances of the women. Some time after at another trading House, in the month of July, two of [us] went off to hunt and early walked off to the Horse tent, on account of the flies all the horses were crowded round the smoke of the fires; we saddled two of the best, and rode

2 Rocky Mountain House.

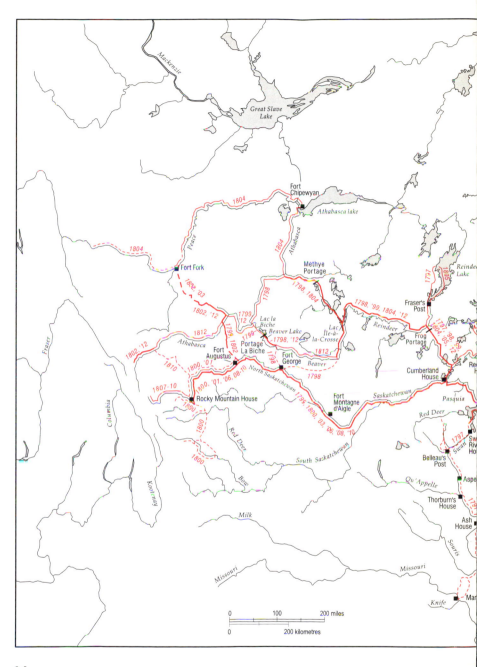

Map 4

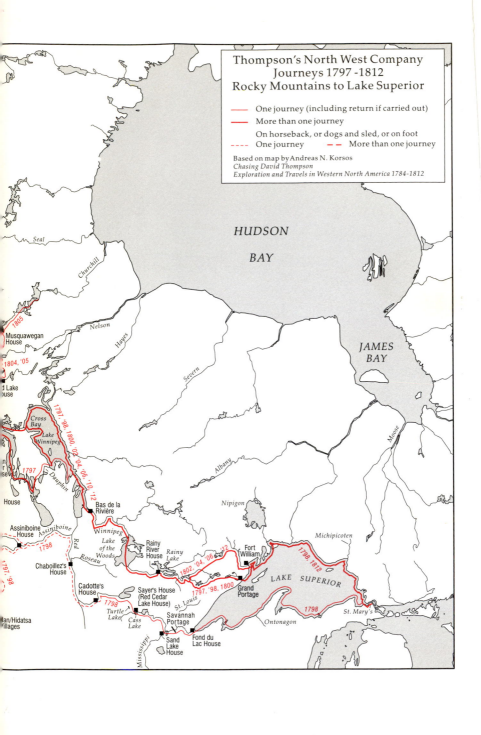

**Thompson's North West Company
Journeys 1797-1812
Rocky Mountains to Lake Superior**

—— One journey (including return if carried out)

━━ More than one journey

On horseback, or dogs and sled, or on foot

- - - One journey   – – More than one journey

Based on map by Andreas N. Korsos
*Chasing David Thompson
Exploration and Travels in Western North America 1784-1812*

Seal

Churchill

HUDSON

BAY

JAMES
BAY

1805

Musquawegan
House

Nelson

1804, '05

d Lake
ouse

Hayes

Severn

Moose

*Cross
Bay*

1797, '98, 1800, '02, '04, '06, '10, '12

Lake
Winnipeg

Albany

1797

se

Dauphin

Nipigon

House

Bas de la
Rivière

Michipicoten

Assiniboine
House

Assiniboine

1798

Winnipeg

Rainy
River
House

*Rainy
Lake*

1802, '04, '06, '12

Fort
William

1798, 1812

Red

Roseau

*Lake
of the
Woods*

1797, '98

Chaboillez's
House

Cadotte's
House

Sayer's House
(Red Cedar
Lake House)

St. Louis

1797, '98, 1800

Grand
Portage

LAKE SUPERIOR

1798

St. Mary's

1798

Turtle
Lake

*Cass
Lake*

Savannah
Portage

an/Hidatsa
illages

Mississippi

Sand
Lake
House

Fond du
Lac House

Ontonagon

off a few miles but the flies were so numerous the horses were frequently for throwing themselves on the ground to get rid of them, and seeing nothing we returned to the Horse tent, where we found the three men in a violent passion and swearing with all their might. On looking at them, one of them[3]

[iv.311] pass part of the summer at one of the trading houses. In the latter end of August he took his outfit for the winter's hunt, and with his two horses carrying his traps and baggage set off for his winter quarters. A few days after we were surprised to see him return: he informed us that as he proceeded on his journey the Horses with their loads struck a wasp's nest and were severely stung by the wasps, that in running away and rolling themselves on the ground, they had lost one of his steel traps and broke another, and spoilt some of his gunpowder, which he wanted to be replaced and informed us this was not the first time he had suffered from them. The old man sat very serious smoking his pipe, and shaking his head, said "I can never get my Horses accustomed to the Wasps." When removing their Tents, the Men going before destroy the wasps and nest before the Women and children come on.

I have already remarked the tribe of the Pee a gans have their country along the east foot of the Mountains from the Saskatchewan southward to the Missisourie, and are the frontier people and their enemies on the west side of the Mountains must break through them to make war on their allies, who thus live in security in their rear. This station has given to this Tribe something of a chivalrous character and their war parties carry on their predatory excur-

---

3 Page iv.310 is missing. The anecdote begun on iv.309 appears in Thompson's Montreal *Gazette* article of 15 August 1848. In that version the story concludes as follows:

> we had to return to the tent, where we found the men swearing with all their might: two of them had each an eye closed up, and the third had both his closed. They told us that three Stone Indians suddenly made their appearance; one of them came close to the smoke and dashed a wasp's nest on the head of one of the horses at the fire, close to which they were standing. The wasps, in revenge for their nest being broken, fell on them and the horses, and stung them without mercy. The horses all scampered away, snorting and kicking as if possessed; and before they could get rid of the wasps, seize their guns, and go after the horses, some time was lost. At length, when they had collected the horses and brought them to the smoke, they found these Indians had gone off with five of the best horses: pursuit could not be followed, for no one knew which way they had gone. The horses thus stolen are accounted the property of the person who stole them, yet many regard them as common property; and the horses are ridden until they are in a manner ruined.
>
> Voyageur, "I have already informed you ..." Montreal *Gazette*, 15 August 1848

sions to a distance scarcely credible in search of their enemies, the Snake Indians.[4]

¶ In the year 1807, in the early part of September a party of about two hundred and fifty Warriors under the command of Koo ta nae Appe went off to war on the Snake Indians; they proceeded southward near the east foot of the Mountains, and found no natives, they continued further than usual, very unwilling to return without having done something, at length the scouts came in with word that they had seen a long file of Horses and Mules led by Black Men (Spaniards) and not far off. They wer[e] soon ready [iv.312] and formed into one line about three feet from each other, for room to handle their Bows and Shiel[d]s, having but a few guns; the ground was a rough undulating plain, and by favor of the ground they approached to near the front of the file before they were discovered, when giving the war whoop, and making a rush on the front of the file, the Spaniards all rode off, leaving the loaded Horses and mules to the war party, each of whom endeavoured to make prize of a Horse or Mules. They were loaded with bags containing a great weight of white stone (Silver) which they quickly threw off the animals on the ground; in doing which the saddle girths were cut except a few, and then rode off.

¶ I never could learn the number of the animals, those that came to the camp at which I resided were about thirty hor[s]es and a doze<n> mules with a few saddles, and bridles. The Horses w<ere> about fourteen hands high finely shaped, and though very tired yet lively, mostly of a dark brown color, head neat and small, ears short and erect, eyes fine and clear fine manes and tails with black hoofs. The sadd<les> were larger than our english saddles, the side leath<er> twice as large, of thick well tanned leather of a choc<o>late color with the figures of flowers as if done by a hot iron, the bridles had snaffle bits,[5] heavy and coarse as if made by a blacksmith with only his hammer the weight and coarseness of these bits had made the Indians throw most of them away. The place this war party started from is in about 53°·20' N and the place where they met the Spaniards conveying the silver from the mines is about the latitude of 32 degres north, a distance of 1500 miles in a direct line, and without seeing[6]

∽

4 For these Piegan raids, see note on 27u (66).
5 A simple form of bridle bit, without a curb.
6 Page iv.313, which Thompson records in his daily journal as having written on 29 June 1849, is missing. Thus the 1850 version of the *Travels* concludes, as befits its unfinished nature, in mid-sentence.

APPENDIX I: DISCARDED PAGE 22

This page is heavily worn, and torn in several places, which may account for its replacement by iv.22 (41–2). The content is close to that of the new page but is worthy of special note because Thompson includes Cree names for seven mammals absent in the later version. A list of fish, birds, berries, and mammals written on the verso of this page was used in composition of pages iv.30–5.

{par}t of the day of Kabow, Kabow, Kow á é. The Hens hav{e the sa}me call, but in a low note. {In bad weather the willow grouse shelters itself under the snow, b}ut{the rock gr}ouse{run about}as{if enjoyin}g the{snow} During winter and spring, wh{at} ever may be the number of the flock, each bird singly burrows in the snow, the feathers are of a brilliant white, if possible whiter than the snow. In the months of march, and April, part of the feathers particularly about the neck and fore part of the body, change color to a glossy brown, or deep chocolate, upon a ground of brilliant white, most beautiful; and a{re} often stuffed and sent to London: no dove is more m{eek} than the white grouse. I have often taken them fro{m} under the net, and provoked them all I could, wi{thout} hurting them, but all was submissive meekness. Ro{ugh} beings as we were, sometimes of an evening, we could no{t} help enquiring, why such an angelic bird should be doomed to be the suffering prey of every carnivorous animal; the ways of Providence are unknown to us. Their nests are under the low spreading branches of a pine tree, on the ground, they lay from 11 to 13 Eggs. Their young from the shell are active. There is a third species of Grouse, called the Pine, or Swamp grouse, of dark brown feathers. It feeds upon the leaves of the pine tree, and it's flesh tastes of the pine on which it feeds. It is not numerous; it is found sitting on the branches of the pine tree, ten, or twelve feet above the snow, or ground. It is a stupid bird: a snar{e} is tied at the end of a stick, put on it's neck and pulled to the ground, it is only eaten for want of better. A few Pheasants are shot, they are something larger than the willow grouse, of a fine dark plumage, but not to be compared to the English Pheasant. The carnivorous animals are the Ermine (Seekoose) the Marten (Wop pe stan) the Mink, lives on Fish, Mice and Birds. The Fisher, as strong as the Fox tho' not so tall, he lives on all he can master. The Mink the Fox in it's varieties of color (Mak e shoo); the Wolf

(Miha gan) the black Bear (Mus quah) the Fisher the Wolverine Ome thar chis or Que-que hauk is.

The trapping of Martens is of some importance, as their skins are valuable, two male, or three female skins, bring of the value of a Beaver Skin in trade: they are caught in traps made of light logs of wood, with a bait of the head and neck of the white grouse, with the feathers on: ranges of traps for the Marten sometimes extends to forty miles, at about five, or eight traps per mile; at the end of each twenty traps, a strong trap of falling logs is made to take the Wolverene, which is baited with an entire willow grouse; the number of Martens caught per day throughout the winter, may be, from four to six as the forest is more, or less, favourable: their general prey is small birds and mice {a}nd sometimes {...sq}uirrel these require dry ground. They cannot be tamed, so as to be trusted and are a most determined little animal. I have seen them run up along the pole on which a Hare was suspended by a snare which near the top,

APPENDIX 2: BRIEF BIOGRAPHIES

JEAN-BAPTISTE CADOTTE *fils* (1761–1818) was the eldest son of the French Canadian fur trader Jean-Baptiste Cadotte *père* and the Ojibwa woman Equawaice. He studied at the Collège Saint-Raphaël in Montreal from 1773 to 1780, and in 1796 he and his brother Michel (*c.v.*) took over their father's business. Thompson was at Cadotte's post on the Red Lake River from 25 to 27 March and 31 March to 9 April 1798 (iv.189–203, 228–40). Jean-Baptiste became an NWC partner in 1801 but was expelled two years later for alcoholism. His two shares were awarded to Thompson. In later life Cadotte worked as an interpreter in Upper Canada. David A. Armour, "Jean-Baptiste Cadot" *père*, DCB, 5:128–30; Wallace, *Documents*, 428.

MICHEL CADOTTE *le grand* (1764–1837), the second son of Jean-Baptiste Cadotte *père* and Equawaice, entered the fur trade in 1782 and spent his long career on the south shore of Lake Superior, usually based at La Pointe. When Thompson encountered him in May 1798, Cadotte was trading at the mouth of the Ontonagan River (iv.233–7, 262–5), and in 1803 he signed an agreement with the NWC to trade at Chequamagon. Nelson, *My First Years*, 205; Wallace, *Documents* 1934, 429.

CHARLES CHABOILLEZ (1772–1812) joined the NWC as a clerk in 1791, becoming a partner in 1796. Chaboillez was active in the regions of the Red and Assiniboine Rivers and hosted Thompson at his Pembina trading post 14–21 March 1798 (iv.184–9, 225–8); Chaboillez's journal for this time has been published in *Ethnohistory* 6 (1959): 265–316, 363–427. Between 1804 and 1807, Chaboillez promoted the expansion of NWC trade into the Upper Missouri. He retired from the fur trade in 1809 and settled, as would Thompson, at Terrebonne. Gratien Allaire, "Charles Chaboillez," DCB, 5:178–9; Wallace, *Documents*, 432.

GEORGE CHARLES (c. 1771–1807) was, like Thompson, a graduate of Westminster's Grey Coat School. He was bound apprentice to the HBC in 1785, and Thompson describes his arrival at Churchill on iii.9b (28) and iv.117 (172–3). After serving for several years as a writer, Charles became an inland trader in 1796, and in this capacity opposed Thompson at Musquawegan Lake in 1804–05. Charles succumbed to fever in 1807 while at Nelson

House. Anne Morton, "George Charles," HBCA, http://www.gov.mb.ca/chc/archives/hbca/biographical/c/charles_george.pdf.

JOSEPH COLEN (c. 1751–1818) joined the HBC as a writer in 1785 and the next year was made resident chief at York Factory. Colen promoted the exploration of new routes to the Athabasca region, quarrelling constantly with inland master William Tomison, who disdained this project. Thompson writes that in 1796 he asked permission from Colen to explore a route to Athabasca (iv.85, 137) and that Colen sent him a letter the next year stating that he could sanction no more surveys (iv.114, 169). Neither claim has been substantiated. Colen was recalled to London in 1798 and his contract terminated. Shirlee Anne Smith, "Joseph Colen," DCB, 5:194–5.

PETER FIDLER (1769–1822) joined the HBC as a labourer in 1788 and was quickly promoted to writer. Fidler had kept the South Branch House post journal for Mitchell Oman in 1789–90, and after Thompson lost his sight that winter, Fidler was summoned to Cumberland to learn astronomy under Philip Turnor, whom he accompanied in his explorations of the Athabasca region over the next two years (27zd, 74). Fidler's distinguished HBC career included exploration, surveying, mapmaking, and often difficult trading assignments, in which he was vigorously opposed by the NWC. On 12 August 1805 Thompson and Fidler passed each other on the Churchill River and, in Fidler's words, "did not speak together." While J.B. Tyrrell and A.S. Morton read this as a sign of enmity and estrangement, there is no positive evidence that such feelings existed between the two; indeed, in a 1793 letter, Thompson asked Joseph Colen to convey his regards to Fidler. J.G. MacGregor, *Peter Fidler: Canada's Forgotten Surveyor, 1769–1822* (Toronto: McClelland & Stewart, 1966); Morton, *History of the Canadian West*, 444, 447; J.B. Tyrrell, "Peter Fidler, Trader and Surveyor, 1769 to 1822," *Royal Society of Canada Transactions*, 3rd series, 7 (1913): ii:117–27.

SIR JOHN FRANKLIN (1786–1847), a Royal Navy officer, led overland expeditions to the Arctic coast in 1819–22 and 1825–27. The first expedition achieved little before culminating in a desperate southward trek, while the second charted a substantial portion of the coastline. Franklin and his fellow expedition members produced narratives of both of these voyages. After colonial service in Van Diemen's Land (Tasmania), Franklin was selected to lead a third Arctic expedition, which would attempt to find a Northwest Passage by sea. The ships *Terror* and *Erebus* departed from England in 1845 but disappeared soon after entering Arctic waters. At the time Thompson was writing, Franklin's fate was still unknown, and in May 1848 he wrote to the Montreal *Gazette* on the explorer's likely whereabouts (see Volume III). In 1854 Inuit informed John Rae that Franklin's expedition had ended in disaster, the ships locked fast in ice off King William's Island. Franklin is one of the *Travels'* touchstones, and Thompson appeals to him for information about the igloo (iii.6–6a, 17–18), the aurora borealis (iv.104a–f, 153–8), and fossils (iv.133, 187). Clive Holland, "Sir John Franklin," *DCB*, 7:323–8.

ALEXANDER FRASER (1763–1837) entered the NWC as a clerk before 1789, by 1799 was the proprietor of the English (Churchill) River district, and was a signatory of the NWC agreement of 1804. In 1802 Fraser had purchased the seigneury of Rivière-du-Loup, where he settled upon his retirement in 1806. When Thompson left the HBC for the NWC in 1797, he travelled first to Fraser's post at the south end of Reindeer Lake (iv.114, 169), and in 1810 he addressed a letter to Fraser, anticipating his retirement from the fur trade (see Volume III). Coues, ed., *Early History of the Great Northwest*, 2:897; Wallace, *Documents*, 443–4; "Alexander Fraser," in *Dictionary of Canadian Biography*, 2nd edn., ed. Wallace (Toronto: Macmillan, 1945), 1:214.

CUTHBERT GRANT (d. 1799) served the NWC in the Athabasca district during the late 1780s. In 1793 he established Fort La Souris at the junction of the Souris and Assiniboine Rivers, assuming responsibility for NWC activities in the Upper Assiniboine region. Grant became an NWC partner in 1795, by which time he was resident at Aspen House on the Assiniboine. Here he hosted Thompson from 25 September to 14 October and 2 to 9 November 1797 (iv.134–5, 188–9). Hartwell Bowsfield, "Cuthbert Grant," *DCB*, 4:310; Wallace, *Documents*, 449.

SAMUEL HEARNE (1745–92) joined the HBC in 1766. His accomplishments included an arduous journey of exploration to the mouth of the Coppermine River in 1770–72 and the founding of Cumberland House in 1774, which initiated the HBC's trading presence on the Saskatchewan. Hearne was chief factor at Prince of Wales's Fort from 1776 until its surrender to a French naval force in 1782. He returned to the bay in 1783 to establish Churchill Factory, which he administered until his retirement in 1787. He is the author of *A Journey from Prince of Wales's Fort in Hudson's Bay to the Northern Ocean* (London: A. Strahan and T. Cadell, 1795). Thompson spent his first year as an HBC apprentice at Churchill under Hearne, for whom he had little regard (see iv.8–9, 10–12 and notes). Kenneth McGoogan, *Ancient Mariner: The Amazing Adventures of Samuel Hearne, the Sailor Who Walked to the Arctic Ocean* (Toronto: HarperCollins, 2004).

ROBERT HOOD (c. 1797–1821) joined the Royal Navy in 1809 and in 1819 was appointed midshipman on Sir John Franklin's first expedition. During early 1820 he studied the aurora borealis at Cumberland House, and the results of these observations were published as appendices to the narrative of the journey. Having participated in the charting of the Arctic coastline in 1821, Hood was murdered on 20 October 1821, during the expedition's desperate return to Fort Enterprise. Thompson refers to Hood's observations on the aurora in his own writings on the subject (iv.104a, 154). Jim Burant, "Robert Hood," *DCB*, 6:327–9.

WILLIAM JEFFERSON (c. 1740 – after 1796) of the city of York entered HBC service in 1770 as a writer. He worked in this capacity at Prince of Wales's Fort until 1776, when he became Hearne's deputy. Like Hearne, Jefferson was taken prisoner by La Pérouse in 1782, returning to Hudson Bay the following year to help establish Churchill Factory. Upon Hearne's retirement in 1787, Jefferson was named chief factor of the post. He retired from HBC employ in 1792, leaving behind at least two children at Churchill.

RENÉ JUSSEAUME (fl. 1790–1806) became a free trader in the region of the Mandan-Hidatsa villages around 1790 and in 1794 built a trading post near the villages. Jusseaume participated in Thompson's 1797–98 journey as interpreter (iv.148–79, 198–221). He was at the Mandan-Hidatsa villages when Lewis and Clark arrived in 1804 and two years later accompanied the explorers to Washington as interpreter for the Mandan chief Shahaka (*c.v.*). Coues, ed., *Early History of the Great Northwest*, 1:401; Wood and Thiessen, *Early Fur Trade*, 45–6.

KOOTANAE APPEE (c. 1750 – after 1807) served as Piegan war chief. Much of what is known about him is derived from the *Travels*, in which he is mentioned several times. Thompson first met Kootanae Appee when wintering with the Piegan in 1787–88. According to Thompson, Kootanae Appee was a respected and successful military strategist, and he led the Piegan in campaigns against the Shoshone and Kootenai, and in raids on Spanish convoys. Thompson encountered Kootanae Appee again in the fall of 1807, when he forestalled an attack by a Piegan war party under the chief's direction. It is unclear when Kootanae Appee died, since his name was later borne by a succession of Piegan figures.

HUGH McCRACHAN (fl. 1797–1808) was active as a trader on the northern Plains, working both independently and on behalf of the NWC and HBC. He participated in Thompson's 1797–98 journey to the Mandan-Hidatsa villages (iv.148–79, 198–221) and is described in the *Travels* as a "good hearted Irishman." Although Thompson reports that McCrachan was murdered in 1799 (iv.180, 221), his presence on trading missions to the Mandan-Hidatsa villages is attested as late as 1808. Wood and Thiessen, *Early Fur Trade*, 317.

JOHN MACDONNELL (1768–1850) joined the NWC in 1793. He became a partner in 1797, at which time he ran a post on the Assiniboine River, where he hosted Thompson 23–28 November 1797 (iv.147–8, 197–8) and 3–26 February 1798 (iv.179–81, 221–2). For his part, Thompson called Macdonnell "my hospitable friend." Macdonnell spent much of his fur trade career in the Qu'Appelle region, and upon his retirement in 1815 settled on the Ottawa River. His reputation for piety earned him the nickname *le prêtre*. Wallace, *Documents*, 465–6; Wood and Thiessen, *Early Fur Trade*, 77–9.

HUGH McGILLIS (c. 1767–1848) joined the NWC as a clerk in 1790. In late October 1797, Thompson visited McGillis's post on the Red Deer River (iv.135, 189). Four years later McGillis became an NWC partner and he spent most of his career in the region of Lake Superior. After being tried and acquitted in 1816 in connection with the events at Seven Oaks, McGillis retired from the fur trade. He settled in Williamstown, where he and Thompson were neighbours for about twenty years. In 1836 McGillis managed the sale of Thompson's Glengarry properties. Wallace, *Documents*, 468–9.

WILLIAM McGILLIVRAY (1764–1825) joined the NWC as a clerk in 1784 and in 1790 became a partner in the firm by buying Peter Pond's share. McGillivray rose steadily in the NWC and in 1793 was given responsibility for managing the depot at Grand Portage. On the death of his uncle Simon McTavish in 1804, McGillivray became the NWC's director. In this capacity he encouraged Thompson's explorations west of the Continental Divide in 1807–12 and commissioned the drafting of his great "Map of the North-West Territory of the Province of Canada" in 1812–15. In addition to his role as head of the NWC, McGillivray served as a justice of the peace and a member of the House of Assembly of Lower Canada. Fernand Ouellet, "William McGillivray," DCB, 6:454–7.

ALEXANDER MACKENZIE (1764–1820) joined the fur trade in 1779 and by 1785 was a wintering partner with Gregory, McLeod and Company. After this firm joined the NWC in 1787, Mackenzie became one of the most prominent and active Nor'west partners, taking charge of the Athabasca Department in 1788. Anxious to find a trading route to the Pacific Ocean, in 1789 he journeyed down the Mackenzie River to the Arctic Ocean, and in 1792–93 travelled from Fort Chipewyan to the Pacific at Bella Coola. His NWC partnership expired in 1799, and in 1800 he acquired shares in the rival XY Company, which he dominated until it united with the NWC in 1804. Mackenzie served in the House of Assembly of Lower Canada before retiring to his native Scotland in 1810. He is the author of *Voyages from Montreal ...* (London: T. Cadell and W. Davies, 1801). Roy Daniells, *Alexander Mackenzie and the North West* (Toronto: Oxford University Press, 1971).

NICOLAS MONTOUR (1756–1808) entered the fur trade in 1777 and spent most of his career on the Saskatchewan. He owned two of the sixteen shares in the 1783–84 NWC agreement, which he retained in the 1787 agreement. Thompson encountered Montour in 1786, when the trader was in charge of the NWC post on the South Saskatchewan (not the Gregory, McLeod post, as Thompson states), although as Montour was an anglophone it is curious that Thompson refers to him as a "French gentleman" (27f, 52). He retired about 1792, later purchasing a seigneury and serving as a member of the House of Assembly of Lower Canada. François Béland, "Nicholas Montour," DCB, 5:602–4; Wallace, *Documents*, 487–8.

MITCHELL OMAN (b. c. 1753), of Stromness, Orkney, entered HBC service as a labourer in 1771. Oman spent most of his career inland, where he was first employed as a canoeman, eventually working his way up to become a trader. In 1786–87 Thompson kept the South Branch House post journal for Oman, who provided the young apprentice with a vivid account of the 1781–82 smallpox epidemic (iv.257–9, 283–5). He retired in 1799. Tyrrell, ed., *Journals of Hearne and Turnor*, 237n1.

PETER PANGMAN (1744–1819) was involved in the fur trade by 1767 and by the mid-1770s was trading on the Saskatchewan. In 1784 Pangman was admitted to partnership in Gregory, McLeod and Company, and in this capacity he supervised the construction of a post at South Branch in 1786, where Thompson first encountered him (27f, 52). In 1787 Pangman became a partner in the twenty-share NWC. He left the West in 1793, becoming a seigneur in Lower Canada. Collaborative authorship, "Peter Pangman," DCB, 5:656–7.

SIR WILLIAM EDWARD PARRY (1790–1855) directed four voyages of exploration to the Arctic during his long career with the Royal Navy. During the first of these, in search of the Northwest Passage, Parry's ships, the *Hecla* and *Griper*, passed the winter of 1819–20 at Winter Harbour on Melville Island. The narrative of this voyage was published as *Journal of a Voyage for the Discovery of a North West Passage from the Atlantic to the Pacific* (London: John Murray, 1821). In the *Travels*, Thompson refers to the observations on the aurora borealis that Parry made on this expedition (iv.104.b–e, 154–6). J.K. Laughton, "Sir (William) Edward Parry," ODNB, 42:869–71.

JEAN-FRANÇOIS DE GALAUP, COMTE DE LA PÉROUSE (1741–88?) joined the French navy in 1756 and saw action in the Seven Years War. His service in the American Revolutionary War included the capture of Prince of Wales's Fort and York Factory; the former event is described by Thompson on iv.8 (10–11). In 1785 La Pérouse was chosen to command an expedition to the Pacific Ocean. Two years of exploration ensued before he ran aground on the Melanesian island of Vanikoro in March 1788. His ultimate fate is unknown. Bohlander, ed., *World Explorers*, 266–9.

PETER POND (1739/40–1807), from Milford, Connecticut, joined the fur trade in 1765 and worked for several years in the area of the Great Lakes. By 1778 he was in the Athabasca region, where he traded vigorously on behalf of the NWC. Pond left the West in 1788, pursued by a reputation for violence and intimidation, and exited the NWC in 1790. Thompson writes of Pond's map of 1784–85, and of two murders in which he was implicated, on iv.116–19 (171–4). Barry M. Gough, "Peter Pond," DCB, 5:681–6; Wallace, *Documents*, 492.

SIR JOHN RICHARDSON (1787–1865), a Royal Navy surgeon, served in this capacity on Sir John Franklin's first two Arctic expeditions. He was also a leading naturalist and wrote many of the natural history appendices in the expedition's narratives. Richardson's writings were influential and widely cited, and the *Travels* contains an extract from his account of an 1826 visit to an Inuit village (iii.6b, 18–19). In later life Richardson worked as a senior navy physician and published widely on biology, and in 1848–49 he led an unsuccessful search for the lost third Franklin expedition. R.E. Johnson, "Sir John Richardson," DCB, 9:658–61.

MALCHOM ROSS (c. 1754–99) joined the HBC as a labourer in 1774 and spent most of his early career serving at inland posts. In 1790–92 he and Peter Fidler accompanied Philip Turnor on his Athabasca expedition, and in 1793 Ross was assigned to carry out the HBC's planned expansion into this fur-rich region, a task in which he was to be aided by Thompson. After Thompson's 1796 expedition to Athabasca, he and Ross passed the winter of 1796–97 at Bedford House on Reindeer Lake (iv.101–14, 150–65). Shortly after his appointment as inland master in 1799, Ross was drowned while bound for the interior. Jennifer S.H. Brown, "Malchom Ross," DCB, 4:684–5.

SAUKAMAPPEE (c. 1700–93), for whom the *Travels* is virtually the only biographical source, was born a Cree, distinguished himself in wars against the Shoshone, and was subsequently adopted by the Piegan. Thompson lodged with Saukamappee when wintering with the Piegan in 1787–88, during which time he listened to the elder's stories. The written relation of these discourses (iv.264–78, 289–98) contains an account of Piegan-Shoshone warfare that reaches back to the 1730s, and a description of the arrival of smallpox in 1781. Thompson admired Saukamappee deeply, stating that "he has always been a friend to the weak" (iv.290, 306). Peter Fidler, who met Saukamappee when he wintered with the Piegan in 1792–93, reported that he died in June 1793; his leg had become infected after it had been bitten by a beaver. E.3/2, fol. 15, HBCA.

JOHN SAYER (c. 1750–1818) spent his entire fur-trading career in the region south and west of Lake Superior. Active by the late 1770s, he joined the NWC in 1791, becoming a partner in 1798, the same year in which Thompson visited his post on Cass Lake (iv.210–13, 245–7). Sayer signed subsequent NWC agreements and played a prominent coordinating role in the Upper Mississippi fur trade, but seems to have been forced to retire from the NWC in 1807, at which time he moved to Lower Canada. Douglas A. Birk, "John Sayer," DCB, 5:741–2; Wallace, *Documents*, 497.

SHESHEPASKUT (fl. 1798) was an Ojibwa chief in the vicinity of Red Lake, in what is now northern Minnesota. He is referred to variously in the *Travels* and Thompson's journals with the cognates Sheshepaskut, Sugar, and Sucre (sometimes preceded by the adjective "Old"). He first appears in Thompson's journals on 28 March 1798 when, travelling east from Cadotte's House, Thompson sends to him for a guide. On 2 April, Sheshepaskut visited Jean-

Baptiste Cadotte's post, where he conversed with Thompson about Ojibwa-Cheyenne warfare (iv.198–203, 236–9, and iii.67–9 in Volume II); he then hosted Thompson at Red Lake, 17–20 April (iv.205, 241). He is probably the same figure referred to as "Sweet," "Wiscoup," or "We-esh-coob" (literally, "sweet" in Ojibwa) in the writings of William W. Warren, Alexander Henry the Younger, and Henry R. Schoolcraft. Coues, ed., *Early History of the Great Northwest*, 1:163, 190; Henry R. Schoolcraft, *Narrative Journal of Travels* (Albany: E. & E. Hosford, 1821), 252; William W. Warren, *History of the Ojibway People* (St Paul: Minnesota Historical Society Press, 1984), 231, 376.

WILLIAM THORBURN (fl. 1789–1805) entered NWC service before 1789. During the early 1790s he traded at a series of posts in the vicinity of Nipawin on the Saskatchewan River and in 1793 became an NWC partner. While Thompson asserts that Thorburn was present at South Branch House in 1786–87 (27f, 52), he is not mentioned in the HBC post journal. Beginning in 1794, Thorburn shifted his trading activities to the region of the Swan, Qu'Appelle, and Assiniboine Rivers, where Thompson encountered him in November 1797 (iv.147, 197). Thorburn was included in successive NWC partnership agreements but relinquished his shares in 1805. In 1792, Malchom Ross reported of Thorburn that he "understands the Natives & exceeding well." B.161/a/1, fol. 3, HBCA; Innis, *The Fur Trade in Canada*, 253; Johnson, ed., *Saskatchewan Journals*, xxvii; Wallace, *Documents*, 503.

WILLIAM TOMISON (c. 1739–1829) joined the HBC in 1760 as a labourer and worked his way up to become inland master in 1778. The apex of his career came in 1786 when he was named chief of York, with the proviso that he reside inland to oversee trade. As inland master, Tomison was responsible for Thompson during his years on the Saskatchewan, 1786–90. As part of his strategy to compete with the North West Company, Tomison promoted links between the HBC and the Piegan, a policy that would see Thompson sent to winter with the Piegan in 1787–88. Tomison took leave in Britain in 1789 but returned to the inland trade the following year and did not retire definitively until 1810. John Nicks, "William Tomison," DCB, 6:775–7.

PHILIP TURNOR (c. 1751–1799/1800) joined the HBC as an inland surveyor in 1778. He arrived at Cumberland House on 7 October 1789 and during the winter taught astronomy, first to Thompson and then to Peter Fidler. Turnor's survey of Athabasca (which Thompson mentions at iv.97, 146, and iv.117–18, 173) lasted from September 1790 to July 1792, after which he returned to England. E.E. Rich, "Philip Turnor," DCB, 4:740–2.

BIBLIOGRAPHY

MANUSCRIPT MATERIAL BY THOMPSON

Archives of Ontario, Toronto
David Thompson Fonds, F443
Notebooks 1–84 (96 volumes, including notebooks numbered 3a, 28a, 34a, 48a, 48b, 49a, 59a, 61a, 61b, 66a, 70a, 73a), three unnumbered notebooks, field books 1–9 (11 volumes, including field books numbered 4b and 6b)
Travels, pages 27a–zd
"Map of the North West Territory of the Province of Canada," 1812–1815, F443–6

Hudson's Bay Company Archives, Provincial Archives of Manitoba, Winnipeg
Duck Portage, Post Journal, 6 September 1795 to 3 May 1796, B.55/a/1
Hudson House, Post Journal, 24 May to 19 September 1788, found in Manchester House, Post Journal, 1788–1789, B.121/a/3
South Branch House, Post Journal, 13 September 1786 to 30 May 1787, B.205/a/1

The National Archives of the United Kingdom (formerly PRO), London
"Map of the North West Territory of the Province of Canada," 1812–1815, FO925/4622: 1–10

Thomas Fisher Rare Book Library, University of Toronto
David Thompson Papers, MS21

OTHER MANUSCRIPT MATERIAL

Archives of Ontario, Toronto
Macaulay Family Fonds, F32

City of Westminster Archives, London, England
Grey Coat School Records
Poor Rate Books, St Margaret's and St John's, 1759–1772
The Register Book of Births and Baptisms Belonging to the Parish of Saint John the Evangelist Westminster in the County of Middlesex, vol. 2, 1755–1791
A Register of the Burials in the Parish of St John the Evangelist Westminster, 1754–1775

Hudson's Bay Company Archives, Provincial Archives of Manitoba, Winnipeg
London Correspondence Book Outwards, H.B.C. Official, 1781–1786, A.6/13

London Correspondence Book Outwards, H.B.C. Official, 1787–1791, A.6/14
London Correspondence Book Outwards, H.B.C. Official, 1792–1795, A.6/15
London Inward Correspondence from HBC Posts, Churchill, 1774–1791, A.11/15
Officers' and Servants' Ledger, York, 1797–1813, A.16/34
Officers' and Servants' Account Book: Servants' Commissions, 1787–1802, A.16/111
Register Book of Wills and Administrations of Proprietors, 1717–1819, A.44/1

Bedford House, Post Journal, 1796–1797, B.14/a/1
Churchill, Post Journal, 1784–1785, B.42/a/104
Churchill, Post Journal, 1785–1786, B.42/a/106
Cumberland House, Post Journal, 1789–1790, B.49/a/21
Edmonton House, Post Journal, 1796–1797, B.60/a/2
Edmonton House, Post Journal, 1798–1799, B.60/a/4
Fairford House, Post Journal, 1795–1796, B.66/a/1
Manchester House, Post Journal, 1787–1788, B.121/a/2
Manetoba District Report, 1820, B.51/e/1
Hudson House, Post Journal, 1788–1789, B.121/a/3
Petaigan River, Post Journal, 1792–1793, B.161/a/1
Reed Lake, Post Journal, 1794–1795, B.178/a/1
Reed Lake, Post Journal, 1795–1796, B.178/a/2
York Factory, Post Journal, 1784–1785, B.239/a/85
York Factory, Post Journal, 1785–1786, B.239/a/86
York Factory, Post Journal, 1791–1792, B.239/a/92
York Factory, Post Journal, 1792–1793, B.239/a/93
York Factory, Post Journal, 1796–1797, B.239/a/100
York Factory, List of Servants, 1783–1795, B.239/f/1

Governor's Incoming Correspondence, 1847, D.5/20; 1850, D.5/28
"Journal of a Journey over Land from Buckingham House to the Rocky Mountains
    in 1792 – a 3 by Peter Fidler," E.3/2
Ship's Log, *Prince Rupert*, 1784, C.1/906

Library and Archives Canada, Ottawa
McGillivray Papers, MG24 I3
Joseph Burr Tyrrell Papers, MG30 D49
State Book U, RG1 E1
Register of Provincial Secretary's Correspondence, RG4 C1
British Military and Naval Records, RG8 C250
1852 Census: Canada East, Subdistrict 430, Melbourne Township, Brompton Gore

The National Archives of the United Kingdom (formerly PRO), London
Colonial Office, British North America, Original Correspondence, 1842, CO 42/502;
    1843, CO 42/504

Foreign Office, United States of America, General Correspondence, 1845, FO5/441

Thomas Fisher Rare Book Library, University of Toronto
J.B. Tyrrell Papers, MS26

PUBLISHED WORKS

Anderson, Gary Clayton. *Kinsmen of Another Kind: Dakota-White Relations in the Upper Mississippi Valley, 1650–1862*. Lincoln: University of Nebraska Press, 1984

"Auction Sale of Real Estate ... Belonging to the Est. of Mr. D. Thompson." Montreal: Starke and Company, 2 September 1836

Ballantyne, Robert Michael. *Hudson's Bay; or, Life in the Wilds of North America*. Edinburgh: W. Blackwood, 1848

Barrington, Daines. "Observations on the Lagopus, or Ptarmigan." *Philosophical Transactions* 63 (1773–74): 224–30

[Barrow, John]. Review of *Narrative of a Journey to the Shores of the Polar Sea, in the Years 1819, 20, 21, and 22*, by John Franklin. *Quarterly Review* 28 (January 1823): 372–409

Barrow, John, and William Gifford. Review of *Account of an Expedition from Pittsburgh to the Rocky Mountains* by Edwin James, *Narrative Journey of Travels from Detroit Northwest* by Henry Rowe Schoolcraft, and *A Journal of Travels into the Arkansa Territory* by Thomas Nuttall. *Quarterly Review* 29 (April 1823): 1–25

Belyea, Barbara. "The 'Columbian Enterprise' and A.S. Morton: A Historical Exemplum." *BC Studies* 86 (Summer 1990): 3–27

Bentley, D.M.R. "UnCannyda." *Canadian Poetry* 37 (Fall/Winter 1995): 1–16

Berger, Carl. *Science, God, and Nature in Victorian Canada*. Toronto: University of Toronto Press, 1983

Bigsby, J.J. *The Shoe and Canoe; or Pictures of Travels in the Canadas*. 2 vols. London: Chapman and Hall, 1850

Binnema, Theodore. *Common and Contested Ground: A Human and Environmental History of the Northwestern Plains*. Toronto: University of Toronto Press, 2004

Bird, Louis. *Telling Our Stories: Omushkego Legends and Histories from Hudson Bay*. Edited by Jennifer S.H. Brown, Paul W. DePasquale, and Mark F. Ruml. Peterborough: Broadview, 2005

Birk, Douglas A. "John Sayer and the Fond du Lac Trade: The North West Company in Minnesota and Wisconsin." In *Rendezvous: Selected Papers of the Fourth North American Fur Trade Conference, 1981*, edited by Thomas C. Buckley, 50–61. St Paul: North American Fur Trade Conference, 1984

Bohlander, Richard E., ed. *World Explorers and Discoverers*. New York: Macmillan, 1992

Brightman, Robert. *Grateful Prey: Rock Cree Human-Animal Relationships.* Regina: Canadian Plains Research Centre, 2002

British Museum Catalogue of Printed Maps, Charts, and Plans. 15 vols. London: Trustees of the British Museum, 1967

Brown, George W., David M. Hayne, Francess G. Halpenny, and Ramsay Cook, gen. eds. *Dictionary of Canadian Biography.* 15 vols. to date. Toronto: University of Toronto Press, 1966–

Brown, Jennifer. "Charlotte Small Thompson Personified: Identities in Motion." Paper presented at the American Society for Ethnohistory, November 2006

Burch, Ernest. "The Caribou Inuit." In *Native Peoples: The Canadian Experience*, edited by R. Bruce Morrison and C. Roderick Wilson, 106–33. Toronto: McClelland & Stewart, 1986

Burnham, Dorothy K. *Cut My Cote.* Toronto: Royal Ontario Museum, 1973

Burpee, Lawrence J., ed. *Journals and Letters of Pierre Gaultier de Varennes de la Vérendrye and his Sons.* Toronto: Champlain Society, 1927

Campbell, Marjorie Wilkins. *Northwest to the Sea: A Biography of William McGillivray.* Toronto: Clarke, Irwin, 1975

Carman, Bliss. *Far Horizons.* Toronto: McClelland & Stewart, 1925

Catalogue of Books in the Montreal Library. [Montreal: J. Starke, 1842]

Clark, Peter. *British Clubs and Societies 1580–1800: The Origins of an Associational World.* Oxford: Clarendon, 2000

Clutton-Brock, Elizabeth. *Woman of the Paddle Song.* Vancouver: Copp Clark, 1972

Cochrane, Charles Norris. *David Thompson the Explorer.* Toronto: Macmillan, 1924

Coues, Elliott, ed. *New Light on the Early History of the Greater Northwest: The Manuscript Journals of Alexander Henry and David Thompson.* Minneapolis: Ross and Haines, 1965

Cross, Tom Peete. *Motif-Index of Early Irish Literature.* Bloomington, IN: Indiana University Press, 1952

Daniells, Roy. *Alexander Mackenzie and the North West.* Toronto: Oxford University Press, 1971

Defoe, Daniel. *Robinson Crusoe.* London: W. Taylor, 1719

Dickens, Charles. *American Notes for General Circulation.* London: Chapman and Hall, 1842

Dugas, Georges. *The Canadian West.* Montreal: Librarie Beauchemin, 1905

Erichsen-Brown, Charlotte. *Use of Plants for the Past 500 Years.* Aurora, ON: Breezy Creeks Press, 1979

Evans, Hubert. *North to the Unknown: The Achievements and Adventures of David Thompson.* Toronto: McClelland & Stewart, 1949

Fenn, Elizabeth. *Pox Americana: The Great Smallpox Epidemic of 1775–82.* New York: Hill and Wang, 2001

Fenton, William N. *The Iroquois Eagle Dance: An Offshoot of the Calumet Dance.* Syracuse: Syracuse University Press, 1991

Fidler, Peter. "Journal of a Journey with the Chepawyans or Northern Indians ..." In *Journals of Samuel Hearne and Philip Turnor between the Years 1774 and 1792,* edited by J.B. Tyrrell, 493–555. Toronto: Champlain Society, 1934

Forster, J.R. "An Account of the Birds Sent from Hudson's Bay." *Philosophical Transactions* 62 (1772): 382–433

Franchère, Gabriel. *Narrative of a Voyage to the Northwest Coast of America, in the Years 1811, 1812, 1813, and 1814.* New York: Redfield, 1854

Franklin, John. *Narrative of a Journey to the Shores of the Polar Sea, in the Years 1819–20–21–22.* 2 vols. London: John Murray, 1824

– *Narrative of a Second Expedition to the Shores of the Polar Sea in the Years 1825, 1826, and 1827.* London: John Murray, 1828

Friesen, Gerald. *The Canadian Prairies: A History.* Toronto: University of Toronto Press, 1987

Frye, Northrop. Conclusion to *Literary History of Canada: Canadian Literature in English.* Edited by Carl F. Klinck. Toronto: University of Toronto Press, 1965

Fulford, Tim, Debbie Lee, and Peter J. Kitson. *Literature, Science, and Exploration in the Romantic Era.* Cambridge: Cambridge University Press, 2004

Garrod, Stan. *David Thompson.* Toronto: Grolier, 1989

Gates, Charles M., ed. *Five Fur Traders of the Northwest.* Minneapolis: University of Minnesota Press, 1933

Gibbon, Guy. *The Sioux: The Dakota and Lakota Nations.* Malden, MA: Blackwell, 2003

Glover, Richard. "The Witness of David Thompson." *Canadian Historical Review* 31 (1950): 25–38

Grabowski, Jan, and Nicole St-Onge. "Montreal Iroquois *engagés* in the Western Fur Trade, 1800–1821." In *From Rupert's Land to Canada,* edited by Theodore Binnema, Gerhard Ens, and R.C. Macleod, 23–58. Edmonton: University of Alberta Press, 2001

Green, W.A. *Pedigree of Acworth of Bedfordshire.* London: Mitchell Hughes and Clarke, 1905

Greenfield, Bruce. *Narrating Discovery: The Romantic Explorer in American Literature, 1790–1855.* New York: Columbia University Press, 1992

Hackett, Paul. *A Very Remarkable Sickness: Epidemics in the Petit Nord, 1670 to 1846.* Winnipeg: University of Manitoba Press, 2002

Hallowell, A. Irving. "The Spirits of the Dead in Saulteaux Life and Thought." *Journal of the Royal Anthropological Institute of Great Britain and Ireland* 70, no. 1 (1940): 29–51

– *The Ojibwa of Berens River, Manitoba: Ethnography into History.* Fort Worth: Harcourt Brace Jovanovich, 1992

Hearne, Samuel. *A Journey from Prince of Wales's Fort, in Hudson's Bay, to the Northern Ocean.* London: A. Strahan and T. Cadell, 1795

Henry the Elder, Alexander. *Travels and Adventures in Canada, 1760–1776.* Edited by James Bain. New York: Burt Franklin, 1969

Hickerson, Harold. "The Genesis of a Trading Post Band: The Pembina Chippewa." *Ethnohistory* 3 (Fall 1956): 289–345

– *The Chippewa and Their Neighbours.* Rev. edn. Prospect Heights, IL: Waveland, 1988

Hitsman, J. Mackay. "David Thompson and Defence Research." *Canadian Historical Review* 40 (December 1959): 315–18

Hopwood, Victor G. "David Thompson: Mapmaker and Mythmaker." *Canadian Literature* 38 (Autumn 1968): 5–17

Howard, Henry. *The Anatomy, Physiology, and Pathology of the Eye.* Montreal: Armour and Ramsay, 1850

Innis, Harold Adams. *The Fur Trade in Canada: An Introduction to Canadian Economic History.* New Haven: Yale University Press, 1930

Jablow, Joseph. *The Cheyenne in Plains Indian Trade Relations, 1795–1840.* New York: J.J. Augustin, 1950

James, Edwin. *A Narrative of the Captivity and Adventures of John Tanner.* Minneapolis: Ross and Haines, 1956

Jefferson, Thomas. *Notes on the State of Virginia.* Edited by David Waldstreicher. New York: Palgrave, 2002

Jenish, D'Arcy. *Epic Wanderer: David Thompson and the Mapping of the Canadian West.* Scarborough, ON: Doubleday Canada, 2003

Johnson, Alice M., ed. *Saskatchewan Journals and Correspondence, 1795–1802.* London: Hudson's Bay Record Society, 1967

Keating, William H. *Narrative of an Expedition to the Source of St. Peter's River, Lake Winnepeek, Lake of the Woods, &c., performed in the year 1823.* Minneapolis: Ross and Haines, 1959

Keith, W.J. *Canadian Literature in English.* London: Longman, 1985

Landau, Barbara R. *Essential Human Anatomy and Physiology.* 2nd edn. Glenview, IL: Scott, Foresman and Company, 1980

Lewis, Henry T. *A Time for Burning.* Edmonton: Boreal Institute for Northern Studies/University of Alberta, 1982

Lindsey, Charles. *An Investigation of the Unsettled Boundaries of Ontario.* Toronto: Hunter, Rose and Company, 1873

Long, Stephen H. *The Northern Expeditions of Stephen H. Long: The Journals of 1817 and 1823 and Related Documents.* Edited by Lucile M. Kane et al. St Paul: Minnesota Historical Society Press, 1978

Lyell, Charles. *Principles of Geology.* 3 vols. London: John Murray, 1833

Lynch, William Francis. *Narrative of the United States' Expedition to the River Jordan and the Dead Sea.* Philadelphia: Lea and Blanchard, 1849

Lytwyn, Victor. *Muskekowuck Athinuwick: Original People of the Great Swampy Land.* Winnipeg: University of Manitoba Press, 2002

McCafferty, Michael. "Correction: Etymology of *Missouri.*" *American Speech* 79 (Spring 2004): 32

McGillivray, Duncan. *The Journal of Duncan M'Gillivray of the North West Company at Fort George on the Saskatchewan, 1794–5.* Edited by Arthur S. Morton. Toronto: Macmillan, 1929

McGoogan, Kenneth. *Ancient Mariner: The Amazing Adventures of Samuel Hearne, the Sailor Who Walked to the Arctic Ocean.* Toronto: HarperCollins, 2004

MacGregor, J.G. *Peter Fidler: Canada's Forgotten Surveyor, 1769–1822.* Toronto: McClelland & Stewart, 1966

MacLaren, Ian. "David Thompson's Imaginative Mapping of the Canadian Northwest, 1784–1812." *Ariel* 15 (1984): 89–106

MacLulich, T.D. "The Explorer as Sage: David Thompson's Narrative." *Journal of Canadian Fiction* 4, no. 4 (1976): 97–107

McMorran, G.A. "Souris River Posts in the Hartney District." *Manitoba Historical Society Transactions*, series 3, 5 (1948–49): 46–62

Malaher, David. "David Thompson's Surveys of the Missouri/Mississippi Territory in 1797–98." Paper presented at the 9th North American Fur Trade Conference and Rupert's Land Colloquium, St Louis, 25 May 2006

Malainey, Mary E. "The Gros Ventre/Fall Indians in Historical and Archaeological Interpretation." *Canadian Journal of Native Studies* 25, no. 1 (2005): 155–83

Mandelbaum, David G. *The Plains Cree: An Ethnographic, Historical, and Comparative Study.* Regina: Canadian Plains Research Centre, 1979

Martin, Calvin. "Wildlife Diseases as a Factor in the Depopulation of the North American Indian." *Western Historical Quarterly* 7 (January 1976): 47–62

Matthew, H.C.G., and Brian Harrison, eds. *Oxford Dictionary of National Biography.* 60 vols. Oxford: Oxford University Press, 2004

Matthews, Maureen, and Roger Roulette. "Fair Wind's Dream: *Naamiwan Obowaajigewin.*" In *Reading Beyond Words: Contexts for Native History*, 2nd edn., edited by Jennifer S.H. Brown and Elizabeth Vibert, 262–92. Peterborough: Broadview Press, 2003

Meyer, Roy W. *The Village Indians of the Upper Missouri: The Mandans, Hidatsas, and Arikaras.* Lincoln, NE: University of Nebraska Press, 1977

Moore, John Bassett. *History and Digest of the International Arbitrations to Which the United States Has Been a Party.* 6 vols. Washington: Government Printing Office, 1898

Moore, John H. *The Cheyenne.* Cambridge, MA: Blackwell, 1996

Moreau, Bill. "The Death of Père Aulneau, 1736: The Development of Myth in the Northwest." *Canadian Catholic Historical Association Historical Studies* 69 (2003): 52–63

Morton, Arthur Silver. *David Thompson.* Toronto: Ryerson Press, 1930

– "The North West Company's Columbian Enterprise and David Thompson." *Canadian Historical Review* 17 (1936): 266–88

– *A History of the Canadian West to 1870–71: Being a History of Rupert's Land (The Hudson's Bay Company's Territory) and of the North-West Territory (including the Pacific Slope)*. London: T. Nelson and Sons, 1939

Murray, Laura J. "The Uses of Literacy in the Northwest." In *History of the Book in Canada*. Vol. 1: *Beginnings to 1840*, edited by Patricia Fleming et al., 187–93. Toronto: University of Toronto Press, 2004

Nelson, George. *"The Orders of the Dreamed": George Nelson on Cree and Northern Ojibwa Religion and Myth, 1823*. Edited by Jennifer S.H. Brown and Robert Brightman. Winnipeg: University of Manitoba Press, 1988

– *My First Years in the Fur Trade: The Journals of 1802–1804*. Edited by Laura Peers and Theresa Schenck. Montreal & Kingston: McGill-Queen's University Press, 2002

Nesper, Larry. *The Walleye War: The Struggle for Ojibwe Spearfishing and Treaty Rights*. Lincoln: University of Nebraska Press, 2002

Nicks, Trudy. "The Iroquois and the Fur Trade in Western Canada." In *Old Trails and New Directions: Papers of the Third North American Fur Trade Conference*, edited by Carol M. Judd and Arthur J. Ray, 85–101. Toronto: University of Toronto Press, 1980

Nisbet, Jack. *Sources of the River: Tracking David Thompson across Western North America*. Seattle: Sasquatch, 1994

– "Smoke." In *Visible Bones: Journeys across Time in the Columbia River Country*. Seattle: Sasquatch, 2003

– *The Mapmaker's Eye: David Thompson on the Columbia Plateau*. Pullman, WA: Washington State University Press, 2005

– "Breaking a Leg," *Pacific Northwest Inlander*, 11 April 2007

Palliser, John. *A General Map of the Routes in British North America Explored by the Expedition under Captain Palliser*. London: Stanford's, 1865

Parker, James. *Emporium of the North: Fort Chipewyan and the Fur Trade to 1835*. Regina: Alberta Culture and Multiculturalism/Canadian Plains Research Centre, 1987

Payne, Michael. *The Most Respectable Place in the Territory: Everyday Life in Hudson's Bay Company Service, York Factory, 1788 to 1870*. Ottawa: Minister of Supply and Services Canada, 1989

Peers, Laura. *The Ojibwa of Western Canada, 1780–1870*. Winnipeg: University of Manitoba Press, 1994

Pennant, Thomas. *Arctic Zoology*. 2 vols. London: Henry Hughs, 1785

Picard, Liza. *Dr. Johnson's London: Life in London, 1740–1770*. London: Weidenfeld and Nicolson, 2000

Plutarch. "Marcus Cato." In *Parallel Lives*, 11 vols., edited by Bernadotte Perrin. Loeb Classical Library. Cambridge: Harvard University Press, 1914–26

Podruchny, Carolyn. *Making the Voyageur World: Travelers and Traders in the North American Fur Trade*. Lincoln: University of Nebraska Press, 2006

Pole, Graeme. *David Thompson: The Epic Expeditions of a Great Canadian Explorer.* Canmore, AB: Altitude Pub Canada, 2003

Porter, Roy. *London: A Social History.* London: Hamish Hamilton, 1994

Prior, Sir James. *Memoir of the Life and Character of the Right Hon. Edmund Burke.* 2 vols. London: Baldwin, Cradock and Joy, 1826

Review of John Franklin, *Narrative of a Second Expedition to the Shores of the Polar Sea, in the Years 1825–26–27,* by John Franklin. *Quarterly Review* 38 (October 1828): 335–58

Rich, E.E. *The Fur Trade and the Northwest to 1857.* Toronto: McClelland & Stewart, 1967

Richards, J. Howard. *Atlas of Saskatchewan.* Regina: University of Saskatchewan, 1969

Robertson, Colin. *Colin Robertson's Correspondence Book, September 1817 to 1822.* Edited by E.E. Rich. Toronto: Champlain Society, 1939

Robson, Joseph. *An Account of Six Years' Residence in Hudson's-Bay, from 1733 to 1736, and 1744 to 1747.* London: J. Payne and J. Bouquet, 1752

Ruggles, Richard I. "Hospital Boys of the Bay." *Beaver* 308 (Autumn 1977): 4–11

Schoolcraft, Henry Rowe. *Narrative Journal of Travels.* Albany: E. & E. Hosford, 1821

– *Narrative of an Expedition through the Upper Mississippi to Itasca Lake ... in 1832.* New York: Harper and Brothers, 1834

Scott, Hew, et al. *Fasti Ecclesiae Scoticanae.* 7 vols. Edinburgh: Oliver and Boyd, 1928

Sellers, David. *The Transit of Venus: The Quest to Find the True Distance of the Sun.* Leeds: Magavelda Press, 2001

"Shahaka." In *Biographical Dictionary of American Indian History to 1900,* rev. edn., edited by Carl Waldman, 346. New York: Checkmark, 2001

Shardlow, Tom. *David Thompson: A Trail by Stars.* Lantzville, BC: XYZ Publishing, 2006

Smith, James K. *David Thompson: Fur Trader, Explorer, Geographer.* Toronto: Oxford University Press, 1971

– *David Thompson.* Don Mills: Fitzhenry & Whiteside, 1975

Smith, Marion R. *Koo-koo-sint: David Thompson in Western Canada.* Red Deer, AB: Red Deer College Press, 1976

Smyth, David. "David Thompson's Surveying Instruments and Methods in the Northwest, 1790–1812." *Cartographica* 18, no. 4 (1981): 1–17

Spry, Irene. "The Tragedy of the Loss of the Commons in Western Canada." In *As Long as the Sun Shines and the Water Flows,* edited by Ian A.L. Getty and Antoine S. Lussier, 203–28. Vancouver: University of British Columbia Press, 1983

Sturtevant, William C., gen. ed. *Handbook of North American Indians.* 13 vols to date. Washington: Smithsonian Institution, 1978–

Swift, Jonathan. *Gulliver's Travels*. Edited by Claude Rawson. New York: Oxford University Press, 2005

Thistle, Paul C. "The Twatt Family, 1780–1840: Amerindian, Ethnic Category, or Ethnic Group Identity?" *Prairie Forum* 22 (Fall 1997): 193–212

Thompson, David. *David Thompson's Narrative of His Explorations in Western America, 1784–1812*. Edited by J.B. Tyrrell. Toronto: Champlain Society, 1916

– *David Thompson's Narrative, 1784–1812*. Edited by Richard Glover. Toronto: Champlain Society, 1962

– *Travels in Western North America 1784–1812*. Edited by Victor G. Hopwood. Toronto: Macmillan of Canada, 1971

Thomson, W.P.L. *History of Orkney*. Edinburgh: Mercat Press, 1987

Thoreau, Henry David. *A Yankee in Canada*. Boston: Ticknor and Fields, 1866

Tyrrell, J.B. *A Brief Narrative of the Journeys of David Thompson in North-Western America*. Toronto: Copp, Clark, 1888

– "Peter Fidler, Trader and Surveyor, 1769 to 1822." *Royal Society of Canada Transactions*, 3rd series, 7 (1913): ii:117–27

– ed. *Journals of Samuel Hearne and Philip Turnor*. Toronto: Champlain Society, 1934

Udal, John O. *The Nile in Darkness: Conquest and Exploration, 1504–1862*. Norfolk: Michael Russell, 1998

Umfreville, Edward. *The Present State of Hudson's Bay*. London: Charles Stalker, 1790

Vecsey, Christopher. *Traditional Ojibwa Religion and Its Historical Changes*. Philadelphia: American Philosophical Society, 1983

Wallace, William Stewart, ed. *Documents Relating to the North West Company*. Toronto: Champlain Society, 1934

– "Alexander Fraser." In *Dictionary of Canadian Biography*, 2nd edn., 2 vols., edited by Wallace, 1:214. Toronto: Macmillan, 1945

Warkentin, Germaine. "David Thompson." In *Profiles in Canadian Literature*, vol. 1, edited by Jeffrey M. Heath, 1–8. Toronto: Dundurn Press, 1980

– ed. *Canadian Exploration Literature: An Anthology, 1660–1860*. Toronto: Oxford University Press, 1993

– "John McDonald of Garth and the Dream of a Native North-West." In *Gathering Places: Essays on Aboriginal and Fur Trade Histories*, edited by Laura Peers and Carolyn Podruchny. Forthcoming. Vancouver: University of British Columbia Press

Warren, William W. *History of the Ojibway People*. St Paul: Minnesota Historical Society Press, 1984

Watkins, Edwin Arthur, and Richard Faries. *A Dictionary of the Cree Language as Spoken by the Indians in the Provinces of Quebec, Ontario, Manitoba, Saskatchewan, and Alberta*. Toronto: General Synod of the Church of England in Canada, 1938

Webster, Noah. *An American Dictionary of the English Language.* Philadelphia: J.B. Lippincott, 1857

White, Bruce. *The Fur Trade in Minnesota: An Introductory Guide to Manuscript Sources.* St Paul: Minnesota Historical Society Press, 1977

White, Catherine M., ed. *David Thompson's Journals relating to Montana and Adjacent Regions, 1808–1812.* Missoula, MT: Montana State University Press, 1950

White, Richard. *The Middle Ground: Indians, Empires, and Republics in the Great Lakes Region, 1650–1815.* Cambridge: Cambridge University Press, 1991

Wishinsky, Frieda. *David Thompson: Map-Maker.* Don Mills, ON: Pearson Educational, 2005

Wood, Kerry. *The Map-Maker: The Story of David Thompson.* Toronto: Macmillan, 1955

Wood, W. Raymond, and Thomas D. Thiessen, eds. *Early Fur Trade on the Northern Plains: Canadian Traders among the Mandan and Hidatsa Indians, 1738–1818.* Norman: University of Oklahoma Press, 1985

WEBSITES

Insults.net. "Historical Insults." Insults.net. http://www.insults.net/html/historical/curses_2.html

Louisbourg Institute. "Spruce Beer." Louisbourg Institute. http://fortress.uccb.ns.ca/behind/beer.html

Morton, Anne. "George Charles." HBCA. http://www.gov.mb.ca/chc/archives/hbca/biographical/c/charles_george.pdf

– "William Budge." HBCA. http://www.gov.mb.ca/chc/archives/hbca/biographical/b/budge_william.pdf

Native American Repatriation Review Committee. "Assessment of a Request for the Repatriation of the Ontonagon Boulder by the Keweenaw Bay Indian Community." Smithsonian National Museum of Natural History. http://anthropology.si.edu/repatriation/reports/regional/northeast/ontonagon.htm

INDEX

Where terms used by Thompson differ from those in familiar usage, Thompson's term is provided in square brackets.

MAP 5 AND EXCERPTS
FROM THE KEY MAP

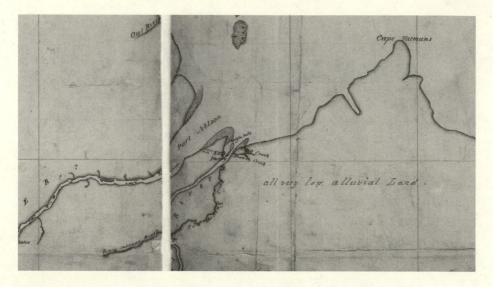

Map 5A   York Factory and Vicinity (approximate scale: 1 centimetre to
18 kilometres)

Thompson's description of life at York Factory on Hudson Bay can be found on pages
iv.13–27 (32–47). The Nelson River is on the north and the Hayes River on the south.
The vertical white band is the dividing line between two sections of Thompson's map.

Map 5B (*facing page*)   Reindeer Lake–Lake Athabasca route (approximate scale:
1 centimetre to 26 kilometres)

Thompson followed this route in his explorations of the summer of 1796, described
on pages iv.85–101 (137–49). There is a great contrast in the detail of the route
Thompson followed on the western shores of Reindeer Lake and Lake Wollaston (his
Manito Lake) and the other shores of those lakes. Thompson notes that he based the
course of the Reindeer River on a "Chipawayn drawing," and marks the portage used
by the Chipewyan to reach the "Moss lands," i.e., the Barren Grounds. The pattern at
the top marks the northern boundary of the great map, and the white vertical band is
the dividing line between two sections of the map.

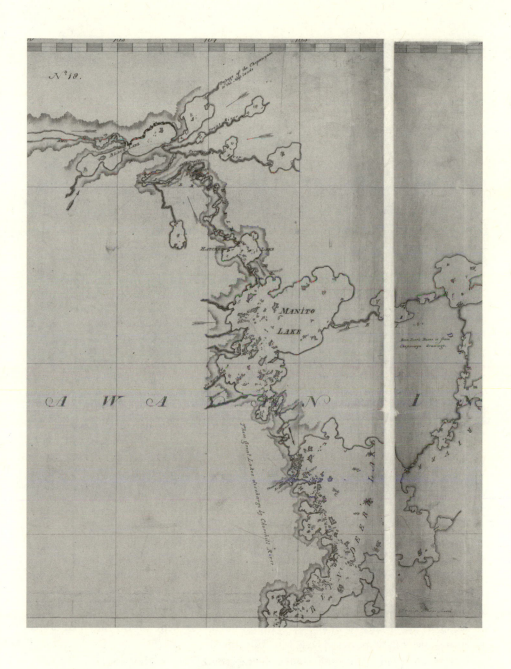

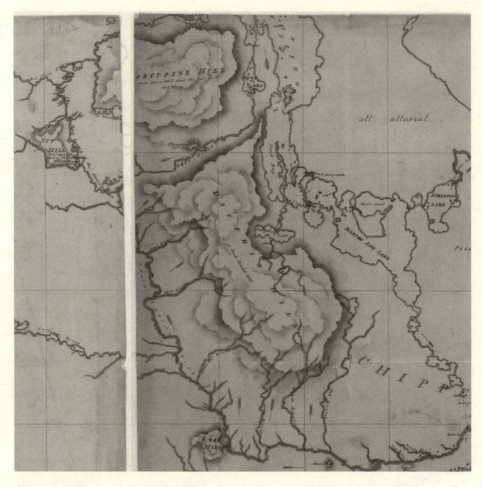

Map 5C   Upper Assiniboine and Swan River Country (approximate scale:
1 centimetre to 38 kilometres)

Thompson travelled through these regions during the autumn of his first year with the
NWC; see pages iv.133–48 (187–98) and iv.179–82 (221–3). The modern Manitoba-
Saskatchewan boundary roughly coincides with the white vertical band dividing two
sections of Thompson's main map. The Manitoba Escarpment follows the trend of the
eastern slope of Porcupine and Dauphin Hills (the latter now known as Duck Mountain at its north end and Riding Mountain at its south). The outlines of Dauphin and
Manitoba Lakes, which Thompson never visited, are highly inaccurate. Thompson's
"Stone Indian River" and "Calling River" are the Assiniboine and Qu'Appelle, respectively.

Map 5D   Journey to the Mandan Villages (approximate scale: 1 centimetre to 22 kilometres)

This journey, which took place between 28 November 1797 and 2 February 1798, is described on pages iv.148–79 (198–221). Thompson's route is shown by a dashed line, and the places where he made astronomical observations are marked "Obs." At the Mandan-Hidatsa settlements on the Missouri he notes that the villages can muster "1200 Warriors." The 49th parallel runs east-west through Turtle Mountain. Note also that Thompson has signed one of the map sections.

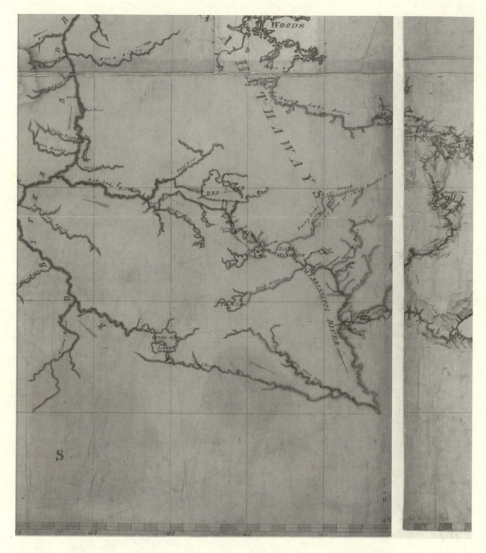

Map 5E   Pembina–Fond du Lac route (approximate scale: 1 centimetre to
40 kilometres)

Thompson traversed this region in the spring of 1798, visiting NWC posts and
searching for the source of the Mississippi; for this journey, see pages iv.184–223
(225–54). The Red River is on the western side of the section, and the western tip of
Lake Superior appears on the eastern side. In the northeast is part of the great arterial
fur trade route between Lake Superior and Lake of the Woods. The pattern at the
bottom marks the southern boundary of the great map, and the vertical white band is
the dividing line between two sections of the map.